The Petroff Defence

Lasha Janjgava

Translated by Graham Burgess

D1344466

First published in the UK by Gambit Publications Ltd 2001

ISBN 1 901983 46 3

DISTRIBUTION:
Worldwide (except USA): Central Books Ltd, 99 Wallis Rd, London E9 5LN. Tel +44 (0)20 8986 4854 Fax +44 (0)20 8533 5821.
E-mail: orders@Centralbooks.com
USA: BHB International, Inc., 41 Monroe Turnpike, Trumbull, CT 06611, USA.

For all other enquiries (including a full list of all Gambit Chess titles) please contact the publishers, Gambit Publications Ltd, P.O. Box 32640, London W14 0JN.
E-mail Murray@gambitchess.freeserve.co.uk
Or visit the GAMBIT web site at http://www.gambitbooks.com

Edited by Graham Burgess
Typeset by Petra Nunn
Printed in Great Britain by The Cromwell Press, Wiltshire.

10 9 8 7 6 5 4 3 2 1

Gambit Publications Ltd
Managing Director: GM Murray Chandler
Chess Director: GM John Nunn
Editorial Director: FM Graham Burgess
German Editor: WFM Petra Nunn

Contents

Symbols

+	check	Wcht	world team championship
++	double check	Ech	European championship
#	checkmate	Echt	European team championship
!!	brilliant move	ECC	European Clubs Cup
!	good move	Ct	candidates event
!?	interesting move	IZ	interzonal event
?!	dubious move	Z	zonal event
?	bad move	OL	olympiad
??	blunder	jr	junior event
+−	White is winning	wom	women's event
±	White is much better	mem	memorial event
⩲	White is slightly better	rpd	rapidplay game
=	equal position	sim	game from simultaneous display
∞	unclear position	adv	Advanced chess (human + computer)
∓	Black is slightly better	corr.	correspondence game
∓	Black is much better	1-0	the game ends in a win for White
−+	Black is winning	½-½	the game ends in a draw
Ch	championship	0-1	the game ends in a win for Black
Cht	team championship	(*n*)	*n*th match game
Wch	world championship	(*D*)	see next diagram

Transpositions are displayed by a dash followed by the moves (in *italic*) of the variation to which the transposition occurs. The moves start with the first one that deviates from the line under discussion. All the moves to bring about the transposition are given. Thus, after 1 e4 e5 2 ♘f3 ♘f6 3 d4 ♘xe4 4 ♗d3 d5 5 ♘xe5 ♘d7 6 ♘f3 the comment "6...♗d6 7 0-0 0-0 8 c4 c6 9 ♘c3 ♘xc3 10 bxc3 − *5...♗d6 6 0-0 0-0 7 c4 c6 8 ♘c3 ♘xc3 9 bxc3 ♘d7 10 ♘f3* ±" signifies that the reader should locate material on 1 e4 e5 2 ♘f3 ♘f6 3 d4 ♘xe4 4 ♗d3 d5 5 ♘xe5 ♗d6 6 0-0 0-0 7 c4 c6 8 ♘c3 ♘xc3 9 bxc3 ♘d7 10 ♘f3, to which play has transposed. The '±' sign indicates the overall assessment of that line; such signs are only given when it is meaningful to do so.

Introduction

1 e4 e5 2 ♘f3 ♘f6 *(D)*

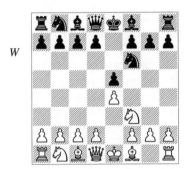

W

The Petroff Defence (also known as the Russian Game) is one of the most popular opening systems. This method of defence was introduced into practice in a correspondence game contested in St Petersburg in 1837 where Petroff played as White against a team of consultants.

The first detailed investigation of this system was made by the Russian master Karl Jaenisch in his book *Analyse Nouvelle des Ouvertures de Jeu des Echecs* (1842/3). The famous English master Staunton named it the Russian Game in his *Chess-Player's Handbook* (London, 1847), noting that, although this method of defence had been known about for a long time, it had "never received the consideration it was entitled to until Mr. Petroff, the celebrated Russian player, introduced it again a few years back". Further, Staunton drew attention to Petroff's role in developing White's attacking line 3 d4. The Petroff Defence was tried in practice and analysed by some of the best players of the 19th and early 20th century: Morphy, Steinitz, Tarrasch, Chigorin, Marshall and others.

The Petroff experienced a new wave of popularity in the 1980s and the 1990s. Those leading this wave included well-known players such as Karpov, Yusupov, Hübner, Hort, Ivanchuk, Short, Shirov, Makarychev, Rozentalis and others.

In recent years the Petroff has been extremely popular, and it is often used in top-class events, with its adherents including both Kramnik and Anand.

In this book I have sought to present a complete picture of the modern theory of the Petroff Defence, with especial emphasis on the most critical variations. I hope that this book helps readers to play the Petroff successfully, whether they defend it as Black or face it as White. I also hope that my work encourages more chess-players to take up this interesting and dependable opening.

1 Unusual Third Moves for White

1 e4 e5 2 ♘f3 ♘f6

This move characterizes the Petroff Defence. Instead of defending the attacked e5-pawn with 2...♘c6, Black counterattacks White's own pawn on e4. The Petroff is often played by beginners who simply mimic their opponent's moves (these beginners usually get a shock after 3 ♘xe5 ♘xe4 4 ♕e2 ♕e7 5 ♕xe4). Moving up a few classes, the Petroff is popular at virtually all levels of chess. It is solid and forces White to fight hard for the initiative. It is especially appropriate when facing a dangerous attacking player, who may find the resulting positions not to his taste. At grandmaster level, where a draw with Black is regarded as a good thing, it is particularly popular, and in recent years has been a workhorse of many of the world's top players.

In most lines the e4- and e5-pawns disappear, which reduces the tension in the centre. The question then is whether White can use his extra tempo to gain a tangible advantage. If White does not succeed, then the symmetrical pawn-structure and open e-file may lead to early exchanges and dead equality. However, if White chooses one of the critical lines then very sharp play can result. Indeed, in these sharp lines it is often Black who sacrifices material for the initiative (see, for example, Line A21 of Chapter 10). Thus a certain amount of concrete knowledge is important when playing the Petroff with either colour. The theory of this opening has developed substantially in recent years with several new lines being developed, in addition to new finesses in older variations.

White's main options are now 3 d4 and 3 ♘xe5, which are the subject of later chapters. However, there are a few other possibilities that must be considered:

A:	**3 ♗c4**	6
B:	**3 ♘c3**	10
C:	**3 d3**	16

A)

3 ♗c4 (D)

This move was investigated in the 19th century and enjoyed a new wave of popularity at the beginning of the 1990s. White must be prepared to sacrifice a pawn, gaining real attacking chances in return. However, readers who might be tempted by this line should note that Black can decline the offer (see note 'b' to Black's 5th move) and defuse much of White's attacking potential.

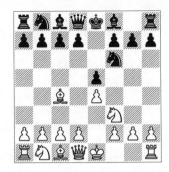

B

3...♘xe4

3...♘c6 transposes to the Two Knight's Defence.

4 ♘c3

Or:

a) After 4 d3 ♘d6 (4...♘f6 was played in the old game Williams-Löwenthal, London 1851; 5 ♘xe5 d5 =) 5 ♘xe5 ♘xc4 6 ♘xc4 d5 7 ♘e5 ♗d6 8 d4 0-0 Black's game is slightly preferable due to his bishop-pair.

b) White has also tried 4 ♕e2 d5 5 d3 (5 ♗b3 ♘c6 6 d3 ♘c5 7 ♘xe5 ♘d4 ∓) 5...dxc4 6 dxe4, and now:

b1) 6...♗g4 7 ♘c3 ♗b4? (7...♘c6 =; 7...♗d6 =) 8 ♕xc4 ♗xf3 9 ♕xb4! ♗xg2 10 ♖g1 ♘c6 11 ♕xb7 ♘d4 12 ♖xg2 ♘xc2+ 13 ♔f1 ♘xa1 14 ♕c6+ ♔f8 15 ♘d5 ♖b8 16 ♖xg7 ♕d6 17 ♗h6!! 1-0 Pradzhanov-Pinkas, Sofia 1922.

b2) 6...♘c6! 7 ♕xc4 ♗e7 8 ♘c3 0-0 9 0-0 ♗g4 ∓.

c) 4 ♘xe5 and now:

c1) 4...d5 is fully possible:

c11) 5 ♕f3 ♗e6 6 ♗b3 (6 d4 ♘d7 7 ♘xd7 ♕xd7 ∓) 6...♘d7 7 ♘xd7 ♕xd7 8 d3 ♘c5 ∓.

c12) 5 ♕e2 ♗c5 (5...dxc4?! 6 ♕xe4 ♕e7 7 ♘c3 f5 8 ♕e2 ♗e6 9 0-0 ♘d7

10 ♖e1 ±; 5...♗e6!? 6 d3 ♘xf2 7 ♘xf7 ♔xf7 8 ♕xf2+ ♕f6 9 ♕xf6+ gxf6 10 ♗b3 ♘c6 11 ♘c3 ♘d4 =) 6 d3 dxc4 7 ♕xe4 0-0 8 ♕xc4 ♕e7 9 d4 ♗xd4 10 ♕xd4 ♘c6 = Steinitz.

c2) 4...♕e7! 5 d4 d6 6 ♗xf7+ ♔d8 7 0-0 dxe5 8 dxe5+ ♗d7 9 ♗d5 ♘c5 10 b4 c6 11 bxc5 cxd5 ∓/∓; White has no real compensation for the sacrificed material.

We now return to 4 ♘c3 *(D)*:

B

4...♘xc3

Or:

a) 4...d5 5 ♗xd5 ♘f6 6 ♗b3 ♗d6 7 d3 0-0 (7...h6!?) 8 ♗g5 ± Yusupov.

b) 4...♘d6!? 5 ♗b3 ♘c6 6 0-0 ♗e7 7 ♖e1 (it is more dangerous, but also riskier, to make a true gambit of it by playing 7 d4!? exd4 8 ♘d5) 7...e4! 8 ♘xe4 ♘xe4 9 ♖xe4 d5 10 ♖e1 0-0 = Albin-Hodges, New York 1893.

c) 4...♘f6!? 5 ♘xe5 d5 6 ♗b3 c6 7 d4 and then:

c1) 7...♗e7 8 0-0 0-0 (8...♘bd7 9 f4 ♘b6 10 ♕f3 ± Morphy-Potier, Paris sim 1858) 9 ♗g5! ♘bd7 10 f4 ±.

c2) 7...♗d6 8 0-0 0-0 (8...h6 9 ♘e2 ♘bd7 10 ♘g3 0-0 11 f4 ♘e4 12 ♘xe4 dxe4 13 ♕e2 {13 ♕h5! ±} 13...♘f6

14 c3 c5 15 ♗e3 ± Roeberg-Meijers, Giessen 1992) 9 ♗g5! (9 ♘e2 ♘g4 10 f4 f6 11 ♘xg4 ♗xg4 12 ♕d2 ♗xe2 13 ♕xe2 f5 = Pavlov-Solovtsov, Moscow 1904) 9...♘bd7 10 f4 ±.

5 dxc3 c6!?

Or:

a) 5...d6? is bad in view of 6 ♘g5 ♗e6 7 ♗xe6 fxe6 8 ♕f3 ±.

b) 5...♗e7!? is interesting: 6 ♘xe5 0-0 7 ♕h5 (7 0-0 c6 {7...d6!?} 8 ♗d3 d5 9 ♗f4 ♘d7 =) 7...d5 8 ♗d3 g6 9 ♘xg6 (9 ♕h6 ♗f6 =) 9...fxg6 10 ♗xg6 hxg6 11 ♕xg6+ =.

c) Black often plays 5...f6:

c1) 6 0-0 and here:

c11) 6...♕e7 7 ♘h4 c6!? (7...d6 8 ♕h5+ ♔d8 9 f4 ♗e6 10 ♗xe6 ♕xe6 11 fxe5 dxe5 12 ♘g6 ♗c5+ 13 ♔h1 ♖e8 14 ♕xh7 ♕g8 15 ♕h5 ± Morphy-Barnes, London 1859) and then:

c111) 8 ♕h5+ ♔d8 9 ♘f5 ♕c5 (9...g6?! 10 ♘xe7 gxh5 11 ♘xc8 d5 12 ♗e2 ±) 10 ♕f7 d5 11 ♘xg7 ♕e7! –+.

c112) 8 ♘f5 ♕c5 9 ♗b3 d5 10 ♗e3 ♕a5 11 ♕g4 ♕c7 ∓.

c12) 6...g6 7 ♖e1 d6 is an interesting idea, since 8 ♘g5?! fxg5 9 ♖xe5+ dxe5 10 ♗f7+ ♔xf7 11 ♕xd8 ♘c6 12 ♕xc7+? ends in disaster for White after 12...♔g8, intending ...h6 followed by ...♖h7.

c13) 6...♘c6 7 ♘h4 and now:

c131) 7...♘e7?! 8 ♗d3! g6 (8...d5 9 ♕h5+ ♔d7 10 f4 ♕e8 11 ♕d1 ±) 9 f4 exf4 (9...♗g7 10 fxe5 fxe5 11 ♗g5 ±) 10 ♗xf4 ±.

c132) 7...g6 8 f4 f5 (8...♗c5+ 9 ♔h1 d6 10 b4 ♗b6 11 f5 ♘e7 12 ♗d3 gives White compensation, Ja Afar-Grassi,

Thessaloniki OL 1984) 9 ♘f3 e4 10 ♘g5 ♗c5+ 11 ♔h1 ♕e7 12 ♗f7+ ♔f8 13 b4 ♗d6 14 ♗b3 ♘d8 15 ♗e3 ♘e6 16 ♘xe4! fxe4 17 f5 gives White a strong attack.

c133) 7...♕e7 8 ♘f5 ♕c5 9 ♗b3 d5 10 ♗e3 ♕a5 11 ♘h4 ♗e6 12 ♕h5+ ♗f7 13 ♕g4 ♘e7 is slightly better for Black.

c14) 6...d6 7 ♘h4 g6 8 f4 and here:

c141) 8...f5? 9 ♘xf5! (9 ♘f3 d5 10 ♗xd5 ♗c5+ 11 ♔h1 c6 12 ♗c4 ♕xd1 13 ♖xd1 e4 14 ♘e5 ♘d7 ∞) 9...♗xf5 10 ♕d5 ♗e7 11 fxe5 ♖f8 (11...♘c6 12 ♖xf5! ♘xe5 13 ♖xe5 dxe5 14 ♕f7+ ♔d7 15 ♗g5 1-0 Spitzer-Szen, Pest 1857) 12 ♕xb7 ♘d7 13 e6 +–.

c142) 8...♘c6 9 f5 ♘e7 10 fxg6 hxg6 11 ♖xf6 and now Black should try 11...d5 rather than 11...♖xh4? 12 ♗f7+ ♔d7 13 ♗g5 ±.

c143) 8...♕e7! 9 f5 ♕g7! 10 ♕f3 (10 ♗e3 ♘c6 11 ♕f3 ♗e7 12 b4 ♘d8 ∞) 10...♗e7 ∓ intending ...c6 and ...d5.

c2) 6 ♘h4 g6 7 f4 ♕e7 (7...d6?! 8 f5 ±; 7...c6!? 8 f5 d5 9 fxg6 dxc4 10 ♕h5 ♔d7 11 g7 ♗xg7 12 ♕g4+ ♔d6 13 ♕xg7 ♕f8, Göbel-Koskivirta, corr. 1988-90, 14 ♕g3! with the initiative) 8 f5 *(D)* and then:

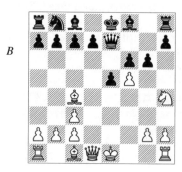

B

c21) 8...c6!? 9 fxg6 d5 10 ♕h5 ♔d8 11 0-0 (this may well be wrong) 11...♕g7 (11...♕c5+ 12 ♔h1 ♕xc4 13 ♖xf6 was given as winning for White by I.Kuznetsov, but it is not clear how White is even surviving after 13...♕g4) 12 ♖xf6 hxg6 (12...♗e7 13 ♖f7 hxg6 14 ♗g5! ±) 13 ♕xe5 ♗c5+ 14 ♔h1 ♘d7 15 ♖f8+! ♕xf8 16 ♗g5+ ♗e7 17 ♗xe7+ (I.Kuznetsov-Dementiev, Russia 1992) 17...♔e8 18 ♕d4 c5 (or 18...♖xh4? 19 ♗xh4 +−) 19 ♗xc5! +−.

c22) 8...♕g7 9 fxg6 (9 ♗d3?! g5 10 ♕h5+ ♕f7 11 ♘g6 d5 {11...♖g8!?} 12 g4 ♖g8 ∓) 9...hxg6 10 ♕g4 and now:

c221) 10...g5 11 ♘f5 ♕g6 12 ♗d3 ♕h5? (better is 12...♕g8) 13 ♕xh5+ ♖xh5 14 ♘g7+ ♗xg7 15 ♗g6+ ± Szell-Fedorov, West Berlin 1987.

c222) 10...♔d8 11 ♕g3 g5 12 ♘f5 and here:

c2221) 12...♕g6 13 ♗d3 (13 0-0!?) 13...d5 (13...♕g8 14 ♗e3 d6 {14...d5 15 0-0-0 ±} 15 0-0 gives White compensation) 14 ♘e7 ♕f7 15 ♘xc8 e4 (15...♔xc8 16 ♗f5+ ♘d7 17 ♗e3 intending 0-0-0 ±) 16 ♗e2 ♔xc8 17 ♗e3 (17 ♗g4+?! ♘d7 18 ♗e3 f5! 19 0-0 f4 ∓) 17...♗d6 18 ♕f2 ♕e6 (not 18...♖xh2? 19 ♖xh2 ♗xh2 20 g3 ♕h7 21 ♗g4+ ♘d7 22 0-0-0 c6 23 ♖h1 ♗xg3 24 ♖xh7 ♗xf2 25 ♗xd7+ +−) 19 h3 ♘d7 20 0-0-0 ♘e5 21 ♖hf1 and now 21...♗e7! ± is better than either 21...♖f8?! 22 ♗xg5 (22 c4 dxc4 23 ♗xg5 ♗e7 ∞) 22...fxg5 23 ♕xf8+ ♗xf8 24 ♖xf8+ ♔d7 25 ♖xa8 ± or 21...♖h6? 22 c4! c6 (22...dxc4 23 ♖d4 ±) 23 cxd5 cxd5 24 h4! ± Szell-Autenrieth, Hungary 1987.

c2222) 12...♕h7!? 13 0-0 d5!? (13...c6?! 14 ♗d3 d5 15 ♘d6 e4 16 ♖xf6 exd3 17 ♗xg5 ♗e7 18 ♖f7 1-0 Rublevsky-Sketinin, Pardubice 1992) 14 ♗xd5 ♗xf5 15 ♖xf5 (15 ♗xb7? ♗e4 −+) 15...♕xf5 16 ♗xb7 c6 17 ♗xa8 ♖h7 (∞ Rublevsky) 18 ♗e3 ♕c8 (18...♔c8 19 ♖f1 ♕e6 20 ♕f2 ±) 19 ♕f3 ±.

c223) 10...♘c6 11 ♕xg6+ ♕xg6 12 ♘xg6 ♖h5 13 g4 ♖h3 14 ♗f1 (14 ♘xf8 ♔xf8 15 0-0 ♔g7 16 ♔g2 ♖h8 ∞; 14 0-0 d5! 15 ♘xf8 dxc4 16 ♖xf6 ♗xg4 17 ♗g5 0-0-0 18 ♘g6 ∞ I.Kuznetsov) 14...♖h7 15 ♗d3 ♖h3 (½-½ I.Kuznetsov-Potapov, Russia 1992; 15...♗c5? 16 ♘f4 ♖g7 17 ♘h5 ±) 16 0-0 d5 17 ♔g2 ♖xd3!? 18 cxd3 ♗xg4 19 ♖xf6 ♗g7 20 ♖f2 ±.

6 ♘xe5 d5 7 0-0 ♗d6 8 ♖e1 ♗e6 *(D)*

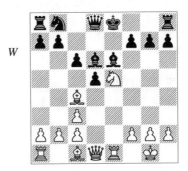

W

9 ♕h5!?

This is a new move that I am recommending. I believe that it deserves serious attention.

9 ♗d3 ♘d7 10 f4 ♘xe5 11 fxe5 ♗c5+ 12 ♔h1 ♕h4 13 ♗e3 = Boden-Morphy, London 1858.

9...♗xe5

Or:

a) 9...♕f6? 10 ♗g5 ♕f5 11 ♗d3 +−.

b) 9...0-0?! 10 ♗d3 ±.

c) 9...g6?! 10 ♘xg6 fxg6 11 ♕g4 (11 ♕h3! ±) 11...♕d7 (not 11...dxc4?? 12 ♕xe6+ +−) 12 ♖xe6+ ♔f7 13 ♕d4 gives White interesting play.

10 ♕xe5

Not 10 ♖xe5? g6 11 ♕e2 dxc4 12 ♗g5 ♕c8 −+.

Now (after 10 ♕xe5):

a) 10...dxc4? loses to 11 ♗g5.

b) 10...0-0 11 ♗d3 ♘d7 12 ♕g3 ±.

B)

3 ♘c3

One of the most common ways to avoid the main lines of the Petroff.

3...♗b4 *(D)*

If he wishes, Black can transpose to the Four Knights by 3...♘c6, and this is a sound option because the Four Knights gives Black few theoretical problems.

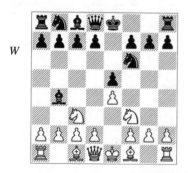

W

The text-move is a playable alternative, but probably offers White slightly more chances for an advantage. In the main line, Black is forced to surrender the bishop-pair by exchanging on c3. Although the almost symmetrical pawn-structure makes it hard work for White to make progress, the bishop-pair offers White a small but nagging edge. Black's main problem is the lack of secure outposts for his knights. He starts off with a knight on e4, but this usually has to move at some point and then Black may run into the typical problem of the player facing the bishop-pair − if he sits tight then White can gradually improve his position, but if he tries direct action, the position may become more open, which enhances the power of the bishops.

4 ♘xe5

Or:

a) 4 ♘d5 ♘xd5 5 exd5 e4 6 ♘d4 0-0 (6...♕g5!? 7 ♘b5 ♕e5 8 ♘c3 0-0 9 ♗c4 d6 intending ...♘d7 ∞ Pavlović) 7 c3 ♗c5 gives Black a slight advantage.

b) 4 d3 d5 5 exd5 ♘xd5 6 ♗d2 0-0 7 ♗e2 ♘c6 8 0-0 ♗xc3!? (8...♖e8!?; 8...♘xc3!? 9 bxc3 and now Black can play 9...♗a5!? or 9...♗e7!?; 8...♗e6 9 ♖e1 h6 10 ♘xd5 ♗xd2 11 ♘xd2 ♗xd5 12 ♗f3 ♕d6 13 ♘e4 ♗xe4 14 ♗xe4 ♖ae8 15 ♗xc6 ♕xc6 = Maroczy-Marshall, New York 1924) 9 bxc3 ♕d6!? ∞ Alekhine.

c) 4 a3?! ♗xc3 5 dxc3 d6 (5...♘xe4 6 ♕d5 ♘f6 7 ♕xe5+ ♕e7 8 ♕xe7+ ♔xe7 9 ♗f4 d6 10 0-0-0 ♘c6 11 ♗b5 ♗e6 12 ♖he1 ± Yandemirov-Daniliuk, Voronezh 1991) 6 ♗c4 h6 7 h3 ♘c6 8 ♕e2 ♕e7 (intending ...♗e6) is equal, M.Přibyl-Raetsky, Pardubice 1987.

d) 4 ♗c4 *(D)* and then:

d1) 4...d6!? and here:

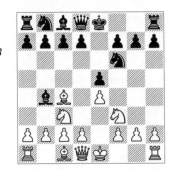

B

d11) 5 ♘d5 ♘xd5 6 ♗xd5 0-0 7 c3 ♗a5 8 d3 c6 = Becker-Euwe, Karlsbad 1929.

d12) 5 d3 and now:

d121) 5...♘c6 – 4...♘c6 5 d3 d6.

d122) 5...0-0 and then:

d1221) 6 a3?! ♗xc3+ 7 bxc3 ♗e6 8 ♗b3 ♘c6 9 0-0 ♕e7 10 ♖e1 (10 ♗g5!? h6 11 ♗h4 g5 ∞) 10...♘d7 11 ♗g5 f6 12 ♗e3 ♘c5 13 d4 ♘xb3 (13...♗xb3 14 cxb3 ± intending to meet 14...♘xe4?! with 15 dxe5 ±) 14 cxb3 ♗g4 15 d5 ♘d8 16 h3 ♗h5 17 g4 ∞.

d1222) 6 ♗g5 ♗xc3+ 7 bxc3 ♗e6 8 ♗b3 ♘bd7 =.

d123) 5...c6 6 ♗b3 0-0 7 0-0 ♘a6 8 ♘e2 ♘c5 9 c3 ♘xb3 10 axb3 ♗a5 11 ♘g3 and now Black should play 11...h6! =, rather than 11...♗c7?! 12 ♗g5 h6 13 ♗h4 g5?! 14 ♘xg5 hxg5 15 ♗xg5 ±.

d13) 5 0-0 0-0 and then:

d131) 6 d4 exd4 7 ♕xd4 ♘c6 8 ♕d3 ♗xc3 9 bxc3 ♖e8 (9...h6 10 ♖e1 ♗g4 11 e5 dxe5 12 ♘xe5 ♘xe5 13 ♖xe5 ♖e8 14 ♗f4 ♖xe5 15 ♗xe5 ♕e7 16 ♕d4 ♖d8 17 ♕f4 ♖d1+ is equal) 10 ♖e1 ♗g4 11 ♗g5 (11 ♘g5 ♘e5) 11...h6 12 ♗h4 ♗xf3 13 ♕xf3 ♘e5 14

♕e2 ♘g6 and Black has a slight advantage.

d132) 6 d3 ♗xc3 (6...♗e6 7 ♗b3 ♘bd7 8 ♘e2 ♗xb3 9 axb3 d5 10 ♘g3 ♖e8 11 c3 ♗f8 12 b4 c6 =) 7 bxc3 ♗e6 (7...♗g4!? 8 h3 ♗h5 9 g4 ♗g6 10 ♗g5 ♘bd7 ∞) 8 ♗b3 ♘bd7 9 ♕e2 ♕e7 10 h3 a5 11 ♖e1 a4 ½-½ Lanc-Banas, Trnava 1986.

d2) 4...♘c6 and now:

d21) 5 d3 and then:

d211) 5...0-0 6 ♗g5 ±.

d212) 5...d6 6 0-0 (6 h3 ♗e6 7 ♗xe6 fxe6 8 0-0 ♗xc3 9 bxc3 0-0 10 ♖b1 b6 11 c4 ♕e8 is equal, Walbrot-Blackburne, Vienna 1898) 6...♗xc3 (6...♗g4!? 7 ♘e2 ♗xf3 8 gxf3 ♕d7 = Rausis-Goria, St Martin 1991) 7 bxc3 and here:

d2121) 7...0-0 8 h3 (8 ♗g5!? is an alternative) 8...♗e6 9 ♗b3!? (9 ♗xe6 fxe6 10 ♘g5?! ♕e7 11 f4 exf4 12 ♗xf4 h6 13 ♘f3 ♘xe4 14 ♗xh6 ♘g3 15 ♗g5 ♖xf3! ∓ Delmar-Pillsbury, Cambridge Springs 1904) 9...a5 10 ♕e2 a4 11 ♗xe6 fxe6 12 d4 ± Pillsbury.

d2122) 7...h6 8 ♕e2 ♗e6 9 ♗b3 ♕c8 10 ♘h4 ♗xb3 11 axb3 ♕g4 = Hartston-Romanishin, Buenos Aires OL 1978.

d213) 5...d5 6 exd5 ♘xd5 7 ♗d2 (7 0-0 ♗xc3 8 bxc3 0-0 leads to equality, Schmid-Klein, Hamburg 1987) 7...♗xc3 (7...♗e6?! 8 0-0 f6 9 ♕e1 ♗c5 10 ♘a4 ♗d6 11 d4 0-0 12 ♘c3 ± Chajes-Black, New York 1918) 8 bxc3 ♗g4 =.

d22) 5 ♘d5 ♗a5 6 c3 (6 0-0 d6 7 ♕e2 0-0 8 d3 ♘xd5 =) 6...0-0 7 d3 h6 8 a4 ♗b6 9 b4 a6 10 ♘xb6 cxb6 11 ♕b3 with a slight advantage for White,

Rohaček-Šefc, Trenčianske Teplice 1949.

d3) 4...0-0 *(D)* and here:

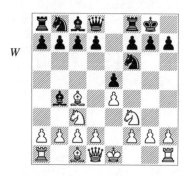

d31) 5 d3 d5 (5...c6!? 6 0-0 d5 7 ♗b3 a5 8 a3 ♗xc3 9 bxc3 a4 10 ♗a2 ♗g4 =) 6 exd5 ♘xd5 7 ♗d2 ♘xc3 (7...c6 8 0-0 ♖e8 9 ♖e1 ♗xc3 10 bxc3 ♗g4 11 h3 ♗xf3 12 ♕xf3 ♘f6 13 a4 ♘bd7 ∞ Tartakower-Marshall, Moscow 1925; 7...♗xc3 8 bxc3 ♘c6 9 0-0 ♗g4 =) 8 bxc3 ♗d6 9 ♘g5 h6 10 ♘e4 ♕e7 11 ♕h5 ♗e6 12 ♗g5 f6 13 ♗xe6+ ♕xe6 14 ♗xh6 = Tartakower-Kostić, Bled 1931.

d32) 5 ♕e2 d6 6 a3 ♗xc3 7 dxc3 ♗e6 8 ♗g5 ♘bd7 = Rogers-Finegold, Prague 1990.

d33) 5 ♘d5 ♘xd5 6 ♗xd5 c6 7 ♗b3 d5 8 0-0 ♗g4 9 h3 ♗h5 10 d3 dxe4 11 dxe4 ♘d7 12 ♕e2 ♕c7 (12...♔h8 13 ♖d1 ♕e7 14 g4 ♗g6 15 ♗g5 f6 16 ♗d2 ♗xd2 17 ♘xd2 ♘c5 = Spielmann-Marshall, Berlin 1928) 13 g4 ♗g6 14 ♘h4 ♘c5 15 ♘xg6 hxg6 16 ♗c4 ♘d7 = Spielmann-Marshall, Budapest 1928.

d34) 5 0-0 and now:

d341) 5...♗xc3 6 dxc3 (6 bxc3?! ♘xe4 7 ♘xe5 d5 8 ♗e2 ♖e8 9 ♘f3 c5

10 ♗b2 ♕f6 11 ♖e1 ♘c6 12 ♗b5 ♗g4 ∓ Gurieli-Alterman, Katerini 1992) 6...d6 7 ♗g5 (7 ♕e2 ♘bd7 8 ♗g5 h6 9 ♗h4 ♘c5 10 ♖ad1 ♕e7 11 ♘d2 g5 = Kofidis-Alterman, Komotini 1992) 7...h6 8 ♗h4 ♗g4 9 h3 ♗h5 10 ♕d3 ♘bd7 11 b4 ♕e8 12 ♕e3 ♗g6 13 ♘d2 ♘h5 14 a4 = Lev-Alterman, Israel 1992.

d342) 5...♘c6 and then:

d3421) 6 ♘d5 ♘xd5 (6...♗a5 7 d3 h6 8 h3 d6 9 ♘h2 ♘xd5 10 exd5 ♘e7 11 f4 ♗b6+ ∞ Rubinstein-A.Rabinovich, Prague 1908) 7 ♗xd5 d6 8 c3 ♗a5! 9 d3 ♗g4 10 h3 ♗d7 = Ed.Lasker-Marshall, New York 1924.

d3422) 6 d3 ♗xc3 7 bxc3 d5 8 exd5 ♘xd5 9 ♖e1 (9 ♘g5 ♘a5 10 ♗xd5 ♕xd5 11 ♗a3 ♖e8 12 c4 ♕d7 13 f4 f6 14 ♘e4 ∞) 9...♗g4 (9...♖e8 10 ♘g5 ♗f5 11 ♖b1 ±) 10 ♗d2 (10 h3 ♘xc3 11 ♕d2 ♗xf3 12 ♕xc3 ♗d5 13 ♖b1 ♗xc4 14 ♕xc4 ♖e8 ∓ Gilg-Marshall, Prague 1931) 10...♕d6 11 ♖b1 ♘b6 = Bernstein-Alekhine, Paris 1933.

4...0-0 *(D)*

This is clearly the strongest continuation. Black experiences problems after 4...♕e7:

a) 5 ♘f3!? and now:

a1) 5...♗xc3 6 dxc3 ♕xe4+ 7 ♗e2 0-0 8 0-0 d5 9 ♖e1 ♗g4 10 h3 gives White a slight advantage, Beraha-S.Müller, Dornbirn 1988.

a2) 5...♘c6 is best met by 6 ♗e2 ± rather than 6 ♗b5 ♗xc3 7 dxc3 ♕xe4+ 8 ♕e2 ♕xe2+ 9 ♔xe2 0-0 =.

a3) 5...♘xe4!? 6 ♗e2 (6 ♘xe4 ♕xe4+ 7 ♗e2 0-0 8 0-0 d5 9 d4 ♗g4 10 h3 ♗h5 11 ♗e3 ♘c6 12 c3 ♗d6 13 ♘g5 ♗xe2 14 ♘xe4 ♗xd1 15 ♘xd6

♗e2 16 ♖fe1 ♗a6 with equality, Von-thron-M.Braun, Bundesliga 1988/9)
6...♗xc3 (6...♘xc3!? 7 dxc3 ♗c5 ∞) 7 dxc3 d6 8 0-0 ♗e6 9 ♖e1 ♘d7 10 ♗b5 ♘ef6 ± Janowski-Blackburne, Vienna 1898.
   b) 5 ♘d3! ♗xc3 6 dxc3 ♘xe4 (6...♕xe4+ 7 ♗e2 0-0 8 0-0 d6 9 ♗f3 ♕h4 10 g3 ♕h3 11 ♘f4 ± Yusupov) 7 ♗e2 d5 8 0-0 0-0 9 ♘f4 c6 10 c4 dxc4 11 ♗xc4 ♗f5 (11...♘d6?! 12 ♖e1 ± Istratescu-Wijesundara, Manila OL 1992) 12 ♕e2 and White has a slight advantage, Alapin-Alekhine, Karlsbad 1911.

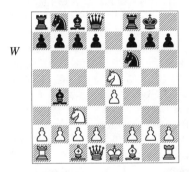

W

5 ♗e2
Or:
   a) 5 ♘f3 ♗xc3 (5...♖e8!? 6 ♗e2! {6 d3?! d5 ∓} 6...♘xe4 7 ♘xe4 ♖xe4 8 c3 ♗f8 =) 6 dxc3 ♘xe4 7 ♗d3 d5 8 h3 ♘c6 9 0-0 ♗f5 = Perlis-A.Rabino-vich, Karlsbad 1911.
   b) 5 ♘d3 ♗xc3 6 dxc3 ♘xe4 7 ♗e2 (7 ♗e3 d6 8 ♕f3 ♖e8 9 0-0-0 ♘d7 10 h3 b6 11 ♕f4 ♗b7 12 f3 ♘g3 with equality, Mainka-Michaelsen, Bad Wörishofen 1992; 7 ♘f4 ♖e8 8 ♗e2 – 5 ♗e2 ♖e8 6 ♘d3 ♗xc3 7 dxc3 ♘xe4 8 ♘f4) 7...d5 8 0-0 and then:

b1) 8...♗f5 9 ♗e3 (9 ♘f4!? c6 10 c4 ∞) 9...♘d7 10 f3 ♘d6 11 ♖e1 ♖e8 = Nimzowitsch-Spielmann, Baden-Baden 1925.
   b2) 8...♘d7 9 ♘f4 c6 10 c4 dxc4 11 ♗xc4 ♘e5 12 ♕xd8 ♖xd8 13 ♗e2 ♗f5 14 g4! ♗c8 15 f3 ♘d6 16 ♖d1 ± Alapin-A.Rabinovich, Karlsbad 1911.
   b3) 8...c6 9 ♘f4 and here:
   b31) 9...♖e8 – 5 ♗e2 ♖e8 6 ♘d3 ♗xc3 7 dxc3 ♘xe4 8 0-0 d5 9 ♘f4 c6.
   b32) 9...♗f5 10 ♗e3 (10 c4!?) 10...♘d6 11 ♖e1 ♘d7 12 ♗f1 ♖e8 13 b3 ♘f6 (13...♘e4 14 c4 ±) 14 f3 ♕c7 15 ♕d2 ♖ad8 16 ♗d4 ± Kreuzer-Navratil, Budapest 1992.
   b33) 9...♘d6 10 ♔h1 ♘d7 11 g4 b6 12 f3 ♖e8 13 ♘g2 ♗b7 14 ♗f4 ♘c5 15 ♕d2 ♕d7 16 ♖ae1 ♖ad8 17 b3 ♘e6 18 ♗g3 c5 ∞ Ye Jiangchuan-Ye Rongguang, Shenzhen 1992.
   5...♖e8 (D)
If 5...d6, then:
   a) 6 ♘c4 ♗xc3 7 dxc3 ♘xe4 =.
   b) 6 ♘f3!? ♗xc3 7 dxc3 ♘xe4 8 0-0 ♘d7 9 ♖e1 ♘df6 10 ♗d3 ♘c5 11 ♗g5 h6 12 ♗h4 ♗g4 13 h3 ♘xd3 14 ♕xd3 ± Janowski-Pillsbury, London 1899.
   c) 6 ♘d3 ♗xc3 7 dxc3 ♘xe4 8 0-0 and then:
   c1) 8...♘c6 9 ♘f4 (9 f3!? ♘f6 10 ♗g5 M.Pavlović) 9...♘f6 10 c4 ♗f5 11 b3 ♘b4 (11...♘e7 12 ♗b2 ♘g6 {M.Pavlović} 13 ♘d5 ±) 12 a3 ♘c6 (12...♘xc2 13 ♖a2 ±) 13 ♗b2 ♖e8 14 f3 ± Svidler-Delanoy, Groningen 1990.
   c2) 8...♖e8 9 ♘f4 and here:
   c21) 9...♘c6 10 ♘d5 (10 ♗e3 ♗f5 11 ♖e1 h6 12 ♗f1 intending f3 ±; 10 c4 a5 11 ♘d5 ♘c5?! {11...♗e6!?} 12

b3 ± Marciano-Mirallès, Montpelier 1991) 10...♘e5 11 f3 ♘c5 12 b4 ± intending f4, Golubev-Meiers, Biel 1992.

c22) 9...♘d7 10 ♗e3 (10 ♗d3 ♘dc5 11 ♕f3 ♗d7 12 c4 ♘g5 13 ♕h5 ♘xd3 = Spielmann-A.Rabinovich, Karlsbad 1911; 10 ♖e1 ♘df6 11 ♗e3 ♗f5 12 a4 {12 c4 ±/=} 12...d5 = Ka.Müller-Schulte, Bundesliga 1989/90) 10...♘e5 (10...♘df6 11 c4 ♗f5 12 ♖e1 ± intending ♗f1 and f3) 11 f3 ♘f6 12 ♗f2 ± Tarrasch-Grünfeld, Vienna 1922.

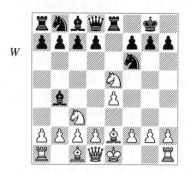

6 ♘d3

It is easy for Black to equalize after other moves:

a) 6 ♘f3 ♗xc3 (6...♘xe4 =) 7 dxc3 (7 bxc3 ♘xe4 8 0-0 d5 =) 7...♘xe4 8 0-0 d6 (8...d5 9 c4 ±) 9 ♖e1!? ♘d7 10 ♗c4 ♘df6 11 ♘g5 ♘xg5 12 ♗xg5 ♖xe1+ 13 ♕xe1 ♗f5 =.

b) 6 ♘c4 ♘xe4 (6...♗xc3 7 dxc3 ♘xe4 8 ♘e3 d6 9 0-0 ♘c6 {9...♘d7 10 ♕d4 ±} 10 ♘d5 ♗f5 ∞) 7 ♘xe4 ♖xe4 8 c3 and now:

b1) 8...d5!? 9 d3 (9 ♘e3 ♗f8 10 d4 ♖e8 =) 9...♖e8 10 cxb4 dxc4 11 dxc4 ♕e7 12 b5 (12 a3 ♕e4 ∞) 12...♕e4 13 ♔f1 ♗h3 14 ♖g1 ±.

b2) 8...♗f8 9 d4 ♖e8 10 ♗f4 d5 11 ♘e3 (11 ♘e5 ♘d7 and now both 12 0-0 ♗d6 and 12 ♘d3 c5 are equal) 11...c6 12 ♗d3 ♗e6 13 ♕h5 (13 0-0 ♘d7 =; 13 ♕c2!? leads to unclear play after 13...h6 or 13...g6 14 h4) 13...g6 14 ♕f3?! (better is 14 ♕e2) 14...c5! 15 dxc5 (15 ♗b5 ♘c6 ∓) 15...d4! 16 cxd4 ♕xd4 17 ♖d1 ♕b4+ 18 ♔f1 (18 ♖d2 ♗xa2 ∓) 18...♘c6 ∓ Reinderman-Alterman, Tilburg 1994.

6...♗xc3 7 dxc3 ♘xe4 8 ♘f4

Or 8 0-0, and now:

a) 8...♘c6 9 ♖e1 (9 ♘f4!?; 9 c4!?; 9 f3 ♘d6!? 10 ♖e1 ♘f5 11 ♗f1 d6 12 ♗g5 ♖xe1 13 ♕xe1 ♕f8 = Taborov-Yusupov, Baku 1979) 9...d6 10 ♗f1 ♗f5 11 f3 ♘f6 12 ♗g5 ♘e5 13 ♕d2 ± Shtyrenkov-Tolstykh, Katowice 1993.

b) 8...d6 9 f3!? (9 ♘f4 – 8 ♘f4 d6 9 0-0 ±) 9...♘f6 10 ♗g5 h6 11 ♗h4 ♘bd7 12 c4 ♘f8 13 ♕d2 ± Ostermeyer-Schulte, Bundesliga 1989/90.

c) 8...d5 and then:

c1) 9 ♗e3 c6 (9...♘d7 10 ♘f4 ♘df6 11 c4 dxc4 12 ♕xd8 ♖xd8 13 ♗xc4 ♘d6 and now White should prefer 14 ♗b3 ± to 14 ♗d3?! ♗f5 15 ♖ad1 ♗xd3 16 ♖xd3 ♘f5 17 ♖fd1 ♖xd3 18 ♖xd3 ♖e8 = Maroczy-Pillsbury, Vienna 1898) gives White a choice between 10 ♖e1!?, intending ♗f1 and f3, and 10 ♘f4 – 9 ♘f4 c6 10 ♗e3.

c2) 9 ♘f4 c6 (9...♘f6!? deserves attention: 10 ♗e3 {intending to play c4} 10...♘c6 11 ♗f3 ♗e6 12 ♘xe6 ♖xe6 13 ♗f4 ♕e7 14 ♖e1 ♘e5 = Torre-Borik, Bochum 1981) and here:

c21) 10 ♕d4!? ♕f6 11 f3 ♕xd4+ 12 cxd4 ♘d6 13 ♔f2 ± Polovodin-Glianets, Leningrad 1981.

c22) 10 ♗e3 ♘d6! (10...♘d7?! 11 c4 dxc4 12 ♗xc4 ♘e5 13 ♕xd8 ♖xd8 14 ♗e2 ♗f5 15 g4! ♗d7 16 f3 ♘f6 17 ♖ad1 ♘g6 18 ♘xg6 hxg6 19 c4 ♗e6 20 b3 ± S.Popov-Onishchuk, Leningrad jr tt 1991) 11 ♗d3 (11 ♖e1 ♘d7 12 ♘h5 ♘f8 13 ♗f1 ♗f5 14 b3 ♗g6 15 ♘f4 = Heidrich-K.Lehmann, Bundesliga 1985/6) 11...♗f5 12 ♕h5 g6 13 ♕h6 ♗xd3 14 cxd3 ♘f5 15 ♕h3 ♘d7 16 ♖ae1 ♕f6 17 ♗d2 ♘e5 18 d4 ♘c4 19 ♗c1 ♖e4 20 ♖xe4 dxe4 21 ♖e1 ♖e8 22 ♘d3 h5 23 ♘c5 ♘cd6 24 ♗f4 b6 25 ♗xd6 ♘xd6 26 ♘d7 ♕e6 ½-½ Benjamin-Yusupov, Munich 1994.

c23) 10 c4 d4 11 ♗f3 (11 ♖e1 ♘a6 12 ♘d3 ♗f5 =) 11...♘g5 (11...♘a6 12 c3 ±) 12 ♗g4 ♘e6 (12...♘a6!? 13 ♗xc8 ♖xc8 =) 13 ♖e1 and then:

c231) 13...♘xf4 14 ♖xe8+ (but not 14 ♗xc8? ♖xe1+ 15 ♕xe1 ♘xg2 ∓) 14...♕xe8 15 ♗xc8 ♘e2+ 16 ♔h1 ♕xc8 17 ♕xe2 ±.

c232) 13...♘a6 14 ♗xe6 ♗xe6 15 ♘xe6 ♖xe6 16 ♖xe6 fxe6 17 ♗d2 ♕f6 18 ♕e2 ♕f5 19 c3 d3 20 ♕e3 ♘c5 21 ♖e1 ♖d8 22 f3 b6 23 b3 (23 b4 ♘a4 24 ♕xe6+ ♕xe6 25 ♖xe6 ♔f7!? 26 ♖xc6!? {26 ♖e4 ♘xc3 27 ♗xc3 d2 28 ♗xd2 ♖xd2 29 a4 ♖a2 =} 26...♖e8 27 ♖d6 ♘b2 gives Black compensation according to Dolmatov, but 28 c5 may favour White) 23...h6 24 ♔f1 ± Adams-Hübner, Dortmund 1996.

We now return to 8 ♘f4 *(D)*:

8...d6

White is better after 8...c6 9 c4 d6 10 0-0 ♗f5 11 a4! (intending ♖a3) 11...a5 12 ♖a3 ♘d7 13 ♗e3 ♘dc5 14 g4! ♗e6 15 f3 ♘f6 16 ♕d4 (16 b3 h6 17 ♕d4 ± Psakhis-Yusupov, USSR Ch

(Vilnius) 1980/1) 16...♕c7 17 b3 h6 18 ♗b2 ♖ad8 19 ♖f2! ± Õim-Pililian, corr. 1982-3.

9 0-0 ♘d7

If 9...♘c6, then:

a) 10 ♗e3 ♗f5 11 ♖e1 h6 (Bastian-G.Röder, Bundesliga 1985/6) 12 ♗f1!? ± intending f3.

b) 10 c4!? a5 11 a4 (intending ♖a3-e3) 11...b6 12 ♖a3 ♗b7 13 ♖h3 ♘e5 14 ♘d5 ♘c5 (14...c6 15 ♘c3 ♘xc3 16 ♖xc3 ♕c7 17 b3 ♖ad8 18 ♖e3 ♖e6 19 f4 ♘g6 20 ♖xe6 fxe6 21 f5 ±) 15 b3 ♘g6 16 ♗g4 ♗c8 17 ♗b2 ♘e4 18 ♖e3 c6?! 19 ♕d4! ♖e5 20 ♗xc8 cxd5 (20...♖xc8 21 f4! cxd5 22 fxe5 dxe5 23 ♕xd5 ♕xd5 24 cxd5 ♖xc2 25 ♗xe5 ♘xe5 26 ♖xe4 +−) 21 ♗b7 +− Shabalov-Gawehns, Bonn 1994.

10 c4

10 f3!? deserves attention:

a) 10...♘ec5!? 11 c4 a5 (11...♘f8 12 b3 ♕f6 13 ♖b1 ±) 12 b3 ♕f6 (or 12...a4 13 ♗b2 ±) 13 ♖b1 c6 gives White a pleasant choice between 14 g3!? ± and 14 ♘h5!?.

b) 10...♘ef6 11 c4 ♘f8 12 b3 ♕e7 13 ♖f2 ♕e5 14 ♖b1 ♗d7 and then:

b1) 15 ♘d3 ♕e7 16 ♗b2 ♕e3! (alternatively, 16...♘g6 17 ♕d2 ♕e3 18

♕c3 ±) 17 ♘b4 (17 ♕f1 ♘g6 18 ♖e1 ♕b6 =) 17...a5 18 ♘d5 ♘xd5 19 cxd5 ± Shirov-Akopian, Linares 1995.

b2) 15 ♘d5 ♘xd5 16 cxd5 ±.

10...a5

Or:

a) 10...c6!? 11 ♗e3!? (11 f3?? ♕b6+ −+) 11...♘dc5 12 ♖e1 ♕f6 13 c3 ♗d7 14 ♕d4 ±.

b) 10...♘df6 11 f3 ♘c5 12 b3 ♕e7 13 ♖f2 ♕e5 14 ♖b1 ♗d7 15 ♗f1 (15 g3!?) 15...♘e6 16 ♘d3 ♕h5 17 ♗b2 (17 ♘b4? ♘e4!) 17...a5 18 ♕d2 ♗c6 and now 19 ♖e1!? ± is an improvement over 19 ♗xf6?! gxf6 20 ♕c3 ♕h6 21 ♖e1 b6 22 f4 f5 23 ♖e3 ♘f8 24 ♖fe2 ♖e6 is equal, Nijboer-Piket, Dutch Ch 1994.

11 f3 ♘ec5 12 b3 ♕f6 13 ♖b1 c6 14 ♘h5!

14 g3!? ±.

14...♕g6 15 ♘g3

White has a slight advantage, Shirov-Yusupov, Bundesliga 1994/5.

C)

3 d3

White chooses to play a Philidor Defence with a tempo in hand. However, as so often happens when a passive opening is played with an extra tempo, the free move doesn't change the essential characteristics of the position. It may make it easier to equalize, but one move won't change an opening like the Philidor into an aggressive attacking system. Therefore this move is totally harmless and presents Black with no problems.

3...♘c6 4 g3

Other possibilities:

a) 4 ♘bd2 g6 5 c3 d5 6 b4 a6 7 ♗b2 ♗g7 8 a3 0-0 9 ♕c2 ♖e8 with an equal position, Planinc-Garcia Martinez, Portorož/Ljubljana 1975.

b) 4 c3 d5 5 ♘bd2 a5!? (5...g6 − 4 ♘bd2 g6 5 c3 d5) 6 ♗e2 g6!? 7 b3! (7 0-0 ♗g7 ∓) 7...♗g7! 8 ♗a3 ♘h5! 9 0-0 (9 g3 ♗h3 ∞) 9...♘f4 10 ♖e1 ♘xe2+ 11 ♕xe2 ♗e6 (11...d4!? 12 cxd4 exd4 13 ♖ac1 ♘b4 =) 12 exd5 (12 ♖ad1? d4 ∓) 12...♕xd5 13 c4! ♕d7 14 ♗b2 and here:

b1) 14...0-0-0 15 ♗xe5! (15 ♘xe5? ♗xe5! 16 ♗xe5 ♗g4 ∓) 15...♘xe5 16 ♘xe5 ♕d6 17 ♘df3 ♖he8 18 d4 f6 19 ♘d3 ♗g4? 20 ♕xe8!.

b2) 14...♗g4! 15 d4!? (15 h3 ♗xf3 16 ♘xf3 0-0-0 ∓ with the point 17 ♘xe5 ♘xe5 18 ♗xe5 ♖he8 19 ♕b2 ♖xe5 20 ♖xe5 ♕xd3) 15...0-0-0 16 dxe5 ♖he8 ∞ Morozevich-Makarychev, Moscow 1992.

4...d5

Black has another plan at his disposal: 4...♗c5 5 ♗g2 d6 6 ♘c3, transposing to a line of the Four Knights.

5 ♘bd2

White has also tried 5 exd5 ♘xd5 6 ♗g2 g6 (6...♗d6!? 7 0-0 0-0 8 ♘c3?! {8 ♘bd2!?} 8...♘xc3 9 bxc3 ♗g4 10 h3 ♗h5 11 ♗d2 f6 ∓ Seret – Santo-Roman, France 1990) 7 0-0 ♗g7 8 ♖e1 0-0 9 ♘bd2 ♖e8 10 ♘c4 ♘b6! 11 ♗g5 f6 12 ♘xb6 axb6 13 ♗d2 ♗e6 = Zaichik-Bagirov, Tallinn rpd 1988.

5...♗e7 6 ♗g2 0-0 7 0-0 ♗e6 8 ♖e1 dxe4 9 dxe4 a5 10 ♕e2

10 a4!? =.

10...a4 11 c3 ♗c5 12 ♘c4 ♘g4 13 ♘e3 ♘xe3 14 ♗xe3 ♗xe3 15 ♕xe3 f6

= Haas-Flear, Mondorf 1991.

2 3 d4 without 3...♘xe4

1 e4 e5 2 ♘f3 ♘f6 3 d4 *(D)*

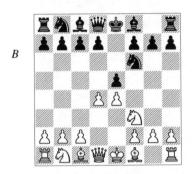

B

Black must now choose between two main continuations.

3...exd4

The most popular move is 3...♘xe4, which is considered in Chapters 3-5.

At one time, 3...exd4 was quite a popular continuation. It very often leads to the liquidation of all the central pawns, when the resulting open files and symmetrical pawn-structure might seem to foretell an early draw. However, the defect of the move is that it affords White a significant lead in development. It turns out that it is not easy for Black to complete his development and execute his plan of a general liquidation in the face of the pressure exerted by White's active pieces. In most cases Black is forced to make some sort of concession in order to complete his development. This concession can take many forms. In some lines where Black plays ...♗d6 or ...♗e6, White is able to inflict a central isolated pawn on Black by exchanging one of these bishops; in other variations White is able to break up Black's queenside pawn-structure by playing ♗b5 and then taking a knight on c6; in yet others White gains the bishop-pair, which is a significant plus in such an open position. In any case, Black is left with a permanent positional weakness, which may indeed become more pronounced if a liquidation to an endgame occurs. Few players are happy with the idea of voluntarily accepting a long-term positional weakness without compensation, and so the popularity of 3...exd4 has severely declined in recent years.

There are a few less common moves:

a) 3...♗e7?! 4 dxe5 ♘xe4 5 ♕d5 (5 ♗c4 ±) 5...♘c5 6 ♘c3 ♘c6 7 ♗f4 ±/±.

b) 3...d6 transposes to a line of the Philidor Defence.

c) 3...d5 is an aggressive and little-explored continuation:

c1) 4 ♘xe5 ♘xe4 5 ♗d3 – *3...♘xe4 4 ♗d3 d5 5 ♘xe5.*

c2) 4 ♗g5!? dxe5 5 ♘xe5 ♗e7 6 ♗c4 0-0 7 0-0 ♘fd7 and now White has a choice:

c21) 8 ♗xe7 ♕xe7 9 ♖e1 ♘xe5 10 ♖xe4 ♖d8 (10...♕b4 11 dxe5 ∞) 11 ♕e1 ∞.

c22) 8 ♗f4 ♘xe5 9 dxe5 ♕xd1 10 ♖xd1 ♗e6 11 ♗b3 (11 ♗xe6!? fxe6 12 ♗g3 ±) 11...♗xb3 12 axb3 f5 13 ♘c3 ♔f7 14 ♘b5 ♘a6 15 e6+ (15 ♖d7!? might be a better try) 15...♔f6! (15...♔xe6?! 16 ♖xa6+ bxa6 17 ♘xc7+ ♔f7 18 ♘xa8 ♖xa8 19 ♖d7 ±) 16 ♗d2 c5 17 ♗c3+ ♔xe6 18 ♗xg7 ♖fd8 = Smirin-Akopian, Vilnius 1988.

c3) 4 exd5 exd4 (4...e4?! 5 ♘e5 ♘xd5 6 ♗c4 ±) 5 ♗b5+ c6 (5...♗d7 6 ♘xd4 ♘xd5 7 0-0 ♗e7 8 ♗xd7+ ♕xd7 {8...♘xd7? 9 ♘f5 ±} 9 ♕f3 0-0 10 ♖d1 ±) 6 dxc6 and then:

c31) 6...♕a5+ 7 ♘c3 bxc6 8 ♘xd4 cxb5 9 ♕f3 ♕c7 10 ♗f4 ♕b7 11 ♘cxb5 ♘a6 12 ♕e2+ ♕e4 13 ♕xe4+ ♘xe4 14 0-0-0 ♗e6 (14...f5!?) 15 ♖he1 ± Lepsenyi-Butler, corr. 1964.

c32) 6...bxc6 7 ♗e2 ♗c5 8 c3 dxc3 9 ♕xd8+ ♔xd8 10 ♘xc3 ♔e7 11 0-0 ♖d8 12 ♖e1 ♔f8 13 ♗f4 ± Stein-Bronstein, USSR Ch (Tbilisi) 1966/7.

4 e5 ♘e4 *(D)*

Instead, both 4...♕e7?! 5 ♗e2 ± and 4...♘d5?! 5 ♕xd4 ♘b6 6 ♘c3 ± are bad for Black.

5 ♕xd4

This is the main continuation. However, White has also tried other moves:

a) 5 ♘xd4 d5 6 ♗f4 ♗c5 =.

b) 5 ♗d3 d5 (5...♘c5!? 6 ♗c4 d5 =) 6 ♘xd4 c5 7 ♗e2 ♘c6 8 f3 ♘g5 9 f4 ♘e6 10 0-0 (Morphy-Löwenthal, London 1858) 10...c4 11 ♗f5 ♗c5+ 12 ♔h1 0-0 =.

c) 5 ♗b5 is a tricky move that Black should certainly be aware of:

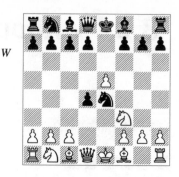

c1) 5...♘c6 transposes to a line of the Ruy Lopez.

c2) 5...♗b4+ 6 c3 (6 ♔f1!? has the point that 6...♘c6?! is met by 7 ♕e2 ±) 6...dxc3 7 0-0 ♗e7 8 ♖e1 ♘c5 9 ♘xc3 c6 10 ♗c4 b5 (10...0-0 11 ♗f4 and White has compensation) 11 ♗f1 0-0 12 ♗f4 gives White compensation.

c3) 5...a6!? is a new move that I am recommending:

c31) 6 ♗a4 b5 7 ♗b3 (7 ♕xd4 ♗b7 intending ...♗c5) 7...♗b7 8 0-0 and now Black can choose between 8...c5 ∓ and 8...♗c5 ∓.

c32) 6 ♕xd4 ♘xf2 (6...♘c5 7 ♗c4 ±/±; 6...axb5 7 ♕xe4 ♗e7 {7...♖a4?! 8 ♕d3 ±} 8 ♘c3 b4 9 ♘d5 ♘c6 10 ♗f4 ±) 7 ♗c4 ♘xh1 ∞.

c4) 5...c6 6 ♕xd4 and here:

c41) 6...♘c5 7 ♗c4 and then:

c411) 7...b5 8 ♗b3 ♗e7 (8...a5!?) 9 ♕g4 g6 10 ♕f4 ♘xb3 (10...d5 11 exd6 ♘xb3 12 axb3 ♕xd6 13 ♘c3 ♗f5 14 0-0 ♕xf4 15 ♗xf4 ♗xc2 16 ♖fe1 gives White compensation) 11 axb3 d6!? (11...0-0?! 12 ♕h6 f6 13 h4 ♖f7 14 h5 ♗f8 15 hxg6!! ♗xh6 16 gxf7+ ♔xf7 17 ♖xh6 fxe5 18 ♘c3 d5 19 ♗g5 ± Jansa-Kolarov, Luhačovice 1971) 12 ♘c3 (12 ♕h6 dxe5 13 ♘xe5

♗f6 ∞) 12...0-0 13 ♘e4 dxe5 14 ♕xe5 ♘d7 ∞.

c412) 7...♘e6 8 ♕e4 ♘a6 (8...d5?! 9 exd6 ♗xd6 10 ♘g5 ±) 9 ♗xa6 (9 0-0 ♘ac5 10 ♕e2 a5 11 ♘c3 d5 12 exd6 ♗xd6 13 ♘e4 0-0 14 ♘xd6 ♕xd6 15 ♖d1 ♕c7 16 ♗e3 {16 a4!?} 16...b5 17 ♗xe6 ♘xe6 18 c4 ♗a6 = Jansa-Kholmov, Moscow-Prague 1968) 9...♕a5+ 10 ♘bd2 ♕xa6 11 ♘c4 ±.

c42) 6...♕a5+ 7 c3 ♘xf2 and now:

c421) 8 0-0?! ♘h3+ 9 gxh3 ♕xb5 gives Black a clear advantage.

c422) 8 ♗c4? ♘xh1 (8...♗c5?! 9 ♕f4 d5 10 exd6 ♗e6 11 b4! {11 ♖f1?! ♗b6 12 b4 ♕d5 13 ♗xd5 ♘d3+ 14 ♔d1 ♘xf4 15 ♗xc6+ ♘xc6 16 ♗xf4 =} 11...♗xc4 12 ♕e5+ ♗e6 13 ♕xg7 ♘d3+ 14 ♔d2 ♘xb4 15 ♕xh8+ ♔d7 is unclear, Kuijf-Hartoch, Wijk aan Zee 1984) 9 ♘g5 (9 ♕f4 d5 10 exd6 ♕f5 and Black has a winning position) 9...♗c5 ∓.

c423) 8 ♕xf2 ♕xb5 9 a4 ♕d5 10 ♗e3 ♗e7 (10...d6?! 11 0-0 h6 12 ♘a3 dxe5 13 ♖ad1 ♕b3 14 ♘c4! ± Kosten-Mirallès, France 1988) 11 0-0 0-0 12 ♘a3 gives White compensation.

d) 5 ♕e2 *(D)* and now Black has two possible ideas:

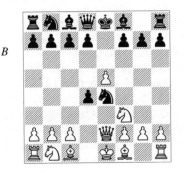

B

d1) 5...♗b4+ and then:

d11) 6 ♘bd2 ♘xd2 7 ♗xd2 ♕e7 8 0-0-0 ♘c6 9 ♗xb4 (9 ♗g5 ♕e6 10 ♔b1 ♗c5 11 ♕b5 b6 12 ♗c4 a6 13 ♕b3 ♕g6 14 h4 ♘a5 15 h5 ♕f5 ∞ Grechikhin-Nikitin, USSR 1964) 9...♕xb4 10 ♕e4 b6 11 ♘xd4 ♗b7 12 ♗b5 0-0-0 13 a3 ♘xd4 14 axb4 ♘b3+ 15 cxb3 ♗xe4 = An.Rodriguez-Ginzburg, San Martin 1995.

d12) 6 ♔d1 d5 7 exd6 f5 and here:

d121) 8 dxc7 ♕xc7 9 ♘xd4 ♘c6 10 ♘xc6 (10 c3 ♘xd4 11 cxd4 ♕d6 12 f3 ♕xd4+ 13 ♘d2 ♗xd2 14 ♗xd2 ♕xd2+ 15 ♕xd2 ♘xd2 16 ♔xd2 is equal, Steinitz-Pillsbury, St Petersburg 1895/6) 10...bxc6 11 c3 ♗e7 gives Black compensation.

d122) 8 ♘g5 0-0 9 ♕c4+ ♔h8 10 ♘xe4 (10 ♕xb4?! ♘c6 11 ♘a3 ♘xf2+ 12 ♔e1 ♘xh1 13 dxc7 ♕e8+ 14 ♗e2 f4 15 ♔f1 ♗d7 16 ♘d2 ♘e5 17 ♘df3 ♘g4 18 ♗d3, Steinitz-Pillsbury, St Petersburg 1895/6, 18...h6 ∓ Polugaevsky) 10...fxe4 11 dxc7 (11 ♕xb4?! ♗g4+ 12 ♗e2 ♗xe2+ 13 ♔xe2 ♘c6 14 ♕e1 ♕xd6 gives Black compensation) 11...♗g4+ (11...♕e7 ∞; 11...♕f6 12 cxb8♕ ♕xf2? and now 13 ♗e2? ♖xb8 14 ♕xb4 d3 15 cxd3 exd3 16 ♗xd3 ♖d8 gave Black compensation in Kharus-D.Gurevich, USSR 1975, but 13 ♕g3! +− makes better use of the extra queen) 12 ♗e2 ♗xe2+ 13 ♔xe2 ♕h4 14 c8♕ ♘c6!? 15 ♕h3 (15 ♕xa8!? ±) 15...♕xf2+ 16 ♔d1 d3 17 cxd3 ♘d4 ∞ Yusupov.

d2) 5...♘c5 6 ♘xd4 ♘c6 and now:

d21) 7 ♘f5 g6 8 ♘h6 ♕e7 ∞.

d22) 7 ♘xc6 dxc6 (7...bxc6?! 8 ♘c3 {8 ♗e3 ♕h4 9 ♕c4 ±} 8...♖b8 9

f4! ♗e7 10 ♕f2 d5 11 ♗e3 ♘d7 12
0-0-0 0-0 13 g4! ♗b4 14 ♘e2 ±
Fischer-German, Stockholm IZ 1962)
8 ♘c3 ♗f5 9 g3 ♘e6 10 ♗e3 ♘d4 11
♗xd4 ♕xd4 12 a3 ♗g4 13 f3 ♗e6 14
f4 ♗e7 15 ♕e4 ♗c5 = Tal-Szabo, Havana OL 1966.

d23) 7 ♗e3 ♘xd4 8 ♗xd4 and now:

d231) 8...♕h4!? 9 ♗e3 ♕b4+ 10
c3 ♕e4 11 f4 d5 12 ♘d2 ♕g6 13 ♘f3
c6 14 0-0-0 ♗e7 15 ♖g1 h5 16 ♕f2
♘e4 17 ♕c2 b5 18 ♗d3 f5 (18...a6!?
intending ...c5) 19 exf6 ♗xf6 20 ♗c5
∞ Tal-Kholmov, USSR Ch (Alma-Ata)
1968/9.

d232) 8...♘e6 9 ♗c3 d5 10 exd6
♕xd6 (10...♗xd6?! 11 ♗xg7 ♖g8 12
♗c3 ♗d7 13 ♘d2 ♗c6 14 ♘e4 ±
Barcza-Calvo, Havana OL 1966) 11
♘d2 ♗d7 12 0-0-0 (12 ♘c4!? and
now 12...♕a6 ∞ should be preferred
over 12...♕f4?! 13 g3 ±) 12...0-0-0 13
♘c4 ♕f4+ 14 ♗d2 ♕f6 =.

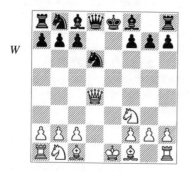

5...d5 6 exd6 ♘xd6 (D)
Now:
A: 7 ♗d3   21
B: 7 ♘c3   24

White has some alternatives:

a) 7 ♗f4 ♘c6 8 ♕d2 (8 ♕e3+ ♕e7
9 ♘c3 ♕xe3+ 10 ♗xe3 ♗g4 11 ♘d4
♘xd4 12 ♗xd4 ♘f5 = Hübner-Timman, Tilburg 1986) and now:

a1) 8...♕e7+!? leads to unclear
play: 9 ♗e2 ♘e4 10 ♕e3 ♘b4 11 ♕c1
♕c5 12 0-0 ♗e6 (12...♘xc2?! 13 ♘c3
♘xc3 14 ♕xc2 ♘xe2+ 15 ♕xe2+ ♕e7
16 ♕c2 ♗e6 17 ♖fe1 ♕c5 18 ♕e4
♗d6 19 ♖ac1 ♕b4 20 ♘d4 ± Schmidt-
Kinzel, Siegen OL 1970) 13 c4 is unclear.

a2) 8...♗g4 9 ♘c3 ♕e7+ 10 ♕e3 =
Sznapik-Smyslov, Berlin 1979.

b) 7 ♗g5 and now two moves deserve attention:

b1) 7...♘c6 8 ♕e3+ ♗e7 9 ♘c3
♘f5 (9...0-0 10 0-0-0 ♗xg5 11 ♘xg5
♗f5 12 ♕f4 ♕d7 13 ♘ge4 ± Konstantinopolsky-Rauzer, corr. 1934-5) 10
♗xe7 ♘cxe7 (10...♕xe7?! 11 ♕xe7+
♘cxe7 12 ♘b5 ±) 11 ♕e5 0-0 12 ♖d1
♘d6 13 ♗d3 ♘g6 14 ♕g3 and then:

b11) 14...♕e7+!? 15 ♔d2 (15 ♔f1!?)
15...♘f5 16 ♗xf5 ♗xf5 17 ♔c1 ♖ad8
18 ♘d4 ± Konstantinopolsky-Smyslov, Sverdlovsk 1943.

b12) 14...♖e8+ 15 ♔f1 (15 ♔d2
♕f6! ∞) 15...♗e6 (15...♕f6? 16 ♘d5
♕xb2 17 ♘xc7 ±) 16 h4 ♕f6 17 h5
♘f4 ∞.

b2) 7...f6 8 ♗f4 and here:

b21) 8...♘c6 9 ♕e3+ (9 ♕d2 ♗f5
10 ♗e2 ♕e7 11 0-0 0-0-0 12 ♖e1 and
now Black should play 12...♕f7! ∞,
intending ...g5, rather than 12...♘e4?!
13 ♕c1 g5 14 ♗d3 ♗h6 15 ♗d2 ±)
9...♕e7 10 ♕xe7+ (10 ♘c3 ♗g4 11
♗e2 ♕xe3 12 ♗xe3 ♘f5 13 ♘d5
0-0-0 14 0-0-0 ♘xe3 15 ♘xe3 ♗d7 16
♗d3 ♗c5 ∓ Stoltz-Alekhine, Munich

1941) 10...♗xe7 11 ♘c3 ♗f5 12 0-0-0 0-0-0 13 ♘d4 ♘xd4 14 ♖xd4 ♘f7 15 ♖xd8+ ♖xd8 16 ♗e2 ♗d6 17 ♗g3 ♘g5 18 ♖d1 ½-½ Spielmann-Marshall, Baden-Baden 1925.

b22) 8...♕e7+!? 9 ♗e2 ♘c6 10 ♕a4 ♗d7 (10...g5?! 11 ♗xd6 ♕xd6 12 ♘c3 ♕b4 13 ♕b5 ♗d7 is best met by Romanishin's 14 h4! ±, rather than 14 0-0-0?! ♕xb5 15 ♗xb5 0-0-0 16 ♘d5 g4 17 ♘d2 f5 18 ♖he1 a6 19 ♗d3 ♘b4 = Romanishin-Smyslov, Lvov 1978) 11 0-0 (11 ♘c3 ♘e5) 11...♕xe2! 12 ♖e1 ♘e5 13 ♕xd7+ ♔xd7 14 ♖xe2 ♘xf3+ 15 gxf3 ♘f5 16 ♘c3 ♗d6 =/∓.

A)

7 ♗d3 (D)

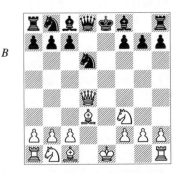

At one time this was considered the main line, but now 7 ♘c3 is thought to cause Black more problems. However, even against 7 ♗d3 Black does not have an easy time achieving equality.

7...♘c6

Or:

a) Black should avoid 7...♗f5?! 8 0-0 ♗xd3 9 cxd3 ±.

b) 7...♕e7+ is also inadvisable, in view of 8 ♗e3:

b1) 8...♘f5?! 9 ♗xf5 ♗xf5 10 ♘c3 is much better for White, Bonch-Osmolovsky – Baranov, Moscow 1954.

b2) 8...♗f5 9 ♘c3 ♘c6 10 ♕f4 ♗xd3 11 cxd3 ♕e6 (11...♕d7 12 ♘e5! ♘xe5 13 ♕xe5+ ♕e6 14 ♕a5 b6 15 ♕a4+ ♕d7 16 ♕d4 ± Suetin-Mikenas, USSR 1959) 12 0-0-0 ♗e7 13 d4 ♕f5 14 d5 ♘b8 15 ♕xf5 ♘xf5 16 ♗f4 ♘a6 17 g4 ♘h4 18 ♘xh4 ♗xh4 19 d6! ± Spassky-Kholmov, USSR 1960.

b3) 8...♘c6 9 ♕f4 and then:

b31) 9...f6? 10 ♘c3 ♗e6 11 0-0-0 0-0-0 12 ♕a4 ♔b8 13 ♗c5 ♕f7 14 ♘d4 ♘c8 15 ♘xc6+ bxc6 16 ♗a6 ♗d7 17 ♖xd7 ♕xd7 18 ♖d1 ♘d6 19 ♗b7! 1-0 Bonch-Osmolovsky – Kamyshev, USSR 1949.

b32) 9...h6!? 10 ♘c3 ♗e6 11 0-0 g5 12 ♕a4 ♗g7 13 ♗d4 (13 ♘d4!?) 13...0-0 14 ♗xg7 ♔xg7 15 ♖ae1 ♕f6 = Pavlov-Breazu, Romania 1959.

b33) 9...g6 10 ♘c3 ♗e6 (10...♗g7 11 0-0 ♗e6 12 ♖fe1 0-0 13 ♗c5 b6 14 ♗a3 ± Matanović-Kieninger, Hamburg 1955) 11 ♘d4! ♗g7 12 ♘xc6 (12 ♘xe6!?) 12...bxc6 13 ♕a4 (13 0-0 0-0 14 ♗d4 ♖ab8 15 ♗xg7 ♔xg7 16 b3 ♕f6 17 ♕xf6+ ♔xf6 18 ♘a4 is a little better for White, Spassky-Rossetto, Amsterdam 1964) 13...♗d7 14 0-0 0-0 15 ♕a5 ♗f5 16 ♗xf5 ♘xf5 17 ♗c5 ♘d6 18 ♘a4 ♖fc8 19 ♕a6 ± Korchnoi-Averbakh, Sverdlovsk 1957.

8 ♕f4 ♗e7

Or:

a) 8...♕e7+ 9 ♗e3 – 7...♕e7+ 8 ♗e3 ♘c6 9 ♕f4.

b) 8...♗e6 9 ♘c3 (9 ♘g5!?) 9...♕d7 (9...g6 10 ♘d4 ♗g7 11 ♘xe6 fxe6 12 ♘e4 ♘b4 13 ♘f6+ ±) and then:

b1) 10 0-0 0-0-0 11 ♗d2 h6 (11...♗e7 should be compared with 8...♗e7) 12 ♕a4 ♔b8 13 ♗e3 ♕e8 14 ♖ad1 ± Evans-Rossetto, Amsterdam IZ 1964.

b2) 10 ♗e3 ♘f5 (10...♗f5?! 11 0-0-0 ±; 10...0-0-0 11 0-0-0 ±) 11 ♗xf5 ♗xf5 12 ♘e5 ♘xe5 13 ♕xe5+ ♗e6 14 ♘b5 ♗d6 15 ♘xd6+ ♕xd6 16 ♕xd6 cxd6 17 0-0-0 ± Adorjan-Kostro, Wijk aan Zee 1971.

c) 8...g6 (D) and then:

c1) 9 ♗d2?! ♕e7+ 10 ♗e2 (10 ♔d1 ♗g7 11 ♖e1 ♗e6 ∓) and then:

c11) 10...♘e4!? 11 ♘c3 ♘xd2 is at least OK for Black, since 12 0-0-0? (Kotkov-Vistaneckis, Vilnius 1961) fails to 12...♘xf3! 13 ♘d5 ♘fd4!.

c12) 10...♗g7 11 ♘c3 (11 ♘c3 ♗e6 =) 11...0-0 12 ♗xg7 ♔xg7 13 ♘c3 ♗e6 = intending ...♕f6.

c2) 9 0-0 ♗g7 and here:

c21) 10 ♗d2 ♗xb2 (10...♕f6 11 ♕xf6 ♗xf6 12 ♘c3 ♗e6 13 ♘g5 ±; 10...0-0 11 ♗c3 ♗f5 12 ♖d1! ♕e7 13 ♗xg7 ♔xg7 14 ♘c3 ♗e6 15 ♘b5 ± Matsukevich-Chesnauskas, Leningrad 1964) 11 ♗c3 ♗xc3! 12 ♘xc3 0-0! 13 ♖fe1 (13 ♕h6 ♕f6 14 ♘d5 ♕g7 =; 13

♘d5 ♗e6 14 ♕h6 ♗xd5 15 ♘g5 ♖e8 16 ♖ae1 ♕f6 ∓) 13...♔g7 14 ♖ad1 gives White compensation.

c22) 10 ♖e1+ ♗e6 and now:

c221) 11 ♘g5?! is risky owing to 11...0-0! 12 ♘xe6 fxe6, and then:

c2211) 13 ♕g4 ♗d4!? (13...♕f6 14 ♕g3?! ♘b4 15 ♖f1 ♘f5 16 ♕xc7 ♖ac8 17 ♕xb7 ♘xd3 18 cxd3 ♘g3 19 hxg3 ♖xc1 -+ Hübner-Al.Segal, Dresden U-26 Wcht 1969) 14 ♕xe6+ ♔h8 15 ♖f1 (15 ♖e2 ♕h4 16 g3 ♕h5 -+) 15...♖xf2!? 16 ♖xf2 ♗xf2+ 17 ♔xf2 ♕h4+ 18 ♔g1 ♖e8 ∓.

c2212) 13 ♕g3 ♗d4 14 ♖e2 (not 14 ♖f1? ♘e4! 15 ♗xe4 ♗xf2+ -+) 14...♕f6 ∓.

c222) White gains no advantage from 11 ♕a4 0-0 12 ♗g5 ♕d7 13 ♘c3 h6 14 ♗f4 a6 = Milić-Trifunović, Yugoslavia 1958.

c223) 11 ♘c3 0-0 and here:

c2231) 12 ♗e3 ♕f6 13 ♕a4 h6 (intending ...a6 and ...b5) 14 ♗c5 a6 15 ♗xd6 cxd6 =.

c2232) 12 ♗d2 ♗f5 (12...♕f6!? 13 ♕xf6 ♗xf6 14 ♘g5 ♗f5 =) 13 ♗xf5 ♘xf5 14 ♖ad1 ♕d6 15 ♘e4 ♕xf4 16 ♗xf4 ♘cd4 17 ♘xd4 ♘xd4 18 c3 ♘e6 ½-½ Boleslavsky-Trifunović, Zagreb 1958.

c3) 9 ♘c3 ♗g7 10 ♗e3 (10 ♗d2 is unpleasantly met by 10...♕e7+! 11 ♔f1 ♗e6 12 ♖e1 0-0 13 h4 ♕f6 ∓ Yudovich-Gusakov, USSR 1960) 10...♗e6 (D) (10...0-0?! 11 0-0 {11 0-0-0! ♗e6 – 10...♗e6 11 0-0-0! 0-0?! ±} 11...♖e8! 12 ♖ad1 ♘e5 13 ♗b5 ♗d7 14 ♗d4 ♘xf3+ 15 ♕xf3 ♗xd4 16 ♗xd7 ♕xd7 17 ♖xd4 ♕f5 18 ♕xf5 ♘xf5 19 ♖d7 ♖e7 20 ♖xe7 ♘xe7 21 ♖d1 ♔f8 22

♖d7 ♖c8 23 ♘e4 h6 24 h4 ♘g8! = Geller-Smyslov, Biel IZ 1976) and now:

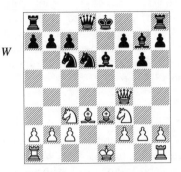

c31) 11 h4?! ♘f5!? 12 ♗c5 ♗xc3+ 13 bxc3 ♕d5 14 ♗a3 ♕a5! 15 ♗b4 ♘xb4 16 cxb4 ♕b6 17 h5 0-0-0! ∞.

c32) 11 ♘d4?! ♘xd4 12 ♗xd4 g5! 13 ♕e3 ♘c4 14 ♗xc4 ♕xd4 15 ♗xe6 ♕xe3+ ∓ M.Mihaljčišin-Trifunović, Yugoslav Ch (Zagreb) 1961.

c33) 11 0-0!? 0-0 (11...♕f6?! 12 ♕a4! ± h6?? 13 ♗d4 +–) and here:

c331) 12 ♖ad1 ♖e8 (12...♕f6 13 ♕xf6 ♗xf6 14 ♘g5 ♘b4 {14...♗f5!?} 15 ♘xe6 fxe6 16 ♗c5 ♘xd3 17 ♖xd3 ♖fd8 18 ♖e1 b6! ± Short-Murei, Hastings 1982/3) 13 ♗c5 – *12 ♗c5!? ♖e8 13 ♖ad1* ∞.

c332) 12 ♗c5!? ♖e8 (12...♕f6?! 13 ♕xf6 ♗xf6 14 ♘b5 ± Unzicker-Jimenez, Leipzig OL 1960) 13 ♖ad1 ♕f6 14 ♗xd6 cxd6 15 ♕xd6 and now 15...♖ad8 gives Black compensation, while 15...♖ed8 16 ♕g3 ♕e7 17 ♘g5 ♗xc3 18 bxc3 ♗xa2 is unclear, Hermlin-Maslov, USSR 1970.

c333) 12 ♘g5 ♖e8 13 ♖ad1 ♕f6 14 ♕xf6 ♗xf6 15 ♘xe6 fxe6 16 ♘b5 ± Larsen-Trifunović, Dortmund 1961.

c34) 11 0-0-0! and now:

c341) 11...0-0?! 12 ♗c5! (12 h4 ♕f6 13 ♕xf6 ♗xf6 14 ♘g5 ♗xc3!? 15 bxc3 ♗xa2 16 h5 f6 17 ♘xh7 ♚xh7 18 hxg6++ ♚g8 19 ♖h7 ♘e5 20 ♗h6 ♖fc8 21 ♖g7+ ♚h8 22 ♖h7+ ½-½ Bannik-B.Nikolić, corr. 1966) 12...♕f6 (12...♖e8 13 ♗b5! a6 14 ♗xc6 bxc6 15 ♘e4 ±) 13 ♕xf6 ♗xf6 14 ♘b5 is much better for White, Matanović-Trifunović, Yugoslavia 1958.

c342) 11...♕f6 and here:

c3421) 12 ♕xf6 ♗xf6 13 ♘e4 (13 ♘g5 ♗xc3 14 ♘xe6 ♗xb2+ 15 ♚xb2 fxe6 16 h4 gives White compensation) 13...♗g7 14 ♘fg5 (14 ♘xd6+ cxd6 15 ♗e4 ±) 14...0-0 15 ♘xe6 fxe6 16 ♘g5 ♖ae8 17 ♖he1 ♘e5 = Parma-Trifunović, Bled 1961.

c3422) 12 ♕a4 h6 13 ♘d4 0-0 14 ♘xc6 bxc6 15 ♕xc6 ♗xa2 ∞ Mikenas.

c3423) 12 ♘g5!? ♕xf4 13 ♗xf4 ♗xc3 (13...0-0-0 14 ♘xe6 fxe6 15 ♖he1 ±) 14 bxc3 (14 ♘xe6!? ♗xb2+ 15 ♚xb2 fxe6 16 ♖he1 gives White compensation – Keres) 14...0-0-0 (14...0-0 15 c4 ±; 14...♗xa2 15 ♖he1+ ♚f8 16 c4! ♘xc4 17 ♘e4 ♘4e5 18 ♘c3! ♘xd3+ 19 ♖xd3 ♗e6 20 ♗h6+ intending ♘d5 ± Keres) 15 ♘xe6 fxe6 16 ♖he1 ♖hf8 17 ♗g3 ♖de8 (17...♘f5 18 ♖xe6 ♘xg3 19 fxg3 ±/±) 18 f3 ±. White has an advantage in the endgame due to his two strong bishops.

9 ♘c3

9 0-0 ♗e6 10 ♘c3 0-0 11 ♗e3 (11 ♘g5 ♗xg5 12 ♕xg5 ♕xg5 13 ♗xg5 ♘b4 =) 11...h6 12 h4?! (12 ♖ad1!?) 12...a5 13 a3 ♖b8 14 ♖ad1 ♚h8 15 ♘b5 ♕d7 16 ♘bd4 ♗f6 = Kuzmina-Fedorov, St Petersburg 2000.

9...♗e6 (D)

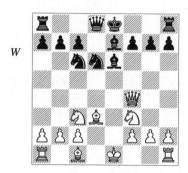

Now:

a) 10 ♗d2!? is interesting:

a1) 10...♕d7 11 0-0-0!? and now:

a11) 11...0-0-0 12 ♗e3 f5 (12...♕e8 13 ♕a4 ± Matanović-Krivec, Yugoslavia 1952) 13 ♕a4 ♗f6 14 ♗b5 a6 15 ♗xa6 ♗xc3 16 ♗b5! ♕e7 17 ♗xc6 bxc6 18 bxc3 ± Kindermann-Tischbierek, Bundesliga 1990/1.

a12) 11...0-0!? 12 ♖he1 (12 h4 ♗f5 ∞) 12...♖ad8 13 h4 ♗f5 ∞.

a2) 10...0-0 11 0-0-0 (11 0-0 ♗f6 12 ♖fe1 ♕d7 13 ♖ad1 ♗f5 14 ♘d5 ♗xb2 15 ♗xf5 ♕xf5 16 ♘xc7 ♖ad8 = Murei-Vasiukov, USSR 1967) 11...a5 12 a3 ♕d7 ∞.

b) 10 ♗e3 and then:

b1) 10...0-0 11 0-0-0 a5 ∞.

b2) 10...♕d7!? and here:

b21) 11 0-0 0-0 12 ♖ad1 ♖ad8!? 13 ♘g5 (13 ♗c5 ♕c8 14 ♘g5 ♗xg5 15 ♕xg5 ♖fe8 16 ♗xd6 ♖xd6 17 ♘e4 ♕d8! = Broadbent-Hooper, London 1954) 13...♗xg5 14 ♕xg5 f6 15 ♕h4 ♗f5 16 ♗c5 ♗xd3 17 ♖xd3 ♕e6 18 ♘d5 ♖f7 = Smyslov-Kan, Moscow 1939.

b22) 11 0-0-0!? 0-0 12 ♖he1 ±.

b3) 10...♗f6 11 0-0 0-0 12 ♖ad1 ♘e7 (12...♕d7 13 ♘e4!? ♗xb2 14 ♘xd6 cxd6 15 ♘g5 g6 16 ♕h4 h5 17 ♘xe6 ♕xe6 18 ♗c4 gives White compensation) 13 ♗c5 ♘g6 14 ♕g3 (14 ♕b4!?) 14...♗xc3 15 bxc3 ♕f6 16 ♘g5! gives White the initiative. Note that 16...♕xc3?? loses to 17 ♗xd6! cxd6 18 ♗xg6.

B)

7 ♘c3

The main advantage of this move is its flexibility. In some lines White will develop his bishop to d3, with a transposition to Line A, but in others he will make use of the option to develop his bishop to b5, so as to shatter Black's queenside pawns by exchanging on c6.

7...♘c6

7...♗f5 is dubious in view of 8 ♗g5 (also interesting is 8 ♕e5+ ♕e7 9 ♘d5 ♕xe5+ 10 ♘xe5 f6 11 ♘f3 ♔d7 12 ♗f4 ♘c6 13 0-0-0 ± Bronstein-Borisenko, USSR Ch (Moscow) 1961) 8...♘c6 (8...f6 9 ♗f4 ♘c6 10 ♕a4 ♗e7 11 0-0-0 0-0 12 ♘d5 ♔h8 13 h4 ± intending h5 and ♘h4, Stein-Shakarov, USSR 1960) 9 ♕e3+ ♗e7 10 ♘d5 ♗e6 11 0-0-0 and White has a slight advantage.

8 ♕f4 (D)

This is the principal position of this variation. Black has several ways to organize his defence:

B1: 8...♗f5   25
B2: 8...♗e6   27
B3: 8...♗e7   27
B4: 8...♘f5   28
B5: 8...g6   29

B

B1)

8...♗f5

This continuation is insufficient for equality, because White can make use of the option of developing his bishop to b5.

9 ♗b5! ♕e7+ *(D)*

Or:

a) 9...♗xc2? 10 ♘e5 ±.

b) 9...♗d7 is well met by 10 ♗d3!.

c) 9...♗e7 and now:

c1) 10 ♗e3 0-0 11 0-0-0 ♕c8 12 ♗a4 ♗e6 13 ♘g5 ♗f6 14 ♘d5 ♗xd5 15 ♖xd5 ♘e7 16 ♖dd1 ♘g6 17 ♕f3 ♘e5 18 ♕f4 ♕g4 = Matulović-Kholmov, USSR-Yugoslavia 1968.

c2) 10 ♘d4!? ♗d7 11 ♗xc6 ♗xc6 (11...bxc6 12 ♕f3 ±) 12 ♘xc6 bxc6 13 ♕a4!? ♕d7 14 0-0 0-0 15 ♘d5 ♖fe8 16 ♗f4 ♗f8 17 ♖ad1 ♖ed8 18 ♘e3 ± Gligorić-Badzić, Sarajevo 1951.

c3) 10 ♗xc6+! bxc6 11 ♘e5! (11 ♘d4 ♕d7 12 ♘xf5 ♕xf5 =) 11...0-0 (11...♗d7 12 ♕f3!; 11...♗xc2 12 ♗e3 0-0 13 ♘xc6 ♕d7 14 ♘xe7+ ♕xe7 – *11...0-0 12 ♘xc6 ♕e8 13 ♘xe7+ ♕xe7+ 14 ♗e3 ♗xc2*) 12 ♘xc6 ♕e8 13 ♘xe7+ ♕xe7+ 14 ♗e3 ♗xc2 (or 14...♖ab8 15 0-0-0) 15 ♖c1! ♗d3 16 ♘d5 ♕d8 (16...♕e6? 17 ♘xc7 ♕g6

18 ♘xa8 ♕xg2 19 ♔d2! +–) 17 ♕d4! and then:

c31) 17...♗a6? 18 ♘xc7 ♖b8 (alternatively, 18...♖c8? 19 ♘xa6 ♕a5+ 20 ♘b4 ♘f5 21 ♖c5! +–) 19 ♘xa6! (more accurate than 19 ♖c6?! ♗b7 20 ♖xd6 ♕xc7 21 0-0 ± Sax-Yusupov, Rotterdam 1988) 19...♕a5+ 20 ♘b4 ♖xb4 (20...♘f5 21 ♖c5! ♘xd4 22 ♖xa5 ♖xb4 23 0-0 +–) 21 ♕xd6! ♖d4+ 22 b4! +–.

c32) 17...♗g6 18 0-0 ♘f5 19 ♕c5 ♘xe3 20 ♘xe3 ±.

W

10 ♔f1

This is the sharpest and most consistent continuation. However, 10 ♗e3 ♘xb5 11 ♘xb5 ♕b4+ 12 ♕xb4 ♗xb4+ 13 c3 is also possible:

a) 13...♗a5 14 b4 ♗d3!? (14...a6 15 ♘bd4) 15 a4 a6 and now:

a1) 16 ♘a3 ♗b6 =.

a2) 16 0-0-0?! ♗e2! (this gives Black equality; the alternatives are inferior: 16...♗xb5? 17 axb5 +– or 16...axb5?! 17 ♖xd3 ♗b6 18 ♗xb6 cxb6 19 ♖e1+! ±) 17 bxa5 (17 ♖d2?! ♗xf3 18 ♘d4 ♗xg2 19 ♖g1 ♗b6 20 ♖xg2 ♘xd4 21 ♗xd4 ♗xd4 22 ♖xd4 0-0 23 ♖d7 ♖ac8 24 ♖g5 ♖fd8 ∓

Matanović-A.Antunes, Zagreb 1964) 17...axb5 18 罝de1 奧xf3 19 axb5 奧d5 20 bxc6 奧xc6 21 奧g5+ 含f8 22 奧e7+ 含g8 23 奧b4 b6 24 axb6 cxb6 25 含b2 h5! = Stein-Kholmov, Moscow Z 1964.

a3) 16 ②bd4! 奧b6 (16...②xd4? 17 奧xd4 奧b6 18 0-0-0! 奧xd4 19 罝xd3 奧f6 20 罝e1+ 含f8 21 罝d7 奧xc3 22 罝ee7 +− Parma-Trifunović, Amsterdam 1965) 17 ②xc6 bxc6 (17...奧xe3? 18 ②ce5 +−) 18 奧xb6 cxb6 19 0-0-0 0-0-0 20 ②e5 奧e4 21 ②xf7 奧xg2 22 罝xd8+! (22 ②xd8 奧xh1 only leads to equality) 22...罝xd8 23 ②xd8 奧xh1 24 ②e6 ±.

b) 13...奧d6 14 ②xd6+ (14 0-0-0 0-0-0 15 ②xd6+ cxd6 16 ②d4 ②xd4 17 奧xd4 含c7 18 奧xg7 罝hg8 19 奧f6 罝de8 20 g3 罝e2 21 罝d2 罝ge8 22 罝hd1 罝xd2 23 含xd2 奧g4 ±/= S.Hassan-T.Hassan, Tanta City 2000) 14...cxd6 15 0-0-0 奧e6 16 罝xd6 奧xa2 17 奧c5!? (17 ②d4 ②xd4 18 奧xd4 0-0 19 罝d7 罝fb8 20 罝e1 a5 21 罝e5 奧c4 = Liberzon-Kholmov, USSR Ch (Moscow) 1969) 17...0-0 18 罝xc6 bxc6 19 奧xf8 含xf8 20 ②d2 奧d5 21 f3 罝e8 22 含c2 罝e3 23 罝a1 罝e2 24 罝g1 罝e3! limits White to a slight advantage, Matulović-Kholmov, USSR-Yugoslavia (Sochi) 1968.

10...奧e4 11 奧xc6+
Or:

a) 11 奧d2 ②xb5 12 ②xb5 0-0-0 13 罝e1 f5 14 ②c3 奧c5 15 ②xe4 fxe4 16 奧xe4 奧b5+ 17 c4 奧xb2 18 奧g5 奧b4 gives Black compensation, Mukhin-Borisenko, Tashkent 1968.

b) 11 奧a4!? 0-0-0 12 奧e3 f6 (or 12...奧xf3!? 13 奧xf3 {13 gxf3!?}

13...②e5 14 奧h3+ ∞) 13 ②xe4 奧xe4 14 罝d1 ±.

11...奧xc6 12 ②e5 (D)

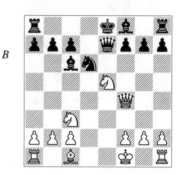

12...0-0-0
Other moves are worse: 12...奧d7? 13 ②d5 +−; 12...奧b5+? 13 ②xb5 ②xb5 14 ②xf7 奧xf7 15 奧e5+ ±; 12...奧e6? 13 ②xc6 bxc6 14 奧f3 奧d7 15 ②a4! ±.

13 ②xc6 bxc6 14 奧a4!
14 奧e3?! is met by 14...奧e6, eyeing the weak c4-square.

14...②b5
Black should avoid 14...奧e6 15 奧xa7! (15 奧xc6 奧c4+ 16 奧xc4 ②xc4 gives Black compensation) 15...奧c4+ 16 含g1 ②b5 17 奧a6+ 含d7 18 a4! and White is much better.

15 奧a6+ 含b8 16 奧e3 奧b4 17 奧xc6
White gets no advantage from either 17 ②xb5 奧xb5+ 18 奧xb5+ cxb5 19 a4 bxa4 20 含e2 a3 = or 17 a3 奧c4+ (17...奧xb2? 18 罝b1 奧xc3 19 罝xb5+ +−) 18 含g1 奧c5 19 奧xc6 ②d4, when Black has compensation due to his active pieces.

17...②d4 18 奧a6!
Or:

a) 18 ♕e4 ♗c5 19 a3 ♕c4+ 20 ♕d3 ♕xd3+ 21 cxd3 ♘c2 with a clear advantage for Black.

b) 18 ♗xd4 ♕xd4 (18...♖xd4!? and Black has compensation) 19 ♖d1 (19 ♘b5 ♕c5! gives Black compensation; 19 ♕b5+!? intending g3 and ♕e2) 19...♕xd1+ 20 ♘xd1 ♖xd1+ 21 ♔e2 ♖xh1 22 g4 ♖xh2 23 ♕e8+ ♔b7 24 ♕b5+ = Suetin-Kholmov, Moscow 1964.

18...♗c5

Not 18...♖d6? 19 ♕d3! ± ♘b3 20 ♗xa7+!.

19 a3 ♕b7 20 ♕xb7+ ♔xb7 21 ♖c1 ♗b6 22 g3 h5 23 h4 ♘e6 24 ♗xb6 axb6 25 ♔g2 ♖d2 26 ♖he1

White has a clearly advantageous endgame with an extra pawn, Klovans-Herman, corr. 1967.

B2)

8...♗e6 *(D)*

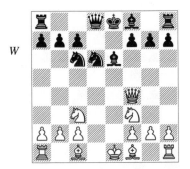

An interesting continuation, upon which White's wisest course is probably 9 ♗d3 – *7 ♗d3 ♘c6 8 ♕f4 ♗e6 9 ♘c3*; White is a little better in that line. Otherwise...

9 ♗e3

9 ♗d2 can be met by 9...g6, while 9 ♗b5 is ineffective in view of 9...♘xb5 10 ♘xb5 ♗d6 11 ♕e4 (11 ♘xd6+ ♕xd6 =) 11...♕d7 12 ♗f4 ♗xf4 13 ♕xf4 0-0-0 = Boleslavsky-Maslov, USSR 1963.

9...♘f5!

Freeing the d6-square for the dark-squared bishop.

10 ♘b5

10 ♗d3 ♗d6 11 ♕e4 ♘xe3 12 ♕xe3 ♕f6 (12...♕e7 =) 13 ♘e4 ♕xb2 14 0-0 ♕b6 15 ♕g5 ♕a5 16 ♗b5 ♕b4 17 ♖fe1 gives White compensation, Simagin-Vistaneckis, Moscow 1961.

10...♗b4+ 11 ♗d2

11 c3 is met by 11...♗a5.

11...♗xd2+ 12 ♘xd2 0-0 13 0-0-0 ♖c8 14 ♘f3 ♕e7 15 ♗d3 a6 16 ♘c3 ♕b4

The game is equal. Fuderer-Bronstein, USSR-Yugoslavia (Kiev) 1959 concluded 17 ♘e4 ♘fe7 18 a3 ♘g6 19 ♕g5 ♕a5 20 ♘c5 ♗g4 21 ♗xg6 fxg6 22 ♖d5 ½-½.

B3)

8...♗e7 9 ♗e3

9 ♗d3 transposes to the line *7 ♗d3 ♘c6 8 ♕f4 ♗e7 9 ♘c3*.

9...♗e6 10 0-0-0 0-0 11 ♘g5

11 g4!?.

11...♗xg5 12 ♕xg5 ♕e7 13 ♕xe7

13 ♗e2 f6 14 ♕c5 ♕f7 leads only to equality, Sveshnikov-Oll, Norilsk 1987.

13...♘xe7 14 ♗c5 ♘ef5

14...♖fd8 can be met by 15 ♗e2 ± or 15 ♗xd6 ♖xd6 16 ♖xd6 cxd6 17 ♗e2 ±.

15 ♘b5!

Instead 15 g3 b6! is equal, since 16 ♗a3 c5 exploits the looseness of the a3-bishop.

After the text-move, White has slightly the better chances in the end-game. Not only does White have the long-term advantage of the bishop-pair, but also Black faces immediate problems with his clumsily placed knights.

B4)
8...♘f5!? *(D)*

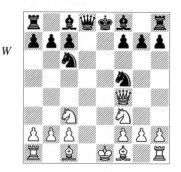

One of the interesting inventions of Igor Zaitsev.

9 ♗b5

Here too the development of the bishop to b5 causes Black the most difficulty. The alternatives for White are:

a) 9 ♗c4!? ♗d6 10 ♕e4+ ♗e7 (10...♕e7!?) 11 ♗d5 0-0 12 ♗d2 ♗f6 13 0-0-0 ♘cd4 14 g4 ♖e8 15 ♕f4 ♘xf3 16 ♕xf3 ♘d4 17 ♕g2 c5 18 ♗e3 ♕b6 19 ♘e4 ♗e7 20 c3 ♗e6 21 ♗xe6 ♘xe6 ∞ Tiviakov-Ye Rongguang, Groningen FIDE 1997.

b) 9 ♘b5!? is an interesting possibility:

b1) 9...♗d6 10 ♘xd6+ ♕xd6 (or 10...♘xd6 11 ♗d3 ♕e7+ 12 ♗e3 ±) 11 ♕xd6 ♘xd6 12 ♗f4 ± intending to meet 12...♘b4 with 13 ♗xd6 ♘xc2+ (13...cxd6 14 ♔d2 ♗f5 15 ♘d4 ±) 14 ♔d2 ♘xa1 15 ♗b5+ ±.

b2) 9...♗b4+ 10 c3 and now:

b21) 10...♕e7+ 11 ♗e2 ♗d6 (Black also fails to equalize after 11...♗a5 12 0-0 0-0 {12...a6?! 13 ♘a3 ±} 13 ♗d3 g6 14 ♖e1 ±) 12 ♘xd6+ ♘xd6 13 0-0 ♗f5 14 ♗e3 0-0 15 ♖ad1 ±.

b22) 10...♗a5 11 ♗e2 (11 ♗c4 ♕e7+! ∞) 11...0-0 12 0-0 ♖e8 (12...a6 13 ♘a3 intending ♘c4 ∞) 13 ♗c4 ∞.

c) 9 ♕e4+ ♗e7 (9...♕e7!?) 10 ♗b5 0-0 11 ♗xc6 bxc6 12 ♕xc6 ♖b8 gives Black compensation.

9...♗d6 10 ♕e4+ ♕e7 *(D)*

10...♘fe7 11 ♗g5 h6 12 ♗h4 ♗f5 13 ♕a4 0-0 14 0-0-0 ♕c8 15 ♗g3 ♖d8 16 ♗xd6 ♖xd6 17 ♖xd6 cxd6 18 ♖e1 ± Ulybin-Sorokin, USSR Ch (Moscow) 1991.

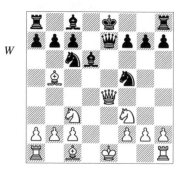

11 ♗d2
Or:

a) 11 0-0 0-0 (11...♕xe4 12 ♘xe4 0-0?! 13 ♘xd6 cxd6 14 ♖d1 ± Mainka-Panzer, Lippstadt 1992; 11...♗d7!? 12

♗xc6 bxc6 =) 12 ♗xc6 bxc6 13 ♕xc6 ♖b8, intending ...♗b7, gives Black compensation.

b) 11 ♕xe7+ ♘fxe7 12 ♘e4 ♗b4+ 13 c3 ♗a5 =.

c) 11 ♗xc6+ bxc6 12 0-0 ♕xe4 (12...0-0!?) 13 ♘xe4 ♗e6 =.

d) 11 ♗g5 f6 (11...♕xe4+ 12 ♘xe4 ♗e7 13 ♗xc6+ bxc6 14 ♗xe7 ±) 12 ♗d2 ♗d7 13 0-0-0 ♕xe4 (13...0-0-0? 14 ♗xc6 ±) 14 ♘xe4 ♗e7 15 g4 (15 ♖he1 0-0-0 = Azmaiparashvili-G.Georgadze, San Sebastian 1991) and now:

d1) 15...♘h6? 16 ♘xf6+! gxf6 17 ♗xh6 ♗xg4 18 ♖d3 ±.

d2) 15...a6? 16 ♗xc6! (16 ♗c4? ♘d6 17 ♘xd6+ ♗xd6 18 ♖de1+ {½-½ Kasparov-Karpov, New York/Lyons Wch (10) 1990} 18...♗e7! 19 ♗d5 0-0-0 20 ♗xc6 ♗xc6 21 ♖xe7 ♗xf3 22 ♖g1 ♖d7 =) 16...♗xc6 17 ♖he1 ♗xe4 (17...♘d6? 18 ♘xd6+ cxd6 19 ♘d4 ±) 18 ♖xe4 ♘d6 19 ♖e2 intending ♘d4-e6 ±.

d3) 15...♘d6! 16 ♘xd6+ ♗xd6 17 ♖de1+ (17 ♖he1+ ♔f8!) 17...♔f8! 18 ♖hg1 ♖e8 19 ♖xe8+ ♔xe8 =.

11...♗d7 12 0-0-0 ♕xe4 13 ♘xe4 ♗e7

13...0-0-0?! 14 g4! ♘fe7 15 ♘xd6+ cxd6 16 ♘g5 ♗xg4 17 ♘xf7 ♗xd1 18 ♖xd1 ± Schulze-C.Hacker, Dortmund 1992.

14 ♖he1

14 g4!? is best met by 14...♘h6! =, rather than 14...a6 15 ♗c4 ♘d6 16 ♘xd6+ ♗xd6 17 ♖de1+ ♗e7 18 ♘e5 ± or 14...♘d6 15 ♘xd6+ ♗xd6 16 ♖de1+ ♔f8 17 ♗c3! ±.

14...0-0-0 15 ♗c4

15 ♘eg5?! ♖df8 and then:

a) 16 g4 ♗xg5 17 ♗xg5 ♘d6 18 ♗xc6 ♗xc6 19 ♘d4 (19 ♘e5 f6 20 ♘xc6 fxg5 =) 19...♗d7 20 ♗e7 ♖e8 21 ♗xd6 cxd6 22 f3 ♖e5 =.

b) 16 ♗c4 ♘d6 17 ♗d5 h6 18 ♗xc6 ♗xc6 19 ♖xe7 hxg5 20 ♗xg5 ♘f5 21 ♖e5 ♗xf3 22 gxf3 g6 23 ♖ed5 f6 24 ♗f4 ♖d8 25 ♖xd8+ ♖xd8 26 ♖xd8+ ♔xd8 27 ♗e3 (27 ♔d2 ♘d4! is equal) 27...♘h4 28 f4 (28 ♗xa7? b6 favours Black) 28...a6 = Hellers-Hector, Malmö 1993.

15...f6 16 ♗c3 ♘d6

Black neutralizes White's initiative, achieving equality.

B5)

8...g6 (D)

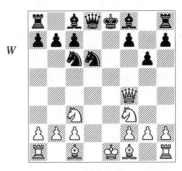

Black aims to develop his bishop actively on the long diagonal, but it takes two tempi instead of one to bring the bishop into play.

9 ♗e3

White has several other possibilities here:

a) 9 ♘d4 ♗g7 (9...♗d7!?) 10 ♘xc6 bxc6 11 ♗e2 0-0 12 0-0 ♖b8 13 ♕a4 ♗f5 14 ♗f3 ♖b6 (14...♗b5 15 ♘e2! c5 16 c3 ♗d3 17 ♖d1 c4 18 ♘f4 ♗xc3

19 ♘xd3 cxd3 20 bxc3 ♘xc3 21 ♕f4 ♘xd1 22 ♗xd1 ♖b5 23 ♗b3 ± Khalifman-Zysk, Groningen jr Ech 1985/6) 15 ♗xc6 ♗xc2 =.

b) 9 ♗b5 (here this is less effective; although White doubles Black's pawns, the two bishops become rather active) 9...♗g7 10 ♗xc6+ bxc6 11 0-0 0-0 12 ♗e3 ♖b8 (12...a5 13 ♗d4 ±) 13 ♖ab1 a5 14 a3 ♖e8 15 ♗a7 ♖b7 16 ♗c5 (16 ♗d4!? ±) 16...♗f5 17 ♕a4 ♘e4 18 ♖bd1 ♕c8 19 ♗d4 ♘xc3 20 ♗xc3 ♗xc3 21 bxc3 ♖b5 is best met by 22 ♖fe1 =, rather than 22 ♘d4 ♖c5 23 ♖fe1 ♗e4 24 ♘e2 ♖ce5 25 h3 ♗d5 ∓ Romanishin-Smyslov, USSR Ch (Leningrad) 1977.

c) 9 ♗d2 and now:

c1) 9...♗g7 10 0-0-0 and then:

c11) 10...0-0 11 h4 h6! and here:

c111) 12 ♘d5!? ♗e6 13 ♗c3 ♗xd5 14 ♖xd5 ♗xc3 15 bxc3 ♔g7 16 h5 ♕f6 (16...g5? 17 ♘xg5 wins for White, Zatulovskaya-Morguliov, USSR 1966) 17 ♕xf6+ ♔xf6 18 hxg6 ♔xg6 19 ♖dh5 ♖h8 20 ♗d3+ ♔g7 21 ♖1h4 is slightly better for White.

c112) 12 ♗d3 ♗e6 13 ♖he1 ♖e8 14 a3 a6 15 ♘e4 ±.

c12) 10...♗e6 and here:

c121) 11 ♘b5?! a6! 12 ♘xd6+ (the alternative 12 ♗c3 axb5! 13 ♗xg7 ♖xa2 14 ♖xd6 cxd6 15 ♗xh8 ♕a5 16 b3 ♘b4 17 ♕xd6 ♖xc2+ 18 ♔d1 ♖c6! 19 ♕e5 ♘d5 gives Black compensation) 12...cxd6 =/∓.

c122) 11 ♘g5 0-0 12 h4 ♗e5 (or 12...h6 13 ♘xe6 fxe6 14 ♕g4 ♕f6 15 ♗d3 ♘e5 16 ♕h3 b5 17 ♖de1 ♖ae8 ∞) 13 ♕a4 ♗d7 14 h5 ♘d4 15 ♕a5 ♖e8 ∞.

c123) 11 h4!? h6! 12 ♗d3 ♕f6 13 ♕xf6 ♗xf6 14 ♖he1 0-0-0 – 9...♕e7+ 10 ♗e2 ♗e6 11 0-0-0 ♗g7 12 h4 h6 13 ♖he1 0-0-0 14 ♗d3 ♕f6 15 ♕xf6 ♗xf6 =.

c124) 11 ♗d3 0-0 (11...♕f6?! 12 ♕xf6 ♗xf6 13 ♘g5 0-0-0 14 ♘xe6 fxe6 15 ♖he1 ♖he8 16 ♘e4 ± Tal-Rossetto, Amsterdam IZ 1964) 12 h4 ♕f6 13 ♕h2 (13 ♕xf6 ♗xf6 14 ♘g5 ♘b4 =) 13...♘e5 14 ♗g5 (14 ♘xe5 ♕xe5 15 ♕xe5 ♗xe5 16 h5 ♖fe8 17 b3 ♗f5 18 ♗xf5 ♘xf5 19 ♘d5 c6 20 ♘e3 ♘xe3 21 ♗xe3 ♖ad8 ½-½ Boleslavsky-Alatortsev, USSR Ch (Moscow) 1945) 14...♘xf3 15 gxf3 ♕xf3 16 h5 ♕xh5 17 ♕xh5 gxh5 18 ♖xh5 f5 19 ♖g1 (19 ♖dh1 ♖f7 ∓ Krogius-Kholmov, USSR Ch (Tbilisi) 1959) 19...♖f7 20 ♘e2 gives White compensation; Black's best course is 20...♗c4 =, rather than 20...♖e8 21 b3 ♘e4 22 ♗e3 ♔h8 23 ♘f4 ± Medina Garcia-Miagmasuren, Skopje OL 1972.

c2) 9...♕e7+ 10 ♗e2 ♗e6 with another branch:

c21) 11 ♘g5?! ♗h6 12 0-0-0 f6 13 ♘xe6 ♗xf4 14 ♘xf4 0-0-0 15 ♖he1 ♕f7 16 ♗f3 ♘c4 (16...♖de8 17 ♗d5 ∓) 17 ♗d5 ♖xd5 18 ♘fxd5 ∓ Geller-Trifunović, Bled 1961.

c22) 11 ♘d4 ♗h6! 12 ♘xc6 (½-½ Geller-Smyslov, Moscow 1971; 12 ♕xh6 ♘xd4 =) 12...♗xf4 13 ♘xe7 ♗xd2+ 14 ♔xd2 ♔xe7 =.

c23) 11 0-0 ♗g7 12 ♖ae1 0-0-0 13 ♕a4 ♔b8 14 ♗d3 ♘c8 15 ♗g5 f6 16 ♗e3 ♕b4 17 ♗xa7+ ♘8xa7 18 ♕xb4 ♘xb4 19 ♖xe6 ♘xd3 20 cxd3 ♖xd3 21 ♖e7 ♖g8 22 ♖fe1 ½-½ Geller-Smyslov, Lvov 1978.

c24) 11 0-0-0 ♗g7 and then:

c241) 12 h4 h6 13 ♖he1 and here:

c2411) 13...♕f6!? 14 ♗d3 (14 ♕a4 a6 ∞ intending ...b5) 14...♕xf4 15 ♗xf4 0-0-0 16 ♘e5 ♘xe5 17 ♗xe5 ♗xe5 = Keres-Trifunović, Bled 1961.

c2412) 13...0-0-0 14 ♗d3 ♕f6 15 ♕xf6 ♗xf6 16 ♗xg6 ♖hg8 (the alternative 16...♖dg8!? should maintain equality) 17 h5 ♗g4 18 ♗h7 ♖h8 19 ♗d3 ♗xh5 20 ♗e2 ♗g6 21 ♘d5 ♗g7 22 ♗c3 ♗xc3 23 ♘xc3 ♖he8 24 ♘h4 ♗h7 25 g3 ± Geller-Smyslov, Moscow 1991.

c242) 12 ♖he1 0-0-0 13 ♗d3 ♕f6 14 ♕xf6 ♗xf6 15 ♗g5 ♗xc3 16 ♗xd8 ♗xe1 17 ♗f6 ♖e8 18 ♘xe1 ♘b4 = Ivanchuk-Kamsky, Linares 1994.

9...♗g7 10 0-0-0 *(D)*

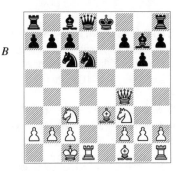

10...0-0

10...♗e6 can be met by 11 ♗b5!? ♕f6 12 ♗xc6+ bxc6 13 ♕xf6 ♗xf6 14 ♗d4 ♗xd4 15 ♘xd4 ♗d7 16 ♖he1+ ± Bertok-Rabar, Yugoslavia 1962 or 11 ♘e4!? 0-0 12 ♘xd6 cxd6 13 ♖xd6 ♕a5 14 a3 ±.

11 h4

11 ♗b5!? is possible, but the text-move is most energetic. Again we can

see the advantage in leaving the bishop on f1. Here the most effective plan is to delay developing the bishop, and to play for direct threats.

11...h6

11...♗e6 is dubious in view of 12 ♘g5 ♕f6 13 ♕xf6 ♗xf6 14 ♘xe6 fxe6 15 ♘b5 ♘xb5 16 ♗xb5 ± Sveshnikov-Kholmov, Moscow 1995.

12 ♗c5!

The most energetic move. Weaker are 12 ♗c4 ♗f5 13 ♗b3 ♖e8! 14 ♘d4 ♘xd4 15 ♗xd4 ♗e6 16 ♖he1 g5! = Gligorić-German, Stockholm IZ 1962, and 12 ♘b5 ♗e6 13 a3 ♖e8! 14 ♘xc7 ♕xc7 15 ♕xd6 ♕a5 16 ♕c5 ♕xc5 17 ♗xc5, whereupon both 17...♖ac8 and 17...♗g4 give Black compensation.

12...♗e6

12...♖e8!? Ivanchuk.

13 ♗b5 a6

13...♘e7 14 ♗d4 f6 15 ♗c5 ±.

14 ♗xc6 bxc6 15 ♗d4!

15 ♗xd6 cxd6 16 ♖xd6 ♕b6 17 ♘d4 ♖ab8 gives Black counterplay.

After the text-move (15 ♗d4!) White has a definite advantage, as Black has nothing to show for his weakened pawns and White's pressure along the central files. Play can continue:

a) 15...f6?! 16 ♗c5 ♖f7 (16...♖e8 17 ♖he1 ♖b8 18 ♗xd6 cxd6 19 ♘d4 ♗d7 20 ♕xd6 ±) 17 ♖he1 (17 ♘d4!? ♗d7 18 ♕g3 g5 19 ♗xd6 cxd6 20 ♕xd6 ±) 17...♗d7 18 ♘d4 ♕c8 19 ♕g3! (19 ♗xd6 cxd6 20 h5 g5 21 ♕xd6 ♖b8 22 ♘e4 ♕b7 23 ♘b3 ±) 19...♘b7 20 ♘a4! ± Ivanchuk-Akopian, Lucerne Wcht 1997.

b) 15...♖b8 16 ♗xg7 ♔xg7 17 ♘d4 ♗d7 18 ♖he1 ±.

3 3 d4 ♘xe4: Sidelines for White and Black

1 e4 e5 2 ♘f3 ♘f6 3 d4 ♘xe4 *(D)*

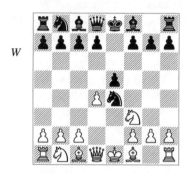

W

This is the currently fashionable continuation, and the starting point for a massive body of theory. Black executes the threat behind his second move, and challenges White to prove that the knight is exposed on e4.

Now:

A: 4 dxe5   32
B: 4 ♗d3   35

The latter continuation is the main line.

Or:

a) 4 ♕e2?! seeks a dull game: 4...d5 5 ♘xe5 ♗e7 6 ♘d2 ♘xd2 7 ♗xd2 ♘d7 (7...0-0 =) 8 ♘xd7 ♕xd7 (8...♗xd7 9 ♗b4 and now both 9...♗e6 10 ♕b5+ and 9...♔f8 10 ♗d2 are unclear) 9 0-0-0 0-0 10 ♗f4 ♗f6 =

Mnatsakanian-Mihailović, Budapest 1991.

b) 4 ♘xe5 d5 5 ♗d3 transposes to the main line, i.e. *4 ♗d3 d5 5 ♘xe5.*

A)

4 dxe5

A rather harmless continuation.

4...d5 *(D)*

4...♗c5?! seems dubious:

a) 5 ♕d5!? ♗xf2+ and now:

a1) 6 ♔d1 f5 7 ♗c4 ♕e7 (7...♖f8 8 ♘bd2 c6 9 ♘xe4! cxd5 10 ♘d6+ ♔e7 11 ♗g5+ ♔e6 12 ♗xd8 ♖xd8 13 ♗b3 gives White excellent compensation) 8 ♘bd2 c6 9 ♕d3 d5 10 exd6 ♘xd6 11 ♖f1 ∞.

a2) 6 ♔e2 f5 7 ♘c3 (7 ♘bd2!? c6 8 ♘xe4 cxd5 9 ♘d6+ ♔f8 10 ♔xf2 may give White enough compensation, but no more than that) 7...c6 (7...♘xc3+ 8 bxc3 ♗h4 ∞) 8 ♕d3 ♘xc3+ (8...0-0 9 ♘xe4 fxe4 10 ♕xe4 d5 11 exd6 ♖e8 12 ♕xe8+ ♕xe8+ 13 ♔xf2 ♗g4 14 ♗c4+ ♔h8 15 ♖e1 ± Lozenko-Titlianov, Sverdlovsk 1974) 9 bxc3 ♗c5 ∞ intending to meet 10 ♕xf5 with 10...d5.

b) 5 ♗c4 ♘xf2 6 ♗xf7+ ♔xf7 (6...♔f8 7 ♕d5 ♘xh1 8 ♗h5 ♕e7 9 ♗g5 ♗f2+ 10 ♔e2 ♕e6 11 ♘c3! gives White a very dangerous initiative) 7

♕d5+ ♔e8 8 ♗g5!? (8 ♕xc5 ♘xh1 9
♗g5 d6 10 ♕e3 ♕d7 ∞ Vargha-Ostru-
ken, corr. 1978-9) 8...♗e7 9 ♗xe7
♕xe7 10 ♔xf2 ♘c6 11 ♘c3 b6 12
♘b5 ±.

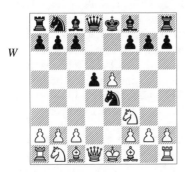

After the text-move, the position
slightly resembles an Open Spanish,
but here Black's position is consider-
ably more comfortable. One of Black's
main problems in the Open Spanish is
that his c-pawn is blocked by a knight.
This prevents him both from supporting the d5-pawn by ...c6, and from
bringing his pawns line-abreast by
playing ...c5. Here Black's c-pawn is
not blocked by a knight, and the additional option of playing ...c5 before
...♘c6 gives him a much easier time.

5 ♘bd2

5 ♗e3?! is no good in view of
5...♗g4! 6 ♘bd2 ♘d7! 7 ♗e2 ♕e7 8
0-0 0-0-0 9 ♗xa7 ♘xe5 10 ♘xe5 ♗xe2
11 ♕xe2 ♕xe5 12 c4 (12 c3 ♗d6 13
♘f3 ♕h5 14 h3 g5 ∓/∓) 12...♗d6 13
♘f3 ♕h5 ∓ Westerinen-Bednarski,
Eksjö 1976.

5 ♗d3 transposes to *4 ♗d3 d5 5
dxe5*.

5...♘xd2

Black has also tried other methods
of defence:

a) 5...f5 6 exf6 ♘xf6 7 c4!? d4 8
♗d3 ♗e7 9 0-0 0-0 10 ♖e1 ± Svesh-
nikov-Raetsky, Podolsk 1992.

b) 5...♘c6 6 ♘xe4 dxe4 7 ♕xd8+
♘xd8 8 ♘d4! (8 ♘g5 ♗f5) 8...♗c5
(8...♘e6 9 ♗e3 ±) 9 ♗e3! (9 ♘b5
♗b6 10 ♗e3 ♗a5+ 11 ♗d2 ♗b6 =)
9...0-0! (9...♗b6 10 ♗c4 ±) 10 ♗c4
(10 0-0-0 ♖e8 11 ♘b5 ♗xe3+ 12 fxe3
♘e6 13 ♗c4 offers Black a choice
between 13...a6, with equality, and
13...♖e7) 10...♗xd4 (10...♖e8? 11
♘b5 ±) 11 ♗xd4 ♗e6 and then:

b1) 12 ♗e2 ♗d5 =.

b2) 12 ♗xe6 fxe6 (12...♘xe6!? 13
0-0-0! f5! 14 ♗c3 ∞) 13 0-0 ♘c6 14
♗c3 (14 c3 ♖ad8 15 ♖ad1 ♖d5 16
♖fe1 ♗f4! 17 g3 ♖f5 18 ♖xe4 ♘xe5 ∓)
14...b5 15 a3 a5 16 ♖fe1 (16 b4 axb4
17 axb4 ♖fd8 ∞) 16...b4 17 ♗d2! (17
axb4 axb4 18 ♗d2 ♘d4! ∓) 17...♖ad8
(17...♘d4 18 ♖ac1 ±) 18 ♗g5 (18
♖ad1 ♘d4! ±) 18...♖d4 19 axb4 axb4
20 b3 (20 ♖a6 ♖c4! ∓) 20...♘xe5 21
♖e2 ♘f7! 22 ♗e7 ♖b8 23 ♖ae1 ♘d6
½-½ Sveshnikov-Yudasin, USSR Cht
(Podolsk) 1990.

b3) 12 ♗b5 a6 13 ♗e2 ♘c6 14
0-0-0 ♖fe8 15 ♗c3 ♖ad8 16 f4 exf3
17 ♗xf3 h6 18 b3 ♗f5 19 ♖xd8 ♖xd8
20 ♖f1 ♗e6 21 ♗xc6 bxc6 22 ♖f4
♖b8 23 ♖a4 ♖a8 24 ♗a5 ♖c8 25 g3
♔h7 26 ♖b4 ± Sveshnikov-Rõtšagov,
Tallinn Keres mem rpd 2000.

c) 5...♗e7!? and here:

c1) 6 ♘xe4!? dxe4 7 ♕xd8+ ♗xd8
8 ♘g5 ♘c6 (8...♗xg5 9 ♗xg5 ♘c6 10
0-0-0 0-0 11 ♗b5 h6 12 ♗f4 ± Zel-
čić-Delanoy, Geneva 1993) 9 ♘xe4

♗f5!? (9...♘xe5 10 ♗f4 ♘g6 11 ♗e3 0-0 12 0-0-0 ±) 10 ♘c5 ♗e7 11 ♗d3 ♗c8! =.

c2) 6 ♗b5+ c6 (6...♗d7!? 7 ♕e2 ♗xb5 8 ♕xb5+ c6 and now White can settle for 9 ♕e2 =, while 9 ♕xb7 ♘c5 is unclear) 7 ♗d3 ♘c5 8 ♗e2 and then:

c21) 8...♗g4?! 9 ♘d4 ♗xe2 10 ♕xe2 ♘bd7 11 0-0 ♘e6?! (11...0-0!? 12 f4 ♘e6 13 c3 ♘xd4 14 cxd4 f5 ±) 12 ♘xe6 fxe6 13 ♕g4! ± Smirin-Alterman, Haifa 1995.

c22) 8...♘e6 9 ♘f1 c5 10 ♘g3 g6 11 0-0 ♘c6 ∞.

c23) 8...0-0 9 0-0 ♘bd7 intending ...f6 =.

d) 5...♗f5!? 6 ♘xe4 (6 ♘b3!?) 6...♗xe4 7 ♗d3 ♘c6 8 0-0 ♗e7 9 ♖e1 ♘b4 10 ♕e2 ♘xd3 11 cxd3 ♗xf3 12 ♕xf3 ♕d7 = Balashov-Mikhalchishin, Minsk 1985.

e) 5...♘c5 6 ♘b3 (D) and now:

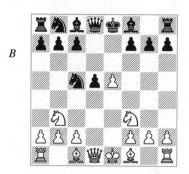

e1) 6...♘xb3 7 axb3 ♗e7 8 ♗d3 (8 ♗f4 ♗g4 9 ♗d3 ♘c6 =; 8 ♗b5+ c6 9 ♗d3 ♘d7 10 c3 ♘c5 11 ♗c2 ♗g4 12 0-0 0-0 13 b4 ♘d7 14 ♖e1 g6 15 ♕d4 ♗xf3 16 gxf3 ♕b6 17 ♕g4 f5 18 ♕g3 ♔h8 = Nunn-Schüssler, Vienna 1986)

8...♘d7 (8...♘c6!? 9 ♗f4 ♗g4 10 h3 ♗h5 11 0-0 0-0 12 ♖e1 ♕d7 ±/=) 9 c3 ♘c5 10 ♗c2 ♗g4 11 b4 ♘e6 12 ♕d3 ♕d7 13 0-0 g6 14 ♗h6 ♗f5 15 ♕e2 ♗xc2 16 ♕xc2 ♗f8 17 ♕d2 ♗xh6 18 ♕xh6 a6 19 ♖fd1 ♖d8 20 h4 ± Ivanchuk-Kasimdzhanov, Elista OL 1998.

e2) 6...♗g4 7 h3 ♗h5 8 ♗e2 ♘c6 9 ♘fd4 ♗xe2 10 ♕xe2 ♘xb3 11 ♘xb3 (11 ♘xc6? ♘xc1 12 ♕b5 bxc6 13 ♕xc6+ ♔e7 intending ...♖b8-b6 −+) 11...♕d7 12 ♗f4 0-0-0 13 0-0-0 ♕e6 14 ♖d2 ♗e7 15 ♖hd1 and here:

e21) 15...h5?! 16 c3! g6 17 ♘d4 ♘xd4 (17...♕d7 18 ♘xc6 ♕xc6 19 ♕f3 ♕a4 20 ♔b1 c6 21 ♗e3 ±) 18 cxd4 ♔b8 19 ♖c2 ± Kharlov-Akopian, USSR Ch (Moscow) 1991.

e22) 15...g6! 16 ♕g4 h5 =.

We now return to 5...♘xd2 (D):

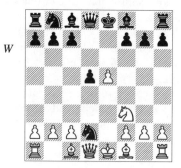

This move is the simplest option. Although White gains a slight lead in development, all Black's pieces can move directly to natural squares.

6 ♗xd2

6 ♕xd2!? is original, but achieves nothing special: 6...♗e7 7 ♕f4 c5 8 ♕g3 g6 9 ♗b5+ ♗d7 10 ♗xd7+ ♕xd7 11 0-0 ♘c6 12 ♗g5 0-0-0 13 ♖fe1

♖he8 14 ♗xe7 ♖xe7 15 ♖e2 ♕f5 16 ♖ae1 ♖de8 17 ♘h4 = Zelčić-Alterman, Dresden Z 1998.

6...♗e7 7 ♗d3

7 ♗f4 can lead to a sharp fight: 7...c5 8 c3 ♘c6 9 ♗d3 ♗e6 (9...♗g4!?) 10 h3 g5 11 ♗g3 ♕b6 12 ♕d2 h6 13 0-0 0-0-0 14 ♖fb1 a6 15 ♗c2 d4 16 ♗e4 h5 ∞ Short-Seirawan, Lugano 1986.

7...c5

Of course, this move should come before ...♘c6. However, 7...♗g4 is entirely possible: 8 0-0 ♘d7 9 ♗f4 ♘c5 10 ♗e2 ♘e6 = Sznapik-Schüssler, Helsinki 1978.

8 c4 ♘c6 9 cxd5

9 ♕b3?! dxc4!? (9...d4 10 0-0 ♕c7 11 ♖fe1 ♗e6 =) 10 ♗xc4 0-0 11 0-0-0 gives Black a pleasant choice:

a) 11...♕c7 12 e6 fxe6 13 ♗xe6+ ♗xe6 14 ♕xe6+ ♔h8 15 ♗c3 with equality.

b) 11...♘d4!? 12 ♘xd4 cxd4 13 ♔b1 ♗f5+ 14 ♔a1 ♖c8 with an initiative.

c) 11...b5! 12 ♗xb5 ♗e6 13 ♕a4 (13 ♗c4 ♖b8 14 ♕a4 ♕b6 favours Black) 13...♘d4 gives Black the initiative.

d) 11...♕b6 12 e6 fxe6! 13 ♗xe6+ ♔h8 14 ♖he1 ♗xe6 15 ♖xe6 (15 ♕xe6 ♗f6 16 ♗c3 ♗xc3 17 bxc3 ♕a5 ∓) 15...♕xb3 16 axb3 ♖ad8 17 ♖de1 ♗f6 ∓ Smirin-Alterman, Israel 1998.

9...♕xd5 10 ♕e2 ♗g4 11 ♗e4 ♕e6 12 ♗c3 0-0 13 h3 ♗f5

The game is level.

B)

4 ♗d3 *(D)*

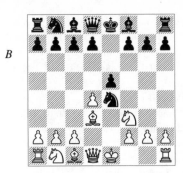

B

The main line. Now Black has a choice:

B1: 4...♘c6   35
B2: 4...d5   39

The former is one of the most interesting ideas of recent years, while the latter is the classical move and still overwhelmingly the main line.

B1)

4...♘c6

It is a tribute to the depth of chess that the Petroff Defence had been played for over 150 years before this move was first seen, in the game Timman-Murei (see note 'c122' to Black's 6th move). Unfortunately for Murei, his amazing idea did not put Timman off his stride, and the Dutch grandmaster won the game. Since then, there has been a flurry of interest in Murei's idea and currently no really effective reply is known. However, despite the relatively positive theoretical status, there still seems to be a certain amount of suspicion regarding Murei's idea. A more objective reason, perhaps, is that the ending arising in note 'b' to White's 6th move is slightly unpleasant for Black while offering no winning chances. Nevertheless, 4...♘c6 is an interesting way to avoid the main variations. Of course, it is not a real piece sacrifice, as Black will regain the material.

5 ♗xe4

White has other ways to fight for the advantage:

a) 5 0-0 d5 6 c4 ♘xd4! leads to equality.

b) 5 d5 and then:

b1) 5...♘f6!? 6 dxc6 e4 7 cxb7 ♗xb7 8 ♗e2 exf3 9 ♗xf3 ♗xf3 10 ♕xf3 d5 11 0-0 ♗e7 12 ♘c3 0-0 13 ♗g5 c6 14 ♖fe1 h6 15 ♗h4 ♖e8 16 ♖e2 ♕d7 17 ♖ae1 ± Ziukin-Liiva, Tallinn 2000.

b2) 5...♘c5 6 dxc6 (6 ♗c4 e4! =; 6 ♗e2 e4! =) 6...e4 7 cxb7 ♗xb7 8 ♗e2 exf3 9 ♗xf3 ♗xf3 (9...d5 10 0-0 ♗e7 11 ♗e3! 0-0 12 c4! ±) 10 ♕xf3 and then:

b21) 10...♗e7 11 0-0-0 and now:

b211) 12 ♖d1?! ♗f6 13 c4 (13 ♘c3 c6!) 13...♗e5! 14 ♘d2 (14 ♘c3? ♕h4) 14...♖e8 15 ♖b1 a5 16 ♘f1 (16 ♕d5!? d6 17 ♘f3 ♗f6 18 ♗e3 ±) 16...♕f6 17 ♕xf6 ♗xf6 18 ♘e3 ± Short-Timman, Groningen 1996.

b212) 12 c4 ♗f6 13 ♘c3 ♗e5 14 ♗f4 ±.

b213) 12 ♗e3 ±.

b22) 10...♕e7+ 11 ♗e3 ♕e4 12 ♘d2 ♕xf3 13 ♘xf3 ♘e6 (13...d5? 14 0-0-0 c6 15 ♖he1 ±) 14 0-0-0 ♗c5 15 ♗xc5 ♘xc5 16 ♖he1+ ♘e6 17 ♖e3 (17 ♘e5? d6 18 ♘c6 ♔d7 =) 17...d6 and now 18 ♖d5 ±, as played in Dolmatov-Howell, Calcutta 1996, is better than 18 ♘g5 0-0! 19 ♘xe6 fxe6 20 ♖xe6 ♖xf2 =.

b23) 10...♗d6 11 ♗e3 (11 0-0 0-0 and now White should prefer 12 ♘c3 ♖b8! = to 12 g3 ♗e5 13 ♖d1 ♕f6 14 ♕xf6 ♗xf6 15 c3 ♖fd8 ∓ Milov-Ye Rongguang, Dieren 1997) 11...0-0 12 ♘d2 ♕h4 (12...♘e6 13 ♖d1 c6 14 0-0 ♗c7 15 ♘b3 ♗e5 16 c3 d5 17 g3 a5 18 c4 ♗xb2 19 cxd5 cxd5 20 ♖xd5 ♕c7 21 ♖b1 ± Short-Timman, Wijk aan Zee 1997) 13 ♗xc5 ♗xc5 14 0-0 ♗d6 15 g3 ♕d4 16 ♕d3 ♕xb2 = Nijboer-Kroeze, Leeuwaarden 1997.

c) 5 dxe5 (D) and now:

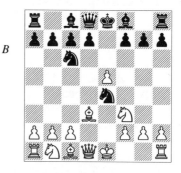

c1) 5...♘c5 and then:

c11) 6 ♗c4 d6 7 ♗e3 ♘e6 (or 7...♗e6 8 ♗b5 ±) 8 exd6 ♗xd6 9 0-0 0-0 10 ♘c3 ±.

c12) 6 ♗g5!? ♘xd3+ 7 ♕xd3 ♘xe5 (7...♗e7 8 ♗xe7 ♕xe7 9 0-0 ♘xe5 10 ♘xe5 ♕xe5 11 ♘c3 gives White compensation) 8 ♕e2 f6 9 ♘xe5 ♕e7 ∞ Ivanchuk.

c2) 5...d5 6 exd6! ♘xd6 7 ♘c3 (7 0-0 ♗e7 8 ♘c3 ♗e6 =) 7...♗e7 (or 7...♘b4!? 8 0-0 ♗e7 9 ♗e2 0-0 10 a3 ♘c6 11 ♘d5 ♖e8 12 ♗f4 ♗e6 13 ♖e1?! {13 ♘xe7+ ±} 13...♗f8 14 c4 ♗xd5 15 cxd5 ♘e7 16 ♕b3 ♖b8 17 ♖ac1 ♘g6 18 ♗g3 ♕d7 19 h4 ♖e4 ∞

Vysochin-Rozentalis, Bydgoszcz 2000) and then:

c21) 8 0-0 and here:

c211) 8...0-0 9 ♘d5 ♗f5 10 ♗f4 ♗g6 11 c4 ♘e8 12 ♗xg6 hxg6 13 ♕e2 (13 ♖e1 ♗d6 14 ♗g5 ♘f6 15 a3 a5) 13...♗d6 14 ♗g5 f6 15 ♗e3 ♖f7 16 ♕c2 g5 17 ♖ad1 ♕c8 18 c5 ± Movsesian-Hráček, Germany 1997.

c212) 8...♗g4 9 ♘d5 ♘d4 10 ♗e2 ♘e6 11 h3 ♗h5 12 ♖e1 0-0 13 ♘xe7+ ♕xe7 14 ♘g5 ♗xe2 15 ♕xe2 ♕f6 16 ♘xe6 ♖fe8 17 ♕g4 ♖xe6 18 ♖xe6 fxe6 19 c3 ± Yakovich-Makarychev, Russia 1995.

c213) 8...♗e6!? 9 ♖e1 0-0 10 ♗f4 ♗f6 ∞.

c22) 8 ♘d5 and then:

c221) 8...0-0 9 0-0 ±.

c222) 8...♘f5?! 9 ♗e4 (another interesting line is 9 ♗c4!? ♘b4 {9...♘d6 10 ♗b3} 10 ♘xe7 ♕xe7+ 11 ♗e2 ±) and now:

c2221) 9...0-0 10 0-0 ±.

c2222) 9...♘b4?! 10 ♘xe7 ♕xe7 11 0-0 ♘d6 (11...0-0 12 ♖e1 ♖d8 13 ♗d2 ♕f6 14 ♗g5 ♖xd1 15 ♖axd1 ♕d6 16 ♖xd6 ♘xd6 17 a3 ±) 12 ♗g5! f6 (12...♕d7 13 ♕d4!; 12...♕e6 13 ♖e1 ♘xe4 14 ♕d8#) 13 ♗d5 ♘xd5 14 ♖e1 ♗e6 15 ♘d4 0-0-0 16 ♘xe6 ♖de8 (16...fxg5 17 ♘xd8 ♕xd8 18 ♕xd5 +−) 17 ♕xd5 fxg5 18 ♕d4 ± Ivanchuk-Anand, Linares 1994.

c2223) 9...♘d6 10 ♗f4 0-0 (White meets 10...♘xe4 by 11 ♘xc7+ ♔f8 12 ♘xa8 g5 13 ♗e3; 10...g5 11 ♗xd6 ♗xd6 12 ♘d4 ±) 11 ♗d3 ♗f6 12 0-0 ♗xb2 13 ♘xc7! ±.

c223) 8...♗e6 9 ♘xe7 ♕xe7 10 0-0 0-0-0 (10...0-0 11 ♖e1 ♕d7 12 ♗f4 ±)

11 ♖e1 ♕d7 (11...h6!? 12 ♗d2 ♕d7 13 ♗c3 f6 14 ♕d2 ♗f5 15 ♖ad1 ♖he8 =) 12 ♘g5 ♗g4 (12...♗f5!? 13 ♗f4 f6 14 ♗xf5 ♕xf5 15 ♘e6 ♖de8 16 g4 ♕g6 17 ♗xd6 cxd6 ∞) 13 f3 ♗f5 14 ♗f4 (14 c3 h6 15 ♗xf5 ♕xf5 16 ♘h3 ♘e5 17 ♘f4 ♖he8 ∞) 14...h6 15 ♘e4 ♘xe4 16 ♗xe4 (Morgado-Finocchiaro, corr. 1996) 16...♕e6 17 ♕e2 ♗xe4 (17...♘d4 18 ♕f2 ∞) 18 ♕xe4 ♕xe4 19 ♖xe4 g5 (19...♖he8 =) 20 ♗e3 f5 21 ♖c4 f4 22 ♗f2 (22 ♗c5 ♖d2 23 ♖c1 ♖e8 ∓) 22...♖d2 23 ♖e1 ∞.

5...d5 *(D)*

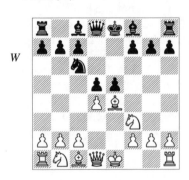

6 ♗g5

Two other moves deserve attention:

a) 6 ♗xh7 ♖xh7 7 dxe5 (7 ♘xe5!?) 7...♗g4 8 ♗f4 ♕d7 (intending ...♕f5) 9 ♘bd2 ♕f5 10 ♗g3 0-0-0 11 0-0 ♗c5 gives Black compensation; e.g., 12 a3 (12 h3 ♗xh3!; 12 c3 d4!) 12...♗b6 13 b4 ♕h5 14 ♖e1 ♘d4 15 a4 a6 16 ♖a3 ♘f5 ∓ Tiviakov-Forintos, Porto San Giorgio 1994.

b) 6 ♘xe5 ♘xe5 7 dxe5 dxe4 8 ♕xd8+ ♔xd8 and here:

b1) 9 ♗g5+!? ♔e8!? (9...♗e7?! 10 ♗xe7+ ♔xe7 11 ♘c3 ♔e6 12 0-0-0 ± Lakos-Gorshkova, Zagan girls Wch

1997) 10 ♘d2 ♗f5 11 0-0 h6 12 ♗h4 g5 13 ♗g3 ♖d8 14 ♘c4 ∞.

b2) 9 ♘c3 and then:

b21) 9...♗f5 10 ♗e3! (10 ♗g5+ ♔c8 11 0-0-0 ♗c5 12 ♖hf1 ♖e8 ∞) 10...♔c8 (10...c6 11 0-0-0+ ♔c7 12 ♗f4!) 11 0-0-0 and now Black should play 11...♗e7, rather than 11...b6?! 12 ♖d4! ♗c5 (12...♕b7 13 ♘xe4 c5 14 ♘d6+ ♗xd6 15 ♖xd6 ♖hd8 16 ♖hd1 is also good for White) 13 ♖c4 ♗xe3+ 14 fxe3 ♔b7 (14...♖e8? 15 ♘b5! +–) 15 ♖f1 ♗g6 (15...♗e6 16 ♖xe4 ±) 16 ♘d5! ± Leko-Timman, Ubeda 1997.

b22) 9...♗b4! and here:

b221) 10 ♗d2 ♖e8! (10...♗xc3 11 ♗xc3 ♗f5 12 0-0-0+ ♔e7 =) 11 ♗g5+ ♔d7 12 0-0-0+ ♔c6 13 ♘xe4 ♖xe5 14 f3 ♗f5 15 ♗f4 ♖ee8 ∓ Camacho-Otero, Cuba 1997.

b222) 10 ♗g5+ ♔e8 11 0-0-0 ♗g4! 12 ♖d4 ♗xc3 13 bxc3 h6! (13...♗f5? 14 ♖hd1) 14 ♖xe4 (14 ♗e3 ♗f5 =) 14...♗h3! (14...♗f5 15 ♖h4 ±; 14...♗e6 15 ♗e3 ±) 15 gxh3 hxg5 16 ♖g1! ♖xh3 17 ♖xg5 ♔f8 (17...g6 18 e6 ♖xh2 19 ♖f4! ±) 18 ♖eg4 ♖e8! and Black should be able to hold this ending, albeit with some difficulty, Shirov-Timman, Wijk aan Zee 1998.

6...♕d6

Or:

a) 6...f6?! 7 ♘xe5! ♘xe5 (7...dxe4 8 ♕h5+ g6 9 ♘xg6 hxg6 10 ♕xg6+ +–) 8 dxe5 dxe4 9 ♕xd8+ ♔xd8 10 exf6 ±.

b) 6...♗e7 7 ♗xe7 ♘xe7 8 ♗xd5 (8 ♗xh7 e4 9 ♗xe4 dxe4 10 ♘e5 ♗e6 ∞) 8...♕xd5 9 dxe5 ±.

c) 6...♕d7!? 7 ♗d3 (7 ♗xd5 ♕xd5 8 ♘c3 ♗b4 =; 7 ♘xe5 ♘xe5 8 dxe5

dxe4 9 0-0 can be met by 9...♗e7 = or 9...h6 10 ♗h4 g5 11 ♗g3 ♗g7) 7...e4 8 0-0 f6 and now:

c1) 9 ♖e1 and then:

c11) 9...♔f7!? 10 ♗xe4! (10 ♗f4? exf3 11 ♕xf3 ♘xd4 12 ♕h5+ ♔g8 ∓) 10...dxe4 11 ♖xe4 fxg5 12 ♘xg5+ ♔g8 13 ♕e2 ♘b4! 14 ♖e8 (14 c4 ♕f5 15 ♘f3 {15 ♖e5 ♕f4} 15...♗d7 ∞) 14...h6 ∞ intending ...♘bd5.

c12) 9...♗e7 10 ♗f4 exd3 11 ♕xd3 0-0 12 ♘c3 ♗b4 (12...♘d8? 13 ♗xc7 ±; 12...♗d8!?) 13 ♖e2 and here:

c121) 13...a6 14 a3 ♗a5 15 ♖ae1 ±.

c122) 13...♘e7 14 ♕b5 ♘g6 15 ♕xd5+ (15 ♕xd7?! ♗xd7 16 ♘xd5 ♘xf4 17 ♘xf4 ♗d6 gives Black compensation) 15...♖f7 16 ♗d2 ♗xc3 17 ♕xd7 ♗xd7 18 ♗xc3 ♘f4 19 ♖e3 ± Timman-Murei, France 1993.

c123) 13...♕f7!? 14 ♘b5 ♗a5 =.

c2) 9 ♗f4 exd3 10 ♕xd3 ♗d6 (or 10...♗e7 11 ♘c3 0-0 12 a3! intending ♖fe1 ±) 11 ♖e1+ ♔f7 (11...♘e7 12 ♗xd6 ♕xd6 13 ♕e2 ♔f7 14 ♘h4! intending ♕h5 ±) 12 ♕d2 (Milu-Ionescu, Romania 1995) 12...♖f8 13 ♘c3 ♗b4 (13...♗xf4? 14 ♕xf4 ± intending 14...♔g8 15 ♘b5 ♖f7 16 ♘xc7!) 14 ♖e2 ±.

We now return to 6...♕d6 *(D)*:

7 dxe5

If 7 ♗d3, then 7...e4:

a) 8 0-0 exd3 9 ♖e1+ ♗e7 10 ♕xd3 f6 11 ♗h4 ♗g4 12 ♘c3 0-0 13 ♗g3 (13 h3 ♘b4 14 ♕e2 ♗xf3 15 ♕xe7 ♕xe7 16 ♖xe7 ♘xc2 17 ♖c1 ♘xd4 18 ♖xc7 ♖f7 19 ♖xf7 ♔xf7 20 gxf3 ♘xf3+ 21 ♔f1 ♘xh4 22 ♘xd5 ♖d8 23 ♖c7+ ♔e6 24 ♘f4+ ½-½

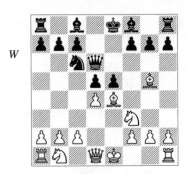

Sax-J.Horvath, Hungarian Ch (Budapest) 1995) 13...♕d7 =.

b) 8 ♘c3 exd3 and now:

b1) 9 ♕xd3 ♘b4!? 10 ♕e2+ (10 ♕d2 ♕a6!?) 10...♕e6 with an equal position.

b2) 9 0-0 a6 (9...dxc2!? 10 ♕e2+ ♗e6 11 ♕b5 f6! 12 ♗f4 ♕d7 13 ♕xb7 ♖b8 14 ♕a6 ∞) 10 ♕xd3 f6 11 ♖fe1+ ♗e7 12 ♗h4 0-0 (12...♗g4!?) 13 ♖e3?! (13 ♗g3 is better) 13...♗g4!? 14 ♖ae1 (14 h3 ♗h5 15 ♕f5 ♗f7 ∓) 14...♕d7 15 a3 ♖f7 16 h3 ♗f5 17 ♕e2 ♗f8 18 ♗g3 h6 and Black is slightly better, Wedberg-Shvidler, Biel open 1993.

7...♕b4+ 8 ♘c3 dxe4 9 a3 ♕a5 *(D)*

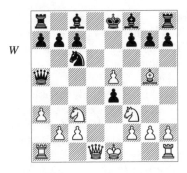

10 ♘d4

10 ♘d2? ♕xe5 11 ♘dxe4 f5 12 ♕h5+ g6 13 ♕h4 ♗g7! gives White severe difficulties:

a) 14 f4 ♕e6 15 0-0-0 fxe4 16 ♘xe4 (16 ♘d5 0-0 17 ♘xc7 ♕a2! 18 c3 ♘a5! 19 ♖d5 ♘c4 20 ♖b5 ♗xc3! –+) 16...0-0 17 ♖he1 ♕g4! 18 ♕f2 h6 19 h3 ♕f5 20 ♗h4 ♗d4 –+.

b) 14 ♗f4 ♕e6 15 0-0-0 fxe4 16 ♘xe4 (16 ♘b5 0-0! 17 ♘xc7 ♕g4 –+) 16...♕a2 17 c3 0-0 18 ♗xc7 ♗f5 –+.

c) 14 0-0-0 fxe4 15 ♗f4 (15 ♖he1 0-0 16 ♖xe4 ♕a5 17 ♖a4 ♕c5 18 ♗e3 ♕f5 19 ♖f4 ♕h5 20 ♖xf8+ ♔xf8 –+) 15...♕e7 16 ♗g5 ♕e6 17 ♘d5 (17 ♖he1 ♗xc3 18 ♖xe4 ♗e5 19 ♖xe5 ♕xe5 20 ♗f6 ♕e2 21 ♗xh8 ♗f5 22 ♖d2 ♕e1+ 23 ♖d1 ♕e4 24 ♕xe4+ ♗xe4 25 ♖e1 ♔f7 wins for Black) 17...0-0! (17...♗e5? 18 ♖he1 gives White compensation) 18 ♘xc7 ♕e5 19 ♘xa8 ♕xb2+ 20 ♔d2 ♕c3+ 21 ♔e2 (21 ♔c1 ♗f5! intending ...e3 and Black wins) 21...♗e6! –+.

10...♗d7

Or: 10...♕xe5 11 ♘xc6 ♕xg5 12 ♘xe4! ♕h4 13 ♕e2 gives Black some problems; 10...♘xd4? 11 ♕xd4 ±; 10...♘xe5!? 11 ♘b3 ♘d3+ 12 ♕xd3 ♕xg5 13 ♘xe4 ♕e5 14 0-0 (14 0-0-0 ♗e7) 14...♗e7 15 ♖fe1 is slightly better for White.

11 ♘db5 ♖c8 12 b4 ♕a6 13 ♗f4 ♘d8

∞ Mateo-Bick, Linares open 2000.

B2)

4...d5 *(D)*

Now:

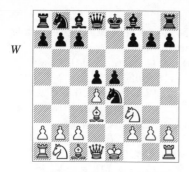

5 ♗xe4 dxe4 6 ♘xe5 ♗d6 7 ♕e2
♗xe5 8 dxe5 ♗f5 9 ♘c3 0-0 10 ♘xe4
♘c6 11 0-0 ♖e8 12 f4 ♘d4 13 ♕d3
♘xc2 14 ♕xc2 ♕d4+ = Capablanca-
Rading, New York 1905.

B21)
5 dxe5

A rare continuation. Just as in Line
A (from which this line can arise by
transposition), the structure in the resulting positions is highly reminiscent
of the Open Spanish. However, even
though Black is unable to play an early
...c5, this line presents no problems for
him. There is no pressure against d5,
as there is in the Open Spanish, and
Black's development can proceed
without difficulty.

5...♘c6! *(D)*

This is the strongest continuation,
as we can see from a consideration of
the alternatives:

a) 5...c5? 6 ♗xe4 dxe4 7 ♕xd8+
♔xd8 8 ♘g5 costs Black a pawn. This
is why Black cannot make use of the
possibility of playing ...c5 before
...♘c6 in this particular line.

b) 5...♘c5 6 ♗e2 ♗e7 7 0-0 0-0 8
♗e3 ♗g4 9 h3 ♗xf3 (9...♗h5 10 ♗d4

±) 10 ♗xf3 c6 11 c4! dxc4 12 ♘d2 b5
13 a4! ♘xa4 14 ♘xc4 ♕c7 15 ♘d6
♘d7 16 ♘xb5 cxb5 17 ♖c1 ± Roman-
ishin-Arkhipov, Tbilisi 1986.

c) 5...♗e7 is worse in view of 6 0-0
0-0:

c1) 7 ♘c3 ♘xc3 (7...♗f5!?) 8 bxc3
♘c6 9 ♖e1 f6 (9...♗g4!?) 10 e6 (10
exf6 ♗xf6) 10...f5 11 ♗b5 ♕d6 12
g3! ♗f6 13 ♗f4 ♕c5 14 ♖b1 ♗xc3 15
♖e2 ♗f6 16 ♗d3 ♘e7 ∞ Horvath-
Forintos, Budapest 1985.

c2) 7 c4! ♘c6 (7...c6 8 ♕c2 ± Zag-
orovsky-Shamaev, Leningrad 1949) 8
cxd5 ♕xd5 9 ♕e2 ♗f5 (9...♘c5 10
♗c4 ♘d4 11 ♘xd4 ♕xd4 12 ♖d1 ♕e4
13 ♘c3 ♕xe2 14 ♗xe2 ±) 10 ♗c4 ±.

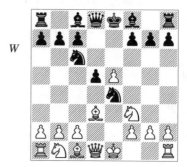

6 0-0

If 6 ♗f4, then 6...♗g4 7 ♘bd2 ♘c5
8 ♗e2 ♘e6 9 ♗g3 ♗c5 gives Black
easy development.

6...♗e7

6...♗g4 is also entirely feasible:

a) 7 ♗f4 ♗e7 8 ♘c3 ♘xc3 9 bxc3
g5 10 ♗g3 h5 11 h3 ♗e6 12 ♘d4
♘xd4 13 cxd4 ♕d7 ∓ Beliavsky-Mak-
arychev, USSR 1973.

b) 7 ♘bd2 ♘xd2 8 ♗xd2 ♘d4 9
♗e2 ♘xe2+ 10 ♕xe2 ♕d7 11 h3 ♗xf3

12 ♕xf3 ♗c5 13 c4 0-0-0 = Roman-ishin-Makarychev, Frunze 1985.

c) 7 ♘c3 ♘xc3 8 bxc3 ♗e7 9 ♖e1 0-0 (9...♕d7 10 h3 ♗h5 11 ♖b1 ♘d8 12 ♗e2 c6 13 c4! dxc4 14 ♕xd7+ ♔xd7 15 e6+ ♔c7 16 exf7 is good for White, Romanishin-Ehlvest, Erevan 1988) 10 h3 ♗e6 11 ♖b1 ♖b8 12 ♘d4 ♘xd4 13 cxd4 ♕d7 14 ♕f3 b6 15 ♕g3 ♗f5 16 ♖b3 ♖bc8 17 ♗g5 ♖fe8 18 ♗xe7 ♖xe7 ½-½ Romanishin-Akopian, Barcelona 1992.

7 ♘bd2

7 c4?! is strongly met by 7...♘b4, while 7 c3?! can be answered with 7...♗g4 8 ♗f4 0-0 (8...g5!?) 9 h3 ♗h5 10 ♘bd2 (10 ♕c2 ♗xf3 11 gxf3 ♘g5 ∓ Miladinović) 10...♘xd2 11 ♕xd2 ♗xf3 12 gxf3 f6! 13 exf6 (13 e6 ♘e5 ∓) 13...♖xf6 ∓ Miladinović-Skembris, Greece 1995.

7...♘c5 8 ♗e2

8 ♗b5 0-0 9 ♘b3 ♗g4 =.

8...0-0 9 ♘b3 ♘xb3 10 axb3 f6 11 exf6 ♗xf6 12 ♖a4 ♘e7

= Romanishin-Karpov, Moscow 1981.

B22)

5 ♘xe5 *(D)*

This is the basic starting position for the main lines. The situation in the centre is symmetrical, but White still has the advantage of moving first. Much depends on Black's ability to maintain his knight on e4. If he is forced to spend a tempo retreating it to f6, then White's lead in development could become serious. Black may use various measures to maintain his knight on e4; for example, he may

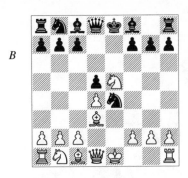

B

counterattack White's pawn on d4, he may support the knight by ...f5, or in extreme cases he may even offer a pawn sacrifice on e4.

White has two basic plans. He can either opt for simple development, or can undermine the e4-knight directly by c4. It is worth noting that playing c4 may result in the exchange of the pawns on c4 and d5, whereupon an isolated d-pawn situation arises. Which plan is more appropriate depends on the specifics of the position. Simple development can itself take many forms, but usually White plays to exchange the e4-knight by ♘d2 or ♘c3.

Black has a number of important continuations:

B221: 5...♗e7 42
B222: 5...♘c6 44

The two most popular continuations are 5...♘d7, which is the subject of Chapter 4, and 5...♗d6, which is covered in Chapter 5.

5...♗e6?! is rarely seen: 6 ♕e2 ♘d6 7 0-0 ♗e7 8 ♘d2 (8 ♖e1 ♘d7 9 ♗f4 ♘xe5 10 ♗xe5 0-0 11 ♘d2 ± Fuchs-Malich, Leipzig 1965) 8...0-0 9 ♖e1 ♗f5 10 ♘b3 ♗xd3 11 ♕xd3 ♘d7 12

♘c5 ♘xc5 13 dxc5 ♘e4 14 c6 ±
Minić-Rogoff, Zagreb 1971.

B221)
　5...♗e7 (D)

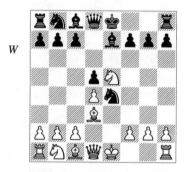

This somewhat passive line makes
little attempt to challenge White's advanced knight on e5. In this case both
plans (simple development or undermining the e4-knight with c4) offer
White good prospects, but the most direct is to aim for c4.

6 0-0
The alternatives, which are based on
simple development, are worth inves-
tigating:
　a)　6 ♘c3 ♘xc3 7 bxc3 ♘d7 8 0-0
♘xe5 9 dxe5 0-0 (9...♗e6 10 ♖b1 ♖b8
11 f4 ±) 10 ♖b1 b6 11 f4 ±.
　b)　6 ♘d2!? and then:
　b1)　6...♘d6?! 7 ♕f3 (7 ♕h5!?)
7...♗e6 (7...c6 8 ♘f1 intending ♘g3 ±
Kapengut) 8 0-0 0-0 9 ♖e1 ±.
　b2)　6...♘f6?! 7 0-0 0-0 8 ♘df3 (8
c3 c5 9 dxc5 ♗xc5 10 ♘b3 ♗d6 11
♘f3 ♘e4 12 ♕c2 ± Kapengut-Roiz-
man, USSR 1968) 8...♘c6 9 ♘xc6
bxc6 10 ♘e5 ±.
　b3)　6...♘xd2 7 ♗xd2 and here:

b31)　7...♘d7 8 f4!? ♘xe5 9 dxe5
g6 10 ♕f3 ♗e6 11 0-0-0 ♕d7 12 h3 h5
13 g4 hxg4 14 hxg4 ♖xh1 15 ♖xh1
♗xg4 16 ♖h8+ ♗f8 17 ♕f2 ♕e7 18
a3 ± Gurgenidze-Travnicek, Olomouc
1976.
　b32)　7...0-0 8 ♕h5!? (Bronstein
suggested 8 ♕f3 intending 0-0-0 ±)
8...g6 9 ♕f3 ♗f6 10 0-0-0 ± intending
h4-h5.
　b33)　7...♘c6 8 ♘xc6 bxc6 9 0-0
0-0 10 ♕h5 g6 11 ♕h6 ♖b8 12 b3
♗f6 13 c3 and now:
　b331)　13...♗g7 14 ♕f4 ♕d6 15
♕f3 ♗e6 (15...c5 16 ♗f4 ♕c6 17 ♕g3
cxd4 18 cxd4 ♗xd4 19 ♖ac1 intending ♖c7 ±) 16 ♗f4 ♕d7 17 ♕g3 ±.
　b332)　13...♖e8 14 ♖fe1 ♖xe1+ 15
♖xe1 ♗e6 16 ♕f4 ♗e7 17 ♕g3 ♗d6
18 ♗f4 ♗xf4 19 ♕xf4 ± Spassky-
Hort, Reykjavik Ct (14) 1977.
　6...0-0 (D)
Or:
　a)　6...♘c6 7 ♘xc6 bxc6 – 5...♘c6
6 ♘xc6 bxc6 7 0-0 ♗e7.
　b)　6...♘d7 7 c4 (7 ♘xd7! ♗xd7 –
5...♘d7 6 ♘xd7 ♗xd7 7 0-0 ♗e7;
White is probably a little better in that
line) 7...♘xe5 (7...c6 8 cxd5 cxd5 9
♘c3 ♘xc3 10 bxc3 ♘xe5 11 dxe5 0-0
12 ♗e3 b6 13 ♗d4 ♗c5 14 ♕h5 h6
15 f4 ± Gligorić-F.Olafsson, Hastings
1956/7) 8 dxe5 c6 (8...♗e6 9 cxd5
♗xd5 10 ♕c2 ♘c5 11 ♖d1 ♘xd3 12
♖xd3 c6 13 ♘c3 ♕a5 14 ♗d2 ♗c4 15
♖d4 ♕a6 16 ♘e4 ♗e6 17 ♗g5 ± Cio-
caltea-Rogoff, Malaga 1971) 9 cxd5
(9 ♗c2 ♗e6 10 ♕e2 ♘c5 11 ♖d1 d4!
12 b3 ♕b6 13 ♘d2 0-0-0 14 ♘f3 ♗g4
∞ Tseshkovsky-Ovchinnikov, USSR
1968) 9...♕xd5 and then:

b1) 10 ♕e2 ♘c5 11 ♗c2 (11 ♗c4 ♕e4 =) 11...♗e6 12 ♘c3 (12 ♘d2!?) 12...♕c4 13 ♕e3 0-0-0 14 b3 ♕a6 15 ♕g3 occurred in Nunn-I.Jones, England-Wales 1975 and now, according to Nunn, Black could have obtained the better chances by 15...h5! ∓.

b2) 10 ♕f3 ♗f5 (10...♘c5!? 11 ♕xd5 cxd5 12 ♗e2 0-0 13 ♖d1 ♖d8 14 ♗e3 ♘e6 =) 11 ♘c3 ♘xc3 12 ♕xf5 g6 13 ♕h3 ♖d8 =.

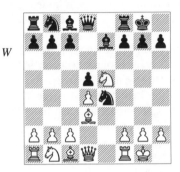

W

7 c4

7 ♘c3!? deserves serious attention. Then Yusupov assessed 7...♘xc3 8 bxc3 ♘d7 9 ♘xd7 ♕xd7 as equal, but the game Kengis-Larsen, Århus 1997 challenged this evaluation: 10 ♖e1 ♗f6 (10...♗d6!?) 11 ♗a3 ♖d8 12 ♕h5 g6 13 ♕f3 ♔g7 14 h3! b6 15 ♗c1 (intending ♗h6+) 15...♕c6 16 ♖b1 a6 17 c4 ±.

7...♘f6

It is usually a bad sign for Black when he must voluntarily retreat this knight to f6 without having some compensating pressure against d4. Here there is no such pressure and White is able to develop his minor pieces without any hindrance.

If 7...c6, then:

a) 8 ♘c3!? ♘xc3 (8...♘f6 – 7...♘f6 8 ♘c3 c6) 9 bxc3 ♘d7 10 cxd5 (10 f4 ±) 10...cxd5 11 ♘xd7 ± Stein-Udovčić, East Berlin 1962.

b) 8 ♕c2 ♘f6 9 c5 ♘bd7 10 ♘c3 ♘xe5 11 dxe5 ♘d7 12 ♗xh7+ ♔h8 13 ♗f5 ♘xe5 14 ♖e1 ♗f6 15 ♗f4 ♖e8 16 ♖e3 ± Tseitlin-Karasiov, Leningrad 1970.

8 ♘c3 c6

Unfortunately for Black, he has little choice but to continue with this passive move, because exchanging on c4 gives White an ominous lead in development and dangerous pressure against f7. The alternatives do not yield equality:

a) 8...♗e6 9 c5! ♘c6 10 ♘xc6 bxc6 11 ♗f4 ±.

b) 8...♘c6 9 ♘xc6 bxc6 10 c5 a5 11 ♖e1 ♖e8 12 ♗f4 ♗e6 13 h3 ♕d7 14 ♕f3 ♖eb8 15 b3 ♘e8 16 ♗e5 ♗f6 17 ♗c2 ♗xe5 18 ♖xe5 gives White a slight advantage, Sveshnikov-Kholmov, Moscow 1987.

c) 8...dxc4 9 ♗xc4 and then:

c1) 9...♘bd7?! 10 ♕b3 ♘xe5 11 dxe5 ♘g4 12 ♗f4 c6 (12...♕d4 13 ♘d5 +−) 13 h3 ± Em.Lasker-Mason, Paris 1900.

c2) 9...♘fd7? 10 ♗f4 ♘b6 11 ♗b3 ♘8d7 12 ♕f3 ♘f6 13 ♖fe1 c6 14 ♗g5 a5 15 ♖e3 a4 16 ♗xf7+ ♖xf7 17 ♘xf7 ♔xf7 18 ♖ae1 ♗f8 19 ♘e4 ± Short-Tempone, Mexico 1981.

c3) 9...♘c6 10 ♗e3 (10 ♘xc6 bxc6 and now 11 ♗f4 ± is better than 11 ♗e3 ♘d5 =) 10...♗d6 (10...♘a5? 11 ♗d3 b6 12 ♕f3 ♗b7 13 ♕h3 ♖e8 14 ♖ad1 ♘c6 15 ♘xf7 +−) 11 f4 ♘e7 12

♕b3! ♕e8 13 ♖ae1 ± Dührssen-Batik, corr. 1930.

d) 8...♘bd7 9 ♗g5 dxc4 10 ♗xc4 ♘b6 11 ♗b3 c6 (11...♗e6 12 ♗xf6 ♗xf6 13 ♗xe6 fxe6 14 ♕g4 ♕e7 15 ♖ae1 ♖ad8 16 ♘f3 ♖fe8 17 ♖e2 ± Matulović-Malich, Lugano OL 1968; 11...♘bd5 12 ♕f3 ♗e6 13 ♗xf6! ♘xf6 14 ♗xe6 fxe6 15 ♕xb7 ♕xd4 16 ♘c6 ±; 11...♘fd5 12 ♗xe7 ♘xe7 13 ♕f3!? ♗e6!? 14 ♗xe6 fxe6 15 ♕xb7 ♕xd4 16 ♕xc7 ♘ed5 17 ♕d6 ♖f6 18 ♖ad1 ± Gligorić-Gudmundsson, Amsterdam 1950) 12 ♖e1 ♘bd5 13 ♕f3 ♗e6 14 ♖ad1 and now, rather than 14...♖e8 ± Jacek-Polaković, corr. 1981, Yusupov suggests 14...♕a5!?.

9 ♖e1

White obtained the better ending in Bordonada-Balinas, Manila 1975 after 9 ♕b3!? ♕b6 10 c5 ♕xb3 11 axb3 ±.

9...♗e6 10 cxd5 cxd5

10...♘xd5 11 ♕h5 ♘f6 12 ♕h4 intending ♗g5 ±.

11 ♗g5 ♘c6 12 ♖c1

12 ♘xc6 bxc6 13 ♘a4 is also fully possible: 13...h6 14 ♗h4 ♘d7 15 ♗xe7 ♕xe7 16 ♖c1 ± Nagy-Lengyel, Balatonturist 2000.

12...♖c8 13 ♗b1 ♖e8 14 ♕d3
± Rechlis-Brook, Oakham 1988. White has a strong outpost on e5 and attacking prospects against the black king.

B222)
5...♘c6 (D)

This is the old move, which is considered insufficient for equality. Although Black manages to remove the

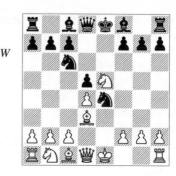

knight from e5, the cost is quite high – his queenside pawn-structure is damaged. In the main line White opens up the position by playing c4, after which several avenues of attack are available against the weakened pawns. In recent years the Petroff expert Artur Yusupov has attempted to rehabilitate this variation, but current theory gives White good chances of retaining the advantage.

6 ♘xc6 bxc6 7 0-0

The alternative 7 ♕e2 was played in the old game Showalter-Marshall, Paris 1900: 7...♕e7 8 0-0 ♘d6 9 ♖e1 ♕xe2 10 ♖xe2+ and now, according to Dolmatov, Black could have equalized by 10...♗e6, but then there is the possible continuation 11 ♘d2 ♔d7 12 ♘b3 (12 ♘f3 f6 13 ♗f4 g5 14 ♗g3 and now 14...h5 15 ♖ae1 ♗g4 ∞ or 14...♗g4!? 15 ♖e3 ♖e8 = Forintos) 12...♘b7 (12...♘c4 13 ♘c5+ ♗xc5 14 dxc5 f6 15 f4! intending b3 ±) 13 ♗e3 ±, keeping a grip on the c5-square.

7...♗e7 8 c4

This is the main continuation, but other moves have also been tried:

a) 8 ♘c3 ♘xc3 9 bxc3 0-0 10 c4 dxc4! (10...♗a6 11 c5 ♗xd3 12 ♕xd3

♗f6 13 c3 ♖e8 14 ♕a6 ♖e6 15 ♖b1 ♕e7 16 ♗f4 ± Rauzer-Dubinin, USSR Ch (Leningrad) 1934) 11 ♗xc4 ♗f6 12 c3 c5 =.

b) 8 ♖e1 and now:

b1) 8...♗f5 9 c4 0-0 10 f3 *(D)* and then:

b11) 10...♘d6 11 c5 ♗xd3 12 ♕xd3 (12 cxd6 ♗h4 13 g3 ♗xb1 is equal) 12...♘e8 (12...♘b5?? 13 a4 wins for White; 12...♘c4? 13 b3 ♘a5 14 ♕a6! ♗xc5! 15 dxc5 ♕f6 16 ♕xa5 ♕xa1 17 ♗f4 ±) 13 ♘c3 ±.

b12) 10...♗b4 11 ♖e2 ♖e8 (not 11...♘d6? 12 c5 ♕f6 13 ♗e3 ♗xd3 14 ♕xd3 ♘f5 15 a3 ♘xe3 16 ♖xe3 ♗xc5 17 dxc5 ♕xb2 18 ♕c3 +−) 12 fxe4 dxe4 13 ♗c2 ♗g4 14 ♗e3 ♗d6 15 c5 (15 ♘c3 ♕h4!) 15...♗f4 16 ♗xf4 ♗xe2 17 ♕d2? (there is no reason for White to avoid 17 ♕xe2 ♕xd4+ 18 ♕e3 +−) 17...♗d3 18 ♗e3 ♗xc2 19 ♕xc2 f5 20 ♕f2 ♖f8 21 ♗f4 ♖b8 22 ♘c3 e3 23 ♕xe3 ♖xb2 24 ♖d1 ± Dirr-Zaura, Munich 1991/2.

b2) 8...0-0 9 ♗xe4 dxe4 10 ♖xe4 c5 (Dolmatov's recommendation; previously Black had tried 10...♖b8 11 ♘d2 {11 c4 ±; 11 ♖e1 ±} 11...f5 12

♖e1 f4 13 c3?! {13 ♘f3!?} 13...♔h8 14 b4 ♖b5 15 ♘f3 ± Schmid-Bhend, Venice 1953) 11 d5 (11 ♕e1 ♗f6 12 dxc5 ♗b7 13 ♖e2 ♖e8 gives Black compensation) 11...♗b7 12 c4 c6 13 ♘c3 ♗f6 and here Yusupov gave the following variation: 14 ♗e3 ♗xc3 15 bxc3 cxd5 16 cxd5 ♕xd5 17 ♕xd5 ♗xd5 18 ♖e5 ♖fd8 19 ♗xc5 ♗xa2 =. However, the question arises: why 14 ♗e3?! (my marking) rather than 14 d6!, when Black has problems? For example: 14...♗d4 15 ♗f4 ± (or 15 ♖xd4!? ±/±); 14...♕d7 15 ♗e3 ±; or 14...♗c8 15 ♗e3 ♗f5 16 ♖f4 ±. Thus 8 ♖e1 deserves serious attention.

The text-move not only serves to help undermine the knight on e4, but also allows for ♕a4, taking immediate aim at Black's queenside pawns.

8...0-0 *(D)*

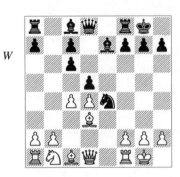

9 ♘c3

9 c5 (there is no need to release the tension so early) 9...f5 (9...♗f6 = Dolmatov, Yusupov) 10 f3 ♘g5 11 ♘c3 ♗f6 12 ♗e3 ♖b8 13 ♕c2 g6 14 a3 ♘e6 15 ♘e2 ♕e7 16 ♗f2 a5 17 b3 ♗d7 18 ♖ab1 ♖fe8 19 ♕c3 ♕g7 20 ♖fd1 ♖e7 21 b4 a4 22 b5 cxb5 23 c6

♗e8 24 ♖xb5 ± Sveshnikov-Smyslov, Tilburg 1992.

9...♘xc3

On 9...f5 there may follow 10 ♕a4 ♘xc3 11 bxc3 ♗d7 12 ♕a5 with a slight advantage for White.

10 bxc3 dxc4

10...♗a6 is suspect due to 11 ♕a4 ±, as is 10...♗e6 due to 11 c5! a5 12 ♕a4 ♕d7 13 ♖b1 ±.

11 ♗xc4 (D)

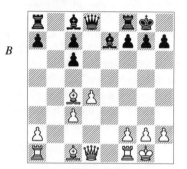

This is a critical position for the 5...♘c6 variation. In practice Black has had problems equalizing.

11...♗d6!?

Or:

a) Maybe it is time to investigate Dolmatov's recommendation 11...c5!? 12 ♕f3 (12 d5 should probably be met by 12...♗d6!?, rather than 12...♗f6 13 ♕f3 ±) 12...♖b8 and now 13 ♖d1 ♗b7 ∞ or 13 d5 ♗d6 =.

b) Black does not manage to equalize after 11...♗f5:

b1) 12 ♖e1!? ♗d6 13 ♕f3 ♕d7 14 ♗f4 ♖fe8 15 h3! (intending ♗b3-a4) 15...a5! 16 ♗e5 (intending ♖e3 and ♖ae1) 16...♗e6 17 ♗xe6 ♖xe6 18 ♕g4! ± Herrera-Rod.Perez, Havana 1998.

b2) 12 ♗f4 ♗d6 13 ♗g3 ♖e8 (or 13...♕d7 14 ♕a4 c5 15 ♕xd7 ♗xd7 16 dxc5 ♗xc5 17 ♖ad1 ±) 14 ♕a4 ♗e4 15 ♖ae1 ± Ivanchuk-Yusupov, Novgorod 1995.

12 ♕f3

Black equalized quickly after 12 ♕d3 in Holzke-Yusupov, Bundesliga 2000: 12...♖b8 13 h3 c5 14 dxc5 ♗xc5 15 ♗f4 ♕f6 16 ♕g3 ♗d6 ½-½.

12...♖b8 13 ♖e1

13 ♕xc6 is very risky in view of 13...♗b7. However, 13 ♗f4!? deserves attention.

13...c5 14 ♗e3 cxd4 15 ♗xd4 c5

15...♗b7 is unpleasantly met by 16 ♕g4, while after 15...♕g5 16 ♗xa7 ♗b7 17 ♕h3 ♖be8 18 ♗e3 ♕g6 19 ♗d4 ♗e4 20 f3 ♗f5 21 ♕h4 c5 22 ♗f2 ♖b8 23 ♖ad1 ♖b2 24 a4 h5 25 a5 ♖c2 26 ♖c1 ♖d2 27 a6 ♗b8 28 ♖e2 ♖fd8 29 ♖ce1 ± Black is heading for an early bath, Rublevsky-Yusupov, Frankfurt rpd 2000.

16 ♗e5

White is somewhat better due to his generally more active pieces and Black's weak pawn on c5.

It appears that in the 5...♘c6 variation Black needs to seek out new possibilities.

4 3 d4 ♘xe4 4 ♗d3 d5 5 ♘xe5 ♘d7

1 e4 e5 2 ♘f3 ♘f6 3 d4 ♘xe4 4 ♗d3 d5 5 ♘xe5 ♘d7 *(D)*

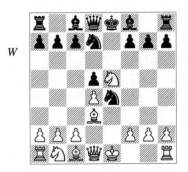

W

This has been the most popular continuation in recent years. Black seeks to challenge the e5-knight at the earliest opportunity, and by playing ...♘d7 rather than ...♘c6 he avoids having his queenside pawns damaged if White exchanges knights. This logical continuation may be regarded as one of the key lines of the Petroff, and many white-players have pondered over the best way to try to gain the advantage. Although it might appear that White should leave Black to exchange, it turns out that allowing ...♘xe5 gives Black excellent equalizing chances. Instead, White should fall in with Black's wishes and exchange himself, the point being that he gains time to

undermine Black's knight with c4. As so often in the Petroff, the key question then is whether Black has to retreat his knight or whether he can ignore White's efforts to displace the knight from e4. The resulting lines are quite complex and tactical.

Now:

A: 6 ♘xf7   48
B: 6 0-0   49
C: 6 ♘c3   50
D: 6 ♕e2   51
E: 6 ♘xd7   55

All these moves are important, but the last is without any doubt the main line.

There are also a few other moves:

a) 6 ♗f4 ♕f6 7 ♕f3 ♘xe5 8 dxe5 ♕b6 9 ♗c1 ♘c5 10 ♗e2 ♗e6 11 0-0 ♘d7 12 ♕g3 h5 = Tulin-Khramov, corr. 1985-6.

b) 6 ♘d2 ♘xe5 7 dxe5 ♘c5 8 ♗e2 ♗e7 9 0-0 0-0 10 ♘f3 ♘e6 (10...♗g4 11 ♘d4 ±) 11 ♗e3 c5 12 c3 b6 =.

c) 6 ♘f3 ♘df6 (6...♗d6 7 0-0 0-0 8 c4 c6 9 ♘c3 ♘xc3 10 bxc3 – *5...♗d6 6 0-0 0-0 7 c4 c6 8 ♘c3 ♘xc3 9 bxc3 ♘d7 10 ♘f3 ±*) 7 0-0 ♗d6 8 ♖e1 0-0 9 c4 c6 10 ♘c3 ♖e8 11 cxd5 cxd5 12 ♘xd5 ♗xh2+ 13 ♘xh2 ♕xd5 14 f3 ♘d6 15 ♖xe8+ ♘dxe8 16 ♗c2 ♗f5

17 ♗b3 ♕d6 18 ♗e3 ♖d8 = Melnikov-Savchenko, St Petersburg 2000.

A)

6 ♘xf7

Despite its superficially aggressive appearance, this is a very limp move since even if Black simply takes the knight, White has no more than perpetual check. If Black wants to avoid an immediate draw he also has the option of declining the offer, and in fact this amounts to a pawn sacrifice by Black. In the resulting complications Black has sufficient compensation, but not more than that.

6...♕e7!? (D)

6...♔xf7 7 ♕h5+ ♔e6 (7...♔e7 8 ♕e2 ♔f7 =) 8 ♕e2 (8 ♗xe4 dxe4 9 d5+ ♔e7 10 ♗g5+ ♘f6 11 ♘c3 ♕e8! ∓) 8...♗d6 (8...♔f7 =) 9 f3 ♕h4+ 10 ♔f1 ♖f8 11 ♔g1 ♔f7 12 fxe4 ♔g8 13 g3 ♗xg3 14 hxg3 ♕xg3+ 15 ♕g2 ♕e1+ = Yusupov.

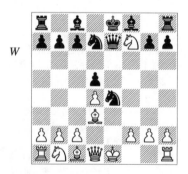

W

7 ♕e2

Or 7 ♘xh8? ♘c3+ 8 ♔d2 ♘xd1 9 ♖e1 ♘xf2 10 ♗xh7 (10 ♖xe7+ ♗xe7 ∓) 10...♘e5!! (better than 10...♘e4+? 11 ♖xe4 dxe4 12 ♗g6+ ♔d8 13 ♘f7+

= A.Zaitsev-Karpov, Leningrad 1966) 11 ♖xe5 ♗e6 12 ♗g6+ (12 ♗g8 ♕h4! 13 ♘g6 ♕xd4+ 14 ♔e2 ♗d6 0-1 Pronheim-Kristensen, corr. 1984) 12...♔d7, and here:

a) 13 ♗f7 ♘e4+ 14 ♔e3 (14 ♔d3 ♘c5+! 15 dxc5 ♗f5+ 16 ♖xf5 ♕e4+ 17 ♔c3 ♕xf5 18 ♗e3 d4+! wins for Black) 14...♘g5 ∓.

b) 13 ♗f5 ♕g5+ 14 ♔e2 ♕xc1 15 ♗xe6+ ♔c6 16 ♗xd5+ ♔b6 −+ Yusupov.

7...♕xf7

Now it is too late to accept the sacrifice: 7...♔xf7? 8 ♕h5+ ♔f6 9 0-0 ♕f7 10 ♕h4+ g5 11 ♗xg5+ ♘xg5 12 f4 ♔e6 13 fxg5 ♕g7 14 ♘c3 ♘b6 15 ♖f6+ ♔d7 16 ♖af1 +− Gurgenidze-Bellin, Tbilisi/Sukhumi 1977.

8 f3 ♘df6 9 ♘d2

9 fxe4 ♗g4 10 ♕e3 dxe4 11 ♗xe4 0-0-0 12 0-0 ♕h5 13 h3 ♖xd4!? 14 hxg4 ♘xg4 15 ♗f5+ ♔b8 16 ♗xg4 ♖xg4 ∓ Yusupov.

9...♕h5

Other moves cannot be recommended: 9...♗f5? 10 fxe4 dxe4 11 0-0 ♕d5 12 ♖xf5 ♕xf5 13 ♘xe4 ♘xe4 14 ♗xe4 ♕e6 15 ♗g5 ♗e7 16 ♗g6+! 1-0 Krantz-Kiorz, corr. 1987-92; 9...♗g4?! 10 fxg4 0-0-0 11 0-0 ±.

10 fxe4 ♗g4 11 ♕e3

11 ♕f2 dxe4 12 ♘xe4 ♘xe4 13 ♗xe4 0-0-0 ∓.

11...dxe4 12 ♘xe4 0-0-0

Black's lead in development and threats against the white king provide him with adequate compensation for the pawn.

13 ♘xf6 gxf6 14 0-0

Now:

a) 14...♔b8 15 h3 ♗d7 16 ♖xf6 ♖g8 (16...♗g7? 17 ♕g5! ± Harding-Kristensen, corr. 1989) 17 ♕f3 ♕h4! 18 ♖f4 ♕e1+ 19 ♕f1 ♕g3 20 ♖f3 ♕h4 gives Black compensation.

b) 14...♗d6 15 h3 ♖hg8!? (the alternative 15...♗d7!? gives Black compensation) 16 hxg4 ♕h2+ 17 ♔f2 ♕h4+ 18 ♔e2 ♖de8 19 ♗f5+ ♔b8 20 ♗e6 ♖xg4 21 ♔d3 ♖xe6 22 ♕xe6 ♖xd4+ 23 ♔e3 (23 ♔c3 is met by 23...♗e5!) 23...♗c5 24 ♔f3 ♕h5+ 25 ♔g3 ♕g6+ = Yusupov.

B)

6 0-0 ♘xe5 7 dxe5 *(D)*

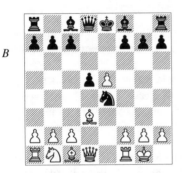

We saw in Chapter 3 (Lines A and B21) that positions in which the d4-pawn is transferred to e5 usually do not offer White any advantage. Here White has slightly more chances than in the positions from the previous chapter, since his f-pawn is not blocked by the knight on f3 and can advance to support its colleague on e5. However, Black has no problems developing his pieces and with a few accurate moves he can steer the game towards equality.

7...♘c5
Or:

a) 7...♗e7?! 8 ♗xe4 dxe4 9 ♕xd8+ ♗xd8 10 ♘c3 ♗f5 11 ♖e1 ±.

b) 7...♗e6!? 8 ♗xe4 dxe4 9 ♕e2 ♕d5 10 ♗f4 ♕c6 11 ♘d2 ♗e7 12 ♖fe1 (12 ♕xe4?! ♗d5; 12 ♘xe4?! ♗c4) 12...g5 13 ♗g3 h5 14 h3 h4 15 ♗h2 ♕xc2 ∞ Djurhuus-Gu.Hernandez, Thessaloniki OL 1988.

8 ♘c3!
White now threatens ♘xd5. Other ideas:

a) 8 ♕f3 ♗e6 9 ♘c3 ♘xd3 10 ♕xd3 (10 cxd3 ♕d7 11 ♗d2 0-0-0 ∓) 10...♕d7 11 ♖d1 c6 12 ♕g3 ♗f5! 13 ♗e3 ♗xc2 14 ♖d2 ♗g6 15 h4 ♗e7! ∓ Kovaliov-Ionov, Moscow 1990.

b) 8 ♗e2 ♗e7 (8...♗f5 9 ♘d2 ♗e7 10 ♘f3 ♘e6 11 ♗e3 0-0 12 c3 c6 13 ♘d4 ♘xd4 14 cxd4 f6 = Blatny-Gi.Hernandez, Thessaloniki OL 1988) 9 b3 (9 f4 g6 =; 9 ♘c3 c6 10 f4 d4 11 ♘b1 ♗f5 12 ♗g4 ♕d7 13 ♗xf5 ♕xf5 14 b4 ♘a6 15 a3 ♖d8 ∞ Minić-H.Eng, West Berlin 1984) 9...0-0 10 ♗b2 c6 11 ♘d2 a5 12 a3 ♕c7 13 ♘f3 ♗d7 = J.Polgar-Szmetan, Buenos Aires 1992.

8...c6
Or 8...♘xd3 9 ♕xd3 (9 cxd3 ♗e6 10 d4 ♕d7 11 ♕b3 c6 12 ♘e2 ♗e7 13 ♕g3 0-0-0 = Velimirović-Davidović, Yugoslavia 1989) 9...c6 10 ♘e2, and now:

a) 10...♗e7!? 11 ♕g3 g6 12 ♗h6 (12 c3 0-0 13 ♗h6 ♖e8 14 f4 ♗f5 = Adams-Petrović, Paris 1989) 12...♗e6 13 ♘d4 ±.

b) 10...g6 11 ♕g3 ♗g7 12 ♘f4 0-0 13 ♘h5 gxh5 14 ♗h6 ♗g4 15 ♗xg7 ♔xg7 16 f3 ♕g5 17 h3 ♖ae8 18 ♖ae1

± De Vreugt-Bykhovsky, Tel-Aviv 2000.

9 ♕f3

9 ♖e1 ♗e7 10 ♕h5 ♘xd3 11 cxd3 ♗e6 =.

9...♕h4

9...♗e7 10 ♕g3 g6 11 ♗h6 ±.

The text-move (9...♕h4) is a key idea, preventing White from playing ♕g3, which would otherwise impede the development of Black's kingside. Now White cannot gain the advantage:

a) 10 h3 ♗e7 11 ♖e1 ♘xd3 12 cxd3 0-0 13 ♗f4 ♖e8 14 a3 ♗f8 = Geller-Smejkal, Moscow 1981.

b) 10 ♘e2 ♗e7 11 ♘f4 0-0 12 h3 ♘e6 13 ♗e3 f6 14 ♘xe6 ♗xe6 15 ♗f5 ♗xf5 16 ♕xf5 fxe5 17 ♕xe5 occurred in Geller-Plaskett, Sochi 1984. Now, according to Yusupov, Black can achieve equality by 17...♖f7. 17...♕f6 18 ♕c7 b6 is also interesting.

c)

6 ♘c3 *(D)*

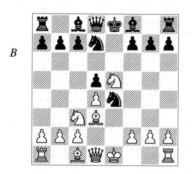

If White is going to allow the exchange on e5 then this is probably the best way to go about it. White aims to liquidate the e4-knight straight away and then hope for an advantage based on his lead in development.

6...♘xe5

If he wishes, Black can transpose by 6...♘xc3 7 bxc3 ♗d6 to the satisfactory line *5...♗d6 6 ♘c3 ♘xc3 7 bxc3 ♘d7*. Since the main line is not completely plain sailing for Black, this is an option he should seriously consider.

Also interesting is 6...♘ef6!? 7 0-0 ♗e7 8 ♗f4 0-0 9 ♕f3 c6 10 ♖fe1 ♖e8 11 ♘xd7 ♘xd7! 12 ♖e3 ♘f8 13 ♖ae1 ♗e6 is equal, Kostyra-Kiseliov, Krakow 1993.

7 dxe5 ♗b4

Or:

a) 7...♕h4? is bad in view of 8 ♗xe4! dxe4 9 ♘d5 ♕d8 10 ♗g5! ♕d7 (10...♗b4+ 11 c3 ♕xg5 12 ♘xc7+ ♔e7 13 ♕d4 1-0 Kremenetsky-Khachaturov, Moscow 1977) 11 e6! fxe6 12 ♕h5+ g6 13 ♘f6+ ♔f7 14 ♕h4 ±.

b) Black has a viable option in 7...♘xc3 8 bxc3:

b1) 8...♗e7 9 0-0 0-0 10 f4 f5 ∞.

b2) 8...♗e6!? 9 ♗e3 ♕d7 10 0-0 ♗e7 (10...g6 11 ♖b1 b6 12 ♗g5 ♗g7 13 f4 0-0 14 ♗f6 ♗f5 15 ♗xf5 ♕xf5 16 ♗e7 ♖fe8 17 ♕xd5 ♖ac8 18 ♗h4 ♕xc2 19 ♖bc1 ♕f5 20 ♖cd1 ± Sax-Arlandi, Lugano 1989) 11 f4 and now Black should certainly prefer 11...g6 = to 11...f5 12 exf6 ♗xf6 13 ♗c5! ±.

b3) 8...♕h4 9 0-0 ♗g4 10 ♕d2 ♗d7 11 ♕e3 b6 12 a4 ♗c5 13 ♕f3 c6 14 a5 0-0 15 ♗e3 ♕g4 16 ♕xg4 ♗xg4 17 ♗d4 ♗xd4 18 cxd4 c5 19 c3 ± Iordachescu-Motylev, Romania 2000.

b4) 8...♗c5 9 0-0 and now:

b41) 9...c6 10 ♔h1 ♕h4 11 ♕e2 (11 ♖b1?! 0-0 12 ♕e2 ♖e8! is level, Nevednichy-Schwartzman, Odorheiu Secuiesc 1993) 11...0-0 12 ♗e3 ±.

b42) 9...♗e6 10 ♖b1 (10 ♔h1!?) 10...♕d7 11 ♕e2 (11 ♖xb7 ♗b6 12 ♕e2 0-0 13 ♗a3 ♕c6 gives Black compensation) 11...0-0 12 ♗e3 ♗xe3 13 ♕xe3 b6 14 f4 ♗f5 =.

The text-move aims to eliminate the c3-knight with the bishop, and thereby maintain the knight on e4. However, the exchange of Black's dark-squared bishop makes the c1-bishop a potentially powerful piece and so there is an element of risk to Black's plan.

8 0-0 ♗xc3

8...♘xc3 9 bxc3 ♗xc3 10 ♖b1 (adventurous players can investigate 10 ♗a3 ♗xa1 11 ♕xa1 ♗e6 12 ♕b2) 10...♕e7 (after 10...0-0 11 ♗xh7+ ♔xh7 12 ♕d3+ ♔g8 13 ♕xc3 b6 14 ♕g3 ± White has the better chances in the middlegame with opposite-coloured bishops) 11 ♖b3 ♗b4 (Black blundered in Sax-Nunn, Brussels 1985: 11...♗xe5? 12 ♖e1 0-0 13 ♕h5 f5 14 ♗f4 1-0) 12 f4 gives White compensation for the pawn.

9 bxc3 ♗e6

Or:

a) 9...0-0 10 ♕h5 f5 11 exf6 ♘xf6 12 ♕e5 ± Zarnicki-Spangenberg, Buenos Aires 1991.

b) 9...♘xc3 10 ♕e1 d4 11 f4 g6 12 ♗b2 ♘a4 13 ♗a3 ♗e6?? 14 ♗b5+ ♗d7 15 e6! ♗xb5 16 ♕e5 +−.

10 f4

Now:

a) 10...♕d7 11 ♕f3 g6 12 c4 (12 ♗xe4 dxe4 13 ♕xe4 0-0-0 =) 12...♘c5

13 ♗e2 ♕c6! and now 14 ♕a3 ± (intending ♗f3 and ♗e3) is better than 14 ♖d1?! 0-0-0 15 ♗a3 ♘a4! 16 ♕e3 ♘b6 17 cxd5 ♗xd5 18 ♗e7 ♖d7 19 ♗g4 ♗e6 20 ♗f3 ♕a4 21 ♖xd7 ♗xd7 = Sax-Nikolić, Brussels 1988.

b) 10...f5 11 exf6 ♕xf6 12 f5! (12 ♗xe4?! dxe4 13 ♕h5+ ♕f7 14 ♕b5+ c6 15 ♕b4 ♗d5 16 a4 b6 = Palac-Arkhipov, Belgrade 1988) 12...♗d7 (12...♗xf5? 13 ♗b5+ c6 14 ♕xd5 ♘xc3 15 ♖e1+ ♘e4 16 ♖xe4+ ♗xe4 17 ♕xe4+ ♔d7 18 ♖b1 +−; 12...♗f7 13 ♗xe4 dxe4 14 ♗e3 ±) 13 ♕h5+ ♕f7 14 ♕xf7+ ♔xf7 15 c4 ♗c6 16 cxd5 ♗xd5 17 ♗b2 ±.

D)

6 ♕e2 *(D)*

B

This leads to interesting play where White gets an extra pawn, but Black has compensation in the form of his bishop-pair and superior development. White has been unable to prove any advantage in this line.

6...♘xe5

6...♕e7!? deserves attention, although since the main line is adequate for Black, this possibility is just the icing on the cake so far as Black is concerned:

a) White gains no advantage from 7 0-0 ♘xe5 8 dxe5 ♘c5 9 b3 ♗e6 10 f4 g6 11 ♗b2 0-0-0 12 ♘d2 ♔b8 13 ♘f3 ♕d7 14 a3 ♘xd3 15 cxd3 ♗c5+ 16 ♗d4 ♗xd4+ 17 ♘xd4 c5 18 ♘f3 ♗g4 19 d4! =.

b) 7 ♗f4 ♘xe5 8 ♗xe5 f6 9 ♗f4 ♘d6 10 ♘c3 c6 11 0-0-0 ♕xe2 12 ♘xe2 ♗d7 13 h4 ♔f7 with an equal position, Matanović-Udovčić, Skopje 1962.

c) 7 ♘xd7 ♗xd7 8 0-0 0-0-0 9 c4 ♘f6 10 ♕xe7 ♗xe7 11 c5 is an interesting idea, when White's chances in the ending make his game slightly preferable.

d) 7 ♗xe4 dxe4 8 ♗f4 ♘xe5 9 ♗xe5 ♗f5 10 ♘c3 0-0-0 11 0-0-0 ♕e6 12 ♕e3 and here:

d1) 12...h5 13 h3 f6 14 ♗xc7 (14 ♗h2 g6 15 ♔b1 ♗h6 16 ♕g3 ♖h7 17 ♖he1 ♕b6! = Karpov-Hort, Amsterdam 1980) 14...♔xc7 15 d5 ♕d7 (or 15...♕e5!? 16 ♕xa7 ♗d6 17 ♘b5+ ♔d7 18 ♕xb7+ ♔e8 19 ♕xg7 ♖h7 20 ♘xd6+ ♕xd6 21 ♕g3 ♕xg3 22 fxg3 ♖g7 23 ♖hf1 ♗h7 24 ♖xf6 ♖xg3 ∞) 16 ♕xa7 (D) and now:

B

d11) 16...♔d6? 17 ♕a3+ ♔c7 (or 17...♔e5 18 d6 +− Svec-Wason, corr. 1988-9) 18 ♕a5+ ♔d6 (18...♔b8 19 ♘b5 +−) 19 ♕b4+ ♔c7 20 ♘b5+ +−.

d12) 16...♗d6! 17 ♕a5+ (17 a4? ♖a8 18 ♘b5+ ♕xb5 19 ♕xa8 ♕c5! 20 ♕xh8 e3 −+) 17...♔b8 18 ♘b5 (18 ♖d4 ♗c7) 18...♗c5 19 d6 (19 b4? ♗xf2) 19...♕c6 (19...♖c8 20 ♘c7 and now 20...♗a7 ∞ is far better than 20...♖xc7? 21 dxc7+ ♕xc7 22 ♕xc7+ ♔xc7 23 ♖d5 +−) 20 ♕c7+ (20 ♘c7 b6 ∞) 20...♔a8 21 ♕a5+ =.

d2) 12...♗b4!? 13 ♔b1 (13 ♘b5 ♕xa2) 13...f6 14 ♗g3 ♕c4 ∞ Krakops-Katišonok, Riga 1993.

7 ♗xe4 dxe4 8 ♕xe4 ♗e6 9 ♕xe5

9 dxe5 also has its advocates. Black's best reply is then 9...♗d5 10 ♕g4 (10 ♕a4+ ♗c6 11 ♕g4 h5 12 ♕h3 ♕d5 13 0-0 ♕xe5 14 ♗d2 ♗d7 15 ♕b3 0-0-0 ∓ Tiberkov-Schwartzman, Copenhagen 1990) 10...h5 11 ♕h3, and here:

a) Larsen recommends 11...♕e7!? 12 f4 (12 0-0!? ♕xe5 13 ♘c3 ♗e6 14 ♕f3 c6 15 ♗f4 ♕f5 16 ♘e4 ♗e7 =) 12...♕e6! (it is a curious feature of Black's pawn sacrifice that his initiative persists even after the exchange of queens; the active bishops and pressure against White's kingside provide enough compensation, even in the endgame) 13 ♕xe6+ fxe6 14 ♔f2! (Larsen considered only 14 0-0?! ♗c5+ 15 ♔h1 0-0-0 16 ♘c3 ♗c6 17 f5 ♖d4 18 h3 ♖g4 −+) 14...h4! (14...♗c5+ 15 ♗e3 ♗xe3+ 16 ♔xe3 ♗xg2 17 ♖g1 ±) 15 ♘c3 (15 ♖e1 ♗c5+ 16 ♗e3 ♗xe3+ 17 ♖xe3 0-0 18 g3 g5 ∓; 15 ♖g1!? ♗e4 ∞) 15...♗c5+ 16 ♗e3 ♗xe3+ 17

♔xe3 ♗xg2 18 ♖hg1 h3 19 ♘e4 with equality.

b) 11...♗e6!? 12 ♕e3 (12 ♕f3 ♗d5 =) 12...♕d5 (not 12...h4?! 13 ♘c3 h3 14 g3 ♗b4 15 ♗d2 ♗xc3 16 ♗xc3 ♕d5 17 f3 0-0-0 18 ♔f2 ± Tiviakov-Barua, Calcutta 1994) 13 0-0 ♗c5 14 ♕e2 (14 ♕g5 ♗d4! 15 ♖e1 ♖h6 with a strong initiative) 14...♗d4! 15 ♖e1 h4 gives Black a strong initiative.

9...♕d7 (D)

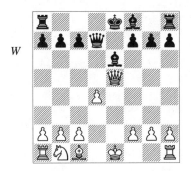

10 ♗e3
Or:

a) 10 ♘c3 ♗b4 (the exchange of the knight on c3 is a key feature of the gambit; Black secures the central square d5 for his bishop, from where it supports a kingside pawn advance; White's extra doubled c-pawn is not especially relevant) 11 0-0 (11 ♕xg7 0-0-0 gives Black adequate compensation) 11...0-0-0 12 ♗e3 f6 and then:

a1) 13 ♕g3 ♗xc3 14 bxc3 h5 15 h4 (15 f3 h4 16 ♕f2 h3 17 g3 ♕c6 18 a4 a5 19 ♖fb1 ♗c4 ∓ Gurgenidze-Rozentalis, Kharkov 1985) 15...g5 16 hxg5 (16 f3 ♖dg8 17 ♖f2 ♕c6 18 ♗d2 g4 19 f4 ♗c4 −+ Karpov-Larsen, Tilburg 1980) 16...h4 17 ♕h2 h3 18 g3

♗d5! (18...♕c6 19 gxf6 ♗d5 20 ♗f4 ♕xc3?! {better is 20...♗f3} 21 ♗e5 ♖h7 22 ♖fe1 c6 23 ♖ac1 b5 24 ♖e3 ♕d2 25 ♖ce1 ♖g8 26 f3 ♕a5 27 c3 ± Nun-Finegold, Prague 1990) 19 gxf6 and after 19...♗f3 White is playing without his queen, while 19...♕g4!? is also interesting.

a2) 13 ♕e4 ♗xc3 14 bxc3 ♗d5 15 ♕d3 ♕c6 16 f3 h5 17 ♖fe1 g5 18 ♗d2 g4 19 ♖e7 gxf3 20 ♗f4 ∞ Sveshnikov-Rozentalis, Riga 1986.

As we can see from these variations, the opposite-coloured bishops mean some danger for White, his extra pawn(s) notwithstanding.

a3) 13 ♕f4 ♗d6 14 ♕f3 ♗g4 15 ♕d5 ♗xh2+ 16 ♔xh2 ♕xd5 17 ♘xd5 ½-½ Unzicker-Rogoff, Amsterdam 1980.

b) 10 0-0-0 0-0-0 11 ♗e3 (11 c3 ♗d6 12 ♕a5 ♗d5 and Black has compensation – I.Zaitsev) 11...♗b4 12 c3 (12 a3 f6 13 ♕g3 ♗d6 gives Black compensation) 12...f6 (12...♗d6!? deserves attention: 13 ♕a5 ♗d5 14 f3 {14 ♘d2? ♗xg2! 15 ♔xg2 ♕g4+ 16 ♔h1 ♕h3 17 f4 ♕xe3 ∓} 14...♖he8 with compensation for Black) 13 ♕g3 ♗d6 (interesting is 13...♗e7!? 14 ♘d2 h5 15 f3 g5 16 c4 f5 17 ♕e5 ♗d6 18 ♕a5 ♗f4 19 ♗xf4 ♕xd4+ 20 ♖f2 gxf4 21 ♘b3 ♕b6 = Ki.Georgiev-Salov, Leningrad 1987) 14 ♗f4 and now:

b1) 14...♗e7!? 15 ♖e1 ♖de8 16 ♘d2 (16 ♗xc7 can be answered by 16...♗d5 17 ♗f4 g5 18 ♗e3 ♗d6) 16...h5 17 h3 and then:

b11) 17...h4 18 ♕e3 ±.

b12) 17...g5 18 ♗xc7 ♗f5! 19 ♗b8! (19 ♗a5 ♗d6 20 ♕f3 g4 ∓) 19...h4 20

♕h2 b5 (intending ...♔b7) 21 ♖e3 ♔b7 22 ♖ae1 ♖h7 23 ♘b3!! ♖xb8 24 ♘a5+! (24 ♖xe7? ♖xe7 25 ♘c5+ ♔a8 −+) 24...♔a6 (24...♔a8 25 ♖xe7 ♖xe7 26 ♖xe7 ♕xe7 27 ♕xb8+! ♔xb8 28 ♘c6+ +−) 25 ♕xb8 ♔xa5 26 a4! with an attack − N.Ninov.

b13) 17...♗f5!? 18 ♕xg7 h4! (not 18...♖hg8 19 ♕f7 ♗xh3 20 ♗g3 h4 21 gxh3 hxg3 22 ♕e6 and White has a clear advantage) 19 ♕f7! ♖h7 20 ♕c4 ♖g7 with compensation for Black, N.Ninović-C.Chandler, corr. 1994-5.

b2) 14...♗f8 15 ♕d3 (15 ♖e1 ♗f7 16 ♘d2 g5 17 ♗e3 ♖g8 gives Black compensation, N.Ninović-Raetsky, Primorsko 1990) 15...g5 16 ♗e3 h5 17 ♘d2 h4 18 f3 ♖g8 19 c4 f5 and Black has compensation, Magem-Macieja, Batumi Echt 1999.

We now return to 10 ♗e3 (D):

This move delays developing the knight in order to avoid its exchange. Since the knight is White's only minor piece capable of controlling some light squares, White would like to retain it if he can.

10...♗b4+

Or:

a) 10...♕c6!? deserves serious attention: 11 ♘c3 ♗b4 12 0-0 ♗xc3 13 bxc3 0-0-0 = Gurgenidze-Dorfman, Volgodonsk 1981.

b) Black has also tried 10...0-0-0 11 ♕a5!, and now:

b1) 11...♕c6?! 12 ♘c3 b6 13 ♕a6+ ♔b8 14 ♘b5 ♗c4 15 a4 ♗b4+ 16 c3 ♗d6 17 ♕xa7+ ♔c8 18 0-0-0 ♕xg2 19 d5! favours White, Hort-Short, Bundesliga 1986/7.

b2) 11...a6 12 ♘c3! f5 13 d5! ± Barcenilla-Barcza, Cebu 1992.

b3) 11...♗d5 12 ♘c3! (12 ♕xa7?! ♕b5 13 ♘d2 ♕xb2 14 0-0 ♕xc2 ∞; 12 0-0? ♗xg2 13 ♔xg2 ♕g4+ 14 ♔h1 ♕f3+ 15 ♔g1 ♖d5 16 ♕c3 ♗d6 17 ♖c1 ♖h5 ∓ Maciejczak-Janocha, Polish corr. Ch 1983) 12...♗xg2 13 ♖g1 b6 14 ♕xa7 ♗b7 15 0-0-0 ± Udalov-Raetsky, corr. 1981-2.

b4) 11...♔b8 12 ♘c3! b6 13 ♕a4 ♕xa4 14 ♘xa4 ♗b4+ 15 c3 ±.

b5) 11...b6!? 12 ♕xa7 ♗d5 13 a4 (13 ♘c3 ♗b4 14 0-0-0 ♗xc3 15 bxc3 ♕c6 16 ♕a3 ♔d7 gives Black compensation) 13...♕c6 and now White should play 14 ♕a6+, since 14 c3?? loses to 14...♔d7! intending ...♖a8.

11 c3

11 ♘d2 0-0-0 12 c3 f6 13 ♕g3 ♗d6 14 ♕f3 ♖he8 15 h3 f5 ∓ Unzicker-H.Eng, Bundesliga 1983/4.

11...♗d6 12 ♕h5

This is an idea of the great Petroff specialist Rozentalis. Other moves:

a) 12 ♕xg7 0-0-0 13 ♘d2 ♕c6! (13...♕b5?! 14 0-0-0 ♕a4 15 ♘e4! ♕xa2 16 ♘xd6+ cxd6 17 ♕f6 ± Oll-Khalifman, Sochi 1984) 14 0-0-0 ♗f5 (threatening ...♕xc3+ −+) 15 ♘b3

♕e4 16 ♔d2 ♕c2+ 17 ♔e1 ♕xb2 with a very strong initiative.

b) 12 ♕a5 ♕c6 (12...b6 13 ♕g5 h6 14 ♕h5 ♕c6 15 0-0 g6 16 ♕h4 ♗e7 17 ♕g3 g5 18 ♘d2 f5 ∓ Shivodov-Kuznetsov, USSR 1987) 13 f3 (13 0-0? ♗d5 14 f3 b6 15 ♕a6 ♗c4 16 d5 ♕xd5 17 ♕a4+ b5 18 ♕d1 ♕e5 −+ Klinger-Wolff, Baguio City jr Wch 1987) 13...♗d5 14 ♘d2 0-0 15 0-0 ♖fe8 and then:

b1) 16 ♗g5 ♖e2! 17 c4 ♗xh2+ 18 ♔xh2 ♕d6+ 19 ♔h1 ♕g3 20 ♖g1 ♕xg5 −+.

b2) 16 ♗f2 b6 17 ♕a6 ♗xh2+! ∓.

b3) 16 ♖fe1 b6 17 ♕a6 ♗xh2+! 18 ♔xh2 ♖xe3 19 ♔g1 (19 ♖xe3 ♕h6+ 20 ♔g3 ♕xe3 ∓ Fedorov-Raetsky, corr. 1983-4) 19...♕e6 20 ♕f1 ♖e8 is slightly better for Black, Barcenilla-Ye Rongguang, Beijing 1992.

c) 12 ♕e4 0-0 13 ♕d3 ♕c6 14 ♘d2 ♕xg2 15 0-0-0 ♕h3 16 d5 ♗f5 17 ♕f1 ♕g4 18 c4 ♖fe8 19 h3 ♕h4 20 c5 ♗e5 21 ♕c4 ♕f6 22 ♕b3 b6 ∓ Hess-Okulsky, corr. 1996.

d) 12 ♕g5 f6 13 ♕h5+ ♗f7 14 ♕f3 0-0-0 (Black has compensation for the pawn) 15 ♘d2 ♕b5 (15...f5!? 16 c4 f4 17 ♗xf4 ♗xf4 18 ♕xf4 ♖he8+ is very dangerous for White) 16 a4 ♕d3 gives Black compensation, Lanc-Haba, Prague 1989.

12...0-0 (D)

Or:

a) 12...♕c6!?.

b) 12...0-0-0 13 0-0 f5 14 f4 ♕b5 (14...♖he8!?) 15 ♘d2 ♕xb2 16 c4 ♕c3 17 ♕f3 ♖he8 18 ♖ab1 ♗xc4 19 ♘xc4 ♕xc4 20 ♕xb7+ ♔d7 21 ♖fc1 ♕xa2 22 ♖a1 ♕e2 23 ♗f2 is winning for White, Rozentalis-P.H.Nielsen, Århus 1997.

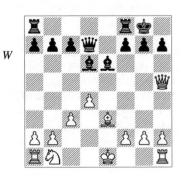

W

13 0-0

Now:

a) After 13...f5!?, 14 f4 is unclear, while 14 ♖e1 f4 15 ♗c1 f3 gives Black compensation.

b) 13...♗g4 14 ♕h4 ♖ae8 (S.Movsesian-Haba, Pardubice 1998) 15 ♖e1!? ♗e7!? (15...♖e6 16 ♘d2 {16 ♕xg4 ♖xe3} 16...♖g6 17 ♘e4 ♗f3 18 ♘g5 ♖h6 19 ♕xh6 gxh6 20 ♘xf3 ±) 16 ♕g3 ♗d6 17 f4 ♖e7 gives Black compensation.

12 ♕h5!? deserves thorough practical testing, even though the general impression is that Black has no problems. His two active bishops, lead in development, and pressure on the light squares provide good compensation for the pawn.

E)

6 ♘xd7 ♗xd7 7 0-0 (D)

Or:

a) 7 ♕e2 ♕e7 8 0-0 0-0-0 9 ♘d2 (9 c4 ♘f6 =) 9...♘g5 10 ♕xe7 ♗xe7 11 f4 ♘e6 12 ♘f3 ♖df8 13 f5 ♘d8 14 ♘e5 ♗e8 15 ♘g4 f6 16 ♗f4 ♗f7 17

♖ae1 ♖e8 18 c3 ♔d7 ½-½ Geller-Arkhipov, Moscow 1986.

b) 7 ♗f4 ♕f6 8 ♗xe4 ♕xf4 9 ♗xd5 0-0-0 10 g3 (10 ♕d2 ♖e8+ 11 ♔d1 ♕f6 gives Black compensation; 10 0-0?! ♗g4 ∓) 10...♖e8+ 11 ♔f1 ♗h3+ 12 ♗g2 ♗xg2+ 13 ♔xg2 ♕e4+ 14 ♕f3 ♕xd4 =.

c) 7 ♘d2 ♕h4 8 0-0 ♘xd2 9 ♕xd2 ♗d6! 10 ♕e2+ (10 ♖e1+ ♔f8 and now 11 g3 ♕xd4 ∓ or 11 f4 ♗xf4 −+) 10...♗e6 (10...♔d8!?) 11 f4 0-0-0 with equality.

This is the key position of the 5...♘d7 line. Exchanging on d7 may appear a concession, because White's active knight disappears and Black's development is slightly accelerated. However, the text-move prepares the advance c4 to undermine the e4-knight (c4 could not be played immediately because of the check on b4). As often happens in the Petroff, if Black is forced to meet c4 by ...♘f6, then White has excellent chances for the advantage. Therefore Black should try to maintain the knight on e4 by means of active play (see Lines E3 and E4 below). Now:

E1:	7...♘f6	56
E2:	7...♗e7	57
E3:	7...♕f6	59
E4:	7...♕h4	60

Note that the very important alternative 7...♗d6 is discussed in the next chapter via the move-order 5...♗d6 6 0-0 ♘d7 7 ♘xd7 ♗xd7.

E1)
7...♘f6
This passive move falls in with White's plan.

8 ♗g5

Or:

a) White gains no advantage by 8 ♖e1+ ♗e7 9 ♗g5 (9 ♗f4 ♗g4 10 ♕d2 0-0 11 ♘c3 c6 =) 9...0-0 10 ♘d2 (10 ♗xf6 ♗xf6 11 ♕h5 g6 12 ♕xd5 ♗e6 13 ♕xd8 ♖axd8 14 c3 c5 =) 10...♖e8 11 ♗xf6 ♗xf6 12 ♕h5 g6 13 ♕xd5 ♗e6 14 ♕xd8 ♖exd8 15 ♘f3 ½-½ Kveinys-Poliakov, corr. 1987.

b) However, 8 c4!? deserves attention, and is in keeping with the general strategy of the position: 8...♗e6 (8...♗e7 transposes to Line E2) 9 c5 (9 cxd5 ♘xd5 10 ♘c3 ♗e7 11 ♖e1 0-0 =) 9...g6 10 ♗f4! (10 ♕a4+?! ♕d7 11 ♕b3 c6 12 ♗f4 ♘h5 13 ♗e5 f6 14 ♗g3 ♘xg3 15 hxg3 ♗g7 slightly favours Black, Prasad-Arlandi, Thessaloniki OL 1988) 10...♘h5 (10...♗g7!? 11 ♕b3 ♕c8 12 ♘c3 0-0 and now 13 ♗e5 ± is better than 13 ♘b5 ♘e8) 11 ♗e3 (11 ♗e5 f6 12 ♗g3 ♘xg3 13 hxg3 ∞) 11...♘g7 12 ♕b3 ♕c8 13 ♗h6! ♘h5 14 ♗xf8 ♔xf8 15 ♖e1 with a clear advantage for White, Atakisi-Detreeuw, Batumi Echt 1999.

8...♗e7 9 c3

Even this rather dull continuation promises White a slight advantage. If 9 ♗xf6, then 9...♗xf6 10 ♖e1+ ♔f8 (10...♗e7 11 ♕h5 c6 12 ♘d2 ±) 11 c3 g6 12 ♘d2 ♔g7 =, while 9 ♘d2 can be met by 9...0-0 10 h3 h6 11 ♗h4 ♖e8 12 ♖e1 ♘h7 13 ♗g3 ♗h4 14 ♖xe8+ ♗xe8 15 ♗xh4 ♕xh4 16 ♘f3 ± Udalov-Poliakov, corr. 1987-8. 9 c4!? remains to be tried.

9...c6

9...0-0?! 10 ♗xf6 ♗xf6 11 ♕h5 ±.

10 ♘d2 0-0 11 ♕c2 h6 12 ♗h4 ♘h5

12...♖e8 13 ♘f3 ♘h5 14 ♗xe7 ♖xe7 15 ♘e5 ±.

13 ♗xe7 ♕xe7 14 ♖fe1 ♕d6 15 ♘f3 ♘f4 16 ♗h7+! ♔h8 17 ♗f5

± Geller-Smyslov, Moscow 1981.

E2)

7...♗e7 *(D)*

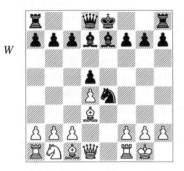

At first sight this is a natural developing move, but it again allows White to force the knight to retreat to f6.

8 c4

Otherwise:

a) 8 ♕f3?! is suspect in view of 8...0-0 9 c3 (9 ♗xe4 dxe4 10 ♕xe4

♗c6 gives Black compensation; 9 c4 ♘f6! 10 cxd5 ♗g4 11 ♕g3 ♕xd5 ∓) 9...♗d6 10 ♘d2 f5 ∓ Timman-Yusupov, Linares Ct (4) 1992.

b) 8 ♖e1 0-0 (8...♘f6!? 9 ♗g5 0-0 10 c3 c6 11 ♘d2 ♖e8 12 h3 h6 13 ♗h4 ♗e6 14 ♗c2 ♘h7 15 ♗g3 ♗d6 16 ♘f1 ♕c7 17 ♕d3 ♘f8 18 ♖e3 ♗d7 19 ♖ae1 ½-½ Rozentalis-Yusupov, Pula Echt 1997) 9 ♗xe4 dxe4 10 ♖xe4 ♗f6! (10...♗c6?! 11 d5! ♗f6 12 c4 ♗d7 13 ♘c3 ± Torre-Rogoff, 1976) and then:

b1) 11 ♗e3 ♗f5 12 ♖f4 ♗g6 13 c3 ♖e8 14 ♕b3 ♕d7 15 ♘d2 c6 is unclear.

b2) 11 ♘c3 ♗c6 12 ♖g4 ♖e8 13 ♗e3 gives White compensation.

b3) 11 ♖e1 ♗c6 12 ♗e3 ♕d5 and now White should play 13 ♕g4 ∞, rather than 13 f3?! (Aseev-Skachkov, St Petersburg 1998) 13...♖fe8!? (intending ...♖xe3) 14 ♘c3 (14 c3 ♗h4 15 ♗f2 ♗xf2+ 16 ♔xf2 ♖xe1 17 ♕xe1 ♖e8 18 ♕d1 ♗b5 19 ♘a3 ♖e2+ 20 ♔g1 ♕g5 with an attack) 14...♕d6 15 ♔h1 ♖ad8 16 ♕d2 ♗xd4 17 ♗xd4 ♕xd4 18 ♖xe8+ ♗xe8 19 ♕xd4 ♖xd4 and Black is slightly better.

c) 8 ♘c3 ♘f6!? 9 ♗g5 c6 10 ♕f3 (10 ♖e1 0-0 11 ♕d2 ♖e8 12 ♖e2 h6 13 ♗h4 ♘h5 14 ♗xe7 ♖xe7 15 ♖ae1 ♖xe2 16 ♘xe2 ♕c7 17 c3 ♖e8 18 ♘g3 ♖xe1+ 19 ♕xe1 ♘xg3 = Am.Rodriguez-Yusupov, Oviedo rpd 1993) 10...0-0 11 ♖ae1 h6 12 ♗f4 ♗e6 13 h3 ♗d6 14 ♖e3 (14 ♗e5!?) 14...♘e8 15 ♘e2 ♕d7 16 ♘g3 ♗xf4 17 ♕xf4 ♕d6 18 ♘h5 ♕xf4 19 ♘xf4 ♘c7 20 ♖fe1 ♖fe8 21 ♔f1 ♗d7 ½-½ Illescas-Beliavsky, Madrid 1997.

8...♘f6 *(D)*

Or 8...c6, and then:

a) 9 cxd5 cxd5 10 ♖e1 0-0 11 ♗xe4 dxe4 12 ♖xe4 ♗c6 13 d5 ♗f6 14 ♘c3 ♗xc3 15 bxc3 ♕xd5 = Mousa-Sorial, Tanta City 2000.

b) 9 ♖e1 ♘f6 10 ♘c3 ♗e6 (Black should consider 10...dxc4!? 11 ♗xc4 0-0 ∞) 11 c5 0-0 12 b4 ± Leko-Casafus, Buenos Aires 1994.

c) 9 ♘c3 ♘xc3 10 bxc3 dxc4 11 ♗xc4 0-0 ± Xu Jun-Lelchuk, Helsinki 1992.

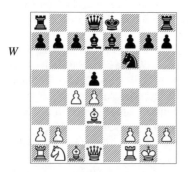

9 ♘c3

Otherwise:

a) 9 ♕b3 needs practical testing.

b) 9 cxd5 ♘xd5 10 ♘c3 should be answered by 10...♗e6 11 ♖e1 0-0 =, rather than 10...♘xc3?! 11 bxc3 0-0 (11...♗c6!?) 12 ♗e4 ♖b8 13 ♕h5 f5 14 ♗d5+ ♔h8 15 ♕f3 c6 16 ♗b3 ♗d6 17 ♗f4 ± Prié-Fritzsche, Strasbourg 1991.

9...♗e6

The alternative is 9...dxc4, although the resulting isolated d-pawn position promises White a slight advantage as he is able to develop all his pieces very easily: 10 ♗xc4 0-0 11 ♖e1 (11 ♗f4 ♗d6 12 ♗e5 ♘g4 13 ♗xd6 cxd6 14 ♕b3 ♖b8 15 a4 ♕h4 16 h3 ♘f6 17 ♕b4 ♖fd8 = Palac-Zaja, Pula 2000) 11...c6 12 h3 ♗f5 13 ♕f3 ♗g6 14 ♗e3 ♖e8 15 d5 (15 ♖ac1 b5 16 ♗b3 b4 17 ♘a4 ♗e4 18 ♕g3 ♗d5 19 ♘c5 a5 ∓ Velička-Konopka, Czech Ch (Opava) 2000) 15...cxd5 16 ♘xd5 ♗e4 17 ♘xe7+ ±.

10 c5 ♕d7

Or 10...0-0 11 ♗f4 c6 (11...♗g4 12 ♕c2 c6 13 ♖fe1 ± Radulov-Kochiev, Sofia 1981), and now:

a) 12 h3!? ♖e8 13 ♖e1 and then:

a1) 13...♕d7 14 ♕c2 (14 g4!?) 14...g6 15 b4 ±.

a2) 13...♘d7 14 ♕d2 (14 b4 ♗g5! 15 ♗g3 ♕f6 intending ...♗f5 equalizes) 14...♗f6 15 ♗c2 ♘f8 16 ♖e2 (16 b4?! ♘g6 17 ♗d6 ♘h4!) 16...b6! (16...♘g6 17 ♗d6 ♕d7 18 ♖ae1 ♖ed8 19 b4 ♗f5 20 ♗a4 ±; 16...♗d7 17 ♖xe8 ♕xe8 18 ♖e1 ♘e6 19 ♗e5 ±) 17 ♖ae1 ± Svidler-Yusupov, Kazan 1997.

b) 12 b4 ♕d7 (12...♗g4!? intends ...♗h5-g6, exchanging off the bad bishop) 13 ♕c2 (13 b5 ♗f5 14 bxc6 bxc6 15 ♕c2 ♗xd3 16 ♕xd3 ♖fe8 =; 13 ♖e1!? ♖fe8 14 ♕c2 g6 15 b5! ±) 13...g6 (13...♗d8!?) and here:

b1) 14 b5 ♖fe8?! (14...♘h5 is a better move) 15 a4 ♘h5 16 ♗e3 ♗d8? (Black should try 16...♘g7!? intending 17...♗f5 or 17...♘f5) 17 a5 a6 18 bxa6 bxa6 19 ♘a4! ± J.Polgar-Van der Sterren, Wijk aan Zee 1998.

b2) 14 ♖fe1 ♘h5 15 ♗e5 f6 (perhaps 15...♘g7!? intending ...♗f5 is better) 16 ♗g3 ♘xg3 (16...♘g7!?) 17 hxg3 ± Tiviakov-Miles, Linares 1998.

11 ♗f4 0-0 12 ♖e1 c6 13 b4 ♖fe8 14 b5

14 h3 ♗f5 15 ♖e5 ♗g6 16 ♕f3 ♗d8 17 ♖xe8+ ♘xe8 18 ♗xg6 (18 ♖d1 ♘c7 19 ♗e5 ♘e6 20 ♗xg6 hxg6 21 a4 ♗c7 22 ♗xc7 ♘xc7 ½-½ J.Polgar-Yusupov, Vienna 1996) 18...hxg6 19 b5 ±.

14...♗f5 15 bxc6 bxc6 16 ♗a6 ♘e4 17 ♘xe4 dxe4 18 ♕a4 ♖ad8 19 ♖ad1

± Hellers-Rozentalis, Malmö 1997. White is better because his bishops are more active than their enemy counterparts. In particular, the f5-bishop is restricted by the e4-pawn and the other bishop must remain where it is to prevent White from playing ♗d6.

E3)
7...♕f6 *(D)*

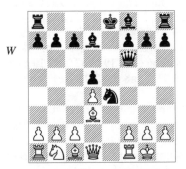

With this move Black aims for rapid development based on queenside castling, and to this end he is willing to sacrifice a pawn. However, this gambit is a poor relation of the one Black offered in Line D above. Perhaps the main difference is that instead of White's knight sitting on b1, here it immediately occupies an active central post at e4. Certainly White

should not underestimate Black's kingside chances, but it is hard to believe that Black has full compensation for the pawn.

8 ♗xe4

Or:

a) 8 c4 ♕xd4 9 ♘c3 0-0-0! (after 9...♘c5?! 10 ♖e1+ Black a choice between 10...♗e6 11 ♖xe6+! ♘xe6 12 cxd5 ♗c5 13 ♗e3 ♕e5 14 dxe6 ♗xe3 15 ♗b5+ ♔f8 16 ♕f3 ♕xe6 17 fxe3 ± Tseshkovsky-Bareev, USSR Ch (Kiev) 1986 and 10...♔d8 11 ♗e2 ♕xd1 12 ♖xd1 dxc4 13 ♗xc4, when White has compensation) 10 ♘xd5 ♘c5 leads to equality.

b) 8 ♘c3 ♕xd4 (8...♘xc3 9 bxc3 0-0-0 10 ♕h5 ♕e6 11 ♗d2 g6 12 ♕f3 f6 13 ♖fe1 ♕f7 14 c4!, Kotronias-Atalik, Pucarevo 1987, 14...♗c6 15 c5 ±) 9 ♕h5 (9 ♘xe4 dxe4 10 ♗xe4 ♕xd1 11 ♖xd1 0-0-0 = Kengis-Rozentalis, USSR jr Ch (Vilnius) 1984) and now:

b1) 9...♘xc3 10 bxc3 ♕xc3 11 ♗g5 ♗e6 12 ♖ae1 gives White compensation.

b2) 9...♘f6 10 ♖e1+ ♗e7 11 ♕g5 ♗e6 (11...♕g4 12 ♖xe7+! ♔xe7 13 ♘xd5+ ♔f8 14 ♘xf6 gxf6 15 ♕xf6 ♖g8 16 ♗h6+ ♔e8 17 ♖e1+ ♗e6 18 g3 ± Shirazi-Kogan, USA Ch (Estes Park) 1985) 12 ♘b5 ♕b6 is unclear since 13 ♗f4 can be met by 13...♘e4!.

b3) 9...0-0-0 10 ♕xf7 (10 ♘xd5 f5 ∞; 10 ♗e3?! ♘f6! ∓) 10...♘xc3 11 bxc3 ♕e5 12 ♗f4 ♕f6 13 ♕xf6 gxf6 14 ♖fe1 ♗c5 15 ♗e3 ♗xe3 16 ♖xe3 ♖de8 = Yusupov.

c) 8 ♗e3!? ♗d6 9 c4 0-0-0 (9...c6 10 cxd5 cxd5 11 ♕h5 – *7...♗d6 8 c4*

c6 9 cxd5 cxd5 10 ♕*h5* ♕*f6 11* ♗*e3*)
10 c5 ♗f4 11 ♘c3 (11 c6!? ♗e6 12
cxb7+ ♔b8 is slightly better for White)
11...♗xe3 12 fxe3 ♕h6!? 13 ♘xd5
♖he8 14 ♖xf7! c6 (14...♕e6? 15 ♗c4
+−) 15 ♗xe4 ♖xe4 16 ♘f4 ♖xe3 17
♕d2 ♖e4 18 ♖e1! ♖xe1+ 19 ♕xe1
♖e8 20 ♕g3 g5! 21 ♘d3 ♕g6 22 ♕f3!
♕h6 23 ♘e5 ± Gufeld-Ye Rongguang,
Kuala Lumpur 1994.

8...dxe4 9 ♘c3 0-0-0 10 ♘xe4 *(D)*

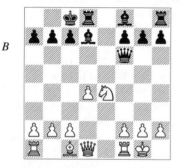

10...♕g6
10...♕b6?! 11 ♖e1! h5 12 ♕d3 h4
13 h3 ♖h5 14 c4 ♖e8 15 ♖e2 ± A.Iva-
nov-Rozentalis, Klaipeda 1985.

11 f3 h5
Black's burden is certainly not eased
by 11...f5?! 12 ♘f2 ♗b5 13 ♖e1 ♗d6
14 ♘h3 ♖he8 15 ♗f4 ♖xe1+ 16 ♕xe1
♖e8 17 ♕g3 ♕f6 18 c3 ♖e2 19 b3 ♖c2
20 ♗xd6 ± A.Koroliov-Glek, USSR
corr. Ch 1986 or 11...♗f5?! 12 c3 h5
13 ♕a4 ♔b8 14 ♗f4 h4 15 ♖ae1 h3 16
g4 ♗d7 (Klovans-Rozentalis, USSR
1985) 17 ♕c4 ♖c8 18 ♘g5! ♗d6 19
♗xd6 cxd6 20 ♕xf7 ♖xg5 21 ♕xd7
♕d2 22 ♕xd6+ ♔a8 23 ♕g3 ± Klo-
vans.

12 ♗f4 h4

12...♕b6?! 13 ♕d2 ♗b5 14 ♖fd1
f5 15 ♘f2 h4 16 c3 ± Am.Rodriguez-
Shirazi, New York 1988.

13 ♕d3 h3
13...♕b6 14 a4 ♗e6 15 ♖fd1 h3
and now White should play 16 g4 ±
rather than 16 a5 ♕c6 17 a6 b6 18 c4!?
f5 19 d5 fxe4 20 ♕xe4 ½-½ Raetsky-
Kveinys, corr. 1987.

14 g4 ♕b6 15 a4 ♗e6 16 ♖fd1 f5!?
Or:

a) 16...♕xb2? 17 ♖ab1 ♕a2 18
♖xb7 ♔xb7 19 ♕b5+ ♔c8 20 ♕c6
+−.

b) 16...a6 17 a5 ♕xb2 (17...♕c6
18 ♕c3! ♕xc3 19 ♘xc3 ±) 18 ♘c3
♕b4 19 ♖a4 ♕e7 20 d5 g5 21 ♗g3 ±
A.Ivanov-Kochiev, Kostroma 1985.

17 a5 fxe4
17...♕c6 18 gxf5 ♗xf5 19 a6 b6 20
♗g3 ♕g6 21 ♕c4 ♖d7 22 d5 ♗xe4 23
♕xe4 ♖h6 24 ♖a4 ♗c5+ 25 ♔f1 ♖e7
26 d6! 1-0 Raetsky-Sivets, corr. 1987.

18 axb6 exd3 19 bxa7 ♔d7 20 a8♕
♖xa8 21 ♖xa8 dxc2 22 ♖c1 ♗b3 23
♗e3
Although the position is quite complicated, the annoying pawn on c2 does
not provide Black with enough compensation for the exchange. Overall,
White has a small advantage.

E4)
7...♕h4 *(D)*
The critical continuation. Black
again aims for rapid development and
queenside castling, but this time without sacrificing a pawn. Play often becomes very sharp in this line, and both
sides have to be on the alert for tactical
possibilities. If it were merely a case

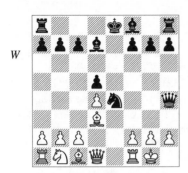

of White's queenside attack racing Black's kingside attack, then the position would not be so tricky, but in fact matters are far more complex. Both sides must take into account the weakening effect of any attacking moves they make. White, for example, usually plays c4-c5, but this leaves his d4-pawn weak. Since this pawn is the linchpin of White's position, it is often worth Black making a positional exchange sacrifice in order to win it. Similarly, Black usually plays ...g5, but this severely weakens Black's kingside, which may be a crucial factor if White can engineer a liquidation. Finally, as always, the e4-knight is critical and if White attacks it with f3, Black may prefer to sacrifice it rather than retreat it to f6.

8 c4

This is the main continuation. The alternatives are not dangerous:

a) 8 ♕e1 0-0-0 9 f3 ♕xe1 10 ♖xe1 ♘d6 = Timoshchenko-Nogueiras, Havana 1981.

b) 8 ♘c3 ♘xc3 9 bxc3 0-0-0 10 ♕f3 ♗e6! (and not 10...♗d6? 11 g3 ♕h3 12 ♕xd5 g6 13 ♗a6 with a clear advantage for White, Smirin-Foisor,

Groningen 1990) 11 ♗f4 ♗d6 = Zusman-Raetsky, USSR 1985.

c) 8 ♘d2 ♘xd2 9 ♗xd2 ♕xd4 (9...0-0-0 =) 10 ♖e1+ ♗e6 11 ♗c3 ♕b6 12 a4 a6 13 ♕d2 c5 14 ♗f5 d4 15 ♗a5 gives White compensation, Gudat-Raetsky, Cuxhaven 1993.

d) 8 g3!? and then:

d1) 8...♕h3 9 f3! ♘f6 (9...♘d6 10 ♖e1+ ♗e7 11 ♗f1 ♕h5 12 ♖e5 ♕g6 13 ♗d3 f5 14 ♘c3 is good for White) 10 ♖e1+ ♗e6 11 ♖e5! (intending ♗f1) 11...g5 12 ♗f5 g4 13 ♗g5 ♗e7 14 ♘c3! (Mi.Pavlović-Konguveel, Benasque 1998) 14...0-0-0 15 ♘e2 ±.

d2) 8...♕f6 9 ♘c3 ♘xc3 10 bxc3 0-0-0 11 ♕h5 ♕e6! (11...h6?! 12 ♗f4 ♗e6 13 ♗e5 ♕g5 14 ♕e2 ♗h3 15 ♖fb1 ± Marinković-Grbić, Serbian Ch (Kragujevac) 2000; White intends ♖xb7) 12 ♗d2 g6 13 ♕f3 f6 14 ♖fe1 ♕f7 15 c4 ♗c6 =.

8...0-0-0

Black seeks counterplay on the kingside. Other moves leave Black with more serious problems:

a) 8...♗d6?! 9 g3 ♕h3 10 ♘c3 (10 c5 ♗e7 11 ♘c3 ♘xc3 12 bxc3 0-0 13 ♗f4 ± Klinger-Bareev, Gausdal jr Wch 1986; 10 ♕c2 0-0 11 f3 ♘f6 12 c5 ♗e7 13 ♘c3 ± Howell-Barua, British Ch (Plymouth) 1989) 10...♘xc3 11 bxc3 0-0-0 12 c5 ♗e7 13 ♖b1 h5 14 ♖e1 ♗f6 15 ♗f4 ± Radulov-Ristić, Smederevska Palanka 1982.

b) 8...♘f6 *(D)* and now:

b1) 9 ♕e2+ ♗e7 and then:

b11) 10 f4!? ♘g4! (10...dxc4? 11 ♗xc4 ♔f8 12 ♘d2! ♗c6 13 ♘f3 ♕g4 14 ♕c2 ± Sax-Arlandi, Catania 1994) 11 h3 ♘h6 12 ♘c3 ∞.

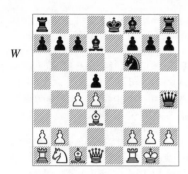

W

b12) 10 cxd5 ♕xd4! (10...♘xd5? 11 ♗e4! ± Leko-J.Horvath, Budapest 1993) 11 ♘c3 ♘xd5 12 ♘xd5 ♕xd5 13 ♖e1 ♕e6 14 ♗f4 ♕xe2 15 ♖xe2 ♗e6 16 ♗xc7 = Adorjan, Leko.

b2) 9 ♘c3!? dxc4 (9...♕xd4? 10 ♖e1+ ♗e7 11 ♗e3 ♕h4 12 ♗c5! ♗e6 13 ♗xe7 ♔xe7 14 cxd5 ♘g4 15 h3! ♕xf2+ 16 ♔h1 +−) 10 ♕e2+! (10 ♗xc4?! 0-0-0! 11 ♗xf7 ♗d6 12 f4 {12 g3 ♕h3} 12...♖hf8 13 ♗c4 g5! 14 g3 ♕h3 with an attack for Black) 10...♗e7 11 ♗xc4 ♕xd4 12 ♖d1 ♕h4! (12...♕c5 13 ♘d5! ♘xd5 14 ♖xd5 ♕b6 {14...♕c6 15 ♗g5 f6 16 ♖ad1! +−} 15 ♗g5 ♗e6 16 ♗xe7 ♔xe7 17 ♖b5 ♕c6 18 ♗d5! ±; 12...♕g4 13 f3 ♕h4 14 ♗e3! intending to counter 14...0-0? with 15 ♗f2! +−) and now:

b21) 13 ♘d5 ♘xd5 14 ♗xd5 0-0-0 is unclear.

b22) 13 g3 ♕h3 14 ♗f4 0-0!! 15 ♕xe7 ♖ae8 16 ♕c5 (not 16 ♖xd7? ♖xe7 17 ♖xe7 ♘g4 18 ♘d1 ♖d8! ∓) 16...♘g4 17 ♗d5! ♗c6! 18 ♖d2! (18 ♗xc6? bxc6 −+) 18...♕xh2+ 19 ♔f1 ♕h3+ 20 ♔g1 ♕h2+ ½-½ Leko-Miles, Cienfuegos 1997.

b23) 13 b3!! ♔f8 14 ♘d5 ♘xd5 15 ♗xd5 and then:

b231) 15...♗g4 16 f3 ♗c5+ 17 ♗e3 ♕e7 18 ♗xc5 ♕xc5+ 19 ♔h1 ♖e8 20 ♖ac1!! ♕b6 (20...♕xc1 21 ♕xe8+ ♔xe8 22 ♖xc1 +−) 21 ♕c4 ±.

b232) 15...c6 16 ♗xf7!? (16 ♗f3!? ♗e6 17 ♗b2 gives White a strong initiative) 16...♗g4 17 f3 ♗c5+! (17...♕f6 18 fxg4 ♕xa1 19 ♗c4! +−) 18 ♔h1 ♕e7 19 ♕xe7+ ♗xe7 20 ♗c4 ♗f5 ± Leko.

b3) 9 ♘d2!? ♕xd4 10 ♘f3 ♕b6 (10...♕c5!? 11 ♗e3 ♕a5 ∞) 11 cxd5! and now:

b31) 11...♘xd5 12 ♗c4 c6!? (the alternatives are worse, e.g. 12...0-0-0? 13 ♕xd5 +− or 12...♗e6?, which loses to 13 ♗xd5 in view of 13...0-0-0 14 ♗xe6+ or 13...♖d8? 14 ♕a4+ +−) 13 ♗xd5 cxd5 14 ♘e5 gives White the initiative.

b32) 11...♗e7 12 ♖e1 ♕d6 13 ♗g5! h6 (13...0-0 14 ♘e5 ±) 14 ♗h4 ♕xd5 (14...0-0 15 ♗g3 +−) 15 ♖c1 and then:

b321) 15...♗e6 16 ♕a4+ ♔f8 (16...♕d7 17 ♗b5 c6 18 ♖xc6! +−; 16...c6 17 ♗c4 ±) 17 ♗c4 ♕d7 18 ♕b3 gives White a strong initiative.

b322) 15...♗c6 16 ♕e2 ♕d8 (or 16...0-0 17 ♗c4 ♕h5 18 ♕xe7 ♗xf3 19 ♗xf6 ♕g4 20 ♗f1 gxf6 21 ♖c3 +−) 17 ♖cd1! ♔f8 18 ♗b5! ♗d6 19 ♗xc6 bxc6 20 ♕c4! g5 21 ♘e5! +− Z.Almasi-C.Horvath, Budapest 1997.

9 c5! (D)

White limits the scope of Black's dark-squared bishop and seizes space on the queenside. Otherwise:

a) If 9 cxd5, then 9...♗d6 10 g3 (10 h3? ♗xh3! ∓) 10...♘xg3 11 hxg3 ♗xg3 12 fxg3 ♕xg3+ =.

b) 9 ♘c3 ♗d6 and now:

b1) 10 g3 ♘xg3 11 fxg3 ♗xg3 12 ♕c2 (12 ♕d2 ♕xd4+ 13 ♕e3 ♗xh2+ 14 ♔xh2 ♕h4+ 15 ♔g1 ♕g4+ 16 ♔f2 d4 17 ♕g3 dxc3 18 bxc3 ♗e6 = Yusupov, Hübner) 12...♕xd4+ 13 ♔g2 ♗xh2 gives Black compensation.

b2) 10 f4!? ♘xc3 11 bxc3 dxc4 12 ♗xc4 f6 (12...g5? 13 g3 ♕h3 14 ♗d5! ± Tzermiadianos-Skembris, Greece 1998; 12...♗e6!?) 13 ♕b3 ♖he8! (or 13...♗c6 14 ♖b1 b6 15 ♗d5 ♗xd5 16 ♕xd5 ♔b8 17 ♗d2 ♖he8 18 a4 ♖e2 19 ♗e1 ♕g4 20 ♗g3 ♖de8 21 a5 ±; 13...♗f5 14 g3 ♕h3 15 ♗d5 c6 16 ♖b1! ♕d7 17 ♗g2 ♕h6 18 ♖b2 ±) 14 ♖b1 b6 15 ♗d3 (15 ♗a6+ ♔b8 16 ♕d5 ♗c8 17 ♗xc8 ♖xc8 18 c4 ♖e1! ∞) 15...♗c6 16 c4 ± Tzermiadianos.

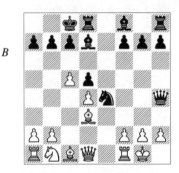

Now:

E41: 9...g6   63
E42: 9...g5   66

The latter is the principal move, by which Black begins his counterplay most rapidly.

Or:

a) 9...♘xf2? 10 ♖xf2 ♕xd4 11 c6! is good for White.

b) 9...♘f6 10 ♘c3 and now:

b1) Black's best course is 10...g5 – *9...g5 10 ♘c3 ♘f6* ±.

b2) 10...♕xd4? 11 c6! ±.

b3) 10...g6 11 ♘e2 ♗h6 12 ♗xh6 ♕xh6 13 ♖c1 ♖he8 14 b4 ♔b8 (or 14...c6?! 15 ♕a4 intending ♖c3-a3 ±) 15 b5 ♗f5 16 ♖c3 ♗e6 (16...♘e4 17 ♗xe4 ♗xe4 18 ♖a3 intending ♕a4 ±) 17 ♗xf5! gxf5 18 ♖a3 ♖g8 19 c6! ♘e4 (19...b6 20 ♖xa7 ♔xa7 21 ♕a4+ ♔b8 22 ♕a6 +–) 20 ♕a4 a6 21 cxb7! f4 22 bxa6 ♔a7 23 ♖b1 +– Prasad-Ravikumar, Indian Ch 1987.

E41)
9...g6

This aims to develop Black's dark-squared bishop, but without creating the serious weaknesses entailed in playing ...g5. However, it also offers Black fewer chances for counterplay and it turns out that this factor is more significant, because without adequate kingside counterplay there is little to stop White developing serious threats on the queenside.

10 ♘c3 ♗g7 (D)

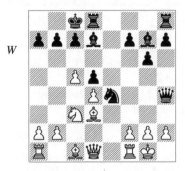

11 g3
Or:

a) 11 ♘e2!? ♖he8! (11...♘f6? 12 b4 ♘h5 13 b5! ± Timman-Hübner, Tilburg 1983) and then:

a1) 12 a4 ♘g5! 13 ♖a3 h6! 14 ♗e3 (14 ♗c2?! ♖xe2! 15 ♕xe2 ♘e6 ∓ Ivanchuk-Rozentalis, Manila OL 1992) and here both 14...♗g4 and 14...♘e6 lead to unclear play.

a2) 12 f3 (this move, not previously suggested, demands careful analysis) 12...♘g5 13 ♔h1 ♘e6 (13...♖xe2!?) 14 ♗e3 ♗xd4! (14...♘xd4? 15 ♗f2 +−) 15 ♘xd4 ♘xd4 16 ♕d2 (16 ♗f2 ♕f6; 16 ♗xd4 ♕xd4 17 c6! ♗e6 18 ♗a6 {18 cxb7+ ♔b8 ∞} 18...♕xd1 19 ♗xb7+ ♔b8 20 ♖axd1 d4 =) 16...♘e6 (16...h6? loses material to 17 ♗f2) 17 ♕a5 ♔b8 18 c6 b6 19 ♕b5 ♗c8 20 a4 ♘d4! 21 ♗xd4 ♕xd4 22 ♖fc1 a5! 23 b4 ♕xb4 24 ♕xb4 axb4 25 a5 ♖e3! 26 axb6 ♖xd3 27 ♖a7 ♖d6 28 ♖ca1 (28 b7 ♖xc6! −+) 28...♖a3 −+ Analysis.

a3) 12 ♗e3!? and here:

a31) 12...♘f6?! 13 ♕d2 ♘g4 14 ♗f4 ♗h6 15 c6! ♗xc6 16 h3 ♗xf4 17 ♕xf4 ± Xie Jun-Ye Rongguang, Shenzhen 1992.

a32) 12...♗h6 13 ♗xh6 (13 ♖c1 ♗xe3 14 fxe3 f5 15 c6 ♗xc6 16 ♖xc6 bxc6 17 ♕a4 gives White compensation − Yusupov) 13...♕xh6 14 ♕c1 (14 ♘c3 ♗c6 ∞) 14...♕xc1 15 ♖axc1 ♗f5 16 ♖fe1 ±.

a33) 12...g5!? is a new move that I am recommending:

a331) 13 ♕c1 ♖e6 14 ♗xe4!? (14 f3 ♖h6! 15 fxe4 dxe4 16 ♗c4 ♕xh2+ 17 ♔f2 ♗g4! 18 ♗xg5 ♗xe2 gives Black a dangerous attack) 14...♕xe4 15 ♘g3 ♕g6 16 ♗xg5 ♖g8 17 ♖d1! (17 ♕d2 ♗xd4 18 ♕xd4 ♕xg5 19

♖ad1 {19 f4 ♕f6 20 ♕xd5 ♗c6 is unclear} 19...h5! gives Black counterplay) 17...h6! (17...h5 18 h4!? {18 ♕f4 f6 19 ♗h4 ♗h6 20 ♕f3 ♕g4 ∞} 18...f6 19 ♗f4 ♕g4 20 f3 ♕g6 {not 20...♕xh4 21 ♘f5 +−} 21 ♕b1 ±) 18 ♗f4 h5 19 h4 ♕g4 ∞.

a332) 13 f3 ♘c3 14 bxc3 ♖xe3 15 ♖b1 ♖de8 16 ♖b4!? (16 ♕b3? ♖xd3 17 ♕xb7+ ♔d8 18 ♕xd5? ♖xe2 19 c6 ♖xg2+! −+; 16 ♘g3? ♗xd4! 17 cxd4 ♕xd4 18 ♘f5 ♕xd3 will give Black too much for the exchange; 16 ♔h1 ♖8e6 ∞) 16...a5!? (16...♖8e6? 17 ♘g3 ♖h6 18 ♗f5! ±) 17 ♖b2 ∞ Analysis.

b) 11 ♗e3!? *(D)* and now:

b1) 11...♘f6 12 ♕d2 h6 ±.

b2) 11...♖he8? 12 ♘xd5 ♗g4 (or 12...♗c6 13 ♘b4 ±) and now, rather than 13 ♕b3 ♗e6 14 ♗c4 ♗xd4 (not 14...c6? 15 g3! ±) 15 ♗xd4 ♘d2 16 ♗f6 ♘xb3 17 ♗xh4 ♘xa1 18 ♗xd8 ♖xd8 19 ♘e7+ ♔d7 20 ♗xe6+ ♔xe6 21 ♘xg6 ±, White should continue 13 ♕a4! ±.

b3) 11...♘xc5 12 g3 ♕h3 13 ♗e2! (13 dxc5? d4) and now:

b31) 13...♘e6?? 14 ♗g4 wins for White.

b32) 13...♔b8 14 ♗f3 (14 ♘xd5 ♕f5 ∞) 14...♘e4 15 ♘xd5 ♘f6 16 ♘f4 ±.

b33) 13...♘e4 14 ♘xd5 ♘f6 (or 14...♖he8 15 ♖c1 ±) 15 ♘f4 ♕f5 16 ♗d3 ♕a5 17 ♕c2 ±.

b34) 13...h5 14 ♘xd5 (14 dxc5 d4 15 ♗xd4 ♗c6 16 ♗f3 ♖xd4 17 ♕e2 ♖e8 −+) 14...♗a4 (14...♘e6 15 ♗f3 ±) 15 b3 ♖xd5 16 bxa4 ♖e8!? (16...♖hd8?! 17 ♗f3 ♖xd4 18 ♕c2!! ± J.Polgar-Skembris, Moscow OL 1994) leads to unclear play after either 17 ♕c2!? or 17 ♗f3 ♘e4 intending ...♕d7.

We now return to 11 g3 *(D)*:

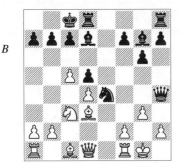

11...♕f6
Or:

a) 11...♘xc3?! 12 bxc3 ♕h3 13 ♕b3!? (13 ♖b1 h5 14 ♗f4 ♗c6 15 ♕b3 ± Geenen-Handoko, Manila OL 1992) 13...h5 14 ♖b1 ♗c6 15 ♗b5 ♔d7 16 ♗f4! ±.

b) 11...♕h3?! 12 ♘xd5 ♗g4 (alternatively, 12...♖he8 13 ♘f4 ♕f5 14 ♗e3!? ±) 13 ♘e7+ (13 ♘f4? ♗xd1 14 ♘xh3 ♗f3 ∓) 13...♔b8 (13...♔d7? 14 ♕a4+ +−) 14 ♘c6+! ♔c8 (14...bxc6 15 ♕b3+ +−) 15 ♘xa7+ ♔b8 16 ♘c6+ ♔c8 17 f3 (17 ♗e2? ♗xe2 18 ♕xe2 ♖he8 intending ...♘g3; 17 ♘e7+ ♔b8 intending to counter 18 ♗e2? with 18...♗xe2 19 ♕xe2 ♕e6!) and then:

b1) 17...bxc6 18 ♗a6+ ♔d7 19 fxg4 +−.

b2) 17...♘xg3 18 fxg4 ♗xd4+ 19 ♘xd4 ♖xd4 20 ♖f4! ♖hd8 21 ♖xd4 ♖xd4 22 ♕e1!! ♖xd3 (22...♕xg4 23 hxg3 ♖xd3 24 ♗e3! +−) 23 ♗g5! +−.

b3) 17...♖xd4 18 ♗e3 ♖xd3 19 ♕xd3 ♘xg3 20 ♗f4 1-0 Ivanchuk-Rozentalis, Debrecen Echt 1992.

12 ♗e3
12 ♘xe4 dxe4 13 ♗xe4 ♗h3 (another possibility is 13...♗b5!?) 14 ♕b3 c6! (14...♕a6? 15 ♖e1 ♖xd4 16 ♗f4 ♗e6 17 ♕f3 c6 18 ♗d6 ♖d2 19 ♕f4 ± Sax-Skembris, Burgas 1992) 15 d5!? cxd5 16 ♗xd5 ♖xd5 17 ♕xd5 ♖d8 18 ♕b3 (18 ♕e4?! ♗xf1 19 ♕g4+ ♕e6 20 ♕xe6+ fxe6 21 ♔xf1 ♖d1+ 22 ♔e2 ♖h1 23 a4 ♗h6 ∓ Tsvetkov-Kalinichenko, corr. 1993) 18...♗c6 19 f3 ♗d4+ 20 ♗e3 ♗xf1 21 ♖xf1 ♕xc5 with equality.

12...♘g5!
Playing the knight to h3 is obviously a high-risk strategy, but the alternative offers Black no hope at all: 12...♗f5? 13 ♘b5! a6 (13...♗h3 14 ♘xa7+ ♔b8 15 ♘b5 ♗xf1 16 ♗xf1 ♖he8 17 ♕a4 ♕a6 18 ♕b4 ± Anand-Hübner, Dortmund 1992) 14 ♘xc7 ♔xc7 (14...♕c6 15 ♘a8! ♔b8 16 ♘b6 ♖he8 17 ♖e1 favours White) 15 ♗f4+ ♔d7 (15...♔c8 16 ♗e5 ♕c6 17 ♗xg7 ♖hg8 18 ♗e5 f6 19 ♗f4 g5 20 ♗e3 +−) 16 ♗e5 ± Har-Zvi – Lev, Tel-Aviv 1995.

13 f4
Or:

a) 13 ♘xd5 ♘h3+ 14 ♔g2 (14 ♔h1 ♗c6 15 ♕g4+ ♕e6) 14...♗c6 15 ♕g4+ ♔b8 16 ♕xh3 ♖xd5 ∓.

b) 13 ♗e2 h5! 14 a4 (better is 14 ♖e1) 14...♗h3 15 ♖e1 (15 c6?! ♗xf1 16 cxb7+ ♔b8 17 ♔xf1 h4 ∓ Caplan-Pavasović, Bled 1994) 15...♘e6! ∓.

13...♘h3+

13...♕e6 14 ♖e1 ♘e4 15 ♗xe4 dxe4 16 d5 ♕a6 17 ♗d4 ♗xd4+ 18 ♕xd4 f5 19 b4 ±.

14 ♔g2 ♖he8 15 ♕d2

Now:

a) 15...h5 16 b4 ±.

b) 15...c6 16 b4 ♗f5 17 ♗xf5+ ♕xf5 18 b5 ♕e6 19 ♖fe1 ±.

c) 15...♗f5!? 16 ♖ae1 h5 17 ♗xf5+ ♕xf5 18 ♕d1 ♖e7 19 ♕b1 ♕g4 ∞.

d) 15...♖xe3 16 ♕xe3 ♖e8 17 ♕d2 ♕xd4 18 ♖ae1 ♖xe1 19 ♖xe1 ♔d8 (19...♕xc5? 20 f5! +–; 19...♗h6? 20 ♖e8+! ♗xe8 21 ♗f5+ gxf5 22 ♕xd4 +–) 20 ♖d1 ♗g4 21 ♗b5! ± Leko-S.Farago, Budapest 1993.

E42)

9...g5 *(D)*

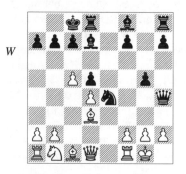

The critical move. Black advances on the kingside as quickly as possible,

in order to deflect White from his queenside ambitions. Now:

E421: 10 f3 66
E422: 10 ♗e3 69
E423: 10 ♘d2 70
E424: 10 ♘c3 71

E421)

10 f3

A logical move, because at this early stage Black is unable to sacrifice his knight and so must simply retreat it to f6. However, the move does slightly weaken White's kingside, and lends added force to the advance ...g4. The pros and cons are hard to assess, but it is White's second most common move in the position after 9...g5, and if the analysis below holds up, it could be set to become even more popular.

10...♘f6

10...♗g7?! 11 ♗e3! (not 11 fxe4? ♗xd4+ 12 ♔h1 ♗e5 ∓) and then:

a) 11...♘f6 12 ♘c3 (12 ♗f2 ±) 12...♖de8 13 ♗f2 ♕h6 (Van Riemsdijk-Finegold, Dieren 1990) 14 h3 ±.

b) 11...f5 12 fxe4 dxe4 13 ♗c2 ♕h6 14 ♘c3 f4 15 ♗xf4 gxf4 16 ♗xe4 ♖he8 17 ♕d3 f3 18 ♖xf3 ♗g4 19 ♗f5+ ± Kotkov-Benuenir, corr. 1993.

11 ♗e3 *(D)*

11...♖e8!?

Or:

a) 11...g4!? and now:

a1) 12 ♕d2!? gxf3 13 ♖xf3 (13 c6?! ♗xc6 14 ♗f5+ ♘d7 15 ♗g5 ♕h5) 13...♘g4 14 ♗f4 ♗g7 15 ♗f1 ♕f6 16 ♗e5 ♕h6 17 ♕xh6 ♗xh6 18 ♗xh8 ♖xh8! 19 ♘c3 ♗e3+ 20 ♖xe3 ♘xe3 21 ♗d3 ± Kheit.

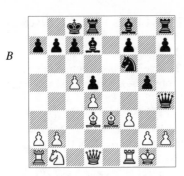

B

a2) 12 g3 ♕h5 (12...♕h3?! 13 f4 ♖e8 14 ♖e1 ±) 13 f4 and then:

a21) 13...♗g7 14 ♘c3 ♖he8 15 ♖e1 (Almasi-Hellsten, Malmö 1994) and now:

a211) 15...♘g8?! 16 ♗f2! ♖xe1+ (not 16...♘e7? 17 ♗f1 ♘c6 18 ♖xe8 ♖xe8 19 ♗g2 ♗e6 20 ♕a4 ±) 17 ♕xe1 ♖e8 18 ♕d1 ♘e7 19 ♗f1! ±.

a212) 15...♖e7!? 16 b4 (16 ♗f2 ♖xe1+ 17 ♕xe1 ♗f5 =; 16 ♕d2 ♖de8 17 ♗f2 ♖xe1+ 18 ♖xe1 ♖xe1+ 19 ♕xe1 ♗f5 20 ♗f1 ±) 16...♖de8 17 ♕d2 ±.

a22) 13...♖e8 14 ♖e1 and now:

a221) 14...♘e4?! 15 ♘c3! (15 ♘d2 ♘xd2 16 ♕xd2 ♗g7 ±) 15...♘xc3 (not 15...♘xc5? 16 dxc5 ♖xe3 17 ♖xe3 ♗xc5 18 ♕c1! +− Z.Almasi-Schwartzman, Wijk aan Zee 1995) 16 bxc3 ♗g7 (16...♗f5? 17 ♕a4 +−) 17 ♕c2 ±.

a222) 14...♗f5 15 ♘c3 ♗xd3 16 ♕xd3 ♘e4 ±.

b) 11...♖g8!? 12 ♘c3 (12 ♕e1!? ♖e8 13 ♘d2 ♕h5 14 ♕f2 g4 15 ♖ae1 ± Wedberg-Timpani, St Martin 1991) 12...g4 (12...♖e8!? 13 g3 ♕h5!? {not 13...♕h3? 14 ♖e1 g4 15 f4 ± Tiviakov-Schwartzman, Wijk aan Zee 1995} 14 ♕d2 g4 15 f4 ♗f5 ∞) and now:

b1) 13 ♗f2 ♕h6 ∓.

b2) 13 ♕e1? g3! 14 hxg3 ♖xg3 and here:

b21) 15 ♗f2? ♖xg2+ 16 ♔xg2 ♕h3+ 17 ♔g1 ♗d6 intending ...♖g8+ −+.

b22) 15 ♘e2!? ♗d6! (15...♖xg2+? 16 ♔xg2 ♕h3+ 17 ♔g1 ♗d6 18 cxd6 ♖g8+ 19 ♗g5! +−) 16 cxd6? ♖xg2+ 17 ♔xg2 ♖g8+ 18 ♗g5 (18 ♘g3 ♕h3+ −+) 18...♖xg5+ 19 ♘g3 ♗h3+! −+.

b23) 15 ♕d2 ♗xc5! 16 dxc5 ♖dg8! −+ Dolmatov-Makarychev, Palma de Mallorca 1989.

b3) 13 g3 ♕h3 (13...♕h5!? 14 f4 ♖e8 ∞) 14 f4 ♘h5 and then:

b31) 15 ♗f2? ♘xf4! 16 gxf4 g3 ∓.

b32) 15 ♘e2 ♖e8 16 ♗f2 and here 16...♗xc5? 17 dxc5 d4 has been recommended, but looks none too convincing. True, White must avoid 18 ♘xd4? ♘xf4! 19 gxf4 g3 −+, but after 18 ♗xd4 Black has no way through.

b33) 15 ♕e1 ♖e8 16 ♕f2 ♘f6 17 ♖fe1 ♗g7 18 ♕c2 ♖e7 19 ♗f2 ♖ge8 20 ♖e5 c6 (Van Riemsdijk-Casafus, Buenos Aires 1990) 21 b4! ±.

c) 11...♗g7 and here:

c1) 12 g3!? leads to interesting play: 12...♕h5 13 ♘c3 ♖he8 14 ♖e1 g4 15 f4 ♘e4!? 16 ♘xe4 dxe4 17 ♗e2 ♕g6 18 ♕b3 ♗c6 19 ♗c4 ♕f5 20 ♖ed1 ♗d5 21 c6!? bxc6 22 ♖ac1 ♖e6 23 ♕a3 ♗xc4 24 ♖xc4 ♕b5 25 ♖dc1 gives White compensation for the pawn, in view of the poor position of the black king, Tiviakov-Rozentalis, Groningen FIDE 1997.

c2) 12 ♘c3 ♘h5!? (12...♖de8 13 ♗f2 ♕h6 14 h3! ±) 13 ♘e2 ♘f4 14 g3

(14 ♘xf4!? gxf4 15 ♗f2 ♕g5 16 ♔h1 ♖dg8 17 ♖g1 intending b4 and b5 ∞) 14...♘xe2+ 15 ♗xe2 ♕h6! (15...♕h5?! 16 f4 ♕g6 17 fxg5 ♕e4 18 ♗f2 ♗h3 19 ♗f3 ♕f5 20 ♗e3 ±) 16 ♕d2 ♖de8 17 ♖fe1 (17 ♗xg5!? ♗xd4+ 18 ♕xd4 ♕xg5 19 f4 ♕e7 20 ♗f3 ±) 17...♖hg8 18 ♗f1 (Am.Rodriguez-Borras, Terrassa 1997) 18...♕f6 19 ♗g2 h5 ∞.

We now return to 11...♖e8 (D):

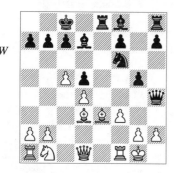

12 ♕d2

12 ♗f2 ♕h6! (12...♕h5 13 ♘c3 g4 14 fxg4 ♘xg4 15 h3 ±) 13 ♘c3 (13 ♕d2 ♘h5 ∞) 13...g4 14 f4! (14 ♖c1 ♖g8! 15 f4? g3 16 ♗xg3 ♖xg3! 17 hxg3 ♘g4 –+) and now:

a) 14...♕xf4 15 ♗h4 ♕xd4+ 16 ♔h1 ♘e4! (16...♗g7 17 c6! ±) 17 c6! ♗e6 18 ♘b5 ♕b6 19 ♖c1! ♔b8! 20 cxb7 c6 21 ♗xe4 ♕xb5 22 ♗d3 ♕xb7 23 ♗g3+ ♔a8 24 ♕a4 ±.

b) 14...g3! 15 ♗xg3 ♖g8 16 ♕f3 (Makarychev-Ye Rongguang, Belgrade 1988) 16...♘h5!? 17 ♕xd5 ♗c6 18 ♕f5+ ♔b8 19 ♗e4! (19 ♖ae1? ♗g7!! gives Black compensation) 19...♘xg3 20 hxg3 ♕g7 21 ♗xc6 ♕xd4+ 22 ♔h2 bxc6 23 ♖ad1 (23 ♕xf7 ♗c5 24 ♖ad1 ♕e3 25 ♖f3 ♕e6! ∞ 26 ♖d8+?

♔b7!! and Black wins) 23...♕xc5 24 ♕xc5 ±.

12...♖g8

12...♖xe3? is bad, though this is far from obvious at first. 13 ♕xe3 ♘h5 (13...♗g7? 14 g3 ±) and now:

a) 14 ♗f5? ♗g7 15 ♗xd7+ ♔xd7 16 g4 (16 ♖d1 ♖e8 17 ♕f2 ♗xd4! 18 ♖xd4 ♖e1+ –+) 16...♖e8 17 ♕d2 ♖e2!! 18 ♕xe2 ♗xd4+ 19 ♖f2 ♘f4 –+.

b) 14 ♕f2? ♕xf2+ 15 ♖xf2 ♗g7 ∓.

c) 14 ♘a3 ♗g7 15 ♘c2 ♖e8 16 ♕f2 ♘f4 17 ♖fd1 ♔d8! gives Black compensation.

d) 14 ♖d1?! ♗g7 15 ♗f1 g4! is equal, Dolmatov-Makarychev, Reykjavik 1990.

e) 14 ♘d2 ♗g7 15 ♘b3 ♖e8 16 ♕f2 ♘f4 17 ♖fd1 ♕xf2+ 18 ♔xf2 ♗a4 ∞.

f) 14 ♘c3 ♗g7 15 ♘e2 ♖e8 16 ♕f2 ♖xe2!? 17 ♕xh4 gxh4 18 ♗xe2 ♗xd4+ 19 ♔h1 ♘f4! 20 ♖ad1 (20 ♖ae1 ♗xb2 21 ♗d1 ♗b5 22 ♖f2 ♘d3 ∞) 20...♗xb2 21 ♖d2 ♗c3 22 ♖c2 ♘xe2 23 ♖xe2 ♗b5 ∞.

g) 14 g3!! ♘xg3 15 ♕e5!! ♖g8 (15...♘xf1 16 ♕xh8 ♕xh2+ 17 ♔xf1 ♗h3+ 18 ♔e1 ♕g1+ 19 ♔d2 ♕f2+ 20 ♔c3 ♕e1+ 21 ♘d2 +–) 16 hxg3 ♕h3 17 ♖d1 ♗g7 18 ♗f1 1-0 Tomasević-Kondali, corr. 1991.

13 ♗f2 ♕h6 (D)
14 ♘c3

This is a new move that I am recommending. White does not allow himself to be diverted from completing his development.

Hitherto, White has played 14 ♕a5 ♔b8 15 ♗g3 ♖c8 16 ♘c3 ♘h5 (not

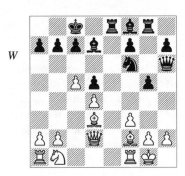

W

16...g4? 17 ②f5!! ②xf5 18 ②b5 a6 19 ②xc7+ ③a8 20 ♕b6 +–) 17 ②e5 ②g7 18 ②xd5 ②xe5 19 dxe5 g4 (19...♕e6 20 ②e4 ♕xe5 ∞) 20 f4 (a game between two computers developed in interesting fashion: 20 ②e4!? g3 21 h4 ②f4 22 ②xf4 ♕xf4 23 ②fd1 ②e6 24 ②xb7 ③xb7 25 ♕b5+ ③a8 26 ♕c6+ = *Junior-Hiarcs*, Cadaques 2000) 20...c6! 21 ②b6 (21 ②e7 ②xf4 22 ②xg8 ②xg8 ∓ intending 23 ♕c3 g3 24 h3 ②xh3+!! 25 gxh3 ♕e3+ 26 ③g2 ②xh3+! 27 ③xh3 g2+ 28 ③h2 g1♕+ 29 ②xg1 ♕h6#) 21...②cd8 and now White should play 22 ♕b4!? ∞ rather than 22 ②xd7+ ②xd7 23 ②f5 g3!! ∓ Am.Rodriguez-Lima, Guarapuava 1991.

14...g4

If 14...③b8, then 15 ②ae1 ②xe1 16 ②xe1 g4 17 ♕xh6 ②xh6 18 fxg4 ②xg4 19 ②xd5 ±.

15 ♕xh6 ②xh6 16 fxg4 ②xg4

If 16...②xg4, then 17 ②ae1 ②eg8 (17...②e4 18 ②xe4! dxe4 19 ②e3 ±) 18 g3 intending ③g2 and ②g1 ±, while 16...②xg4 can be met by 17 ②ae1 ②xe1 (17...②h3 18 ②xe8+ ②xe8 19 ②g3 ±) 18 ②xe1 (18 ②xe1 ②d2 ∞) 18...②e3+ (18...②h3 19 ②xf6 ②e3+ 20 ③f1 ②xg2 21 ②f5+! +–) 19 ②f2 ±

intending to meet 19...②h3 with 20 ②f5+ ②xf5 21 ②e3 ±.

17 ②xd5 ②c6

17...②xf2 18 ②xf2 ②g4 (18...②c6 19 ②f6 ②e3 20 d5 ±) 19 c6! ±.

18 ②f5+ ③b8 19 ②b4

Now:

a) After 19...②xf2 20 ②xc6+ bxc6 21 ③xf2 ②e3+ 22 ③f3 ②xd4 23 ②ae1 ±/± Black is faced with a difficult defence – Analysis.

b) 19...②xg2 (Nunn) 20 ③xg2 ②e3++ 21 ③h1 ②xf5 22 ②g1!? ②g5 23 ②ae1 ±.

E422)

10 ②e3 *(D)*

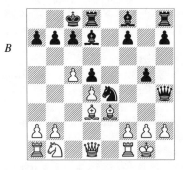

B

This is an interesting idea from Makarychev. White first of all supports the important d4-pawn, and then aims to displace or exchange the e4-knight by playing ②d2.

10...②e8

Or:

a) 10...②g7 11 f3 ②f6 – *10 f3 ②f6 11 ②e3 ②g7*.

b) 10...②f6 11 ②d2 (11 f3 – *10 f3 ②f6 11 ②e3*) 11...②g8 (11...②g4 12 ②f3 ②xe3 13 fxe3 ♕h5 14 ②e5 +–)

12 ♘f3 ♛h5 13 ♘e5 ♛xd1 14 ♖axd1 ± I.Gurevich-Barua, Hastings 1993/4.

c) 10...f5!? 11 f3 f4!? (11...♘f6 12 c6 ♗xc6 13 ♗xf5+ ♗d7 14 g3 ♛h5 15 ♗xd7+ ♖xd7 16 ♘c3 ± Yusupov) 12 ♗c1 ♘f6 13 ♘c3 ♗g7 ∞.

11 ♘d2!

This move stems from Kasparov. Otherwise: 11 ♘c3 is met by 11...♗e6! intending ...♖h6; 11 f3 ♘f6 – *10 f3 ♘f6 11 ♗e3 ♖e8*.

11...♗g7

11...f5 12 ♘f3 ♛h6 (12...♛h5? 13 ♘xg5 ±) 13 ♘e5 (13 ♗xe4 fxe4 14 ♘xg5 ♛g6 gives Black compensation) 13...f4 14 ♗c1 ±.

12 ♘f3 ♛h5 13 ♘xg5

13 ♗xe4? ♖xe4 (13...dxe4 14 ♘xg5 ♗g4 15 ♛a4 h6 ∓) 14 ♘xg5 ♗g4 15 ♘f3 ♖xg2+ 16 ♔xg2 ♗h3+ 17 ♔h1 ♗g4 18 ♔g2 ♛h3+ −+.

13...♛xd1

13...♗g4 14 f3 ♘xg5 15 fxg4 ♛h6 16 ♛d2 ♘h3+ (16...♗xd4 17 ♗f5+ +−) 17 gxh3 ♛xe3+ (17...♖xe3!? 18 ♔h1 may be a little better for White) 18 ♛xe3 ♖xe3 19 ♖ad1 ±.

14 ♖fxd1

14 ♖axd1 ♘xg5 15 ♗xg5 ♗xd4 16 c6! ♗g4 17 ♗f5+ ♗xf5 18 ♖xd4 ±.

14...♘xg5 15 ♗xg5 ♗g4!?

15...♗xd4 deserves attention: 16 c6! ♗e6 (16...♗g4 17 cxb7+ ♔xb7 18 ♗a6+ ♔xa6 19 ♖xd4 ±) 17 cxb7+ ♔xb7 (17...♔b8 18 ♖d2 ±) 18 ♗a6+ ♔xa6 19 ♖xd4 c5 and White has only a slight advantage.

16 ♖d2 ♗xd4 17 c6 ♗e5

17...♖hg8 18 ♗f4 ±; 17...♗b6 18 ♗b5 ±.

18 ♗b5 b6 19 ♗h4!

Kasparov-Ivanchuk, Debrecen Echt 1992. White has a small but permanent advantage in view of Black's inferior pawn-structure combined with the fact that the black king will remain out of play for a long time. Although 10 ♗e3 is not often played, it deserves more attention as it is not clear how Black can equalize against it.

E423)

10 ♘d2 *(D)*

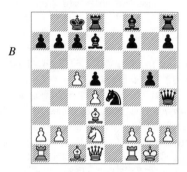

A rare but interesting continuation; White at once sets about eliminating the e4-knight. The defect of this move is that it leaves the d4-pawn weak.

10...♘xd2 11 ♗xd2 ♖g8

11...♗g7 12 ♗e3 ♖he8 (12...♗xd4?? 13 g3 and White wins) 13 ♛d2 h6 14 ♖ae1 ± intending 14...♗xd4? 15 c6! ± Palivalov-Bunenar, corr. 1993.

12 ♖c1

12 ♗e3 f5 ∞.

12...♛xd4 13 ♗c3 ♛h4 14 ♗f6 ♗g7!?

14...♖e8 15 f4 ♗e7 is possible, as 16 c6 ♗xc6 17 ♖xc6 bxc6 18 ♗f5+ ♔d8 doesn't appear to give White more than a draw.

15 ♗xd8 ♖xd8

The game is unclear. 10 ♘d2 needs thorough testing in practice.

E424)

10 ♘c3 *(D)*

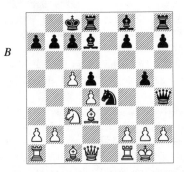

The main line. White simultaneously strikes at the e4-knight and the d5-pawn. If Black exchanges on c3, then the b-file is opened for White's attack.

10...♗g7

This is the principal move, taking aim at the d4-pawn, but other continuations are often used in practice:

a) 10...f5 11 ♘xd5 and then:

a1) 11...♗e6 12 ♘c3 ♖xd4 13 ♗e3 ♖d8 14 ♕c2! (14 c6 can be met by 14...♗d6!? ∞ or 14...♘c5!? ∞) 14...♘xc5 (14...♘xc3 15 ♕xc3 ±) 15 ♗xf5 ♗d6 (15...♕h6 16 h4 ±) 16 g3 ♕c4 17 ♗xg5 ± Glek-Raetsky, Zillertal 1993.

a2) 11...♘xf2!? 12 ♖xf2 ♕xd4 13 ♗xg5 (13 c6?! ♕xd5 14 cxd7+ ♖xd7 15 ♖d2 and now 15...♗d6! ∞ is better than 15...♗b4? 16 ♗c4 ♕c5+ 17 ♔h1 ♗xd2 18 ♗e6 +−) 13...♗xc5 14 ♘e3 f4! 15 ♗xf4 ♖hf8 16 ♕f1! ♕xe3!? (16...♗g4? 17 ♔h1!; 16...♗e6 17 ♖d1!) 17 ♗xe3 ♗xe3 18 ♕e2 (18 ♗xh7

♖xf2 19 ♕xf2 ♗xf2+ 20 ♔xf2 ♖h8 =) 18...♗xf2+ 19 ♔h1 ♖de8 20 ♕c2 ♗b6? (20...h5! ±) 21 ♗e4! ± Wedberg-Schneider, Torshavn 1987.

b) 10...♖g8 and here:

b1) 11 ♘e2?! ♖g6! 12 f3 ♖h6 13 fxe4 dxe4 14 ♗c2 ♕xh2+ 15 ♔f2 ♕h4+! 16 g3 (16 ♔g1? ♕h1+ 17 ♔f2 ♖f6+ −+; 16 ♔e3 ♗g4! intending 17 ♗xe4 ♖e6) 16...♕g4! 17 a4 ♖h2+ 18 ♔e1 (18 ♔e3 ♗c6! intending ...♖xe2+ −+) 18...♗e6!! −+ An.Rodriguez-Casafus, Buenos Aires 1990.

b2) 11 ♘xd5 ♖g6! 12 f3 ♖h6 13 ♗xe4 (13 fxe4 ♕xh2+ 14 ♔f2 ♖h3!) 13...♕xh2+ 14 ♔f2 ♕h4+ 15 ♔g1 (15 ♔e2 ♗b5+; 15 ♔e3 f5 ∞) 15...♕h2+ with a draw.

b3) 11 g3! and here:

b31) 11...♗h3?! 12 ♕f3 ♕h6 13 ♘xd5 (13 ♘xe4 ♗xf1 14 ♔xf1 dxe4 15 ♗xe4 gives White compensation) 13...f5! (13...♗xf1 14 ♗xe4 intending ♘f6 and ♕f5+ ±; 13...♖xd5 14 ♗xe4 ♖xd4 15 ♗e3 ±) 14 ♗c4 (14 ♘e3?! ♖xd4 15 ♘xf5 ♖xd3! 16 ♕xe4 ♕c6 ∓; 14 ♗xe4?! fxe4 15 ♕xe4 ♗xf1 16 ♔xf1 ♕c6 ∓) 14...♖g6! (14...♗xf1 15 ♕xf5+ ±) 15 ♖e1 ♗g4 16 ♕a3! ♕h5 (16...♔b8 17 f3 ±) 17 ♕xa7 ♗f3 18 h4 ♕g4 (18...gxh4 19 ♗b5! +−; 18...♘xf2 19 ♕a8+ mates) 19 ♗b5! ♖a6 20 ♗xa6 ♕h3 21 ♘b6+! 1-0 Sveshnikov-Ionins, Latvia 1992.

b32) 11...♕h3!? 12 ♘xe4 dxe4 13 ♗xe4 ♗b5 14 ♗g2 ♕e6 15 ♗e3 (15 ♕f3 c6! ∞) 15...♗xf1 (15...♗xc5!?) 16 ♕xf1 c6 17 b4 f5 ∞.

b33) 11...♘xc3 12 bxc3 ♕h3 13 ♖b1 (13 ♕f3!? ± Sveshnikov) 13...f5 (13...♗c6 14 ♕f3 ♔b8 15 ♗xg5!

Xg5 16 ₩f6 ♗e7 17 ₩xc6 +−; 13...h5 14 ₩b3 ♗c6 15 ₩c2! g4 {15...♗d7? 16 c6! +−} 16 Xe1 intending ♗f1 +−) 14 Xxb7! ♔xb7 15 ₩b3+ ♔a8 16 ₩xd5+ c6 17 ₩xg8 h6 18 Xe1 +− Hellers-Engedal, Skei 1993.

c) 10...♘f6 *(D)* and now:

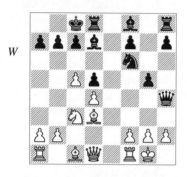

c1) 11 ♘e2 ♘g4! 12 h3 ♘h6 13 ♗d2 Xg8! (13...g4? 14 g3! {intending h4} 14...₩xh3? 15 ♘f4 +−) 14 f3 (14 b4 g4! 15 g3 gxh3 ∓) 14...f5 15 ₩e1 ₩h5 (15...₩xe1 16 Xaxe1 f4 17 h4! ±) 16 b4 Xe8 17 ₩f2 (17 b5!? g4 18 c6 ∞) 17...f4! (17...g4? 18 ♘f4! {18 ♘g3 ₩h4 19 ♗xh6 gxh3! ∓} 18...₩f7 19 g3! ± Am.Rodriguez-Arkhipov, Belgrade GMA 1988) 18 h4 ±.

c2) 11 ₩f3 ♗g7 (11...g4?! 12 ₩g3! ₩xg3 13 fxg3 ±) 12 ♗f5 and then:

c21) 12...h6 13 ♘xd5 ♘xd5 (13...g4 14 ♘e7+ ♔b8 15 ₩b3 ±; 13...₩xd4 14 ♘e7+ ♔b8 15 c6 ♗xc6 16 ♘xc6+ bxc6 17 ₩b3+ ₩b6 18 ₩xf7 Xhg8 19 ♗e3 ±) 14 ₩xd5 ₩xd4 =.

c22) 12...♔b8!? 13 g3 ₩xd4 14 ♗xg5 ₩e5 15 ♗xd7 Xxd7 16 h4 ♘e4 17 ♗f4 ₩e6 18 Xfe1 f5 19 ♘b5 a6 20 a4 ♗e5 21 Xa3 d4 with an unclear position.

c23) 12...Xhe8 13 ♗e3 h6 14 h3 and here:

c231) 14...♗xf5 15 ₩xf5+ ♔b8 16 Xae1 (16 g3 ₩h5 17 ♔g2 ₩g6 =) 16...g4 (16...c6 17 b4 ±) 17 ♗f4! gxh3 18 g3 ₩g4 (18...₩h5 19 Xxe8 Xxe8 20 ♗xc7+! ♔xc7 21 ₩f4+ ♔c8 22 ♘b5 Xe7 23 ♘xa7+ ♔d7 24 ₩d6+ ♔e8 25 ₩b8+ ♔d7 26 ₩c8#) 19 ₩xg4 ♘xg4 20 ♘b5 ±.

c232) 14...₩h5 15 g4 (15 ₩xh5?! ♘xh5 16 ♗xd7+ Xxd7 ∓ intending ...f5; 15 ♗xd7+ Xxd7 16 ₩f5 =) 15...₩h4 16 ♔g2 h5 and now 17 Xh1! ± should be preferred over 17 ♘xd5?! ♘xg4! (17...♘xd5? 18 ₩xd5 hxg4 19 hxg4 ♗e5 20 ₩xd7+! Xxd7 21 Xh1 1-0 Nogueiras-Am.Rodriguez, Havana 1991) 18 hxg4 (18 c6 bxc6 19 ♘b4 ♘xe3+ 20 fxe3 g4 ∓) 18...hxg4 19 ₩g3 ₩h3+! 20 ♔g1 ₩xg3+ 21 fxg3 c6! ∓ with the point that 22 ♗xg5? fails to 22...♗xd4+ 23 ♔h1 ♗xf5! −+.

c3) 11 g3 ₩h3 12 ₩f3 ♘g4 (or 12...♗g7 13 ♗xg5 ♗g4 14 ₩g2 ₩h5 15 h4 h6 16 ♗f4 ♗f3 17 ₩h3+ ♘g4 18 ♗e2 ♗xe2 19 ♘xe2 Xhe8 20 Xae1 ±) 13 ₩g2 ₩xg2+ (13...₩h5 14 h3 ♘h6 15 g4 ₩h4 16 ₩g3 ±) 14 ♔xg2 f6 (14...h6 15 f4 ±) 15 f4 Xe8 16 ♘d1!? (16 Xf3 gxf4 17 ♗xf4 c6 18 b4 ♘e5! 19 Xe3 ♘xd3 20 Xxd3 h5 = Kozakov-Mikhalchishin, Lvov 1997) 16...♗e7 17 h3 ♘h6 18 fxg5 fxg5 19 ♘c3 ±.

We now return to the position after 10...♗g7 *(D)*:

11 g3

Or:

a) 11 ♘xd5 ♗xd4 12 ♗e3 ♗xe3 13 fxe3 ♘xc5 14 Xxf7 ♔b8 ∞ Yusupov.

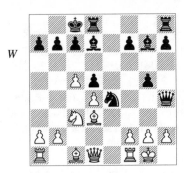

W

b) 11 ♗e3!? ♗c6 (11...♘xc5!? 12 ♘xd5 ♘xd3 13 ♕xd3 ♖he8 ∞) 12 ♘e2 f5 13 f3 f4 with an unclear position – Yusupov.

c) 11 ♘e2 and now:

c1) 11...♘f6?! 12 ♗d2 ♔b8 (Black also fails to equalize after 12...♖he8 13 ♗e1 ± and 12...♖hg8 13 ♖c1 ♘g4 {13...c6 14 f3 intending ♗e1-g3 ±} 14 h3 ♘h6 15 c6! ♗xc6 16 ♖xc6 bxc6 17 ♕a4 ± Makarychev-Kuijpers, CSKA-Eindhoven ECC 1986) 13 f3 ♖de8 14 ♗e1 ♕h6 15 b4 ♘h5 16 b5 ♘f4 17 ♗f2 g4 18 c6 ± Tiviakov-Barua, Tilburg 1992.

c2) 11...♖de8!? 12 f3 (12 a4 ♖e6 13 f3 ♖h6 14 fxe4 dxe4 15 ♗c4 ♕xh2+ 16 ♔f2 ♖f6+ 17 ♔e1 ♕xg2 18 ♖xf6 ♗xf6 19 ♗e3 ♗g7 ∞ Ioseliani-Gaprindashvili, Borzhomi wom Ct 1990) 12...♘f6 13 ♗d2 ♖xe2 14 ♕xe2 ♘h5 15 ♕f2 ♕xf2+ 16 ♖xf2 ♘f4 17 ♗xf4 gxf4 18 c6!? ♗e6 19 cxb7+ ♔b8 20 ♔h1 ♗xd4 21 ♖c2 ♗e3 22 b4 ♔xb7 23 g3 fxg3 24 hxg3 h5 gives Black compensation, Ulybin-Akopian, Borzhomi 1988.

c3) 11...♖he8!? and then:

c31) 12 ♗e3?! ♖e6 intending to continue ...♖h6.

c32) 12 ♕e1 ♘f6 (12...♗xd4? 13 ♘xd4 ♘xc5 14 ♕c3 ♘a4 15 ♘f5! +–) 13 ♕d2 ♘e4! 14 ♕a5 (14 ♕e1 =) 14...♔b8 15 f3 ♘f6 and now White should play 16 ♗d2!?, rather than 16 g3?! ♕h5 17 a4?! (17 ♗d2 ♘g8 ∓) 17...♘g4! ∓ 18 fxg4 ♗xg4 19 ♘f4 (19 ♘c3 ♗xd4+ 20 ♔g2 ♕h3+ 21 ♔h1 ♗f3+ 22 ♖xf3 ♖e1+ –+; 19 c6 ♖xe2 20 ♗xe2 ♗xd4+ 21 ♔g2 {21 ♔h1 ♗xe2 –+} 21...♗h3+ 22 ♔h1 ♕xe2 –+) 19...♗xd4+ 20 ♔g2 gxf4 –+ J.Polgar-Gaprindashvili, Novi Sad wom OL 1990.

c33) 12 f3 ♘f6 13 ♗d2 (13 ♕e1 ♕xe1 14 ♖xe1 =) 13...♖xe2! (this motif is worthy of close attention; Black is willing to give up the exchange in order to further his attack against the d4-pawn) and here:

c331) 14 ♕xe2 ♘h5 (14...♕xd4+? 15 ♗e3 ±) 15 ♕f2 (15 ♗e1 ♕xd4+ 16 ♗f2 ♘f4 ∓) 15...♕xf2+ 16 ♔xf2 (16 ♖xf2!? ♗xd4 17 ♗xg5 ∞) 16...♘f4! 17 ♗xf4 gxf4 18 ♖fe1 ♗xd4+ 19 ♔f1 ♗xb2! (19...♗xc5 20 ♖e5! ∞) 20 ♖ab1 ♗d4! ∓ Howell-Makarychev, Frunze 1989.

c332) 14 ♗xe2 ♘g4!? (more accurate than 14...♕xd4+?! 15 ♔h1 h6 16 b4 ±) and now:

c3321) 15 fxg4 ♗xd4+ 16 ♔h1 ♗e5 is very good for Black: 17 h3 ♕g3 18 ♔g1 ♕h2+ 19 ♔f2 ♗d4+ 20 ♔f3 (20 ♗e3 ♕f4+ ∓) 20...f5 ∓; 17 g3 ♗xg3 18 ♔g2 ♕xh2+ 19 ♔f3 ♖e8! –+; or 17 ♗f4 ♗xf4 18 ♖xf4 gxf4 19 ♕xd5 ♖e8! –+ Sherzer-Halasz, Budapest 1990.

c3322) 15 ♗f4! ♘f2 (15...♘xh2? 16 ♗xh2 ♗xd4+ 17 ♔h1 ♗e5 18 f4

♗xf4 19 ♖xf4 +–; 15...gxf4!? 16 fxg4 ♕f6 17 ♔h1 ♖e8! gives Black compensation) 16 ♗g3 (16 ♗xg5 ♘h3+! 17 gxh3 ♕xg5+ 18 ♔h1 ♕f4 ∓; 16 g3? ♘xd1 17 gxh4 ♗xd4+ is good for Black) 16...♘xd1 17 ♗xh4 ♗xd4+ 18 ♔h1 ♘e3 19 ♗xg5 ♖e8 20 ♗xe3 ♖xe3 gives Black compensation.

c4) 11...f5!? 12 f3 ♖hf8 *(D)* (the alternative 12...♘f6!? deserves serious attention: 13 ♗e3 {13 b4!? ♘h5 14 ♗e3 g4 15 c6 ♗xc6 16 ♗xf5+ ♗d7 17 fxg4 ♗xf5 18 gxf5 ♖de8 and Black has enough compensation, Short-L.Schneider, 1982} 13...f4 14 ♗f2 ♕h5!? {14...♕h6?! 15 ♕d2 ♖he8 16 ♖ac1 ♘g8 17 b4 ♔b8 18 b5 ♘e7 19 ♘c3 ♘f5 20 c6! ± Tiviakov-Raetsky, USSR 1987} 15 ♕d2 ♗h6 16 b4 ♖hg8 17 b5 g4 18 ♘xf4 gxf3 19 ♘xh5 ♖xg2+ 20 ♔h1 ♘g4! 21 ♕xh6 ♖xh2+ =) and now:

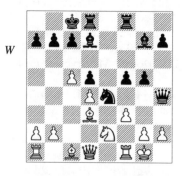

c41) 13 fxe4? fxe4 14 ♗c2 ♖xf1+ 15 ♕xf1 ♖f8 16 ♕d1 ♕f2+ 17 ♔h1 ♗g4 –+.

c42) 13 g3?! ♕h5 14 fxe4 fxe4 15 ♗c2 ♖xf1+ 16 ♕xf1 ♖f8 17 ♕e1 ♗h3 18 ♗e3 ♖f1+ 19 ♕xf1 ♗xf1 20 ♔xf1 ♕f3+ –+ Yusupov.

c43) 13 ♗e3!? f4 14 ♗xe4 and now rather than 14...dxe4 15 ♗f2 ♕h5 16 fxe4 ♗g4 17 ♖e1 ♗xe2 18 ♖xe2 f3 (18...♗xd4!?) 19 ♖d2 ♕g4 20 ♕f1 ♕xe4 21 ♖e1 ♕f4 22 ♗e3 fxg2 23 ♕xg2 ♕h4 24 ♖ed1 ♖fe8 ± Rodin-Fedorov, corr. 1987-90, Black could try 14...fxe3!? 15 ♗xd5 ♗b5, when he has compensation.

c44) 13 a4!? and then:

c441) 13...♖f6 14 ♕e1 ♕h5 15 fxe4 ♖h6 (15...dxe4 16 ♗b5 c6 17 ♘f4! gxf4 18 ♗xf4 ♖e6 19 d5 cxd5 20 ♕a5 ♗e5 21 ♗xe5 ♖xe5 22 ♕xa7 ♖e6 23 c6 ± Grünfeld-Davidović, Tel-Aviv 1989) 16 ♕g3 dxe4 17 ♗c4! (17 ♗xg5 ♖g6 18 ♗xd8 ♖xg3 19 ♘xg3 ♕g6 20 ♗b5 c6 ∞ Oll-Vladimirov, Tallinn 1988) 17...f4 18 ♗xf4! gxf4 19 ♖xf4 ±.

c442) 13...♖de8!? and now:

c4421) 14 fxe4? fxe4 ∓.

c4422) 14 ♖a3?! and then:

c44221) 14...f4?! 15 c6 (15 fxe4!? dxe4 16 ♗b5 c6 17 d5 f3!? {17...cxb5?! 18 c6! ±} 18 dxc6 ♗xc6! 19 ♗xc6 bxc6 20 ♗e3! ±) 15...♗xc6 16 fxe4 dxe4 17 ♗b5 f3 18 ♗xc6 (18 ♘g3 ♖e6 19 ♗xc6 ♖h6!) 18...fxe2 19 ♗xb7+ (19 ♕xe2!? ♖xf1+ 20 ♕xf1 ♖f8 21 ♕e2! ♗xd4+ 22 ♗e3 ±) 19...♔xb7 20 ♕xe2 ♖xf1+ (20...♗xd4+? 21 ♗e3 ±) 21 ♕xf1 ♗xd4+ 22 ♗e3 ± Sveshnikov-Makarychev, Moscow 1987.

c44222) 14...♘f6! 15 ♕e1 ♕xe1 16 ♖xe1 f4! ∓.

c4423) 14 g3 ♘xg3 15 hxg3 ♕h3! 16 ♖f2 ♗xd4!? 17 ♘xd4 ♕xg3+ =.

c4424) 14 ♕e1! and here:

c44241) 14...♕h5!? 15 fxe4 (15 c6 ♗xc6 16 fxe4 dxe4 17 ♗b5 ♖e6 18

♕d1 f4 19 d5 ♖d6 20 ♘c3 f3 21 ♘xe4 {½-½ Van der Wiel-Mirallès, Lyons 1988} 21...♖xd5 22 ♕e1 ∞) 15...dxe4 16 ♗b5! c6 17 ♗c4 f4 18 ♖a3 ♖f6 19 ♖b3 ♖h6 20 h3 ♗g4 21 ♘xf4 gxf4 22 ♗xf4 ♗xd4+ is equal, Elizarov-Beshukov, Belorechensk 1989.

c44242) 14...♕xe1 15 ♖xe1 f4! (not 15...♘f6? 16 ♗xg5 +–) 16 fxe4 dxe4 17 ♗c4 f3 (17...e3? 18 ♖f1!) 18 ♗e3! fxe2 19 ♖xe2 c6! 20 d5! cxd5 21 ♗xd5 h6 22 ♖d2! ♖d8 = Sax-Salov, Brussels 1988.

c45) 13 ♕e1!? and then:

c451) 13...♕h5 and here:

c4511) 14 ♕a5!? ♔b8 15 ♕b4 ♖f6 16 fxe4 dxe4 (16...♖h6? 17 exf5 ♕xh2+ 18 ♔f2 ±) 17 ♘g3 ♕h4 18 ♗xe4! (18 c6? ♖xc6 19 ♖xf5 exd3 20 ♗xg5 ♕xd4+ –+; 18 ♗e2 ♖h6 ∓) 18...fxe4 19 ♖xf6 ♗xf6 20 ♗e3 ∞ Van der Wiel-Sisniega, Thessaloniki OL 1988.

c4512) 14 fxe4 fxe4 (14...dxe4 15 ♗c4 f4 16 c6! ♖xc6 17 ♕a5 is good for White, Am.Rodriguez-P.Hernandez, Pinar del Rio 1990) 15 ♘g3 ♕h4 16 ♖xf8 ♖xf8 17 ♗f1 ♗xd4+ 18 ♗e3 ♗e5 ±.

c452) 13...♕xe1 14 ♖xe1 f4 (the alternatives are 14...♖de8 15 fxe4 dxe4 16 ♗c4 f4 17 ♔f1 f3 18 ♗e3! fxe2++ 19 ♔xe2 ± and 14...♗c6 15 ♖d1 f4 16 fxe4 dxe4 17 ♗c4 ±) 15 fxe4 dxe4 16 ♗xe4 ♖de8 17 ♘c3 ♗xd4+ 18 ♔f1 f3 19 gxf3 g4 20 c6 bxc6 21 f4 g3 22 ♔g2 c5 23 hxg3 ♗xc3 24 bxc3 ♖xe4 25 ♖xe4 ♗c6 26 ♗e3 ♗xe4+ 27 ♔h3 gives White slightly the better ending, Kveinys-Fedoseev, corr. 1987-90.

We now return to the position after 11 g3 *(D)*:

11...♕h3

11...♕h6!? 12 ♘xe4 dxe4 13 ♗xe4 f5 14 ♗g2 f4 15 a4!? (this is a new move that I am recommending as an improvement over 15 d5?! ♖hf8 16 ♖e1 ♔b8 ∞ Arencibia-Vladimirov, Lyons 1991) and here are some sample lines from my analysis:

a) 15...♗c6? 16 d5 ♗xd5 17 ♗xd5 c6 18 ♕g4+ +–.

b) 15...♗xd4 16 ♕xd4 ♗c6 17 ♕c3 +–.

c) 15...♕g6 16 ♕b3! (16 ♖a3 h5 ∞) 16...c6 17 a5 a6 18 ♖a4! ♗e6 19 ♕b6 and now 19...♗d5 20 ♖b4 ♕f7 21 ♕a7 ♕c7 22 ♗h3+ +– or 19...♖d5 20 ♖b4 ♕f7 21 ♕a7 ♕c7 22 ♕a8+ ♕b8 23 ♕xb8+ ♔xb8 24 ♗xd5 ♗xd5 25 gxf4 +–.

d) 15...♕f6 16 d5 h5 17 ♖a3 ♗g4 (17...h4 18 g4! ±) 18 ♕b3 f3 (18...h4 19 c6 ±) 19 ♗xf3 ♗xf3 20 ♕xf3 ♕xf3 21 ♖xf3 ♖xd5 22 b4 a5 (22...g4 23 ♖f4) 23 bxa5 ♖xc5 24 ♗e3! (24 ♖f7 ♗d4! ±) 24...♖xa5 25 ♖f7! ±.

e) 15...c6 16 d5 (16 a5!?) 16...♔b8 (16...cxd5 17 ♕xd5 ♗c6 18 ♕f5+ ♗d7 19 ♕c2 ♖hf8 20 ♖a3 ±) 17 d6!? ♕g6 18 ♖a3! h5 19 ♕d3! ♗f5 20 ♕b3 ♗e6 21 ♕b4 ♔a8 22 a5 ±.

f) 15...♖hf8 16 ♖a3 and then:

f1) 16...♗xd4? 17 ♕xd4 ♗c6 18 ♕c4! ♗xg2 19 ♔xg2 f3+ (19...♕c6+ 20 f3) 20 ♖xf3 ♕c6 21 ♕g4+ and White wins.

f2) 16...♗h3! 17 d5! ♗xg2 18 ♔xg2 ♕g6 19 ♖d3 ♕e4+ (19...fxg3 20 hxg3 ♕e4+ 21 f3 ♕b4 22 ♗xg5 +–) 20 f3 (20 ♕f3!?) 20...♕b4 21 c6! (21 ♕c2 ♗d4 22 ♗d2 ♕xc5 23 ♕xc5 ♗xc5 24 b4 ♗d6 25 ♖e1 =) 21...bxc6 22 dxc6 ♗xb2 23 ♗xb2 (23 ♖xd8+ ♖xd8 24 ♕c2 ♗xc1 25 ♕f5+ ♔b8 26 ♖xc1 ♔a8! ∞) 23...♕xb2+ 24 ♖f2 ♕b6 25 ♖c2 fxg3 26 hxg3 h5 27 ♖xd8+ ♖xd8 28 ♕h1!? ♕b3 29 ♖f2 ♕xa4 30 ♕xh5 ♕xc6 31 ♕xg5 ±.

12 ♘xe4

Sometimes White decides to take the pawn on d5: 12 ♘xd5 ♖he8 (not 12...♗g4? 13 ♗xe4! ♗xd1 14 ♗f5+ +–) 13 ♕f3 ♗f5 14 ♘e3 ♗g6 15 d5 (15 c6?! ♖xd4 16 ♗e2 h5 17 cxb7+ ♔b8 18 ♖e1 ♕d7 ∓ Smagin-H.Olafsson, Sochi 1988) 15...♘d2! 16 ♗xd2 ♗xd3 17 ♕xf7 ♗xb2 18 d6 ♕d7 19 ♕b3 ♕b5 20 ♕f7 ♕d7 21 ♕b3 ♗xf1 22 ♖xf1 ♗d4 ∞ Ioseliani-Howell, Spijkenisse 1989.

12...dxe4 13 ♗xe4 ♗b5 (D)

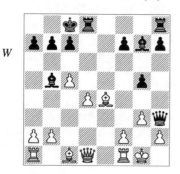

This is a critical position for this variation. Further investigations into it will most likely determine the overall fate of this whole line. Now:

E4241: 14 ♗xg5　　76
E4242: 14 ♗g2!　　78

It is worth mentioning that White is obliged to sacrifice the exchange, as 14 ♖e1? is no good due to 14...♖xd4 15 ♕f3 ♖xe4! 16 ♕xe4 ♗c6 –+.

E4241)

14 ♗xg5

It is tempting to grab the pawn which Black advanced on move 9, but this gives Black time to develop counterplay.

14...♖xd4

14...♗xf1? 15 ♗xd8 ♖xd8 16 ♕xf1 ♕xf1+ 17 ♖xf1 ♖xd4 18 ♗xh7 ±.

15 ♗g2

15 ♕b3 ♖xe4 16 ♕xb5 h6! 17 ♗e3 (17 c6 hxg5 18 ♕xb7+ ♔d8 19 ♖ad1+ ♗d4 –+) 17...♖h4! 18 ♖fd1 (not 18 gxh4?? ♗e5 –+) 18...♗xh2+ 19 ♔f1 ♕h3+ 20 ♔e1! (20 ♔e2? ♕g4+ –+) 20...♖e4 (20...♖h5!? is unclear) 21 c6! = ♖xe3+ 22 fxe3 ♕xg3+ 23 ♔e2 (23 ♔d2 ♖d8+ –+) 23...♕g2+ 24 ♔e1 ♕g3+ ½-½ Dolmatov-Akopian, Erevan 1988.

15...♕f5

Or:

a) 15...♗xf1? 16 ♗xh3+ ♗xh3 17 ♕f3 c6 18 ♕xf7 +–.

b) 15...♕e6?! 16 ♕f3 ♗c6 17 ♕b3!? (17 ♕e3 ♗xg2 18 ♔xg2 ♖e4 19 ♕b3 ♕c6!? {19...♕xb3!? 20 axb3 a6} 20 ♔g1 ♕xc5 21 ♗f4 ± Nunn-Barua, London Lloyds Bank 1990)

17...♗xg2 18 ♔xg2 ♛c6+ 19 ♔g1 with a clear advantage for White.

16 ♛b3 c6 17 ♗e3 ♗xf1 18 ♖xf1 *(D)*

18 ♗xd4 ♗xd4 19 ♖xf1 ♗xc5 20 ♛c4 ♔b8 21 b4 ♗b6 22 a4 a5 23 bxa5 ♗xa5 24 ♛b3 ♛e6 25 ♛c2 f6 26 ♖b1 ♔a8 27 ♛c5 ♛e5 28 ♛c4 ♖c8 = *Junior-Hiarcs*, Cadaques 2000.

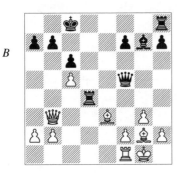

18...♖hd8!

Attempting to retain the extra material by 18...♖d7 is very risky for Black:

a) 19 ♛a3 ♔b8 (19...a6 20 b4 intending b5 gives White compensation) 20 b4 and now:

a1) 20...♗d4!? 21 b5 ♗xe3 22 fxe3 ♛d3 23 ♛xd3 ♖xd3 24 bxc6 bxc6 25 ♖xf7 (25 ♗xc6 ♖c8 26 ♖b1+ ♔c7 27 ♗g2 ♖b8 28 ♖f1 ♖b2 29 ♖xf7+ ♖d7 is unclear) 25...♖d1+ 26 ♔f2 ♖d2+ =.

a2) 20...♖d3 21 ♗f4+ ♔a8 22 ♛a4 ♛d7 23 ♛c2 ♖c3 24 ♛b1 ♛d3!? (24...♖c4?! 25 ♗d6 ♖e8? {25...h5!? 26 a4 intending b5 ±} 26 ♛xh7 ♗e5 27 ♗h3 ♛d8 28 ♛xf7 +− A.Ivanov-Makarychev, Reykjavik 1990) 25 ♛xd3 ♖xd3 26 b5 ♖c8 27 bxc6 bxc6 28 ♖b1 a5 ∞.

a3) Black should try 20...♖hd8! intending ...♖d1.

b) 19 ♛a4! a6 (19...♔b8 20 b4 ♛d3 21 ♗f4+ ♔a8 22 ♗d6! ♖xd6 {22...♛b5 23 ♛b3 a5 24 ♗h3 +−; 22...♗f8 23 ♗xc6 +−; 22...♖hd8 23 ♖d1 +−} 23 cxd6 ♛xd6 24 b5 c5 {24...cxb5? 25 ♛xb5 +− Geller-Howell, Reykjavik 1990} 25 ♛e4 ♛c7 26 ♖c1! ±) and here:

b1) 20 b4!? and now:

b11) 20...♔b8 21 ♗f4+ ♔a8 (the alternatives are no better: 21...♗e5 22 ♗h3 +− or 21...♔c8 22 ♗xc6 +−) 22 b5 ♖d4 23 ♛xa6+!! bxa6 24 ♗xc6+ ♔a7 25 b6#.

b12) 20...♖hd8 21 ♗xc6 bxc6 22 ♛xc6+ ♔b8 23 ♛b6+ ♔c8 (23...♔a8 24 c6 +−) 24 ♛xa6+ ♔b8 25 c6 ♖e7 (25...♖c7 26 ♗f4 ♗e5 27 ♛b5+ +−) 26 ♗a7+! ♖xa7 27 ♛b6+ ♔c8 28 ♛xa7 +−.

b13) 20...♗d4 21 ♗xc6 bxc6 22 ♛xc6+ ♔b8 23 ♛b6+ ♔c8 24 ♛xa6+ ♔b8 (24...♔d8 25 ♗xd4 ♖xd4 26 ♛b6+ +−) 25 c6 ♖a7 26 c7+! +−.

b14) 20...♛d3 21 ♗f4 ♛b5 (or 21...♖e8 22 ♗xc6 bxc6 23 ♛xc6+ ♔d8 24 ♛a8+ ♔e7 25 ♖e1+ +−) 22 ♛xb5 axb5 23 ♗h3 ±.

b2) 20 ♗xc6!? bxc6 21 ♛xc6+ and then:

b21) 21...♔b8? 22 ♛b6+ ♖b7 (White also wins after 22...♔a8 23 c6 ♖e7 24 c7 or 22...♔c8 23 c6) 23 ♛d6+ ♔c8 24 ♛xa6 ♔b8 25 c6 +−.

b22) 21...♖c7? 22 ♛xa6+ ♔b8 (or 22...♔d8 23 ♗f4 ♛xc5 {23...♗e5 24 ♖d1+ ♖d7 25 ♛a8+ ♔e7 26 ♖xd7+ ♛xd7 27 ♛e4 +−} 24 ♖d1+ ♖d7 25 ♛a8+ ♔e7 26 ♖e1+ ♔f6 27 ♛f3 +−)

23 c6 +− Hraček-Haba, Czech Cht 1997/8.

b23) 21...♔d8 22 ♖e1 with a final branch:

b231) 22...♗e5 23 ♕xa6 ♖e8 (alternatively, 23...♕g4 24 c6 ♖d1 25 ♗g5+ f6 {25...♔c7 26 ♔g2 ♖xe1 27 ♕b7+ ♔d6 28 ♗e7+ ♔d5 29 c7+ +−} 26 ♗xf6+ ♔e8 27 ♕f1 +−) 24 ♕a5+! ♖c7 (24...♔e7 25 c6 ♖d3 26 f4 +−) 25 c6 ♕e6 26 ♗f4 ♗xf4 27 ♖xe6 ♖xe6 28 gxf4 +−.

b232) 22...♕f6 23 ♕a4 ♕xb2 (or 23...♖e8 24 c6 ♖xe3 25 ♖xe3 ♕d4 26 ♕a5+ ♖c7 27 ♕g5+ f6 28 ♕h5 ♖xc6 29 ♖e8+ +−) 24 c6 ♗c3 (24...♖d5 25 ♕c4! ♖d6 {25...♕b5 26 ♗b6+ +−} 26 ♕xa6 ±) 25 cxd7 ♗xe1 26 ♕c6 ♗xf2+ 27 ♗xf2 ♕b1+ 28 ♔g2 ♕b2 29 ♔f3 ♕a3+ 30 ♔g4 with a clear advantage for White.

Thanks to the text-move (18...♖hd8), this whole line has more or less disappeared from practice. Black returns the exchange in order to defuse White's attacking chances. If White accepts, then the c5-pawn falls, and with material equal the opposite-coloured bishops exert an almost irresistible drawish influence. Now:

a) 19 ♗xd4 ♗xd4 =.

b) 19 ♕a3 ♖d1 (19...♔b8 20 ♗xd4 ♖xd4 21 b4 ±) 20 ♕xa7 ♖xf1+ 21 ♗xf1 ♗e5 (21...♖d1 22 ♕a8+ ♔c7 23 ♗f4+ ♗e5 24 ♕a4 ∞) 22 ♕a8+ ♔c7 23 ♕a5+ =.

c) 19 h4!? ♗e5 20 ♗xd4 ♗xd4 21 ♔h2 ♔c7 = 22 ♕c4 ♗xc5 23 b4 ♗b6 24 b5 ♖d4 25 ♕b3 ♖d3 26 ♕c4 ♖d4 ½-½ Ivanchuk-Anand, Monaco rpd 1992.

E4242)
14 ♗g2! *(D)*

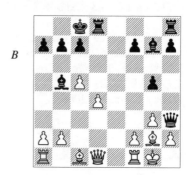

This appears to be the best continuation. Rather than waste time taking the g5-pawn, White concentrates on supporting the key point in his position – the d4-pawn.

14...♕f5 15 ♗e3!?
15 ♕b3 c6 16 ♖d1 (16 d5 ♗xf1 17 dxc6 ♗a6! −+) 16...♖xd4 (16...♗xd4 17 ♗e3 =) 17 ♖xd4 (17 ♗e3? ♗a4 −+) 17...♗xd4 18 ♗e3 =.

15...♗xf1 16 ♗xf1
White has good compensation for the exchange. From the material point of view, White's sacrifice is not all that large since he already has one extra pawn. Moreover, now that the d4-pawn is defended, Black's rooks have limited active possibilities. White's king is secure for the moment, which gives him time to start an attack against the enemy king. The immediate threat is ♕a4, followed by ♖d1-d3. This plan enables White to proceed with his attack while keeping the d4-pawn securely defended. Despite this, with accurate defence Black can liquidate to an endgame in which White has an

extra pawn, but the opposite-coloured bishops offer Black fair drawing prospects.

16...♖he8

If 16...♔b8, then 17 ♕a4 c6 18 ♖d1 ♖d7 19 ♖d3 ♖hd8 20 ♖a3 a6 21 ♖b3! (21 ♗xa6? ♖xd4! 22 ♗xd4 ♗xd4 ∓) 21...♗xd4 (21...♖xd4 22 ♕xc6 ±) 22 ♗xd4 ♕e4 (22...♖xd4 23 ♕xc6 ♖8d7 24 ♗xa6 ♖d1+ 25 ♔g2 ♕d5+ 26 ♕xd5 ♖1xd5 27 c6 +−) 23 ♕xa6 ♕xd4 24 ♕b6! ♖e8 25 ♖a3 ♖d5 (25...♖e1? 26 ♕a7+ ♔c8 27 ♕a8+ ♔c7 28 ♕a5+ +−) 26 ♕a7+ ♔c7 27 ♖b3 ± Zarnicki-Howell, Cuba 1993.

17 ♕a4 ♔b8 18 ♖d1 c6 19 ♖d3 ♕e4 20 ♖a3 a6 21 ♗d3 *(D)*

21 ♗xa6 ♖xd4 22 ♗xd4 ♕xd4 ±.

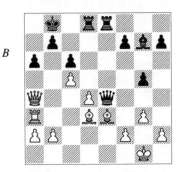

21...♕d5

21...♕g4? is bad due to 22 ♖b3! ♖e7 (22...♖d7 23 ♗xa6 ♗xd4 24 ♕xc6 ♕d1+ 25 ♔g2 ♕xb3 26 ♕xd7 +−; 22...♗xd4? 23 ♖xb7+ ♔xb7 24 ♕xa6+ ♔b8 25 ♕b6+ ♔a8 26 ♕xc6+ ♔b8 27 ♕b6+ ♔a8 28 ♗b5 1-0 Anand-Ivanchuk, Linares 1993) 23 ♖b4! ±.

22 ♗xa6 ♗xd4 23 ♗xb7

23 ♖b3 ♖e7 24 ♗xd4 ♕xd4 25 ♕xc6? ♕d1+ 26 ♔g2 ♕xb3 −+.

23...♗xc5 *(D)*

23...♔xb7?? 24 ♕b4+ ♔c8 25 ♖a7 +−.

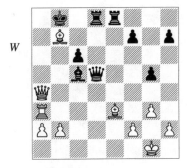

24 ♗xc6!

24 ♕a8+ ♔c7 25 ♕a5+ ♔xb7 26 ♗xc5 ♕d1+ 27 ♔g2 ♕d5+ =.

24...♕d1+ 25 ♔g2 ♕xa4 26 ♖xa4 ♖xe3 27 fxe3 ♖d2+ 28 ♔f3 ♖xb2 29 h3

The ending is quite unpleasant for Black, although objectively White's winning chances are not too great, Gi.Hernandez-Howell, Cuba 1993.

5 3 d4 ♘xe4 4 ♗d3 d5 5 ♘xe5 ♗d6

1 e4 e5 2 ♘f3 ♘f6 3 d4 ♘xe4 4 ♗d3 d5 5 ♘xe5 ♗d6 (D)

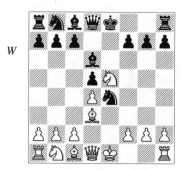

W

This symmetrical reply is also very popular in top-class chess. Black copies White's play, and challenges him to prove that the extra move has some genuine value. Two of the lines in this chapter deserve a special mention. Firstly, the continuation 6 0-0 ♘d7!? (Line A) is currently a hot topic, although Black's pawn sacrifice may not be the solution to all his problems. Secondly, the long tactical line B3 leads to a double-edged endgame which has been debated for decades. Until recently, White's winning chances have appeared rather slim, but the latest theory suggests that it may be more favourable for White than hitherto believed.

6 0-0

This is the main line, but sometimes White prefers other moves:

a) 6 ♕e2 ♗xe5 7 dxe5 ♘c5 =.

b) 6 c4 and then:

b1) 6...0-0 7 0-0 (7 cxd5!? ♗b4+ 8 ♘d2 ±) – *6 0-0 0-0 7 c4*.

b2) 6...♗xe5 7 dxe5 ♘c6 8 0-0 ♗e6 =.

c) 6 ♘d2 ♗xe5 (6...♗f5?! 7 ♕f3 ±; 6...♘xd2?! 7 ♗xd2 ♘d7 8 ♕h5 ♕e7 9 0-0-0 ♘f6 10 ♕g5 0-0 11 ♖he1 ♗e6 12 ♖e3 ± Alexandria-Litinskaya, Riga 1974) 7 dxe5 ♘c5 8 ♘f3 (8 ♗e2 ♘c6 9 ♘f3 ♗g4 10 ♗f4 0-0 11 0-0 ♖e8 12 ♖e1 ♕d7 = Mateu-Yusupov, Skien jr Wch 1979) and now:

c1) 8...♘xd3+ 9 ♕xd3 c6 (9...♘c6 10 ♗g5 ♘xe5!? 11 ♕e3 f6 12 ♘xe5 ♕e7 13 0-0-0 ♕xe5 14 ♕xe5+ fxe5 15 ♖xd5 ♔f7 16 ♖xe5 ♗e6 17 ♖he1 ± Hort-Toth, San Bernardino 1982) 10 0-0 (10 ♗g5!?) 10...♗g4 11 ♘g5 h6 12 ♕d4 ♗e6 13 ♘xe6 fxe6 14 c4 ♕e7 15 ♗d2 c5 16 ♕g4 d4 17 f4 0-0 = Raetsky-Alexandrov, corr. 1983-4.

c2) 8...♗g4 9 h3 ♘xd3+ (9...♗h5?! 10 ♗f5! 0-0?! {10...♘e6!?} 11 g4 ♗g6 12 ♗g5 f6 13 exf6 gxf6 14 ♗e3 ♕d6 15 ♕d4 ♘ba6 16 0-0-0 ± Gurgenidze-Yusupov, Kislovodsk 1982) 10 ♕xd3 ♗xf3 11 ♕xf3 and then:

c21) 11...0-0 12 ♕g3 (12 ♗f4 ♘c6
13 0-0-0 d4 14 ♖he1 ♕e7 15 ♔b1 ♕e6
16 a3 ♖fe8 17 ♗h2 ♖ad8 18 ♕d3 ♘e7
∓ Nunn-Toth, Lugano 1984) 12...♔h8
13 ♗g5 ♕d7 14 0-0-0 ∞.

c22) 11...♘c6 12 ♗f4 (12 ♕g3!?
♕e7 13 ♕xg7 ♕xe5+ 14 ♕xe5+♘xe5
15 ♗f4 f6 16 0-0-0 ±) 12...♘d4 13
♕d3 ♘e6 14 ♗e3 d4 15 0-0-0 ♕d5
with an unclear position, Ratnikov-
Belov, corr. 1985-7.

d) 6 ♘c3 and here:

d1) 6...0-0?! 7 ♘xe4! dxe4 8 ♗xe4
and here:

d11) 8...f6? 9 ♕h5 g6 10 ♗d5+
and White wins.

d12) 8...c5 9 0-0 cxd4 10 ♘f3 ±.

d13) 8...♕e7 9 0-0 (9 f4? loses material to 9...♗xe5!; e.g., 10 ♕h5 g6 11
♕xe5 ♖e8!) 9...♗xe5 10 dxe5 ♕xe5
11 ♖e1 ±.

d14) 8...♗xe5 9 dxe5 ♕e7 10 ♕e2
♘c6 (10...♖e8 11 f4 f6 12 0-0 fxe5 13
fxe5 ♕xe5 14 ♗d5+ +−) 11 f4 ♘d4
12 ♕f2 (12 ♕d3!? ♖d8 13 0-0 ♗g4 14
♕e3 ±) 12...♘b3 13 ♗xh7+ ♔xh7 14
cxb3 ± Am.Rodriguez-Sariego, Cienfuegos 1989.

d2) 6...♘xc3 7 bxc3 ♘d7 (7...0-0 8
0-0 – *6 0-0 0-0 7 ♘c3 ♘xc3 8 bxc3*) 8
0-0 ♘xe5 9 dxe5 ♗c5 10 ♕h5 g6 11
♕h6 ♗f8 12 ♕e3 c6 13 c4 ♗e6 14
cxd5 ♕xd5 ∞ Tseshkovsky-Av.Bykh-
ovsky, Irkutsk 1983.

We now return to the position after
6 0-0 *(D)*.

Now:

A: 6...♘d7!?   81
B: 6...0-0   88

Or:

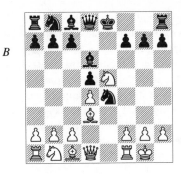

a) 6...c5?! 7 ♗b5+ ♘d7 8 dxc5
♗xe5 9 ♕xd5 ♕e7 10 c6! ± Khalip-
etsky-Wagner, corr. 1934.

b) 6...♘c6 7 ♘xc6 bxc6 8 c4 ♕h4
(8...0-0 – *6...0-0 7 c4 ♘c6 8 ♘xc6
bxc6*) 9 g3 ♕h3 10 c5 ♗g4 11 ♗e2
♗xe2 12 ♕xe2 ♗e7 13 f3 ♘f6 14 ♗f4
♕d7 15 ♘c3 0-0 16 ♖fe1 ±.

c) 6...♗xe5?! 7 dxe5 ♘c5!? (7...♘c6
8 ♗xe4 dxe4 9 ♕xd8+ ♘xd8 10 ♘c3
±) and then:

c1) 8 ♘c3 c6 9 ♘e2 0-0 10 b3
♗g4!? 11 ♗a3 ♘bd7 12 f3 ♗h5 13
♘f4 ♗g6 14 ♗xg6 hxg6 15 ♘d3 b6 =
Borge-Rozentalis, Reykjavik 1996.

c2) 8 f4 0-0 9 ♘c3 (9 ♗e2!?) 9...c6
10 f5 ♘bd7 11 ♗f4 ♖e8 12 ♖e1 ♕b6
13 ♔h1 ♕xb2 14 f6 g6 15 ♕d2 ♘xd3
∓ Kindermann-Rozentalis, Bundesliga
1995/6.

c3) 8 ♗e2 0-0 9 f4 ♘c6 10 b3 ♘e7
11 ♗a3 b6 12 ♘c3 c6 13 ♕d2 f6 14
exf6 ♖xf6 15 ♗xc5 bxc5 16 ♘e4 ±
Rozentalis-Meiers, Berne 1992.

A)

6...♘d7!?

A currently fashionable continuation. Black immediately dislodges the
knight from e5, even though this early

action entails the sacrifice of the d5-pawn. In return, Black obtains a lead in development and active piece-play. The jury is still out on the assessment of this idea, but at the moment it appears that it does not completely equalize, although it is hard to say whether White can obtain significant winning chances in the ensuing play.

7 ♘xd7 ♗xd7 *(D)*

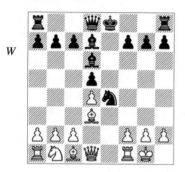

We should note that this position arises more frequently via the move-order *5...♘d7 6 ♘xd7 ♗xd7 7 0-0 ♗d6*.

8 c4

Or:

a) 8 ♖e1?! allows Black, if he so chooses, to take an immediate draw by 8...♗xh2+ 9 ♔xh2 ♕h4+, etc.

b) 8 ♕h5 ♘f6!? 9 ♖e1+ ♔f8 10 ♕h4 ♘g4 11 ♕xd8+ ♖xd8 12 h3 ♘f6 13 ♘d2 g6 14 ♘f3 ♔g7 15 ♘e5 ♗c8 = Movsesian-Akopian, Las Vegas FIDE 1999.

c) 8 ♘c3!? and now:

c1) 8...♘xc3!? 9 bxc3 0-0 10 ♕h5 f5 (this appears weakening, but the exchange of all the knights has removed White's best chance of exploiting the

weakness of e5 and so Black does not have any real problems) 11 ♖b1 (11 c4 dxc4 12 ♗xc4+ ♔h8 13 ♖b1 b6 14 ♖e1 ♗e8 15 ♕f3 ♖b8 = Boudy-Dvoretsky, Varna 1980; 11 ♖e1 ♕f6 12 ♕f3 ♔h8 13 ♖b1 {13 ♕xd5 ♗c6 is risky for White} 13...b6 14 ♗f4 ♖ae8 15 ♖xe8 ♗xe8 16 ♖e1 ♗h5 is equal, M.Pavlović-Mikhalchishin, Lenk 1999) 11...b6! (11...♖b8?! 12 ♖e1 ♕f6 13 ♕f3 c6 14 ♗f4 b6 15 ♕g3 ♗xf4 16 ♕xf4 b5 17 ♕c7! ± Adorjan-Toth, Budapest 1970) 12 ♖e1 (12 ♕f3 c6 13 ♗f4 ♕c7 14 ♗xd6 ♕xd6 15 ♖fe1 ♖ae8 = Shirov-Kramnik, Belgrade 1997; 12 ♗g5 ♗e8 13 ♕h4 ♕d7 14 ♗f4 ♗g6 15 ♕g3 ♗xf4 16 ♕xf4 ♖ae8 17 ♖fe1 ♕c6 18 ♖xe8 ♗xe8 19 ♕e5 g6 20 ♗b5 ♕d6 = Timoshchenko-Schüssler, Bayamo 1981) and then:

c11) 12...♕f6 13 ♕f3 c6! (13...♔h8 14 ♗f4 ±) 14 ♗f4 b5 15 ♕g3 (15 h4!?; 15 ♗xd6 ♕xd6 16 ♖e5 ♖ae8 17 ♖be1 ♖xe5 intending 18 ♖xe5?! ♕a3 ∓) 15...♗xf4 16 ♕xf4 ♖f7 17 ♔f1! (17 h4 ♖e7 =) 17...♖af8! (17...♖e7 18 ♖xe7 ♕xe7 19 ♖e1 ±) 18 ♖e2 ♕d8! ∞ Shirov-Anand, Groningen FIDE 1997.

c12) 12...c6! 13 ♗g5 ♕c7 14 c4!? (14 ♗e7 ♖fe8 15 ♗xd6 ♕xd6 16 h3 {16 ♕g5!?} 16...♖e7 17 f4 g6 18 ♕h4 ♖ae8 19 ♖xe7 ♖xe7 20 ♔f1 ♖e8 = Geller-Yusupov, USSR Ch (Minsk) 1979) 14...♗e8! 15 ♕h3 dxc4 and then:

c121) 16 ♗xf5?! h6! 17 ♗e4 (17 ♗xh6?! gxh6 18 ♕xh6 ♖xf5 19 ♖xe8+ ♖xe8 20 ♕g6+ ♕g7 21 ♕xe8+ ♔h7 ∓) 17...♗xh2+! ∓.

c122) 16 ♗xc4+ ♗f7 17 ♗e6 (17 ♗xf7+ ♕xf7! =) 17...♗xe6 18 ♖xe6 ♖ae8 19 ♕b3 (19 ♖be1 ♖xe6! 20 ♖xe6

♕d7 =) 19...♖xe6 20 ♕xe6+ ♖f7 21 ♕e8+ (21 ♖e1?! ♕d7 22 ♕b3 h6 23 ♗c1 ♔h7 ∓) 21...♖f8 22 ♕e6+ ♖f7 23 ♕e8+ ♖f8 ½-½ Shirov-Kramnik, Cazorla (2) 1988.

c2) 8...♕h4!? (this is a double-edged move; in the main line Black has to forfeit his right to castle, although it is hard for White to exploit this factor) 9 g3 (9 h3?! ♗xh3 10 gxh3 ♕xh3 11 f4 =) 9...♘xc3 10 bxc3 (D) (10 ♕e1+ ♕e7 11 ♕xc3 0-0 {11...0-0-0?! 12 ♕a5 ±} 12 ♕b3 ♗c6 =) and now:

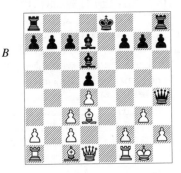

c21) 10...♕h3?! 11 ♖e1+ ♗e6 12 ♖b1 0-0-0 13 ♕f3 intending c4.

c22) 10...♕f6?! 11 ♕h5 ♕e6 (or 11...h6? 12 ♖e1+ ♔f8 13 ♕xd5 c6 14 ♕b3 b6 15 ♗a3 ±) 12 ♗f4 g6 13 ♕h6 ♗f8 14 ♕g5 f6?! (14...♗e7 15 ♕e5 is unclear) 15 ♕h4 0-0-0 16 ♗xg6 hxg6 17 ♕xh8 ♕f7 18 ♗h6 ♗d6 19 ♕g7 ♕e7 20 ♕xg6 1-0 Kveinys-Maciejewski, Gdynia 1989.

c23) 10...♕g4! 11 ♖e1+ and here:

c231) 11...♔f8 12 ♗e2 ♕f5 13 c4 (13 ♖b1!? b6 14 c4 ∞) 13...dxc4 14 ♗xc4 h5!? 15 h4 ♖e8 16 ♖xe8+ ♗xe8 17 ♗e3 b5 18 ♕d3 ♕xd3 = Magem-Illescas, Pamplona 1995/6.

c232) 11...♔d8!? 12 ♗e2 (12 f3?! ♕h3) 12...♕f5 13 ♖b1 (13 c4!? is also possible) 13...b6 14 c4 dxc4 (14...c6?! 15 c5! bxc5 {15...♗c7 16 c4 ±} 16 c4 ±) 15 ♗xc4 ♖e8 (15...h5!?) and now:

c2321) 16 ♖xe8+ ♔xe8 17 ♗d3 (17 ♕e2+ ♔f8 =) 17...♕d5! (17...♕h3?! 18 ♕f3 ♖d8 {18...♖c8 19 ♗f4 ±} 19 ♗g5 ±) 18 c4 (18 ♕e2+ ♔f8 ∓ intending to meet 19 ♗e4? with 19...♖e8 ∓) 18...♕xd4 19 ♗b2 ♕g4 20 ♕xg4 ♗xg4 21 ♗xg7 h5 ∞.

c2322) 16 ♗e3 ♗c6! (16...♖e7?! 17 ♗f1 ♔e8 18 ♗g2 ♖d8 19 c4 ±) 17 d5 ♗d7 18 ♗f1 (18 ♗d3!? ♕g4! {18...♕xd5?! 19 c4 and now 19...♕c6 20 ♕h5 or 19...♕a5 20 ♕f3 ±} 19 ♗e2 ♕g6 ∞) 18...h6 (18...♗a4!? 19 ♖e2 ♖e5 20 ♗g2 ♔d7 intending ...♖ae8 ∞) 19 c4 ♖e7! ∞ Kamsky-Karpov, Elista FIDE Wch (6) 1996.

8...c6 (D)

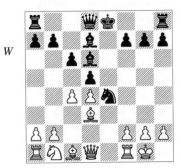

9 cxd5

9 ♘c3 can be met by:

a) 9...♘xc3 10 bxc3 0-0! (better than 10...dxc4?! 11 ♖e1+ ♗e7 12 ♗a3 ♗e6 13 ♗xe7 ♕xe7 14 ♗xc4 0-0 15 ♖e5 ♕a3 16 ♗xe6 fxe6 17 ♕e1 ♖ad8 18 h3 ± Short-Hübner, Wijk aan Zee

1986) 11 cxd5 cxd5 – *9 cxd5 cxd5 10 ♘c3 ♘xc3 11 bxc3 0-0!*.

b) 9...0-0! 10 ♕h5 (10 cxd5 ♘xc3 11 bxc3 cxd5 – *9 cxd5 cxd5 10 ♘c3 ♘xc3 11 bxc3 0-0!*) 10...♘f6 11 ♕h4 dxc4 12 ♗xc4 ♖e8 13 ♗g5 h6 14 ♗xf6 ♕xf6 15 ♕xf6 gxf6 = Sveshnikov-Mikhalchishin, Kuibyshev 1986.

9...cxd5 10 ♕h5

Or 10 ♘c3!? ♘xc3 (10...0-0!? 11 ♘xd5 {11 ♕h5 ♘f6 12 ♕h4 ♗e6 =} 11...♕h4 ∞) 11 bxc3, and here:

a) 11...a6?! 12 ♖e1+ ♗e6 13 ♕h5 ♕d7 14 c4! 0-0-0 (14...g6 15 ♕xd5 0-0-0 16 ♕a5! {16 ♕f3 ♗b4 is unclear} 16...♗c7 17 ♕c3 ♕xd4 18 ♕xd4 ♖xd4 19 ♗b2 ±; 14...♗b4!? 15 cxd5! ♗xe1 16 dxe6 ♕xe6 17 ♗a3 with a dangerous initiative) 15 c5 ♗c7 16 ♗g5 ♖de8 17 c6! ± Hellers-Wolff, Baguio City jr Wch 1987.

b) 11...0-0! (just as in the main line, Black does best to sacrifice the weak d5-pawn) 12 ♕h5 g6! (12...f5?! 13 ♕f3 ♗e6 14 ♖e1 ±) 13 ♕xd5 ♕c7 14 ♗h6 ♖fe8 and now:

b1) 15 c4 ♗e6 (not 15...♕xh2+? 16 ♔h1 ±) 16 ♕f3 ♗xc4 17 ♕f6 (17 ♖ac1 b5 =) 17...♗f8 18 ♗f4 (18 ♗xf8 ♖xf8 19 ♖ac1 b5 =) 18...♕d8 19 ♕xd8 ♖exd8! (19...♖axd8? 20 ♗xc4 ♖xd4 21 ♗b5 ±) 20 ♗xc4 ♖xd4 with an equal position.

b2) 15 f4 ♗e6 (15...♖e3!? ∞) 16 ♕g5 (16 ♕f3 ♕xc3) 16...♕xc3 17 ♕f6 ♗f8 18 ♗xf8 ♖xf8 ∞ intending 19 f5?! ♕xd3 20 fxe6 ♕e3+.

b3) 15 h3!? ♗e6 16 ♕f3 ♕xc3 17 ♕f6 ♗f8 18 ♗xf8 ♖xf8 ±/=.

b4) 15 h4!? ♗e6 16 ♕f3 ♕xc3 17 ♕f6 ♗f8 18 ♗xf8 ♖xf8 and then:

b41) 19 ♗e4 ♖ad8 20 ♖fd1 ♗d5 21 h5 (21 ♖ac1 ♕a3 22 h5 ♕d6) 21...♕c6 is level.

b42) 19 ♖fd1 and here:

b421) 19...♖ad8? 20 ♗xg6! hxg6 21 h5 gxh5 (21...♔h7 22 ♖ac1 +–) 22 ♕g5+ ♔h7 23 ♕xh5+ ♔g7 24 ♕g5+ ♔h7 25 ♖ac1 +–.

b422) 19...♖fd8 20 ♗e4 ♗d5 21 ♖ac1 ♕a5 (21...♕a3 22 ♖c7) 22 ♕e5 is good for White.

b423) 19...♕a5! 20 ♗e4 ♕d8 (or 20...♗d5?! 21 h5 ♕d8 22 ♕e5 ♗xe4 23 h6 f6 24 ♕xe4 ±) 21 ♖xd8 (21 ♕e5 ♖e8! {21...♕xh4? 22 ♗xb7 ±} 22 ♗xb7 ♖b8 23 ♗c6 ♗d7 24 ♕c5 ♗xc6 25 ♕xc6 ♕xh4 =; 21 ♕f4 ♗d5 22 h5 ♖e8 23 ♗xd5 ♕xd5 = with the point that 24 h6 is met by 24...♖e6 intending ...g5; 21 ♕f3!? ∞) 21...♖axd8 22 d5 (22 ♗xb7 ♖d7 23 ♗c6 ♖d6 24 d5 ♖fd8 =) 22...♗f5! (22...♗c8 23 ♖ac1 ±) 23 ♗xf5 (23 ♗f3 h5 =) 23...gxf5 24 d6 ♖d7 = Tiviakov-Yusupov, Groningen 1994.

b5) 15 ♕f3!? should be considered.

We now return to 10 ♕h5 *(D)*:

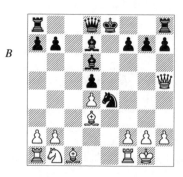

10...0-0

Black sacrifices a pawn for speedy development.

10...♕f6 is the alternative, but this appears less reliable than the text-move:

a) 11 ♕xd5 ♗c6 12 ♗b5?! 0-0-0! 13 ♗xc6? ♗xh2+ −+.

b) 11 ♘c3 ♕xd4 12 ♕xd5 ♕xd5 13 ♘xd5 ♘c5 (13...f5 was recommended by Sveshnikov as ±, but this remains untested) 14 ♖e1+ ♘e6 (or 14...♗e6 15 ♗b5+ ±) 15 ♗g5!? 0-0?! (15...f6? 16 ♗f4 ♗xf4 17 ♘xf4 ♔f7 18 ♗c4 ♖he8 19 ♖ad1 ±; 15...h6!?) 16 ♗e7 ♗xe7 17 ♘xe7+ ♔h8 18 ♖ad1 ♖ad8 (18...♖ae8 19 ♘f5 ♘c5 20 ♖xe8 ♖xe8 21 ♘d6 ±) 19 ♗e4 ± Sveshnikov-I.Zaitsev, USSR Ch (Moscow) 1991.

c) 11 ♗e3!? is a new idea; here is my analysis:

c1) 11...♗c6?? 12 f3 +−.

c2) 11...♕f5?? 12 ♕xf5 ♗xf5 13 f3 ♘g3 14 ♗b5+ +−.

c3) 11...0-0?! 12 ♘c3 ±.

c4) 11...g6 12 ♕xd5 ♗c6 13 ♕c4 with a clear advantage for White.

c5) 11...♕g6 12 ♕xd5 ♗c6 13 ♗xe4 ♗xd5 14 ♗xg6 hxg6 15 h3 ±.

c6) 11...♕e6 12 ♘c3 ♘f6 (after 12...♘xc3 13 bxc3 ± White intends to meet 13...♕g4? with 14 ♕xd5 ♗c6 15 ♗b5 +−) 13 ♕h4 ♕g4 (13...0-0 14 ♗g5 ±; 13...♘g4 14 ♖fe1 ±) 14 ♕xg4 ♗xg4 15 ♗g5 ♗e6 16 f4 ♗e7 17 f5 ♗d7 18 ♖ae1 ±.

c7) 11...0-0-0 12 ♗xe4 (12 ♘c3!? ♘xc3 13 bxc3 ±; 12 f3!?) 12...dxe4 13 ♕a5 ♔b8 14 ♘c3 ♗c7 (14...♕h4 15 g3 ♕h3 16 d5 ±) 15 ♕xc7+ (15 ♕a3!?) 15...♔xc7 16 ♘d5+ ±/±.

c8) 11...♗f5 is possible, as 12 f3 (12 ♗b5+ may be better) can be met by 12...g6 13 ♕h6 ♗f8 14 ♕f4 ♗d6, etc.

11 ♕xd5

11 ♘c3 ♘f6 (11...g6!? 12 ♕xd5 ♗c6 13 ♕b3 ♘xc3 14 bxc3 and now Black can force a draw by 14...♗xh2+ 15 ♔xh2 ♕h4+ 16 ♔g1 ♗xg2 – Ivanchuk) 12 ♕h4 ♗e6 13 ♗g5 h6 14 ♗xf6 ♕xf6 =.

11...♗c6 12 ♕h5 g6

Or:

a) 12...♗c7 13 ♗e3 g6 14 ♕h3 ♘g5!? (14...f5?! 15 ♘c3 ♘g5 16 ♗xg5 ♕xg5 17 d5 ± Sveshnikov-Meiers, Riga 1991) 15 ♕h6 ♘e6 16 ♘c3 ♘xd4 17 ♖ad1 ♗e5 18 ♖fe1 ± Yusupov.

b) 12...♗b4!? is interesting: 13 ♗e3 ♖e8 14 ♗xe4 ♖xe4 15 ♘c3 ♖h4 16 ♕f5 g6 17 ♕d3 ♗xc3 18 ♕xc3 (18 bxc3? ♕d5 intending ...♗b5) 18...♕d6 19 h3 ♖e8 20 ♖ad1 ♕e6 21 d5 ♗xd5 22 ♗xa7 ♗xa2 23 ♖fe1 ♖e4 24 ♖xe4 ♕xe4 25 ♗d4 ♕c6 = *Nimzo-Junior*, Cadaques 2000.

13 ♕h3 *(D)*

13 ♕h6 ♖e8 14 ♘c3 (14 ♗e3 ♗f8 15 ♕h3 gives Black various possibilities, including 15...♗b4 – *13 ♕h3 ♗b4 14 ♗e3 ♖e8*) 14...♗f8 15 ♕f4 ♕xd4 = Yusupov.

This is a critical position. In return for the pawn, Black has a lead in development and has driven White's queen offside. In addition, White's extra pawn is isolated and weak. On the other hand, White's concessions are of a temporary nature; once he develops his remaining pieces he will be well on the way to consolidating the extra pawn. Currently Black has not proved

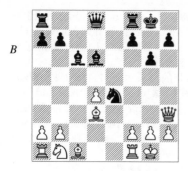

full compensation for the pawn, although there are a number of unexplored possibilities and it could be that the solution to Black's problems lies in one of them.

13...♘g5

This move was suggested by Yusupov, and enjoyed some popularity in high-level games in the late 1990s without, it must be said, achieving very good results.

Other possibilities are certainly worth considering:

a) 13...♕b6!? 14 ♘c3 ♕xd4 15 ♗xe4 ♗xe4 16 ♕h4 (16 ♖d1 ♕e5 = with the point that 17 ♖e1? fails to 17...♗xg2! ∓) 16...f5 17 ♖d1 (17 ♘b5 ♕f6 18 ♕xf6 ♖xf6 19 ♗g5 ♖e6 20 ♘xd6 ♖xd6 21 ♖ad1 ½-½ J.Polgar-Yusupov, Madrid 1995; 17 ♗h6 may give White an edge, Palac-Marciano, Cannes 1998) 17...♕e5 18 ♘xe4 fxe4 19 ♗e3 ± *ECO*.

b) 13...♖c8 and here:

b1) 14 ♗h6 ♖e8 15 ♘d2 ♗d7 (15...♘xd2!? 16 ♗xd2 ♗f8 17 ♗c3 b5 gives Black compensation according to Ivanchuk) 16 ♕f3 ♕h4 17 g3 ♘xd2 18 ♗xd2 ♕xd4 19 ♗c3 ♕g4 20 ♕f6 (20 ♕xg4 ½-½ Ivanchuk-Yusupov,

Linares 1993) 20...♖xc3 21 bxc3 (21 ♕xc3 ♗c6 gives Black enough compensation for the exchange – Yusupov; e.g., 22 f3 ♕h5) 21...♗e5 22 ♕h4 ♕xh4 23 gxh4 ♗xc3 24 ♖ac1 ♗a5 gives Black compensation.

b2) 14 ♗xe4 ♗xe4 15 ♘c3 ♖e8 (15...♗f5?! 16 ♕f3 ♕h4 {16...♖e8 ± Yusupov; this doesn't look very pleasant for Black though} 17 g3 ♕xd4 regains the pawn, but 18 ♖d1 ♕b6 19 ♘d5 gives White too much play) and now:

b21) 16 ♗e3 ♗f5 17 ♕f3 ♗b8 18 ♖fe1 b5 19 g4!? b4 (19...♖xc3? 20 bxc3 ♗e4 21 ♕h3 h5 22 gxh5 ♖e6 23 f3 +– Timman-Yusupov, Linares 1993) 20 ♘d5 ♖e4! 21 gxf5 ♕xd5 22 ♖ec1 ±.

b22) 16 ♗g5!? ♕xg5 17 ♘xe4 ♕e7 18 ♖ae1 ±.

c) 13...♗b4!? *(D)* seeks to hinder White's queenside development. Then:

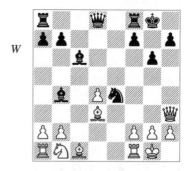

c1) 14 ♘c3 ♗xc3 15 ♗xe4 ½-½ Smirin-Yusupov, Dresden Z 1998.

c2) 14 ♗xe4!? ♗xe4 15 ♘c3 ♕xd4 16 ♖d1 ♕e5 17 ♗h6 gives White a slight advantage, since 17...♖fd8? may be met by 18 ♕h4!.

c3) 14 ♗e3 ♖e8 15 a3 ♗a5 16 ♖c1 ♖c8 (16...h5? is based on ideas of trapping the white queen, but it proves impossible to do so without the cost for Black being too great: 17 ᐤc3 ♗d7 18 ♕f3 ♗g4 19 ♕f4 ± Svidler-Anand, Dortmund 1998) and now:

c31) Lukacs advocated returning the pawn by 17 ᐤc3, but then 17...♗d7 seems best, hitting the queen while the g3-square is unavailable to it, before regaining the pawn on c3.

c32) 17 ♕h6 ♗b6 18 ᐤc3 ᐤxf2!! 19 ♗xf2 ♗xd4 20 ♖d1 ♗xf2+ 21 ♔xf2 ♕b6+ 22 ♔f1 ♕xb2 (22...♖e6!? 23 ♕h4 ♖f6+ 24 ♕xf6 ♗xg2+ 25 ♔xg2 ♕xf6 gives White a good deal of material for the queen, but his king remains exposed) 23 ♕d2 ♕xc3 (½-½ Svidler-Yusupov, Bad Homburg 1998) 24 ♕xc3 ♗xg2+ 25 ♔xg2 ♖xc3 =.

c33) 17 ♗xe4 ♗xe4 (17...♖xe4 was suggested by Anand) 18 ᐤc3 ♗xc3 19 ♖xc3 ♖xc3 20 bxc3 ♕c8 21 ♕xc8 ♖xc8 22 ♗d2 ♗d5 seems to give Black sufficient positional compensation for the pawn, Sadvakasov-Kasimdzhanov, Lausanne jr 1999.

14 ♕g4 *(D)*

This is the critical reply. Other moves:

a) 14 ♕e3?! ᐤe6! intending ...♗f4 and ...ᐤxd4.

b) 14 ♕h6 ᐤe6 15 ♗e3 ♗f4 (the alternative 15...♖e8 gives Black compensation) 16 ♕h3 ♕f6 17 ᐤc3 ᐤxd4 18 ♕g4 ᐤe6 19 ♗e4 ½-½ Sermek-Timoshenko, Ljubljana 2000.

c) 14 ♗xg5 (giving up the bishop-pair is a long-term concession, which White should be trying to avoid in this

position; now Black has no problems) 14...♕xg5 15 ᐤc3 and then:

c1) 15...♖fe8?! 16 d5! (16 ♖ad1?! ♖e7 gives Black enough compensation) 16...♗xd5 17 f4 ♕d8 18 ᐤxd5 ♗c5+ 19 ♔h1 ♕xd5 20 ♖ac1! ♗e3 (20...♖e3?! 21 ♗c4 ±) 21 ♖c3! (21 ♗c4? ♕f5 22 ♕xf5 gxf5 = Shirov-Kramnik, Cazorla (4) 1998) 21...♗d4 (21...♖ad8 22 f5 ±) 22 ♖c7 ±.

c2) 15...♖ae8! 16 ♖ad1 (16 d5 ♗xd5 17 f4 ♕d8 18 ᐤxd5 ♗c5+ 19 ♔h1 ♕xd5 =; 16 ♖ae1 ♖xe1 17 ♖xe1 ♕d2 =) 16...♖e7 17 d5 ♗d7 18 ᐤe4 ♖xe4 19 ♕xd7 ♕e7 20 ♕xe7 ♖xe7 = Luther-Delchev, Gorica 2000.

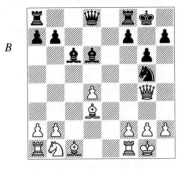

B

14...ᐤe6

14...♗e7!? deserves to be tried:

a) 15 ᐤc3 h5! 16 ♕g3 h4 17 ♕g4 ♗d7!? 18 ♕f4 h3 19 g3 (19 ᐤd5 hxg2 20 ᐤxe7+ ♕xe7 21 ♔xg2 ♗h3+ ∓) 19...♗c6 20 ♗e2 ᐤe6 intending to play ...ᐤxd4 ∓.

b) 15 ♗xg5 ♗xg5 16 ᐤc3 and now 16...♗f6 gives Black compensation, which is an improvement over 16...h5?! 17 ♕g3 ♕xd4 18 ♗xg6 ♗f4 19 ♕d3 ±.

15 ♗h6

15 ♘c3 h5 16 ♕h3 ♘xd4 17 ♘e4
♘e2+ 18 ♗xe2 ♗xe4 19 ♗h6 ♖e8 =.
15...♖e8
15...f5?! 16 ♕h3 ♘f4 17 ♗c4+ ♔h8
18 ♗xf4 ♗xf4 19 d5 ±.
16 ♘c3 ♗f4!?
16...♘xd4 deserves attention. 17
♖ad1 ♗e5 18 f4 f5 and now:
a) 19 ♕g3 ♕b6 20 ♔h1 ♗f6 21
♗c4+ ♔h8 22 ♖d2 (22 ♗g5 ♗g7 ∞)
22...♕c5 ∞ Isaev-Barua, India 2000.
b) 19 ♕h3 ♗f6 20 ♗g5 ♗xg5 21
♗c4+ ♔h8 22 fxg5 ♕b6 23 ♔h1
♕xb2 (23...♖ad8!?) 24 ♖xd4 ♖e3! 25
♘d1 ♕xd4 26 ♘xe3 ♖e8 27 ♕h6
♕xe3 28 ♖xf5! ♗d5! 29 ♖f8+ ♗g8
30 h3 ♕e7 31 ♖xe8 ♕xe8 32 ♕h4
♕e5! 33 ♗xg8 ♔xg8 34 ♕c4+ ♔g7
35 ♕a4 ♕xg5 = Nijboer-Van der Sterren, Rotterdam 1999.
17 ♗xf4 ♕xd4 18 ♗e4
Now:
a) 18...f5 and here:
a1) 19 ♗xf5?! ♘xf4 20 ♖ad1 (20
♖fd1 ♕e5 21 ♗d7? h5 −+; 20 g3 h5
21 ♕xf4 ♕xf4 22 gxf4 gxf5 is equal)
20...♕e5 21 g3 (not 21 ♗d7? ♗xg2)
21...♕xf5 22 ♕xf5 gxf5 23 gxf4 ♔f7
with equality.
a2) 19 ♕d1!? ♕xd1 (19...♗xe4 20
♕xd4 ♘xd4 21 ♖ad1 ±) 20 ♖fxd1
fxe4 21 ♗e3 ♔f7 (21...a6!? 22 ♘d5
♔f7 23 ♘b4 ±) 22 b4! b6 23 a4 ♖ed8
24 h3! ± Kasparov-Piket, Wijk aan
Zee 1999.
a3) 19 ♕g3!? ♘xf4 20 ♗xc6 bxc6
and here:
a31) 21 ♖ad1 ♕xc3 22 ♕xf4 ♕xb2
23 ♕c4+ ♔h8 24 ♖d7 ♖ed8! (not
24...♕f6? 25 ♖f7 ♖e4 26 ♕b3 ±) 25
♖c7 ♖dc8 =.

a32) 21 ♕f3! ♘d5 (21...♕c4 22 b3
♕xc3 23 ♕xf4 ±) 22 ♖fd1 ♕g4 23
♘xd5 ♕xf3 24 gxf3 cxd5 25 ♖xd5
♖ad8 26 ♖ad1 ♖xd5 27 ♖xd5 ♖e2
(27...♖e7 28 b4 ♔g7 29 ♖a5 ± Anand-Karpov, Leon adv (4) 1999) 28 ♖b5 a5
29 ♖b7 f4 30 a4 ♖e1+ 31 ♔g2 ♖a1 32
b3 ♖a2 33 h4 ± Anand-Karpov, Leon
adv (6) 1999.
b) 18...♘xf4 19 ♕xf4 ♗xe4 and
now:
b1) 20 ♖fe1?! ♗b1! 21 ♕c1 ♗f5 22
♕h6 (22 ♖d1 ♕e5 ½-½ Alonso-Zarnicki, Mar del Plata 2000) 22...♖ad8
23 h3 ♕b6 = Vescovi-Benares, Brasilia 2000.
b2) 20 ♖ae1 f5 21 ♖e3 ♖ad8 22
♖fe1 was given as ± by Blatny.

B)
6...0-0 *(D)*

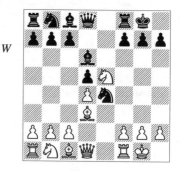

7 c4
This is the main line, though White
has tried other moves:
a) 7 f3 ♘c5! =.
b) 7 ♖e1 ♖e8 (7...♘c6!?) 8 ♘c3
♗xe5 9 dxe5 ♘xc3 10 bxc3 ♕h4! ∞.
c) 7 ♕f3 ♕e7 (7...c5 8 ♗xe4 dxe4
9 ♕xe4 ♕e7 10 ♖e1 ♖e8 11 ♘d2 cxd4

12 ♘ef3 ♘c6 13 ♕xe7 ♖xe7 = Raetsky-Mironov, corr. 1985-6) 8 ♘c3 ♘xc3 9 bxc3 ♗xe5 10 dxe5 ♕xe5 11 ♗f4 ♕f6 12 ♕g3 ♘c6 13 ♗g5 ♕d6 14 ♗f4 ♕f6 ½-½ I.Zaitsev-Yusupov, Erevan 1982.

d) 7 ♘d2 (this and line 'e' aim to remove the e4-knight by attacking it with a knight; although careful play is required from Black, these ideas are perhaps too straightforward to promise White an advantage) and now:

d1) 7...♘f6?! 8 ♘df3 h6 9 c4 c6 10 ♕b3 ♗e7 11 ♖e1 ♘bd7 12 ♗d2 is much better for White, Richardson-Marsh, Spain 1969.

d2) 7...♘xd2 8 ♗xd2 ♘c6 (also possible is 8...♘d7!?) 9 ♘xc6 bxc6 10 ♕h5 g6 11 ♕h6 ♖e8 (11...♕f6 12 c3 ♖e8 13 ♖ae1 ♗d7 14 ♗g5 ♕g7 15 ♕h4 c5 16 ♗f6 ± Fedorov-Dragomaretsky, Moscow 1972) 12 ♗g5 ♗e7 13 ♖ae1 ♗xg5 14 ♖xe8+ ♕xe8 15 ♕xg5 ♗e6 16 f4 ♕d8 17 ♕g3 ± Nunn-Hort, London 1979.

d3) 7...♗xe5 8 dxe5 ♘c5 (Black's soundest reply; unless White is prepared to lose time, he must allow the exchange on d3, but then the simplification of the position and the opposite-coloured bishops give Black good equalizing prospects) and here:

d31) 9 ♘f3 ♗g4! 10 ♗e2 ♘e6! 11 c4? dxc4 12 ♕a4 ♘c6 13 ♖e1! ♘ed4 14 ♘xd4 ♕xd4 15 ♗e3 ♕e4 ∓ Fedorov-Makarychev, Moscow 1974.

d32) 9 ♕h5 ♘xd3 10 cxd3 c5 11 b4!? cxb4 12 a3 bxa3 13 ♗xa3 ♖e8 14 ♗d6 ♘c6 15 ♖a4 ♕d7! 16 ♖f4 ♕e6 17 d4 ♕g6 18 ♕f3 ♗e6 ∓ J.Polgar-Kamsky, Groningen PCA 1993.

d33) 9 ♗e2!? ♘c6 10 ♘f3 ♗g4 11 h3 (11 ♗f4 ♕d7 =) 11...♗h5 12 c3 ♕d7 13 ♗e3 ♘e6 14 ♕b3 ♘a5 15 ♕b4 ♘c6 16 ♕b3 ♘a5 = Korneev-Rozentalis, Groningen 1995.

d34) 9 ♘b3 ♘xd3 10 ♕xd3 ♘c6 *(D)* and then:

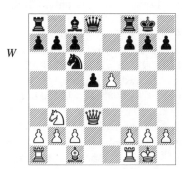

d341) 11 f4 f6 (11...g6 12 f5 ♘xe5 13 ♕g3 f6 14 fxg6 ♘xg6 15 ♗h6 ♖f7 16 ♖ae1 ♗d7 17 ♘d4 c6 18 h4 gives White compensation, Wedberg-I.Jones, Haifa Echt 1989) 12 exf6 ♕xf6 (or 12...♖xf6 13 ♗e3 {13 f5!?} 13...♗f5 14 ♕d2 b6 15 ♘d4 ♗e4 16 ♘e2 ♕e8 17 ♘g3 ♖d8 18 ♖ae1 d4 19 ♗f2 ♖e6 20 f5 ♖e5 ∞) 13 ♕xd5+ ♗e6 14 ♕c5 ♖ad8 15 ♗d2!? ♕xb2 16 ♗c3 ♕xc2 17 ♗xg7 ♕xc5+ 18 ♘xc5 ♖fe8 19 ♗c3 (19 ♘xe6?! ♖xe6 20 f5 ♖e4! 21 ♗h6 ♘d4 ∞ Maeder-Morgado, corr. 1978-84) 19...♗c4! (19...♖d5? 20 ♘e4! ♖f8 21 ♘f6+ ♖xf6 22 ♗xf6 ♔f7 23 ♗b2 ± Ljubojević-Razuvaev, Amsterdam 1975) 20 ♖f3 b6 with an equal position.

d342) 11 ♗f4 ♕d7 (11...♕h4 12 ♕d2 h6 13 c3 a5 14 a4 ♖d8 15 ♘d4 ♕e7 16 ♖fe1 ± Gufeld-Kochiev, USSR 1978) and now:

d3421) 12 ♖ad1 ♕g4 13 ♕e3 (13 ♕g3 ♕xg3 14 ♗xg3 ♗e6 15 f4 ♘e7 ½-½ Motwani-Yusupov, Skien jr Wch 1979) 13...♘e7 14 ♕c5!? (14 h3?! ♕g6 15 c3 b6 ∓ Timoshchenko-Yusupov, Frunze 1979; 14 f3!? ♕g6 15 ♕c5 ♕b6! 16 ♗e3 ♖e8 17 ♕c3 ♕c6 18 ♕d2 ♕g6 19 ♖fe1, Grünfeld-Toth, Biel 1986, 19...b6! intending ...c5 =) 14...♘g6 15 ♗g3 h5 ∞ Yusupov.

d3422) 12 ♗g3 b6 13 ♖fe1 ♘b4! (13...♗b7 14 c3 ♘e7 15 ♘d4 c5 16 e6 ± Tseshkovsky-Yusupov, USSR Ch (Minsk) 1979) 14 ♕d2 c5 15 ♘d4 ♕g4 16 c3 cxd4 17 cxb4 d3 18 ♕xd3 ♕xb4 19 a3 ♕c4 20 ♕d2 ½-½ Grünfeld-Yusupov, Amsterdam 1982.

e) 7 ♘c3 (D) is more dangerous for Black than line 'd', but even here White cannot count on an advantage if Black defends accurately:

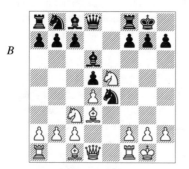

e1) 7...♘f6?! 8 ♗g5 ±.

e2) 7...♗xe5?! 8 dxe5 f5 9 ♕h5 ♗e6 10 ♖d1 ♕e8 11 ♕h4 c6 12 ♗e3 ♘d7 13 f4 ♕f7 14 ♘e2 ± Réti-Spielmann, Stockholm 1919.

e3) 7...f5!? 8 f3 (8 ♘xd5 ♗xe5 9 ♗xe4 ♗xh2+ 10 ♔xh2 fxe4 11 ♘e3 ♘c6 12 d5 ♕h4+ ∓) 8...♗xe5 (8...♘xc3

9 bxc3 c5 10 f4 c4 11 ♗e2 ♘d7 12 a4 ♘f6 13 ♗a3 ♗xa3 14 ♖xa3 ♕d6 15 ♖a1 ± Tseshkovsky-Reshevsky, Moscow 1989) 9 dxe5 ♘xc3 10 bxc3 ♕e7 11 ♖e1 ♗e6 12 a4 c5 13 ♗b5 a6 14 ♗f1 ♘c6 15 ♖b1 ♕c7 16 ♗f4 ♖fd8 17 ♕c1 d4 18 cxd4 (18 ♕b2 ∞) 18...♘xd4 19 c3 ♘b3 20 ♖xb3 ♗xb3 21 e6 gives White compensation, Geller-Yusupov, USSR Ch (Vilnius) 1980/1.

e4) 7...♘xc3 8 bxc3 ♘d7 (the safest reply) and now:

e41) 9 ♘xd7 ♕xd7 (Black's best reply is 9...♗xd7! – 6...♘d7 7 ♘xd7 ♗xd7 8 ♘c3 ♘xc3 9 bxc3 0-0) 10 ♕h5 (10 ♖b1!? ♖e8 11 ♕h5 g6 12 ♕f3 ♖b8 13 h3 c6 14 ♗g5 ♕c7 15 ♖be1 ♗d7 16 ♕f6 ♗f8 17 ♖e3 ♗g7 18 ♕f3 ♕a5 19 ♗f6 ♕xa2 ∞ A.Ivanov-Vladimirov, Pavlodar 1987) 10...g6 and here:

e411) 11 ♕f3 ♖e8 12 ♗h6 (12 h3 c5 13 dxc5 ♗xc5 14 ♗f4 b6 15 ♖fe1 ♗b7 16 ♗e5 ♖e6 17 ♕g3 ♕e7 18 ♔f1 ♖e8 19 f4 f6 ½-½ Kveinys-Glek, corr. 1987; 12 a4 c6 13 ♗f4 ♕c7 =) 12...♗f8 13 ♗xf8 ♖xf8 14 ♖fe1 ♕c6 15 h4 ♕xc3 16 ♕xd5 ♗e6 ½-½ Short-Yusupov, Plovdiv Echt 1983.

e412) 11 ♕h6 ♖e8 12 ♗d2 ♕e7 13 ♖ae1 ♕f8 14 ♕xf8+ ♖xf8 15 ♗h6 ♖d8 16 ♗g5 ♗f8 17 ♗e7 ♗xe7 18 ♖xe7 c6 19 ♖fe1 ± Ziatdinov-Tashkodzhaev, Tashkent 1984.

e42) 9 ♖e1 and then:

e421) 9...c5 10 ♗f4 (10 ♕f3 c4 11 ♗f1 ♘b6 ∞; 10 ♘xd7 ♕xd7 11 dxc5 ♗xc5 12 ♖e5 ♖e8 13 ♖xe8+ ♕xe8 14 ♗f4 ♕e6 15 ♖b1 b6 16 ♕d2 ♗d7 17 ♖e1 ♕c6 18 c4 ♗e6 = Kremenetsky-Makarychev, Moscow 1976) 10...c4 11

♗f5 ♘f6 12 ♗xc8 ♕xc8 13 ♖e3 ♕f5 14 ♗g3 ♘e4 15 ♕b1 ± U.Carlsson-Schaufelberger, corr. Echt 1972-81.

e422) 9...♗xe5 10 dxe5 ♘c5 and then:

e4221) 11 ♕h5!? ♘xd3 12 cxd3 ♕d7 13 ♕f3 d4 (13...c6 14 ♖b1 ♕f5 15 ♕xf5 ♗xf5 16 ♖xb7 ♗xd3 17 ♗f4 ±) 14 ♖b1 dxc3! 15 ♖b3 ♕f5 with equality.

e4222) 11 ♗f1 and here:

e42221) 11...♘e6 12 f4 f5 13 exf6 ♖xf6 14 ♗d3 g6 15 f5 gxf5 16 ♖e5 ± Raetsky-Skotorenko, corr. 1985.

e42222) 11...♖e8 12 ♕h5 (12 ♗e3!? b6 13 c4 ±; 12 ♗a3 b6 13 c4 d4 is equal, Gufeld-Makarychev, Tbilisi 1973) 12...♕d7 13 ♗e3 ♕c6 14 ♖ab1 a6 15 ♖b4 b6 16 ♖h4 ± Chiburdanidze-Schüssler, Haninge 1988.

e42223) 11...♗f5 12 ♗a3 b6 13 c4 d4 14 f4 ♕d7 (14...d3!? ∞) 15 h3 d3! ∞ Yusupov.

e43) 9 f4 c5 and now:

e431) 10 dxc5 ♗xc5+ (10...♘xc5!? 11 ♗e3 ♕c7 =) 11 ♔h1 ♘f6 =.

e432) 10 a4 ♘f6 11 f5 c4 12 ♗e2 ♘e4 13 ♕e1 ♕c7 14 ♗a3 ♗xa3 15 ♖xa3 ♖e8 16 ♖a1 f6 17 ♗h5 ♖e7 18 ♘g4 ♗d7 19 ♖f3 ♗e8 ∞ Pyhälä-Toth, Thessaloniki OL 1984.

e433) 10 ♘xd7 ♗xd7 11 ♕h5 f5 12 ♕f3 ♗c6 13 ♕h3 ♕f6 14 ♗a3 b6 = Janošević-Toth, Caorle 1973.

e434) 10 c4 cxd4 11 cxd5 ♘f6 12 ♗c4 ♗c5 (12...♕a5!?) 13 ♘d3! (13 ♕f3 ♗f5 14 ♖e1 ♕a5! 15 ♗b2 d3+ 16 ♔h1 d2 ∓ Kupreichik-Dvoretsky, USSR Ch (Leningrad) 1974) 13...♗e7 and now both 14 ♕f3!? and 14 ♖e1!? are unclear.

e435) 10 ♕f3 and then:

e4351) 10...♘f6?! 11 g4!? (or 11 dxc5!? ♗xc5+ 12 ♗e3 ♕b6 13 ♖ae1 ±; 11 f5? ♕a5 12 ♘g4 ♘xg4 13 ♕xg4 ♕xc3 14 ♗e3 ♖e8 15 dxc5 ♗xc5 16 ♗xc5 ♕xc5+ 17 ♔h1 ♗d7 with a clear advantage for Black, Tseshkovsky-Makarychev, Lvov 1973) 11...c4 12 ♗e2 ± Barry-Showalter, Boston 1889.

e4352) 10...c4 11 ♗e2 ♕a5 12 a4 (12 ♗d2 f6 13 ♗xc4 ♘b6! 14 ♗d3 fxe5 15 ♕h5 e4 16 ♗xe4 h6 17 ♖ae1 ♗g4! ∞) 12...f6 13 ♘g4 (13 ♗xc4 should be met by 13...♘b6! rather than 13...fxe5?! 14 ♕xd5+ ♕xd5 15 ♗xd5+ ♔h8 16 fxe5 ♖xf1+ 17 ♔xf1 ♘xe5! 18 dxe5 ♗xe5 19 ♖b1 ♗xh2 20 ♗a3 ♖b8 = Tal-Benko, Hastings 1973/4) 13...f5 14 ♘e5 ♘f6 with equality – Tal.

We now return to the position after 7 c4 *(D)*:

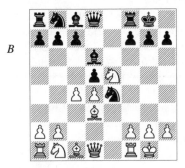

Now:
B1: 7...c6   91
B2: 7...♘c6   93
B3: 7...♗xe5   97

B1)
   7...c6

This rather passive response allows White to liquidate the e4-knight while retaining pressure against d5.

8 ♘c3

Or:

a) 8 ♕e2 ♕h4! =.

b) 8 ♕c2!? and now:

b1) 8...f6?? 9 cxd5 cxd5 10 ♗xe4 +−.

b2) 8...♘f6?! 9 ♗g5 h6 10 ♗h4 ♘bd7 11 ♖e1 dxc4 12 ♗xc4 ♘b6 13 ♗b3 ♘bd5 14 ♘c3 ♗e6 15 a3 ± Sarwat-Andolo, Cairo Z 2000.

b3) 8...♘a6!? and Black has compensation after 9 a3 ♘ac5! 10 dxc5 ♗xe5 11 ♗xe4 dxe4 12 ♕xe4 ♖e8 or 9 ♗xe4 dxe4 10 ♕xe4 ♖e8.

b4) 8...♕h4!? 9 ♘f3 ♕h5 10 c5 (10 cxd5 cxd5 11 ♗xe4 dxe4 12 ♕xe4 ♘c6 gives Black enough compensation) 10...♗c7 11 ♗xe4 dxe4 12 ♕xe4 ♗g4 13 ♘e5 ½-½ Timman-Hort, Bugojno 1980.

c) 8 ♘d2!? ♘xd2 9 ♗xd2 ♗xe5 (9...dxc4 10 ♗xc4 ♘d7 11 ♖e1 ♘xe5 12 dxe5 ♗c5 13 ♕c2 ♕e7 14 ♗d3 g6 15 h4 ♗b6 16 ♗g5 ± Sveshnikov-Kveinys, Kiev 1989) 10 dxe5 dxc4 11 ♗xc4 ♕d4 12 ♕c2! (12 ♕e2? ♗g4!) 12...♕xe5 13 ♖fe1 gives White compensation.

8...♘xc3

8...♘d7 9 ♘xe4 dxe4 10 ♗xe4 ♘xe5 11 dxe5 ♗xe5 12 ♗xh7+ (12 ♕h5?! f5!) 12...♔xh7 13 ♕h5+ ♔g8 14 ♕xe5 ♖e8 (14...♕d3 15 b3 ♕f5 16 ♕g3 ±) 15 ♕c3 (15 ♕g3 ♕d4!) 15...♕h4 16 b3 ♖e6 17 ♗b2 ♖g6 18 ♖fe1 ±.

9 bxc3 *(D)*

9...♘d7

Or:

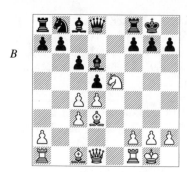

a) 9...♗e6?! 10 ♕h5! g6 11 ♕h6 ♘d7 12 f4 ±.

b) 9...♕h4 10 f4 ♘d7 11 ♗d2 ±.

c) 9...♗xe5?! 10 dxe5 dxc4 11 ♗xc4 and then:

c1) 11...♕xd1?! 12 ♖xd1 ♗e6 (or 12...♗f5 13 ♗a3 ♖e8 14 f4 ± Maroczy-Marshall, Paris 1900) 13 ♗xe6 fxe6 14 ♖b1 b6 15 ♖d6 ♖e8 16 ♗e3 c5 17 a4 ♘a6 18 a5 +− Klinger-Stanojević, Dortmund 1987.

c2) 11...♕e7 and now:

c21) 12 ♖e1 ♕c5 (12...b5?! 13 ♗d3 ♖d8 14 ♕f3 ±; 12...♗e6!?) 13 ♕b3 b5 14 ♗d3 ♗e6 15 ♕c2 h6 16 a4 ♖d8 17 ♗e3 ♕xe5 18 ♗e4! ± Botterill-De Veauce, Islington 1971.

c22) 12 a4!? and here:

c221) 12...♕xe5 13 ♗a3 (13 ♖e1!? ♕c7 {13...♕xc3? 14 ♗a3 +−} 14 ♗a3 c5 and now 15 ♕f3 ± or 15 ♕h5 ±) 13...c5 (13...♖e8 14 ♖e1 ♕xe1+ 15 ♕xe1 ♖xe1+ 16 ♖xe1 ♗e6 {16...♗d7 17 ♖e7 ±} 17 ♗xe6 fxe6 18 ♖xe6 ♘d7 19 ♖e7 ±) 14 ♖e1 ♕c7 15 ♕h5 b6 16 ♖e3 ±.

c222) 12...♗e6 13 ♗a3 c5 14 ♗d3 ♘c6 15 f4 ♖fd8 16 ♕c2 g6 (16...h6 17 ♖ae1 ±) 17 ♖ae1 ♘a5 18 f5 ± Pogats-Androvitsky, Hungary 1962.

10 f4

This is the most forthright move, but it is likely that White can retain an edge with some of the alternatives:

a) 10 ♘f3!? dxc4 11 ♗xc4 ♘b6 (11...♗e7?! – *3 ♘xe5 d6 4 ♘f3 ♘xe4 5 d4 d5 6 ♗d3 ♗e7 7 0-0 0-0 8 c4 c6 9 ♘c3 ♘xc3 10 bxc3 dxc4 11 ♗xc4 ♘d7 ±*) 12 ♗b3 ± Gufeld-Sokolin, New York 1996.

b) 10 ♖e1!? ♗xe5 11 dxe5 ♘c5 12 ♗c2 dxc4!? (12...♗e6?! 13 cxd5 cxd5 14 ♕h5 g6 15 ♕h6 f5 16 exf6 ♕xf6 17 ♗e3 ♘e4 18 ♗d4 ± B.Ivanović-Kurajica, Bar 1980) 13 ♗a3 ♕xd1 14 ♖axd1 b6 15 ♗xc5! (15 ♖d6 ♘d3 =) 15...bxc5 16 ♖d6 ±.

c) 10 ♘xd7!? ♗xd7 (10...♕xd7!?) 11 cxd5 cxd5 12 ♕h5 g6 (12...f5 13 ♕f3! ♗e6 14 ♖e1 ♕d7 15 ♖b1 ♔h8 16 ♗f4! ♗xf4 17 ♕xf4 ± Prüss-Laursen, corr. 1961-4) 13 ♕xd5 ♕c7 and then:

c1) 14 h3 ♗e6 15 ♕f3 ♕xc3 16 ♗h6 ♖fd8 17 ♖ad1 ♗f8 (17...♗xa2!?; 17...♗d5!?) 18 ♗xf8 ♔xf8 19 ♕xb7 is unclear.

c2) 14 ♗h6!? ♖fd8 15 ♕f3 ♗xh2+ (15...♕xc3 16 ♕f6 ♗f8 17 ♗xf8 ♖xf8 18 ♗e4 ±) 16 ♔h1 ♗d6 17 c4 is slightly better for White.

c3) 14 ♗d2 ♗xh2+ 15 ♔h1 ♗c6 16 ♕g5 ♖fd8 17 f4!? (17 ♕h4?! ♖d5 18 ♗g5 ♕a5 19 f4 ♕xc3 20 ♗e4 ♗g3 ∞ Antonio-Handoko, Asian Ch 1995) 17...♖d5 18 f5 with an initiative.

Now we return to 10 f4 *(D)*:

a) 10...♘f6 and here:

a1) 11 f5 should be answered by 11...♖e8! ∞, rather than 11...c5?! 12 ♗g5 ♖e8 13 ♖e1 cxd4 14 cxd4 ♗xe5 15 dxe5 ♕b6+ 16 ♗e3 d4 17 ♖b1 ♕c7

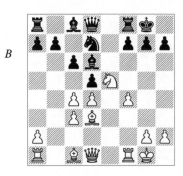

B

18 ♗xd4 ± Jansa-Kupka, Czechoslovakia 1962.

a2) 11 ♕f3 ♖e8 12 ♗b2 ♘e4 13 cxd5 cxd5 14 ♗xe4 dxe4 15 ♕xe4 f6 16 ♔h1! fxe5 17 fxe5 ♗e6 18 d5 ♗xe5 19 dxe6 ♖xe6 20 ♕xb7 ♖e7 ∞ Tiviakov-Handoko, Gausdal 1992.

a3) 11 ♕c2 dxc4 12 ♘xc4 ♗e7!? (12...♗e6?! 13 ♘xd6 ♕xd6 14 f5 ± Chigorin-Pillsbury, Paris 1900) 13 ♖e1 b6 (13...c5 14 ♗a3 b6 15 dxc5 ±; 13...♗e6?! 14 ♘e5 c5 15 f5 {15 ♗a3!? ♕c7 16 c4! ±} 15...♗c8 16 ♕b3! ± Almasi-Forintos, Hungary 1994) 14 a4 c5 15 ♗a3 ♗b7 16 ♖ab1 ±.

b) 10...dxc4 11 ♗xc4 ♕c7 12 a4 c5 13 ♕e2 b6 14 a5 (14 ♘xf7!?) 14...♖b8 15 ♗d2 bxa5 16 ♗d3 ♘f6 17 g4 ♖b2 18 g5 ♗xe5 19 fxe5 ♘d5 (19...c4? 20 gxf6 cxd3 21 ♕g2 g6 22 ♕g5 ♕d7 23 ♖f4! 1-0 Am.Rodriguez-Sisniega, Bayamo 1981) 20 ♕e4 g6 21 ♗c1! ♘xc3 22 ♕e1 ♖b3 23 ♗c2 c4 24 ♗xb3 cxb3 25 ♗b2 ± Am.Rodriguez.

B2)

7...♘c6 *(D)*

This move has become fashionable thanks to the efforts of Yusupov. Black is willing to accept doubled c-pawns

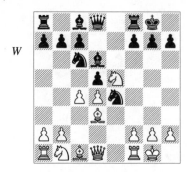

in return for liquidating the e5-knight. The resulting positions can become quite tactical, as Black attempts to generate kingside play to compensate for his long-term weaknesses.

8 ♘xc6

Or:

a) 8 f4 ♗xe5! 9 dxe5 – 7...♗xe5 8 dxe5 ♘c6 9 f4; Black has a number of satisfactory options in that line.

b) 8 cxd5 ♘xd4 9 ♗xe4 (9 ♘c4 ♕h4!? 10 ♘xd6 ♘xd6 11 ♘c3 ♗f5 = Euwe) 9...♗xe5 and then:

b1) 10 f4 ♗f6 11 ♕d3 (11 ♘c3 ♗f5 = Alekhine-Alexander, Hastings 1933/4) 11...♖e8! 12 ♘c3 g6 13 ♗d2 ♗g7 14 ♖ae1 ♗f5 = Henley-Wheeler, Bristol 1960.

b2) 10 ♘c3 and here:

b21) 10...f5!? could be considered.

b22) 10...♗f5 11 ♗e3 ♗xe4 12 ♗xd4 ♗xd4 (12...♗c2 13 ♕d2! ♗xd4 14 ♕xd4 ♕d7 15 ♖fe1 a6 16 ♖e2 ± Tal-Osnos, USSR Ch (Kiev) 1964/5) 13 ♕xd4 ♗f5 (13...♗g6 14 ♖ac1 a6 15 ♕b4 ± Matulović-Hecht, Belgrade 1969) 14 ♖ac1 ♗d7 15 ♕b4 b6 ±.

b23) 10...♕f6!? 11 ♗xh7+! (11 ♕d3?! ♘f5 12 ♔h1 h6 13 f4 ♗d4 14 ♗d2 ♘d6 15 ♖ae1 ♗d7 ∓) 11...♔xh7

12 f4 ♕b6 13 ♗e3 (13 ♘a4 ♘e2+ 14 ♔h1 ♘g3+ 15 hxg3 ♕h6+ 16 ♔g1 ♗d6 ∓) 13...♗f6 14 ♘e4 c5 15 dxc6 ♕xc6 16 ♘xf6+ ♕xf6 17 ♗xd4 ±/±.

8...bxc6 9 c5

9 ♘c3 f5 10 f3 ♘g5 11 ♗e3 ♗e6 = Parma-Trifunović, Belgrade 1964.

9...♗e7 *(D)*

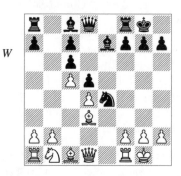

10 ♘c3

Or:

a) 10 ♘d2!? and then:

a1) 10...♘xd2?! 11 ♗xd2 ♗f6 12 ♗c3 a5 13 ♗c2 ♕d7 14 h3 g6 15 ♖e1 ♗g7 16 ♗a4 ♖a6 17 ♕f3 ♕d8 18 ♖e2 ♗d7 19 ♖ae1 ± Geller-Naranja, Palma de Mallorca IZ 1970.

a2) 10...♗f6 and here:

a21) 11 ♘b3 a5!? (11...♖e8!? 12 ♕c2 a5 13 a4 ♗a6 14 ♗xa6 ♖xa6 15 ♖e1?? ♘xc5! ∓ Kasperski-Bysina, corr. 1990-1) 12 a4 ♕d7 = intending ...♗a6 and ...♖fb8.

a22) 11 ♘xe4! dxe4 12 ♗xe4 ♗a6 (12...♕xd4 13 ♕c2 is slightly better for White) 13 ♖e1 (13 ♗xc6 ♖b8 14 ♖e1 ♗xd4 = Keres) 13...♗xd4 14 ♕c2 ♖e8! 15 ♗e3 ♗xb2 16 ♗xh7+ ♔h8 17 ♖ad1 ♕f6 18 ♗d3 ♗xd3 19 ♖xd3 ± Sanchez-Morgado, corr. 1977-8.

a3) 10...♗f5!? 11 ♘b3 ♕d7 =.

b) 10 f3 ♘g5 11 ♘c3 and here:

b1) 11...f5?! 12 ♗e3 ♘e6 13 b4 f4 14 ♗f2 ♗h4 15 b5 ♗d7 16 ♕c2 ± Matulović-Zuidema, Hamburg 1965.

b2) 11...♗f6 12 ♗e3 ♖e8 13 ♗f2 ♖b8 14 ♕c2 g6 15 a3 ♘e6 16 ♘e2 ♘g7 17 g4 is slightly better for White, Lupu-Delanoy, Torcy 1991.

b3) 11...♖e8!? 12 ♕a4 (12 ♗e3? ♗xc5; 12 f4 ♘e6 13 ♗e3 ♗f6 14 ♘e2 ♘xc5) 12...♗d7 (12...♗f6 13 ♕xc6 ♖b8 {13...♗xd4+? 14 ♔h1 ♘e6 15 ♕xa8 +−} 14 ♔h1 ±) and now:

b31) 13 ♗d2 ♖b8! 14 ♖ab1 ♗f6 15 ♔h1 h5! (15...a5?! 16 ♘e2 ±) 16 ♘e2 h4 17 h3 ♕c8?! (better is 17...g6! ∓ intending ...♘e6-g7-f5) 18 ♗a6 ♕d8 19 ♗d3 ♕c8 20 ♗a6 ♕d8 ½-½ Kasparov-Yusupov, Horgen 1995.

b32) 13 f4 ♘e4 14 ♘xe4 dxe4 15 ♗xe4 ♗f6 16 ♗f3 ♗f5 17 ♗xc6 ♗e4 and at this point Yusupov gave 18 ♗xe8 ♗xd4+ 19 ♔h1 ♕d5 with an attack, but 18 d5! ± is better.

We now return to 10 ♘c3 *(D)*:

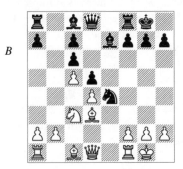

B

10...f5

A very committal move, seriously weakening e5 but staking a claim to some space on the kingside. However, this move does not appear to equalize so Black should take a look at the alternatives:

a) 10...♗f6 and then:

a1) 11 ♘xe4 – *10 ♘d2 ♗f6 11 ♘xe4!* ±.

a2) 11 ♗e3!? ♘xc5 12 dxc5 d4 13 ♗f4 dxc3 14 bxc3 ♕e7 15 ♖e1 ♗e6 ±.

a3) 11 ♕c2!? ♗xd4 (11...♗f5 12 ♘xe4 dxe4 13 ♗xe4 ♗xe4 14 ♕xe4 ♕xd4 15 ♕xc6 gives White the advantage) 12 ♘xe4 dxe4 13 ♗xe4 ♕h4 (13...g6 14 ♗xc6 ±; 13...♗a6 14 ♖d1 ♗xf2+ 15 ♔xf2 ♕h4+ 16 g3! ♕xh2+ 17 ♗g2 +−) 14 g3 ♕f6 (14...♕h5 gives White a choice between 15 ♗e3! ± and 15 ♗f4!? ♖b8 16 ♖ab1 ♖b5 17 b4 ±) 15 ♗e3! and here:

a31) 15...♗xb2? 16 ♖ab1 ♖b8 (or 16...♗d4 17 ♗xh7+ ♔h8 18 ♖b4 ♗xe3 19 fxe3 ♕h6 20 ♖h4 ±; 16...♗c3 17 ♗xh7+ ±) 17 ♗c1! +−.

a32) 15...g6 16 ♗xd4 ♕xd4 17 ♖ad1 ♕f6 18 b4 ±.

a33) 15...♗xe3 16 fxe3 (the alternative is 16 ♗xh7+!? ♔h8 17 fxe3 ♕e5 18 ♗e4 ♖b8 ±) 16...♕h6 17 ♖f4 g5 (17...♖b8 18 ♖af1 ±) 18 ♖f2 ♗h3 19 ♗f5 ♗xf5 (19...♖ae8? 20 ♕c3! ± Ivanchuk-Yusupov, Horgen 1995) 20 ♖xf5 ♕g7 ±.

b) 10...♗f5 and then:

b1) 11 ♕c2 ♗g6 12 ♘xe4 (12 ♘e2!? ♘g5 ±) 12...dxe4 13 ♗xe4 ♕xd4 14 ♗xg6 hxg6 15 ♗e3 ♕b4! (15...♕d5 16 ♖fd1 ♕e6 ±) 16 a3 ♕b5 with equality, Shirov-Yusupov, Bundesliga 1995/6.

b2) 11 ♕f3 ♗g6 12 ♘xe4 dxe4 13 ♗xe4 ♕xd4 14 ♗xg6 (14 ♗xc6 ♖ab8)

14...hxg6 15 ♗e3 (15 ♕xc6 ♕xc5 16 ♕xc5 ♗xc5 17 ♗f4 ♗d4 18 ♖ab1 and now both 18...c5 and 18...♖fe8 are equal) 15...♕a4 16 b3 ♕a6 17 ♕f4 ♗f6 18 ♗d4 ♗xd4 19 ♕xd4 ♖ad8 20 ♕f4 ♖d7 21 ♖fe1 ½-½ Kindermann-Yusupov, Nussloch 1996.

b3) 11 f3 ♘xc3 12 bxc3 ♗xd3 13 ♕xd3 ♗g5?! (Black should try either 13...a5 or 13...♕c8, denying the queen access to a6) 14 ♕a6! ♗xc1 15 ♖axc1 ♕d7 16 ♖fe1 ♖fe8 17 ♖xe8+ (17 h3!?) 17...♖xe8 18 h3 h5 (18...♕e6 19 ♔h1 ♕e3 20 ♖g1 ♕xc3 21 ♕xc6 ±) 19 ♕xa7 ± Shirov-Hübner, Frankfurt rpd 1996.

11 f3

11 ♘e2 deserves attention: 11...♗f6 12 ♕a4 ♗d7 13 f3 ♘g5 14 ♘f4 ♕e7 15 ♗d2 (15 ♘h5!? is also slightly better for White) 15...g6 16 ♖ae1 ♕g7 17 ♗c3 ± Timman-Yusupov, Linares 1992.

11...♘g5 12 ♕a4 ♗d7

12...♕d7 and now 13 ♗f4 ± is better than 13 ♘e2 ♘e6 14 ♘f4 ♘d8 15 ♖e1 ♗f6 = Schmid-Krebs, German corr. Ch 1950-2.

13 ♗f4!

The natural move, seeking control of e5. 13 b4 ♘e6 14 ♗e3 a6 15 ♕c2 g6 ∞.

13...♗f6 14 ♖ae1 ♘e6!?

14...♘f7!? ±.

15 ♗e5 ♗xe5 16 ♖xe5 ♕h4 (D)

A critical moment. White has occupied e5 but Black has managed to set up a counterattack against the slightly weak d4-pawn.

17 f4!?

Or:

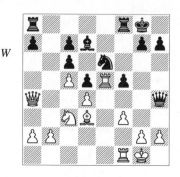

W

a) 17 ♖xf5 ♕xd4+ (17...♖xf5? 18 ♗xf5 ♘xd4 19 ♗g4! ♘f5 20 ♘xd5 +−) 18 ♕xd4 ♘xd4 =.

b) 17 ♗xf5 (it is rather depressing for Black that in addition to the complicated text-move, White also has this safe route to a modest advantage) 17...♖xf5! (17...♘xc5? 18 dxc5 ♕xa4 19 ♗xh7+ ♔xh7 20 ♘xa4 ±) 18 ♖xf5 ♘xc5 (18...♘xd4? 19 ♖e5 ±) 19 dxc5 ♕xa4 20 ♘xa4 ♗xf5 21 ♖d1! ♖b8! 22 b3 ♖b4! ±.

17...♘xf4 18 g3 ♘h3+ 19 ♔g2 ♕h6 20 ♘xd5 ♕d2+

Black should avoid 20...f4? 21 ♘e7+ ♔h8 22 ♘f5! ± Shirov-Yusupov, Ter Apel 1997, while 20...♔h8? comes to the same thing after 21 ♘e3! f4 22 ♘f5.

21 ♗e2

Now:

a) 21...♘g5? 22 ♘xc7 ♖ab8 (22...f4? 23 ♕c4+ ♔h8 24 ♖xg5 +−; 22...♖ac8 23 ♖f2 +−) 23 ♖f2! with a clear advantage for White.

b) 21...f4?! 22 ♕b4! f3+?! (alternatively, 22...♕xb4 23 ♘xb4 ±) 23 ♖xf3 ♕c1 24 ♘e7+ ♔h8 25 ♘f5 ♖ab8 and now 26 ♕c3! (Stohl) is very good for White.

c) 21...♖ae8 22 ♘e7+ (22 ♕b4? ♕xe2+ 23 ♖xe2 ♖xe2+ 24 ♔xh3 cxd5 gives Black strong threats) 22...♔h8 23 ♕d1! (23 ♔xh3 ♖f7! 24 ♔g2 ♖fxe7 25 ♖f2 ♖xe5 26 dxe5 ♕d5+ 27 ♗f3 ♕xe5) 23...♕g5 24 ♕c1! ♕f6 25 ♕e3 f4 26 gxf4 ♘xf4+ 27 ♔h1 with a small advantage for White – Shirov.

B3)

7...♗xe5 8 dxe5 ♘c6 (D)

Or:

a) 8...c6 9 ♕c2 f5 10 exf6 ♘xf6 11 ♗g5 ± Honfi-Bartos, Budapest 1954.

b) 8...♗e6 9 cxd5 ♕xd5 10 ♕c2 f5 11 exf6 ♘xf6 12 ♘c3 ♕e5 (12...♕c6 13 ♗g5 ♘bd7 14 ♖fe1 ♗c4 15 ♗f5! ±) 13 ♘e4 (13 ♗d2!?; 13 ♘e2 ♘bd7! 14 ♗f4 ♕c5 = Honfi-Malich, Kecskemet 1968) 13...♘g4 14 ♘g3 h5 (14...h6 15 ♗d2 ±) 15 ♗d2 ♗d5 16 ♗c3 ♕g5 17 ♗h7+ ♔h8 18 ♕g6 +– Liberzon-Hennings, Debrecen 1968.

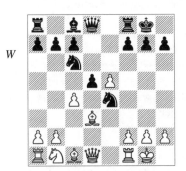

W

The text-move introduces a long sequence leading to a highly unbalanced endgame. While this sequence is not absolutely forced, the various alternatives appear inferior to the main line.

9 cxd5

The main continuation, although there are some meaningful alternatives:

a) 9 ♖e1 ♘xe5 10 cxd5 ♘xf2!? (10...♘xd3 11 ♕xd3 ♗f5 =) 11 ♔xf2 ♘g4+ gives Black attacking chances.

b) 9 ♗c2 ♗e6 (9...♘b4!?) 10 cxd5 ♕xd5 11 ♕xd5 ♗xd5 12 f3 ♘c5 13 ♗e3 ♘e6 14 ♖d1 ♘b4 15 ♗a4 ♗xa2 16 ♗d2 ♗xb1 17 ♗xb4 c5 18 ♗c3 ♗f5 ∞ Wedberg-Schüssler, Malmö 1988.

c) 9 f3 ♘c5 10 cxd5 ♘xd3! 11 ♕xd3 ♘xe5! (11...♘b4?! 12 ♕b3 ♘xd5 13 ♖d1 c6 14 ♘c3 ♕b6+ 15 ♕xb6 ♘xb6 and now White should play 16 ♘e4! ±, rather than 16 b3 ♗e6 17 ♔f2 ♖fd8 = Raetsky-Kuznetsov, corr. 1983) 12 ♕d4 ♘c6 (12...♕f6 13 ♗e3 ±) 13 ♕c5 ♘e7 14 ♘c3 (14 ♖d1 c6 15 d6 ♘d5 ∓) 14...b6 15 ♕c4 c6! 16 dxc6 ♗e6 17 ♕e4 ♕d6 = Zhidkov-Dvoretsky, USSR 1973.

d) 9 ♗f4 ♘b4 (9...♗e6!? 10 ♘a3 ♘c5 11 cxd5 ♕xd5 12 ♗b5 ♖fd8 ½-½ Haygarth-Clarke, British Ch (Brighton) 1972) 10 ♘a3 (10 cxd5 ♕xd5 11 ♗e2 ♗f5 12 ♘a3 ♖fd8 13 ♗c4 ♕xd1 14 ♖fxd1 c6 15 ♗e3 b5 16 ♖xd8+ ♖xd8 17 ♗e2 ♘d5 = Ivanović-Forintos, Bar 1980; 10 ♗e2 dxc4 11 ♗xc4 ♕xd1 12 ♖xd1 ♗e6 13 ♘a3 ♖fd8 14 f3 ♘c5 15 ♗d2 ♘c6 = Arbakov-Mikenas, USSR 1967) 10...♘c5 (10...♗f5 11 ♗b1 ♗g6 12 ♗e3 ♕e7 13 f4 f5 14 cxd5 ♖ad8 15 d6 cxd6 16 ♕b3+ d5 17 ♘b5 ± Van der Wiel-Zsu.Polgar, Brussels 1985) 11 ♗b1 dxc4 (11...d4 12 ♘c2 ♘bd3 13 ♕d2 ♗f5 14 ♗g3 ♘xb2 15 ♘xd4 ♗xb1 16 ♖axb1 ♘ba4 17 ♕e3 ± Schmidt – Medina-Garcia, Gstaad 1973) 12 ♘xc4 ♗e6 13 b3 ♕xd1 14 ♖xd1 ♖ad8 ∓.

e) 9 f4 and now:

e1) 9...♘c5!? 10 cxd5 ♘xd3 11 ♕xd3 ♘b4 12 ♕b3 ♘xd5 13 ♖d1 c6 14 ♘c3 ♗g4 15 ♖d4 ♕b6 16 ♕xb6 ♘xb6 17 ♘e4 ±.

e2) 9...f5!? 10 ♘c3 ♘xc3 11 bxc3 ♗e6 12 ♕e2 ♘a5 = Yusupov.

e3) 9...♘b4 10 cxd5 ♕xd5 11 ♗xe4 ♕xe4 12 ♘c3 ♕g6 13 ♗e3 ♗g4! and then:

e31) 14 ♘d5 ♘xd5 (14...♗xd1!? 15 ♘e7+ ♔h8 16 ♘xg6+ hxg6 17 ♖axd1 ♖fd8 18 a3 ♘d5 =) 15 ♕xd5 ♗f5! 16 ♖ad1 ♗e4 17 ♕d2 ♖ad8 = Palciauskas-Morgado, corr. 1978-80.

e32) 14 ♕b3 ♘c2 15 ♘d5 ♕e4 16 ♖ac1 ♘xe3 17 ♘xe3 ♗e6 18 ♕c3 ♖ad8 ∞ Kraut-Forintos, Kecskemet 1987.

e4) 9...♗f5 (a safe reply, which often leads to the exchange of light-squared bishops; the general simplification makes life easier for Black) and here:

e41) 10 g4?! dxc4!.

e42) 10 ♗e3 d4! ∓.

e43) 10 cxd5 ♕xd5 11 ♗xe4 ♕xe4 = Kostro-Dvoretsky, Polanica Zdroj 1973.

e44) 10 ♕e1?! ♕d7!? (10...♘d6!? 11 ♗xf5 ♘xf5 12 g4 ♘fd4 13 cxd5 ♕xd5 14 ♘c3 ♕f3! 15 ♕d1! ♕xd1 16 ♖xd1 ♖ad8 = Wikman-Slot, corr. 1984-5) 11 g4 (11 ♘a3 ♖ad8 =) 11...♗xg4 12 cxd5 ♘c5 13 ♗c4 ♗h3 (13...♘d4!? ∞) 14 dxc6 ♕xc6 15 ♕e2 ♕g6+ 16 ♔h1 (16 ♔f2?! ♘e4+ 17 ♔e1 ♖ad8 ∓ Hess-Salminsch, corr. 1989) 16...♗xf1 17 ♕xf1 ♕e4+ =.

e45) 10 ♘c3 ♘xc3 (10...♘b4?! 11 ♗b1 ♕e7 12 cxd5 ♕c5+ 13 ♔h1 ♘xc3

14 bxc3 ♕xc3 15 ♗b2! ♕xb2 16 ♗xf5 ♖ad8 17 ♖b1 ± Janošević-Toth, Madonna di Campiglio 1974) 11 bxc3 ♗xd3 12 ♕xd3 dxc4 13 ♕xc4 ♕e7 (13...♕d7 14 ♖b1 b6 15 ♖b2 ♖ad8 = Jansa-Makarychev, Amsterdam 1975) 14 ♖b1 ♖ab8 15 ♗e3 ♕e6 = Valkesalmi-Dolmatov, Groningen jr Ech 1978/9.

9...♕xd5 (D)

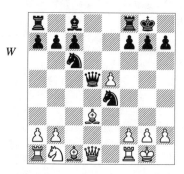

10 ♕c2

White achieves nothing with other moves:

a) 10 ♖e1 is met by 10...♖d8 or 10...♗f5 11 ♕f3 ♖ad8.

b) 10 ♕f3 and then:

b1) Not 10...f5?! in view of 11 exf6 ♘xf6 12 ♕xd5+ ♘xd5 13 ♗c4 ♗e6, and then:

b11) 14 ♘c3!? ♘f4! (14...♘ce7?! 15 ♗g5 ♗f7 16 ♘b5 ±) 15 ♗xe6+ ♘xe6 16 ♗e3 ♖fd8 17 ♖fd1 ♔f7 with equality, Malishauskas-Pavlovicius, Vilnius 2000.

b12) 14 ♖d1 ♘ce7 15 ♘c3 c6 16 ♗g5 ♗f7 17 ♘e4 ± Gufeld-Mikenas, Tallinn 1965.

b2) 10...♗f5 11 ♕xf5 ♕xd3 12 ♘c3 ♘c5 13 ♕h5 (13 ♕xd3 ♘xd3 ∓)

13...♖fe8! 14 f4 (14 ♖e1 ♕d4!? 15 ♗e3 ♖xe5! ∓) 14...♕d4+ 15 ♔h1 ♖ad8 16 ♕f3 ♕c4 ∓ Gergetti-Mileto, Venice 1989.

10...♘b4

Black goes in for hand-to-hand combat. Other continuations are insufficient for equality:

a) 10...♘c5?! 11 ♗xh7+ ♔h8 12 ♗e3 ♘e6 13 f4 ± Petkevich-Kuzmichev, USSR 1968.

b) 10...♗f5?! 11 ♘c3 ♘xc3 12 ♗xf5 ♘d4 13 ♗xh7+ ♔h8 14 ♕d3 ♘ce2+ 15 ♔h1 ♕xe5 16 ♕h3 ♘f4 17 ♗xf4 (17 ♕h4 ±) 17...♕xf4 18 ♖ad1 (18 ♗e4+ ♕h6 ±) 18...♖fd8 (18...c5!?; 18...♕h6!?) 19 ♗e4+ ♕h6 20 ♕c3 ♘c6 21 ♖d5 ± Mi.Tseitlin-Kondali, corr. 1990.

11 ♗xe4 ♘xc2 12 ♗xd5 ♗f5! *(D)*

Black cannot afford to grab the exchange at this point: 12...♘xa1?! 13 ♗e4! ♖e8 (13...♖d8 14 ♗e3 ♗e6 15 ♘c3 ♘b3 16 axb3 ♗xb3 17 ♖a1 c6 18 ♖a3 ♗e6 19 f4 ± Mi.Pavlović-Männer, Berne 1989) 14 ♘a3! (14 ♘c3 ♖xe5 15 ♗d2 ♖xe4 16 ♘xe4 ♘c2 17 ♖c1 ♗f5 18 f3 ♘d4 ±) 14...♖xe5 15 f3 g5 (15...f5 16 ♗f4 ±) 16 ♗d2 f5 17 ♗c3 ♖c5 18 ♗d3 ♗e6 19 ♖xa1 ♖d8 20 ♗e2 c6 21 ♔f2 ± Klovans-Forintos, Münster 1992.

This is the first critical moment. Black is temporarily a piece down, but White stands to lose a whole rook on a1. The first prerequisite for White is to prevent the knight from escaping from a1 by jumping back to c2. Once this has been achieved, White can set about the second task of rounding up the trapped knight.

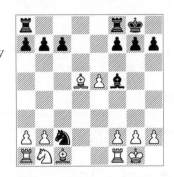

13 g4

White's play is based on this tactical point. If Black retreats the bishop to g6, then the reply f4 causes some problems, so he is more or less forced to take the pawn. Then, however, White is able to occupy the b1-h7 diagonal himself and control the critical c2-square. This move sets the pattern for the following play. It turns out that White can usually win the knight on a1, but it costs a pawn or two and quite a lot of time. In the resulting position, White has two minor pieces for a rook and pawn(s). Such positions can be quite hard to assess and a lot depends on the specific details of each situation.

13...♗xg4

Or:

a) 13...♗d3?! is suspect in view of 14 ♖d1 ♗a6 15 e6 fxe6 16 ♗xe6+ ♔h8 17 ♘a3 ±.

b) 13...♗g6 also cannot be recommended: 14 f4 ♗d3 (14...c6 15 ♗c4 b5 16 f5 ♘xa1 17 ♘a3 bxc4 18 ♗d2 ♖fd8 19 ♗c3 ♘b3 20 axb3 cxb3 21 ♘c4! ± Ghinda-Witt, Galati 1973) 15 ♖d1 ♗a6 16 e6! (16 ♘c3? ♘xa1 17 b4 c6 18 ♗e4 ♖ad8 19 ♖d6 ♖xd6 20 exd6 ♖d8 21 ♗b2 ♘b3 22 axb3 ♖xd6 23 ♗a3 ♖d4 ∓ Browne-Acers, USA 1971) 16...fxe6 17 ♗xe6+ ♔h8 18 ♘a3 ♘xa1 19 ♗e3 ± Popov-Riski, corr. 1969.

14 ♗e4

White has the choice between controlling c2 with the knight, bishop or rook. The alternatives are:

a) 14 ♘a3?! is dubious. Although White wins the a1-knight, his knight is seriously misplaced on a3 and Black can use the time to activate his rooks: 14...♘xa1 15 b4 (15 ♗e3?! ♖ad8 16 ♗xb7 ♖d1 ∓ rescues the knight; 15 ♗e4 ♗e2! 16 ♖e1 ♖ad8 ∓) 15...♗e6 16 ♗xe6 fxe6 17 ♗b2 ♖f4 18 ♗xa1 ♖af8 ∓ Analysis.

b) Sveshnikov's idea 14 ♗f4!? is interesting, aiming to control c2 with the rook. However, with accurate play Black can steer the game towards equality: 14...♘xa1 15 ♖c1!? (15 ♗e4 – 14 ♗e4 ♘xa1 15 ♗f4), and now:

b1) 15...♖fd8 16 ♘c3 is much better for White.

b2) 15...♖ad8 16 ♘c3 b5 (16...c6 17 ♗e4 ±) 17 ♗e4 b4 18 ♘d5 ♖d7 19 f3 (19 ♖xa1 a5 20 b3 ♗e6 21 ♘e3 ♖fd8 22 ♖c1 ♖d2 23 ♖xc7 ♖xa2 24 ♘c4 a4 ∞) 19...♗e6 20 ♘xb4 ♖b8 21 ♘d3 ♗d5 22 ♘c5 ♖dd8 23 b3 ♗xe4 24 fxe4! ± Sveshnikov-Belov, Moscow 1987.

b3) 15...c6 and then:

b31) 16 ♗e4 and now:

b311) 16...f6!? 17 ♘c3 fxe5 18 ♗xe5 (18 ♗e3!?) 18...♖ae8 19 f4 g5 20 ♖xa1 gxf4 21 ♗d4 ♖d8 is slightly better for Black.

b312) 16...f5 and here:

b3121) 17 exf6 ♖xf6 18 ♗e3 ♗e6 (18...♖e8 19 ♘c3 b5! 20 ♗g2 (20 b4? a5 21 a3 ♘b3 22 ♖b1 a4 −+) 20...♖g6 21 ♔h1 is good for White) 19 ♘d2 ♗xa2 20 ♖xa1 ♗f7 (20...♗d5?! 21 ♗xd5+ cxd5 22 ♖xa7 ♖xa7 23 ♗xa7 ♖f4 24 ♔f1 ± Sveshnikov-Tischbierek, Budapest 1988) 21 ♖xa7 ♖xa7 22 ♗xa7 ♖d6 23 ♗e3 c5 led to a draw in Lanc-Morgado, corr. OL 1987-94.

b3122) 17 ♗g2 ♖fd8 18 ♘c3 ♖d4 19 ♗e3 ♖b4 20 ♖xa1 ♖xb2 21 ♖c1 ♔f7 =.

b32) 16 ♗g2!? and here:

b321) 16...♖fd8 17 ♘d2! (17 f3 ♗f5 18 ♘a3 ♖d4 19 ♗e3 ♖b4 =; 17 ♘c3 ♖d4 18 ♗e3 ♖b4 =) 17...♖d4 18 ♗e3 ♖b4 19 b3 ♘xb3 20 axb3 ±.

b322) 16...f6!? 17 ♘c3 (17 exf6!? is another idea) 17...fxe5 18 ♗xe5 (18 ♗e3!?) 18...♖ae8 19 f4 g5 20 ♘e4 ♗f5! =.

14...♘xa1 *(D)*

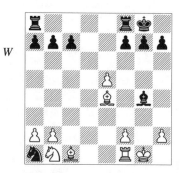

15 ♗f4

I believe this should be regarded as the main line, although some other moves are also popular in practice:

a) 15 ♗e3?! f5 16 ♗d5+ ♔h8 17 ♘a3 c6 18 ♗g2 f4 ∓.

b) 15 f3?! ♗h3 16 ♖e1 f5 17 ♗d5+ (17 exf6 ♖ae8 18 ♘a3 gxf6 19 ♗h6 f5 20 ♗d5+ ♔h8 21 ♖xa1 ♖f6 22 ♗f4 ♖g6+ ∓) 17...♔h8 18 ♘a3 ♖ad8 19 ♗xb7 f4 ∓.

c) 15 b3?! ♗e6 16 ♗b2 ♘xb3 17 axb3 ♗xb3 ∓.

d) 15 ♘a3 ♗e2! 16 ♖e1 ♖ad8 and here:

d1) 17 b3 ♖d1 18 ♖xd1 ♗xd1 19 ♗b2 ♘xb3 ∓.

d2) 17 f3 ♗d3 18 ♗g5 f6 (18...♗xe4 19 ♗xd8 ♗f5 =) 19 exf6 gxf6 20 ♗h6 ♖fe8 21 ♔f2 ♔f7 ∓ Damjanović-Toth, Greece 1977.

d3) 17 b4 ♖d4 18 f3 ♗d3 19 ♖d1 ♖fd8 20 ♗b2 ♗xe4 21 ♖xd4 ♖xd4 22 ♗xd4 ♘c2 = Analysis.

e) 15 ♘c3 is the main alternative to the text-move, but with accurate defence Black has good equalizing prospects:

e1) 15...f5!? 16 exf6 and now Black should continue 16...♗h3! 17 ♖e1 – *15...♗h3 16 ♖e1 f5 17 exf6*. Otherwise: 16...♖xf6 17 ♗e3 ♗f3 18 ♗xf3 ♖xf3 19 ♖xa1 ♖d8 20 ♖c1 ± Shteinberg-Peshina, Riga 1968; 16...♖ae8?! is inaccurate due to 17 ♗d2! ♖xe4 18 ♘xe4 ♘c2 19 ♗c3! ♖e8 20 f3 ♘e3 21 ♖e1 ♗xf3 (21...♘c2 22 ♖e2) 22 f7+ +– Analysis.

e2) 15...♗h3 16 ♖e1 f5 (16...♖fe8?! 17 ♗f4 g5 18 ♗xg5 ♖xe5 19 ♗xh7+ ♔xh7 20 ♖xe5 ± Georgescu-Clarke, corr. 1972) 17 exf6 ♖ae8 *(D)* and then:

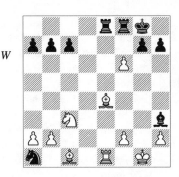

e21) 18 fxg7? ♖f7 19 ♗h6 ♖e6 ∓.

e22) 18 ♗d2 ♖xe4 19 ♘xe4 ♘c2 20 ♖c1 ♘d4 21 ♖xc7 ♘f3+ (21...♖f7!? 22 ♖xf7 ♘f3+ 23 ♔h1 ♔xf7 24 fxg7 ♔xg7 25 ♗e3 b6 26 ♘d2 ♘xd2 27

♗xd2 a5 28 f3 a4 = Tal-Karpov, Milan 1975; 21...gxf6 22 ♗h6 ♖f7 23 ♖c4 ±) 22 ♔h1 ♘xd2 23 ♖xg7+ ♔h8 24 ♘g5 ♗f5 (24...♖xf6 25 ♖xh7+ ♔g8 26 ♖xh3 ♖xf2 ±) 25 ♘f7+ ♖xf7 26 ♖xf7 ♗e4+! (26...♔g8? 27 ♖g7+ ♔f8 28 f3! ♘xf3 29 ♖xb7 +– Klovans-Levchenkov, Riga 1971) 27 f3 ♗xf3+ 28 ♔g1 ♔g8! 29 ♖g7+ ♔f8 30 ♖xh7 ♗c6 =.

e23) 18 ♖e3!? and here:

e231) 18...♖xe4 19 ♘xe4 ♗f5 20 ♘g3 (20 fxg7?! ♖d8! 21 ♘g3 ♗h3! ∓) 20...♖xf6 (20...♗b1 21 fxg7!? ♔xg7 {21...♖d8 22 ♖c3 intending 23 ♗h6} 22 b4! ♘c2 23 ♖b3 +–) 21 ♘xf5 ♖xf5 22 ♖c3 ♖a5 (22...c6?! 23 b4 ♖d5 24 ♔g2 ♖d1 25 ♔f3 ±) 23 ♖xc7 ♖xa2 24 ♖xb7 ♘c2 25 ♗d2 ♘d4 26 ♗e3 ♘c6 27 ♔g2! ±/± Analysis.

e232) 18...♗d7 19 ♗d5+ ♖f7 20 fxg7 ♘c2 21 ♖xe8+ ♗xe8 22 ♗f4! (22 ♗h6 ♗c6 23 ♗xf7+ ♔xf7 24 ♗f4 ♘b4! 25 ♗xc7 ♘d5 =) 22...♘b4! 23 ♗xf7+ ♗xf7 24 ♗h6! (24 ♗e5 ♘d3 {24...♘xa2 =} 25 ♗f6 ♘f4 =; 24 ♗xc7 ♘d5 =) 24...♘d5 25 ♘e4 ♗g6 (intending ...♘e7-f5) 26 f3 ♗xe4 27 fxe4 ♘f6 28 e5 ♘e8 again with equality – Analysis.

e24) 18 ♗e3 ♖xe4 19 ♘xe4 ♘c2 20 ♖c1 ♘xe3 (20...♗f5!? 21 ♖xc2 ♗xe4 22 ♖xc7 ♖xf6 23 ♗xa7 ♖c6 ½-½ Makarychev-Karpov, Oslo 1984) 21 fxe3 and now:

e241) 21...c6 22 f7+! (22 ♘g5 ♗f5 23 f7+ ♔h8 24 ♖f1 ♗g6? 25 e4? {25 ♖d1! wins material} 25...h6 26 e5 hxg5 27 e6 ♔h7 28 ♖f3 g4 29 ♖f4 ♗xf7 30 ♖xf7 ♖e8 31 ♖xb7 ♖xe6 32 ♖xa7 ♖e2 ½-½ Tal-Timman, Reykjavik 1987) 22...♔h8 23 ♘d6 ±/±.

e242) 21...♗f5 22 ♘g3 ♖xf6 (or 22...♗c8 23 ♖xc7 gxf6 24 ♘e4 ±) 23 ♖xc7 ♗h3 24 ♖xb7 h5 25 ♖xg7+! ±.

e243) 21...♖c8!? 22 f7+ ♔f8 23 ♘g5 ♗f5 24 ♖f1 h6 25 ♖xf5 hxg5 ½-½ Butnorius-Makarychev, Cheliabinsk 1975.

We now return to 15 ♗f4 *(D)*:

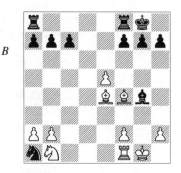

15...f5

15...♗h3? is bad due to 16 ♖c1! f5 17 ♗d5+ ♔h8 18 ♘c3 c6 19 ♗f3 ♖ad8 20 ♖xa1 g5 21 ♗e3 ♖fe8 22 ♖e1 and White wins, Trabattoni-Toth, Milan 1987.

However, there are those who prefer 15...f6!? 16 ♘c3 (16 ♗xb7 ♘c2 17 ♗d5+ ♔h8 18 ♗xa8 ♖xa8 19 exf6 gxf6 20 ♗xc7 ♗h3 21 ♖c1 ♖e8 22 ♘c3 ♘d4 gives Black compensation) 16...fxe5, and now:

a) 17 ♗xe5 ♖ae8 18 f4!? (18 ♗xc7 ♖xe4 19 ♘xe4 ♘c2 =) 18...♖xe5 19 fxe5 ♖xf1+ 20 ♔xf1 c6 21 ♔e1 ♔f7 ∞ Herman-Savostianov, corr. 1989.

b) 17 ♗g3 ♖ad8 18 ♖xa1 and then:

b1) 18...♖d2 19 b4 (19 ♗xb7!? ♖xb2 20 ♗d5+ ♔h8 21 ♗b3 c5 intending ...c4 ∞) 19...♗f3 20 a3! ± Smagin-Schüssler, Copenhagen 1988.

b2) 18...♗f3 19 ♗xe5 (19 ♗xf3 ♖xf3 20 ♔g2 ♖f7!? =) 19...♖d2! gives Black compensation.

c) 17 ♗e3!? ♗f3 18 ♖xa1 ♗xe4 19 ♘xe4 (in this case Black even has two extra pawns, but White's minor pieces occupy secure squares in the centre of the board and this gives him the advantage) 19...b6 20 b4 a5 21 b5 ♖ad8 22 ♖c1 ♖f7 23 a4 h6 24 ♔g2 ♖d3 25 ♖c4 ♔f8 26 ♘d2 ♔e8 27 ♘f3 ♖e7 28 ♖e4 ♖b3 29 ♘xe5 ± Kasparov-Timman, Paris Immopar rpd 1991.

The text-move attempts to drive the bishop off the b1-h7 diagonal, but it has the defect of being rather committal – Black can no longer eliminate White's e-pawn by playing ...f6.

16 ♗d5+

An important intermediary move. 16 ♗xb7 gives White nothing real in view of 16...♘c2 (16...♖ab8!? 17 ♗d5+ ♔h8 18 f3 ♗h5 19 ♘a3 ♖fd8 20 ♗c4 ♖d4 21 ♗e3 ♘c2! is a good alternative) 17 f3 ♗h5 18 ♗d5+ ♔h8 19 ♗xa8 ♖xa8 20 ♖d1 c5 21 ♔f2 ♘d4 = Romanishin-Kochiev, Ordzhonikidze 1987.

16...♔h8 17 ♖c1!

Thus in this line White also ends up using the rook to defend c2. 17 ♘a3 ♖ad8 18 ♗xb7 ♖d1 =.

17...c6 *(D)*

17...♖ad8? is bad in view of 18 ♘c3 b5 19 e6 ♖fe8 20 ♗xc7 ♖c8 21 ♘xb5 ♖e7 22 ♖xa1 +− Glek-Varlamov, corr. 1987.

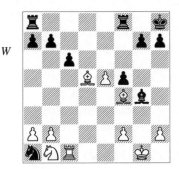

W

18 ♗g2

This is the main line. 18 ♗e6 yields no advantage in view of 18...g5! (the best move; Black must take active measures before White captures the a1-knight; 18...h6?! is too slow; e.g., 19 ♗d7 g5 20 ♗d2 ♗h5 21 ♗b4 ♖fd8 22 e6 ♗e8 23 ♗xe8 ♖xe8 24 e7 ♖ac8 25 ♗d6 ± Lacasse-Cantin, corr. 1989) 19 ♗xg5 ♖ae8, and now:

a) 20 ♗c4 b5!? (20...f4?! 21 ♗f6+ ♖xf6 22 exf6 b5 23 ♗d3 ±) 21 ♗f1 and then:

a1) 21...♖xe5?! 22 ♗d2 ♔g8! (the alternatives are 22...♖g8 23 f3! and 22...♖e6 23 ♗c3+ ♔g8 24 ♘d2 ♖d8 25 ♖xa1 ♖ed6 26 h3 ♗h5 27 ♘b3 ♖d1 28 ♖xd1 ♖xd1 29 ♔g2 ± Van der Wiel-Mikhalchishin, Lugano 1987) 23 ♘c3 ♗f3 24 ♗g2 ♗xg2 25 ♔xg2 b4 26 ♘a4 ♖d8! ∞.

a2) 21...f4! and here:

a21) 22 ♘d2? (Rozentalis-Ivanchuk, Minsk 1986) 22...♖xe5!? 23 f3 (23 h4 can be met by 23...♖xg5 24 hxg5 ♖d8 25 ♘e4 ♖d1 ∓ or 23...♖d5 24 ♗e7 ♖e8 25 ♗b4 ♖ed8 ∓) 23...♗h5 24 h4 (24 ♗h6 ♖f6 ∓; 24 ♗h4 ♖d5 25 ♗e1 ♖e8 ∓) 24...♖d5 25 ♘e4 ♗xf3 26 ♘f2 ♖d2 27 ♖xa1 ♖xb2 ∓.

a22) 22 ♗f6+ ♖xf6 23 exf6 ♗f5 24 f7 ♖f8 25 ♖xc6 ♗xb1 26 ♖c1 =.

b) 20 ♗h6 ♖xe6 21 ♗xf8 ♗h3 22 ♖c3 ♖g6+ 23 ♖g3 ♔g8 (23...f4 24 ♖xg6 hxg6 25 ♗h6 ♘c2 26 ♗xf4 ♘b4 is slightly better for White, Ioseliani-Browne, Baden-Baden 1988) 24 ♗e7 f4! (24...♘c2 25 f4 ±) 25 ♖xg6+ hxg6 26 ♘a3 f3 27 ♗c5 b6 28 ♗d4 ♗f5 29 b4 ♘c2 30 ♘xc2 ♗xc2 ½-½ Oll-Khalifman, Vilnius 1988.

18...♖fd8!

Other moves are no good; for example, 18...♖ad8? 19 ♘c3 ♖d4 20 ♗e3 ♖b4 21 ♗c5 +− or 18...h6? 19 ♘c3 ♖fe8 20 ♖xa1 ♔h7 21 ♖e1 g5 22 ♗c1 ♖ad8 23 f4 ♔g6 24 ♔f2 ♖d4 25 ♗e3 giving White a clear advantage, Pirrot-Browne, Baden-Baden 1988.

19 ♘d2 *(D)*

Or:

a) 19 f3 ♗h5 20 ♘a3 ♖d4 21 ♗e3 ♖b4 22 ♘c4 ♖a4 (22...♗f7 23 ♘d6 ♗xa2 24 ♖xa1 ♖xb2 ∞) 23 ♘a3 ♖b4 24 ♘c4 ½-½ Sax-Yusupov, Thessaloniki OL 1988.

b) 19 ♘c3 ♖d4! 20 ♗e3 ♖b4 21 f3 (21 ♖xa1 ♖xb2 22 ♘a4 ♖c2! ∞) 21...♗h5 22 ♘d1 ♖d8 23 ♖xa1 b6 24 e6 ♖e8 25 ♗d2 ♖b5 is unclear − Yusupov.

19...♖xd2

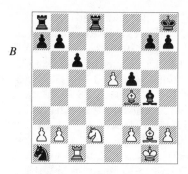

B

With this counter-sacrifice, Black tries to steer the game into an equal endgame. The other idea is 19...h6!? (19...♖d4?! 20 ♗e3 ♖b4 21 ♖xa1 f4 22 ♗c5 ♖xb2 23 ♘b3 ±) 20 h4 ♖d3, and now:

a) 21 ♖xa1 g5! (21...♖ad8 22 ♘c4 ±) 22 hxg5 hxg5 23 ♗xg5 (23 ♗f1 gxf4! 24 ♗xd3 ♖d8 25 e6 ♖xd3 26 e7 ♗h5 27 ♘b3 b6 28 ♖e1 ♗e8 29 ♖e5 ♔g7 30 ♖xf5 ♖d1+ 31 ♔g2 ♖e1 =) 23...♖g8 24 ♗f6+! (24 ♘f1? ♖xg5 25 f4 ♖g7 26 ♔f2 ♖d4 27 ♔e3 ♖gd7 28 ♖e1 ♖d3+ 29 ♔f2 ♖7d4 0-1 Rozentalis-Gelfand, Vilnius 1988) 24...♔h7 25 ♘f1 f4! (25...♗f3?! 26 ♘g3 f4 27 ♗xf3 ♖xf3 28 ♔g2 ♖d3 29 ♖h1+ ♔g6 30 ♘e4! ♔f5+ 31 ♘g5 ♖xg5+ 32 ♗xg5 ♔xg5 33 ♖e1 +−) 26 ♔h2 (26 ♘g3 ♔h6!?) 26...♖g6! (26...♗f3?! 27 ♗h3 ♗g4 28 ♗xg4 ♖xg4 29 ♔h1! ± intending ♘h2) 27 ♖e1 (27 ♗e4? ♖h3+) 27...♖h6+ 28 ♔g1 ♖g6 29 ♔h2 ♖h6+ 30 ♔g1 ♖g6 31 ♔h2 ½-½ Timman-Yusupov, Linares Ct (2) 1992.

b) 21 ♗f1! (an important finesse, driving Black's rook into a less active position before taking the knight) 21...♖d4 22 ♗e3 ♖d5 23 ♖xa1! (23 f4 ♖ad8 24 e6 ♖8d6! ∞) 23...♖xe5 (this

is another situation where Black has rook and two pawns for the minor pieces, but White certainly has the advantage; his pieces are very active, while the g4-bishop isn't doing much) 24 ♘c4 ♖d5 (24...♖e4 25 ♗d3 ♖e6 26 f4 ♖d8 27 ♗c2 ±; 24...♖e6 25 f4! ±) 25 ♗g2 ♖b5 (25...♖d1+ 26 ♖xd1 ♗xd1 27 ♘a5 ♗c2!? and now 28 b3! +− is even better than 28 ♘xb7 ♖b8 29 ♗xc6 ♗e4 30 ♗xe4! fxe4 31 ♘c5 ♖xb2 32 a4 ±) 26 ♖e1! ± Timman-Yusupov, Linares Ct (6) 1992.

20 ♗xd2 ♖d8 21 ♗c3

21 ♗e3 ♖d1+ 22 ♖xd1 ♗xd1 23 ♗xa7 ♘c2 24 e6 ♔g8 25 ♗c5 ♘e1 26 ♗f1 ♘f3+ 27 ♔g2 ♘d2 28 ♗d3 ♗f3+ 29 ♔g1 ♘e4 30 ♗e7 ♘f6 = Yusupov.

21...♖d1+ 22 ♖xd1 ♗xd1 *(D)*

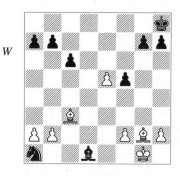

W

Here we see how far modern opening theory extends into the game in certain variations – we are well into the endgame, and yet this is a deeply investigated position. White is a pawn down, but he has two powerful bishops and a passed e-pawn, which threaten to cause Black a great deal of trouble. Furthermore, the black knight is a long way from the main theatre of battle.

23 ♗f1! *(D)*

The bishop is doing nothing on the h1-a8 diagonal and White needs urgently to improve its position.

White continued unsuccessfully in Kasparov-Anand, Linares 1991: 23 f4?! ♘c2 24 ♔f2 ♔g8 25 a4 a5! 26 ♗xa5 ♘d4 27 ♗f1 ♗b3 ½-½. No advantage is to be found in other directions either: 23 b4 ♘c2 24 b5 cxb5 25 ♗xb7 b4! 26 ♗b2 b3! 27 axb3 ♘b4 28 ♗c3 a5 =; 23 ♗h3 g6 24 ♗f1 ♔g7! 25 ♗c4 ♘c2 26 ♗b3 c5 27 e6+ ♔f8 28 ♗f6 b5 29 ♗d5 ♘d4 =.

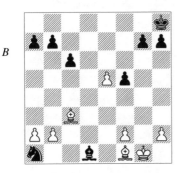

23...♔g8

This is Yusupov's recommendation. Other moves lead to more unpleasant situations for Black:

a) 23...b5? 24 ♗g2 c5 25 b4! +–.

b) 23...♘c2? 24 ♗c4 b5 (24...♗h5 25 ♗d3 ♘a1 26 b4 ±) 25 ♗b3 (25 ♗f7?! ♗f3 intending ...♗d5) 25...b4 (25...g6? 26 e6+) 26 ♗d2 ± intending e6.

c) 23...g6 24 ♗c4 ♔g7 (24...b5? 25 e6+ +–) 25 b4!? (25 e6+ ♔f8 26 ♗f6 ♔e8 27 e7 ♘c2 ∞; 25 ♗e6!? intending ♗c8 and e6) 25...♘c2 26 ♗b3 is much better for White.

d) 23...♗f3 24 ♗d3! (intending b4) 24...♗e4 25 ♗c4! (25 ♗xe4!? fxe4 26 ♔f1 ♘c2 27 ♔e2 c5 28 ♔d2 ♘d4 29 ♔e3 +– Rizzio-Battistini, Italy 1990) 25...♗d5 (25...b5? 26 e6 +–) 26 ♗xd5! cxd5 27 ♔f1 ± Zapata-Zarnicki, São Paulo 1992.

24 ♗c4+!

Yusupov only gave 24 ♗d3 f4 25 ♗f5 ♘c2 26 ♗c8 c5 27 ♗xb7 ♘d4 =. However, the text-move is far stronger and presents Black with difficult problems.

24...♔f8 25 b4

Interesting is 25 ♗b4+!? ♔e8 26 ♗g8 h6 27 ♗h7 intending ♗g6+.

25...♘c2 26 ♗b3 *(D)*

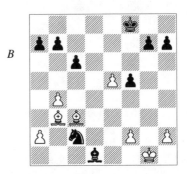

Black still has an extra pawn, but the cost has been high – both his minor pieces are paralysed and White's e-pawn is dangerous. It only requires a few lines to be opened and White's bishops will be able to usher the e-pawn home while Black's bishop and knight remain stuck on the sidelines. It would be going too far to claim that this position is winning for White, but Black faces an uphill defensive task in which a mistake will bring the game to an abrupt end, while even correct defence will leave White in the driving seat.

26...b6!

26...g5 is bad in view of 27 h4!:

a) 27...gxh4 28 ♗d2! ♔e8 (28...b6 29 ♗g5! h3 30 ♔h2 ♔e8 31 e6 a6 32 f3! intending ♔xh3-g3-f4 +–) 29 ♗g5! a6 30 ♔h2 ♔f8 31 e6! intending f3 followed by ♔h3xh4-g3-f4 with a winning position for White.

b) 27...g4 *(D)* and then:

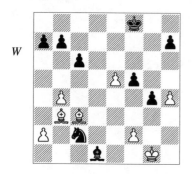

b1) 28 ♔h2!? f4 29 ♗d2 g3+ 30 fxg3 f3 31 ♗h6+ ♔e8 32 ♔g1 b6 33 ♔f2 c5 34 bxc5 bxc5 35 ♗g5! c4 36 ♗xc4 ♘b4 37 ♗d2 ♘c6 38 ♗c3 +–.

b2) 28 ♗d2! b6 29 ♔h2 c5 (29...h5 30 ♔g3 ♔e8 31 ♔f4 a6 32 ♗c3 ♔e7 33 e6 c5 34 bxc5 bxc5 35 ♔g5 +–) 30 bxc5 bxc5 31 e6 c4 32 ♗xc4 ♗f3 33 ♔g3 ♘d4 34 ♔f4 ♔e7 35 ♔e5 ♘c6+ 36 ♔xf5 ♘d4+ 37 ♔e5 ♘c6+ 38 ♔f4

a5 39 ♗c3 ♔d6 40 a3 ♗d5 41 ♗xd5 ♔xd5 42 ♔f5 +–.

c) 27...h6 28 e6! b6 (28...gxh4 29 ♗d2! h5 30 ♔h2 b6 31 ♗g5 h3 32 f3! ♔e8 33 ♔xh3 a6 34 ♔g3! ♔f8 35 ♔f4 ♔e8 36 ♔e5 +–; 28...♔e7 29 h5 ♔f8 30 f4! gxf4 31 ♗d2 ♘e3 32 ♗xe3 fxe3 33 ♗xd1 ♔e7 34 ♔g2 ♔xe6 35 ♔f3 b6 36 ♔xe3 ♔e5 37 ♗a4! c5 38 b5! +–) 29 hxg5 hxg5 30 ♗f6 g4 31 ♗g5! ♔e8 (31...g3 32 e7+! ♔e8 33 fxg3 ♘e3 34 ♗xe3 ♗xb3 35 axb3 ♔xe7 36 ♔f2 +–) 32 ♔h2 intending ♔g3-f4-e5 +–.

27 h4 c5 28 bxc5 bxc5 *(D)*

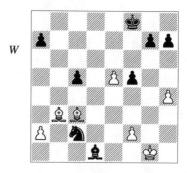

29 e6! ♔e7 30 ♔h2! f4

30...g6?! 31 ♗d2! c4 32 ♗xc4 ♘d4 33 ♗b4+ ♔e8 34 ♔g3 ±.

31 ♗xg7 c4 32 ♗xc4 ♘a3 33 ♗d5!

± Vojna-Rumiantsev, corr. 1996-8. In this variation the next move is up to Black.

6 3 ♘xe5: Sidelines

1 e4 e5 2 ♘f3 ♘f6 3 ♘xe5 *(D)*

This is White's other main third move. In fact, the difference between 3 d4 and 3 ♘xe5 is less than it might appear. The main lines stemming from these two moves are 3 d4 ♘xe4 4 ♗d3 d5 5 ♘xe5 and 3 ♘xe5 d6 4 ♘f3 ♘xe4 5 d4 d5 6 ♗d3 – the only difference between these two positions (apart from the move-number) is that in the first White's knight is on e5, while in the second it is on f3. However, this small difference results in totally divergent continuations. In general, the knight is more actively placed on e5, but the problem is that Black can immediately challenge (and possibly exchange) it by ...♗d6 or ...♘d7. With the knight on f3, it is secure from such an early challenge, but Black has the additional option of playing ...♗g4 at some point. There is no clear reason to

prefer one move over the other, and in practice both are very popular.

3...d6

Other continuations are very risky for Black:

a) 3...♕e7?! is occasionally played but it is hard to see the attraction of this move; Black exposes his queen without obtaining any compensating advantages:

a1) 4 ♘f3 and then:

a11) 4...♕xe4+?! 5 ♗e2 d5 (5...♗c5 6 0-0 0-0 7 d4 ♗b6 8 c4 c6 9 ♘c3 ♕e7 10 ♗g5 ± Anderssen-Von Kolisch, Paris 1860) 6 0-0 ♗g4 7 ♗b5+ ♔d8 8 ♗e2 ± Anderssen-Göring, Leipzig 1871.

a12) 4...♘xe4 5 ♗e2 ♕d8 6 0-0 ♗e7 7 d4 d5 8 c4 0-0 =.

a2) 4 d4 and here:

a21) 4...♘c6 5 ♘f3 (5 ♘xc6 ♕xe4+ 6 ♗e2 dxc6 7 0-0 ♗e6 8 c3 ♗d6 9 f4 0-0-0 ∞) 5...♘xe4 (5...♕xe4+ 6 ♗e2 d5 7 0-0 ♗d7 8 c4 0-0-0 9 ♘c3 ♕f5 10 ♖e1 dxc4 11 ♗xc4 ±) 6 ♗e2 d5 7 0-0 ♗e6 8 c3 ♕d7 9 ♖e1 0-0-0 10 ♗d3 f5 11 ♗f4 ♗d6 12 ♗xd6 ± Kogan-Kosashvili, Israel 1986.

a22) 4...d6 5 ♘f3 ♕xe4+ (5...♘xe4 6 ♗e3 ♕d8 7 ♗d3 ±) and then:

a221) 6 ♗e3 ♘g4 7 ♕d2 ♘xe3 8 fxe3 c6 (8...d5 9 ♘c3 ♕e6 10 ♗d3 f5 11 0-0-0 ♗e7 12 g4 fxg4 13 ♘e5 is good for White) 9 ♗d3 ♕e7 10 0-0 g6

11 e4 ♗g7 12 ♘c3 ♗g4! with equality.

b222) 6 ♗e2 ♗f5 7 c4 ♗e7 8 0-0 0-0 9 ♘c3 ♕c2 10 ♕xc2 ♗xc2 11 ♗f4 ♘bd7 12 ♖ac1 ♗g6 13 ♘h4 ±.

b) 3...♘xe4?! (this looks like a beginner's move, but it isn't as bad as one might expect; White can gain an advantage in several ways, but there is nothing really crushing) 4 ♕e2 (4 ♕f3?! ♘f6 5 d4 d6 6 ♘d3 ♘c6 =) 4...♕e7 5 ♕xe4 d6 *(D)* and now:

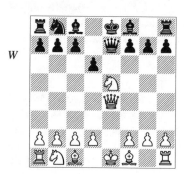

b1) 6 f4!? and then:

b11) 6...♘c6?! 7 ♘c3 (7 ♗b5 ♗d7 8 ♘c3 ±) 7...dxe5 8 ♘d5 f5 9 ♕xe5! gives White the advantage.

b12) 6...dxe5 7 fxe5 f6 (7...♘c6 8 d4 f5 9 ♕f4 ♗e6 10 c3 0-0-0 11 ♗d3 ♕d7 12 ♗c2 g5 13 ♕f2 ♗e7 14 ♘d2 ±) and here:

b121) 8 ♘c3 ♕xe5 9 ♕xe5+ fxe5 10 ♗c4 (10 d4 ♗b4 11 ♗c4 exd4 {11...♖f8 12 ♗e3 ♗g4 13 h3 ♗h5 14 dxe5 ♘c6 gives Black compensation} 12 ♗g5 dxc3 13 0-0-0 gives White compensation) 10...♗c5 11 d3 ±.

b122) 8 d4 ♘d7 (8...fxe5 9 dxe5 ♘c6 10 ♗f4 g5 11 ♗g3 ♗g7 12 ♘c3 ♗xe5 13 ♗xe5 ♕xe5 14 0-0-0 0-0 15 ♗c4+ ♔g7 16 ♖he1 ±) 9 ♗f4 fxe5 10 dxe5 g5 11 ♗g3 ♗g7 12 ♘c3 ♗xe5 13 ♗xe5 ♕xe5 14 0-0-0 ±.

b2) 6 d4!? and now:

b21) 6...♘c6 7 ♗b5 ♗d7 8 0-0 dxe5 9 d5 f5 (9...♘b8 10 d6 cxd6 11 ♕xb7 ♗xb5 12 ♕xa8 ♕c7 13 ♗e3 ±) 10 ♕e2 ♘b8 11 ♖e1 ♗xb5 12 ♕xb5+ c6 13 ♕b3 cxd5 14 ♗g5! ± Speelman-Keogh, Amsterdam Z 1978.

b22) 6...dxe5 7 dxe5 ♘c6 *(D)* and then:

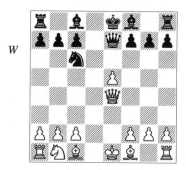

b221) 8 f4!? ♗d7 9 ♘c3 0-0-0 10 ♗c4 ♕h4+ 11 g3 ♕h3 12 ♗f1 ♕e6 13 ♗g2 f6 14 0-0 ±.

b222) 8 ♗b5!? ♗d7 and here:

b2221) 9 0-0 0-0-0 10 ♘c3 ♘xe5 11 ♗e3 a6! (11...♘c6 12 ♕c4! a6 13 ♗xa6! ±; 11...♗xb5 12 ♘xb5 ♘c6 13 ♘xa7+ ♘xa7 14 ♕a4 ♘c6 15 ♕a8+ ♔d7 16 ♖ad1+ ♔e8 17 ♕xb7 ♕e6 18 ♖de1 ♗e7 19 ♗c5 ♖b8 20 ♕a6 ♕d5 21 ♕a3 ♕g5 22 ♖e3 ♔f8 23 ♗xe7+ ♘xe7 24 f4 ♕f6 25 ♖fe1 ♖e8 26 ♖xe7 ± Kholmov-Belousov, USSR 1974) 12 ♘d5 ♕e8 13 ♗xd7+ ♘xd7 14 ♕c4 ♗d6 15 ♗d4 ±.

b2222) 9 ♘c3 and now:

b22221) 9...♕xe5?? 10 ♗xc6 +–.

b22222) 9...♘xe5?! 10 ♘d5 ♕d6 11 ♗f4 f6 (11...0-0-0 12 ♗xe5 ♖e8 13 ♗xd7+ ♔xd7 14 f4 f6 15 0-0-0 +−) 12 ♗xd7+ ♕xd7 13 0-0-0 ±.

b22223) 9...0-0-0 10 ♗f4 g5 (the alternatives are 10...f6 11 exf6 ♕xf6 12 0-0-0 ± and 10...a6 11 ♗c4 ♗e6 12 ♗xa6 ♔b8 13 ♗b5 ♖d4 14 ♕e3 ♘b4 15 ♗a4 ±) 11 ♗g3 (11 ♗xc6?! ♗xc6 12 ♕f5+ ♕d7 13 ♕xd7+ {13 ♕xg5 ♗e7} 13...♖xd7 14 ♗xg5 ♖g8 gives Black compensation) 11...♗g7 (11...f5 12 exf6 ♕xf6 13 0-0 ±) 12 0-0-0 ♖he8 (12...♘xe5 13 ♗xd7+ ♖xd7 14 ♖xd7 ♕xd7 15 ♗xe5 ♖e8 16 ♖d1 +−) 13 ♖he1 ♘xe5 14 ♕xh7 ♗xb5 15 ♘xb5 ♖xd1+ (15...♕b4 16 ♕xg7 ♘d3+ 17 cxd3 ♖xe1 18 ♕c3 +−) 16 ♖xd1 ♕f6 17 ♘c3 ± Yusupov.

b223) 8 ♘c3 (this simple move gives White a clear positional advantage without risking any complications) 8...♕xe5 9 ♕xe5+ ♘xe5 10 ♗f4 (10 ♘b5 ♗b4+ 11 c3 ♗a5 12 ♗f4 f6 13 ♗e2 ♗d7 14 a4 ♗xb5 15 axb5 ♗b6 16 ♖d1 ♖d8 17 0-0 ♔e7 18 ♖fe1 ♖he8 19 ♔f1 ± Kr.Georgiev-Trifonov, Sofia 1983) 10...♗d6 11 ♗g3 ♗d7 12 0-0-0 0-0-0 13 ♘e4 ♗c6 14 ♘xd6+ cxd6 15 f3 ♖he8 16 ♖d4 ♔c7 17 a4 f5 18 h4 ± Vasiukov-Chekhov, Kishinev 1975.

After 3...d6 *(D)* the main line is 4 ♘f3, which is the subject of Chapters 7-11. Otherwise, White can choose between:

The former is an interesting knight sacrifice often played by the Latvian IM Vitolinš.

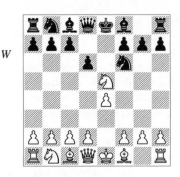

W

4 ♘d3?! is poor: 4...♘xe4 5 ♕e2 (5 g3 d5 {5...♕e7!?} 6 ♗g2 ♗d6 7 0-0 0-0 =) 5...♕e7 6 b3 ♘c6 7 ♗b2 ♗f5 8 g4 ♗d7 9 ♗g2 0-0-0!? 10 0-0 (10 ♗xe4 ♖e8; 10 ♕xe4 ♕xe4+ 11 ♗xe4 ♖e8) 10...♘c5 11 ♕xe7 ♗xe7 12 ♘xc5 dxc5 13 ♖e1 ♗f6! ∓ Glek-Ivanchuk, Pinsk 1986.

A)

4 ♘xf7 ♔xf7 5 d4 *(D)*

5 ♗c4+?! is suspect in view of 5...d5! 6 ♗b3 (6 exd5 ♗d6 7 0-0 ♖f8 8 d4 ♔g8 ∓) 6...♗e6! (6...♕e8!? 7 d3 ♗e6 8 e5 ♗g4 9 ♗xd5+ ♘xd5 10 ♕xg4 ♕xe5+ ∓) 7 e5 (7 ♘c3 dxe4 8 ♗xe6+ ♔xe6 9 ♘xe4 ♘xe4 10 ♕g4+ ♔f7 11 ♕xe4 ♕e7 ∓) 7...♘e4 8 d4 c5 9 ♕f3+ ♔e8 ∓.

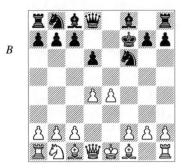

B

At first sight the idea of giving up one's only developed piece for just two pawns looks disastrous, but White does obtain some additional positional compensation. White's central control is quite good, and Black has considerable long-term difficulties in finding a safe haven for his king. Theoretically speaking, there isn't much to commend the sacrifice – Black can equalize without any trouble, and in some lines can play for the advantage – but a tactically minded player might be tempted by this sacrifice.

Now the main lines, or at least those upon which there is the most theoretical and practical material, are:

A1: 5...g6   110
A2: 5...c5!?   113
A3: 5...♗e7   114

As one would expect in such an unexplored and unbalanced position, Black has a great many alternatives:

a) 5...♘xe4? 6 ♕h5+ ♔e7 7 ♕e2 d5 8 ♗g5+ +–.

b) 5...b5 6 ♗xb5 ♗b7 7 ♘c3 c6 8 ♗d3 g6 9 f4 ♔g7 10 ♕e2 ♘bd7 11 0-0 ♗e7 12 e5 ±.

c) 5...♗g4 is a rare continuation. Note that after 6 f3 ♗e6 7 ♘c3 ♗e7 8 ♗d3 ♖f8 9 0-0 ♔g8 10 ♔h1 c5 11 e5 dxe5 12 dxe5 ♘fd7 13 f4, Black should play 13...c4, rather than 13...♘c6? 14 ♕h5 +–.

d) 5...♘c6 6 ♘c3 ♗e7 7 ♗c4+ d5 8 ♘xd5 ♗e6 9 ♘xe7 ♗xc4 10 ♘xc6 bxc6 11 b3 ♗a6 12 e5 ♕d5 13 f3 ♕a5+ 14 ♔f2 ♘d5 15 c4 ♕c3 with an unclear position, Skotorenko-Borisov, corr. 1989-90.

e) 5...c6 6 ♗d3 ♗e7 7 0-0 and now:

e1) 7...g6 8 c4 ♔g7 9 ♘c3 ♘bd7 10 ♗e3 ♘f8 11 h3 d5 12 e5 ♘e8 13 cxd5 cxd5 14 f4 ± Vitolinš-Butnorius, Vilnius 1985.

e2) 7...♘a6 8 ♘c3 ♗e6 9 f4 ♕c7 (9...♕b6!?) 10 e5 ♕b6 11 ♔h1 ♗g4 12 ♕e1 ♘d5 13 ♕g3 ♗c8 14 ♘xd5 cxd5 15 c3 ♕d8 16 f5 ±/+–.

e3) 7...♕a5 8 c3 ♖d8 9 f4 ♕h5 10 ♗e2 ♗g4 11 ♗xg4 ♕xg4 12 ♕b3+ d5 13 ♕xb7 ♘xe4 14 f5 (14 ♕xa8 ♕d7) 14...♕e2 15 ♗f4 ♕a6 16 ♕c7 ♕c8 ∞.

f) 5...♘bd7 6 e5 (6 ♗c4+!? d5 7 ♗xd5+ ♘xd5 8 ♕h5+ g6 9 ♕xd5+ ♔g7 ∞) 6...dxe5 7 dxe5 ♕e7 8 ♗c4+ ♔e8 9 f4 ♘b6 10 ♗e2 ♘e4 11 ♗f3 ♗f5 12 ♕e2 ♕h4+ (12...♘c5 13 0-0 ♘e6 14 ♗e3 ±; 12...♕b4+ 13 c3 ♕c4 14 ♕xc4 ♘xc4 15 g4 ♗g6 16 f5 ♘c5 ∞) 13 g3 ♘xg3 14 ♕f2 ♗c5 15 ♕xg3 ♕e7 16 ♗xb7 ♖d8 17 ♗c6+ ♔f8 ∞ Domuls.

g) 5...♕e8!? 6 ♗d3 (6 ♗c4+ d5 7 ♗xd5+ ♘xd5 8 ♕h5+ g6 9 ♕xd5+ ♕e6 ∞) 6...♘c6 7 c3 d5 8 e5 ♘xe5 9 dxe5 ♕xe5+ 10 ♕e2 =.

h) 5...♗e7 6 ♘c3 g6 (6...♗e6 7 ♕f3 ♔g8 8 e5 ♘fd7 9 ♘d5 ♕d8 10 ♗c4 ♗e7 11 ♘f6+ +–) 7 ♗d3 ♗g7 8 ♗g5 (8 0-0!?) 8...h6 9 ♗h4 g5 10 ♗g3 ♖f8 11 0-0 ♔g8 12 e5 ♘e8 13 ♕h5 ♗f5 14 ♘d5 ♕e6 ∞.

A1)

5...g6 *(D)*

Black frees the g7-square for the king or bishop, but this move does little to challenge White's grip on the centre and as a result White can obtain fair compensation.

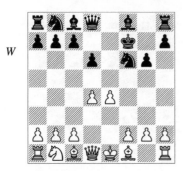

6 ♘c3

6 ♗d3 ♗g7 (6...c5!?) 7 0-0 ♖e8 8 ♘c3 ♔g8 9 h3 is best answered by 9...c5!? ∞, intending to counter 10 d5 with 10...c4, rather than 9...♗e6?! 10 f4 ♘bd7 11 ♕f3 c6 12 ♗e3 ♕a5 13 g4 ♘b6 14 f5 ♗c4 15 g5 ♘fd7 16 f6 ± Skotorenko-Bille Somod, corr. 1985-8.

6...♔g7

Or:

a) 6...♗e7?! and here:

a1) 7 ♕f3?! ♔g7 8 ♗f4 ♘c6 9 ♕e3 ♖e8 10 f3 d5 11 e5 g5! 12 ♗g3 (12 ♗xg5 ♘g4 ∓) 12...♘h5 13 ♗f2 g4 ∓ Strukov-Rodin, corr. 1985-6.

a2) 7 ♗h6! d5 (7...♖e8 8 ♗c4+ ♗e6 9 ♗xe6+ ♔xe6 10 ♕f3 ±/±; 7...♘g4 8 ♗c4+ ♔e8 9 ♗d2 ±) 8 ♘xd5! (8 e5 ♘g4 9 ♕f3+ ♗f5 10 ♗d2 c5 11 h3 h5! ∞) 8...♘xd5 9 ♗c4 c6 10 exd5 cxd5 11 ♕f3+ ±.

b) 6...♕e7 7 ♗d3 ♗g7 8 ♗g5 h6 9 ♗h4 g5 10 ♗g3 ♖f8 11 0-0 ♔g8 12 e5 ♘e8 13 ♕h5 ♗f5 14 ♘d5 ∞ Svenn-Maiorov, Hallsberg 1980.

c) 6...♗g7 7 ♗c4+ ♗e6 8 ♗xe6+ ♔xe6 9 f4 ♔f7 10 e5 and then:

c1) 10...♘e8 11 ♕f3 c6 12 ♘e4 (12 f5?! ♖f8?! {12...♕h4+ looks more natural} 13 fxg6++ ♔g8 14 gxh7+

♔h8 15 ♗f4 ± Rubin-Demidov, corr. 1981-4) 12...♕a5+ (12...♕d7 13 0-0 ♖f8 14 f5! gxf5 15 ♕b3+ d5 16 e6+ +−; 12...♖f8 13 ♕b3+ d5 14 ♘g5+ ♔g8 15 ♘e6 ±) 13 ♗d2 ♕d5 14 f5 and here:

c11) 14...gxf5 15 ♕xf5+ ♔g8 16 0-0 dxe5 17 dxe5 ♘d7 18 ♗c3 ♘f8 19 ♖ad1 ♕e6 20 ♘f6+ ♗xf6 21 ♕xe6+ ♘xe6 22 exf6 +−.

c12) 14...♖f8 15 f6 ♔g8 16 ♕b3 ♕xb3 17 axb3 ♘xf6 18 exf6 ♗xf6 19 ♘xd6 ♗xd4 20 0-0-0 ± Makropoulos-Toth, Rome 1981.

c13) 14...dxe5 15 fxg6+ ♔g8 16 0-0 hxg6 17 dxe5 ♘d7 18 ♗c3 with a dangerous initiative.

c2) 10...♖e8 11 0-0 and here:

c21) 11...♘fd7?! 12 f5 dxe5 (alternatively, 12...gxf5 13 ♕h5+ ♔g8 14 ♗g5 ♕c8 15 ♘d5 ±) 13 fxg6+ ♔g8 14 ♕h5 h6? 15 ♗xh6 ♘f6 16 ♖xf6 ♕xf6 17 ♗g5 +− Didzun-Mikhok, Kombus 1988.

c22) 11...♘c6 12 exf6 (12 d5 dxe5 13 dxc6 ♕xd1 14 ♘xd1 bxc6 15 fxe5 ♖xe5 = Vitolinš-Anikaev, Beltsy 1979) 12...♕xf6 13 ♘b5 ♖e7 14 c3 ± Vaiser-Vysotsky, corr. 1981-4.

d) 6...c6 7 ♗c4+ (7 f4 ♗g7 8 e5 ♖e8 9 ♗c4+ d5 10 ♗d3 ♘g4 11 0-0 gives White compensation, Ginsburg-Gostroevich, USA 1982) 7...d5 8 exd5 cxd5 9 ♘xd5 ♗e6 10 ♘e3 ♗xc4 11 ♘xc4 ♘c6 12 c3 b5 13 ♘e3 a6 14 a4 b4 15 0-0 ♗d6 16 ♘c4 ♔g7 17 f4 ♖c8 18 ♘e5 ∞ Shulman-Ungurs, Riga 1986.

e) 6...♗e6 7 ♗d3 ♗g7 8 0-0 (8 h3 ♖e8 9 ♗e3 ♔g8 10 ♕d2 ♘bd7 11 0-0-0 c5! ∞) 8...♖f8 9 ♗g5 ♕e8 10 f4

♔g8 11 f5 gxf5 12 exf5 ♗f7 ∞ Stamnov-Morgado, Thessaloniki OL 1988.

f) 6...♕e8!? and here:

f1) 7 ♗c4+ ♗e6 8 d5 (8 ♕e2!?) 8...♗c8 (8...♗d7!? intending ...b5-b4) 9 0-0 ♗g7 10 ♖e1 ♖f8 11 f4 (11 e5 dxe5 12 d6+ ♗e6 13 ♖xe5 ♗xc4 14 ♖xe8 ♖xe8 15 dxc7 ♘a6 16 ♗f4 ♖ec8 is slightly better for Black, Vitolinš-Anikaev, Riga 1982) 11...♔g8 12 e5 dxe5 13 fxe5 ♘g4 14 d6+ ♔h8 15 e6 ♘e5 16 d7 ♘bxd7 17 exd7 ♕xd7 18 ♕xd7 ♗xd7 = Popov-Grodzensky, corr. 1982-3.

f2) 7 ♗d3 ♗g7 (7...c5 8 dxc5 d5!?) 8 0-0 ♖f8 9 e5 ♘g4! (9...dxe5?! 10 dxe5 ♕xe5 11 ♖e1 ♕c5 12 ♗e3 ♕c6 13 ♗b5 ♕d6 14 ♗c4+ ♗e6 15 ♗c5 ± Frolova-Lutskene, Leningrad 1989) and now:

f21) 10 h3 ♘h6 11 exd6 ♔g8 (11...cxd6 12 ♖e1 ♕c6 13 ♗e4 +−) 12 dxc7 ♘c6 (12...♘a6!? 13 b3 ♕c6 ∞) 13 d5 ♘e5 14 ♗e4 ♘hf7 (14...♗f5?! 15 ♖e1 ♕d7 16 ♗xh6! ♗xh6 17 d6 ♗xe4 18 ♘xe4 ♕c6 19 b3 ± Vitolinš-Domuls, Riga 1983) 15 d6 ♕d7 16 ♗e3 ♘xd6! 17 ♗d5+ ♔h8 18 ♗c5 ♖f6 19 ♖e1 (19 ♕e2 ♕xc7 20 ♗d4 ♖f5 21 g4 ♖g5 ∓) 19...♖f5! 20 ♗xd6 ♕xd6 21 ♗e4 ♕xc7 22 ♘d5 ♕c5 23 ♗xf5 ♗xf5 24 ♘e3 ♗e6 ∓.

f22) 10 ♗c4+! should be tried.

We now return to 6...♔g7 (D):

7 ♗e2

Or:

a) 7 ♗c4?! ♗e7 8 ♗g5? (8 f3 c5 9 d5 ♘bd7 10 ♗e3 ♘e5 11 ♗e2 b5 ∓) 8...c6 (8...♘xe4 wins for Black) 9 ♕d2 h6 10 ♗xf6+ ♗xf6 11 0-0 ♖e8 ∓ Poletov-Kapusin, corr. 1981-4.

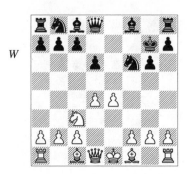

b) 7 ♗g5?! ♗e7 (7...h6!?) 8 ♕d2 h6 9 ♗e3 ♗e6 10 h3 ♘bd7 11 f4 d5 12 e5 ♘h5 ∓ Amirov-Obukhov, corr. 1981-2.

c) 7 f4 ♕e8 (7...d5 8 e5 ♘g4 9 ♕f3 ♗b4 10 h3 ♘h6 11 ♗e3 ♗xc3+ 12 bxc3 ♘f5 13 ♗f2 h5 14 g3 c5 15 ♗g2 gives White compensation) 8 e5 dxe5 9 fxe5 ♗b4 10 a3 (10 ♗d3 ♘d5 11 ♕d2 ♖f8 12 ♕h6+ ♔g8 13 ♗d2 ♘xc3 14 bxc3 ♗a3 15 h4 ♘c6 16 h5 ♘xe5! ∓ Lazarev-Grozdensky, corr. 1981-4) 10...♗xc3+ 11 bxc3 ♘c6 12 ♗e2 ♘xe5 13 dxe5 ♕xe5 14 0-0 ♗f5 15 ♗f4 ♕xc3 16 ♗d3 and White has compensation, Vitolinš-Kveinys, Jurmala 1981.

7...♕e8

Or:

a) 7...♗e7 8 ♗e3 ♗e6 9 ♕d2 h6 (9...♕e8!?) 10 f3 ♘bd7 11 0-0-0 c6 12 g4 gives White compensation.

b) 7...d5!? 8 e5 ♘e4 9 ♘xe4 dxe4 10 0-0 ♘c6 11 ♗e3 h5 (11...♗e7!? 12 ♕d2 ♖e8 ∞) 12 f3 exf3 13 ♖xf3 with compensation for White, Vitolinš-Meiers, Latvia 1989.

Now (after 7...♕e8):

a) 8 ♗f3?! c5 9 ♗e3 ♘c6 ∓ Bessonov-Grozdensky, corr. 1981-4.

b) 8 f3 c5 9 ♗e3 ♘c6 10 d5 ♘e5 11 0-0 a6 12 a4 gives White compensation. If White can set his central pawns in motion and push Black's knights away, then he could develop a dangerous attack.

A2)
5...c5!?
Black takes immediate steps to break up White's centre, at the cost of leaving his king in an exposed position for the time being.
6 dxc5 *(D)*
6 ♗c4+?! d5 7 exd5 ♗d6 8 0-0 ♖e8 9 dxc5 ♗xc5 10 ♘c3 (10 ♗g5!?) 10...♗g4 11 ♕d3 ♘bd7 12 ♗f4 ♘e5 13 ♗xe5 ♖xe5 14 ♖ae1 ♕e8 15 ♕d2 ♖c8 16 ♘b5 ♔g8 17 d6+ ♔h8 ∓ Yandemirov-Plisetsky, Moscow 1983.

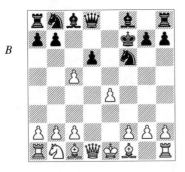

6...♕a5+
Or:
a) 6...♗e6?! 7 e5 ♘fd7 8 ♕f3+ ♔g8 9 ♕xb7 ±.
b) 6...♗g4!? 7 ♗e2 ♗e6 8 0-0 ♘c6 9 f4 ♔g8 (9...d5 10 f5 ♗xc5+ 11 ♔h1 ♗c8 12 exd5 ♘d4 ∞) 10 ♘c3 dxc5 11 e5 ♕d4+ 12 ♔h1 ♕xd1 13 ♖xd1 ♘g4 14 ♘e4 ♗e7 (14...♘d4? 15 ♖xd4 cxd4

16 ♘g5 ± Vitolinš-Kveinys, Kuldiga 1987) 15 h3 ♘h6 and now 16 c3 gives White compensation, and should definitely be preferred to 16 g4? ♘d4, when Black has a clear advantage.
c) 6...♕e8 7 ♘c3 d5 (7...♘xe4?? 8 ♕d5+ +−; 7...dxc5 8 ♗g5!? ∞) 8 ♗g5 and then:
c1) 8...dxe4? 9 ♗xf6! gxf6 (alternatively, 9...♔xf6? 10 ♘d5+ ♔g6 11 ♘c7 +−) 10 ♕h5+ ♔e7 11 ♘d5+ ♔d8 12 ♕xe8+ ♔xe8 13 ♘c7+ +−.
c2) 8...♘bd7 9 ♗b5 ♕e6 (9...♗xc5? 10 ♗xf6 gxf6 11 ♕xd5+ ♕e6 12 ♕h5+ ♔g7 13 ♗xd7 +− Vitolinš-Viksin, Riga 1985) 10 0-0 and here:
c21) 10...♗xc5?! 11 exd5 ♕f5 12 ♕d2 ♘e5 13 ♖ae1 a6 (13...♖d8 14 ♗xf6 ♕xf6 15 ♘e4 +−) 14 ♗e2 ♖d8 15 ♔h1 ♗b4 16 f4 ♘g6 17 ♗d3 ♕d7 18 f5 ♘f8 19 d6! ♔g8 20 ♗c4+ ♔h8 21 ♗xf6 gxf6 22 ♕d5 ♕g7 23 ♖e7 +− Savko-Meiers, Riga 1994.
c22) 10...♘xe4 11 ♘xd5 intending to meet 11...♘xg5 with 12 ♘c7.
c23) 10...dxe4 11 ♕e2 gives White compensation.
d) 6...d5!? 7 e5 ♕e8 8 f4 ♗g4 (not 8...♗xc5 9 ♗e2 ♘fd7 10 ♕xd5+ ♕e6 11 ♕e4 ♘b6 12 f5 ±) 9 ♗e2 ♗xe2 10 ♕xe2 ♗xc5 (10...♘e4!? 11 ♗e3 ♘a6 ∞) 11 exf6 ♕c6 12 ♔d1 g6 and now:
d1) 13 g4? ♕xf6 14 f5 ♘c6 15 c3 ♖he8 16 ♕g2 ♔g7 17 ♖f1 d4 18 c4 ♖ad8 19 g5 ♕f7 20 ♘d2 d3 ∓ Vitolinš-Khalifman, Borzhomi 1984.
d2) 13 f5 ♘d7 (13...♖e8!? gives Black compensation) 14 ♕e6+ ♕xe6 15 fxe6+ ♔xe6 16 ♖e1+ ♔xf6 17 ♘c3 ♘b6 18 ♗e3 ♗xe3 19 ♖xe3 ♖he8 is equal.

d3) 13 ♘c3 ♘d7 14 ♕f3 ♖ad8 (or 14...♘xf6 15 f5) 15 ♖e1 ♘xf6 (White also has an advantage after 15...♖he8 16 ♖xe8) 16 f5 ♘e4 17 fxg6++ ♔xg6 18 ♖f1 ±.

e) 6...♘c6!? (a rather risky idea, as it allows White to draw Black's king even further forward) 7 ♗c4+ ♗e6 8 ♗xe6+ ♔xe6 9 0-0 (9 cxd6?! ♗xd6 10 0-0 ♔f7 ∓; 9 ♘c3 dxc5 10 ♕e2 ♘d4 11 ♕c4+ ♔d7 12 0-0 ♔c8 ∓) 9...d5! (9...dxc5?! 10 ♕e2 ♘d4 11 ♕c4+ ♔d7 12 c3 ±) and then:

e1) 10 ♘c3 d4 (10...dxe4?! 11 ♕e2 ♔f7 12 ♗g5 h6 13 ♖ad1 ♕e8 14 ♗xf6 gxf6 15 ♘xe4 ♖g8 16 ♕c4+ ♔g7 17 ♘xf6! +− Savko-Enin, Riga 1989) 11 ♕e2! (11 ♘d5 ♘xd5 12 exd5+ ♕xd5 13 ♖e1+ ♔f7 ∓) 11...dxc3 12 ♕c4+ ♔e7 13 e5 ♘xe5 14 ♖e1 ∞.

e2) 10 e5 ♘e4 11 ♕g4+ ♔f7 and here:

e21) 12 ♕f5+? ♔e8 13 ♘c3 ♘d4 14 ♕h3 ♕d7 15 e6 (15 ♕xd7+ ♔xd7 16 ♘xe4 ♘xc2! 17 ♖b1 {17 e6+ ♔c6} 17...dxe4 18 ♖d1+ ♔e6 19 b4 ♗e7 −+ intending ...♖hd8) 15...♕xe6 16 ♕d3 ♘xc3 17 bxc3 ♘e2+ 18 ♔h1 ♘xc1 19 ♖axc1 ♔f7 20 ♖ce1 ♕c6 21 ♕f5+ ♔g8 ∓ Vitolinš-Dautov, Minsk 1988.

e22) 12 ♘c3! ♘xc3 (12...♘xe5? 13 ♕h5+ ♘g6 14 ♘xe4 dxe4 15 ♗e3 gives White compensation) 13 ♕f5+ ♔e8 14 bxc3 g6 (14...♗xc5? 15 e6! ±) 15 ♕h3 ♗xc5 16 ♗h6 ♕d7 17 e6 is unclear.

7 ♘c3 ♕xc5 8 ♗e3

Now:

a) 8...♕b4?! 9 a3 (9 ♕d2 ♗e6 10 ♗d3 ♗e7 11 a3 ♕a5 leaves White with compensation, Savko-Roskho, Riga

1989) has the point that 9...♕xb2? fails to 10 ♗d4 +−.

b) 8...♕a5 9 ♗c4+ ♗e6 10 ♗xe6+ ♔xe6 11 0-0 (11 ♕e2!? ♗e7 12 g4 ♖c8 13 0-0 ♖xc3 14 bxc3 ♘c6 15 g5 ± Zelinsky-Volchok, corr. 1988) 11...♘c6 12 f4 ♖d8 13 g4 d5 14 g5 (14 f5+?! ♔f7 15 g5 ♗c5! 16 gxf6 ♗xe3+ 17 ♔h1 d4 18 fxg7 ♖hg8 favours Black, Novozhilov-Raetsky, corr. 1981-4) 14...dxe4 (14...♘xe4 15 ♕g4+ ♔d6 16 ♘xd5 ♕xd5 17 ♖ad1 ±) 15 ♕e2 ♘d5 16 f5+ ♔e7 (16...♔f7!?) 17 ♘xe4 and White is much better.

c) 8...♕c7! ∓ Bezgodov-R.Vasiliev, Ufa 1993. This solid move prevents the annoying check on c4 and leaves White with some problems in demonstrating enough compensation for the piece.

A3)
5...♗e7 *(D)*

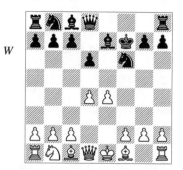

In this line Black aims for rapid development, even at the cost of giving White a third pawn for the piece.

6 ♘c3

Or: 6 ♗c4+ d5 7 exd5 ♗d6 ∓; 6 ♗d3 ♖e8 7 0-0 ♔g8.

6...c6
Or:

a) 6...♗e6 7 f4 ♖e8 8 f5 ♗d7 9 ♗c4+ ♔f8 10 0-0 ±.

b) 6...♖e8 7 ♗c4+ and here:

b1) 7...d5 8 ♘xd5 ♗e6 9 ♘xf6 ♗xf6 10 ♗xe6+ ♖xe6 11 e5 ♕d5 (or 11...♗xe5 12 dxe5 ± Fedorov-Salnikov, Leningrad 1977; 11...c5!? 12 0-0 ♗e7 13 ♕f3+ ♔g8 14 ♕b3 ♕b6 15 c3 cxd4 16 cxd4 gives White compensation) 12 0-0 ♗e7 13 ♕d3 ♖g6 14 g3 ♘c6 15 ♗e3 ♖d8 16 c3 ♕f3 17 ♕d1 ♘xe5? 18 ♕b3+ +−.

b2) 7...♗e6 8 ♗xe6+ (8 d5 ♗c8 9 e5 dxe5 10 d6+ ♗e6 =) 8...♔xe6 and now:

b21) 9 ♕f3 ♔f7 (9...♘bd7 10 g4; 9...♔d7 10 ♕f5+) 10 ♗e3 ♘c6 11 0-0-0 ♕c8 12 h3 ♔g8 13 g4 ±.

b22) 9 g4 ♔f7 10 g5 ♘fd7 11 f4 ♘f8 12 f5 c5 13 0-0 ♔g8 14 ♕h5 favours White.

b3) 7...♔f8 and now:

b31) 8 ♕f3!? ♘c6 (8...♗g4 9 ♕f4) 9 ♗e3 ♘a5 10 ♗d3 ♘c6 (10...♔g8 11 e5) 11 h3 ♗e6 12 g4 ♔g8 ∞ Van der Wijk-Plomp, corr. 1989.

b32) 8 0-0 and then:

b321) 8...c6 9 ♕f3 b5 10 ♗b3 ♕c7 11 ♗f4 b4 12 ♘a4 ♗g4 13 ♕g3 gives White compensation.

b322) 8...♗g4 9 f3 (9 ♕d3!? ♘c6 10 a3 ♗h5 11 f4 ♗g6 12 d5 and White has compensation) 9...♗h5 10 g4 ♗f7 11 ♗xf7 ♔xf7 12 f4 with compensation for White.

b323) 8...♘c6 9 ♗e3 (9 f4 ♗g4 10 ♕d3 ♘b4 11 ♕g3 d5 ∞; 9 f3 d5 {9...♘a5!? 10 ♗d3 ♔g8 ∞} 10 ♘xd5 ♘xd5 11 ♗xd5 ♘xd4 12 ♕xd4 c6 13

♗h6 ♗f6 14 ♕c5+ ♕e7 −+) 9...♘a5 10 ♗d3 ♔g8 ∞.

7 ♗c4+ d5
7...♗e6 8 ♗xe6+ ♔xe6 9 ♕f3 (9 f4 ♔d7 10 e5 ♘e8 11 ♕g4+ ♔c7 ∞) 9...♕a5 (9...♘bd7!? 10 ♕f5+ ♔f7 11 e5 dxe5 12 dxe5 ♘xe5 13 ♕xe5 ♗d6 14 ♕f5 ∞) 10 g4 h6 11 h4 gives White compensation.

8 exd5 cxd5 9 ♘xd5 ♗e6
9...♘xd5 10 ♕h5+ g6 11 ♗xd5+ ♔e8 12 ♕f3 ♖f8 13 ♕b3 ±.

10 ♘e3 ♗xc4 11 ♘xc4 ♘c6 12 c3 ♖e8 13 0-0 ♔g8 14 ♗f4
Or: 14 ♘e5 ♘xe5 15 dxe5 ♕xd1 16 ♖xd1 ♘e4 =; 14 ♕b3 ♕d5 =.

14...♘d5 15 ♗g3
White has three pawns for the piece, but only one is passed and none of them is especially far advanced. White probably has enough compensation for the piece, but certainly not more than that.

B)
    4 ♘c4 *(D)*

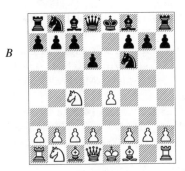

Not a very appealing move. On c4, the knight is vulnerable to attack by ...d5, which costs White more time. If the knight then retreats to e3, the c1-bishop is blocked in. Detailed analysis confirms this instinctive view: Black has few problems equalizing.

4...♘xe4 5 d4

Or:

a) 5 d3 ♘f6 and now:

a1) 6 ♗e2 ♗e7 (6...d5!? 7 ♘e5 ♗d6) 7 0-0 0-0 8 ♘bd2 ♘c6 9 ♘f3 ♗g4 10 ♘e3 ♗e6 11 d4 d5 12 ♘e5 ♘xe5 13 dxe5 ♘e4 14 f3 ♘c5 15 f4 f5 is equal, Udovčić-Bertok, Yugoslavia 1952.

a2) 6 d4 d5 7 ♘e3 c5! 8 ♗b5+ ♘c6 9 0-0 ♗e6 10 b3 ♗e7 11 ♗a3 cxd4 12 ♗xc6+ (12 ♗xe7 ♔xe7! ∓) 12...bxc6 13 ♗xe7 ♕xe7 14 ♕xd4 0-0 15 ♘d2 a5 ∓ Tseshkovsky-Vladimirov, Moscow 1986.

a3) 6 ♗f4 ♗e7 7 d4 0-0 8 ♗d3 ♘c6 9 c3 ♗g4 10 ♕c2 ♗h5 11 ♘e3 ♗g6 12 0-0 ♘h5 13 ♗g3 ♘xg3 ½-½ Spasov-Popchev, Nikšić 1991.

b) 5 ♘c3 and then:

b1) 5...♘f6 6 d4 d5 (6...♗e7 7 ♗d3 ♘c6 8 d5 ♘b4 9 ♗e2 ± Matanović-Udovčić, Yugoslavia 1951) 7 ♘e5 ♗e7 8 ♗d3 0-0 9 0-0 ♘bd7 (9...♖e8?! 10 ♖e1 ♘bd7? 11 ♘xd5! ♘xd5 12 ♗xh7+ ♔f8 13 ♘xf7! ♔xf7 14 ♕h5+ ♔f8 15 ♗g6 ♘7f6 16 ♕h8+ ♘g8 17 ♗h6! +− Shlekis-Maslov, Kaunas 1982) 10 ♖e1 c5!? 11 ♘f3 c4 12 ♗f1 ♗b4 13 ♗d2 ♗xc3 14 ♗xc3 ♘e4 15 ♗b4 ♖e8 16 ♘d2 ♘df6 17 ♘xe4 ♖xe4 18 f3 ♖xe1 19 ♕xe1 ♗f5 = Thipsay-Handoko, Manila OL 1992.

b2) 5...♘xc3 and here:

b21) 6 dxc3 d5 7 ♘e3 ♗e6 8 ♗d3 (8 ♕h5 ♕d6 9 ♗d2 ♘d7 10 0-0-0 0-0-0 11 ♕h4 ♕b6 ∞ Benjamin-Lev,

London Lloyds Bank 1987) 8...g6 9 ♕e2 ♕e7 10 0-0 ♘d7 =.

b22) 6 bxc3 ♘d7!? (also possible is 6...d5 7 ♘e3 c6 8 d4 ♘d7 9 ♗d3 ♘f6 10 0-0 ♗e7 11 ♘f5 ♗xf5 12 ♗xf5 0-0 13 ♕f3 ♘e8!? {13...♖e8 14 ♖e1 g6 ∞ Veličković-Mikhalchishin, Yugoslavia 1992} 14 ♖e1 ♘d6 15 ♗d3 ♗g5 =) 7 d4 d5 8 ♘e3 ♘f6 9 ♗d3 ♗d6 10 0-0 0-0 11 ♕f3 ♖e8 12 ♖b1 c6 13 c4 dxc4 14 ♗xc4 ♕c7 15 h3 b5 16 ♗d3 ♗e6 17 c4 bxc4 18 ♗xc4 ♖ad8 = Gallagher-Delchev, Batumi Echt 1999.

c) 5 ♕e2 ♕e7 *(D)* and then:

c1) 6 b3?! ♘c6 (6...d5 7 ♘e3 c6 8 ♗b2 ♗e6 9 g3 ♘d7 10 ♗g2 0-0-0 11 d3 ♘ef6 12 ♘d2 ♖e8 13 h3 ♕d6 14 d4 h5 = Vasiukov-Kholmov, Voskresensk 1990) 7 ♗b2 d5 8 ♘e3 ♗e6 9 g3 0-0-0 10 ♗g2 ♕d7 11 ♘c3 f5 ∓ Eolian-Kharitonov, Sochi 1978.

c2) 6 ♘e3 ♘f6 7 d4 ♘c6 8 c3 g6 9 g3 ♗g7 10 ♗g2 0-0 11 h3 ♖e8 12 0-0 ♕d8 13 ♕d3 ♘e7 14 ♘d2 ♘f5 15 ♘dc4 c6 16 ♕d1 ♘xe3 17 ♗xe3 d5 with equality, Mnatsakanian-Butnorius, Moscow 1979.

c3) 6 ♘c3 ♘xc3 7 dxc3 ♕xe2+ 8 ♗xe2 ♗e7 9 ♗f4 ♘c6 10 0-0-0 ♗e6

11 ♘e3 0-0-0 = Tseshkovsky-Kuprei-
chik, Erevan 1984.

c4) 6 d3 ♘f6 7 ♗g5 ♕xe2+ (or
7...♗e6!? 8 ♘c3 ♘c6 9 0-0-0 h6 10
♗xf6 ♕xf6 11 ♘d5 ♕g5+ 12 ♘ce3
{½-½ Ljubojević-Hort, Bugojno 1980}
12...♗xd5 13 h4 =) 8 ♗xe2 and now:

c41) 8...♘bd7 9 ♘c3 (9 0-0 h6 10
♗h4 d5 11 ♘e3 g6 12 ♗f3, Ljubo-
jević-Toth, Albufeira 1978, 12...c6 13
♖e1 ±) 9...♗e7 10 ♘b5 ♔d8 =.

c42) 8...♗e7 9 ♘c3 and here:

c421) 9...♘a6?! 10 d4 ♘b4 11 0-0-0
♗e6 12 ♖he1 0-0-0 13 ♘e3 c6 14 ♗xf6
♗xf6 15 a3 ♘a6 16 ♗xa6 bxa6 17
♘e4 ♗e7 18 d5 ± M.Sorokin-Gaga-
rin, Moscow 1986.

c422) 9...♘c6!? 10 ♘b5 (alternatively, 10 0-0-0 ♗e6 11 f4 h6 12 ♗h4
0-0-0 13 ♘e3 ♘d4 14 ♖de1 ♘xe2+ 15
♖xe2 ♖de8 16 ♖he1 ♗d8 17 ♗xf6
½-½ Ljubojević-Christiansen, Linares
1981) 10...♔d8 11 ♘e3 (11 0-0-0 a6
12 ♘c3 ♘d4 = Haag-Kolarov, Kecskemet 1962) 11...♗e6 12 c3 a6 13 ♘a3
♘d5 14 ♗xe7+ ♘cxe7 15 ♘ac2 ♔d7
16 ♘xd5 ♘xd5 17 g3 ♖ae8 18 ♔d2
♘f6 = Carlier-Hartoch, Wijk aan Zee
1987.

c423) 9...♗d7 10 0-0-0 h6 11 ♗xf6
♗xf6 12 ♗f3 ♘c6 13 ♖he1+ ♔d8 14
♗d5 ♖f8 15 ♘e4 ♗e7 16 c3 ♗e6! =
Vitolinš-Kochiev, Frunze 1979.

5...d5 6 ♘e3 *(D)*
6...♕f6

The threat of mate in one is not based
on the hope that White will overlook
it, but rather aims to obstruct White's
natural development. This is an ambitious move which leads to interesting
play, but the fact that there are a number

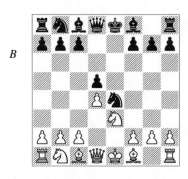

of safe alternatives for Black only
serves to emphasize how harmless this
system is. The other continuations are:

a) 6...♘c6 7 c3 ♗e6 (7...♗e7 8
♘d2 0-0 9 ♗d3 ♘xd2 10 ♗xd2 ♗e6
11 ♕c2 h6 12 f4 ♕d6 13 0-0-0 ♖ab8
14 f5 ± Godena-Vezzosi, Italian Ch
(Chianciano) 1990) 8 ♘d2 ♘xd2 9
♗xd2 ♗d6 10 ♗d3 0-0 11 ♕c2 h6 12
0-0-0 ♘e7 13 g4 with an initiative.

b) 6...♘f6 7 ♗d3 ♘c6 8 c3 ♗d6 9
0-0 ♘e7 10 ♘d2 c6 11 ♘f3 ♕c7 12
♕c2 is slightly better for White,
L.Paulsen-Alapin, Frankfurt 1887.

c) 6...c6 and then:

c1) 7 ♗d3 ♗d6!? (7...♘d6?! 8 0-0
♗e7 9 b3 ♘d7 10 c4 dxc4 11 bxc4
♘f6 12 c5!? ♘b5 13 ♗xb5 cxb5 14
♘c3 a6 15 ♗a3 0-0 16 d5 ± Jansa-
Kristensen, Gausdal 1990) 8 ♘d2 f5
9 c4 f4 10 ♘c2 ♗f5 11 0-0 0-0 12 c5
♗c7 ∓ Vatkinas-Koprasov, Vilnius
2000.

c2) 7 ♘d2 ♘xd2 8 ♗xd2 ♗e6
(8...♘d7?! 9 ♕e2 ♕e7 10 0-0-0 ♘f6
11 ♗b4! ♕e6 12 ♗xf8 ♔xf8 13 f3 g6
14 ♕d2 ♔g7 15 ♖e1 ♕d6 16 g4 ♗e6
17 h4! ± Smagin-Rozentalis, Barnaul
1984) 9 ♗d3 ♗e7?! (better is 9...♘d7)
10 f4 ♘a6 11 0-0 ♕b6 12 c3 0-0-0 13

b4 and White has a clear advantage, Smagin-Arkhipov, Moscow 1986.

d) 6...g6 7 ♘d2 (7 ♗d3 ♗g7 8 0-0 0-0 9 c3 c6 10 ♘d2 f5 11 g3 ♗e6 12 ♘g2 ♘d7 13 f3 ♘d6 14 ♖e1 ♗f7 ∞ Striković-Mikhalchishin, Yugoslavia 1992) 7...♗g7 8 c3 0-0 (8...♘xd2?! 9 ♗xd2 0-0 10 h4 h5 11 ♗d3 ♖e8 12 ♕c2 intending 0-0-0 and g4 ±) 9 ♘xe4 dxe4 10 ♗c4 ♘d7 11 0-0 ♘b6! (11...c5 12 dxc5 ♘xc5 13 ♕c2 ♗e6 14 ♖d1 ± Smagin-Mikhalchishin, USSR Ch (Riga) 1985) 12 ♗b3 c6 13 f3 exf3 14 ♕xf3 ♗e6! = V.Dimitrov-Arlandi, Groningen jr Ech 1985/6.

e) 6...♗e7 7 ♗d3 0-0 8 0-0 ♗e6 9 ♘d2 f5 10 ♘f3 ♘d7 (10...f4? 11 ♘xd5 ♗xd5 12 c4 ±) 11 c4 c6 12 cxd5 cxd5 13 ♕b3 ♘b6 14 ♘e5 ♗d6 = Smagin-Yusupov, Moscow 1980.

We now return to 6...♕f6 (D):

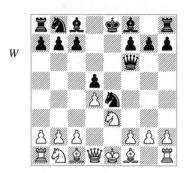

7 ♕e2

Or 7 ♗b5+ c6 8 0-0 cxb5 9 ♘xd5 ♕d8 10 ♖e1 ♕xd5 11 ♘c3 ♕d8 12 ♖xe4+ (12 ♗g5? ♕xg5 13 ♘xe4 ♕g6 −+; the double check achieves little) 12...♗e7, and now:

a) 13 ♕e2?! ♗f5! 14 ♖e5 (the alternative 14 ♕xb5+ ♕d7 15 ♖e5 ♗xc2 is also good for Black) 14...♘c6! and Black is much better.

b) 13 ♗g5 ♘c6 14 ♕e2 ♗f5 (14...f6!?; 14...♗e6 15 ♗xe7 ♘xe7 16 d5 ♘xd5 17 ♖d1 0-0 18 ♘xd5 ♗xd5 19 ♖e5 ♗c4 =) 15 ♗xe7 ♘xe7 16 ♖e5 0-0 17 ♖xe7 (½-½ Smagin-Makarychev, Moscow 1987) 17...b4 18 ♘d1 ♕xd4 19 c3 bxc3 20 ♘xc3 ♗g4 =.

7...♗e6 8 c3 c6

8...♘c6!? 9 ♘d2 0-0-0 and then:

a) 10 ♘xe4 dxe4 11 g3? ♖xd4! ∓.

b) 10 ♘xd5 ♗xd5 11 ♘xe4 ♕g6 12 ♘g3 and now Black can choose between 12...h5! with compensation, and 12...♗b4!? 13 ♗e3 ♖he8 intending ...♘xd4.

c) 10 g3 ♘xd2 (10...♕g6!?) 11 ♗xd2 h5 12 h4 g6 (12...♕g6 13 ♕d3 ±) 13 ♗g2 ♗h6 14 0-0-0 ♖he8 15 ♖he1 ♖e7 16 ♕f1 ± Kholmov-Nikolenko, Moscow 1987.

9 ♕c2

9 g3 ♘d7 10 ♗g2 ♕g6 11 ♘d2 f5 12 0-0 (12 ♗f3 ♕f6 13 ♘xe4 fxe4 14 ♗g2 ♗d6 =) 12...♗d6 and here:

a) 13 f4 h5 ∓.

b) 13 ♘xf5 ♕xf5 14 ♘xe4 dxe4 15 ♗xe4 ♕f6 16 d5 cxd5 17 ♗xd5 ♗e5 (17...♔f7!? 18 ♗xe6+ ♕xe6 19 ♕f3+ ♘f6 ∓) 18 ♗xb7 ♖b8 19 ♗g2 0-0 20 ♗e3 ♘b6 21 ♖fe1 ♗c4 and Black has a slight advantage, Jansa-Forintos, Münster 1992.

c) 13 ♘xe4 fxe4 14 f3 with equality – Yusupov.

9...♘d7 10 ♗d3 ♘d6 11 0-0 g6 12 ♖e1 ♗e7 13 ♘d2 0-0 14 ♘f3 ♖ae8 15 ♗d2 ♕g7 16 h3

= ½-½ Solozhenkin-Ionov, Leningrad 1988.

7 3 ♘xe5 d6 4 ♘f3 ♘xe4: Sidelines

1 e4 e5 2 ♘f3 ♘f6 3 ♘xe5 d6 4 ♘f3 ♘xe4 *(D)*

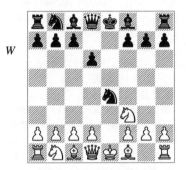

W

At this point White has several possibilities:

A: 5 ♕e2   120
B: 5 ♘c3   126
C: 5 c4   131
D: 5 d3   135
E: 5 d4   137

Of these, A leads to an endgame which offers White only very limited possibilities to play for a win. It is often used by players who are aiming for a draw. Lines B, C and D have had brief periods of popularity, but against correct play offer White few prospects of an advantage. Line E is, of course, far and away the most popular continuation and the only one that really tests Black.

Or:

a) 5 ♗b5+ c6 6 ♕e2 ♕e7 7 0-0 ♘f6 (7...cxb5 is met by 8 ♖e1) 8 ♖e1 ♕xe2 9 ♗xe2 ♗e7 with an equal position, I.Zaitsev-Kochiev, Moscow 1988.

b) 5 ♗d3 and now:

b1) 5...♘c5 6 ♗e2 d5 7 d4 ♘e4 8 0-0 ♗d6 9 c4 c6 10 ♘c3 ♘xc3 11 bxc3 0-0 should be compared with the line *5 d4 d5 6 ♗d3 ♗d6 7 0-0 0-0 8 c4 c6 9 ♘c3 ♘xc3 10 bxc3*. If White plays 12 ♗d3, then there is a direct transposition, but almost certainly White does better by playing 12 ♖b1 first. Therefore this line should be somewhat better for White.

b2) 5...♘f6 6 h3 (after 6 0-0 ♗e7 7 c3 0-0 8 ♗c2 ♗g4 9 d4 ♗h5 the bishop can retreat to g6, neutralizing White's potential kingside pressure) 6...♗e7 7 0-0 0-0 8 c3 d5 9 ♗c2 ♘bd7 10 d4 ♘e4 11 ♘bd2 may give White an edge.

b3) 5...d5 6 ♕e2 ♕e7 7 0-0 ♘d6!? (7...♘c5 8 ♖e1 ♗e6 {8...♕xe2 9 ♗xe2 ♘e6 10 d4 c6 11 c4 gives White some chances of an advantage} 9 ♗b5+ c6 10 d4 cxb5 11 dxc5 ♘c6 12 ♗e3 a6 13 a4 b4 ∞ Morozevich-Shirov, Sarajevo 2000) 8 ♕d1 ♕d8 9 ♘c3 c6 10 ♖e1+ ♗e7 11 ♕e2 ♗g4 12 b3 ♘d7 13 ♗b2 ♘c5 14 ♘a4 ♗xf3 15 ♕xf3 ♘xd3 16

♕xd3 ½-½ Morozevich-Kramnik, Wijk aan Zee 2000.

A)

5 ♕e2 *(D)*

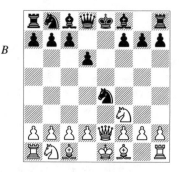

B

Spassky's favourite continuation.

5...♕e7 6 d3

Sometimes White plays 6 ♘c3 ♘xc3 7 dxc3 (7 ♕xe7+ ♗xe7 8 dxc3 ♘c6 9 ♗e3 ♗f5 10 ♗d3 = Hort-Nunn, Bundesliga 1987/8) 7...♕xe2+ (7...♘c6 8 ♗g5 ♕xe2+ 9 ♗xe2 ♗e7 10 ♗xe7 ♔xe7 is equal, Kochiev-Lein, Hastings 1978/9) 8 ♗xe2 ♘c6 9 ♗f4 ♗e7 or (9...♗f5 10 0-0-0 0-0-0 = Tringov-Suetin, Moscow 1967) 10 0-0-0 (10 ♘d4 ♘xd4 11 cxd4 c6 with an equal position, Prandstetter-Knežević, Prague 1983) 10...♗g4 11 ♖he1 0-0-0 = Hübner-Seirawan, Manila IZ 1990.

6...♘f6

6...♘c5 7 ♘c3 and now:

a) 7...c6 8 d4 ♕xe2+ (8...♘e6?! 9 ♗d2 d5 10 0-0-0 ♘d7 11 ♕d3 ±; 8...♘ca6 9 ♗g5 ♕xe2+ 10 ♗xe2 d5 11 0-0-0 ♗d6 12 ♖he1 ♘c7 13 ♗h4 f6 14 ♗g3 ♗xg3 15 hxg3 ♔f7 16 ♖h1 ♘d7 17 ♗d3 ♘f8 = Cifuentes-Piket, Netherlands 1993) 9 ♗xe2 ♘e6 10 d5

♘c7 11 ♗f4 cxd5 12 0-0-0 ♗e6 13 ♘d4 ± Davies-Barua, London 1992.

b) 7...♗g4 8 ♗e3 c6 9 h3 ♗h5 10 g4 ♗g6 11 ♗g2 ♘bd7 12 ♘d4 (12 0-0-0 ±) 12...♘e6 13 f4 ♘xd4 14 ♗xd4 f5 15 0-0-0 ± Hodgson-Barua, London Lloyds Bank 1986.

7 ♗g5 *(D)*

Or:

a) 7 ♕xe7+ ♗xe7 8 ♘c3 (8 d4 ♗f5 9 c3 = Marco-Pillsbury, Budapest 1896) 8...c6 9 ♗g5 ♘a6 10 0-0-0 ♘c7 11 d4 ♗e6 12 ♗d3 0-0 = G.Mohr-Radulov, Maribor 1990.

b) 7 ♘c3 and then:

b1) 7...♘bd7!? 8 ♗e3 (8 ♘b5 ♘e5! 9 ♘xe5 dxe5 10 ♗d2 a6 11 ♘a3 ♘d5 {11...♗f5!?} 12 ♘c4 f6 13 g3 ♗e6 14 ♗g2 ♕d7 15 0-0 ♗c5 = Dely-Toth, Budapest 1968) 8...♘b6 9 0-0-0 ♘bd5 10 ♘xd5 ♘xd5 11 ♗d2 ♕xe2 12 ♗xe2 ♗e7 13 ♖he1 0-0 = Van der Wiel-Yusupov, Groningen 1994.

b2) 7...♕xe2+ 8 ♗xe2 g6!? (or 8...♗e7 9 0-0 ♘c6 10 ♘b5 ♔d8 11 ♗d2 ♗d7 12 ♖fe1 h6 13 h3 ♖e8 14 ♗f1 a6 15 ♘c3 ♗f8 16 ♖xe8+ ♗xe8 = Forintos-Kholmov, Moscow 1975) 9 ♘d4 a6 10 h3 ♗g7 11 g4 ♗d7 (after 11...♘xg4 12 hxg4 ♗xd4 13 ♘d5 White has compensation) 12 ♗f3 (12 g5 ♘g8 ∞) 12...♘c6 13 ♘xc6 ♗xc6 14 ♗xc6+ bxc6 15 ♗d2 h5! 16 g5 ♘d5 17 ♘xd5 cxd5 18 0-0-0 ♔d7 ½-½ Shirov-Kramnik, Cazorla (8) 1998.

The text-move aims to induce Black to exchange on e2, when White is two development tempi ahead. In this respect, White can boast that he has gained one tempo over the initial position; unfortunately, the symmetrical

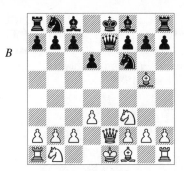

B

and static nature of the position means that this extra move doesn't translate into enhanced winning prospects.

Now:

A1: 7...♘bd7!? 121
A2: 7...♕xe2+ 124

Both these moves are satisfactory. The former continues to play a waiting game with respect to the queen exchange, but Black will probably have to concede White his tempo sooner or later in any case. The latter provides very reliable equality.

7...♗e6 8 ♘c3 leaves Black with more problems:

a) 8...♘c6 9 ♘e4! d5 10 ♘xf6+ gxf6 11 ♗e3 0-0-0 12 d4 ♗g4 (12...♗f5 13 c3 ♖g8 14 ♘h4 ±) 13 ♕d2 ♕e6 14 ♗e2 ± Zhukov-Shifman, corr. 1953.

b) 8...♘bd7 9 0-0-0 h6 (9...0-0-0 10 d4 d5 11 ♘e5 ±) 10 ♗h4 0-0-0 11 ♘d4 ±.

c) 8...h6 and here:

c1) 9 ♗d2?! ♘c6 10 0-0-0 0-0-0 11 g3 g5 12 ♗g2 ♗g7 ∓ Boe-Handoko, Gausdal 1992.

c2) 9 ♗h4 g5 10 ♗g3 ♗g7 11 d4 ♘c6 12 0-0-0 ♘d5?! 13 ♘xd5? (White should play 13 ♕b5 ♘xc3 14 bxc3)

13...♗xd5 14 ♕b5 ♗xf3 15 gxf3 0-0-0 and Black is slightly better, Kupchik-Marshall, New York 1915.

c3) 9 ♗xf6 ♕xf6 10 d4 ♗e7 11 0-0-0 0-0 12 ♕e4 (12 ♕d2 d5 13 ♔b1 ♘d7 = Mieses-Marshall, Baden-Baden 1925) 12...c6 13 ♗d3 g6 14 ♕e3 (14 d5 cxd5 15 ♘xd5 ♗xd5 16 ♕xd5 ♘c6 ± Malevinsky-Gusev, USSR 1970) 14...♔h7 15 h4 ±.

A1)
7...♘bd7!? *(D)*

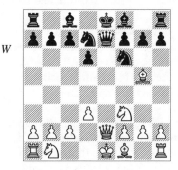

W

This is Bronstein's suggestion, and is the best hope if Black wishes to sharpen the play.

8 ♘c3

Or:

a) 8 c4?! h6 9 ♗d2 ♘c5! 10 ♕xe7+ ♗xe7 11 b4 ♘a4 12 ♘c3 ♘xc3 13 ♗xc3 0-0 = Kurajica-Hulak, Banja Luka 1983.

b) 8 ♘bd2 ♕xe2+ 9 ♗xe2 h6 10 ♗h4 g5 (10...g6 11 0-0 ♗g7 12 ♖fe1 0-0 13 ♗f1 ♘b6 = Johanssen-Trifunović, Halle 1963) 11 ♗g3 ♘b6 (or 11...♗g7 12 ♘c4?! ♘d5 13 h4?! g4 14 ♘fd2 f5 15 0-0-0 f4 16 ♗h2 h5 ∓ Watson-Rozentalis, Mondorf 1991) 12

♘d4 (12 ♘e4!?) 12...♗g7! 13 ♘b5?! ♘fd5 14 c4 ♗d7! 15 a4 (15 ♘xd6+ cxd6 16 cxd5 ♗xb2 17 ♖b1 ♗e5 18 ♗xe5 dxe5 19 ♘c4 ♘xc4 20 dxc4 b6 ∓ intending to meet 21 c5 with 21...bxc5 22 ♖b7 ♔e7!) 15...a6 16 ♘xd6+ cxd6 17 cxd5 0-0 gives Black the initiative, Fernandez Garcia-Alterman, Katerini 1992.

8...♕xe2+

Black should not delay any longer. For example, 8...h6?! is less satisfactory: 9 ♗e3! (intending 0-0-0, ♕d2 and ♖e1) 9...♘b6 10 0-0-0, and here:

a) 10...♗e6 11 ♘d4 0-0-0 (another idea is 11...♘bd5!?) 12 ♘xe6 ♕xe6 13 g3 ♘bd5 14 ♗d2 ♘xc3 15 ♕xe6+ fxe6 16 ♗xc3 e5 17 ♗h3+ ♔b8 18 ♗e6 ♗e7 19 f4 ± Gufeld-Lein, USSR Ch (Tbilisi) 1966.

b) 10...♘g4 11 ♕d2 ♘xe3 12 ♖e1! ♗e6 13 ♖xe3 ♕f6 14 ♘b5 ♔d7 15 c4 g5 16 ♘fd4 ♗g7 17 ♘xe6 fxe6 18 ♗e2 ± Radovici-Penrose, Budapest 1959.

c) 10...♘fd5 11 ♘xd5 ♘xd5 12 ♕d2 ♘xe3 13 ♖e1! ♗e6 14 ♖xe3 0-0-0 15 d4 d5 16 ♕a5 ±.

9 ♗xe2 h6 *(D)*

Or:

a) 9...g6 10 0-0-0 ♗g7 11 ♖he1 0-0 12 ♘b5 ♘d5 13 c4 a6 14 ♘xd6 (14 ♘bd4!? ±) 14...cxd6 15 cxd5 ♘f6 gives Black compensation, Suetin-Petran, Olmutz 1975.

b) 9...c6 10 0-0-0 (White can consider 10 ♘e4!?) 10...♗e7 (10...h6 11 ♗d2 ♗e7 12 d4 ±) 11 ♖he1 (11 ♘e4 d5 12 ♘xf6+ ♗xf6 13 d4 {13 ♗f4!?} 13...♗xg5+ 14 ♘xg5 0-0 = Kirpichnikov-Klovans, Jurmala 1978) 11...♘f8 (11...♘c5?! 12 d4 ♘e6 13 ♗xf6 ♗xf6

14 ♘e4 ♗e7 15 d5 ±) 12 ♘e4 ♘xe4 13 dxe4 ♗xg5+ 14 ♘xg5 h6 15 ♘f3 ♔e7 16 ♘d4 g6 17 f4 ♘e6 18 ♘xe6 ♗xe6 ½-½ Hazai-Lechtynsky, Vrnjačka Banja 1984.

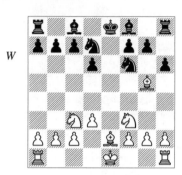

W

10 ♗d2

Or:

a) 10 ♘b5? ♘d5 11 c4 a6! ∓.

b) 10 ♗e3 ♘b6 =.

c) 10 ♗xf6 ♘xf6 11 0-0-0 ♗d7 12 d4 ♗e7 13 ♖de1 0-0 14 ♗b5 ♗xb5 15 ♖xe7 ♗d7 16 ♖he1 ♖fe8 = Čirić-Kholmov, Belgrade 1983.

d) 10 ♗f4 and here:

d1) 10...g6!? 11 0-0-0 (11 ♘d4 a6 12 0-0 ♗g7 13 ♖fe1 0-0 14 ♗f3 g5 15 ♗d2 ♘e5 16 ♗d1 c5 17 ♘b3 ♘c6 18 ♗f3 ♗e6 19 ♘a4 ♘d7 ∓ Ki.Georgiev-Plaskett, Plovdiv 1984) 11...♗g7 12 h3 ♘b6 13 ♘d2 ♘fd5 14 ♘xd5 ♘xd5 15 ♗h2 0-0 = Trifunović-Bronstein, Leningrad 1957.

d2) 10...♘c5!? 11 d4 ♘e6 12 ♗e3 d5 13 ♘e5 c6 14 f4 g6! 15 0-0-0 (15 g4 h5!?) 15...h5 16 g3 ♗h6 ∞ Nijboer-Skembris, Wijk aan Zee 1995.

d3) 10...♘b6 11 0-0-0 (11 ♘b5 ♘fd5! intending ...a6 ∓) 11...♗d7 12 ♖he1 (12 h3 0-0-0 13 ♘d4 g5 14 ♗g3

♗g7 15 ♘b3 ♗c6 = Campora-Zarnicki, Buenos Aires 1993; 12 ♘d4 0-0-0 13 ♗g3 g6 14 ♗f3 ♗g7 = Janssen-Yusupov, Graz tt 1981) 12...0-0-0 13 ♘d2?! (13 h4!?; 13 ♔b1 g5 14 ♗c1 ♗g7 ∞) 13...g5 14 ♗g3 ♗g7 15 ♘c4 ♖de8 ∓ Kuporosov-Mikhalchishin, Brno 1991.

e) 10 ♗h4 g5 11 ♗g3 ♘b6 (the alternative 11...♘h5 is worse in view of 12 ♘d5 ±) 12 0-0-0 (12 h4 g4 13 ♘d2 ♘h5 14 ♗h2 ♗d7 15 0-0-0 0-0-0 16 ♘c4 ♖e8 17 ♖he1 ♗g7 ∓ Sherzer-Wolff, USA 1987) 12...♗d7 and now:

e1) 13 h4 g4 14 ♘d2 and at this point Black should play 14...♘h5!? (rather than 14...♗g7 15 f3 {15 h5!?} 15...0-0-0 and White is slightly better, Arulaid-Vistaneckis, USSR 1964) preventing the move f3 and intending ...0-0-0, and in some cases ...f5 with an initiative on the kingside.

e2) 13 ♘d2 h5 14 h4 g4 15 ♘de4 ♗h6+ 16 ♔b1 ♘h7 17 f4 0-0 18 d4 ♖fe8 19 ♖he1 ♖e7 20 ♗d3 ♖ae8 21 ♖e2 f5 22 ♘g5 ♘a4 23 ♗c4+ ♔h8 = Apicella-Motyliov, Romania 2000.

e3) 13 ♖he1 0-0-0 14 ♗f1 (14 ♘d4!? ♗g7 is equal) 14...♗g7 15 ♔d2 ♖de8 = Ermenkov-Makarychev, Lublin 1976.

We now return to 10 ♗d2 *(D)*:

10...♘b6

Or:

a) 10...c6 11 0-0-0 (11 0-0 ♗e7 12 ♖fe1 0-0 13 d4 ♘b6 14 ♗d3 ♖e8 is level) 11...♗e7 12 ♘e4!? (12 ♖he1 0-0 13 ♘e4 d5 14 ♘xf6+ {14 ♘g3!?} 14...♘xf6 15 h3 ♗d6 16 ♗f1 ♗d7 = Panchenko-Kaidanov, Irkutsk 1983) 12...d5 13 ♘g3 ±.

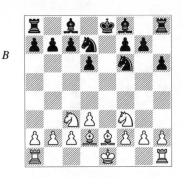

b) 10...g6 11 ♘b5 ♔d8 12 c4 ♗g7 13 0-0 ♘c5 14 b4 ♘e6 15 ♖ac1 ♗d7 16 ♘c3 ♖e8 17 ♖fe1 a6 and now White should play 18 h3 ± instead of 18 g3 ♘g4 19 h3 ♘e5 = Lukin-Sokolin, St Petersburg 1992.

11 ♘b5

Or:

a) 11 a4 ♗d7 12 a5 ♘bd5 ∞.

b) 11 0-0-0 ♗d7 12 ♘d4 (12 ♘e4 ♗e7 13 ♖he1 0-0 14 h3 ♖ae8 15 ♗f1 ♗d8 = Panchenko-Makarychev, Sochi 1983) 12...0-0-0 13 ♗f3 ♗e7 14 ♖de1 ♖he8 15 ♘b3 ♗e6 = Malishauskas-Rozentalis, Vilnius 1988.

11...♘bd5

11...♔d8 12 0-0 (12 c4 ±) 12...♗d7 13 d4 a6 (13...♘e4 14 ♗a5 ±) 14 ♘c3 ♗f5 15 ♖fc1 g5 16 a4 ♗g7 ± Kholmov-Mikenas, USSR 1967.

12 c4

Now:

a) 12...a6 13 ♘bd4 ♘b6 14 0-0 g6 15 ♖fe1 ♗g7 16 ♗d1+ ♔d8 17 b4! ♘bd7 18 ♖c1 ± Taimanov-Suetin, Leningrad 1967

b) 12...♗d7 13 a4 c6 14 ♘bd4 ♘c7 15 0-0 ♗e7 16 b4 0-0 17 ♘b3 ♖fe8 18 ♖fe1 ♘h7 19 ♘fd4 ♗f6 20 ♖ab1 ♖ad8 = Spassky-Yusupov, Moscow 1981.

A2)

7...♛xe2+ (D)

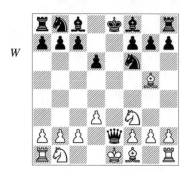

This is Petrosian's plan, which leads to equality.

8 ♗xe2

8 ♚xe2 ♗e7 9 ♘c3 h6 10 ♗e3 c6 11 g3 ♘a6 12 ♗g2 0-0 13 ♖he1 ♖e8 14 ♚f1 ♗f8 = Ivkov-Petrosian, Yugoslavia-USSR 1972.

8...♗e7

8...♘d5?! 9 c4 ♘b6 (9...♘b4 10 ♚d2 ♗e7 11 ♗xe7 ♚xe7 12 ♘c3 h6 13 a3 ♘4c6 14 ♖he1 ♚d8 15 b4 ±) 10 ♚d2 h6 11 ♗e3 ♗e7 (11...♘c6 12 ♘d4 ± intending ♗f3) 12 ♗d4 0-0 13 g4 ± Mukhin-Voronov, USSR 1975.

9 ♘c3

Or: 9 ♘bd2 ♘d5 =; 9 c4 h6 10 ♗f4 ♘c6 11 ♘c3 ♗f5 12 0-0-0 0-0-0 13 ♖he1 g5 14 ♗e3 ♘g4 15 ♘d5 ♘xe3 16 ♘xe7+ ♘xe7 17 fxe3 ♖de8 = Spassky-Karpov, Hamburg 1982.

9...c6

Or:

a) 9...♘c6 10 ♘b5 ♚d8 11 0-0-0 a6 12 ♘bd4 ±.

b) 9...♗g4 and then:

b1) 10 h3 ♗h5 11 ♘d4 ♗xe2 12 ♚xe2 h6 13 ♗h4 (13 ♗e3!?) 13...♘c6

14 ♘f5 ♘h5! 15 ♘xe7 ♘xe7 16 ♗xe7 ♚xe7 17 ♘d5+ ♚d7 with equality, Smyslov-Kogan, Moscow 1938.

b2) 10 ♘d4 ♗xe2 and now 11 ♚xe2 ± is an improvement over 11 ♘cxe2 ♘d5 12 ♗xe7 ♘xe7 13 0-0-0 ♘bc6 14 ♘xc6 ♘xc6 = Botvinnik-Smyslov, Leningrad/Moscow 1941.

c) 9...♗d7 and here:

c1) 10 0-0 and then:

c11) 10...0-0 11 ♖fe1 ♘c6 12 d4 (12 ♘b5 ♖ac8 13 ♘fd4 ♘xd4 14 ♘xd4 ♖fe8 15 ♗f3 c6 16 ♖e2 ♘d5 = Szabo-Barcza, Marianske Lazne Z 1951) 12...♖fe8 13 ♗b5 a6 14 ♗a4 b5 15 ♗b3 ♘a5 16 ♖e3 c6 17 ♖ae1 ♚f8 18 ♗f4 ♘b7 19 h3 ± Capablanca-Kostić, Havana (1) 1919.

c12) 10...♘c6!? 11 ♖fe1 0-0-0 is level.

c2) 10 0-0-0 ♘c6 and here:

c21) 11 ♖he1 0-0-0 12 ♗xf6 (12 ♘e4 ♘xe4 13 dxe4 ♖de8 is equal, Hennings-Bilek, 1970) 12...♗xf6 13 ♘d5 ♗d4 14 ♘e7+ ♘xe7 15 ♘xd4 ½-½ I.Zaitsev-Kholmov, USSR Ch (Alma-Ata) 1968/9.

c22) 11 d4 h6 (11...0-0?! 12 ♖he1 ♘g4 13 ♗xe7 ♘xe7 14 ♗b5 ♗xb5 15 ♖xe7 ♗a6 16 ♖xc7 ± Em.Lasker-Teichmann, Cambridge Springs 1904) 12 ♗xf6 ♗xf6 13 d5 ± intending ♘e4.

d) 9...h6!? and now:

d1) 10 ♗e3 ♘c6 11 0-0 ♗d7 12 a3 0-0 13 d4 a6 = Gligorić-Rossetto, Amsterdam 1954.

d2) 10 ♗d2 c6 11 0-0 0-0 12 ♖fe1 d5 13 h3 ♗d6 =.

d3) 10 ♗f4 ♗g4 11 h3 ♗h5 12 0-0-0 (12 ♘d4!?) 12...♘bd7 13 ♖he1 0-0-0 14 ♘d4 ♗xe2 15 ♖xe2 ♖he8 16

♖de1 ♗f8 ½-½ Kavalek-Smyslov, Tilburg 1977.

d4) 10 ♗h4 ♗d7 11 0-0-0 ♘c6 12 d4 (12 h3 0-0-0 13 d4 ♖de8 14 ♗c4 ♖hf8 15 ♗g3 ♗d8 16 d5 ♘e7 17 ♗h2 a6 18 a3 ♘g6 = Short-Anand, Wijk aan Zee 2000) 12...0-0-0 (12...0-0 13 ♖he1 ±) 13 ♗c4 ♖hf8 14 ♖he1 ♗g4 (14...♖de8 15 d5! {15 h3 a6 16 a3 ♗d8 =} 15...♘b8 16 ♘b5 a6 17 ♘bd4 ± Katalymov-Baranov, Sochi 1952) 15 d5 ♗xf3 16 dxc6 ♗xd1 17 ♖xe7 gives White compensation.

We now return to the position after 9...c6 *(D)*:

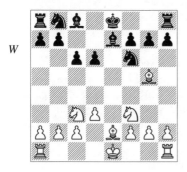

10 0-0-0

Other continuations give White no advantage either:

a) 10 ♘d4 ♘a6 11 0-0 ♘c7 12 ♖fe1 ♘e6 =.

b) 10 b4 ♘bd7 11 0-0 ♘f8 12 b5 ♘e6 13 bxc6 bxc6 = Spassky-Karpov, Linares 1981.

c) 10 ♘e4 ♘xe4 (10...♘bd7 11 0-0-0 ♘xe4 12 dxe4 ♘c5 = Dreev-Arkhipov, Moscow 1985) 11 dxe4 ♗xg5 12 ♘xg5 h6 13 ♘f3 ♔e7 14 0-0 ♘d7 15 ♖fe1 ♘e5 = Kurajica-Knežević, Sarajevo 1981.

d) 10 d4 ♗e6 (10...♗g4 11 0-0-0 ♘bd7 ½-½ Timman-Hort, Amsterdam 1978) 11 h3 ♘bd7 12 0-0-0 h6 13 ♗h4 ♘b6 14 ♖he1 ♔d7 15 ♗d3 ½-½ Short-Karpov, Tilburg 1988.

e) 10 0-0 ♘a6 11 ♖fe1 ♘c7 12 d4 (12 ♗f1 ♘e6 13 ♗e3 0-0 14 d4 d5 15 ♘e5 ♘d7 16 ♘d3 ♗f6 = Spassky-Timman, London 1982; 12 ♘d4 ♘e6 =) and now:

e1) 12...♘e6 13 d5!? ♘xg5 (after 13...♘xd5 14 ♘xd5 ♗xg5 15 ♘xg5 cxd5 16 ♗f3 0-0 17 ♘h3 White has compensation) 14 ♘xg5 ♘xd5 15 ♘xd5 cxd5 16 ♗b5+ ♔f8 17 ♘f3 gives White compensation – Yusupov.

e2) 12...d5 13 ♗d3 ♘e6 14 ♗e3 0-0 15 ♖ad1 ♗d6 16 ♘e5 ♘e8! 17 ♘e2 f6 18 ♘f3 ♘8c7 19 b3 b5!? (19...♗d7 20 c4 ♖fe8 21 c5 ♗f8 22 ♘c3 b5 = Spassky-Yusupov, Toluca IZ 1982) 20 c4 bxc4 21 bxc4 ♗a6 is equal.

10...♘a6 11 ♖he1

Or:

a) 11 ♖de1 ♘c7 12 ♘d4 ♘e6 13 ♗e3 ♘xd4 14 ♗xd4 ♗e6 =.

b) 11 ♘d4 ♘d5 12 ♘e4 f5 13 ♗xe7 ♔xe7 14 ♘d2 ♘b6 15 ♖de1 ♔f6 with equality, Karpov-Smyslov, Moscow 1981.

c) 11 h3 ♘c7 and now:

c1) 12 d4 ♘cd5 =.

c2) 12 ♖he1 ♘fd5 (12...♘e6 13 ♗d2 0-0 = Plachetka-Knežević, Keszthely 1981) 13 ♘xd5 ♘xd5 14 ♗xe7 ♘xe7 15 d4 h6 16 ♗d3 ♗e6 17 b3 ♔d7 = Kholmov-Dvoirys, Voronezh 1988.

c3) 12 ♘e4 ♘xe4 13 dxe4 ♗xg5+ 14 ♘xg5 ♔e7 15 ♖he1 ♘e6 16 ♘f3 f6

17 ♗f1 ♖d8 18 g3 g6 19 ♖e3 a5 20 a3 ♘c5 = Matanović-Zsu.Polgar, Vienna 1986.

d) 11 ♘e4 ♘xe4 12 dxe4 ♘c5 and then:

d1) 13 ♗xe7 ♔xe7 14 ♖he1 ♗e6 (14...♖e8 15 ♘d4 ♔f8 ½-½ Spassky-Salov, Barcelona 1989) 15 ♘d4 ½-½ Spassky-Korchnoi, Brussels 1985.

d2) 13 ♖he1 ♗xg5+ (13...♘xe4? 14 ♗xe7 ♔xe7 15 ♗d3 d5 16 ♗xe4 dxe4 17 ♖xe4+ ♗e6 18 ♘d4 ±; 13...f6!? 14 ♗f4 ♘xe4 15 ♗d3 d5 16 ♗xe4 dxe4 17 ♖xe4 ♗f5 18 ♖e2 ♔f7 19 ♘d4 ♗d7 =) 14 ♘xg5 ♗e7 15 ♘f3 ♖d8 16 ♘d4 g6 17 ♗f1 ♔f8 18 b4 ♘e6 19 ♘b3 b6 = Spassky-Petrosian, Moscow Wch (13) 1969.

11...♘c7 (D)

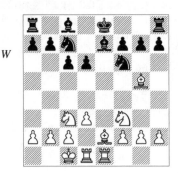

12 ♘e4

Or:

a) 12 ♘d4 ♘e6 13 ♘xe6 ♗xe6 14 ♗f3 ♔d7 15 ♘e2 h6 ½-½ Spassky-Karpov, USSR Spartakiad 1979.

b) 12 ♗f1 ♘e6 13 ♗d2 (13 ♗h4 ♘h5!? =) 13...♗d7 14 d4 h6 15 ♗d3 d5 16 h3 ♖d8 17 a3 0-0 18 ♗e3 ♗c8 19 ♘h4 ♖fe8 ½-½ Spassky-Petrosian, Moscow Wch (15) 1969.

c) 12 d4 ♗e6!? 13 ♗d3 h6 14 ♗h4 0-0-0 15 a3 ♖he8 16 h3 ♘cd5 17 ♘xd5 (17 ♘e2!? g5 18 ♗g3 g4 19 hxg4 ♘xg4 20 c4 ♘c7 21 ♘f4 ♗d7 ½-½ Osis-O.Lauridsen, corr. 1989) 17...♗xd5 18 ♗e3 ♗xf3 19 ♖xf3 ♘h5 20 ♗g3 ♘xg3 21 fxg3 ♗f6 = Přibyl-Dvoretsky, Tbilisi 1980.

12...♘xe4 13 dxe4 ♗xg5+

13...♘e6?! 14 ♗e3! b6 15 ♘d2 ♗b7 16 f4 0-0 17 ♗f3 ± Kr.Georgiev-Pergericht, Haifa 1991.

14 ♘xg5 ♔e7 15 f4

15 ♗c4 ♘e6 16 ♗xe6 ♗xe6 ½-½ Gipslis-Tal, Jurmala 1985.

15...♘e6 16 ♘xe6

16 ♘h3 ♘c5 17 ♘f2 ♖d8 18 ♗f3 f6 19 h4 ♗e6 = Spassky-Hort, Reykjavik Ct (5) 1977.

16...♗xe6

16...fxe6 17 ♖d3 ♗d7 18 ♖ed1 d5 19 ♖e3 ♖hf8 20 exd5 cxd5 21 g3 ♔d6 should also be enough for a draw, Spassky-Van der Wiel, Volmac-Lyons ECC 1991.

17 f5 ♗d7 18 ♖d2 ♖ad8 19 ♖ed1 ♗c8

The position is dead equal.

B)

5 ♘c3 (D)

This system aims simply for rapid development. It is somewhat crude but offers White dangerous attacking possibilities against careless play. Black must continue very accurately to neutralize it.

5...♘xc3

Or:

a) 5...♗f5?? is disastrous in view of 6 ♕e2 +−.

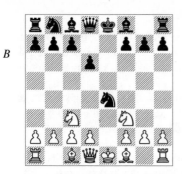

B

b) 5...d5?! is dubious due to 6 ♕e2 ♗e7 7 ∆xe4 dxe4 8 ♕xe4 0-0 9 ♗c4! (9 ♗d3? g6 10 ♕d4 ♗d6 11 ♕h4 {11 0-0 ∆c6 12 ♕h4 ♕xh4 13 ∆xh4 ∆b4 ∓} 11...♖e8+ 12 ♗e2 ♕xh4 13 ∆xh4 ∆c6 14 c3 g5 15 ∆f3 g4 ∓ Gunsberg-Schlechter, Monte Carlo 1902) 9...♗d6 (9...♖e8? 10 ∆e5) 10 0-0 ♖e8 11 ♕d3 ∆c6 12 b3 ♕f6 13 ♗b2!! ♕xb2 14 ∆g5 ♗e6 15 ♗xe6 fxe6 16 ♕xh7+ +– Alekhine-Rabinovich, Moscow 1918.

c) 5...∆f6!? 6 d4 ♗e7 is entirely feasible:

c1) 7 ♗g5 ♗f5 =.

c2) 7 h3 0-0 (7...♗f5 8 ∆h4 ♗g6 9 ∆xg6 hxg6 10 d5 ∆bd7 11 ♗e3 c6 12 ♗e2 ∆b6 13 ♗f3 ∆bxd5 14 ♗xd5 cxd5 15 0-0 ♕a5 16 ♖e1 ± Kupreichik-Butnorius, Riga 1975) 8 ♗d3 ∆c6 9 a3 ♖e8 10 0-0 h6 11 ∆e2 ♗f8 12 ∆g3 d5 = Tseshkovsky-Smyslov, Odessa 1974.

c3) 7 ♗f4!? 0-0 8 ♕d2 ♗f5 9 0-0-0 d5 (9...c6!? intending ...b5 and ...♕a5) 10 ∆e5 c6 11 f3 ♕a5 12 g4 ♗e6 13 ♔b1 ♗b4 14 ∆d3 ± Chekhov-Villareal, Yugoslavia 1975.

c4) 7 ♗d3 and then:

c41) 7...♗g4 8 h3 ♗h5 9 ♗f4 0-0 10 0-0 (10 g4 ♗g6 11 ♕d2 ∆c6 12

♗xg6 hxg6 13 d5 ∆a5 14 0-0-0 ♕d7 15 ♖he1 ♖fe8 16 ♕d3 b6 17 ♕b5 a6 18 ♕xd7 ∆xd7 = Tal-Smyslov, Aker Brygge rpd 1989) 10...∆bd7 11 ♖e1 ♖e8 12 g4 ♗g6 13 ♔g2 ∆b6 14 ♗xg6 hxg6 15 ♕d3 ♕d7 16 ♖e2 ♗f8 = Fuchs-Hennings, East Berlin 1968.

c42) 7...0-0 8 ∆e2 (8 ♗f4 ♖e8 9 ♕d2 ∆c6 10 h3 ♗f8+ 11 ∆e2 d5 12 c3 ∆e4 13 ♕c2 ♗d6 14 0-0 ♗f5 15 ♖fe1 ♕f6 16 ♗xd6 ♕xd6 17 ∆d2 ♗g6 = Kupreichik-Kholmov, Rostov 1976) 8...♖e8 (8...c5 9 h3 b6 10 d5 ♗b7 11 c4 b5 12 b3 a5 13 a4 ± Ulybin-Sorokin, Minsk 1990) 9 0-0 ∆c6 10 c3 ♗f8 11 ∆g3 d5 (11...h6 12 ♗c2 {12 ♗f4!?} 12...d5 13 ♗f4 ♗d6 14 ♗xd6 ♕xd6 15 ♕d3 ♗d7 = Kochiev-Kholmov, USSR 1978) 12 ♕c2 h6 13 ∆h4 ♔h8 14 b4 ∆g8 15 ∆hf5 ∆ce7 16 ∆e3 ∆f6 17 a4 ∆eg8 18 b5 ∆g4!? 19 ∆xg4 (19 c4?! ♖xe3! 20 fxe3 ♕h4 21 h3 ♕xg3 22 hxg4 ♗d6 ∓ Ulybin-Akopian, Tbilisi 1989) 19...♗xg4 20 ♗a3 is equal.

6 dxc3 ♗e7 *(D)*

6...♗f5 7 ♗e3 ∆c6 8 ♕d2 a6 9 0-0-0 ♗e7 10 ♖g1 ♕d7 11 ♗e2 with a slight advantage for White, Kosten-Hingst, Paris 1989.

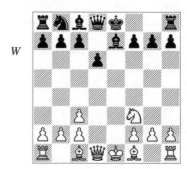

W

The exchange on c3 has allowed White to develop his dark-square bishop without loss of time, and indeed all White's pieces can be developed without difficulty. His plan is to develop the c1-bishop to e3 or f4, and then play ♕d2 followed by 0-0-0. The other bishop will probably stay at home for the moment until it becomes clearer where it will be best posted. The opposite-side castling situation means that play can become quite sharp and White hopes that with his quick development he will be well placed to develop a kingside attack. The defect of White's plan is that it is very one-dimensional. White no longer has a central pawn, so structurally speaking he has little to play for; his chances for an advantage lie solely in piece-play. With accurate play Black can prevent White from developing a serious initiative, and then equality is not far away.

Now:

B1: 7 ♗f4!?   128
B2: 7 ♗e3   129

Or:

a) 7 ♕d5?! ♘d7 8 ♗e3 0-0 9 0-0-0 ♘f6 10 ♕d2 ♘e4 = Galdunts-Janjgava, Erevan 1985.

b) 7 ♗d3 ♘c6 (7...0-0 8 h3 ♘d7 9 0-0 ♘e5 =) 8 ♗f4 (8 ♗e3 ♗g4 9 ♗e4 ♕d7 = Nimzowitsch-Marshall, Karlsbad 1911) 8...♗g4 9 h3 ♗h5 10 g4 ♗g6 =.

B1)

7 ♗f4!?

White intends ♕d2 and 0-0-0.

7...0-0

Or:

a) 7...♗g4 8 ♗e2 0-0 9 ♕d2 ♘d7 10 0-0-0 ♘f6 11 h3 ♗h5 12 g4 ± Dzindzichashvili-Young, Philadelphia 1992.

b) 7...♘c6 8 ♕d2 ♗g4 9 ♗e2 ♕d7 10 h3 ♗e6 (10...♗h5 11 0-0-0 0-0-0 12 ♖he1 ♖he8 13 ♕d5 ♗g6 14 g4 ♕e6 15 ♗c4 ♕xd5 16 ♗xd5 ♗f6 17 ♗g5 ± Osachuk-Raetsky, Belorechensk 1989) 11 0-0-0 0-0-0 12 ♖he1 (12 ♘g5 ♗xg5 13 ♗xg5 f6 14 ♗e3 h5 15 c4 ♘e5 = Santo-Roman – Mirallès, Lyons 1988) 12...a6 13 ♘g5 ♗xg5 14 ♗xg5 f6 15 ♗e3 ♘e5 16 b3 g5 17 f4 gxf4 18 ♗xf4 h5 19 ♗f1 ± Tseshkovsky-Makarychev, Tbilisi 1973.

8 ♕d2 ♘d7!

8...♘c6 allows White some advantage: 9 0-0-0 ♗f6!? (9...♗g4 10 ♗e2 ♗f6 11 h3 ♗xf3 12 ♗xf3 ♘e5 13 ♗xb7 ♖b8 14 ♗d5 c5, Kupreichik-Schüssler, Reykjavik 1980, 15 ♗xe5 ±) 10 ♗d3 ♘e5 11 ♗xe5 dxe5 12 ♕e3 (12 ♘xe5?! ♗xe5 13 ♗xh7+ ♔xh7 14 ♕xd8 ♖xd8 15 ♖xd8 b6 16 ♖e1 ♗f4+! 17 ♔b1 ♗b7 18 ♖xa8 ♗xa8 19 g3 ♗d6 ∞) 12...♕e7 13 h4 ♖e8 (Kholmov-Majorovas, USSR 1979) 14 ♕e4!? g6 15 g4 ♗d7 16 ♗c4 ♗c6 17 ♗d5 ♗xd5 18 ♖xd5 c6 19 ♖d3 ♖ad8 20 g5 ♗g7 21 ♖xd8 ♖xd8 22 ♖e1 ± Kholmov.

The text-move is more accurate. By playing the knight to c5, Black stops the f1-bishop from being developed to d3, and so White finds it harder to develop any attacking chances.

9 0-0-0 ♘c5 (D)

10 ♘d4

10 h3!? ♖e8 11 g4 (11 ♗c4 ♗e6 12 ♗xe6 ♘xe6 13 ♗e3 a5 14 h4 a4 15 a3

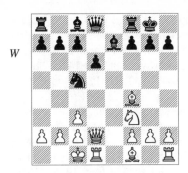

W

♕d7 = Savon-Kochiev, Lvov 1978)
11...♘e4 12 ♕e1 ♗f6 13 ♗e3 and now
Black should choose between 13...b6
intending ...♗b7 ∞ and 13...c5 14 ♘d2
∞, rather than 13...c6 14 ♗d3 ♕a5 15
♗xe4 ♖xe4 16 ♗b6! ± Tseshkovsky-
I.Zaitsev, USSR 1975.

10...♖e8!

10...♘e6 11 ♗e3 ♗g5 (11...♘xd4
12 cxd4 ♗f5 13 f3! {13 h3 ♖e8 =} intending g3, h4 and g4 ±) 12 f4 ♗f6 ±
Valvo-Howell, New York 1990.

11 f3

11 h3?! ♘e4 12 ♕e3 ♗h4 ∓.

11...♘e6 12 ♗e3

Or:

a) 12 h4 ♘xf4 13 ♕xf4 d5 14 ♘f5
♗f6 15 ♗d3 ♗e5 16 ♕d2 ½-½ Kupreichik-Makarychev, USSR Ch (Vilnius) 1980/1.

b) 12 ♘xe6 ♗xe6 13 ♔b1 ♕d7 =.

12...♗g5!

Or 12...♘xd4 13 cxd4 ♗f6 (13...♗f5
should be compared with *10...♘e6 11
♗e3 ♘xd4 12 cxd4 ♗f5 13 f3!*), and
now:

a) 14 ♗d3 ♗e6 15 h4 (15 ♔b1!?)
15...c5! 16 ♗g5 (16 dxc5 dxc5 17
♗xc5 ♕c7 gives Black compensation)
16...h6 17 d5 ♗d7 18 ♗f4 b5 19 c3

(19 ♗xd6? can be met by 19...♗xb2+
or 19...c4) 19...c4 is good for Black,
Sveshnikov-Kochiev, Lvov Z 1978.

b) 14 g3! intending h4 and g4 ±.
Now (after 12...♗g5):

a) 13 f4 ♗f6 14 ♘f3 b6! (14...♘c5?
15 ♗xc5 dxc5 16 ♕f2 ♕e7 17 ♖e1
♕f8 18 ♖xe8 ♕xe8 19 ♕xc5 ± Sveshnikov-Kochiev, USSR 1977) 15 ♗c4
(15 g4?! ♗b7) 15...♘c5!? 16 ♗d5 ♖b8
17 ♘d4 ♗xd4! 18 cxd4 ♘e4 19 ♕d3
♘f6 ∓ Dolmatov-Yusupov, USSR Ch
(Vilnius) 1980/1.

b) 13 ♗xg5 ♕xg5 14 ♕xg5 ♘xg5
15 ♘b5 ♘e6 16 ♖e1 ♗d7 17 ♖xe6
♗xb5 18 ♖xe8+ ♗xe8 = Ivanović-
Yusupov, Vrbas 1980.

B2)

7 ♗e3 *(D)*

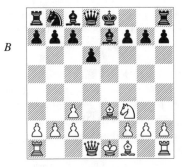

B

This move can lead to play similar
to that in Line B1.

7...0-0

Or:

a) 7...d5?! is suspect in view of 8
c4! dxc4 9 ♕xd8+ ♗xd8 10 ♗xc4
♗f6 11 0-0-0 0-0 12 ♖he1 ♗g4 13
♗c5 ♖c8 14 ♗e7 ♘d7 15 h3 ± Nunn-
Mascariñas, Thessaloniki OL 1984.

b) 7...♘d7 deserves attention. 8 ♕d2 ♘e5 (8...0-0 – 7...0-0 8 ♕d2 ♘d7) and now:

b1) 9 ♘d4 is well met by 9...c5!.

b2) 9 ♗e2 0-0 10 ♘d4 c5 11 ♘b3 ♗e6 12 ♖d1 ♕b6 13 0-0 a5 ∓/∓ Sznapik-Borik, Dortmund 1981.

b3) 9 ♗d4 ♗f6 (9...♘xf3+ 10 gxf3 ♗f6 ∞) 10 0-0-0 ♗e6 11 ♕e3 ♘xf3 12 ♕xf3 ♗xd4 13 cxd4 ♕g5+ = Taulbut-Speelman, Brighton 1980.

b4) 9 0-0-0 ♘xf3 10 gxf3 ♗e6 11 ♔b1 (11 ♗d4!?) 11...♗f6 12 ♗d3 c6 13 a3 ♕a5 14 f4 0-0-0 15 c4 ½-½ Van der Wiel-Barua, Novi Sad OL 1990.

8 ♕d2

White prepares to castle queenside.

8...♘c6

Just as in the previous line, 8...♘d7 9 0-0-0 ♘c5 (9...c6?! 10 c4!? ♘e5 11 c5 ♘xf3 12 gxf3 dxc5 13 ♕c3, intending ♖g1, gives White the initiative; 9...♘e5 – 8...♘c6 9 0-0-0 ♘e5) proves satisfactory for Black:

a) 10 ♘d4 ♘e4!? (10...♖e8 11 f3 c6 12 g4 ♗f8 13 h4 ♕a5 14 ♔b1 ♗e6 15 ♘xe6 ♘xe6 and now, instead of 16 g5 d5 17 h5 d4! = Podlesnik-Rukavina, Kladovo 1990, White could try 16 c4!? ±) 11 ♕d3 d5 ∞.

b) 10 h4 and then:

b1) 10...♖e8?! 11 ♘g5! (threatening 12 ♘xf7 ♔xf7 13 ♗xc5 dxc5 14 ♕f4+) 11...♗xg5 and here:

b11) 12 hxg5?! ♘e4 13 ♕e2 (13 ♕d5?! c6) 13...♘xg5 14 ♕h5 ♖xe3! (14...h6 15 ♗d4 intending ♗xg7) 15 fxe3 ♕e7 is equal, Kupreichik-Yusupov, USSR Ch (Vilnius) 1980/1.

b12) 12 ♗xg5! ♕d7 (12...f6 13 ♗e3 ♗e6 14 a3 ♕e7 15 ♗b5 ♘d7 16

h5 a6 17 ♗e2 ♘e5 18 h6 g6 19 ♖he1 ± Kupreichik-Szymczak, Polanica Zdroj 1981) 13 f3! a5! and now 14 ♔b1! ± is a big improvement over 14 h5?! h6 15 ♗f4 ♕a4 16 a3 ♗f5 17 ♖h4 ♕b3!! –+ (Black can meet 18 ♔b1 by 18...♘a4) Supatashvili-Janjgava, Tbilisi 1985.

b2) 10...♗g4! 11 ♗e2 ♖e8!? (or 11...♕c8 12 ♘d4! ♗xe2 13 ♕xe2 ♖e8 14 ♕f3 ± ♗f6 15 h5 ♘e4 16 h6 g6 17 ♖he1 ♗h8 18 ♗f4 ♘c5 19 ♗g5 ♘e6 20 ♗f6 ♘xd4 21 cxd4 ½-½ Pinal-Siero, Havana 1983) 12 ♘g5 ♗xg5 13 hxg5 (13 ♗xg5 ♖xe2) 13...♘e4 14 ♕d3 ♗xe2 15 ♕xe2 ♘xg5 16 ♕h5 and now Black should choose 16...h6! ∓, rather than 16...♖xe3?! 17 fxe3 ♕e7 with equality, Supatashvili-Janjgava, Borzhomi 1985.

We now return to 8...♘c6 (D):

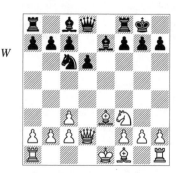

9 0-0-0 ♘e5

This move highlights the defect of 7 ♗e3. 9...♗e6 10 ♔b1 ♘e5 11 ♘d4 ♗c4 12 b3 ♗xf1 13 ♖hxf1 ♗f6 14 h3 ♕d7 15 g4 ♘c6 = Arnason-Makarychev, Reykjavik 1990.

10 ♘d4 c5

Or 10...a6 11 f4 ♘g4 12 ♗d3, and now:

a) 12...c5 13 ♘f5 c4?! (13...♖e8!?) 14 ♗e4 ♗xf5 15 ♗xf5 ♘xe3 16 ♕xe3 d5 17 ♔b1! ± Van der Wiel-Yusupov, Sarajevo 1984.

b) 12...♘xe3 13 ♕xe3 ♗f6 14 ♕f3 c5 (14...♕d7?! 15 ♔b1 ♖b8 16 h3 g6 17 g4 ±) 15 ♘b3 a5 (15...♗e6 16 ♗e4 ♕b6 17 g4 a5 18 g5 ♗e7 19 ♗d5 a4 20 ♘d2 a3 21 b3 ♗xd5 22 ♕xd5 ♕a5 23 ♘e4 ♖fe8, Van der Wiel-Piket, Amsterdam 1989, 24 ♖hg1! ±) 16 ♗c4 a4 17 ♘d2 a3 18 b3 d5! 19 ♗xd5 ♗xc3 20 ♘c4 ♕f6 21 g4 g6 22 g5 ♕g7 23 ♗xb7 ♗d2+!! (23...♗xb7? 24 ♕xb7 ♗b4 25 ♔b1 ♖ad8 26 ♕f3 ± Dolmatov-Anikaev, USSR Ch (Minsk) 1979) 24 ♔xd2 ♕d4+ 25 ♔c1 =.

11 ♘b5 ♗e6

11...♕a5 12 a3 ♗e6 (12...a6 13 ♘xd6 ♖d8 14 ♘xc8 ♖xd2 15 ♘xe7+ ♔f8 16 ♖xd2 ♔xe7 17 ♖d5 ♘d7 18 ♗e2 gives White compensation) 13 ♘xd6 ♕b6 14 f4! ♘g4 15 f5 ♕xd6 (15...♖ad8 16 fxe6 ♖xd6 17 exf7+ ♖xf7 18 ♗d3 ±) 16 ♕xd6 ♗xd6 17 ♖xd6 ♘xe3 18 fxe6 ♘xf1 (18...fxe6 19 ♗d3 ± Kramnik-Kasparov, New York blitz 1995) 19 ♖xf1 fxe6 20 ♖xf8+ ♖xf8 21 ♖xe6 ♖f2 ∞.

12 ♘xd6 ♕b6 13 b4

13 ♘e4 is met by 13...♖ad8.

13...♗xd6 14 ♕xd6 ♕xd6 15 ♖xd6 cxb4 16 cxb4 ♗xa2 17 ♗f4 f6

= Nunn-Zsu.Polgar, Brussels 1985.

C)

5 c4 (D)

The idea behind this move is to obstruct ...d5, so that when White finally does attack the e4-knight (by d4 followed by ♗d3) it will be forced to

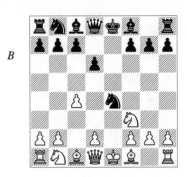

B

retreat to f6. The problem is that it is rather slow, and additionally Black can retreat the knight to g5 rather than f6. After the exchange of knights, Black will be less worried by White's space advantage and shouldn't have many problems equalizing.

5...♗e7

Black has other possibilities:

a) 5...d5 (it is quite tempting to play the move White was trying to prevent, but this doesn't completely equalize) 6 ♘c3 (6 cxd5 ♕xd5 7 ♘c3 ♘xc3 8 bxc3 c5 =) and now:

a1) 6...♘xc3 7 dxc3 c6 8 ♕d4 ♗e6 9 ♘g5 ± Keres-Ribero, Leipzig OL 1960.

a2) 6...♘f6 7 d4 and then:

a21) 7...♗e7 8 cxd5 (8 ♗g5!? is possible) 8...♘xd5 9 ♗c4 ♘xc3 (not 9...c6? 10 ♗xd5 cxd5 11 ♕b3 ±) 10 bxc3 0-0 11 0-0 ♘d7 12 ♖e1 ±/± Marco-Goncharov, Moscow 1907.

a22) 7...♗b4!? 8 ♗g5 0-0 9 ♗xf6 (9 cxd5 ♕e8+! intending ...♘xd5) 9...♕xf6 10 cxd5 ♗g4! 11 ♗e2 ♗xf3 12 ♗xf3 ♖e8+ 13 ♗e2 and now Black has a choice between 13...c6 ∓ and 13...c5!?.

a3) 6...♗c5 7 d4 ♗b4 (D) and then:

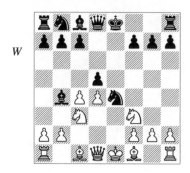

W

a31) 8 ♗d2 ♘xd2 9 ♕xd2 0-0 10 cxd5 ♘d7 (10...♗xc3 11 bxc3 ♕xd5 12 ♗e2 c5 13 0-0 cxd4 14 ♘xd4 intending ♗f3 and ♖b1 ±) 11 a3 ♖e8+ 12 ♗e2 (Keres-Keller, Zurich 1959) 12...♗xc3 13 bxc3 ♘b6 14 0-0 and now 14...♕xd5 ∞ should be preferred to 14...♘xd5 15 c4 ±.

a32) 8 ♕c2 ♕e7!? (8...♗e6 9 a3 ♗xc3+ 10 bxc3 ± Rantanen-Toth, Nice OL 1974) 9 ♗e3 ♗f5 10 ♕b3 0-0 is unclear.

a33) 8 ♕b3 ♕e7 (8...c5? 9 ♗d3 ♕a5 10 0-0 ♘xc3 11 bxc3 ♗xc3 12 ♗b2 ♗xb2 13 ♖ae1+! ± Evans-Bisguier, USA Ch (New York) 1958/9) 9 ♗e3 and now:

a331) 9...0-0?! 10 cxd5 ♗f5 (alternatively, 10...♖e8 11 ♘e5 ♘d7 12 ♗b5 ♘xe5 13 dxe5 ±) 11 ♗e2 ±.

a332) 9...dxc4 10 ♗xc4 0-0 11 0-0 ♘xc3 12 bxc3 ♗d6 13 ♖fe1 ♘c6 14 ♕c2 ±.

a333) 9...♗e6 and then:

a3331) 10 a3?! ♗xc3+ 11 bxc3 c6 12 cxd5 cxd5 13 c4 ♘f6 14 ♘g5 (14 ♖b1 0-0!) 14...dxc4 15 ♕b5+ ♘c6 16 ♘xe6 fxe6 17 ♗xc4 ♖d8 with a balanced position, Dolmatov-Forintos, Budapest 1982.

a3332) 10 cxd5 ♗xd5 11 ♕xd5 ♘xc3 12 ♕xb7 ±.

a334) 9...c6 10 ♗d3 (10 cxd5 cxd5 11 ♗b5+!? ±; 10 a3 ♗xc3+ 11 bxc3 0-0 12 ♗e2 dxc4 13 ♗xc4 ♘d6 14 0-0 ♘xc4 15 ♕xc4 ♗e6 16 ♕d3 ± Tolnai-Anka, Budapest 1989) 10...dxc4 (10...♗e6?! 11 0-0 ♘xc3 12 bxc3 ♗d6 13 c5 ♗c7 {13...♗xc5 14 dxc5 d4 15 ♗g5 +−} 14 ♘g5! ± Kindermann-Forintos, Berlin 1987) 11 ♗xc4 ♗xc3+ 12 bxc3 ♘d6 13 0-0 ♘xc4 14 ♕xc4 0-0 15 ♕d3 ±.

b) 5...g6 is a sound and solid move:

b1) 6 d4 ♗g7 7 ♗d3 ♘f6 8 0-0 (8 ♕e2+!?) 8...0-0 9 h3 ♖e8 10 ♘c3 ♘c6 11 ♗f4 d5 = Kindermann-Knežević, Budapest 1986.

b2) 6 d3 ♘f6 7 ♘c3 ♗g7 8 ♕e2+ ♕e7 9 ♕xe7+ ♘xe7 10 ♗g5 ♖e8 11 0-0-0 ♘f8 12 h3 a6 = Keres-Rossetto, Buenos Aires 1964.

b3) 6 ♘c3 ♘xc3 7 dxc3 ♗g7 8 ♕e2+ (8 ♗g5!?) 8...♕e7 9 ♕xe7+ ♘xe7 10 ♗e3 b6 11 0-0-0 ♘c6 12 ♗d3 (12 ♖e1 ♘d7) 12...♗b7 13 ♖he1 ♘d7 14 c5 bxc5 15 ♗xc5 ♖he8 16 ♖xe8 ♖xe8 17 ♗e3 ♘e5 = G.Kuzmin-Grember, Paris 1986.

c) 5...♘c6 (D) is also quite a good move. Now White's idea of d4 followed by ♗d3 doesn't work; the fact that Black has several reasonable replies to 5 c4 makes it a rather unattractive plan. Now:

c1) 6 d4 d5! 7 ♘c3 (7 ♗d3 ♗b4+) 7...♗b4 8 ♕c2 (8 ♕b3 ♕e7 ∓; 8 ♗d2 ♘xd2 9 ♕xd2 0-0 10 cxd5 ♖e8+ 11 ♗e2 ♘e7 12 0-0 ♘xd5 13 ♗c4 ♘b6 14 ♗b3 ♗e6 = Prasad-Ye Rongguang, Calcutta 1991) 8...♕e7 9 ♗e3 (9 ♔d1!?

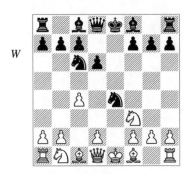

W

♗xc3 10 bxc3 ∞) 9...♗f5! 10 a3 (10
♕c1? ♘xc3 11 bxc3 ♗a3 12 ♕d2 ♘b4!
13 ♔e2 ♘c2 14 ♖d1 dxc4 15 ♘e5 0-0
16 f3 b5 17 g4 ♘xe3 18 ♕xe3 ♗d7 ∓
Kupreichik-Mikhalchishin, Kuibyshev
1986) 10...♗xc3+ 11 bxc3 ♘d6 12
♕b3 dxc4 13 ♗xc4 ♘xc4 14 ♕xc4
♗e4 15 d5 ∞.

c2) 6 ♗e2 ♗e7 7 0-0 and then:

c21) 7...♗e6!? 8 ♘c3 (8 d4 d5 9
cxd5 ♗xd5 10 ♘c3 ♘xc3 11 bxc3 0-0
12 ♗e3 ♗f6 = Sharif-Mirallès, French
Ch (Val Thorens) 1988) 8...♘xc3 9
bxc3 0-0 10 ♖b1 b6 11 d3 ♗f6 12 ♕c2
d5 13 ♘d2 ♕d7 ½-½ Benjamin-
Seirawan, New York 1989.

c22) 7...0-0 8 d4 (8 d3 ♘f6 9 ♘c3
d5 =) 8...♗f6 and now:

c221) 9 ♗d3 ♗f5 10 ♖e1 ♖e8 is
level.

c222) 9 h3 ♖e8 and now:

c2221) 10 ♘c3?! gives Black a
pleasant choice between the simple
line 10...♘xc3 11 bxc3 ♗f5 and the
sharper 10...♗xd4 11 ♘xe4 ♖xe4 12
♗d3; however, Black should avoid
10...♘xd4? 11 ♘xd4 ♗xd4 12 ♘xe4
♖xe4 13 ♗f3 ♖h4 14 g3.

c2222) 10 ♗e3 ♘g3! ∓.

c2223) 10 ♖e1 =.

c2224) 10 ♗f4 ♗f5 11 ♖e1 ♕d7 =
Chiburdanidze-Makarychev, Frunze
1985.

c223) 9 d5 ♘e7 10 ♘a3 (10 ♗d3
must be met by 10...♘c5, rather than
10...♗f5?? 11 ♕c2 +−) 10...♖e8 11
♘c2 h6 12 ♖e1 a5 13 ♖b1 ♗f5 14
♗e3 ♗h7 (14...♕d7?! 15 ♘fd4! ♗h7
16 ♗g4 ♕d8 17 ♕e2 c6 18 dxc6 bxc6
19 f3 ♘c5 20 ♖bd1 ± Kholmov-Raet-
sky, Voronezh 1988) 15 ♘fd4 ♘f5 16
♘xf5 ♗xf5 17 ♗d3 ♕d7 =.

c224) 9 ♘c3 ♘xc3 10 bxc3 and
then:

c2241) 10...♖e8 11 ♗e3 ♘e7 (or
11...♗f5 12 h3 h6 {12...♕d7!?} 13
♕d2 ♗h7 14 ♖ad1 ♕d7 15 ♘h2 ♕f5
16 ♘g4 ♗g5 and now 17 ♖b1!? ± is
better than 17 f4?! ♗h4 18 ♖b1 ♕c2
19 ♕xc2 ♗xc2 20 ♖b2 ♗e4 ∞ Kuprei-
chik-Forintos, Budapest 1988) 12 ♕d2
♗g4?! (12...b6!?) 13 h3 ♗xf3 14 ♗xf3
c6 15 ♖ab1 ♖b8 16 ♕c2 ± Kupreichik-Schüssler, Malmö 1987/8.

c2242) 10...♘a5! 11 ♗e3 (11 ♗f4
♖e8 12 ♘d2 c5 13 ♘b3 ♗f5 14 ♗d3
♗xd3 15 ♕xd3 cxd4 16 cxd4 d5 is
equal, Perenyi-Michaelsen, West Berlin 1988) 11...b6 12 ♘d2 ♗a6 13 ♖e1
(13 ♗d3?! ♖e8 14 ♕a4 d5 15 ♖fd1 c6
16 ♘b3 dxc4 17 ♘xa5 b5 18 ♕a3?!
cxd3 with a clear advantage for Black,
Voichekhovsky-Raetsky, Makhachkala
1989) 13...♖e8 =.

c225) 9 ♗e3 ♖e8 (9...d5!? 10 ♘c3
♘xc3 11 bxc3 dxc4 12 ♗xc4 ♗g4 13
h3 ♗h5 14 ♗e2 ♘a5 15 ♕a4 c6 16 c4
c5 17 ♖ad1 ♗xf3 18 ♗xf3 cxd4 19 c5
♕e8 = Kindermann-Tischbierek, Budapest 1987) 10 ♘bd2 (10 ♘a3 ♗g4
11 ♘c2 d5 12 c5 a6 =; 10 ♕b3 ♘g5 11

♕d3 g6 12 ♘xg5 ♗xg5 13 ♘c3 ♗e6 14 ♕d2 ♗xe3 15 fxe3 d5 ∞ Mainka-Davidović, Dortmund 1988) 10...♗f5 (10...♗g4 11 h3 ♗h5 12 ♘xe4 ♖xe4 13 ♗d3 ∞) and then:

c2251) 11 ♘b3?! d5 12 ♖c1 (12 cxd5 ♘b4 ∓) 12...dxc4 13 ♗xc4 ♘d6 14 ♗e2 ♘b4 ∓ Kupreichik-Makarychev, Frunze 1985.

c2252) 11 ♖c1 ♕d7 (11...a5!? 12 d5 ♘b4 13 a3 ♘a6 ∞) 12 d5 ♘e7 13 ♗d4 ♘xd2 14 ♕xd2 ♗xd4 15 ♘xd4 ♗g6 = Nijboer-Finegold, Wijk aan Zee 1991.

c2253) 11 ♘xe4 ♗xe4 12 d5 ♗xf3 13 ♗xf3 ♘e5 14 ♗e2 =.

c3) 6 ♘c3 ♘xc3 7 dxc3 and now:

c31) 7...♗g4 8 ♗e2 (8 ♗d3!?) 8...♗e7 9 h3 ♗f5 10 ♗f4 ♕d7 11 ♕d2 ♗f6! 12 0-0-0 0-0-0 13 g4 ♗g6 14 ♖he1 ♖he8 = Marjanović-Mikhalchishin, Sarajevo 1985.

c32) 7...♗e7 8 ♗d3 ♗g4 9 ♗e4 ♕d7! (9...0-0 10 ♕c2 h6 11 ♗e3 ♗e6 12 b3 ♗f6 13 0-0-0 a5 14 a4 ± Stefansson-I.Sokolov, Reykjavik 2000) 10 ♗e3 ♗f5 11 ♗xf5 ♕xf5 12 ♕d5 ♕xd5 13 cxd5 ♘e5 14 ♘xe5 dxe5 15 ♔e2 ♔d7! = Timman-Yusupov, Hilversum (4) 1986.

We now return to 5...♗e7 (D):

6 d4

6 ♘c3 ♘xc3 7 dxc3 (7 bxc3 0-0 8 d4 ♖e8 9 ♗e2 ♘d7 10 0-0 ♘f8 11 ♘e1 ♗f5 12 ♗d3 ♗xd3 13 ♕xd3 ♕d7 = Marco-Maroczy, Monte Carlo 1904) and now:

a) 7...♘d7!? 8 ♗e2 0-0 9 0-0 ♘c5 10 ♘d4 (10 ♗e3 ♗f6 11 ♕c2 g6 12 ♖ad1 ♗f5 = Ivanov-Rozentalis, Vilnius 1983) 10...♗f6 11 ♗f3 ♗e5 12

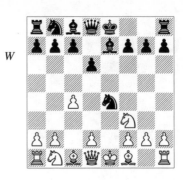

W

♗e3 ♕f6 13 ♗d5 c6 14 f4 ♗xd4 15 ♗xd4 ♕g6 16 ♗f3 ♗f5 = Dolmatov-Rozentalis, USSR 1983.

b) 7...♘c6 8 ♗d3 (8 ♗f4 ♗g4 9 ♗e2 ♕d7 10 ♕d2 0-0-0 11 0-0-0 h6 12 h3 ♗e6 = Teichmann-Marshall, San Sebastian 1911) 8...♘e5 9 ♘xe5 dxe5 10 ♕c2 ♗g5 11 0-0 ♗e6 12 ♖e1 ♗xc1 13 ♖axc1 ♕g5 14 ♖e3 0-0-0 with equality, Maroczy-Marshall, San Sebastian 1911.

6...0-0

6...d5!? 7 ♘c3 (7 ♗d3 ♗b4+ – *5 d4 d5 6 ♗d3 ♗d6 7 c4 ♗b4+*) 7...♘xc3 8 bxc3 0-0 9 cxd5 (9 ♗e2 ♘c6 10 0-0 ♗e6 11 ♖b1 ♘a5 12 cxd5 ♗xd5 13 ♕a4 c6 14 c4!? ♘xc4 15 ♖xb7 ♘b6 16 ♕a6 ♗d6 17 ♖xa7 ♖xa7 18 ♕xa7 ♖e8 19 ♗e3 ♘c4 gives Black compensation, Ferreira-Mirallès, Thessaloniki OL 1988) 9...♕xd5 10 ♗e2 ♗f5 11 0-0 ♘d7 12 ♘d2 ♘b6 13 a4 ♕d7 14 ♗f3 c6 15 a5 ♘d5 16 ♕b3 ♖fe8 17 ♘c4 ♗f6 18 ♗a3 ♖e6 = Kupreichik-Agzamov, Frunze 1985.

7 ♗d3

7 ♗e2 d5 8 0-0 ♘c6 =.

7...♘g5 (D)

The key point. Black need not retreat to f6, where the knight would

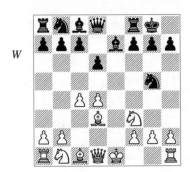

W

obstruct the development of Black's pieces. Instead Black exchanges the knight, and then develops with ...♗f6 and ...♘c6.

8 ♘xg5

Or:

a) 8 0-0 ♘xf3+ 9 ♕xf3 ♘c6 10 ♘c3 f5 (10...♘xd4? 11 ♕e4 ♘f5 12 g4 +−) 11 ♗e3 g5!? 12 ♕h5 ♕e8 13 ♕xe8 ♖xe8 14 ♘d5 ♗d8 15 ♖fe1 f4 16 ♗d2 ♖f8 17 ♗c3 a5 18 ♖e2 ♗g4! 19 f3 ♗h5 20 ♖ae1 ♘b4! 21 ♘xb4 (21 ♗xb4 axb4 22 ♘xb4 c5 =) 21...axb4 22 ♗xb4 ♗f6! 23 ♗c3 ½-½ Chiburdanidze-Kakhiani, Tbilisi 1991.

b) 8 ♘fd2 ♘c6 9 ♘b3 ♘b4 10 0-0 (10 f4?! ♗g4 11 ♕d2 ♘f3+!! 12 gxf3 ♗h4+ 13 ♔f1 ♗h3+ 14 ♔e2 a5! ∓ Kupreichik-Skembris, Debrecen Echt 1992) 10...♘xd3 11 ♕xd3 g6 is unclear.

c) 8 ♘c3 ♗g4 9 ♗e2 ♘xf3+ 10 ♗xf3 ♗xf3 11 ♕xf3 c6!? (11...♘c6?! 12 ♗e3 ♗g5 13 0-0 a5 14 b3 ♗xe3 15 fxe3 ♕d7 16 ♖f2 ♖ae8 17 ♖af1 and White is slightly better, Tseshkovsky-Makarychev, USSR Ch (Minsk) 1979) 12 d5 c5 13 ♗f4 ♘d7 14 ♕g3 ♘f6 15 ♗h6 ♘h5 16 ♕g4 ♕e8! intending ...f5 and ...♗g5+.

d) 8 ♗e3!? ♘c6 9 ♘bd2 ♗g4 10 ♕b3 ♗xf3 11 gxf3 is best answered by 11...a5!? ∞, rather than 11...d5?! 12 cxd5 ♘a5 13 ♕c2 ♗b4 14 0-0-0 ♕xd5 15 ♔b1 ± Malishauskas-Sorokin, Norilsk 1987.

8...♗xg5 9 ♕h5 ♖e8+ 10 ♔d1 h6 11 ♗xg5 ♕xg5 12 ♕xg5 hxg5 13 ♘c3 ♗d7 14 ♔d2

14 ♘d5 ♘a6 15 c5 ♗c6 ∞.

14...♘c6 15 ♘d5 ♖ac8

Black has no trouble neutralizing White's slight initiative.

16 ♔c3

16 h4 g4 17 ♔c3 ♘e7 18 ♘e3 ♔f8 19 g3 ♘g8 20 ♖he1 ♘f6 = Kengis-Akopian, USSR Cht (Podolsk) 1990.

16...♘e7 17 ♘e3 ♔f8

17...a6 18 h4 g4 19 b4 c5 20 bxc5 (20 dxc5 dxc5 21 b5 axb5 22 cxb5 c4! 23 ♗e4 ♗xb5 24 ♗xb7 ♖b8 25 ♗e4 g3! 26 f3 g6 ∞ Kupreichik-Rozentalis, Klaipeda 1988) 20...dxc5 21 d5 b5 22 a3 ±.

18 g4 g6

18...♘g6?! 19 ♗xg6 fxg6 20 h4! ±.

19 h4 gxh4 20 ♖xh4 ♔g7 21 g5 ♖h8

The game is equal, Kupreichik-Akopian, USSR Cht (Podolsk) 1990.

D)

5 d3 *(D)*

White decides to kick the knight back before pushing the pawn to d4. However, this change tends to favour Black because White deprives himself of one of the main themes of his play in the Petroff – gaining time by undermining the e4-knight and forcing it to retreat to f6 voluntarily. Black faces a

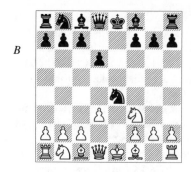

much easier task equalizing here than in the main lines with 5 d4.

5...♘f6 6 d4

6 ♗e2 ♗e7 7 0-0 0-0 8 d4 (8 b3?! ♘c6 9 ♗b2 ♘d5! = intending ...♗f6) 8...c6 (8...♗f5 9 c4 ♖e8 10 ♘c3 ♗f8 11 ♖e1 ♘e4 12 ♘xe4 ♗xe4 13 ♗g5 ♗e7 14 ♗xe7 ♖xe7 15 ♗d3 ♗xf3 16 ♕xf3 ♘c6 17 ♕f4 ♕d7 18 ♖e4 ± Nunn-Plaskett, London 1986) 9 c4 d5 10 cxd5 ♘xd5 11 ♘c3 ♗e6 12 ♖e1 ♘d7 13 ♗d3 ♖e8 = Nunn-Short, London 1986.

6...♗e7

Or:

a) 6...d5 transposes to a line of the Exchange French that is not very frightening for Black.

b) 6...♗g4!? is an alternative:

b1) 7 ♗d3 ♕e7+!? (7...♘c6 8 c3 ♕e7+ 9 ♗e3 ♘d5 10 ♔d2 ♘xe3 11 fxe3 0-0-0 12 h3 ♗h5 13 e4 d5 14 exd5 ♖xd5 = Kruppa-Kochiev, Lvov 1984) 8 ♕e2 (8 ♗e3 ♘d5) 8...♗xf3 9 ♕xe7+ ♗xe7 10 gxf3 ♘bd7 11 ♘c3 0-0-0 12 ♗d2 d5 13 0-0-0 c6 =.

b2) 7 ♘bd2 ♗e7 8 ♗d3 0-0 9 0-0 c5 10 h3 ♗h5 11 dxc5 dxc5 12 ♘e4 ♘c6 13 ♘g3 ♗g6 14 ♗xg6 hxg6 15 ♕xd8 ♖fxd8 is absolutely OK for

Black, Petrenko-Rozentalis, Voronezh 1987.

7 ♗d3

Or:

a) 7 h3 0-0 8 ♗d3 c5 9 0-0 ♘c6 =.

b) 7 c4 d5 8 ♘c3 0-0 9 ♗e3 ♘c6 10 h3 and now:

b1) 10...♗f5 11 ♗e2 ♘b4 12 0-0 ♘c2 13 ♘h4 (13 ♖c1 ♘xe3 14 fxe3 c6 =) 13...♘xe3 14 fxe3 ♗e6 15 ♘f5 dxc4 ∞.

b2) 10...♗b4 11 ♕c2 ♕e7 12 0-0-0 (12 c5? ♗xc5! 13 dxc5 d4; 12 ♗e2 dxc4 13 ♗xc4 ♗e6 is equal) 12...♗xc3 13 bxc3 (Velimirović-Mikhalchishin, Palma de Mallorca 1989) 13...dxc4 14 ♗xc4 ♘a5 15 ♗d3 ♗e6 with an initiative for Black.

7...0-0

Interesting is 7...♗g4 8 ♘bd2 (8 0-0 0-0 – 7...0-0 8 0-0 ♗g4; 8 h3 ♗h5 9 ♘c3 ♘bd7 10 ♗g5 ♘b6 11 ♕e2 0-0 12 g4 ♗g6 13 ♗xg6?! fxg6! 14 ♗d2 ♕d7 15 0-0-0 ♖ae8 16 ♕d3 ♕c6 17 ♘g5 ♘fd5 ∓) 8...0-0 9 ♘f1?! c5 10 ♘e3 ♗h5 11 0-0 ♘c6 12 ♘f5 ♖e8 13 c3 cxd4 14 cxd4 ♗f8 15 ♗g5 h6 16 ♗e3 ♘d5 ∓ Strzeletski-Raetsky, Katowice 1990.

8 0-0 *(D)*

8 h3!? prevents ...♗g4, but gives Black time for a direct strike in the centre:

a) 8...♘c6?! 9 c3 h6 10 0-0 d5 11 ♖e1 ♗d6 12 ♘e5 ± Kosashvili-Zalkind, Israeli Cht 2000.

b) 8...c6 9 0-0 ♘a6 (intending ...♘b4) 10 c3 ♘c7 11 ♗f4 b6 12 ♖e1 ♗b7 13 ♘bd2 ♖e8 14 ♕c2 h6 15 a4 c5 is unclear, Donev-Toth, Swiss Cht 1995.

c) 8...♖e8 9 0-0 ♘bd7 10 ♖e1 (10 c4 c6 11 ♘c3 ♘f8 12 ♗f4 a6 13 ♖e1 b5 14 ♕d2 ♘e6 15 ♗h2 bxc4 16 ♗xc4 ♘c7 17 ♖ac1 ♘cd5 18 ♗b3 ♗f8 19 ♕d3 ♖xe1+ 20 ♖xe1 g6 ± Kosashvili-Lurie, Israeli Cht 2000) 10...♘f8 11 c4 c6 12 ♘c3 ♘g6 13 ♗e3 ♗d7 14 ♕b3 ♕c8 15 ♘e2 ♘h5 16 ♘g3 ♘hf4 17 ♗f1 ♗f6 18 d5 ♕c7 19 ♖ad1 ± Velimirović-Chandler, Sarajevo 1985.

d) 8...c5! 9 0-0 ♘c6 10 ♘c3 (10 c3 d5 11 dxc5 ♗xc5 12 ♘bd2 h6 13 ♘b3 ♗b6 =) 10...♘b4 11 ♖e1 (11 ♗c4 ♗f5 12 ♗b3 ♘e4 =) 11...h6 12 ♗f4 ♗e6 13 ♗f1 ♘bd5 (13...♘fd5 14 ♘xd5 ♗xd5 15 dxc5 dxc5 16 ♘e5 ♗f6 17 c3 ♘c6 18 ♘c4 ♗e6 19 ♕c2 ± Petrenko-Raetsky, Voronezh 1987; 13...♕b6!?) 14 ♘xd5 ♘xd5 15 ♗g3 ♗f6 16 c3 ♕b6 = Psakhis-Mikhalchishin, Minsk 1986.

8...♗g4

8...♘bd7 9 ♖e1 ♖e8 10 ♘bd2 ♘f8 11 ♘f1 ♘g6 12 ♘g3 c6 13 c3 ♗d7 14 h3 ♕c7 15 ♕c2 ♘d5 16 ♗d2 a5 = V.Spasov-Ki.Georgiev, Burgas 1992.

9 h3

9 ♗g5 h6 (9...c5 10 ♘bd2 ♘c6 11 ♘b3?! ♖e8 12 dxc5 dxc5 13 ♗xf6?!

♗xf6 14 ♘xc5 ♘d4 ∓ Adamek-Raetsky, Mlada Boleslav 1992) 10 ♗h4 ♘c6 11 h3 (11 c3 ♘d5 =) 11...♗xf3 12 ♕xf3 ♘xd4 13 ♕xb7 ♕d7 14 ♗xf6 ♗xf6 15 ♘c3 ♖ab8 16 ♕xa7 d5 gives Black compensation, Mukhutdinov-Makarychev, Moscow 1992.

9...♗h5 10 ♖e1

10 ♘c3 c5 11 d5 ♘a6 12 g4 ♗g6 13 ♗xg6 hxg6 14 ♗f4 ♘c7 15 a4 ♖e8 16 ♖e1 ♕d7 17 ♗g3 b6 ∞ Chuprikov-Sedushev, Czestochowa 1991.

10...♘c6

Or:

a) 10...♖e8 11 ♗g5 ♘c6 12 c3 ♘d5 13 ♗xe7 ♖xe7 = Smirin-Ivanchuk, Debrecen Echt 1992.

b) 10...c5!? and now:

b1) 11 dxc5 dxc5 12 g4 (12 ♗g5 ♘c6 13 ♘bd2 ♖e8 14 ♘f1 ♕b6 is slightly better for Black, Velibekov-Raetsky, Baku 1980) 12...♗g6 13 ♗xg6 hxg6 14 ♕xd8 ♗xd8 15 ♗f4 ♗a5! 16 c3 ♖d8 17 ♘bd2 ♘c6 18 ♘e4 (18 ♘c4 ♘d5 19 ♗d6 b5 20 ♘xa5 ♖xd6 21 ♘b7 ♖f6 22 ♘e5 ♘xe5 23 ♖xe5 ♘f4 ∞) 18...♘xe4 19 ♖xe4 d5 = Dolmatov-Raetsky, Podolsk 1992.

b2) 11 d5 ♘bd7 12 g4!? (12 ♘c3 ♘e5 13 ♗e2 ♗xf3 14 ♗xf3 ♘e8 15 ♗e2 f5 16 f4 ♘d7 17 ♗d3 ♘c7 18 ♕f3 ♗f6 19 ♘d1 b5 ∞ Shtyrenkov-Raetsky, Voronezh 1989) 12...♗g6 13 ♗xg6 hxg6 14 ♘c3 ♖e8 15 ♗f4 ±.

11 c3 ♕d7 12 ♘bd2 ♖fe8 13 ♘f1 ♗f8 14 ♖xe8 ♖xe8 15 ♗g5 ♘e4 16 ♗xe4 ♖xe4 17 ♘g3 ♗xf3 18 ♕xf3

½-½ Kavalek-Tal, Tilburg 1980.

E)

5 d4 *(D)*

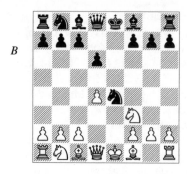

B

The main line is now 5...d5, which is discussed in subsequent chapters. Here we consider the alternatives, of which only one is significant:

5...♗e7

Or:

a) 5...g6?! 6 ♗d3 d5 (6...♘f6?! 7 0-0 ♗g7 8 ♖e1+ ♗e6 9 ♘g5 ±) 7 0-0 ♗g7 8 ♖e1 f5 9 c4 c6 10 ♕b3 ± Weiss-Blackburne, Nuremberg 1883.

b) 5...♘f6 6 c4 ♗e7 7 ♘c3 0-0 8 h3 ♖e8 9 ♗e3 ♗f5 10 g4 ♗g6 11 ♘h4 ♗e4 12 ♖g1 ♘d5 13 cxd5 ♗xh4 14 ♘xe4 ♖xe4 15 ♕f3 ± Velimirović-Reshevsky, Skopje 1976.

c) 5...♗g4 6 h3 ♗h5 7 ♕e2! (7 ♕d3 ♕e7!? 8 ♗e3 {8 ♕b5+? c6} 8...d5 9 a3?! (9 ♕b3!?) 9...♘c6 10 ♘bd2 0-0-0 ∓ Eisenberg-Marshall, Monte Carlo 1902) 7...♕e7 8 ♗e3 intending g4, ♗g2 and 0-0 ± (Polugaevsky).

6 ♗d3 ♘f6 *(D)*

6...♘g5 and now:

a) 7 0-0 ♘xf3+ (7...♗g4 8 ♗xg5 ♗xg5 9 ♕e1+! ♗e7 10 ♕e4 ±) 8 ♕xf3 ♘c6 9 c3 0-0 10 ♘d2 (10 ♘a3!? intending ♘c2-e3) 10...d5 11 ♖e1 ♗g5 (11...♗e6!?) 12 ♘f1 h6 13 ♗xg5 ♕xg5 14 h4! ± Klovans-Arkhipkin, Riga 1980.

b) 7 ♘xg5 ♗xg5 8 ♕e2+ and then:

b1) 8...♗e6 9 f4 ♗h4+ 10 g3 ♗e7 11 f5 ♗d5 12 0-0 0-0 13 ♘c3 ± Kots-Zamykhovsky, USSR 1962.

b2) 8...♔f8 9 ♗e3! (9 0-0 ♗xc1 10 ♖xc1 ♘c6 11 c3 ♕g5 12 ♘d2 ♗g4 13 ♕e3 ♕xe3 14 fxe3 ♖e8 15 e4 g6 ±/= Polovodin-Karasev, Leningrad 1985; 9 ♗xg5 ♕xg5 10 0-0 ♘c6 11 c3 ♗g4 12 ♕c2 ♖e8 13 f4 ♕e7 14 ♘d2 ♗e2 15 ♗xe2 ♕xe2 ∞ Yurtaev-Karasev, Gomel 1984) 9...♘c6 (9...♗xe3 10 fxe3 ♕h4+ 11 g3 ♕g5 12 ♘d2 ♗g4 13 ♕f2 ♘c6 14 c3 ♖e8 15 e4 ♖e6 16 e5 ± Ermolinsky-Karasev, Leningrad 1987) 10 ♘d2 ♘b4 11 ♗e4 ♗xe3 12 fxe3 d5 13 a3 ♘c6 (13...dxe4? 14 axb4 ±) 14 ♗d3 ♕h4+ 15 ♕f2 with a slight advantage for White, Velimirović-Murei, Moscow IZ 1982.

b3) 8...♗e7 9 0-0 0-0 10 ♕e4 f5 (10...g6!?) 11 ♕f3 ♘c6 12 c3 ♗g5 (12...♔h8!?) 13 ♕d5+ ♔h8 14 ♗xg5 ♕xg5 15 f4 ♕e7 16 ♕f3 ♗d7 17 d5 and White has a clear advantage, Makarychev-Bronstein, Moscow 1978.

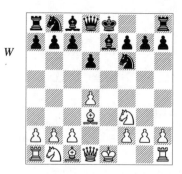

W

7 h3

Limiting the scope of Black's light-squared bishop.

7 0-0 is also very reasonable. 7...♗g4 (7...d5? 8 ♘e5 0-0 9 ♖e1 ♖e8 10 ♗f4 ♘bd7 11 ♘d2 ± Gaprindashvili-de Caro, Medellin 1974) and now:

a) 8 c3 0-0 9 ♘bd2 ♘bd7 (9...c5!? intending ...♘c6) 10 ♖e1 and then:

a1) 10...♖e8 11 ♕b3 ♖b8 12 h3 ♗h5 13 ♗f1! ♗f8 (13...d5!? intending ...♗d6) 14 ♖xe8 ♕xe8 15 g4! ♗g6 16 ♘h4 c6 17 ♘xg6 hxg6 18 ♘f3! ± Lanka-Shvarts, Podolsk 1991.

a2) 10...d5 11 ♘f1 ♖e8 12 h3 ♗h5 13 ♘g3 ♗g6 14 ♗xg6 hxg6 15 ♗f4 ♘f8 16 ♕c2 ♗d6 = Tarrasch-Blackburne, Vienna 1898.

b) 8 ♖e1 0-0 9 ♘bd2 and here:

b1) 9...d5 10 ♘f1 ♖e8 11 ♘g3 ♘bd7 12 h3 ±.

b2) 9...♘bd7 10 ♘f1 ♖e8 (alternatively, 10...♗h5!? 11 ♘g3 ♗g6 12 ♘f5 ±) 11 ♘g3 ♘f8 (11...♗f8!) 12 h3 ± Schlechter-Mason, London 1899.

b3) 9...♘c6 10 c3 ♕d7 11 ♕b3! ♖ab8 12 d5 ♘e5 13 ♘xe5 dxe5 14 ♘c4 (14 ♖xe5?! ♗d6 15 ♖e1 ♘xd5) 14...♕xd5 15 ♘xe5 ♕xb3 16 axb3 ♗c5 17 ♗c4 b5 18 b4 ± Kr.Georgiev-Popchev, Primorsko 1987.

b4) 9...♕d7 10 ♘f1 ♘c6 11 c3 ♖ae8 (11...♗f5 12 d5 ♘e5 13 ♗xf5 ♕xf5 14 ♘xe5 dxe5 15 ♘g3 ♕d7 16 ♖xe5 ♗d6 17 ♖e2 ♗xg3 18 hxg3 ♕xd5 19 ♕xd5 ♘xd5 20 c4 ±/± Stein-Nezhmetdinov, Kislovodsk 1972) 12 ♘g3 ♗d8 ±.

b5) 9...c5!? 10 h3 ♗h5 and then:

b51) 11 c4?! cxd4 12 g4? ♗g6 13 ♗xg6 hxg6 14 ♘xd4 d5 is slightly better for Black, Dvoretsky-Butnorius, Dubna 1970.

b52) 11 dxc5 dxc5 =.

b53) 11 ♘b3 ♘c6 12 ♗e2 ♖e8 13 c3 and now Black can play 13...♖c8!?, intending ...b6 and ...d5, or 13...h6!? intending ...♗f8. Instead, Black has problems after 13...♗f8 14 ♗g5 h6 15 ♗h4 ± or 13...♕b6?! 14 a4!? ♗f8 15 a5 ♕c7 16 ♗g5 ♘e4 17 ♗f4 ± Fedorowicz-Shirazi, USA 1992.

b54) 11 ♘f1 ♘c6 12 ♘g3 ♗xf3 (12...♗g6?! 13 c3! cxd4 {13...♖e8 14 d5 is also good for White} 14 ♘xd4! ♘xd4 15 ♗xg6 hxg6 16 ♕xd4 d5 17 ♗g5 ♕d6 18 ♖e5 ± Beliavsky-Barua, London Lloyds Bank 1985) 13 ♕xf3 ♘xd4 (13...cxd4 14 ♘f5 ±) 14 ♕xb7 ♖e8 15 ♘f5 ± Ljubojević-Smyslov, USSR-RoW (London) 1984.

b6) 9...♖e8 10 ♘f1 ♗f8 11 ♖xe8 ♕xe8 12 ♘g3 (12 ♗g5 ♘bd7 13 ♘g3 g6 14 h3 ♗e6 15 ♕d2 ♗g7 16 ♗h6 ♘f8 is equal, Hübner-Petrosian, Tilburg 1981) 12...♘c6 13 c3 intending h3 ±.

7...0-0 8 0-0 *(D)*

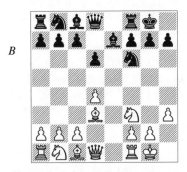

This position is rather awkward for Black. The voluntary retreat of the knight to f6 has given White a free hand with his development, with the result that Black is rather short of space. The move h3 has hindered the development of the c8-bishop, and with all the pieces still on the board Black has little breathing space. It is true that Black's position is without weaknesses, but this is little consolation as he has no real prospects of counterplay. While this position might appeal to those who like cramped positions, objectively speaking it gives White a relatively easy route to a slight advantage.

8...♖e8

Or:

a) 8...♗e6?! 9 c4 c6 10 ♘g5 ♘a6 11 ♘c3 ♘c7 12 f4! ± Tarrasch-Von Bardeleben, Vienna 1898.

b) 8...c6 9 c4 a6?! (9...♖e8 – 8...♖e8 9 c4 c6) 10 ♘c3 b5 11 ♗f4 bxc4 12 ♗xc4 ♘bd7 13 ♖c1 ♘b6 14 ♗b3 a5 15 ♖e1 ♗a6 16 ♗g5 ± Gavrikov-Osnos, Klaipeda 1983.

c) 8...c5 9 ♘c3 ♘c6 and then:

c1) 10 a3 cxd4 11 ♘e2 ♘e5 (11...d5 12 ♘exd4 ♗c5 13 ♗e3 ±) 12 ♘exd4 ♘xd3 13 ♕xd3 ± Short-Asmundsson, Iceland 1985.

c2) 10 ♖e1 and here:

c21) 10...a6 11 d5 ♘a7 (11...♘b4 12 ♗f1 ♗f5 13 ♖e2 ±) 12 a4 ♗d7 13 a5 ♖e8 14 ♗f1 h6 (14...♘b5!?) 15 ♗f4 ♗f8 16 ♖xe8 ♕xe8 17 ♗h2 ♕d8 18 ♘d2 ± Karpov-Smyslov, Moscow 1972.

c22) 10...♘b4 11 ♗f1! (11 ♗g5!?) 11...♗f5 12 ♖e2 ♖e8 13 a3 ♘a6 14 ♗g5 h6 15 ♗f4 ±.

d) 8...♘c6 9 c3 (9 c4 d5 10 ♘c3 – 5...d5 6 ♗d3 ♗e7 7 0-0 ♘c6 8 c4 ♘f6 9 ♘c3 0-0 10 h3; 9 ♖e1!? ♘b4 10 ♗f1 ♗f5 11 c3 ♘bd5 {11...♘c2? 12 ♘h4

+–} 12 ♘h4 ♗g6 13 c4 ♘b6 14 ♘xg6 hxg6 15 ♘c3 ± Thipsay-Barua, Delhi 1982) 9...♖e8 and here:

d1) 10 ♕c2 h6 11 ♘bd2 ♗f8 12 ♘c4 ♘d5 13 ♘e3 (13 a4 ♕f6 is unclear) 13...♘f4 is equal, Riumin-Goglidze, Moscow 1935.

d2) 10 ♗f4!? ♘h5 11 ♗h2 g6 12 ♖e1 ♗f8 (12...♘g7 13 d5 ±) 13 ♖xe8 ♕xe8 14 ♘bd2 ♗g7 15 ♕b3 ± Kavalek-Smyslov, Tilburg 1979.

d3) 10 ♖e1 and then:

d31) 10...h6 11 ♘bd2 ♗f8 12 ♘f1 ♖xe1 (12...d5 13 ♘e5 ♗d6 14 ♗f4 ±/±) King-Barua, London 1982) 13 ♕xe1 g6 14 ♘g3 ±.

d32) 10...♗d7 11 ♘bd2 (11 ♘a3!? h6 12 ♘c4 ♗f8 13 ♘e3 ± Matulović-Toth, Budapest 1972; 11 ♗f4 h6 12 ♘bd2 ♗f8 13 ♕c2 ± I.Polgar-Toth, Kecskemet 1972) 11...♗f8 12 ♘e4!? d5 13 ♘g3 ♗d6 14 ♖xe8+ ♕xe8 15 ♕c2 h6 16 ♗d2 ♕f8 17 ♘f5 ± Bronstein-Smyslov, Moscow 1971.

9 c4 (D)

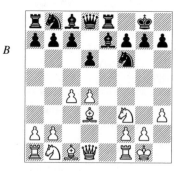

B

9...♘bd7

Or:

a) 9...♘c6 10 ♘c3 h6 11 ♖e1 ♗f8 (11...♘b4 12 ♗b1 c6 ±) 12 ♖xe8 ♕xe8

13 ♗f4 ♗d7 14 ♕d2 ± Fischer-Gheorghiu, Buenos Aires 1970.

b) 9...c5 10 d5 ♗f8 11 ♘c3 a6 12 a4 a5 13 ♗g5 h6 14 ♗h4 ♘a6 15 ♖c1 ♘b4 16 ♗b1 ± Fedorowicz-Smyslov, Dortmund 1986.

c) 9...c6 10 ♘c3 a6?! (10...♘bd7 – 9...♘bd7 10 ♘c3 c6) 11 b4 ♘bd7 12 ♗e3 ♘f8 13 a4 a5 14 b5 ♘g6 15 ♖e1 ♘h5 16 ♕d2 ± Tukmakov-Bronstein, Moscow 1971.

10 ♘c3 (D)

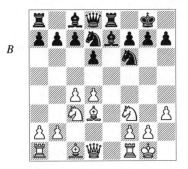

10...c6

10...♘f8!? and now:

a) 11 d5 ♘g6 12 ♖e1 ♗d7 and now 13 ♘d4 ± is better than 13 ♗g5?! ♘h5! = Tal-Smyslov, Moscow 1971.

b) 11 ♗f4!? ♘g6 12 ♗h2 c6 13 b4 a5 14 b5 ♗d7 15 ♖b1 ± Kurajica-Hammer, Biel 1981.

c) 11 ♖e1 ♘g6 (11...♘e6 12 b4 g6 13 ♖b1 c6 14 ♖b2!? ♗f8 15 ♖be2 ♗d7 16 ♗e3 ± Vasiukov-Rossetto, Camaguey 1974) 12 ♕c2 ♗d7 13 ♗g5 ♗c6 14 d5 ♗d7 15 ♖ad1 ± Arnason-Karpov, Oslo 1984.

11 ♖e1 ♘f8 12 ♕c2

Or:

a) 12 ♗e3!? a6 13 a4 a5 14 d5 gives White a slight advantage, Pilnik-Szmetan, Argentina 1972.

b) 12 ♗f4!? a6 and now:

b1) 13 b4?! b5! (13...♘e6 14 ♗h2 ♗f8 15 ♕b3 b5 16 d5! bxc4 17 ♗xc4 cxd5 18 ♘xd5 ♗b7 ±) 14 cxb5 (14 a4 bxc4 15 ♗xc4 d5 ∓) 14...axb5 15 a4 bxa4 16 ♖xa4 ♗e6 ∓.

b2) 13 ♕b3?! ♘e6 14 ♗h2 ♗f8 15 ♖e2 b5 16 ♕c2 ♗b7 17 ♖ae1 (17 a4 ♖b8!) 17...g6! ∞ Fischer-Petrosian, Buenos Aires Ct (5) 1971.

b3) 13 ♕d2 ± intending ♖e2 and ♖ae1.

b4) 13 d5!? ± intending 13...cxd5 14 cxd5 b5 15 b4 ♗b7 16 a4 ±.

12...♘g6 13 ♗g5 ♗d7 (D)

14 ♖e2

14 ♗f5?! ♕c8 15 ♗xd7 ♕xd7 = Prasad-Barua, Calcutta 1986.

14...♘h5 15 ♗d2 ♗f8 16 ♖ae1

± Timman-Radulov, Wijk aan Zee 1974.

8 4 ♘f3 ♘xe4 5 d4 d5 6 ♗d3 ♘c6

1 e4 e5 2 ♘f3 ♘f6 3 ♘xe5 d6 4 ♘f3 ♘xe4 5 d4 d5 6 ♗d3 ♘c6

There are two major alternatives here, which are the subject of later chapters: 6...♗d6 and 6...♗e7.

7 0-0 ♗g4 *(D)*

Note that 7...♗e7 transposes to 6...♗e7 7 0-0 ♘c6.

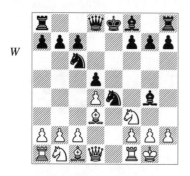

Black's intention behind putting the light-squared bishop on g4 is to increase his influence over the central dark squares. By delaying ...♗e7, Black accelerates his counterplay and exerts serious pressure on d4. Of course, there is an obvious drawback to Black delaying his kingside development: his king will remain in the centre for a while, and this gives White additional tactical possibilities in many lines. It is not so clear who benefits most from

these circumstances, but the effect is to sharpen the play, with White frequently sacrificing a pawn for the initiative.

8 c4

This is the most active continuation, although other moves are sometimes tried in practice:

a) 8 c3 and then:

a1) 8...♗d6 9 ♖e1 f5 10 h3 ♗h5 11 ♕b3 is best met by 11...♕d7! intending ...0-0-0 ∞, rather than 11...♕f6?! 12 ♕xd5 ♗xf3 13 gxf3 0-0-0 14 fxe4 ♗h2+ 15 ♔xh2 ♖xd5 16 exd5 ♕d6+ 17 ♔g1 ± Spraggett-Sieiro Gonzalez, Havana 1986.

a2) 8...♗e7 9 ♘bd2 (9 ♖e1 – 6...♗e7 7 0-0 ♘c6 8 ♖e1 ♗g4 9 c3) 9...♘xd2 (9...f5?! 10 ♕b3 ±) 10 ♗xd2 ♕d6 (10...0-0 11 h3 ♗h5 12 ♖e1 ± ♕d7?, Capablanca-Marshall, Havana 1913, and now Capablanca missed 13 ♘e5! +−) 11 ♖e1 0-0-0 =.

a3) 8...♕d7 9 ♖e1 f5 10 h3 ♗h5 11 ♘e5 ♘xe5 12 ♕xh5+ g6 13 ♕e2 ♘xd3 14 ♕xd3 0-0-0 15 ♘d2 ♗d6 = Csom-Abdul Rahim, Eger 1992.

b) 8 ♘c3 f5 9 h3 (9 ♖e1 ♗e7 10 h3 ♗xf3 11 gxf3 ♘xc3 12 bxc3 0-0 13 ♔h1 ♗d6 14 ♖g1 ♕h4 15 ♕f1 ♗f4 ∓ Ghinda-Forintos, Berlin 1987) 9...♗xf3 10 gxf3 ♘xc3 11 bxc3 ♕f6 12 ♖e1+

♗e7 13 c4 dxc4 14 ♗xc4 0-0-0 (not
14...♕xd4 15 ♕xd4 ♘xd4 16 ♗a3! ±)
15 c3 ♗d6 16 f4 ♖de8 17 ♗e3 h6 is
unclear, Speelman-Seirawan, Reykjavik 1990.

c) 8 ♖e1 and now:

c1) 8...f5?! 9 c4 ♗e7 (9...♗d6?! 10
cxd5 ♗xf3 11 ♕xf3 ♘xd4 12 ♕e3
♕f6 13 ♗xe4 fxe4 14 ♕xe4+ ♔f7 15
♗g5! ± Capablanca-Marshall, New
York 1910; 9...♗b4 10 ♘c3 0-0 11
cxd5 ♗xf3 12 gxf3! ♘xf2 13 ♔xf2
♕h4+ 14 ♔g2 ♗d6 15 f4 ♘xd4 16
♖e3 ± Dončević-Haubt, Bundesliga
1989/90) 10 cxd5 ♕xd5 11 ♘c3 ♘xc3
12 bxc3 0-0 (12...♗xf3 13 ♕xf3 ♕xf3
14 gxf3 ♖f8 15 d5 ♘a5 16 ♗a3 ♖f7
17 ♖e5 ♔d7 18 d6 ♘c6 19 ♖xe7+
♘xe7 20 dxe7 +– Liao-Saliman, Dubai
OL 1986) 13 ♖b1 with a distinct advantage for White.

c2) 8...♗e7 – *6...♗e7 7 0-0 ♘c6 8
♖e1 ♗g4*.

8...♘f6 *(D)*

In this line the retreat to f6 is not a
sign of passivity, but an indication that
Black wants to support d5 in order to
attack d4 undisturbed. The alternatives
are:

a) 8...♘b4? 9 cxd5 ♘xd3 10 ♕xd3
♕xd5 11 ♖e1 ±.

b) 8...♗xf3 9 ♕xf3 ♘xd4 10 ♕e3
♘f5 11 ♕h3 ♕d7 12 cxd5 ♘ed6 13
♘c3 0-0-0 14 ♗f4 ♘e7 15 ♕h5 ♘g6
16 ♗g3 ♔b8 17 a4 ± Psakhis-Martin-
ovsky, Philadelphia 1989.

c) 8...♗e7 – *6...♗e7 7 0-0 ♘c6 8
c4 ♗g4*.

Now:

A: 9 cxd5   143
B: 9 ♘c3   147

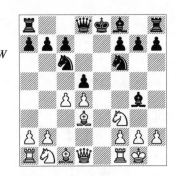

Or 9 ♖e1+ ♗e7 – *6...♗e7 7 0-0
♘c6 8 ♖e1 ♗g4 9 c4 ♘f6*.

A)

9 cxd5

This early exchange does not promise White much.

9...♗xf3 10 ♕xf3 ♕xd5

In general, Black is quite happy to
exchange queens in this line. In that
case, the slightly exposed position of
the black king is less relevant, while in
an endgame White's isolated d4-pawn
can become a serious weakness. Now:

A1: 11 ♖e1+   144
A2: 11 ♕e2+   146

Or:

a) 11 ♕g3?! ♗d6! 12 ♖e1+ ♔f8!
∓.

b) 11 ♕h3 ♕xd4 12 ♘c3 ♗d6 13
♖e1+ ♔f8 14 ♗f5 ♘e7 15 ♗e3 ♕c4 ∓
Saulin-Makarychev, Elista 1995.

c) 11 ♕xd5 ♘xd5 12 ♘c3 0-0-0
13 ♗c4!? (13 ♗e3 ♘ce7 =; 13 ♗e3 g6
=) 13...♘f6 (13...♘ce7 14 ♗d2 ♘xc3
15 bxc3 ♘d5 16 ♖fe1 c6 17 ♗b3 ♗a3
18 c4 ♘f6 19 ♗c3 ♖he8 20 f3 is
slightly better for White, Dvoirys-
Schwartzman, Groningen 1992) 14

♗xf7 ♘xd4 15 ♗g5 ♗b4 ∞ Ugrinović.

A1)
11 ♖e1+ ♗e7 *(D)*

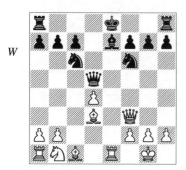

Now:
A11: 12 ♕xd5 144
A12: 12 ♕h3 146

Or 12 ♕g3 ♕xd4 13 ♘c3, and then:
a) 13...♖d8 14 ♗b5! ♗d7 (14...0-0?! 15 ♗h6 ♘h5 16 ♕f3 ±) 15 ♕xg7 ♖g8 16 ♕h6 ♘g4?! (16...♖g6!?) 17 ♕f4 ♔d8 18 ♕xd4 ♖xd4 19 ♗xc6 bxc6 20 f3! (20 h3?! ♘xf2! ∞ Hübner-Smyslov, Velden Ct (1) 1983) 20...♘f6 21 ♗e3 ♖b4 22 ♖ad1+ ♗d6 23 b3 ±.

b) 13...0-0! 14 ♘b5 (14 ♖d1 ♕g4! 15 ♕xc7 ♗c5 16 h3 ♕h4 17 ♕f4 ♕xf4 18 ♗xf4 = Mikhalchishin-Halasz, Budapest 1984) and here:
b1) 14...♕b4 ∞.
b2) 14...♕d7 15 ♖d1 ♗d6 (alternatively, 15...♕g4 16 ♕xg4 ♘xg4 17 ♗e2 ♘f6 18 ♘xc7 ♖ad8 19 ♗e3 ♗d6 20 ♘b5 ♗e5 21 ♘xa7 ♘d4 22 ♗d3 ♘g4 ∞ Kasparov-Wolff, London simul 1984) 16 ♕h4 ♘e5 with an equal position.

b3) 14...♕g4!? 15 ♕xg4 (15 ♕xc7 ♗c5 ∓; 15 ♘xc7!? ♖ad8 16 ♕xg4 ♘xg4 17 ♗e2! ♘f6 =) 15...♘xg4 and now White's best is 16 ♗e2! =, rather than 16 ♘xc7? ♗c5! ∓ or 16 ♗f5?! ♘f6 17 ♘xc7 ♖ad8 ∓ Sax-Yusupov, Thessaloniki OL 1984.

A11)
12 ♕xd5 ♘xd5
The queen exchange has been played quite often, but it presents Black with no problems at all.
13 ♘c3 *(D)*

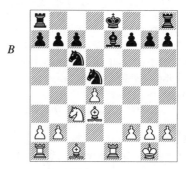

13...0-0-0
Or 13...♘db4!? (the text-move is quite safe for Black, but this sharper continuation is also playable) 14 ♗e4 ♘xd4 15 ♗e3 (15 ♖b1 c6 16 ♗e3 ♘e6 17 a3 ♘a6 18 b4 0-0 19 b5 ½-½ Sax-Ristić, Smederevska Palanka 1982; 15 ♗f4?! ♘e6 ∓), and here:
a) 15...♘dc2? 16 a3.
b) 15...♘bc6? 16 ♗xd4 ♘xd4 17 ♗xb7 ♖b8 18 ♘d5! is much better for White, Wiedenkeller-Schüssler, Swedish Ch 1983.
c) 15...♖d8 16 ♗xd4 ♖xd4 17 a3 ♘c6 18 ♘b5 ♖d2 and then:

c1) 19 ♗xc6+ bxc6 20 ♘xa7 ♔d7 21 ♘xc6 ♗c5! 22 ♘e5+ ♔c8 ∓.

c2) 19 ♘xc7+ ♔d7! (19...♔d8?! 20 ♘b5 ± Abramović-Rukavina, Yugoslavia 1985) 20 ♘b5 ♖d8 21 ♖ad1 ♖xd1 22 ♖xd1+ ♔c8 23 ♖xd8+ ♔xd8 is equal.

c3) 19 ♖ad1! ♖xd1! (19...♖xb2? 20 ♗xc6+ bxc6 21 ♘xc7+ ♔f8 22 ♖d8+!) 20 ♖xd1 h5 21 ♘xc7+ ♔f8 22 ♘b5 a6 23 ♘c3 ♔e8 24 ♗f5 ♖h6 25 ♖d7 g6 26 ♗h3 g5 27 ♗f5 ♖f6 28 ♖d5 ♖d6 29 ♗c8 ± Ivanović-Rukavina, Yugoslavia 1985.

d) 15...c5! and then:

d1) 16 ♘d5? ♘xd5 17 ♗xd5 ♘c2 18 ♗xb7 (18 ♗xc5? ♘xe1 19 ♖xe1 0-0-0! ∓) 18...♖b8 19 ♗c6+ ♔f8 20 b3 h5 ∓.

d2) 16 ♗xb7 ♖d8! 17 ♖ad1 ♘bc2 18 ♖f1 ♖b8 19 ♗e4 ♖xb2 20 ♗c1 ♖b8 21 ♗f4 ♖d8 22 ♖d2 ♘b4 23 ♖e1 0-0! 24 ♗xh7+ ♔xh7 25 ♖xe7 = Beliavsky-Timman, Bugojno 1984.

d3) 16 ♗xd4! cxd4 17 ♘b5 ♖d8 18 a3 ♘c6 19 ♗xc6+ bxc6 20 ♘xa7! ♖d6! 21 ♖ac1 ♔d7 22 ♘xc6 ♗f6! 23 ♘b4 d3 24 ♖cd1 d2! 25 ♖e2 ♖e8! 26 ♖exd2 (26 ♔f1 ♖xe2 27 ♔xe2 ♗xb2 28 a4 ♗c3) 26...♖e1+ 27 ♖xe1 ♖xd2 gives Black compensation, L.Schneider-Forintos, Borås 1986.

14 ♗e4

Or:

a) 14 ♗e3 ♗f6 15 ♖ad1 ♘b6 (Filipenko-Mikhalchishin, Lvov 1995) 16 ♘e2 ♖he8 ∓.

b) 14 ♘xd5 ♖xd5 15 ♗e4 ♖xd4 16 ♗xc6 bxc6 17 ♗e3 ♖d5 18 ♗xa7 ♗f6 19 ♖ac1 ♔b7 20 ♗c5 ♖d2 ∓ Hoffman-Schwartzman, Dortmund 1991.

14...♗b4! *(D)*

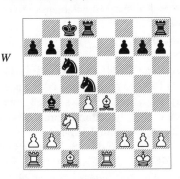

This is the key tactical point which justifies Black's play. By pinning the knight, Black can maintain his blockade on d5.

15 ♗d2

15 ♗xd5 ♖xd5! 16 ♘xd5 ♗xe1 17 ♘xc7 (17 ♗f4 ♗a5 ∓) 17...♗xf2+ (17...♗a5!? 18 d5 ♘d4 19 ♗e3 ♘c2 20 ♖c1 ♘xe3 21 ♘b5+! ♔b8 22 fxe3 ♗d2 23 ♖d1 ♗xe3+ 24 ♔f1 ♖d8! 25 ♔e2 ♗f4 26 ♔f3 ♗e5 27 ♘c3 f5 28 h3 ♔c7 ∓ Borsavolgi-Forintos, Budapest 1990) 18 ♔xf2 ♔xc7 19 ♗f4+ ♔d7 20 ♖c1 ♔e6 = Ljubojević-Tal, Bugojno 1984.

15...♘f6

Or:

a) 15...♘b6!? intending to continue ...♘c4.

b) After 15...♘ce7!? White should settle for 16 a3, with equality, rather than trying 16 ♘xd5 ♘xd5 17 ♗xd5 ♗xd2 ∓.

c) 15...♘xd4!? 16 ♘xd5 (better than 16 ♗xd5?! ♗xc3 17 bxc3 ♘c2! ∓) 16...♗xd2 17 ♖ed1 c6 18 ♖xd2 cxd5 19 ♖xd4 =.

16 ♗xc6

16 a3 ♘xe4 17 ♖xe4 ♗xc3 18 bxc3 ♘a5 = Ehlvest-Mikhalchishin, Lvov 1984.

16...bxc6

Now:

a) 17 a3 ♖xd4! 18 axb4 (18 ♗e3!? ♗xc3 19 bxc3 gives White compensation) 18...♖xd2 19 ♖xa7 ♖e8! and Black is slightly better, Lobron-Mikhalchishin, Dortmund 1984.

b) 17 ♗e3 ♘d5 18 ♖ac1 ♘xe3 (18...♖he8 19 ♖e2 ♘xe3 20 fxe3 c5 is equal, Am.Rodriguez-Seirawan, Biel IZ 1985) 19 fxe3 c5 = Kamsky-Karpov, Linares 1994.

A12)

12 ♕h3 (D)

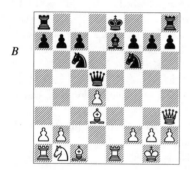

White quite often sacrifices his d-pawn in this line, but this version of the sacrifice is not especially dangerous for Black and he equalizes without difficulty.

12...♘xd4

Alternatively, 12...♕xd4!? 13 ♘c3 ♖d8! (13...0-0?! 14 ♗g5 h6 15 ♖ad1 ±; 13...♕d7?! 14 ♗f5 gives White compensation) 14 ♗f5 (14 ♗b5!?), and then:

a) 14...g6 15 ♗e3 ♕b4 16 a3 ♕b3?! (better is 16...♕c4) 17 ♗h6 gxf5 (not 17...♖g8? 18 ♘e4!) 18 ♗g7 ♖g8 19 ♗xf6 ♕c4 20 ♖e3 ♖g6 21 ♗xe7 ♘xe7 22 ♖ae1 ♖e6 23 ♕xh7 ± Ivanović-Forintos, Metz 1988.

b) 14...h5!? 15 ♕g3 ♔f8 16 ♗e3 (16 ♕xc7!?) 16...♕b4 17 a3 ♕a5 18 ♕f3 g6 19 ♗c2 h4 gives Black a slight advantage, Velimirović-Kurajica, Bela Crkva 1984.

c) 14...0-0 15 ♗e3 ♕b4 ½-½ Korchnoi-Smyslov, Beersheba 1990.

13 ♘c3 ♕d7!?

Now:

a) 14 ♕g3?! 0-0 15 ♗h6 ♘e8 ∓.

b) 14 ♕xd7+ ♔xd7 (14...♘xd7? 15 ♘d5 ♘e6 16 ♖xe6! ±) 15 ♗e3 ♘e6 16 ♖ad1 gives White compensation, Kasparov-Karpov, Moscow Wch (28) 1984/5.

A2)

11 ♕e2+ (D)

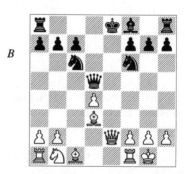

White removes his queen from attack with gain of tempo. However, this line, like Line A1, offers White little against accurate defence.

11...♗e7

Black can even play 11...♕e6, since his rapid development and pressure against d4 compensate for the isolated e6-pawn: 12 ♕xe6+ (12 ♗e3 0-0-0 13 ♗c4 ♕g4 14 ♕xg4+ ♘xg4 15 ♗xf7 ♘xd4 16 ♗xd4 ♖xd4 17 ♘c3 ♗c5 18 ♖ac1 b6 is equal, Schmittdiel-Howell, Biel 1993) 12...fxe6 13 ♗b5 0-0-0 14 ♗xc6 bxc6 15 ♗e3 ♘d5 16 ♖c1 c5 17 dxc5 ♘xe3 18 fxe3, and now:

a) 18...♖d5 19 b4 g6 (19...♖d3!? 20 ♔f2 g6) 20 ♘a3 ∞.

b) 18...♗xc5 19 ♖xc5 ♖d1+ 20 ♔f2 ♖f8+ 21 ♔g3 ♖ff1 ∞.

c) 18...♖d3 19 ♔f2 g6 intending 20 ♔e2 ♖xe3+ 21 ♔xe3 ♗h6+.

12 ♗b5 ♕d6!

Taking the pawn by 12...♕xd4 is too risky, as White replies 13 ♘c3 ± with a dangerous initiative.

13 ♘c3

13 ♖e1 0-0 14 ♗xc6 bxc6 = 15 ♕xe7?? ♖fe8 −+.

13...0-0 14 ♗xc6 bxc6

White's pawn-structure may be marginally superior to Black's, but it is hard for White to gain any advantage from this since Black's pieces are quite active.

15 ♖d1!

Or:

a) 15 ♗g5 h6 16 ♗h4 ♕xd4 17 ♕xe7 ♕xh4 18 ♕xc7 ♕b4 =.

b) 15 ♗e3 ♘d5 16 ♖ac1 (16 ♖fc1 ♘xe3! 17 fxe3 ♖fe8 intending ...♗g5 ∞) and here:

b1) 16...♖ab8?! 17 b3 ♘xe3 18 ♕xe3 ♖fd8 19 ♖fd1 c5 (19...♗f8 20 g3 ± Mestel-Plaskett, London 1986; 19...♗f6 20 ♘e4 ♗xd4 21 ♘xd6 ♗xe3 22 fxe3 ♖xd6 23 ♖xd6 cxd6 24 ♖xc6

♖d8 25 ♖c7 ±) 20 d5 ♗f8 21 ♘e4 ± Short-Plaskett, London 1986.

b2) 16...♖ae8 17 ♕f3! ♕d7 18 ♘xd5 ±.

b3) 16...♖fe8 17 ♘xd5!? (17 ♕f3 ♕d7 18 ♘xd5 cxd5 19 ♗f4 c6 is level) 17...♕xd5! (17...cxd5 18 ♕c2 ±) 18 ♕c4 ♗d6 19 b3 (19 ♕xc6 ♕xa2 =) 19...♗e6! 20 g3 ♕f5!? (20...♖ae8?! 21 ♕xd5 cxd5 22 ♖c6 ±) 21 ♕c2 (21 ♕xc6 ♖ae8 22 d5 ♖e4 23 ♗c5 h5! gives Black compensation) 21...♕h5 22 ♕xc6 ♖ae8 23 ♕g2 ♖e4 with compensation for Black, Timman-Yusupov, Tilburg Ct (2) 1986.

15...♖fe8 16 ♕f3 ♘d5

16...♖ab8 17 b3 (17 ♗f4!? ♕d7 18 d5 cxd5 19 ♘xd5 ♘xd5 20 ♖xd5 ♗d6 21 ♗xd6 cxd6 22 b3 ±) 17...♕d7 18 d5! cxd5 19 ♘xd5 ♘xd5 20 ♖xd5 ♗f6 21 ♗e3 ♕xd5 22 ♕xd5 ♗xa1 23 g3 ± Lobron-Ki.Georgiev, San Bernardino 1987.

17 ♘xd5

Now:

a) 17...♕xd5 18 ♕xd5 cxd5 19 ♗f4 ± c6?! (19...♗d6?! 20 ♗xd6 cxd6 21 ♔f1 ±; 19...♗f6!? 20 ♗xc7 ♖e4 ±; 19...♖ac8!? 20 ♖ac1 c5 ±) 20 ♖ac1 ♖ac8 21 ♔f1 f6 22 ♖d3 ♔f7 23 f3 is slightly better for White, Short-Olafsson, Reykjavik 1987.

b) 17...cxd5 18 ♗f4 ♕d7 19 ♖ac1 c6 intending ...♗f6 and ...♖e6 =. It is true that Black has a backward c-pawn, but his pressure against d4 and more active bishop offer sufficient counterplay.

B)

9 ♘c3 *(D)*

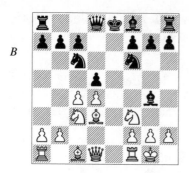

Simple development is a more critical test of Black's system. White is prepared to offer his d-pawn to speed up his development and start an attack against the centralized black king. The resulting play is very complicated and Black must play very accurately to avoid an early disaster. Moreover, even if Black plays precisely White can still retain a modest advantage.

9...♗xf3

Other continuations can lead to serious difficulties for Black:

a) 9...♗e7 10 cxd5 ♘xd5 11 ♗e4 ±.

b) 9...♘xd4 10 ♕e1+! (10 cxd5 ♘xf3+ 11 gxf3 ♗d7 12 ♖e1+ ♗e7 13 ♕e2 is also good) 10...♗e7 (10...♘e6 11 ♘e5 ♗b4 12 ♘xg4 ♘xg4 13 ♗f5 ♗xc3 14 bxc3 ♘f6 15 ♗a3 ±) 11 ♘xd4 dxc4 12 ♘f5 cxd3 13 ♘xg7+ ♔f8 14 ♗h6 ♔g8 15 f3 gives White the initiative.

10 ♕xf3 ♘xd4

This is the critical position, upon which the viability of this variation depends. White now has several possibilities:

B1: 11 ♖e1+	148	
B2: 11 ♕h3	150	
B3: 11 ♕e3+	151	

Or:

a) 11 ♕d1 ♘e6 12 cxd5 ♘xd5 13 ♗b5+ c6 14 ♘xd5 cxb5 ∞.

b) 11 ♕g3 ♘e6 12 ♖e1 ♗e7 13 cxd5 ♘xd5 14 ♗f5 ♘xc3 15 bxc3 ♕d7! 16 ♗xe6 fxe6 17 ♕xg7 0-0-0 18 ♕e5 ♖hf8 =.

B1)
11 ♖e1+ *(D)*

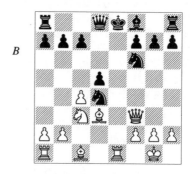

This check is tempting, but after the reply Black is only one move away from castling. Current theory considers it better not to commit the rook to e1, since in some lines it may be better off on d1.

11...♗e7 12 ♕d1!?
Or:

a) 12 ♕e3?! dxc4 13 ♗xc4 ♘c2 is much better for Black.

b) 12 ♕h3?! dxc4 13 ♗xc4 ♘c2 14 ♗g5 ♘xe1 15 ♗xf6 ♗xf6 16 ♖xe1+ ♔f8 17 ♘d5 ∞ Novostruev-Lunev, Oriol 1992.

c) 12 ♕g3 dxc4 (12...♘e6! ∓ Kavalek) 13 ♗xc4 (13 ♕xg7? ♘f3+! 14 ♔h1 ♖g8 15 ♕xf6 ♘xe1 –+) 13...0-0 (13...♘c2? 14 ♕xg7 ♖f8 15 ♗g5 +–; 13...♘f5? 14 ♕h3 ♘d6 15 ♗g5! ♘xc4

16 ♖ad1 ♕c8 17 ♕h4 ±) 14 ♗g5 and now:

c1) 14...♘c2? 15 ♖xe7!.

c2) 14...h6? 15 ♖xe7 ♘f5 (15...♕xe7 16 ♘d5 ♕d6 17 ♘xf6+ ♔h8 18 ♕h3 +–; 15...hxg5 16 ♕xc7 ±) 16 ♖xf7 ♘xg3 (16...♖xf7 17 ♗xf6 ♕xf6 18 ♕xc7 +–) 17 ♖xf6+ ♔h8 18 ♖xh6+ gxh6 19 ♗xd8 ♖axd8 20 hxg3 ±.

c3) 14...♗d6 and here:

c31) 15 ♕h3!? ♕d7 (15...h6 16 ♗xh6 ±) 16 ♕h4 (16 ♕xd7 ♘xd7 17 ♖ad1 ♘c6 = Shteinberg-Voronkov, USSR 1976) 16...♘f5 (16...♕g4? 17 ♕xg4 ♘xg4 18 ♖e4 +–) 17 ♕h3 ♘d4 is equal.

c32) 15 ♕h4 h6! 16 ♗xf6 (not 16 ♗xh6? ♘f5 –+) 16...♕xf6 17 ♕xf6 gxf6 18 ♖e4?! (18 ♘e4? ♘c2 –+; 18 ♖ad1!? ♘c6 ∓) 18...c5! 19 ♖h4 ♔g7 20 ♘e4 (20 ♖g4+ ♔h7 21 ♗d3+ f5) 20...♗e7 21 ♘g3 f5 22 ♖h3 ♗d6 23 f4 b5 24 ♗d3 c4 25 ♗xf5 ♖fe8 ∓ Lobron-Karpov, Hanover 1983.

12...♘e6! *(D)*

Or: 12...0-0 13 cxd5 ±; 12...dxc4 13 ♗xc4 0-0 (13...c5 14 ♕a4+) 14 ♖xe7 ♕xe7 15 ♕xd4 ±; 12...c6 13 ♗e3 ♘e6 14 cxd5 ♘xd5 15 ♘xd5 ♕xd5 16 ♕c2 gives White compensation.

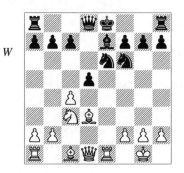

The text-move both removes the knight from an exposed position, and blocks the e-file to prevent White from exploiting the poorly defended bishop on e7. Now White has nothing better than to play to regain the sacrificed pawn, after which the game peters out to sterile equality.

13 cxd5 ♘xd5 14 ♗b5+ c6 15 ♘xd5 cxb5 16 ♕b3

Or:

a) 16 ♗f4 ♘xf4! (16...♗d6?! 17 ♗xd6 ♕xd6 18 ♘f6+ ♔e7 19 ♘d5+ ♔f8 20 ♕f3 gives White compensation; 16...0-0? 17 ♘xe7+ ♕xe7 18 ♗d6 +–; 16...♖c8? 17 ♗e5! ±) 17 ♖xe7+ ♔f8 18 ♖e5 ♕d6! 19 ♖f5 (19 ♕d4? f6) 19...♖d8 20 ♖xf4 (20 ♕f3 ♘xd5 21 ♖d1 ♕e6 22 ♖fxd5 ♖xd5 23 ♕xd5 ♕xd5 24 ♖xd5 ♔e7 =) 20...♕xd5 =.

b) 16 ♕h5!? 0-0 17 ♗e3!? (17 ♘xe7+ ♕xe7 18 ♕xb5 =) 17...♗g5 18 ♖ad1 ♗xe3 19 ♖xe3 ♖c8! (19...♕g5 20 ♕xg5 ♘xg5 21 f4 ±) and then:

b1) 20 ♖ed3 gives White compensation.

b2) 20 ♖h3 h6 (20...♘g5 21 ♖g3 h6 ∞) 21 ♖g3 ♔h8 ∞.

b3) 20 f4 ♖c5 21 b4 (not 21 ♖e5? ♖xd5! –+ Gelfand-Yusupov, Horgen 1994) 21...♖c4 22 f5 (22 ♖ed3? ♘xf4 23 ♘xf4 ♕b6+) 22...♖h4 23 ♕e2 ♘d4 24 ♕f2 ♕xd5 25 ♕xh4 ♘e2+ ∓.

16...0-0

16...a6? is bad in view of 17 ♗e3 0-0 18 ♖ad1 ±.

17 ♘xe7+

17 ♕xb5? ♗c5!.

17...♕xe7 18 ♕xb5

The minor inconvenience of having the knight pinned cannot affect the basic evaluation of the position. Black will bring his rooks to the open files, when further exchanges will make the draw almost inevitable:

a) The immediate 18...♖fd8 fails to equalize: 19 ♗e3 ♕d7 20 ♕xd7 ♖xd7 21 ♖ad1 gives White a slight advantage.

b) 18...a6! is more accurate: 19 ♕b3 (19 ♕e5!?) 19...♖fd8 (19...♖ac8?! 20 ♗d2 ♖fd8 21 ♗c3 ±) 20 ♗e3 ♖ac8 (20...b5 =) 21 ♖ac1 h6 (21...♖xc1 22 ♖xc1 ♕d7 23 h3 h6 24 ♕c3 ♘d4 = Panchenko-Novikov, Lvov 1987) 22 h3 ♘d4! ½-½ Kasparov-Karpov, Moscow Wch (15) 1985; 23 ♗xd4 ♖xc1 24 ♖xc1 ♖xd4 =.

B2)

11 ♕h3 (D)

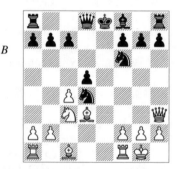

This is a far more dangerous continuation. By attacking h7, White makes it hard for Black to castle kingside, while moves such as cxd5 and ♖e1 will harass the enemy king if it stays in the centre. White has good chances to retain some advantage in this line.

11...dxc4

Or:

a) 11...c6?! 12 ♖e1+ ♗e7 13 ♗g5 ♘e6 (13...dxc4 14 ♗xf6 gxf6 15 ♗xc4 ±) 14 ♗xf6 ♗xf6 15 cxd5 cxd5 16 ♗f5 ±.

b) 11...♗e7 12 cxd5!? (12 ♖e1 dxc4 13 ♗xc4 0-0 ∞; 12 ♗g5 dxc4 13 ♗xc4 – 11...dxc4 12 ♗xc4 ♗e7 13 ♗g5) 12...♘xd5 13 ♖e1 c6 (13...♘e6 14 ♗g6! ♘df4 15 ♗xf4 ♘xf4 16 ♗xf7+ ♔xf7 17 ♕f5+ ±) 14 ♗g5 ♘e6 15 ♗xe7 ♕xe7 16 ♘xd5 cxd5 17 ♗f5 0-0-0 18 ♕g3 ♕d6! 19 ♕xg7 ♔b8 20 ♕xf7 ♘d4 21 ♖e7 (J.Horvath-Forintos, Budapest 1987) 21...♕b6 22 ♗d3 is slightly better for White.

c) 11...♘e6 12 cxd5 ♘xd5 and now:

c1) 13 ♖e1 ♘xc3 14 bxc3 ♕f6 15 ♗f5 0-0-0!? 16 ♗xe6+ fxe6 17 ♖xe6 ♔b8! ∓.

c2) 13 ♗g6!? is a spectacular move, but the consequences are not entirely clear:

c21) 13...♘xc3? 14 ♕xe6+ ♕e7 15 ♗xf7+ ♔d8 16 ♗g5 +−.

c22) 13...♘e7 14 ♖d1 ♕c8 15 ♗c2 is much better for White.

c23) 13...♕f6 14 ♗xf7+ ♔xf7 15 ♘xd5 ♕e5 16 ♕f3+ ♔g8 17 ♗f4 ±.

c24) 13...♘df4 14 ♗xf4 ♘xf4 15 ♕e3+ ♗e7 16 ♗xf7+ ♔xf7 17 ♕xf4+ gives White a clear advantage.

c25) 13...fxg6 14 ♕xe6+ ♘e7 15 ♖d1 ♕c8 16 ♕b3 ±.

c26) 13...♕d7?! 14 ♖e1! (14 ♖d1 c6 15 ♗e4 ♘ec7 is unclear) 14...0-0-0 (14...♗e7 15 ♖xe6 ♘xc3 16 ♗g5 ♘d5 17 ♗xf7+! wins for White) 15 ♘xd5 hxg6 (15...fxg6 16 ♖xe6 ♕xd5 17 ♗g5! +−; 15...♖xd5 16 ♗xf7 +−) 16 ♕xh8 ♗b4 17 ♕xd8+ ♕xd8 18 ♘xb4 a5 19 ♘c2 ♕d3 20 ♘a3 +– Nadanian-Sharbatov, corr. 1992-3.

c27) 13...hxg6! 14 ♕xh8 ♘xc3 15 bxc3 ♕d3 16 ♗a3 0-0-0 17 ♗xf8 ♖xf8 ± Dolmatov, Dvoretsky.

c3) 13 ♗b5+! (this is best; White gains an advantage with absolutely no risk) 13...c6 14 ♖d1 cxb5 (14...♘ec7 15 ♘xd5 ♘xd5 16 ♕b3! ±) 15 ♖xd5 ♕c8 16 ♗e3! ♗b4 (16...♗e7 17 ♖c1 ±) 17 ♘xb5 0-0 18 ♖c1 ♕e8 19 ♕g4 ♗e7 20 ♘c7 ♘xc7 21 ♖xc7 ± Pletanek-Dufek, Czech corr. Cht 1992.

12 ♗xc4 ♗e7

Black cannot conveniently exchange queens: 12...♕d7 13 ♖e1+ (13 ♕xd7+ ♘xd7 14 ♗g5 gives White compensation) 13...♗e7 (13...♔d8 14 ♕xd7+ ♔xd7 15 ♖d1 c5 16 ♗xf7 ±) 14 ♕xd7+ ♘xd7 (14...♔xd7 15 ♗xf7 ±) 15 ♘d5 ♘e6 16 ♖xe6! ±.

13 ♗g5

Now Black has to choose whether to castle kingside or queenside. The former enables Black to keep his extra pawn, but White obtains dangerous attacking chances. It is much safer to castle queenside, but in this case Black has to return the extra pawn.

13...♕c8

Or:

a) 13...♕d7 14 ♕xd7+ ♔xd7 15 ♖ad1 c5 16 ♘b5 ±.

b) 13...0-0 14 ♖ad1 c5 (14...h6 15 ♗xh6! gxh6 16 ♖d3! ♘h7 17 ♕g4+ ±) 15 ♖fe1 h6 (15...♖e8 16 ♗b5! ♘xb5 17 ♖xd8 ♗xd8 18 ♖xe8+ ♘xe8 19 ♗xd8 ♖xd8 20 ♔f1 ±) and then:

b1) 16 ♖xe7?! ♕xe7! (16...hxg5 17 ♖xb7 ±) 17 ♘d5 ♘xd5! 18 ♗xe7 ♘xe7 ∞.

b2) 16 ♗xh6! gxh6 17 ♕xh6 ♘h7 18 ♖d3 ♗g5 19 ♕h5 (19 ♖g3 ♘f5 20 ♕g6+ ♘g7) 19...♕f6 and here:

b21) 20 ♖g3 and now:

b211) 20...♖ae8?! 21 ♘e4 ♔h8? (21...♕g7 22 h4! ±; 21...♔g7!) 22 h4! and White wins, Kupreichik-Yusupov, USSR Ch (Minsk) 1987.

b212) 20...♘f5! 21 ♘e4 ♕g7 22 ♖g4 (22 ♖xg5 ♘xg5 23 ♘xg5 ♘d6!) 22...♘h6! 23 ♖g3 ♘f5 =.

b22) 20 ♖h3! ♕g7 21 f4! ♗xf4 22 ♘d5 ♗g5 (22...♗d6?! 23 ♘e4 ♘e6 24 ♖g4 ♘eg5 25 ♖xg5! ♘xg5 26 ♖g3! +–) 23 ♘e7+ ♗xe7 24 ♖xe7 ♘f6 25 ♕xc5 ± Thesing-Autenrieth, Budapest 1987.

14 ♕d3 ♕g4!?

14...♘e6 and then:

a) 15 ♗xe6?! fxe6 16 ♖fe1 ♕d7 17 ♕c4 0-0-0 18 ♖xe6 (18 ♖ad1 ♕c6 19 ♕xc6 bxc6 20 ♖xd8+ ♔xd8 21 ♖xe6 ♔d7 22 ♖e2 ♖b8 23 g3 ♖b4 ∞ Vehi-Forintos, Barcelona 1987) 18...♘d5! 19 ♗xe7 ♕xe6 20 ♗xd8 ♖xd8 21 ♖d1 c6 22 ♘xd5 b5! 23 ♕f4 (23 ♘b6+ ♔b7!) 23...♖xd5 24 ♕f8+ ♔b7 25 ♕xg7+ ♔b6 = J.Horvath-Forintos, Kecskemet 1987.

b) 15 ♗xf6! ♗xf6 16 ♘d5 ♗d8 17 f4 gives White the initiative.

15 ♗xf6 gxf6

15...♗xf6 is bad in view of 16 ♖fe1+ ♘e6 17 ♗xe6 fxe6 18 ♕b5+ ±.

16 h3 ♕d7 17 ♖ad1 0-0-0 18 ♗xf7

White's chances are slightly better.

B3)

11 ♕e3+ (D)

An interesting idea of Kasparov's. White checks with his queen on the e-file, keeping his rook for a later ♖d1. In this line too White has good prospects of retaining at least a slight advantage.

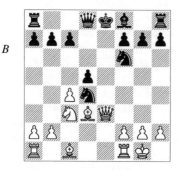

11...♘e6 12 cxd5 ♘xd5

12...♗c5 can be met by 13 ♕f3 ♘d4 14 ♖e1+ ♔f8 15 ♕f4 ♘xd5 16 ♘xd5 ♕xd5 17 ♕xc7 ♘e6 18 ♕g3 ♖d8 19 ♖d1 h5 20 h4 ±.

13 ♘xd5 ♕xd5 14 ♗e4 ♕b5 15 a4

15 ♕f3? ♘d4!.

15...♕a6

Black holds on to his extra pawn and hopes to complete his development in peace.

15...♕c5?! is suspect in view of 16 ♗xb7 ♖b8 17 b4! ♕b6 (17...♕xe3 18 ♗c6+ ♔e7 19 ♗xe3 ±) 18 ♕xb6 cxb6 19 ♗c6+ ♔d8 20 ♖d1+ ♔c7 21 b5 ♖d8 22 ♖xd8 ♘xd8 23 ♗d5 ♘e6 24 ♗xe6 fxe6 25 ♗f4+ ± Ivanchuk-Serper, Sochi jr 1986.

16 ♖d1!

White stops Black castling queenside and establishes control over the d-file. Otherwise:

a) 16 ♕f3 can be met by 16...♘d4! 17 ♕e3, when 17...0-0-0 ∓ is better than 17...♘e2+?! 18 ♔h1 ♘g3+ 19

hxg3 ♕xf1+ 20 ♔h2, when White has compensation.

b) The immediate 16 b4 doesn't give White anything either: 16...♗xb4 17 ♖b1 ♗c5 18 ♕f3 c6 19 ♖xb7 0-0 =.

c) 16 ♗d3 ♕b6 17 ♕h3 with an unclear position.

16...♗e7

Or:

a) Makarychev's recommendation 16...♗d6 (intending ...0-0-0) deserves attention, although 17 b4! gives White the initiative.

b) 16...♗c5 leads to interesting play after 17 ♕f3, and now:

b1) 17...♖d8 18 ♖xd8+ ♘xd8 19 ♗f4 ♘e6 20 ♗e5! has the point that 20...0-0 loses to 21 ♕f5, while 20...♘g5 21 ♕f5 is also winning for White.

b2) 17...c6 18 ♖d7!! (Nunn) and now:

b21) 18...♔xd7? 19 ♕xf7+ and here:

b211) 19...♗e7 20 ♗f5 ♕c4 (20...c5 21 ♗g5 ♕d6 22 ♗xe6+ ♕xe6 23 ♖d1+ +−; 20...♕e2 21 ♗e3 also wins) 21 ♗g5 (21 ♗f4!?) 21...♖he8 22 ♖d1+ ♔c7 23 ♗xe7 +−.

b212) 19...♔d6 20 ♗f4+ ♘xf4 21 ♕xf4+ ♔e7 22 ♕e5+ ♔f7 23 ♕f5+ ♔e8 24 ♕xc5 ±/+−.

b22) 18...0-0! 19 ♗d3 (19 b4 ♗d4) 19...♕b6 (19...♕a5? 20 ♗d2! ♕b6 21 b4 ♗d4 22 a5 +−; 19...b5!? is interesting, since then 20 b4 can be met by 20...♕c8) 20 a5 ♕b4 21 ♗d2 ♕h4! (21...♕xb2? 22 ♗c3! ♕b3 23 ♗xg7 ♔xg7 24 ♕g4+ ♔h8 25 ♕f5 +−) and now 22 ♖xb7?! ♖ad8 23 ♗c3?! was given by Kasparov as favouring White, but Black has the strong response

23...♖xd3! 24 ♕xd3 ♗xf2+ followed by 25...♘c5.

17 b4! *(D)*

White cannot prevent Black from castling, so he uses the time to harass Black's queen. Other moves are less effective:

a) If 17 ♕h3, then 17...♖d8 18 ♖xd8+ ♗xd8 19 ♗e3 ♗f6 with counterplay.

b) 17 b3 ♗f6! 18 ♖a2 0-0 ∞.

c) 17 ♕f3!? and then:

c1) 17...c6?! 18 ♗f5 intending to meet 18...0-0 with 19 ♕h3! ±.

c2) 17...♖b8!? 18 b4 (the two alternatives 18 ♕h3!? and 18 ♕h5!? give White compensation) 18...0-0 19 ♖d7?! (better is 19 ♗b2! with compensation) 19...♖bd8!! ∓ Ivanchuk-Howell, Groningen jr 1986/7.

c3) 17...♖d8 18 ♗d3 (18 ♖xd8+!? ♘xd8 19 ♗f4 gives White compensation) and here:

c31) 18...♘d4 19 ♕g4! ♕f6 20 ♗e3 ♘e6 21 ♕e4 ±.

c32) 18...♕b6!? 19 ♗e3 ♕xb2 20 ♖ab1 and now Black can choose between 20...♕c3 ∞ and 20...♕a3!? 21 ♕xb7 0-0 (21...♖xd3 22 ♕c6+ ♔f8 23 ♖b8+ ♘d8 24 ♖xd8+! +−) 22 ♕e4 g6, when White has compensation, but note that 23 ♗xa7? fails to 23...♗c5! −+.

c33) 18...♕a5! 19 ♗d2 (19 ♕xb7? ♖xd3! −+) 19...♗b4 and now:

c331) 20 ♗b5+?! c6 21 ♗xc6+ bxc6 22 ♕xc6+ ♔f8 23 ♗xb4+ ♕xb4 24 ♖xd8+ ♘xd8 25 ♕d7 (25 ♕d5 ♕b8! ∓) 25...♕e7 26 ♖d1 ♕xd7 27 ♖xd7 ♔e8 28 ♖xa7 h5 ∓.

c332) 20 ♗e3 and here:

c3321) 20...c6 21 ♕e4 (21 ♗c4!? ♖xd1+ 22 ♖xd1 ♕xa4 23 b3 ♕a5 24 ♕e4 gives White compensation) 21...g6 22 ♗c4 ♖xd1+ 23 ♖xd1 ♕f5! 24 ♕xf5 gxf5 25 ♗xa7 ♔e7 26 ♗b6 is slightly better for White.

c3322) 20...0-0 21 ♕xb7 ♘c5 22 ♗xc5 ♗xc5 23 ♕b5 ½-½ Timman-Yusupov, Hilversum (2) 1986.

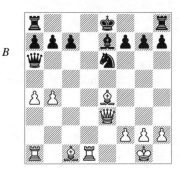

B

17...0-0!

Black calmly finishes his development. Otherwise:

a) 17...♗f6?! 18 b5 ♕b6 19 ♕xb6 axb6 20 ♗xb7 ♗xa1 21 ♗xa8 0-0 22 ♗c6 ♖d8 23 ♖xd8+ ♘xd8 24 ♗d5 ±.

b) Taking the pawn by 17...♗xb4?! is too risky:

b1) 18 ♗b2!? 0-0 19 ♕h3 g6 (19...♘g5 20 ♕g4 ♕h6 21 ♗c1! ♗e7 22 h4 +−; 19...f5 20 ♗xf5 ♘g5 21 ♕b3+ ♔h8 22 ♖d7 +−) 20 ♖d3! h5 (20...♘g5 21 ♕h6 f6 22 ♗xg6! +−) 21 ♕xh5! gxh5 22 ♖g3+ +−.

b2) 18 ♕f3 c6 (18...♖b8 19 ♗b2 has the point that 19...0-0? fails to 20 ♕f5 g6 21 ♕f6 +−; 18...♘c5 19 ♖d4 +−) 19 ♖d7!! and now:

b21) 19...♘d8 20 ♗f5 0-0 21 ♗b2 +−.

b22) 19...♗e7 20 ♖xb7 ♘d4 21 ♖xe7+ ♔xe7 22 ♗a3+ +–.

b23) 19...0-0 20 ♕h3 g6 (20...h6 21 ♗xh6) 21 ♗xg6! hxg6 22 ♗b2 ♘g7 23 ♕h6 +–.

b24) 19...♔xd7 20 ♕xf7+ ♔d6 21 ♗g5!! (21 ♗f4+? ♘xf4 22 ♖d1+ ♘d5 23 ♗xd5 ♕e2 24 ♕f4+ ♔d7 25 ♗f3+ ∞) 21...♘xg5 (21...♖he8 22 ♖d1+ ♔c5 23 ♗e3+ ♔c4 24 ♗d3+ +–) 22 ♖d1+ ♔c5 23 ♕e7+ ♔c4 24 ♗d3+ ♔b3 25 ♖b1+ ♔c3 26 ♕xb4+ +–.

18 ♕h3!

After 18 b5 ♖ad8! White's back rank proves weak, while 18 ♕f3 is also met by 18...♖ad8!.

18...g6

18...h6? is bad in view of 19 ♕f5 g6 20 ♕e5 (20 ♕f3 ±) 20...♘g5 21 ♗xb7! ♕xb7 22 ♗b2 f6 23 ♕xe7 ±.

19 ♕c3!?

Or:

a) 19 b5?! ♖ad8! 20 ♖e1 (20 ♗h6 ♖xd1+ 21 ♖xd1 ♕xa4) 20...♕b6 ∞.

b) 19 ♗b2?! and then:

b1) 19...♗xb4? 20 ♖d3! ♘g7 21 ♕h6 f6 22 ♖d7 +–.

b2) 19...♘g5? 20 ♕h6 ♗f6 21 ♗xb7! +–.

b3) 19...♘f4?! 20 ♕e3 ♕e2 (alternatively, 20...♗g5 21 ♔h1 intending ♕c3) keeps Black in the game since 21 ♕d4 f6 22 ♗f3 ♘h3+ is a draw unless White risks 23 gxh3.

b4) 19...♕c4! and here:

b41) 20 ♗xb7?! ♖ad8! 21 ♕c3 (21 ♖dc1 ♕xb4 22 ♗a3 ♕xb7 23 ♗xe7 ♘f4 24 ♕g4 ♖fe8) 21...♖xd1+ 22 ♖xd1 ♕xc3 23 ♗xc3 ♖b8 ∓.

b42) 20 ♖e1 ♖ad8! 21 ♗xg6 (21 ♖e3 ♗g5) 21...fxg6 22 ♖xe6 ♕c2 ∞.

b43) 20 ♗d5 ♕c2 21 ♗e5?! (21 ♖ab1!? ♖ad8 22 ♖dc1! =) 21...♖ad8! 22 ♖dc1 (22 ♖ac1?? ♖xd5! –+; 22 ♖d3? ♗g5 23 ♖ad1 c6 24 ♕xe6 ♖xd5! –+) 22...♕d2! 23 ♗xe6 fxe6 24 ♕xe6+ ♖f7 ∓.

b44) 20 ♖d7!? ♖ae8! 21 ♗d5 ♕xb4 22 ♗c3 ♘f4! is equal, Kasparov-Karpov, London Wch (6) 1986.

19...♘g5!

This appears to be the only move. 19...f5? fails to 20 ♗d5 ♗f6 21 ♕b3 ♗xa1 22 ♗xe6+ +–, while 19...c5?! is no good due to 20 ♗b2 ♘d4 21 ♗d3 ♕b6 22 a5 ♕c7 23 bxc5 ♗xc5 24 ♗f1 ♖fd8 25 ♖a4 ♖ac8 26 ♖axd4 ♗xd4 27 ♕xc7 ♖xc7 28 ♖xd4 ♖xd4 29 ♗xd4 ± Aseev-Ivanchuk, Irkutsk 1986.

20 ♗xg5

White gains nothing by 20 ♗b2 ♗f6! 21 ♕xf6 ♕xf6 22 ♗xf6 ♘xe4 23 ♗e7 ♖fe8 24 ♖d7 ♘c3!, when Black equalizes.

20...♗xg5 21 ♕xc7

21 a5 ♕e6 =.

21...♖ad8!

The alternatives are less satisfactory: 21...♖ab8? 22 b5 ♕b6 23 ♕xb6 axb6 24 ♖d6! or 21...♖ac8? 22 ♗xb7! ♖xc7 23 ♗xa6, with a clear advantage for White in both cases.

22 ♖xd8 ♖xd8 23 ♗xb7 ♕e2 24 ♗f3 ♕b2 25 ♖f1

White is slightly better, since he has an extra pawn, although Black's active pieces and the opposite-coloured bishops will make it hard for White to exploit it.

As we have seen, Black has certain problems in the 6...♘c6 7 0-0 ♗g4 variation.

9 4 ♘f3 ♞xe4 5 d4 d5
6 ♗d3 ♝d6

**1 e4 e5 2 ♘f3 ♞f6 3 ♘xe5 d6 4 ♘f3
♞xe4 5 d4 d5 6 ♗d3 ♝d6** *(D)*

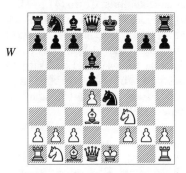

W

This chapter includes some of the
key lines of the Petroff, and it has
formed the battleground for many
games between top grandmasters.
Black's continuation aims for straightforward development. White usually
tries to undermine the knight by c4,
but Black will simply reinforce his d-
pawn with ...c6. As we shall see,
White has the choice between a number of alternative plans, but it is not
clear which is the best.

7 0-0

There is one major alternative:

a) 7 ♘bd2 0-0 8 0-0 ♗f5!? 9 ♖e1
♖e8 10 ♘f1 ♝g6 11 c3 ♘d7 12 ♘g3
c6 13 ♕c2 ♕c7! ∓ Rossetto-Pilnik,
Bahia Blanca (7) 1946. The point is

that 14 ♘xe4 dxe4 15 ♗xe4 ♖xe4 16
♖xe4 is met by 16...♘f6 ∓.

b) 7 c4 and now:

b1) 7...0-0!? and then:

b11) 8 0-0 – *7 0-0 0-0 8 c4.*

b12) 8 cxd5?! ♝b4+ 9 ♘bd2 (9
♔f1? ♕xd5 10 ♕c2 ♖e8 ∓ Janowski-
Marshall, Biarritz (3) 1912) 9...♘xd2
10 ♗xd2 ♖e8+ 11 ♔f1 ♝xd2 12 ♕xd2
♕xd5 ∓ Ricardi-Adla, Buenos Aires
1990.

b13) 8 c5 ♝e7 9 ♘c3 ♘xc3 10
bxc3 b6! 11 cxb6 axb6 12 ♗e3 c5 13
♕c2 h6 14 ♕d2 ♖e8 15 0-0 c4 16 ♗c2
♘d7 17 ♖ae1 ♝f8 ∓ Janowski-Marshall, Biarritz (5) 1912.

b2) 7...♝b4+ 8 ♘bd2 (8 ♗d2 ♘xd2
9 ♘bxd2 0-0 10 0-0 ♝g4 11 ♕b3 ♘c6
12 cxd5 ♝xd2 13 ♘xd2 ♘xd4 14
♕xb7 ♖b8 15 ♕xa7 ♕xd5 gives Black
enough compensation, Göring-Mink-
ewitz, Leipzig 1870) and here:

b21) 8...♘xd2!? 9 ♗xd2 ♕e7+ 10
♕e2 (10 ♔f1 dxc4 11 ♗xb4 ♕xb4 12
♕e1+ ♕xe1+ 13 ♖xe1+ ♔d8 14 ♗xc4
f6 15 d5 ♘d7 16 ♘d4 ♘b6 17 ♗b3
♗d7 18 f4 ½-½ Palac-Forintos, Novi
Sad 1990) 10...♝xd2+ (10...♕xe2+?!
11 ♔xe2 ♗xd2 12 ♔xd2 ♗e6 13 cxd5
♗xd5 14 ♖he1+ ♔d8 15 ♗e4 ♗xe4
16 ♖xe4 ♖e8 17 ♖ae1 ♖xe4 18 ♖xe4
♘c6 19 ♖g4! ± Alekhine-Marshall, St

Petersburg 1914) 11 ♔xd2 ♕xe2+ 12 ♗xe2 dxc4 13 ♗xc4 0-0 14 ♖he1 ♘c6 15 d5?! (15 ♗d5 ±) 15...♘a5 16 ♗d3 c5 17 ♔c3 b6 = Janowski-Marshall, New York 1913.

b22) 8...0-0 9 0-0 and then:

b221) 9...♖e8? 10 cxd5 ♘f6?! 11 ♘e5 ♘bd7 12 ♘df3 ♘xd5 13 ♘xf7! ♔xf7 14 ♘g5+ ♔f8 15 ♕h5 1-0 Capablanca-Black, New York 1913.

b222) 9...♘xd2 10 ♗xd2 ♗xd2 11 ♕xd2 ♘c6 12 ♖fe1 ♗g4 13 ♘e5 ± Capablanca-Marshall, St Petersburg 1914.

b223) 9...♗xd2! 10 ♗xd2 ♗g4 11 ♗f4 (11 ♗e3!? ♘c6 12 h3 ♗h5 13 ♖c1 ♖e8 14 a3 ∞ Short-Adams, Wijk aan Zee 2000) 11...♘c6 12 ♖e1 ♘xd4 (12...♗xf3?! 13 ♕xf3 ♘xd4 14 ♕e3 ♘f5 15 ♕h3 ±) 13 ♗xe4 (13 cxd5?! ♗xf3 14 gxf3 ♘g5! ∓) 13...dxe4 14 ♕xd4 exf3 15 ♕xd8 ♖fxd8 16 ♗xc7 ♖d2 17 b3 fxg2 18 ♔xg2 h6 19 ♗f4 ♖d3 20 ♖e3 ♖xe3 21 ♗xe3 a6 with equality, Tarrasch-Marshall, St Petersburg 1914.

7...0-0 (D)

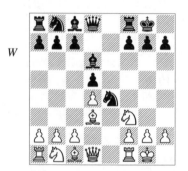

W

8 c4
Or:

a) 8 ♘bd2 f5 9 c4 c6 10 cxd5 cxd5 11 ♕b3 ♔h8 12 ♘e5 ♘c6! ∓ Zakhariev-Skembris, Greece 1992.

b) White sometimes plays 8 ♖e1:

b1) 8...♗f5 9 c4 c6 – *8 c4 c6 9 ♖e1* ♗f5.

b2) 8...♖e8 9 c4 c6 – *8 c4 c6 9 ♖e1* ♖e8.

b3) 8...f5!? 9 c4 c6 10 ♕b3 (10 ♘c3!?) 10...♔h8 11 ♘c3 (11 cxd5 cxd5 12 ♘c3 ♘c6!? ∞) 11...♘a6! ∞ Timman-Skembris, Corfu (4) 1993.

b4) 8...♗g4 9 ♗xe4 dxe4 10 ♖xe4 f5 11 ♖e1 ♘c6 (11...♗xf3?! 12 ♕xf3 ♕h4 13 h3 ♕xd4 14 ♕xb7 ± Lanka-Katišonok, Riga 1983) 12 c3 ♕f6 13 h3 ♗h5 14 ♕b3+ ♔h8 15 ♗g5 ♕g6 16 ♘bd2 ♖ae8 ∞ Lanka-Christiansen, Budapest 1991.

b5) 8...♘c6!? 9 ♗xe4! (9 h3?! ♕f6 10 ♘c3 ♘xc3 11 bxc3 h6 12 ♕e2 ♗d7 13 ♗e3 ♖ae8 14 ♘d2 ♖e7 15 ♕f3 ♕xf3 16 ♘xf3 ♖fe8 gives Black a slight advantage, Teichmann-Schlechter, Monte Carlo 1903) 9...dxe4 10 ♖xe4 ♗f5 11 ♖e1 ∞.

8...c6

This is the main continuation, but the alternatives are also quite important:

a) 8...♗e6 and then:

a1) 9 ♕b3 dxc4 (9...b6 10 cxd5 ♗xd5 11 ♕c2 ♘f6 12 ♗g5 h6 13 ♗h4 ♘bd7 ∞) 10 ♗xc4 (10 ♕xb7?? ♗d5 wins for Black) 10...♗xc4 11 ♕xc4 c6 (11...♘d7!?) 12 ♘c3 ♘f6 13 ♕b3 ♕b6 =.

a2) 9 cxd5 ♗xd5 10 ♘c3 ♘xc3 11 bxc3 ♘d7 (11...♘c6!?; 11...h6 12 c4 ♗xf3 13 ♕xf3 ♘c6 leads to an unclear position, Von Kolisch-Winawer,

Paris 1867) 12 ♘d2!? (intending c4; 12 c4? ♗xf3 13 ♕xf3 ♕h4 14 ♕h3 ♕xh3 15 gxh3 c5! 16 d5 ♘e5 ∓ Mason-Marshall, Paris 1900; 12 ♗b2 ♘b6 ∞; 12 ♖e1!?; 12 ♘e1!?) 12...♕h4 13 h3 =.

a3) 9 ♘c3 ♘xc3 10 bxc3 dxc4 11 ♗e4 (11 ♗xh7+?! ♔xh7 12 ♘g5+ ♔g6! 13 ♘xe6 fxe6 14 ♕g4+ ♔h7 ∓) and now:

a31) 11...♕c8?! 12 ♘g5 ♗f5 13 ♕f3 ♗xe4 14 ♕xe4 g6 15 ♕h4 h5 16 ♘e4 ♘d7 17 ♗g5 ±.

a32) 11...♗c8 12 ♕a4 (12 ♕c2 ∞; 12 ♘g5!?) 12...♕e8 13 ♕c2 h6 14 ♖e1 ♕b5 15 ♖b1 ♕a6 ∞.

a33) 11...♘d7 12 ♘g5 ♘f6 13 ♘xe6 fxe6 14 ♗xb7 ♖b8 15 ♗f3 (not 15 ♗a6? ♗xh2+ 16 ♔xh2 ♕d6+) 15...♘d5 16 ♗d2!? (16 ♕e2 ♘xc3 17 ♕xc4 ♖xf3! 18 gxf3 ♘d5 gives Black compensation, Khalifman-Hübner, Munich rpd 1991) 16...♖b2 17 ♗g4! ♕f6 18 ♕c1 ♖b5 19 ♖b1 ♖xb1 20 ♕xb1 h5!? 21 ♗f3 h4 22 ♗g4 ♗f4 23 ♗xf4 ♘xf4 24 ♕e4 ± Nisipeanu-Hess, Bad Wörishofen 1995.

a4) 9 ♕c2 f5!? (9...♘c6? 10 cxd5 ♘b4 11 ♕e2 ♗xd5 12 ♗xe4 ♗xe4 13 ♕xe4 ♖e8 14 ♕g4 ♘c2 15 ♘c3 ±; 9...♖e8 10 ♘c3 ♘c6 11 ♘xe4 ±) and here:

a41) 10 ♘c3!? should be considered.

a42) 10 ♘bd2?! c6 11 c5?! (11 ♘e5!) 11...♗c7 12 b4 ♘d7 13 b5 g5 14 bxc6 bxc6 15 ♕a4 ♕f6 16 ♕xc6 ♖ac8 17 ♕a6 g4 ∓ Adams-Hübner, Dortmund 1992.

a43) 10 c5 ♗e7 11 ♘e5 (11 b4!?) 11...♘d7 12 ♘xd7 ♕xd7 =.

a44) 10 ♕b3 dxc4 (10...b6? 11 cxd5 ±) 11 ♕xb7 (11 ♗xc4 ♗xc4 12 ♕xc4+ ♔h8 13 ♘c3 =) and then:

a441) 11...c6?! 12 ♗xe4 fxe4 13 ♘g5 ♗f5 (13...♗d5 14 ♘c3 ±) 14 ♘c3 ♕d7 (14...h6 15 ♘gxe4 ♗xe4 16 ♘xe4 ♗xh2+ 17 ♔xh2 ♕h4+ 18 ♔g1 ♕xe4 19 ♕xa8 ♕e7 20 ♗d2 ♕c7 21 ♗b4 ♖d8 22 ♗c5 +−) 15 ♕xd7 ♘xd7 16 ♘gxe4 ±.

a442) 11...♘c6 12 ♕xc6 cxd3 13 ♕b5 d2 14 ♘bxd2 ♖b8 15 ♕d3 ♘xd2 16 ♗xd2 (16 ♘xd2?! ♗d5 ∓) 16...♖xb2 17 ♗c3 ♖b7 18 d5 ♗d7 19 ♘d4 ±.

a443) 11...♘d7!? 12 ♗xe4 ♖b8 and here:

a4431) 13 ♕a6?! fxe4 14 ♘g5 ♖f5! (14...♗d5 15 ♘c3 ♖b6 gives Black compensation) 15 ♘xe6 ♗xh2+ 16 ♔xh2 ♕h4+ 17 ♔g1 ♖h5 18 f3 exf3 is good for Black.

a4432) 13 ♕xa7 fxe4 14 ♘g5 ♗d5 gives Black compensation.

a5) 9 ♖e1 *(D)* and then:

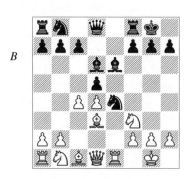

a51) 9...f5!? and here:

a511) 10 cxd5 ♗xd5 11 ♘c3 ♘xc3 12 bxc3 ♘c6 ∞.

a512) 10 c5 ♗e7 11 ♘e5 ♗h4!? (11...♘d7 12 ♘xd7 ♗xd7 {12...♕xd7

13 f3 ♘f6 14 ♕e2 ♗f7 15 ♕xe7 ♖ae8 16 ♕xd7 ♖xe1+ 17 ♔f2 +−} 13 f3 ♘f6 14 ♖e5 ± Capablanca-Michelsen, New York 1915; 11...♗f6!?) 12 g3 ♗f6 ∞.

a513) 10 ♕b3!? dxc4 (10...♘c6 11 cxd5 ♘xd4 12 ♘xd4 ♗xh2+ 13 ♔f1 ♗xd5 14 ♗c4 ♗xc4+ 15 ♕xc4+ ♔h8 16 ♘f3 ±) 11 ♗xc4 ♗xc4 12 ♕xc4+ ♔h8 13 ♘c3 ±.

a52) 9...♖e8 and now:

a521) 10 cxd5 ♗xd5 11 ♘c3 ♘xc3 12 ♖xe8+ ♕xe8 13 bxc3 ♗xf3 14 ♕xf3 ♕e1+ 15 ♗f1 ♘c6 16 ♗b2 ♕d2 17 ♕e2 = Van Baarle-Yusupov, Germany 1992.

a522) 10 ♕c2 ♘c6 11 ♗xe4 dxe4 12 ♖xe4 ♘b4 13 ♕c3 ♗f5 gives Black compensation, Lau-Hübner, Munich 1991.

a523) 10 ♘c3 ♘xc3 11 bxc3 dxc4!? (11...h6 12 c5 ♗f8 13 ♘e5 is slightly better for White) 12 ♗xh7+ ♔xh7 13 ♘g5+ ♔g6 looks risky for Black, but note that 14 h4? is well answered by 14...♗g4!.

a524) 10 c5 and then:

a5241) 10...♗f8 11 ♘c3 f5 (better than 11...♗f5?! 12 ♕b3 ♘c6 13 ♕xb7 ♘xc3 14 ♕xc6 ♗xd3 15 bxc3 ♖xe1+ 16 ♘xe1 ♗e4 17 ♗f4 ± Kuczynski-Gdanski, Polanica Zdroj 1992) 12 ♘e5 (12 ♕b3 b6 ∓) 12...♘d7 13 ♗f4 and White has a slight advantage.

a5242) 10...♗e7 11 ♘c3! ♘xc3 (not 11...f5? 12 ♕b3 ±) 12 bxc3 ♘d7 (12...b6 13 ♕c2 h6 14 cxb6 axb6 15 ♘e5 ♗d6 ±) 13 ♗f4 b6 14 ♕c2 (14 c6 ±) 14...♘f8 15 ♘e5 ♗f6 (15...bxc5?! 16 ♗b5 ♘d7 17 ♘c6 ♕c8 18 ♘xe7+ ♖xe7 19 ♗c6 ♖b8 20 ♗xd5 cxd4 21

cxd4 ♘f6 22 ♗xe6 ±) 16 ♗b5 ♗xe5 17 ♗xe5 ♗d7 18 c6 ♗c8! (18...♗e6 19 ♗a6 +−) 19 ♗g3 a6 20 ♗d3 ♖e6 21 ♖xe6 ♗xe6 22 a4! ± Kamsky-Yusupov, Tilburg 1992.

b) 8...♘f6 (D) and then:

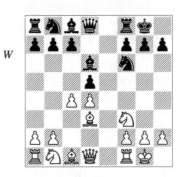

b1) 9 ♕b3!? is worth considering.

b2) 9 c5 ♗e7 10 ♗f4 ♘c6 11 h3 b6 12 ♗b5 ♗d7 13 ♗xc6 ♗xc6 14 b4 ♘e4 = Robey-Barnes, London 1862.

b3) 9 h3 dxc4 10 ♗xc4 ♘c6 (not 10...♘bd7?! 11 ♘c3 c6 12 ♗b3 ♘b6 13 ♖e1 ♘fd5 14 ♕d3! ♖e8 15 ♗g5 ♗e7 16 ♗xe7 ♖xe7 17 ♘g5! g6 18 ♕g3 ♗f5 19 ♖e5! ± Zifroni-Av.Bykhovsky, Israel 1995) 11 ♘c3 – 9 ♘c3!? dxc4 10 ♗xc4 ♘c6 11 h3.

b4) 9 ♘c3!? dxc4 10 ♗xc4 ♘c6 (10...♗g4 11 h3 ♗h5 12 ♖e1 ±) and now:

b41) 11 h3 h6 and then:

b411) 12 a3 ♗f5 13 ♖e1 a6 and here:

b4111) 14 d5 ♘e7, intending to play ...♘g6, is equal.

b4112) 14 ♘e5?! ♗xe5 15 dxe5 ♕xd1 16 ♘xd1 ♘d7 17 e6 (17 f4 ♘b6 18 ♗a2 ♘d4 19 ♘e3 ♗e6 ∓) 17...fxe6 18 ♗f4?! ♘b6 19 ♗a2 ♘d5 20 ♗xd5 exd5 is slightly better for Black, Liogky-Lautier, France 1996.

b4113) 14 b4 ♕d7 15 d5 ♘e7 16 ♘e5 ♗xe5 17 ♖xe5 ♘g6 18 ♖e1 ♖fe8 intending ...♘e5 =.

b412) 12 ♖e1 ♖e8 13 ♗e3 ♗f5 14 a3 a6! 15 ♘h4 ♗h7 16 ♕f3 ♕d7 17 g4 ♖ad8 is equal, Short-Bareev, Pula Echt 1997.

b413) 12 ♗e3 ♗f5 13 ♘h4 ♗h7 14 ♗d3 (14 f4 ♘e4 15 ♘f3 ♘g3 16 ♖f2 = Horwitz-Löwenthal, London 1853) 14...♗xd3 (14...♕d7?! 15 ♗xh7+ ♘xh7 16 ♕f3 f5 17 ♘g6! ± H.Wolff-Pillsbury, Hanover 1902) 15 ♕xd3 ±.

b42) 11 ♗g5 h6 12 ♗h4 ♗g4 13 h3 ♗xf3 14 ♕xf3 ♘xd4 15 ♕xb7 ♘f5 16 ♗xf6 ♕xf6 17 ♕f3 (17 ♖ad1!? ±) 17...♕e5 18 g3 ♖ae8 19 ♖fe1 ♘d4! 20 ♕d5! ♕xd5 21 ♗xd5 ♗b4 22 a3 ♗xc3 23 bxc3 ♘e2+ 24 ♔f1 ♘xc3 25 ♗c6! ± Finkel-Nogueiras, Ubeda 1997.

b5) 9 ♗g5!? and now:

b51) 9...♗e6 10 ♕b3 dxc4 11 ♗xc4 (11 ♕xb7?? ♗d5 12 ♗xf6 gxf6 −+) 11...♗xc4 12 ♕xc4 ♘c6 13 ♘c3 h6 14 ♗h4 g5 15 ♗g3 ± Morphy-Barnes, London 1859.

b52) 9...dxc4 10 ♗xc4 and then:

b521) 10...h6 11 ♗h4 ♘c6 (11...g5 12 ♗g3 ♗g4 13 ♕d3 ♔g7 14 ♘bd2 ♘c6 15 a3 ♗xg3 16 fxg3 ±) 12 h3!? (12 ♘c3 ♗g4 13 ♗d5 ♗e7 14 ♗xc6 bxc6 15 ♖e1 ♖b8 ∓) 12...g5!? 13 ♗g3 and here:

b5211) 13...♗xg3!? 14 fxg3 ♕d6 (14...g4?! 15 hxg4 ♗xg4 16 ♘c3 ♗xf3 17 ♖xf3 ♘xd4 18 ♖f4 c5 19 ♕d3 ±) 15 g4 ♗e6 16 ♗xe6 fxe6 ∞.

b5212) 13...♘e4 14 ♗xd6 ♘xd6 15 ♗d5! (15 ♗b3 ♕f6) 15...♕f6 (15...♘e7

16 ♗b3 ±) 16 ♗xc6 bxc6 17 ♘bd2! and then:

b52121) 17...♗e6 18 ♖c1 ♘b5 (not 18...♗d5? 19 ♘e5) 19 ♖xc6 ♘xd4 20 ♘xd4 ♕xd4 21 ♕c1! ♕f4 (21...♖fd8 22 ♘f3 ♕f4 23 ♕c3 ±) 22 ♘c4 ♕e4 23 ♖c5 ♖fd8 24 ♖e1 ± Bareev-Komarov, Budapest 1996.

b52122) 17...♘b5!? 18 ♘e4 ♕f4 19 ♖e1 g4 20 hxg4 ♗xg4 21 ♕d2 ♕xd2 22 ♘exd2 ♖ad8 23 ♖e4 f5 24 ♖e6 (24 ♖f4!? ∞) 24...♘xd4 (24...♗xf3 25 ♘xf3 ♘xd4 26 ♘xd4 ♖xd4 27 ♖g6+ ♔h7 28 ♖xc6 ±) 25 ♘xd4 ♖xd4 26 ♘b3 ♖d6 =.

b522) 10...♗g4 11 h3 ♗xf3 12 ♕xf3 ♘c6 13 ♖d1 (13 ♘c3?! ♘xd4 14 ♕xb7 and now 14...♖b8! = is better than 14...♕b8?! 15 ♕xb8 ♖axb8 16 ♖ad1 ♘e6 17 ♗c1 ♖fd8 18 ♖fe1 ± O'Kelly-Radulescu, Bucharest 1953) 13...♗e7 14 ♘c3 ♖b8 15 ♘e2 gives White a slight advantage.

c) 8...♗g4 *(D)* and now:

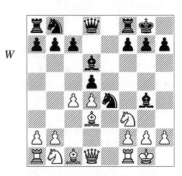

c1) 9 c5? ♗e7 10 h3 ♗xf3 11 gxf3 (11 ♕xf3 f5 ∓) 11...♘g5 ∓ John-Marshall, Hamburg 1910.

c2) 9 ♘c3 ♘xc3 10 bxc3 dxc4 11 ♗xc4 and then:

c21) 11...♕f6!? 12 h3 ♗xf3 (alternatively, 12...♗h5 13 g4 ♗g6 14 ♗g5 ♗c2 15 ♕xc2 ♕xf3 16 ♕d3 ±) 13 ♕xf3 ♕xf3 14 gxf3 ♘d7 ±.

c22) 11...♘d7 12 ♕d3 (12 h3 ♗h5 13 g4 ♘b6 is unclear – Alekhine) 12...c5 (12...♘b6?! 13 ♘g5 g6 14 ♗b3 c5 15 ♕e4 ±; 12...c6 – *8 c4 c6 9 ♘c3 ♘xc3 10 bxc3 dxc4 11 ♗xc4 ♗g4 12 ♕d3 ♘d7*) 13 ♘g5 ♘f6 14 h3 ♗h5 (14...♗d7? 15 dxc5 ♗xc5 16 ♘xf7 ±) 15 f4 (15 dxc5 ♗xc5 16 ♕f5 ♖c8 17 ♘xh7 ♘xh7 18 ♕xh5 ♘f6 19 ♕f3 ♗d6 20 ♗b3 ♕a5 21 ♗d2 ♕e5 22 g3 ♘e4 = Schlechter-Marshall, Hamburg 1910) 15...h6 16 g4! and then:

c221) 16...hxg5 17 fxg5 (17 gxh5!?) 17...♘xg4 (17...b5! is a strong new move here) 18 hxg4 ♕d7 should be compared with *8 c4 c6 9 ♘c3 ♘xc3 10 bxc3 dxc4 11 ♗xc4 ♗g4 12 ♕d3 ♘d7 13 ♘g5 ♘f6 14 h3 ♗h5 15 f4 h6 16 g4 hxg5 17 fxg5 ♘xg4 18 hxg4 ♕d7*.

c222) 16...b5 17 ♗d5 and now 17...♖c8 is far better than 17...♗g6 18 ♕xg6 hxg5 19 ♗xf7+! ± Corzo-Marshall, Havana 1913.

c3) 9 cxd5 f5 10 h3 ♗h5 11 ♘c3 ♘d7 (11...♕e8 12 ♕e2 ♘d7 13 ♘xe4 fxe4 14 ♕xe4 ♕xe4 15 ♗xe4 ♘f6 16 ♘d2 ± Emma-Rossetto, Buenos Aires 1965) 12 ♘xe4 fxe4 13 ♗xe4 ♘f6 (13...♔h8 14 ♕d3 h6 15 ♗d2 ♕f6 16 g4 ♗f7 17 g5 ♕d8 18 gxh6 gxh6 19 ♗xh6 ± Spielmann-Marshall, San Sebastian 1912) 14 ♗f5 ♔h8 (14...♘xd5? 15 ♗e6+ ♗f7 16 ♘g5 +−) and then:

c31) 15 ♗e6!? ♘e4 16 g4 ♗g6 17 ♗e3 (17 ♘e5?! ♕h4 18 ♕e2 ♕xh3 ∓ Mitchell – Milner-Barry, Hastings 1934) 17...♕f6 18 ♘e5 ±.

c32) 15 ♕d3 ♘xd5 16 ♘e5 ♕f6 17 ♗xh7 ♗xe5 18 dxe5 ♕xe5 19 ♗e4 (19 ♗d2!?) 19...♖ad8 20 ♗xd5 ♖xd5 21 ♕e3 ♕d6 gives Black compensation, Maus-Kristensen, Gausdal 1990.

c33) 15 ♕b3!? ♘xd5 16 ♗g5 ♗e7 17 ♗xe7 ♘xe7 18 ♗e4 ♗xf3 19 ♗xf3 ♘f5 and here:

c331) 20 ♗xb7 ♖b8 21 ♕d5 ♕f6 (21...♘d6 22 ♗c6 ♖xb2 23 ♖ae1 ♕h4 24 f4 h6 gives Black compensation, Spielmann-Marshall, San Sebastian 1911) 22 ♖ae1 ♘xd4 23 ♕e4 c6 gives Black compensation, Leonhardt-Marshall, San Sebastian 1912.

c332) 20 ♕xb7 ♘xd4!? (20...♖b8 21 ♕xa7 ♘xd4 22 ♗g4 ± Bernstein-Marshall, San Sebastian 1911) 21 ♖ad1 ♕d6 ∞.

c34) 15 g4! ♘xd5 16 ♗e6 (16 ♘g5 ♖xf5 −+; 16 ♕d3 ♘b4 17 ♕e4 ♗f7 18 ♗g5 ♕e8 ∞ Spielmann-Marshall, Hamburg 1910) 16...♗f7 17 ♘g5 ♗xe6 18 ♘xe6 ♕h4 19 ♕b3! ± (intending ♗g5) Alexander-Mellison, Brighton 1938.

We now return to 8...c6 *(D)*:

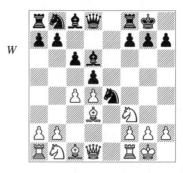

Now there are a number of important continuations for White. All of them attempt to remove the knight from e4, but they are not all equally effective:

A: 9 ♖e1	161
B: 9 ♕c2	165
C: 9 ♘c3	170
D: 9 cxd5	175

Other moves:

a) 9 ♗xe4 dxe4 10 ♘g5 and then:

a1) 10...♗f5 11 ♘c3 ♘d7 (11...h6 12 ♘gxe4 ♗xe4 13 ♘xe4 ♗xh2+ 14 ♔xh2 ♕h4+ 15 ♔g1 ♕xe4 16 ♖e1 ♕h4 17 ♕d3 ♘d7 18 ♖e4 ±) 12 ♖e1 ♖e8 13 c5! ♗c7 14 ♕b3 ♖e7 15 ♘gxe4 ± Corzo-Capablanca, Havana (10) 1901.

a2) 10...f5!? 11 c5 (11 d5 ♘a6 ∓) 11...♗e7 12 ♕b3+ ♕d5 13 ♕xd5+ cxd5 14 ♘c3 ♗xg5 15 ♗xg5 ♗e6 16 b4 ♘c6 17 b5 ♘b4 ∞ Yusupov.

a3) 10...h6 11 ♘xe4 ♗xh2+ 12 ♔xh2 ♕h4+ 13 ♔g1 ♕xe4=.

b) 9 ♕b3 ♗g4 (9...♘a6!?) 10 ♗xe4 (10 ♕xb7? ♗xf3 11 gxf3 ♕h4 ∓; 10 ♘bd2!?) 10...dxe4 11 ♘g5 ♗e7 and here:

b1) 12 ♕xb7 ♗xg5 13 ♕xa8 ♗xc1 14 ♖xc1 and now:

b11) 14...♕g5!? 15 ♖c3 ♗f3 16 g3 ♕h6 17 h4 f5 18 ♕xa7 f4 and now rather than 19 ♘d2? fxg3 20 ♘xf3 gxf2+ 21 ♔g2 exf3+ 22 ♖xf3 ♕g6+ 23 ♔xf2 (23 ♖g3 ♕e4+ 24 ♔h3 g6 25 ♖f1 ♕e6+ 26 ♔h2 ♕xc4 ∞) 23...♕c2+ 24 ♔g3 ♕g6+ 25 ♔f2 =, 19 ♕e7! is very good for White.

b12) 14...♕xd4!? 15 ♕b7 (15 ♘c3 ♕d7! ∓) 15...e3 ∞.

b2) 12 ♘xe4 ♕xd4 13 ♕xb7 ♕xe4 14 ♕xa8 (White should try 14 ♘c3!;

e.g., 14...♕e5 15 ♕xa8 ♕c7 16 ♗e3 +−) 14...♗d6!? 15 ♕xa7 ♗h3! (better than 15...♕e5 16 g3 ♗c5 17 ♗f4! ±) 16 gxh3 ♕e5 17 ♖d1 ♕xh2+ 18 ♔f1 ♕xh3+ 19 ♔e1 (19 ♔e2 ♕h5+ ∓ intending ...♗c5) 19...♗b4+ 20 ♘c3 ♗xc3+ 21 bxc3 ♕xc3+ 22 ♗d2 ♖e8+ 23 ♔f1 ♕h3+ = Dührssen-Batik, corr. 1928.

c) 9 h3 ♘d7 (9...♖e8 10 cxd5 cxd5 11 ♘bd2 ♘c6 = Yanovsky-Kiseliov, Moscow 1986) 10 ♘c3 ♘xc3 11 bxc3 dxc4 12 ♗xc4 ♕a5 (12...♘b6!?) 13 ♘g5?! (13 ♕c2 ♘f6 14 ♗d3 h6 15 ♖e1 ♘d5 =) 13...♕xc3 14 ♕h5 ♘f6 15 ♗xf7+ ♔h8 16 ♕h4 ♗f5! 17 ♗e3 ♘d5 ∓ Aseev-Rozentalis, Vilnius 1984.

A)

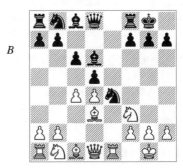

9 ♖e1 *(D)*

White simply attacks the knight a second time, but Black has various acceptable replies. He can either support the knight, or he can offer a pawn to gain time and secure the bishop-pair.

9...♗f5

Or:

a) 9...♘f6?! 10 ♘c3 dxc4 11 ♗xc4 h6?! (11...♗g4 12 h3 ♗h5 13 g4 ±;

11...♘bd7 12 ♗g5 ±) 12 ♘e5 b5?! 13 ♗b3 a6 14 ♕f3 ± Klovans-Levchenkov, Riga 1971.

b) 9...♘a6 10 ♘c3 ♘xc3 11 bxc3 dxc4 12 ♗xc4 ♕a5 13 ♕b3 ♘c7 14 ♘e5 ♘d5 15 ♗d2 ± Renet-Mirallès, Marseilles 1988.

c) 9...♗g4!? is a playable pawn sacrifice:

c1) 10 c5?! ♗xh2+! 11 ♔f1 (11 ♔xh2 ♘xf2 12 ♕c2 ♘xd3 13 ♕xd3 ♗xf3 −+ intending ...♕h4+) 11...f5 12 ♘c3 ♘d7 13 ♘xe4 fxe4 14 ♗xe4 ♗c7 15 ♗g5 ♘f6 16 ♗c2 ♕d7 17 ♕d3 ♘e4 ∓ Emelin-Raetsky, Rostov 1993.

c2) 10 ♗xe4 dxe4 11 ♖xe4 f5 and here:

c21) 12 ♖e3 ♗f4 and now:

c211) 13 ♖d3 ♗xc1 14 ♕xc1 ♗xf3 15 ♖xf3 (15 gxf3 ♕h4 gives Black compensation; he intends ...♖f6-h6) 15...♕xd4 =.

c212) 13 ♖c3 ♗xc1 14 ♖xc1 ♗xf3 15 ♕xf3 ♕xd4 =.

c22) 12 ♖e6 ♗c7! and then:

c221) 13 d5 ♗xf3 14 ♕xf3 (14 gxf3 ♕h4 15 d6 ♕xc4 16 dxc7 ♕xe6 17 cxb8♕ ♖axb8 =/∓) 14...♕h4 15 d6 ♕xc4 16 ♕b3 ♕xb3 17 axb3 ♗b6 18 ♘c3 ♘d7 =.

c222) 13 ♘c3 ♗xf3 14 ♕xf3 ♕xd4 15 b3 (15 ♕e2 ♘d7 16 ♗e3 ♕h4 17 g3 ♕g4 18 f3 ♕h5 ∓) 15...♘d7 16 ♗b2 ♖ae8 17 ♕e2 (17 ♖xe8 ♖xe8 18 ♕xf5 ♕d2 gives Black compensation) 17...♖xe6 18 ♕xe6+ ♖f7 19 ♖d1 ♕e5 is level.

c223) 13 ♘bd2 ♕xd4 14 ♕e2 (14 ♘xd4 ♗xd1 15 b3 ♗h5 16 ♗b2 ±) 14...♕d8 15 b3 ♗d6 16 ♗b2 ♘a6 17 ♖d1 ♘c5 18 h3 ♗h5 ∞ Read-Mohrlok, corr. 1990-2.

c23) 12 ♖e1 ♗xf3 13 ♕xf3 ♕h4 14 h3 ♕xd4 15 ♕b3 ♕b6 = Hjartarson-Ye Rongguang, Novi Sad OL 1990.

d) 9...♖e8 (D) is an alternative way of defending the e4-knight:

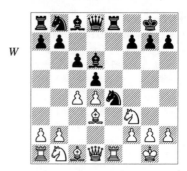

d1) 10 ♘bd2 ♗f5 11 c5 ♗f8 (another idea is 11...♗c7!?) 12 ♕c2 ♘d7 13 ♘f1 (13 ♘xe4?! dxe4 14 ♗xe4 ♖xe4 15 ♖xe4 ♘f6 ∓) 13...♗g6 = Khalifman-Rozentalis, Lvov 1985.

d2) 10 ♕b3 ♘a6 11 cxd5 (11 ♘c3!?) 11...cxd5 12 ♘c3 ♗e6 13 a3 (13 ♕xb7 ♘b4) 13...♘c7 14 ♕c2 (14 ♕xb7 ♖b8 =) 14...f5 15 ♘b5 ♘xb5 16 ♗xb5 ♗d7 = Makarychev-Nikolenko, Moscow 1987.

d3) 10 ♕c2 ♗g4! 11 ♘e5 (11 ♗xe4 dxe4 12 ♖xe4 ♗xf3 13 gxf3 ♘d7 14 ♘c3 ♕f6 gives Black compensation; e.g., 15 c5 ♗c7 16 ♕d1 ♕g6+ 17 ♖g4 ♕h5 18 ♖g2 ♖ad8 ∓ Petrushin-Rozentalis, Barnaul 1984) 11...♗xe5 12 dxe5 ♘a6 13 a3 (13 ♗xe4 dxe4 14 ♕xe4 f5 gives Black compensation) 13...♘ac5! ∞.

d4) 10 h3 ♗f5 11 ♕b3 ♘a6 12 cxd5 (12 c5? ♘axc5 ∓) 12...cxd5 13 ♘c3

♘b4 14 ♗b1 (14 ♗xe4 ♗xe4 15 ♘xe4 dxe4 16 ♘g5 ♕c7 17 ♗d2 ♘c2 18 ♘xf7! ♘xa1 19 ♘h6+ ♔h8 20 ♘f7+ =) 14...♕d7 15 ♘e5 ♘xc3 16 bxc3 (16 ♕xc3 ♗xe5 17 dxe5 gives Black a choice between 17...♗xb1 = and 17...a5!?) 16...♗xe5 17 ♗xf5! (17 ♖xe5?! ♘d3 18 ♖xe8+ ♖xe8 19 ♗e3 ♕c6! ∓ Yudasin-Mikhalchishin, Lvov 1987) 17...♗d6!? (17...♗h2+? 18 ♔xh2 ♕d6+ 19 ♖e5! +–) 18 ♗e3 =.

d5) 10 ♘c3 ♘xc3 (10...♗f5?! 11 ♕b3 ♘a6 12 cxd5 ♘ac5 13 dxc5 ♘xc5 14 ♖xe8+ ♕xe8 15 ♗xf5 ♘xb3 16 axb3 ±) and now:

d51) 11 ♖xe8+ ♕xe8 12 bxc3 and then:

d511) 12...♘d7?! 13 ♕c2 ♘f8 (not 13...g6? 14 c5 ♗c7 15 ♗g5 f6 16 ♖e1 ♕f7 17 ♗h6 ±/± Adianto-Gunawan, Djakarta 1993) 14 ♗g5 ♗g4 15 ♖e1 ♕d7 16 ♘e5 ♗xe5 17 dxe5 dxc4 18 ♗xc4 h6 19 ♗h4 ±.

d512) 12...dxc4 13 ♗xc4 ♗g4 14 ♗g5 (14 ♗e3 ♘d7 15 ♗e2 b5 = Korzubov-Rozentalis, Lvov 1985) 14...♘d7 15 ♕d3 b5 (15...♘b6 16 ♗b3 ♗h5 17 ♖e1 ♕d7 18 ♘e5! ♖e8 19 f4 ♗xe5 20 fxe5 ♗g6 21 ♕f3 ♘d5, L.Schneider-Valkesalmi, Torshavn 1987, 22 c4! ♘b4 23 d5! ±) 16 ♗b3 ±.

d513) 12...♗g4! 13 ♗d2 (13 ♗e3 should be met by 13...h6!? ∞ rather than 13...♘d7? 14 cxd5 cxd5 15 ♗xh7+ ± Levchenkov-Meiers, Riga 1986; 13 h3 ♗h5 14 ♗e3 ♕e7 15 cxd5 cxd5 16 g4 ♗g6 17 ♗xg6 hxg6 18 ♕b3 ♕d7 19 ♔g2 ♕c6 20 ♖b1 b6 21 ♕b5 ♔f8 ± Eskelinen-Utaši, Groningen 1982) and here:

d5131) 13...dxc4 14 ♗xh7+ ±.

d5132) 13...♕d8 14 c5! (14 cxd5!? cxd5 15 h3 ♗h5 16 ♖b1!? ∞; 14 ♖b1 dxc4 15 ♗xc4 ♕c7 16 h3 ♗f5 17 ♘g5 ♗g6 18 ♕e2 ♘d7 19 ♗d3 ♗xd3 20 ♕xd3 ♘f6 = Burn-Marshall, Karlsbad 1911) 14...♗c7 15 ♕b1 ♗xf3 16 ♕xb7 ♘d7 17 gxf3 ♖c8 18 ♖e1! ± Raetsky-Varlamov, corr. 1985.

d5133) 13...h6!? should be considered.

d52) 11 bxc3 and now:

d521) 11...dxc4 12 ♗g5 ♖xe1+ 13 ♕xe1 ♕f8 14 ♗xc4 ♘d7 15 ♗d3 ♘b6 16 c4 c5 17 d5 ♗d7 18 h3 ♖e8 19 ♕d2 ♘c8 20 a4 ± Khalifman-Rozentalis, Minsk 1986.

d522) 11...♖xe1+ 12 ♕xe1 h6 13 h3 ♗e6 14 cxd5 cxd5 15 ♘e5 ♘c6 16 f4 ♕c7 17 ♗d2 ♖e8 = Hawelko-Garcia Gonzales, Polanica Zdroj 1987.

d523) 11...♗g4 12 ♗g5 ♖xe1+ 13 ♕xe1 ♕d7 (13...♕c8? 14 ♗e7 ♗xe7 15 ♕xe7 h6 16 ♘e5 ♗e6 17 f4 ± Novik-Meiers, Leningrad 1989) 14 ♕e3 (14 ♘e5 ♗xe5 15 ♕xe5 f6 16 ♗xf6 gxf6 17 ♕xf6 ♘a6 18 ♖e1 ♖f8 19 ♕h4 ♖f7 ∞) 14...♕e6! (14...♘a6 15 cxd5 cxd5 16 ♖b1 ±) 15 ♖b1 b6 16 cxd5 cxd5 17 c4! ♕xe3 18 fxe3 (18 ♗xe3 ♗xf3 19 gxf3 ♘c6 20 cxd5 ♘e7 =) 18...♘c6!? 19 cxd5 ♘b4 20 ♗c4 ♗f5 gives Black compensation, Hübner-Timman, Rotterdam 1988.

We now return to 9...♗f5 *(D)*:

10 ♕b3

Attempting to exploit the weakness on b7 is the only dangerous line, but it turns out that Black does not have to defend the pawn. The alternatives are:

a) 10 ♕c2 ♗g6 11 c5 ♗c7 12 ♘c3 ♘xc3 13 ♗xg6 hxg6 14 bxc3 ♘d7 15

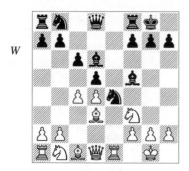

W

♗g5 ½-½ Yudasin-Rozentalis, USSR Ch (Leningrad) 1990.

b) 10 ♘c3 ♘xc3 11 bxc3 ♗xd3 12 ♕xd3 dxc4 13 ♕xc4 ♘d7 and then:

b1) 14 ♖b1 ♕c7 15 ♕d3 ♖ae8 16 ♗e3 b6 17 c4 ♗f4 =.

b2) 14 ♕b3!? ♕c7 15 c4 (15 ♗a3!?) 15...♖fe8 16 ♗b2 h6 17 g3 ♕b6 18 ♕c2 ♕a5 19 ♗c3 ♕h5 20 ♘h4 b5! = Timman-Akopian, Groningen 1996.

b3) 14 ♗g5 and here:

b31) 14...♘b6!? 15 ♕b3 (15 ♕d3 ♕d7 16 ♗h4 h6 17 ♗g3 ♖ae8 18 c4 ♘c8 is equal, Wang Zili-Ye Rongguang, China 1987) 15...♕c7 16 ♖e2 h6 17 ♗d2 c5 (17...♖ae8!?) 18 ♖ae1 (de Firmian-Wolff, Philadelphia 1987) 18...cxd4 19 cxd4 ♕c4 20 ♕b1 ♕d5 with equality.

b32) 14...♕c7 and then:

b321) 15 ♕b3 ♖fe8 (15...c5 16 ♖ab1 b6 17 ♕d5 ♖ae8 18 ♖bd1 ♖xe1+ 19 ♖xe1 ♘b8 20 h3 h6 21 ♗d2 ♖d8 = Bashkov-Haba, Ostrava 1991) 16 c4 c5 17 d5 ♘e5 = Tseshkovsky-Makarychev, Moscow 1992.

b322) 15 ♗e7 ♘b6 16 ♕e2 (16 ♗xd6 ♕xd6 17 ♕b3 ♖ae8 18 c4 ♕c7 19 a4 ♘d7 20 ♖ab1 b6 = Ivanchuk-Gelfand, Lvov 2000) 16...♗xe7 17

♕xe7 ♕xe7 18 ♖xe7 ♖ab8 19 ♖b1 ♖fe8 20 ♖c7 f6 21 ♔f1 ♔f8 22 ♘h4 ♘c4 = Kobaliya-Volzhin, Cuba 2000.

10...♘a6 *(D)*

Or: 10...♕b6 11 ♕c2!; 10...♕d7 11 ♘c3 (11 cxd5 cxd5 12 ♘c3 ♗e6! 13 ♗xe4 dxe4 14 d5 ♗xd5 15 ♘xd5 ½-½ Mikhalchishin-Ionov, Klaipeda 1988) 11...dxc4 12 ♗xc4 ♘xc3 13 bxc3 b5 14 ♗f1 ±.

W

11 ♘c3

White should avoid 11 ♕xb7? in view of the reply 11...♘b4.

The alternative is 11 cxd5 cxd5 (or 11...♘ec5 12 dxc5 ♘xc5 13 ♗xf5 ♘xb3 14 axb3 cxd5 ±) 12 ♘c3, and now:

a) 12...♗b4? 13 ♕xd5! ♕xd5 14 ♘xd5 ♖fe8 15 ♖e3 ± Akopian-Rozentalis, Daugavpils 1989.

b) 12...♘b4 13 ♗xe4 dxe4 14 ♗g5 (14 ♘xe4 ♗e6 gives Black compensation) 14...♕b6 15 ♘xe4 ♖fe8 16 ♘xd6 ♕xd6 17 ♗f4 ♕b6 18 ♗c7 ± Khalifman-Akopian, Groningen PCA 1993.

c) 12...♗e6 and now:

c1) 13 ♕xb7 is met by 13...♘b4 14 ♗xe4 ♖b8 with a draw.

c2) 13 a3 ♘c7 14 ♕c2 (14 ♕xb7 ♖b8 is again a draw since 15 ♕c6?

loses to 15...♗d7) 14...f5 15 ♘e2 ♗f7 16 ♗f4 ½-½ Popović-Fahnenschmidt, Bundesliga 1988/9.

c3) 13 ♘b5!? ♘b4 14 ♘xd6 ♕xd6 15 ♗b1 ♘c6! (15...♖ac8 16 ♗e3 f5 17 g3 f4 18 ♗xf4 ♖xf4 19 gxf4 ♕xf4 20 ♖xe4 ♗h3 21 ♗d3 ♕h6 22 ♖h4 ♖c1+ 23 ♕d1 ♖xd1+ 24 ♖xd1 ♕e6 25 ♗xh7+ ♔f8 26 ♖f4+ 1-0 Ivanchuk-Shirov, Monaco Amber blindfold 2000) 16 ♕xb7 ♖fb8 17 ♕a6 ♘xd4 18 ♕xd6 ♘xf3+ 19 gxf3 ♘xd6 20 b3 ♘f5 with equality.

11...dxc4

Or:

a) 11...♘d2 12 ♗xd2 ♗xd3 13 c5 ±.

b) 11...♘ec5?! 12 dxc5 ♘xc5 13 ♗xf5 ♘xb3 14 axb3 dxc4 (14...d4 15 ♘xd4 ♗xh2+ 16 ♔xh2 ♕xd4 17 ♔g1 ± Vojna-Dempster, corr. 1991) 15 bxc4 ♗b4 16 ♗g5 ♕b6 17 ♗e3 ♕c7 18 g3 ± Khalifman-Rozentalis, Vilnius 1988.

12 ♗xc4

12 ♕xc4?! ♗xh2+! 13 ♔xh2 ♘d6 14 ♕b3 ♗xd3 15 ♗g5 ♕c7 16 ♖e7 ♕c8 17 ♗f4 ♗c4 18 ♕c2 ♘f5 19 ♖e5 ♗e6 20 g4 ♘e7 21 ♔g3 ♘b4 ∓ Emelin-Avrukh, Alma-Ata 1991.

12...♘xc3 13 bxc3 b5

White never got around to taking the b7-pawn and must now simply retreat his bishop. The resulting position offers White no advantage.

14 ♗f1 ♘c7 15 a4

15 ♗a3 ♗e6 16 ♕b2 ♗d5 17 ♘e5 ♖e8 18 ♗xd6 ½-½ Serper-Akopian, Adelaide jr Wch 1988.

15...a5

15...a6 16 ♗g5 (16 ♗a3 ♗e6 17 ♕c2 ♗d5 18 ♗xd6 ♕xd6 19 ♘g5 g6

20 ♘e4 ♗xe4 21 ♕xe4 ♖fe8 is level) 16...♕d7 17 ♘e5 ♗xe5 18 dxe5 ∞.

16 ♗g5 ♕d7 17 ♘e5 ♗xe5 18 dxe5 ♗e6 19 ♖ed1 ♗xb3 20 ♖xd7 ♖fc8

∞ Oll-Rozentalis, Klaipeda 1988.

B)

9 ♕c2 *(D)*

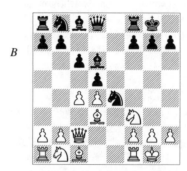

Another direct attack against the e4-knight, but this shares one of the defects of ♖e1, namely that the threat to take on e4 is not especially serious, and so Black can simply ignore it.

9...♘a6

9...f5!? is riskier, since it weakens the a2-g8 diagonal and the e5-square. Then:

a) 10 ♕b3 ♔h8 11 ♘c3 and now:

a1) 11...dxc4 12 ♗xc4 ♘xc3 13 ♕xc3 (13 bxc3!? ±) 13...b5 14 ♗b3 f4 15 ♘e5 ♕f6 16 ♖e1 ±.

a2) 11...♘a6 12 cxd5 (12 ♘e2?! ♘b4 13 ♗b1 dxc4 14 ♕xc4 ♕e8 15 ♗f4 ♘d5 16 ♗xd6 ♘xd6 17 ♕c5 ∞ Rodin-Lopatsky, corr. 1985) 12...cxd5 and here:

a21) 13 ♘xd5?! ♗e6 14 ♕xb7 ♘ac5 15 dxc5 ♘xc5 16 ♕b5 ♖b8 and Black is much better.

a22) 13 ♘e2?! ♘b4 14 ♗f4 a5 15 ♗b5 ♗xf4 16 ♘xf4 g5 17 ♘e2 g4 18 ♘e5 f4 (18...♘d2?! 19 ♕e3 ♘xf1 20 ♖xf1 ♘c6 21 ♗xc6 bxc6 22 ♕h6 ± Kuznetsov-Varlamov, corr. 1986) 19 ♖ad1 ♘d6 (19...f3 20 ♘g3 ♗f5 21 gxf3 ♘xg3 22 fxg3 ♗c2 23 ♕e3 gxf3! 24 ♖d2 ♗e4 25 ♘xf3 ♕b6 gives Black compensation, Peleshev-Borisov, corr. 1985) 20 ♗d3 (20 a3 ♘xb5 21 axb4 f3 22 ♘g3 ♖a6! ∓ Grozdensky-Borisov, corr. 1986) 20...♘xd3 21 ♘xd3 f3 22 ♘g3 ♘c4! ∓ Forsberg-Borisov, corr. 1988.

a23) 13 ♗xa6 bxa6 14 ♕xd5 ♖b8 15 ♕c4 (15 ♘e5 ♗b7 16 ♕e6 ♕h4 17 f4 ♗xe5 18 fxe5 ♘xc3 19 bxc3 ♕e4 is equal, Am.Rodriguez-Sieiro, Cuba 1982) 15...♖b4 16 ♕e2 ♗b7 17 ♗e3 ♖e8 18 a3 ♖b3 19 ♘xe4 ♖xe4 gives Black compensation, Madsen-Kristensen, corr. 1986.

b) 10 ♘c3 and now:

b1) 10...♘xc3? 11 bxc3 b6 (11...h6 12 ♖e1 b6 13 ♘e5 ± Napier-Mason, Hanover 1902) 12 ♖e1 ♕f6 13 ♗g5 ♕g6 14 ♗e7 ± Langier-Neme, Buenos Aires 1991.

b2) 10...♘a6 and here:

b21) 11 a3 – 9...♘a6 10 a3 f5 11 ♘c3.

b22) 11 ♕b3 ♘b4?! (11...♔h8 – 10 ♕b3 ♔h8 11 ♘c3 ♘a6) 12 ♗e2 ♗e7 13 a3 ♘xc3 14 ♕xc3 ♘a6 15 cxd5 cxd5 16 ♗f4 ± Wittmann-Cederlind, corr. Echt 1972-8.

b23) 11 cxd5!? ♘b4 12 ♕d1 ♘xc3 13 bxc3 ♘xd3 14 ♕xd3 cxd5 15 ♕b5 ♔h8 16 ♔h1 ♗c7 17 ♗a3 ± Ernst-Machado, Malmö 1986/7.

We now return to 9...♘a6 *(D)*:

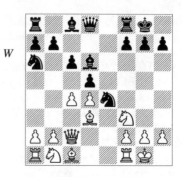

10 a3

10 ♗xe4 dxe4 11 ♕xe4 concedes time and the bishop-pair. Black has more than one way to obtain adequate compensation for the pawn:

a) 11...♘b4!? 12 ♘g5 (12 ♘a3?! ♖e8 13 ♕h4 ♕xh4 14 ♘xh4 – *11...♖e8 12 ♕h4?! ♕xh4 13 ♘xh4 ♘b4 14 ♘a3*; 12 a3?! ♖e8 13 ♘e5 ♘a6 14 ♕c2 ♗xe5 15 dxe5 ♖xe5 ∓ Serovalsky-Fedoseev, corr. 1986) 12...f5 13 ♕e2 f4 and then:

a1) 14 ♘f3 ♗g4 15 a3 ♗xf3 16 gxf3 ♕h4 17 ♕e6+ ♔h8 18 ♕g4 (18 ♕xd6? ♖f6 19 ♕d7 ♘c2 20 ♖a2 ♘xd4 ∓/−+; 18 axb4? ♖f6 19 ♕d7 ♖g6+ 20 ♔h1 ♖d8 21 ♕f5 ♖g5 22 ♕e6 ♕h5 23 ♘d2 ♖g6 −+ Kliets-Grodzensky, corr. 1986) 18...♕xg4+ 19 fxg4 ♘c2 20 ♖a2 ♘xd4 ∓ Kuznetsov-Raetsky, corr. 1986.

a2) 14 ♘e4 f3 15 gxf3 ♗h3 16 ♖e1 ♕c7 17 a3 ♗xh2+ 18 ♔h1 ♘a6 19 ♘g5 ♗f5 gives Black compensation, Khramov-Raetsky, corr. 1986.

b) 11...♖e8 12 ♕d3 (12 ♕h4?! ♕xh4 13 ♘xh4 ♘b4 14 ♘a3 ♖e4 15 ♘f3 ♗g4 16 ♗e3 ♗xf3 17 gxf3 ♖h4 ∓) 12...♗g4! (12...♘b4?! 13 ♕b3 ♗f5 14 ♗g5 ±; 12...c5!?) 13 ♗g5 ♕d7 14

♘bd2 h6 15 ♗e3 f5 16 ♘b3 ♗xf3 17 gxf3 ♕f7 18 f4 ♘b4 19 ♕c3 ♕h5 gives Black compensation, Kruppa-Rozentalis, Lvov 1985.

The text-move prevents ...♘b4 but costs a tempo. The general impression is that White's plan is simply too slow to trouble Black.

10...♗g4

Or:

a) 10...♖e8!? 11 ♘c3 ♗g4 (11...♗f5 12 ♖e1 should be compared with *9 ♖e1 ♖e8 10 ♕c2 ♗f5*) 12 ♘xe4 (12 c5?! ♗c7 13 ♘xe4 dxe4 14 ♗xe4 ♗xf3! 15 ♗xf3 ♕xd4 16 ♗e3 ♖xe3! ∓ Ehlvest-Dokhoian, Tallinn 1986) 12...dxe4 13 ♗xe4 f5!? (alternatively, 13...♗xf3 14 ♗xf3 ♕h4 15 g3 ♕xd4 16 ♗e3 ♕f6 17 ♗e4 ±) 14 ♗xf5 ♗xf3 15 gxf3 ♕h4 ∞.

b) 10...f5 *(D)* (there seems little reason for Black to block in his light-squared bishop with this move, given that 10...♗g4 is possible) and then:

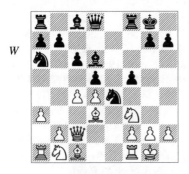

b1) 11 c5 ♗e7 and here:

b11) 12 ♘e5 ♘c7 13 f3 (13 b4!?) 13...♘e6! 14 ♗e3 (14 fxe4? dxe4 ∓) 14...♗g5 15 f4 (15 ♗xg5 ♘4xg5 16 ♕c3 f4 ∓) 15...♗f6 (15...♗h6 16 ♘c3

♗d7 17 b4 ♗e8 18 g4 g6 is unclear, de Firmian-Kogan, USA 1986) 16 b4 g5 17 g3 gxf4 18 gxf4 ♔h8 (18...♗xe5!? 19 dxe5 {19 fxe5 f4 20 ♗f2 ♘6g5 21 ♔h1 ♗h3 22 ♖g1 f3 −+} 19...d4 20 ♗c1 ♔h8 ∓) 19 ♘c3 ♗xe5 20 fxe5 f4 21 ♗f2 ♘6g5! ∓.

b12) 12 b4 ♘c7 13 ♘e5 ♘e6 14 ♗b2 ♘f4 15 f3 ♘g5 16 ♘d2 ± Udalov-Kuzenkov, corr. 1986.

b2) 11 ♘c3 ♘c7 and now:

b21) 12 ♕b3?! ♔h8 13 cxd5 cxd5 ∓ with the point that 14 ♔h1 ♕f6 15 ♘xd5? fails to 15...♕f7 16 ♗c4 b5 ∓.

b22) 12 ♖e1 ♔h8 13 b4 (13 ♗d2 ♗d7, intending ...♗e8-h5, is slightly better for Black, Urday-Duarte, Santiago 1987) 13...♗d7 14 ♗b2 ♗e8 ∞ Gufeld-Kochiev, USSR 1980.

b23) 12 b4!? should be met by 12...♔h8! ∞ rather than 12...♘xc3? 13 ♕xc3 dxc4 14 ♗xc4+ ♘d5 15 ♕b3 ♔h8 16 ♗g5 ± Gaprindashvili-Sternina, USSR 1974.

b24) 12 ♘e2 ♘e6 13 b4 and here:

b241) 13...♔h8 14 ♗b2 ♕e8 (another idea is 14...♖f6!?) 15 ♖ae1 ♕h5 16 ♘e5 f4 17 f3 ♘4g5 18 cxd5 cxd5 19 ♗c1! ♗xe5 20 dxe5 ♗d7 21 ♗b2 and White is much better, Timman-Salov, Saint John Ct (2) 1988.

b242) 13...♗d7 14 ♗b2 ♖f6 (or 14...♘f4 15 ♘xf4 ♗xf4 16 ♘e5 ±) and then:

b2421) 15 ♖ae1?! ♖h6 16 ♗c1 (16 ♘g3 ♘6g5 17 ♘xg5 {17 ♘e5 ♗xe5 18 dxe5 ♘f3+! 19 gxf3 ♕h4 −+} 17...♕xg5 18 ♗c1 f4 19 ♘xe4 ♕h4 20 h3 ♗xh3 ∓ Chandler) 16...♘4g5 17 ♘e5 ♗xe5 18 dxe5 ♘f3+ 19 gxf3 f4 ∓ Chandler-Dive, Wellington 1988.

b2422) 15 ♘e5!?, intending f3, should be considered.

b2423) 15 cxd5 cxd5 16 ♕b3 ♗e8 and here:

b24231) 17 ♘e5?! ♘d2 18 ♕xd5 ♗c6!? 19 ♘xc6 (19 ♕a2? ♗xe5! −+) 19...bxc6 (19...♗xh2+? 20 ♔xh2 ♖h6+ 21 ♔g1 ♕h4 22 ♘e7+ ♔h8 23 f3 +−) 20 ♕xc6 ♖c8! has the point 21 ♕b5 ♗xh2+ 22 ♔xh2 ♖h6+ 23 ♔g1 ♘f3+ 24 gxf3 ♕h4 −+.

b24232) 17 ♖ad1!? intending 18 ♘e5 ±.

b25) 12 c5 ♗e7 13 ♘e2 ♘e6 14 b4 (14 ♘f4 ♘g5 15 ♘xg5 ♘xg5 16 ♖e1 ♗f6 17 ♗e3 g6 18 f3 ♕c7 19 ♕f2 ♕g7 ∓ Sherzer-Wolff, Philadelphia 1987) 14...♗f6 15 ♗b2 a6 16 a4 g6 17 ♘e5 ♗g7 18 f3 ± Kapustin-Kuznetsov, corr. 1986.

We now return to 10...♗g4 *(D)*:

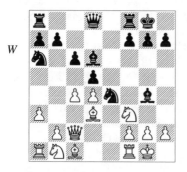

11 ♘e5

Or:

a) 11 ♗xe4?! (this should definitely be avoided; Black regains the pawn and ends up with a lead in development) 11...dxe4 12 ♕xe4 (12 ♘g5 ♗f5 13 ♘c3 {13 ♘xe4? ♕h4 −+; 13 f3 ♗e7 ∓} 13...♖e8 14 ♖e1 ♗c7! ∓

Ljubojević-Timman, Linares 1988) 12...♗xf3 13 ♕xf3 ♕h4 ∓.

b) 11 ♘bd2 ♘xd2 12 ♘xd2 ♕h4 13 f4 ♖ae8 14 c5 ♗b8 (14...♗c7!? intending ...♘b8) 15 ♘b3 ♖e7 16 ♗d2 ♖fe8 17 ♕f2 ♘c7 18 g3 ♕h5 19 f5 f6 20 a4 and here:

b1) 20...♗f3? 21 ♖af1 ♗e4 22 ♘a5 ♘a6 23 ♗xe4 dxe4 24 ♕b3+ ♕f7 25 ♕xf7+ ♔xf7 26 ♖e2 ± Short-Hort, Bundesliga 1987/8.

b2) 20...♘a6 21 ♖af1 (21 ♘a5? ♗f3 22 ♖af1 ♗xg3! −+) 21...♗h3 22 ♖c1 ♗g4 23 ♖cf1 =.

b3) 20...♗e2!? 21 ♖xe2 ♖xe2 22 ♖af1 ∞.

c) 11 c5 ♗c7 12 ♘e5 ♗xe5 13 dxe5 and then:

c1) 13...♘axc5?! is complicated, but the tactics eventually work out in White's favour: 14 f3! (14 ♗xe4 ♘xe4 15 f3 ♕b6+ 16 ♔h1 f5 17 fxe4 fxe4 18 ♖g1 ♖ae8 gives Black compensation) 14...♕b6 (14...♘xd3? 15 ♕xd3 ♘c5 16 ♕c2 +−) 15 ♗e3 d4 16 ♗xd4 ♖fd8 17 ♗xe4 (17 ♗e3 ♖xd3 18 ♕xd3 ♘xd3 19 ♗xb6 axb6 20 fxg4 {20 fxe4 ♗e2} 20...♘xb2 is unclear) 17...♖xd4 18 ♗xh7+ ♔h8 19 fxg4 ♘b3 20 ♔h1 ♘xa1 21 ♕f5 c5 22 ♕xf7! ♔xh7 23 e6 ♕b5 (23...♖d5? 24 ♘c3 ♖e5 25 ♘e4! ♔h8 26 ♘g5!! 1-0 Shakarov-Rozentalis, corr. 1986) 24 ♕f5+ ♔g8 (24...♔h8 25 ♘c3 ♕d3 26 ♕h5+ ♕h7 27 e7 ♕xh5 28 ♖f8+ ♔h7 29 gxh5 +−) 25 ♘c3 ♕e8 26 ♖xa1 ±.

c2) 13...♘exc5! (the correct recapture; even though Black's kingside is weakened, his active pieces enable him to maintain the balance) 14 ♗xh7+ ♔h8 15 b4 ♕h4 (15...♘d7? 16 ♗b2

g6 17 ♗xg6 fxg6 18 ♕xg6 ±) 16 ♗d3
♘xd3 17 ♕xd3 ♘c7 (17...♕h7!?) 18
h3 ♗h5 19 f4 and now:

c21) 19...f5 20 ♘d2 ♘e6 21 ♘b3
∞ d4 (21...b6?! 22 ♘d4 is slightly
better for White, Timman-Salov, Saint
John Ct (4) 1988) 22 ♘xd4 ♖ad8 23
♘xf5 ♕xf4 gives Black compensation.

c22) 19...f6!? 20 ♗b2 fxe5 21 ♗xe5
♘e6 ∞ Salov.

11...♗xe5

Other moves are inferior:

a) 11...♗f5?! 12 b4 ♕h4 13 ♘c3
♘c7 14 ♘f3 ♕h5 15 ♘xe4 dxe4 16
♗xe4 ♗xe4 17 ♕xe4 ♖fe8 18 ♕d3
wins for White, Shirov-Adams, Sarajevo 2000.

b) 11...♗h5?! 12 cxd5 (12 f3 ♕b6
is unclear) 12...cxd5 13 ♗xe4 dxe4 14
♕xe4 ♖e8 15 ♗f4 ♘c7 (15...f6 16
♕d5+ ±/±) and now 16 ♕xb7! ± intending ♘c6 is much better than 16
♕f5 ♗g6 17 ♕g4 ♘e6 18 ♘xg6 ♗xf4
19 ♘xf4 ½-½ Timoshchenko-Mak-
arychev, Moscow 1990.

12 dxe5 ♘ac5 *(D)*

13 f3
Or:

a) 13 cxd5 ♕xd5 14 ♗xe4 ♘xe4
15 ♘c3! (15 f3? ♘c5 ∓) 15...♘xc3 16
♕xc3 ♖fe8 ½-½ Ljubojević-Akopian,
Linares 1995.

b) 13 b4 ♘xd3 14 ♕xd3 ♗f5 15
cxd5 cxd5 = 16 ♕d4 ♖c8 17 f3 (after
17 ♕xa7, 17...b6 gives Black compensation, one possibility being 18 f3?!
♖xc1 19 ♖xc1 ♕g5 20 ♖e1 ♕h4! 21
g3 ♘xg3 22 ♕xb6 d4 with a strong attack; Black can also play 17...d4!?)
17...♘g5 18 ♗xg5 (18 ♕xa7? ♘xf3+
19 gxf3 ♖xc1 −+) 18...♕xg5 19 ♘d2
h5 ∓ Hazai-Vladimirov, Rotterdam
ECC 1988.

c) 13 cxd5 ♕xd5! (13...cxd5? 14
f3 ♕b6 15 ♗e3 d4 16 ♗xd4 ♖fd8 17
♗e3 ♖xd3 18 ♕xd3! +−) 14 ♗xe4
♘xe4 15 f3 ♘c5 16 ♖d1 (16 ♗e3 ♘b3
17 ♘c3 ♘xa1 18 ♖xa1 ♕xe5 ∓; 16
fxg4 ♘b3 ∓) 16...♕b3! 17 ♖d2 ♕xc2
18 ♖xc2 ♘b3 ∓.

13...♘xd3 14 ♕xd3 ♘c5 15 ♕d4

This involves an exchange sacrifice,
but it is the only way to trouble Black.
After other moves, the opposite-
coloured bishops and reduced number
of minor pieces make it easy for Black
to hold the balance; e.g., 15 ♕c2!?
♗h5 16 ♗e3 ♘e6 17 ♖d1 ♕d7 ∞.

15...♘b3 16 ♕xg4 ♘xa1

16...h5!?.

17 ♗h6 g6

17...♕b6+?! 18 ♔h1 g6 19 ♕f4! ±
gives White a dangerous initiative.

18 ♘c3

If White wishes, he can regain the
exchange, but this does not give him
any advantage. The alternative is to
play for the attack, but this is a risky
venture. Perhaps White has enough for

the exchange, but it is unlikely that he has any more than this. The other possibilities are:

a) 18 ♗xf8 ♕xf8 19 cxd5 and then:

a1) 19...cxd5?! is best met by 20 ♖c1! ±, rather than 20 ♕d4 ♘c2 21 ♕f2 (21 ♕xd5? ♘e3 22 ♕xb7 ♘xf1 23 ♔xf1 ♖b8 24 ♕xa7 ♖xb2 25 ♘c3 ♕h6! 26 ♘e2 ♕d2 27 ♕a6 ♕e3! –+) 21...♖c8 22 ♖c1 (22 ♕xa7!?) 22...♘d4 = Ljubojević-Hort, Amsterdam 1988.

a2) Black should play 19...♘c2! ∞.

b) 18 cxd5!? ♕xd5 (18...cxd5 19 ♘c3 ♘b3 20 ♗xf8 ±) 19 ♘c3 ♕c5+ 20 ♔h1 ♘c2!? (20...♘b3 21 ♗xf8 ♖xf8 22 ♕f4! ± Gipslis-Hertz, Biel 1996) 21 ♕e4 ♘xa3!? ∞.

18...♕b6+ 19 ♖f2 ♖fe8 20 ♕f4

Now:

a) 20...f5?! 21 cxd5 ♘b3 22 e6 cxd5 23 ♘xd5 ♕xe6 24 ♘c7 ♕c6 25 ♘xe8 ♖xe8 26 g4 ♕c5 and now White should play 27 ♕a4! ±, rather than 27 ♔g2? ♘d4 28 b4 ♕e5 29 ♖d2 ♕xf4 30 ♗xf4 ♘e6 31 ♗e3 a6 = Shirov-Leko, Linares 2000.

b) Black should prefer 20...♕c7 21 ♖e2 ♖e6 (∞ Shirov); for example, 22 cxd5 cxd5 23 ♕d4 (23 ♘xd5 ♕c5+) 23...♘b3! 24 ♕xd5 ♘a5 25 ♘b5 (otherwise ...♘c6 and ...♖d8 or ...♖ae8) 25...♕b6+ 26 ♗e3 ♖d8! 27 ♗xb6 ♖xd5 28 ♘c3 ♖dxe5 29 ♖xe5 ♖xe5 30 f4 ♖e6! 31 ♗xa5 b6 32 ♗b4 a5 and Black should win (Nunn).

C)

9 ♘c3 (D)

This threatens to take on e4 with the knight, and so Black is forced to exchange on c3. It might seem that White

B

has therefore achieved his fundamental aim and should gain the advantage. However, this isn't quite so. By continuing actively, Black can utilize his quick piece development to harass White. Play then becomes very complicated, with Black sacrificing a piece to expose White's king. As so often with ultra-sharp opening lines, detailed analysis shows that the correct result should be a draw, albeit only after numerous exciting twists and turns.

9...♘xc3 10 bxc3 dxc4

10...♗g4 is an alternative, although it allows a transposition to Line D:

a) 11 cxd5 cxd5 – *9 cxd5 cxd5 10 ♘c3 ♘xc3 11 bxc3 ♗g4.*

b) 11 ♗e2?! dxc4 12 ♗xc4 ♘d7 13 ♕d3 ♗h5 14 ♘g5 ♘f6 (14...♗g6!?) 15 f4 h6 16 ♘f3 ♘d5 leads to an unclear position, Peters-Kochiev, Hastings 1978/9.

c) 11 c5 ♗c7 (11...♗e7!? 12 h3 ♗h5 ∞) 12 ♗g5 ♕xg5 (12...♕c8?! 13 ♖e1 h6 14 ♗e7 ♖e8 15 ♕c2!, Ziatdinov-Galakhov, USSR 1986, 15...♗xf3 16 ♗f5 ±) 13 ♘xg5 ♗xd1 14 ♖fxd1 h6 15 ♘f3 ♘d7 (15...b6 16 c4 bxc5 {16...dxc4?! 17 ♗xc4 ♘d7 18 d5 ±} 17 cxd5 cxd5 18 dxc5 ♘d7 19 ♖ac1 ±)

16 c4 dxc4 17 ♗xc4 ♖ad8 = intending ...b6.

11 ♗xc4 ♗g4 *(D)*
Or:

a) 11...b5?! 12 ♗b3 ♗f5?! 13 ♘e5 ♗xe5 14 dxe5 ♕xd1 15 ♖xd1 a5 16 a4 ± Tal.

b) 11...♗f5?! 12 ♘e5 is slightly better for White.

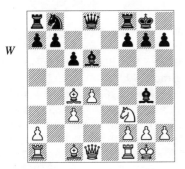

12 ♕d3
Or:

a) 12 a4 ♘d7 13 ♖b1 ♖b8 14 h3 ♗h5 15 ♗e2 ♖e8 16 ♗e3 ♘f6 17 c4 ♘e4 18 ♕b3 c5 = Popović-H.Olafsson, Dortmund 1988.

b) 12 ♗e2 ♘d7 13 ♖b1 ♕c7 14 h3 ♗f5 15 ♗d3 ♗xd3 16 ♕xd3 ♖fe8 17 c4 ♖ad8 18 ♗g5 ♗e7 19 ♗e3 b6 is equal, Beliavsky-Christiansen, Szirak IZ 1987.

c) 12 ♖b1 b5 and then:

c1) 13 ♗e2 ♘d7 14 a4 (14 d5!?) 14...a6 15 c4 bxc4 16 ♕c2 ♗xf3 17 ♗xf3 ♕h4 18 g3 ♕xd4 (Ivanović-Khalifman, Plovdiv 1986) 19 ♖d1 ♕f6 20 ♗xc6 ♖ad8 21 ♗xd7 ♖xd7 22 ♗f4 ♖fd8 =.

c2) 13 ♗d3 ♘d7 and here:

c21) 14 ♗e4 ♖c8 ∞.

c22) 14 ♖e1 ♘b6 15 ♗c2 ♖e8! 16 ♗g5 (16 ♖xe8+? ♕xe8 17 ♗xh7+? ♔xh7 18 ♘g5+ ♔g8 19 ♕xg4 ♕e1#) 16...♕c7 17 ♕d3 g6 18 h3 ♗f5 19 ♕d1 ♖xe1+ 20 ♘xe1 ♗xc2 21 ♘xc2 (Short-Makarychev, Rotterdam 1988) 21...♘d5! ∓.

c23) 14 a4 a6 15 ♗e4 ♖c8 16 axb5 axb5 17 h3 ♗h5 18 ♕d3 ♗g6 19 ♗xg6 hxg6 20 ♘g5 ♗e7 21 h4 ♘b6 with an equal position, Fedorov-Nikolenko, Moscow 1986.

d) 12 h3 ♗h5 *(D)* and then:

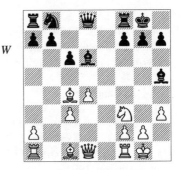

d1) 13 ♖b1 and here:

d11) 13...♘d7 14 ♖xb7 ♘b6 15 ♗a6 ♕f6 16 c4 ♗xf3 17 ♕xf3 ♕xd4 18 ♕xc6 ♖ac8 19 ♕b5 ♘xc4 20 ♖xf7! ♖xf7 21 ♗xc8 ♘e4 (21...♗e7 22 ♗a6 ±) 22 ♗a6 ♘e5 23 ♖d1 ± A.Sokolov-Rozentalis, Sochi 1982.

d12) 13...♕c7 14 ♗d3 ♗g6 15 ♗xg6 hxg6 16 ♘g5 ♘d7 17 f4 ♘f6 18 ♕e1 ♖ae8 19 ♕h4 c5 ∞ Karasev-Frog, USSR Cht (Podolsk) 1990.

d13) 13...b5 14 ♗d3 (14 ♗e2 a6 15 c4 bxc4 16 ♗e3 ♘d7 17 ♘d2 ♗g6 = Kupreichik-Khalifman, Minsk 1985) 14...♘d7 15 a4 (15 ♗e4 ♖c8 16 ♕d3 ♗g6 17 ♗xg6 hxg6 18 c4 a6 19 ♖d1

{19 a4? ♘c5!} 19...♕a5 = Dvoirys-Kochiev, Volgograd 1985) 15...a6 16 ♗e4 ♖c8 17 ♕d3 ♗g6 18 ♗xg6 hxg6 19 ♗g5 (19 c4? ♘c5 ∓; 19 axb5 axb5 =) 19...♕a5 20 c4 (20 ♖a1 ♘b6 21 axb5 ♕xb5 =) 20...bxc4 21 ♕xc4 ♘b6 = Ljubojević-Khalifman, Reykjavik 1991.

d2) 13 ♖e1 ♘d7 and now:

d21) 14 g4?! ♗g6 15 ♘e5?! ♗xe5! 16 dxe5 ♘xe5 17 ♕xd8 ♘f3+ 18 ♔f1 ♖fxd8 19 ♖e3 b5 20 ♗e2 ♘d2+ ∓ Stefansson-Wolff, Baguio City jr Wch 1987.

d22) 14 ♖b1 b5 15 ♗d3 ♘b6 16 ♗e4 ♗g6 17 ♖b2 ♗xe4 18 ♖xe4 ♘d5 19 ♕d3 ♖e8 20 ♖xe8+ ♕xe8 21 ♖e2 ♕d7 = Byrne-Vladimirov, Murcia rpd 1990.

d23) 14 ♗f1 and here:

d231) 14...♖e8 15 ♖xe8+ ♕xe8 16 ♗e3 b5 17 a4 a6 (17...b4!?) 18 axb5 axb5 (18...cxb5!?) 19 ♖xa8 ♕xa8 20 d5 cxd5 21 g4 ♗g6 22 ♗xb5 ± Ehlvest-Anand, Linares 1991.

d232) 14...♕c7 15 c4 ♖fe8 16 ♖xe8+ ♖xe8 17 ♗b2 c5 18 dxc5 ♘xc5 19 ♕d5 ♗xf3 20 ♕xf3 ♗e5 = Kuczynski-Barua, Manila OL 1992.

d24) 14 a4 ♖e8 15 ♖xe8+ ♕xe8 16 ♗d2 ♘f6 17 g4 ½-½ Z.Almasi-Delchev, Batumi Echt 1999.

We now return to 12 ♕d3 *(D)*:

12...♘d7

This is the move that leads to all the complications. Although there is no objective reason to avoid them, more cautious players might prefer the safer 12...♗h5:

a) 13 ♘g5 ♗g6 14 ♕h3 h6 15 ♘f3 ♕f6 =.

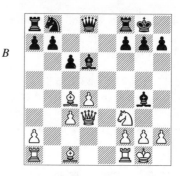

B

b) 13 ♘e5 ♗xe5 14 dxe5 ♕xd3 15 ♗xd3 ♖d8 16 ♗c4 ♘d7 17 f4 b5 18 ♗b3 ♘c5 = Firt-Blatny, Czechoslovak Ch (Brno) 1990.

c) 13 ♖e1 ♗g6 14 ♕e2 (14 ♕d1 ♘d7 15 ♗g5 ♕c7 16 ♕b3 b5 17 ♗e2 h6 18 ♗h4 ♗e4 = Tatai-Ye Rongguang, Manila OL 1992) 14...♘d7 15 ♗g5 ♕a5 16 ♕d2 ♘b6 (16...♕c7!?) 17 ♗b3 ♘d5 18 ♗xd5 ♕xd5 19 ♗e7 ± Armas-Ye Rongguang, Thessaloniki OL 1988.

d) 13 ♗g5 and then:

d1) 13...♕c7 14 ♖ae1 ♘d7 (the alternatives favour White: 14...♗g6 15 ♕e2 ± or 14...♗xf3 15 ♕xf3 ♗xh2+ 16 ♔h1 ♗d6 17 ♖e4 ±) 15 ♗e7 and here:

d11) 15...♖fe8 16 ♘g5 ♗g6? 17 ♗xf7+! +-.

d12) 15...♗g6 16 ♕e2 ♗xe7 (not 16...♖fe8? 17 ♗xd6 ♕xd6 18 ♕xe8+ ♖xe8 19 ♖xe8+ ♘f8 20 ♘e5 +-) 17 ♕xe7 ♕d8 ±.

d13) 15...♗xe7 16 ♖xe7 ♕d6 (not 16...♖ae8? 17 ♘g5 ♗g6 18 ♗xf7+ +-) 17 ♖fe1 b5 18 ♗b3 ♗g6 (or 18...♘c5? 19 ♕f5 ♘xb3 20 ♕xh5 ±) 19 ♕e2 a5 20 c4! ± Chandler-Barua, Thessaloniki OL 1988.

d2) 13...♕a5!? 14 ♗h4 ♘d7 15 ♖ae1 ♗g6 16 ♕d2 (16 ♕e2!?) 16...♖ae8 17 ♗g3 ♗xg3 18 hxg3 ♘f6 19 ♖xe8 ♖xe8 20 ♘e5 ♘d5 21 ♖c1 ♗f5 22 ♗b3 ♗e6 = Boll-M.Schäfer, corr. Echt 1983-92.

13 ♘g5 (D)

This is the most active move. Other moves are less appropriate:

a) 13 ♗g5 ♕a5 14 ♗h4 ♗f5 15 ♕d2 ♘b6 16 ♗b3 h6 17 ♗g3 ♖ad8 = Dvoirys-Donchenko, Smolensk 1991.

b) 13 ♗b3 ♘c5! 14 ♕d1 ♘xb3 15 axb3 ♕f6 = Mainka-Finegold, Dortmund 1990.

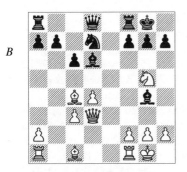

B

13...♘f6

13...g6 14 h3 (or 14 ♘e4 ± Nunn) 14...♗f5 15 ♕f3 ± Short.

14 h3 ♗h5

14...♗d7 15 ♖e1 ±.

15 f4

At first sight the threat to trap the h5-bishop is very awkward, but Black has a tactical way out.

15...h6

15...b5 16 ♗b3 h6 17 ♘f3 (17 g4!? – 15...h6 16 g4 b5 17 ♗b3 ±) 17...♗xf3 18 ♖xf3 a6 19 ♗e3 ♘d5 20 ♗d2 ♕f6 21 ♖af1 ♖fe8 22 g4 ± Kamsky-Barua, 1990.

16 g4

16 ♘f3 ♗xf3 (16...b5 17 ♗b3 ♕d7 18 ♘e5 ±) 17 ♖xf3 (17 ♕xf3 ♕e7 18 ♗d3 ♖fe8 19 ♖b1 and now Black should play 19...♖ad8 with an unclear position, rather than 19...♘d5?! 20 ♗d2 a5 21 f5 ±/± Plaskett-Finegold, Hastings 1988/9) 17...♖e8 18 ♗e3 ♗c7 19 ♖af1 ♕d6 20 ♗f2 ♖e4 21 ♗h4 ♖ae8 22 ♗xf6 ♕xf6 23 ♔h1 ♖e1 = Kamsky-Bareev, Linares 1993.

16...hxg5

Or:

a) 16...♗xg4 17 ♘xf7 ♖xf7 18 ♗xf7+ ♔xf7 19 hxg4 ♘xg4 20 ♕f5+ ± Nunn.

b) 16...b5 17 ♗b3 c5!? 18 ♗d5!? ♗g6 19 ♕xg6 hxg5 20 ♗xf7+! (20 ♕xg5 ±) 20...♖xf7 21 fxg5 ± Corzo-Marshall, Havana 1913.

17 fxg5 (D)

B

This is the critical position for this sharp variation. White has a dangerous initiative, but it appears that Black can hold the position.

17...b5

It looks slightly safer to push the white bishop back first, as it is then less able to take part in the defence of the kingside. However, detailed analysis suggests that 17...♘xg4 18 hxg4 ♕d7 (18...♗xg4 19 g6! ♗e6 20 ♖xf7! 1-0 Ghizdavu-Stanciu, Romania 1972) is also satisfactory:

a) 19 ♕f5 ♗xg4 20 ♕xd7 ♗xd7 21 ♖xf7 ♖xf7 22 g6 ♗e8 =.

b) 19 gxh5 ♕g4+ 20 ♔f2 ♖ae8 21 ♖g1 (21 ♖h1 b5 22 ♕f3 ♕xf3+ 23 ♔xf3 bxc4 24 ♗f4 ♗xf4 25 ♔xf4 c5 =) 21...♕h4+ 22 ♔g2 b5 23 ♗b3 – *17...b5 18 ♗b3 ♘xg4 19 hxg4 ♕d7! 20 gxh5 ♕g4+ 21 ♔f2 ♖ae8 22 ♖g1 ♕h4+ 23 ♔g2 =.*

c) 19 ♕h3!? and then:

c1) 19...♗xg4? 20 ♕h4 ♗f5 (or 20...♗e6 21 ♗d3 g6 22 ♖f6! ♖fe8? 23 ♗xg6! +–) 21 ♗f4! ♗xf4 22 ♖xf4 b5 23 ♗b3 ♖ae8 24 ♔f2! (24 ♖af1?! ♗g6 25 ♕h1 ♖e3! ∓ Morozevich-Ippolito, New York 1997) 24...♕e7 25 ♖xf5 ♕e2+ 26 ♔g1 ♗e4 27 ♕h3 ♖g4+ 28 ♔h1 g6 29 ♖f3 ♖xg5 30 ♖e3 ♕b2 31 ♖g1 +–.

c2) 19...♕xg4+! 20 ♕xg4 ♗xg4 21 ♖xf7 b5! 22 ♖xf8+ (22 ♗b3 ♔h7 =) 22...♔xf8 =.

18 ♗b3

18 gxf6? bxc4 19 ♕d2 ♗g6 20 fxg7 ♔xg7 21 ♕h6+ ♔g8 22 ♗g5 ♗e7 –+ Nunn.

18...♘xg4 19 hxg4 ♕d7! *(D)*

This piece sacrifice is the key to Black's defence. Without it, he would be lost; e.g., 19...♗xg4 20 g6 (20 ♕e4 ♕d7 21 ♖xf7 ♖xf7 22 g6 ♕f5 23 ♗xf7+ ♔f8 24 ♕xf5 ♗xf5 25 ♗g5 ±) 20...♗e6 (20...♕h4 21 ♗f4 ±) 21 ♖xf7! ♕e8 (21...♗xb3 22 ♕h3 ♖xf7 23 ♕h7+ ♔f8 24 ♕h8+ ♔e7 25 ♗g5+ ♔d7 26 ♗xd8 ♖xd8 27 ♕h5 +–) 22

♕h3! ♖xf7 (22...♗xh3 23 ♖f5+! +–) 23 ♕h7+ ♔f8 24 ♗g5 ♖f6 25 ♗xf6 gxf6 26 g7+ +– Nunn.

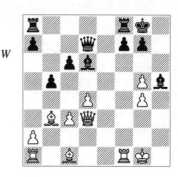

W

20 gxh5

20 ♕f5 ♗xg4 21 ♕xd7 ♗xd7 22 ♖xf7 ♖xf7 23 g6 ♗e8 24 ♗g5! (24 ♗e3? a5 25 ♗e6 ♔f8 26 gxf7 ♗xf7 27 ♖f1 ♖a7 28 c4 bxc4 29 ♗xc4 ♔e8 ∓ Nunn-Salov, Brussels 1988) 24...a5 25 ♖f1 ♖a7 26 ♖f3! a4 27 ♗e6 ♖ac7 28 ♗d8! ♖b7 29 ♗g5 c5 30 dxc5 ♗xc5+ 31 ♔h2 ♔f8 32 gxf7 ♗xf7 33 ♖f5 ♗d6+ 34 ♔g2 = Nunn.

20...♕g4+ 21 ♔f2 ♖ae8 22 ♖g1

22 ♖h1?? ♗g3+ –+.

22...♕h4+ 23 ♔g2 ♕h2+!

Accuracy is required. The alternatives are inferior:

a) 23...c5? 24 ♖h1 (1-0 Short-Hübner, Tilburg 1988) 24...♕g4+ 25 ♔f1 c4 26 ♗d1 ♖e1+ 27 ♔xe1 ♕g2 28 ♕e2 ♕xh1+ 29 ♔d2 +– Short.

b) 23...♕xh5? 24 ♔f1 ♕h2 25 ♗d2 is much better for White.

c) 23...♖e4? 24 ♕f3 ♗h2 and then:

c1) 25 ♖h1?! ♖g4+ 26 ♔f1 ♖g3 and now:

c11) 27 ♕xc6? ♕h3+ 28 ♔f2 (28 ♔e1 ♖g2 intending ...♗g3+ and Black

wins) 28...♕f5+ 29 ♔e1 (29 ♔e2
♕d3+ 30 ♔e1 ♖g2 and Black forces
mate) 29...♗g1! (29...♖c8? 30 ♗e6!
1-0 Psakhis-Mikhalchishin, Klaipeda
1988) 30 ♔d1 (30 ♗d2 ♕f2+ 31 ♔d1
♖d3 −+) 30...♕d3+ 31 ♔e1 (31 ♗d2
♗e3 −+) 31...♖g2!! 32 ♕xg2 ♖e8+
and again Black wins.

c12) 27 ♕f5! ♕xh5 28 ♕e4! (28
♔f2 ♕h4 29 ♔f1 =) may well be very
good for White.

c2) 25 ♗d2! ♖g4+ 26 ♕xg4 ♕xg4+
27 ♔xh2 ♕h4+ (27...♕xh5+ loses to
28 ♔g3) 28 ♔g2 ♕e4+ (28...♖e8 29
♗d1 intending ♗f3) 29 ♔f2 ♕f5+
(29...♖e8 30 ♖g2! +−) 30 ♔e2 ♖e8+
31 ♔d1 ♕f2 32 ♔c2 ♖e2 33 ♖gd1
♕f5+ 34 ♔c1 +−.

24 ♔f1 ♗f4

Now perpetual check is inevitable.

25 ♕f3

White should avoid both 25 ♗d1?
♖e1+ −+ and 25 ♗xf4? ♕xf4+ 26 ♔g2
♖e3 ∓.

**25...♖e1+ 26 ♔xe1 ♕xg1+ 27 ♔e2
♗xc1 28 ♖xc1!**

28 ♔d3 ♕xg5 ∓.

**28...♕xc1 29 g6 ♖e8+ 30 ♔d3
♕b1+**

30...♖e7 31 gxf7+ ♔f8 32 ♕h3
♕b1+ 33 ♗c2 ♕xa2 34 ♕c8+ =.

31 ♔d2 ♕e1+

with perpetual check, A.Sokolov-
Oll, USSR Ch (Odessa) 1989.

D)

9 cxd5 cxd5 10 ♘c3 *(D)*

This is the most challenging line for
Black. Just as in the previous line,
White forces Black to exchange on c3.
The difference is that the preliminary

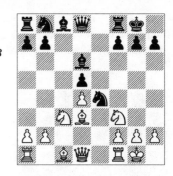

exchange on d5 has broken up Black's
queenside pawns, and White is able to
maintain his bishop on the active diagonal b1-h7.

10...♘xc3

10...♖e8 11 ♗xe4 dxe4 12 ♘g5 ♗f5
13 ♖e1 h6 14 ♘gxe4 ♗xe4 15 ♘xe4
♗xh2+ 16 ♔xh2 ♕h4+ 17 ♔g1 ♖xe4
± Yusupov.

11 bxc3 ♗g4

11...♘c6 12 ♘g5 g6 13 f4 gives
White a slight advantage.

12 ♖b1 *(D)*

White at once tries to exploit Black's
dislocated queenside pawn-structure.
The alternatives are:

a) 12 h3 ♗h5 13 ♕b3 (13 ♖b1 and
now: 13...b6 – *12 ♖b1 b6 13 h3 ♗h5*;
13...♘d7 – *12 ♖b1 ♘d7 13 h3 ♗h5*)
13...♗xf3 14 ♕xb7 ♘d7 15 gxf3 ♘b6
16 ♖b1 ♕f6 17 ♔g2 ♖ac8 18 ♕xa7
(18 ♖b3 ♖c7 gives Black compensation) 18...♖xc3 19 ♖xb6 ♖xd3 20 ♗e3
♕g6+ 21 ♔h1 ♕e6 22 ♔g2 ♕g6+ =
Capablanca-Marshall, New York (20)
1909.

b) 12 ♗b1!? (Tseshkovsky's move)
12...♗h5?! (12...♘c6! ∞) 13 ♕c2 ♗g6
14 ♕b3 b6 15 ♗xg6 hxg6 16 ♔h1
♗c7 17 ♗a3 ♖e8 18 ♖ae1 ♖xe1 19

罝xe1 a6 (19...勾c6 20 彎b5 勾a5 21 奄e7 wins for White) 20 勾e5 罝a7 21 f4 ± Tseshkovsky-Vladimirov, USSR 1987.

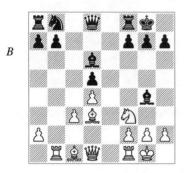

Now:
D1: 12...b6   176
D2: 12...勾d7   180

D1)

12...b6

Black decides simply to save his b7-pawn. The advantages of this are that he doesn't have to worry at each move that White might take on b7, and that the knight can now be developed at c6 instead of b7. The disadvantage is that ...b6 costs Black a tempo which he might otherwise have saved, and that he will be forced to defend the d5-pawn in a rather clumsy way.

13 罝b5

13 h3 奄h5 14 罝e1 (14 罝b5 a6 15 罝b1 勾c6 16 奄e3 奄c7 17 罝e1 勾a5 18 g4 奄g6 19 奄xg6 hxg6 20 勾e5 = Kamsky-Meiers, Dresden 1992) 14...勾c6 15 奄f1 (15 彎a4 彎c7 =) 15...奄h8 16 罝b5 ½-½ Wolff-Akopian, Los Angeles 1991.

13...奄c7 *(D)*

This looks ugly, but if White is unable to make use of his active rook straight away, then he will be forced to retreat. 13...勾c6? 14 罝xd5 奄xh2+ 15 勾xh2 奄xd1 16 罝xd8 罝fxd8 17 罝xd1 ± Short.

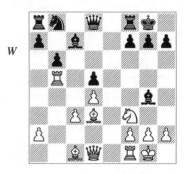

14 h3

Or:

a) 14 罝e1!? a6 15 罝b1 勾d7 16 奄a3 (16 奄g5 勾f6! =) 16...罝e8 17 奄xh7+ 奄xh7 18 罝xe8 彎xe8 19 勾g5+ 奄g6! 20 彎xg4 勾f6 21 彎h4 彎e2 22 罝f1 and now Black should continue 22...罝e8! ∞, rather than 22...奄xh2+?! 23 彎xh2 奄xg5 24 奄e7!! 彎xe7 25 f4+ 奄f5 26 彎h3+ 奄g6 27 彎h4! 彎e3+ 28 奄h1! 勾h5 29 彎g5+ 奄h7 30 彎xh5+ 奄g8 31 彎xd5 ± Ivanchuk.

b) 14 c4 is a major alternative, aiming to open up the fifth rank to swing the rook across for a kingside attack. Then:

b1) 14...彎d6?! 15 罝e1! 奄xf3 (alternatively, 15...dxc4 16 奄e4 勾c6 17 罝d5 彎b4 18 a3! 彎b3 19 奄xh7+ 奄xh7 20 勾g5+ 奄g8 21 彎xg4 ±) 16 彎xf3 彎xh2+ 17 奄f1 勾c6 18 罝xd5 and White is much better, Short-Salov, Amsterdam 1989.

b2) 14...dxc4! 15 ♗e4 ♘c6! 16 ♖g5 (16 ♗xc6? ♕d6 ∓; 16 ♗a3 ♕f6 17 ♗xf8 ♖xf8 18 ♗xc6 ♕xc6 ∓; 16 ♗xc6 ♕d6 17 ♗xa8 ♗xf3 18 ♗f4 ♕xf4 19 g3 ♗xd1 20 gxf4 ♗xf4 gives Black compensation) 16...♗xf3 17 ♕xf3 and then:

b21) 17...♘xd4 18 ♕g4! (the alternative is 18 ♗xh7+ ♔xh7 19 ♕h5+ ♔g8 20 ♖xg7+ =) 18...f5 (18...♘e6 19 ♖d1! ±) 19 ♖xg7+ ♔h8 20 ♗xf5! ♖xf5 21 ♖xc7 ♕xc7 22 ♕xd4+ ♕g7 23 ♕xc4 gives White compensation.

b22) 17...♕d6 is the best defence; Black offers the exchange to defuse White's attack. Now:

b221) 18 ♖h5? g6 19 ♗a3 ♘xd4 20 ♕h3 ♘e2+ 21 ♔h1 ♕d4 ∓.

b222) 18 g3 ♘xd4 19 ♕e3 ♖ae8 20 ♗a3 ♘e2+ 21 ♕xe2! (21 ♔g2 ♕d4 ∓) 21...♕xa3 22 ♗xh7+! ♔xh7 23 ♕h5+ ♔g8 24 ♖xg7+ ♔xg7 25 ♕g5+ with a draw.

b223) 18 ♖g3 ♘xd4 19 ♕g4 g6 (19...♕e5 20 ♗f4 ♘e2+ 21 ♕xe2 ♕xf4 22 ♗xa8 ♖xa8 ∓) 20 ♗xa8 f5 (not 20...♖xa8? 21 ♖d1 ♖d8 22 ♔f1 ∞ Short-Timman, Hilversum (4) 1989) 21 ♕h4! (21 ♕d1?! ♖xa8 22 ♖e1 b5 23 ♗b2 ♖d8 −+; 21 ♗a3? ♕e5 22 ♕d1 ♘e2+ −+) 21...♖xa8 (21...♘e2+? 22 ♔h1 ♘xg3+ 23 hxg3 ♖xa8 24 ♕xc4+ ♔g7 25 ♗f4 +−) 22 ♖h3 h5 23 ♗b2 (23 ♗a3? ♘e2+ 24 ♔h1 ♕c6 ∓ Oll-Akopian, Manila OL 1992; 23 ♔h1!?) 23...♖d8 24 ♖e1 ♖d7! is roughly level. Although Black's king is still somewhat exposed, the two pawns and advanced c-pawn permit Black to keep the balance.

14...a6 *(D)*

Other moves are inferior; for example, 14...♗h5? 15 c4 ±/+− or 14...♗e6?! 15 ♘g5 h6 16 ♕h5 ♕d6 17 g3 ♘d7 18 ♗f4 ± Dvoirys-Rozentalis, Barnaul 1984.

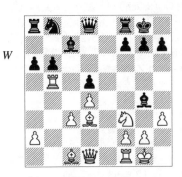

After the text-move, White must sacrifice the exchange if he wants to cause Black any problems. There are two different ways to do so, and it is far from clear which is best.

15 hxg4

A positional exchange sacrifice. Otherwise:

a) If 15 ♖b3, then 15...♗h5 = intending ...♗g6.

b) The alternative exchange sacrifice 15 ♖xd5!? deserves attention. 15...♕xd5 16 hxg4 ♘c6 17 ♘g5 (17 ♕c2!? g6 18 ♕d2 ♕d7 19 ♕h6 f6 20 ♗c4+ ♔h8 21 ♗xa6 ♗d6 22 ♗b5 ♕c7 23 a4 gives White compensation, Kruszynski-Stolte, Germany 1991/2) 17...h6 and now:

b1) 18 ♘h3!? is worth considering.

b2) 18 ♘e4 ♖ad8! (18...♖fe8 19 ♕f3 ♖ad8 20 ♗b1 ♖e6 21 g5 ♘e7 22 gxh6 f5 23 c4 ♕xc4 24 ♘g3 g6 25 ♗g5 ♕d5 26 ♕c3 ± Antonio-Lima,

Novi Sad OL 1990) 19 g5 ♖fe8 20 ♖e1 ♘xd4! 21 cxd4 ♕xd4 22 ♕c2! ♕xd3 23 ♕xc7 ♖c8 24 ♕b7 ♖xc1 25 ♖xc1 ♕xe4 26 ♕xb6 = Dvoirys-Rozentalis, Lvov Z 1990.

b3) 18 ♗h7+!? ♔h8 19 ♗e4 ♕d6 20 ♘f3 ♖fe8 21 ♗c2 b5 (21...♕d7?! 22 g5 ♕g4 {22...h5 23 ♘e5 +−} 23 gxh6 gxh6 24 ♕d3 ♕g7 25 ♘h4 ± Benjamin-Zamora, Philadelphia 1999; 21...♘e7 22 ♘e5 ±) 22 ♕d3 ♕g6 23 ♕xg6 fxg6 24 ♗xg6 ±.

15...axb5 16 ♕c2

16 ♗xh7+? ♔xh7 17 ♘g5+ ♔g8 (17...♔g6? 18 ♕d3+ f5 19 ♖e1 +− Wolff-Miller, USA 1992) 18 ♕d3 ♖e8 (18...g6? 19 ♕h3 ♔g7 20 ♕h7+ ♔f6 21 ♖e1 ± Chandler) 19 ♕h7+ ♔f8 20 ♕h8+ ♔e7 21 ♕xg7 ♔d7 22 ♘xf7 ♕e7 23 ♗g5 ♕f8 ∓ Al Modiahki-Handoko, Doha 1992.

16...g6 (D)

16...h6?! 17 g5 ±.

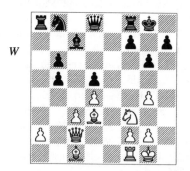

17 ♗xb5

Or 17 ♗h6!? ♖e8 18 ♗xb5, and now:

a) 18...♖e6?! 19 c4 ±.

b) 18...♘d7!? and here:

b1) 19 c4 ♖c8 ∞.

b2) 19 ♗c6 ♖a5 20 ♕b3 ♖e2 21 ♗xd5 ♘e5! ∞ Ivanchuk.

b3) 19 ♕b3 ♖e6 20 ♘g5!? (20 ♕xd5 ♘f6 21 ♕xd8+ ♖xd8 22 ♗g5 ♔g7 23 ♗xf6+ ½-½ Lukin-Ionov, Russia 1992; 20 c4 ♘f6 21 cxd5 ♘xd5 ∞) 20...♖d6 (20...♖e7 21 ♕xd5 ♘f6 22 ♕f3 ±) 21 ♖e1 ♖c8! (21...♘f6!? 22 f3 ♖a7 23 c4 ♗b8 24 c5 bxc5 25 dxc5 ♕a5! ∞) 22 ♗a6 ♖a8 =.

b4) 19 ♗g5 f6 (19...♕c8 20 ♕b3 ±) 20 ♗d2! ± intending 21 ♕b3 or 21 ♗c6 ♖a5 22 c4 − Ivanchuk.

c) 18...♖e4 and then:

c1) 19 g5?! and here:

c11) 19...♕d6 20 ♘e5 and now:

c111) 20...♖xe5? 21 dxe5 ♕xe5 22 g3 ♗d6 23 ♕d2 ♗c5 24 ♔g2 ±.

c112) 20...♕e6? 21 f4! ♘c6 22 ♘xc6 ♖xf4 (22...♗xf4? 23 ♖xf4 ♖xf4 24 ♘e5 ±) 23 ♕d2! (23 ♖xf4? ♗xf4 24 ♘e5 ♗xe5 25 dxe5 ♕xe5 is equal, Short-Gelfand, Brussels Ct (7) 1991) 23...♖xf1+ 24 ♔xf1 ♗g3 25 a4 ♕e4 26 ♗d3 ♕h4 27 ♕e3! ±.

c113) 20...♘c6! 21 ♗xc6 (21 f3?! ♖xe5 22 ♗xc6 ♖e7! −+) 21...♖xe5 22 dxe5 (22 ♗xa8? ♖e2! −+) 22...♕xc6 23 f4 ♖a3! ∓.

c12) 19...♖a3! 20 g3 (20 c4? ♖xf3 21 gxf3 ♕d6 −+; 20 ♘d2 ♕d6 21 g3 ♖e7 ∓) 20...♕c8! is slightly better for Black.

c2) 19 c4 (D) and then:

c21) 19...♗f4? 20 cxd5 ♗xh6 21 ♕xe4 ♖xa2 22 ♖e1 +−.

c22) 19...♕c8 20 g3 (20 ♖c1!? ♗f4 21 ♗xf4 ♖xf4 22 cxd5 ±) 20...♗d6 (not 20...♕xg4? 21 cxd5! ♗xg3 22 fxg3 ♕xg3+ 23 ♕g2 ♕xg2+ 24 ♔xg2 ♖xa2+ 25 ♔g3 +−) 21 ♘g5 and here:

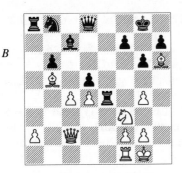

c221) 21...♖xg4 22 ♕e2 ♖xd4 (or 22...♖a3 23 ♖e1 ♖axg3+ 24 fxg3 ♖xg3+ 25 ♔f2 ♕f5+ 26 ♘f3 +−) 23 ♖e1 ♘d7 24 ♕b2 ♗c5 25 ♘f3 +−.

c222) 21...♖e7 22 ♕d1! ♖a3! 23 cxd5 ♕c7 (23...♗xg3 24 fxg3 ♖xg3+ 25 ♔f2 ♖xg4 26 ♘f3 ♕c7 27 ♖g1 ±) 24 ♖e1! ♗xg3 25 ♖xe7 ♕xe7 26 ♕c1! ± Nadanian-Altunian, Erevan 1992.

c23) 19...♖xg4 20 cxd5 ♗f4 (alternatively, 20...♘d7 21 ♕c6 ♘f6 22 ♘e5 ±) 21 ♘e5 (21 ♖e1 ♘d7 22 ♗xf4 ♖xf4 23 ♕d2 ♖xf3 24 gxf3 ♘f6 ∞) and now:

c231) 21...♖h4 22 ♗xf4 ♖xf4 23 ♕c4 (23 ♕d2 ♖f6 24 ♘g4 ♖d6 and now 25 ♖e1!? ♘d7 26 ♕f4 ± is more incisive than 25 ♕f4 ♖a7 26 ♖e1 ♖e7 27 ♖e5, when White merely has compensation, Kotronias-Rozentalis, Debrecen 1991) and then:

c2311) 23...♖a3?? was given as unclear by Yusupov, but it loses to 24 ♕c1 +−.

c2312) 23...♖a7 24 ♖c1 is much better for White.

c2313) 23...♔g7 24 ♖c1 (24 a4!?) 24...♖a3 25 ♖c2 ♖e4 26 ♕b4 ♖a5 27 a4 ♘a6 ∞ Wahls-Rozentalis, Bundesliga 1991/2.

c232) 21...♖xg2+!? 22 ♔xg2 ♗xh6 is unclear.

We now return to 17 ♗xb5 (D):

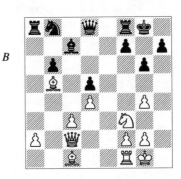

17...♕d6

Or:

a) 17...♘d7 and then:

a1) 18 ♗h6 ♖e8 – *17 ♗h6 ♖e8 18 ♗xb5 ♘d7!?*.

a2) 18 ♕b3 ♘f6 19 ♗h6 ♘xg4! 20 ♗xf8 ♔xf8 =.

a3) 18 g5!? should be considered.

b) 17...♕c8 18 ♗h6 (18 ♕b3 ♕b7 19 ♗h6 ♖c8 20 ♖e1 ♗d6 ∞; 18 ♖e1 ♘d7! 19 ♖e7 ♘f6 20 ♗h6 ♗d6 21 ♗xf8 ♔xf8 = Ivanchuk) 18...♖d8 and now:

b1) 19 ♗g5 ♖d6 20 ♘e5 (20 c4 ♘d7!? ∞ 21 cxd5 ♗d8!) 20...♖a7! (not 20...f6? 21 ♘xg6 +−) 21 f4 ♗d8! ∞ Ivanchuk.

b2) 19 ♕e2! ♗d6 (Tkachev-Ye Rongguang, Djakarta 1994) 20 ♘e5 ♖a7 (20...f6 21 ♘d7!! ♖xd7 22 ♕e6+ ♔h8 23 ♕xf6+ ♔g8 24 ♕e6+ ♔h8 25 ♖e1 ♘c6 26 ♗g5 +−) 21 ♕f3 ♕e6 22 ♗g5 ±.

18 g3

White has only one pawn for the exchange, but his pieces are active, he is slightly ahead in development and he has chances of an attack down the h-file (by ♔g2, ♖h1 and ♕d2-h6, for example). These factors more or less balance each other, so with accurate play Black can achieve equality.

18...♘c6

Or:

a) 18...♖a7 19 ♖e1 ♘d7 (19...♘c6!) 20 g5 ♖d8 21 a4 ± Ivanchuk-Bareev, Linares 1993.

b) 18...♘d7 19 ♗f4 ♕f6 20 ♗xd7 ♗xf4 21 gxf4 ♕xf4 22 ♘e5 ±.

c) 18...♕e6 19 ♔g2 (19 g5 ♘c6 {19...♕e4? 20 ♕xe4 dxe4 21 ♘d2 ±} 20 ♖e1 ♕d7 21 c4 gives White the initiative – Ivanchuk) 19...♕xg4 20 ♖h1 ♖d8 21 ♘g5 h5 22 ♖e1 h4 23 ♗e8 ± Ye Jiangchuan-Nau Oo Kwav Tun, Shanghai 2000.

19 ♔g2 f5

Black must fight for space on the kingside. Not 19...♖fe8? 20 ♖h1! ♖e4 21 ♕d2! ± L.B.Hansen-Danielsen, Valby 1993.

20 ♗f4!?

Or:

a) 20 g5?! f4! ∞.

b) 20 gxf5 ♖xf5 and now:

b1) 21 ♘g5?! ♖af8 22 f4 ♘a7 (22...♖xg5 23 ♗xc6 ♕xc6 24 fxg5 ♖xf1 25 ♔xf1 ♗xg3 26 ♔g2 =) 23 ♗d3 ♖xg5 24 fxg5 ♕xg3+ 25 ♔h1 ♖xf1+ 26 ♗xf1 intending ♕g2 with unclear play.

b2) 21 ♘h4! ♖f7 22 f4 (22 ♗h6 ♘e7!) 22...♘a5 (22...♘e7 23 ♘f3 ♘f5 24 g4!? ∞) 23 ♘f3 ♘c4! intending ...♘a3.

20...♕d7 21 g5 ♗xf4

21...♖a5 22 c4! ±.

22 gxf4 ♕c7 23 ♗xc6! ♕xc6 24 ♘e5 ♕d6

24...♕a4 25 ♕d3 ♕xa2 26 ♖h1 ±.

25 a4 ♖a5!? 26 ♖b1 ♖b8

Intending ...b5; 26...♖fa8? 27 ♖b4 ♖8a6 28 ♕b3 ±.

27 ♖b4 b5 28 ♕b3 ♖xa4 29 ♖xb5 ♖xb5 30 ♕xa4 ♖b7

= A.Sokolov-Nikčević, Yugoslavia 1998.

D2)

12...♘d7 (D)

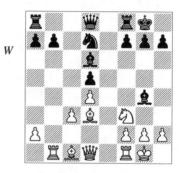

Black concentrates on development, and offers his b7-pawn.

13 h3

It is best to push the bishop back to h5 before undertaking further operations. The alternatives are:

a) 13 ♗c2?! ♗h5 14 ♗b3?! ♘b6 is slightly better for Black, Bademian-Valkesalmi, Dubai OL 1986.

b) 13 ♖b5 ♘b6 14 h3 ♗d7 15 ♖b1 ♗a4 16 ♕e2 ♖e8 17 ♗e3 ♖c8 = Krizinsky-Raetsky, Katowice 1993.

c) 13 ♖e1!? ♘b6 14 a4 ♖c8! (the alternatives are 14...♕d7!? 15 a5 ♘c4 16 h3 ♗f5 17 ♗xf5 ♕xf5 18 ♖xb7 ♘xa5 ∞ and 14...♖e8 15 ♖xe8+ ♕xe8

16 a5 ♘c4 17 ♖xb7 ± Popović-Haba, Austria 1993) 15 a5 ♘c4 16 ♖xb7 (16 ♖b5 ♘xa5 17 ♖xd5 ♖xc3 is unclear) 16...♘xa5 (16...♕xa5!? 17 ♗xh7+ ♔xh7 18 ♘g5+ ♔g8 19 ♕xg4 ♕xc3 =) 17 ♖b5 ♖xc3 18 ♕d2 (18 ♖xd5 ♗xh2+ 19 ♘xh2 ♗xd1 20 ♖xd8 ♖xd8 21 ♖xd1 ♖xd4 22 ♖e1 ♖d8 ∓; 18 ♗b2 ♖c8 19 ♖xd5 ♘c4 =) 18...♖b3 19 ♗xh7+ ♔xh7 20 ♕c2+ ♔g8 21 ♖xb3 ♘xb3 22 ♕xb3 ♗xf3 23 ♕xf3 ♖e8 =.

d) 13 a4 and then:

d1) 13...♘b6?! 14 a5 ♘c4 15 ♖b5 ♗c7 (15...♘xa5 16 ♖xd5 ♗xh2+ 17 ♘xh2 ♗xd1 18 ♖xd8 ♖fxd8 19 ♖xd1 ♖ac8 20 ♗d2 ♘c4 21 ♗xc4 ♖xc4 22 ♘f1 ±; 15...♗e7 16 h3 ♗c8 17 ♗xc4 dxc4 18 ♘e5 ♕c7 19 ♗f4 ♗d6 20 ♕f3 ±) 16 h3 ♕d7 (16...♗e6 17 ♘g5 ±; 16...♗h5? 17 ♗xc4 ♗xf3 18 ♕xf3 dxc4 19 ♗a3 ♖e8 20 ♖xb7 wins for White, Filipenko-Kiseliov, Moscow 1986) 17 ♖c5 ♗h5 18 ♗xc4 ♗xf3 19 ♕xf3 dxc4 20 a6 with a clear advantage for White.

d2) Black should play 13...b6! 14 h3 ♗h5 – *13 h3 ♗h5 14 a4 b6*.

13...♗h5 (D)

Black should not give White the advantage of the two bishops: 13...♗xf3?! 14 ♕xf3 ♘b6 15 g3 ♖c8 16 h4 ♖c7 17 h5 ♖e8 18 ♔g2 g6 19 ♗d2 ♗f8 20 ♖h1 ± Dvoirys-Yakovich, USSR Ch (Kiev) 1986.

Now:

D21: 14 ♖xb7   181
D22: 14 a4   182
D23: 14 ♖b5   183

D21)
    14 ♖xb7

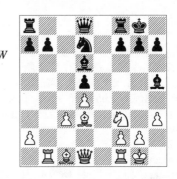

W

White could not have taken the pawn when the bishop was on g4, because Black would have trapped the rook by ...♗c8. Although it is feasible to take the pawn now, White will still be forced to surrender the exchange.

14...♘b6 15 ♗d2

15 ♗a6 ♕e8! 16 ♕e2 (16 ♗d2 ♕c6 intending ...♘c4) 16...♕c6 17 ♕b5 ♕xc3 18 ♗b2 ♕c2 (18...♕c4? 19 ♘e5 ±) 19 ♖c1 ♕e4 (19...♕g6 20 ♕d3 ♕xd3 21 ♗xd3 ♗xf3 22 gxf3 ♖fb8 23 ♖xb8+ ♖xb8 24 ♖c6 ±) 20 ♖e1 ♕g6 21 ♕e2 ♘c4 = A.Sokolov-Rozentalis, Minsk 1986.

15...♗g6

Or:

a) 15...♕c8 16 ♗xh7+! ♔h8 (or 16...♔xh7 17 ♘g5+ ♔g6 18 g4 ♗xg4 19 hxg4 ♕xb7 20 ♖e1! ±) 17 ♖xb6 axb6 18 ♗b1 ±.

b) 15...h6!? 16 ♖e1 (16 ♗a6!?; 16 g4?! ♗xg4 17 hxg4 ♕c8 ∓) 16...♕c8 17 ♗a6 ♕c6 (17...♕f5? 18 ♘h4 +−) 18 ♘e5 ♕xb7 19 ♗xb7 ♗xd1 20 ♗xa8 ♖xe5 (20...♗a4!? 21 ♗c6 {21 ♗b7!? intending ♗a6 ±} 21...♖b8 22 ♗xa4 ♘xa4 23 ♘d3 with a slight advantage for White, Nadyrkhanov-Raetsky, Krasnodar 1995) and now:

b1) 21 dxe5 ♗a4 22 ♗b7 ♗b5! 23 ♖b1 ♗c4 (Black has compensation) 24 a3 (24 ♗e3 ♘a4! 25 ♗d4 ♖b8! 26 ♗xa7 ♘xc3 27 ♗xb8 {27 ♖b2 ♖e8 =} 27...♘xb1 28 a4 d4 =) 24...♖b8 25 ♗c6 ♖c8 26 ♗b5 ♖c5 gives Black compensation, Serper-Akopian, Tbilisi 1989.

b2) 21 ♗b7! ±.

16 ♗xg6

16 ♗a6 can be met by 16...♗f5!? intending ...♗c8. Other possibilities are 16...♕e8 17 ♖e1 and 16...h6 17 ♘e5 ±.

16...hxg6 17 ♕b3

17 ♕e2 ♕c8 18 ♕a6 ♖d8! 19 ♖b1 ♖d7 20 ♖7xb6 axb6 21 ♕xc8+ ♖xc8 22 ♖xb6 ♖a8 ∓.

17...♕c8 18 ♖xb6 axb6 19 ♕xd5 ♖d8 20 ♕b3 ♕a6 21 ♖b1 ♗c7 22 ♖b2

The game is equal, Bodiska-Kaliwoda, Karvina 1989. Although White has two pawns for the exchange, Black's rooks have plenty of scope and White's pieces are not especially active.

D22)

14 a4 *(D)*

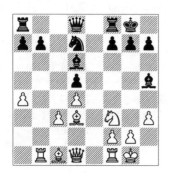

Now White is genuinely threatening to take on b7, because ...♘b6 can be met by a5. However, pushing the a-pawn is rather slow and Black can easily achieve equality.

14...b6

14...♘b6!? is also possible:

a) 15 ♖b5 – *14 ♖b5 ♘b6 15 a4 =*.

b) 15 a5 ♘c4 16 ♗xc4 (16 ♖b5?! ♘xa5 17 ♖xa5 ♗xf3 {17...♕xa5 is best, as 18 ♗xh7+ has little impact} 18 ♕a4 ♗c7 19 ♖xa7 ♕d6 20 g3 ♖xa7 21 ♕xa7 ♕c6 22 ♗a3? ♗b6 −+ Ivanov-Kiseliov, Moscow 1986) 16...dxc4 17 ♖b5 ♗g6 18 ♘e5 a6 19 ♖xb7 ♗xe5 20 dxe5 ♕xa5 21 e6! fxe6 22 ♕d4 ♖f7 23 ♖xf7 ♗xf7 24 ♕xc4 e5 = Krugliakov-Kiseliov, Moscow 1986.

c) 15 ♖e1 ♖b8! 16 a5 ♘c4 17 ♗xc4 dxc4 18 ♖b5 f5! 19 ♕e2 ♔h8! 20 ♕xc4 a6! (20...♗xf3?? 21 gxf3 ♕h4 22 ♔g2 ± A.Sokolov-Skembris, Yugoslavia 1994) 21 ♖b1 (21 ♖d5 ♗f7 −+; 21 ♖b6 ♗c7 ∓) 21...♗xf3 22 gxf3 ♕xa5 ∓.

d) 15 ♔h1!? and here:

d1) 15...♖e8?! 16 a5 ♘c4 17 ♖b5 ♗b8! (17...♘xa5? 18 ♖xd5 ♗xf3 19 ♕xf3 ♕c7 20 ♖xd6 ♕xd6 21 ♕h5 f5 22 ♕xf5 ♕g6 23 ♕d5+ 1-0 Kozlov-Gorelov, Moscow 1986) 18 ♗xc4 ♗xf3 19 ♕xf3 ♕c7 20 ♗f4 ♕xc4 21 ♖fb1 ♗xf4 22 ♕xf4 ♖e1+ 23 ♖xe1 ♕xb5 24 ♕c7! ±.

d2) 15...♗g6 16 a5 ♘c4 17 ♖b5 ♗c7 18 ♗xc4 dxc4 19 ♘e5 a6 =.

15 ♖b5

Or:

a) 15 c4!? dxc4 16 ♗xc4 ♖c8 ∞.

b) 15 ♗f5!? ♗g6 (15...♘f6 16 ♗g5 ♗e7 17 ♕d3 ♗g6 18 ♘e5 ♗xf5 19

♕xf5 ♖c8 20 ♗xf6 ♗xf6 21 ♘d7 ♖e8
22 ♖fe1 ♖xe1+ 23 ♖xe1 ♖xc3 24
♕xd5 ± Kotronias-Arduman, Istanbul
1988) 16 ♕d3 ♕c7 intending ...♖ac8
is unclear.

15...♘f6 16 ♗g5 ♖c8!?

16...♗e7!? 17 g4 (17 ♗xf6 ♗xf6
18 ♗e2 a6 19 ♖b2 ♖e8 = Dolmatov-
Rozentalis, Kharkov 1985) and now:

a) 17...♗g6 and now:

a1) 18 ♘e5 ♖c8!?.

a2) 18 ♗xg6 hxg6 19 ♗xf6 (19
♕b3 ♖c8 20 a5 bxa5 21 ♖a1 ♘e4 22
♖xd5 ♖xc3 23 ♕b7 ♘xg5! 24 ♘xg5
♖c7 ∓ Poliavsky-Raetsky, corr. 1988)
19...♗xf6 20 ♕b3 ♖c8! 21 ♖e1!? (21
a5 bxa5 22 ♖a1 ♕c7 23 ♖axa5 ♕xc3
24 ♕xc3 ♖xc3 25 ♔g2 ♖c7 26 ♖xd5
♖d8 ½-½ Glek-Raetsky, corr. 1987)
21...♕d6! (21...a6 22 ♖xb6 ♖xc3 23
♕xc3 ♕xb6 24 g5 ♗d8 25 ♖e5 ♕b7
26 ♔g2 ±; 21...♕c7? 22 ♖e3 ♕c4 23
♕xc4 ♖xc4 24 a5 ♖fc8 25 axb6 axb6
26 g5 is winning for White, Mikhailov-
Grodzensky, corr. 1987-91) 22 g5 (22
♖xd5 ♖xc3) 22...♕f4! 23 ♕xd5 ♖xc3
with equality.

b) 17...a6!? 18 ♖b3 ♗g6 19 ♘e5
♗d6! 20 ♘xg6 fxg6! 21 ♗h4 ♗c7 22
♖e1 g5! 23 ♗xg5 ♕d6 24 ♖e5 ♕c6 25
♖e7 ♕d6 26 ♖e5 ½-½ I.Semionova-
Chetverik, Balatonbereny 1994.

**17 ♗xf6 ♕xf6 18 ♖xd5 ♗xf3 19
♕xf3 ♕xf3 20 gxf3 ♖xc3 21 ♖xd6**

21 ♗xh7+ ♔xh7 22 ♖xd6 ♖a3 ∓;
21 ♖d1 ♖d8 ∓.

21...♖xd3

= Ivanchuk-Rozentalis, Lvov 1987.

D23)
14 ♖b5 *(D)*

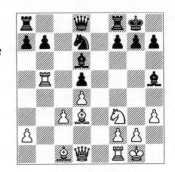

The main continuation. White makes
use of the position of the bishop on h5
to force through c4. This involves a
pawn sacrifice, but in return White obtains a dangerous initiative that can
quickly develop into a deadly kingside
attack if Black plays at all inaccu-
rately. Even against the best defence,
White has chances to maintain a slight
edge.

14...♘b6 15 c4

15 a4 gives Black a choice:

a) 15...♗g6!? 16 ♗xg6 hxg6 17
♕b3 ♖e8 18 ♗g5 ♕d7 19 a5 (19 ♘d2
♕c6 =) 19...♘c4 20 ♖xb7 (20 ♘d2?!
♕c6 ∓ Mestel-Mirallès, Thessaloniki
OL 1988) 20...♗c7! 21 ♕b5 (21 ♗f4?
♘xa5 22 ♖xc7 ♕xc7 23 ♗xc7 ♘xb3
24 ♖b1 ♖ec8 −+) 21...♕d6! 22 ♖a1
(22 a6 ♘a5) 22...a6 23 ♕b4 ♕c6 ∞
Mirallès.

b) 15...a6 and then:

b1) 16 ♖xb6 ♕xb6 17 ♗xh7+ ♔h8!
(17...♔xh7 18 ♘g5+ ♔g6 19 g4) 18
♗d3 (18 g4? ♔xh7 ∓) 18...f5 and
Black is slightly better.

b2) 16 ♗xh7+ ♔xh7 17 ♘g5+
♕xg5 18 ♗xg5 ♗xd1 19 ♖xb6 ♗xa4
20 ♖xd6 ∓.

b3) 16 ♖b1 and here:

b31) 16...♗c7?! 17 ♖e1! ♕d6 18 ♗xh7+! ♔h8 19 ♗d3 f5 20 g3 ♕d7 21 ♘e5! +− Rõtšagov-Kristensen, Gausdal 1991.

b32) 16...♗xf3?! 17 ♕xf3 ♘xa4 18 ♖xb7 ♘xc3 19 ♗xh7+ ♔xh7 20 ♕xc3 ♕c8 (20...♕e8? 21 ♖b6 ± Kozlov-Gorelov, Moscow 1986) 21 ♕xc8 ♖fxc8 22 ♖xf7 a5 23 ♖f5 a4 24 ♖xd5 ♗f8 25 ♗b2 a3 26 ♗a1 ♖cb8 gives Black compensation.

b33) 16...♖e8!? 17 ♗g5 (17 a5 ♘c4 18 ♖xb7 ♘xa5 =) 17...f6 18 ♗h4 ♗c7 19 ♗f5 ♗g6 =.

b34) 16...a5!? 17 ♖e1 ♗c7 18 ♗g5 f6 19 ♗h4 ♖e8 =.

b35) 16...♖b8 17 ♕b3 ♘c4! 18 ♘d2 b5 = Kondali-Ježek, corr. 1987-91.

15...♗xf3

Or:

a) 15...a6?! 16 ♖xb6 ♕xb6 17 c5 ♗xc5 18 dxc5 ♕xc5 19 ♗xh7+ ♔h8 (Bosenberg-Kelbratovsky, corr. 1990) 20 ♗d3 ±.

b) 15...♘xc4 16 ♖xd5 (16 ♗xc4 ♗xf3 17 ♕xf3 dxc4 18 ♖xb7 ♕f6! =) 16...♗h2+ 17 ♘xh2 ♕xd5 18 ♗xc4 ♕xc4 19 ♕xh5 and now:

b1) 19...♕xa2?! 20 d5! ±.

b2) 19...♕xd4 20 ♘f3 ♕c4 (the alternative is 20...♕f6 21 ♗e3 ±) 21 a3 b6 (21...♖ad8 22 ♕a5!) 22 ♗e3 with a slight advantage for White, Dvoirys-Vladimirov, Barnaul 1988.

b3) 19...♖fd8! gives Black compensation, J.Horvath-Greenfeld, Budapest 1989.

16 ♕xf3 dxc4 *(D)*

Black has won a pawn, but has been forced to surrender his light-squared

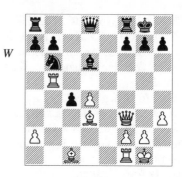

bishop. With two bishops, a rook and a queen well placed to attack Black's kingside, the danger is obvious; indeed, it is perhaps a little surprising that Black has more than one reasonable defence.

17 ♗c2

17 ♗e4 ♕d7 and then:

a) 18 ♖a5?! ♗b4 19 ♖g5 (19 ♖h5? g6 20 ♖g5 ♖ab8 21 ♗f4 ♗d6 22 ♗e3 f5 0-1 Neiman-Borisov, corr. 1990) 19...g6 20 ♗xb7 ♖ab8 21 ♗e4 ♕xd4 is unclear.

b) 18 ♖h5?! g6 19 ♖g5 (19 ♗h6 ♖fd8 20 ♗xb7 gxh5 21 ♕f6 ♗f8 22 ♕g5+ =) 19...♖ab8 20 h4 gives Black a choice between 20...♗e7!? ∞ and 20...f5!?.

c) 18 a4 ♖ab8 19 ♗f5 (19 ♖g5? f6! 20 ♕h5 g6 21 ♗xg6 fxg5 −+; 19 ♗c2 ♖fe8 {19...g6!?} 20 ♗e3 ♘c8?! 21 ♗e4 ♘b6 22 ♖fb1 gives White compensation, Filipenko-Peshiguna, Novi Sad 1989) 19...♕c6 20 ♗e4 with equality, Holmstein-Lelchuk, Helsinki 1992.

17...♕d7

This is the main line, although some of the alternatives may also be playable:

a) 17...f5? 18 ♗xf5 ♕e8 19 a4 g6 20 ♕g4 is much better for White, Robović-Radosavljević, Aschach 1992.

b) 17...g6 18 ♕xb7 ♖e8? (18...♕e8! is very interesting; e.g., 19 a4 ♕e2) 19 ♗g5 ♗e7 20 ♗e3 ♗f6 21 a4 c3 22 ♗b3 ± Yagupov-Dekker, Nagykanisza 1991.

c) 17...a6?! 18 ♗g5 gives Black problems:

c1) 18...♕c7 19 ♗xh7+! ♔xh7 20 ♕h5+ ♔g8 21 ♗f6 ♗h2+ 22 ♔h1 ♕f4 23 ♗xg7 ♔xg7 24 ♖g5+ ♔f6 25 ♕h6+ ♔e7 26 ♖e5+ ♔d7 27 ♕xb6 +−.

c2) 18...f6 19 ♕h5 h6 20 ♗xh6 axb5 21 ♗xg7! f5 22 ♗xf8 ♗xf8 (22...♕xf8 23 ♕g6+ +−; 22...♔xf8 23 ♕xf5+ ♔g7 24 ♕g6+ ♔f8 25 ♖e1 +−) 23 ♗xf5 ±.

c3) 18...axb5 19 ♗xd8 ♖fxd8 20 ♕h5 g6 21 ♕xb5 ♗c7 22 a4 ♖xd4 23 ♕c5 ♖d7 24 g3 ± Beliavsky-Petursson, Reykjavik 1988.

d) 17...♖b8 18 a4 (18 ♗g5!? is possible) 18...a6 19 ♗g5 ♕c7 (19...f6 20 ♕h5 h6 21 ♗xh6 ±) 20 ♗xh7+! ♔xh7 21 ♕h5+ ♔g8 22 ♗f6 ♗h2+! 23 ♔h1 ♕f4! (23...♕d6? 24 ♗xg7 ♔xg7 25 ♖g5+ ♔f6 26 ♖e1 and White wins, Kudrin-Machado, Thessaloniki OL 1988) 24 ♗xg7 ♔xg7 25 ♖g5+ ♔f6 26 ♕h6+ ♔e7 27 ♖e5+ ♔d7 28 ♕xb6 gives White compensation − Kudrin.

e) 17...♕c7!? (Beliavsky) 18 a4 (18 ♗xh7+? ♔xh7 19 ♖h5+ ♔g8 20 ♕f5 f6 21 ♖h7 {21 ♖e1 ♖ae8} 21...♕f7 22 ♗h6 g6 23 ♖xf7 gxf5 wins for Black) 18...a6 (18...♖ab8!? is more ambitious; then 19 a5 ♘c8 20 ♗xh7+?!

♔xh7 21 ♖h5+ ♔g8 22 ♕f5 f6 23 ♖e1 ♘e7! may well be favourable for Black) 19 ♖h5 (19 ♖b1 ♖ab8 =; 19 ♖b2!?) 19...g6 20 ♗h6 ♖fe8 21 ♕f6 ♗f8 22 ♗xf8 ♖xf8 23 ♖c5 ♕d8 24 ♕xd8 ♖axd8 25 ♖b1 ♖d6 26 a5 ♘d7 27 ♖xc4 b5 28 axb6 ♘xb6 = Beliavsky.

We now return to 17...♕d7 *(D)*:

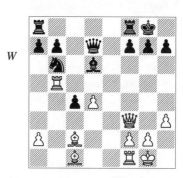

18 a4

18 ♖h5 g6!? (18...h6? 19 ♗xh6 gxh6 20 ♕f6 ♕e6 21 ♗h7+ wins for White; 18...f5? 19 ♗xf5 g6 20 ♗xd7 ♖xf3 21 ♗e6+ ±) 19 d5?! (19 ♖a5 ♗b4 ∓; 19 ♖xh7? ♔xh7 20 ♕h5+ ♔g8 21 ♗xg6 fxg6 −+; 19 ♗f5 gxf5 {19...♕e7!?} 20 ♖xh7 ♔xh7 21 ♕h5+ ♔g8 22 ♕g5+ =) 19...f5!? 20 ♖h4 ♕e7! 21 g3 ♖ae8 ∓ Wittmann-Skembris, Debrecen Echt 1992.

18...g6

This seems to be the strongest move. Other possibilities:

a) 18...♖fe8? 19 ♗f5 ♕c6 (19...♕c7 20 a5) 20 ♗xh7+! ♔xh7 21 ♕xf7 ♗e5 22 ♖xe5 ♖xe5 23 dxe5 +− Howell-Barua, London 1991.

b) 18...♖ae8 19 ♗d2 ♕c6?! 20 d5 ♕c7 21 ♖fb1 ♖b8 22 ♗c3 ♘d7 23 ♗xg7! ♔xg7 24 ♕g4+ ♔h8 25 ♕f5 is much better for White, M.Schlosser-Sarno, Mitropa Cup (Leibnitz) 1990.

c) 18...♗c7 and then:

c1) 19 ♖h5?! is met by 19...g6.

c2) 19 g3 a6 20 ♖h5 g6 21 ♖c5!? (21 ♗h6? f5 22 ♗xf8 ♖xf8 23 ♖h6 ♔g7 24 ♕a3 ♗d6 25 ♕c1 ♗e7 –+ Arakhamia-Akopian, Oakham jr 1990) 21...♗d8 22 a5 ± Kaiumov-Chetverik, Harkany 1991.

c3) 19 ♖c5 ♗d6 20 a5! (20 ♖g5 g6 ∞) 20...♗xc5 (20...♘c8 21 ♗f5 ♕d8 22 a6 ♘e7 23 axb7 ♖b8 24 ♗g5 ± Timman-Anand, Tilburg 1991) 21 dxc5 ♘c8 (21...♘a4 22 c6 ±; 21...♘d5 22 ♖d1 ♖ad8 23 ♗e4 ±) 22 a6 ±.

d) 18...♖ab8 *(D)* and here:

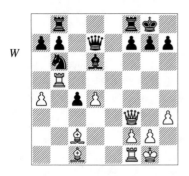

d1) 19 ♗e3 ♘c8 20 ♖fb1 b6 21 h4 ♘e7 22 h5 h6 23 g4 ♗c7 24 g5 a6 25 ♖5b4 b5 26 gxh6 f5 27 axb5 axb5 28 ♕g2 ∞ Shilov-Raetsky, Voroshilovgrad 1989.

d2) 19 ♗g5!? and then:

d21) 19...♖fe8 20 ♕h5 g6 21 ♗f6 ♗f8 22 ♕f3 gives White compensation.

d22) 19...♘c8 20 ♖fb1 (20 ♕h5 f5 21 ♕e2 ♘b6 22 ♖fb1 ♖be8 23 ♕f1 is slightly better for White, Wahls-Haba, Bundesliga 1992/3) 20...b6 21 ♕h5 f5 (21...g6? 22 ♗f6 ♗f4 23 ♕h4 ♕d6 24 g3 a6 25 ♖h5 +–) 22 ♕e2 ♘e7 23 ♕xc4+ ♔h8 24 ♕d3 g6 25 ♕c3 ♖bc8 26 ♕b2 ±.

d23) 19...♗c7 20 ♗f6! and then:

d231) 20...h6? 21 ♖g5! g6 22 ♕h5! wins for White.

d232) 20...gxf6? 21 ♕h5 ♖fe8 22 ♕h6 ♗f4 23 ♗xh7+ ♔h8 24 ♕xf6+ is also winning.

d233) 20...♕e6 21 ♖h5! h6 22 ♖g5! g6 23 ♗xg6 fxg6 24 ♖xg6+ ♔f7 25 ♖g7+ ♔e8 26 ♕h5+ +–.

d234) 20...♕d6! 21 ♗e5 ♕e7 (not 21...♕d7? 22 ♗xg7 +–) 22 a5 ♘a8 (22...♘c8 23 ♗xh7+ ♔xh7 24 ♗xg7 and White wins) 23 ♗xh7+!? (23 ♖xb7 ±) 23...♔xh7 24 ♕h5+ ♔g8 25 ♗xg7 f6 26 ♕h8+ ♔f7 27 ♗xf8 ♖xf8 28 ♕h5+ ♔g8 29 ♕d5+ ± Gavrilov-Frog, corr. 1989-90.

d3) 19 ♗b2 ♘c8 (19...♖fe8!?) 20 ♕c3! a6 and then:

d31) 21 ♖g5?! b5 (21...♕c7? 22 ♖c5! ± Chandler-Haba, Bundesliga 1992/3) 22 axb5 axb5 23 d5 f6 24 ♗f5 ♕c7 25 ♖h5 g6 26 ♗e6+ ♔g7 ∞.

d32) 21 ♖h5!? g6 22 ♖h6 b5 (or 22...♘e7 23 d5 f6 24 ♕xc4 ± Haba) 23 axb5 axb5 24 d5 f6 25 ♗xg6 hxg6 26 ♖xg6+ ♔h7 27 ♕c2 f5! (27...♘e7? 28 ♖g5+! ♔h6 29 ♖h5+! ♔xh5 30 ♕h7+ ♔g5 31 ♗c1+ ♗f4 32 g3 +– Haba) 28 ♖g4 gives White compensation.

19 ♗d2

White has tried virtually every plausible move here:

a) 19 ♗b2!? (intending ♕c3) is met by 19...♖fe8 ∞.

b) 19 h4 ♖fe8 20 h5 ♗f8 with an unclear position.

c) 19 ♗g5!? has the point that 19...♗e7? is met by 20 ♗xe7 ♕xe7 21 a5 ±.

d) 19 ♗e3!? and here:

d1) 19...♖fd8 20 ♖fb1 ♗e7 21 ♗e4 ♖ab8 22 ♗f4 ♗d6 23 a5 ♗xf4 24 ♕xf4 ♘a4 25 ♖xb7 ♖xb7 26 ♖xb7 ♕e6 27 d5 ♕e8 28 d6 ♘c3 29 ♗f3 ♖d7 30 ♖xd7 ♕xd7 31 ♗g4 h5 32 ♕xc4 hxg4! (32...♕xd6?! 33 ♗xh5 ♘d5 34 ♗f3 +− Voitsekhovsky-Kochiev, St Petersburg 1999) 33 ♕c7! ♘e2+! 34 ♔h2 (34 ♔f1 ♕b5!) 34...♕a4!! 35 d7 ♕a1! 36 d8♕+ ♔g7 37 hxg4 ♕g1+ 38 ♔h3 ♕h1+ 39 ♕h2 ♘f4+ 40 ♔g3 ♘e2+ 41 ♔f3 ♕xh2 42 ♔xe2 ♕xg2 43 ♕d4+ ♔g8 44 ♖xa7 (44 a6 ♕a8) 44...♕xg4+ =.

d2) 19...♖ac8! 20 ♖fb1 c3 21 a5 ♘c4 22 ♖xb7 ♕e6 (22...♖c7!? 23 a6 ♘d2 =) 23 ♗b3 (23 ♖a1 ♗b8 ∞ Shirov-Anand, Linares 2000) 23...♗b8 24 ♗h6 c2 25 ♗xc2 ♘xa5 26 ♗xf8 ♘xb7 27 ♗b3 ♕d7 28 ♗h6 ♘d6 29 ♗f4 ♕f5 30 ♗a2 ♘b5 ½-½ Nijboer-Piket, Rotterdam 2000.

e) 19 ♗h6 ♖fe8 20 ♖fb1 (20 ♗e4 ♖ab8 21 ♖fb1? ♕e6! −+ Riand-Delanoy, Geneva 1992) and now:

e1) 20...♕e6 and here:

e11) 21 g4!? ♕e2 22 ♗d1 ♕xf3 (22...♕e1+ 23 ♔g2 ±) 23 ♗xf3 ±.

e12) 21 ♗e3 ♖ab8 22 a5 ♘a8 23 ♖xb7 ♖xb7 24 ♖xb7 ♘c7 25 ♖xa7 ♘d5 ± de Firmian-Appleberry, New York 1994.

e2) 20...♗f8 21 ♗e3 (21 ♗xf8 ♖xf8 22 a5 ♘c8 23 ♖xb7 ♕xd4 24 ♖d1 ♕e5 25 ♖xf7 ♘d6 26 ♖xf8+ ♖xf8 =)

21...♖ad8 22 a5 ♘d5 23 ♖xb7 ♕e6 24 ♗g5 ♗e7 (24...♖d7 25 ♗a4 ♖xb7 26 ♖xb7 ±) 25 ♗d2 ±.

e3) 20...♕c6!? 21 ♔f1 (21 d5?! ♕d7 22 ♗e3 {22 a5?? fails to 22...♕xb5 −+} 22...♗e7 23 ♗xb6 axb6 24 ♖xb6 ∓) 21...♕xf3 22 gxf3 c3! 23 ♗b3 ♖ab8 24 a5 ♘c8 25 ♖c1 ♘e7 26 ♖xc3 ♘f5 =.

e4) 20...♖ad8 21 ♗g5 (21 a5?? ♕xb5! −+; 21 ♗e3?! ♗c7 22 a5 ♘d5 23 ♖xb7 ♕d6 ∓; 21 g4 ♕c6! 22 d5 ♕c7 23 a5 ♘d7 24 ♖xb7 ♕xa5 ∓) 21...♗e7 22 a5 (22 ♗e3 ♕d6! 23 a5 ♘d5 24 ♖xb7 ♘xe3 25 fxe3 ♕f6 =) 22...♗xg5! (22...♘d5? 23 ♖xb7 ♕e6 24 ♗d2 ± Svidler-Akopian, Erevan 1996) 23 axb6 ♗e7! 24 bxa7 b6 25 ♗e4! (25 ♖xb6 ♕xa7 26 ♖b7 ♕a3 =) 25...♕xa7 26 ♗d5 ♗d6 27 ♖xb6 ♖b8! 28 ♖xb8 ♖xb8 29 ♖xb8+ ♗xb8 30 ♗xc4 ♕a1+ 31 ♗f1 ♕xd4 = Svidler.

19...c3

19...♖ac8 20 ♗c3 gives White compensation.

20 ♗xc3

20 ♕xc3 ♖ac8 21 ♕b3 (21 ♕d3 ♘c4 is equal) 21...♖c7 (21...♗b8 22 ♗d1 ♕xd4 23 ♗e3 ♕g7 24 ♗g4 ♖c7 = Topalov-Shirov, Monaco Amber blindfold 2000) 22 ♗d3 ♖fc8 23 ♖e1 ♗f8 24 a5 ♘c4 = A.Sokolov-Finegold, Reykjavik 1990.

20...♖ac8 21 ♗e4 ♖c4 22 ♖bb1

22 ♖fb1 ♖fc8 23 ♖5b3 ♘xa4 24 ♗d2 ♖xd4 25 ♗e3 ♖xe4 26 ♕xe4 ♘c3 27 ♖xc3 ½-½ Topalov-Akopian, Madrid 1997.

22...♖xa4 23 ♗xb7 ♖a3 24 ♖fc1 ♕c7 25 ♖a1

±/= Kasparov-Shirov, Linares 2000.

10 4 ♘f3 ♘xe4 5 d4 d5 6 ♗d3 ♗e7

1 e4 e5 2 ♘f3 ♘f6 3 ♘xe5 d6 4 ♘f3 ♘xe4 5 d4 d5 6 ♗d3 ♗e7 *(D)*

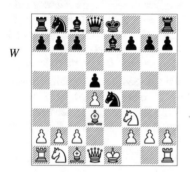

W

This is the third and last of Black's major systems against the 3 ♘xe5 Petroff. Compared to the 6...♗d6 system, Black develops his bishop more modestly, but ...♗e7 has the advantage that the d5-pawn remains guarded by Black's queen. This means that Black does not need to meet c4 with ...c6 and can instead play for pressure against d4 with ...♘c6. White has two basic plans against this set-up. The first is to stick to his basic idea of playing c4, when in many lines an isolated d-pawn position results. This plan can be executed either with or without ♖e1 thrown in. The second possibility is to nullify the pressure against d4 by playing c3, and then try to remove the

e4-knight by attacking it with pieces. To counter this, Black often reinforces his knight with ...f5, although this weakens the squares along the e-file. The battle then develops between the dynamic possibilities afforded by the actively placed knight on e4 and White's longer-term structural advantage. Sharp play can arise in almost all these lines.

7 0-0

7 ♘bd2 ♗f5 8 0-0 ♘xd2 9 ♕xd2 ♗g6 10 ♘e5 0-0 11 ♖e1 ♘d7 = Velikov-Spassov, Pamporovo 1981.

7...♘c6

Or:

a) 7...♗f5 8 c4 dxc4 9 ♗xc4 0-0 10 ♘c3 (10 ♘e5!?) 10...♘xc3 11 bxc3 ♘d7 12 ♖e1 ♘b6 13 ♗b3 ♗f6 14 ♘e5 ♗e6 15 ♗xe6 fxe6 16 ♕g4 ♕d5 17 h4 ♘c4 18 ♗f4 ♖ae8 19 h5 ± A.Sokolov-Tichy, Clichy 1991.

b) 7...♗g4 8 h3 ♗h5 9 c4 ♘f6 10 ♘c3 dxc4 11 ♗xc4 0-0 12 g4 ♗g6 13 ♘e5 c5 14 dxc5 ♕c7 15 ♗f4 ♕xc5 16 ♖c1 ± Ljubojević-Handoko, Indonesia 1983.

c) 7...♘d6 and then:

c1) 8 ♘e5!? 0-0 (8...♘d7 9 ♕f3 ♘f6 10 ♘c3 c6 11 ♖e1 ♗e6 12 ♗g5 ±) 9 ♕f3 c6 (9...♗e6 10 ♘c3 c6 11 ♘e2 ♕c8 12 ♘g3 ♘d7 13 ♖e1 ♖e8 14

♘xd7 ♕xd7 15 h3 ± Tompa-Forgacs, Hungary 1992) 10 ♘d2 (10 ♖e1!?) 10...♘d7 11 ♖e1 g6!? 12 ♘f1 ♘xe5 13 dxe5 ♘f5 14 ♘e3 ♘xe3 15 ♗xe3 ♗e6 ∞ Liss-Skembris, Athens 1995.

c2) 8 ♗f4 *(D)* and now:

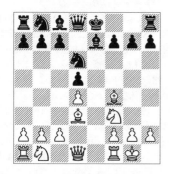

B

c21) 8...♗g4 9 ♘bd2 0-0 10 c3 ♘d7 11 ♕c2 g6 (11...h6!?) 12 ♖ac1! ♖e8 13 h3 ♗e6 (13...♗xf3 ±; 13...♗f5? 14 ♗xd6 ♗xd3 15 ♗xe7 ♗xc2 16 ♗xd8 +−) 14 ♖fe1 ♘f8 15 ♘f1 c6 16 ♘g3 with a slight advantage to White, Balashov-Benko, Lone Pine 1977.

c22) 8...0-0 9 ♖e1 (9 ♘c3!? c6 10 ♘e2 ♖e8 11 ♘g3 ♘d7 12 c3 ♘f8 13 ♕c2 ♘g6 14 ♗d2 ♗e6 15 ♖ae1 ± Torre-Balinas, Melbourne 1975) and here:

c221) 9...♖e8 10 ♘bd2 (10 ♘e5!?) 10...♘c6 11 c3 ♗f6 12 ♖xe8+ ±.

c222) 9...♗e6 10 c3 ♘d7 11 ♕c2 h6 (11...g6? 12 ♗h6 ♖e8 13 ♖xe6 fxe6 14 ♗xg6 ±; 11...♘f6? 12 ♘g5 +−) 12 ♘bd2 ♖e8 13 ♘f1 ♘f8 14 ♘g3 (14 ♕d2!?) 14...♗g5 15 ♕d2 f6 (15...♗xf4 16 ♕xf4 ±) 16 h4 (16 b3!?) 16...♗xf4 17 ♕xf4 ± Timman-Skembris, Corfu (2) 1993.

c223) 9...♗g4 and now:

c2231) 10 h3 ♗h5 (10...♗xf3?! 11 ♕xf3 c6 12 ♘d2 ♘d7 13 ♖e2 ♖e8 14 ♖ae1 ♗f8 15 ♕g3 ♖xe2 16 ♖xe2 ♘f6 17 ♗g5 ± Timman-Hort, Bugojno 1978) 11 ♘c3 (11 ♖e5!? ♗xf3 12 ♕xf3 c6 13 c3 ♘d7 14 ♖e2 ± Lau-Mathe, Munich 1991/2) 11...c6 12 ♕e2 ±.

c2232) 10 ♘bd2 ♘d7 11 c3 and here:

c22321) 11...♗h5 12 ♕b3 ♘b6 13 ♖e2 (13 ♘e5 ♖e8 14 ♕c2 ♗g6 15 ♘xg6 hxg6 16 ♘f3 ♗f6 17 ♖xe8+ ♕xe8 18 ♖e1 ♕d7 19 ♘e5 ♗xe5 20 ♖xe5 ♖e8 ± Byrne-Reshevsky, USA 1975) 13...♗g6 14 ♗xg6 hxg6 15 ♖ae1 ♗f6 (Browne-Benko, Lone Pine 1975) 16 g4! intending ♔g2 followed by h3 ±.

c22322) 11...♖e8 12 ♕c2 (12 ♕b3 ♘b6 13 ♕c2 g6 14 ♘e5 ♗f5 15 ♖e2 ♗g5! 16 ♗xg5 ♕xg5 17 ♖ae1 f6 = Dvoretsky-Khachaturov, USSR 1973) 12...h6 (12...g6 13 ♖ac1! ±) 13 h3 ±.

d) 7...0-0 *(D)* and then:

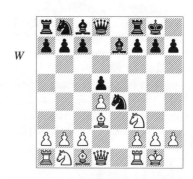

W

d1) 8 h3 ♗f5 9 ♖e1 ♘c6 10 c3 ♖e8 11 ♕c2 ♗g6 12 ♘bd2 ♘xd2 13 ♗xd2 with an equal position, Micheli-Toth, Italy 1973.

d2) 8 ♖e1 and here:

d21) 8...f5 9 c4 c6 10 ♘c3 ♘a6 (10...♔h8 11 ♗f4 ♗b4 12 ♕b3 ♕a5 13 ♖ac1 ♗e6 14 a3 ± Marco-Kaslan, Thessaloniki OL 1984) 11 cxd5 (11 ♗f4!? is another idea) 11...cxd5 12 ♗xa6 bxa6 13 ♕b3 ♗e6 14 ♗f4 ± Tia-Azahari, Kuala Lumpur 1992.

d22) 8...♘f6 9 ♘bd2 c5 10 dxc5 ♗xc5 11 ♘b3 ♗b6 12 ♗e3 ± Lisit-syn-Lilienthal, Moscow 1940.

d23) 8...♗f5 9 c4 c6 10 ♘c3 ♘xc3 11 bxc3 ♗xd3 12 ♕xd3 dxc4 13 ♕xc4 ♘d7 14 ♕b3 b6 (14...♘b6 15 c4 ± Kavalek-Pfleger, Montilla 1973) 15 c4 ♗f6 16 ♗b2 ±.

d3) 8 c4 ♘f6 (8...c6 9 ♘c3 ♘xc3 10 bxc3 dxc4 11 ♗xc4 ♘d7 12 ♖e1 ♘b6 13 ♗d3 ♗e6 14 a4 ♗f6 15 a5 ♘d5 16 ♕c2 h6 17 ♗d2 ± Mrdja-Paoli, Naleczow 1978) and now:

d31) 9 h3!? dxc4 10 ♗xc4 ♘bd7 11 ♘c3 ♘b6 12 ♗b3 ♘bd5 (12...c6 13 ♖e1 ♘fd5 14 ♘e4 ♖e8 15 ♗d2 ♗f5 16 ♘g3 ♗e6 17 ♗c2 ± Timman-Panno, Mar del Plata 1982) 13 ♖e1 c6 (13...♗e6 14 ♘g5 ♘xc3 15 bxc3 ♗xb3 16 ♕xb3 ± h6 ½-½ Vaganian-Tal, Moscow 1982) 14 ♗g5 ♗e6 (14...♗f5?! 15 ♘e5 ♖e8 16 ♕f3 ♗e6 17 ♖ad1 ± Kikolaev-Retsk, St Petersburg 1992) 15 ♖c1 (15 ♘e5!? ♘c7 16 ♗c2 is slightly better for White, Razuvaev-Bagirov, USSR 1982) 15...♖e8 16 ♘e5 and then:

d311) 16...♘xc3 17 bxc3 ♗xb3 18 ♕xb3 ♘d5 19 ♗d2 ±.

d312) 16...♘d7 17 ♗xe7 ♖xe7 18 ♘e4 ♘f8 19 ♘c5 ± Sax-Korchnoi, Wijk aan Zee Ct (6) 1991.

d313) 16...♘c7 17 ♗c2 ♘d7 18 ♕h5 ♘f8 19 ♗xe7 ♖xe7 20 ♖cd1 f6

21 ♘f3 ♕d7 = Yusupov-Hübner, Belfort 1988.

d32) 9 ♘c3 dxc4 10 ♗xc4 and here:

d321) 10...♘c6 11 ♖e1 ♗g4 – *7...♘c6 8 ♖e1 ♗g4 9 c4 ♘f6 10 ♘c3 dxc4 11 ♗xc4 0-0.*

d322) 10...b6?! 11 ♘e5 ♗b7 12 ♕b3 ± Steinitz-Mieses, Hastings 1895.

d323) 10...♗g4 11 h3 ♗xf3 (alternatively, 11...♗h5 12 g4 ♗g6 13 ♘e5 c6 {13...c5!?} 14 f4 b5 15 ♗b3 b4 16 f5 bxc3 17 fxg6 hxg6 18 bxc3 ♘d5 19 ♕f3 ± Henley-Dlugy, New York 1983) 12 ♕xf3 ♘c6 (12...♕xd4 13 ♕xb7 ♘bd7 14 ♗b3 ♗d6 15 ♘b5 ±) 13 ♗e3 ♘xd4 14 ♕xb7 c5 15 ♗xd4 cxd4 16 ♖ad1 ♖c8 17 b3 ♖c7 18 ♕f3 ± Zaichik-Karpeshov, Volgodonsk 1983.

d324) 10...♘bd7 11 ♖e1 (11 ♗b3 c5 12 ♖e1 cxd4 13 ♘xd4 ♘c5 14 ♗c2 ♗g4 15 f3 ♗e6 16 ♗e3 ♘xd4 17 ♕xd4 ♗e6 = Gelfand-Maliutin, Kramatorsk jr 1989) 11...♘b6 12 ♗b3 c6 (alternatively, 12...♗g4 13 h3 ♗h5 14 g4 ♗g6 15 ♘e5 ♘fd7 16 ♘xg6 hxg6 17 ♕f3 ± Tsesarsky-Zakharevich, Kursk 1987) 13 ♗g5 and then:

d3241) 13...♘fd5? 14 ♖xe7! ♘xe7 15 ♕e2 ♖e8 16 ♖e1 ♔f8 17 ♘e5 +–.

d3242) 13...♗f5 14 ♘e5 ♘fd5 15 ♗xe7 ♘xe7 16 ♕f3 ♘bd5 ± S.Ivanov-Mikhalchishin, Uzhgorod 1988.

d3243) 13...♘bd5 14 ♘xd5 cxd5 15 ♘e5 ♗e6 16 ♘d3 ± Browne-Petrosian, Las Palmas IZ 1982.

d3244) 13...♗g4 14 ♕d3 ♗h5 (or 14...♗xf3 15 ♕xf3 ♘fd5 16 ♗xe7 ♘xe7 17 ♖e5 ± Vaganian-Hübner, Tilburg 1983) 15 ♘e5 ±.

We now return to 7...♘c6 *(D)*:

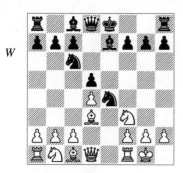

W

White now has two main continuations:

A: 8 ♖e1   191
B: 8 c4   214

Or:

a) 8 ♘bd2 and now:

a1) 8...♘g5 9 ♘xg5 ♗xg5 10 f4 ±.

a2) 8...♘d6 9 c3 ♗f5 10 ♕c2 (10 ♗xf5 ♘xf5 11 ♕b3 ±) 10...♗xd3 11 ♕xd3 0-0 12 ♘e5 ± Em.Lasker-Showalter, Nuremberg 1896 and Savon-Bronstein, Odessa 1976.

a3) 8...♗f5!? 9 ♕e2 ♘d6 10 ♗xf5 ♘xf5 11 ♕d3 ♕d7 12 ♘b3 0-0 = Silva Sanchez-Solomon, Thessaloniki OL 1984.

a4) 8...♘xd2 9 ♗xd2 ♗g4 10 c3 0-0 11 ♗f4 ♗d6! (11...♗f6? 12 ♖e1 ♗h5 13 ♖e3 ♗g6 14 ♕c2 ♕d7 15 ♖ae1 ± Bönsch-Yusupov, Cienfuegos 1979) 12 ♗xd6 ♕xd6 13 ♖e1 (not 13 ♗xh7+? ♔xh7 14 ♘g5+ ♔g6 15 ♕g4 f5 −+) 13...♗h5 14 ♖e3 ♖ae8 15 ♕e2 ♖xe3 16 ♕xe3 ♗xf3 17 ♕xf3 ♖e8 18 g3 ♘b8! = Alburt-Dvoretsky, Minsk 1976.

b) 8 ♘c3 and then:

b1) 8...♘xc3 9 bxc3 with a further branch:

b11) 9...♗g4 10 ♖b1 ♖b8 (and not 10...♘a5? 11 h3 ♗h5? 12 ♖e1 0-0 13 ♖e5 ♗g6 14 ♖b5 ± Adorjan-Miles, Hastings 1973/4) 11 ♖e1 0-0 12 ♗f4 and now Adorjan's 12...h6 =/± is a significant improvement over 12...♕d7? 13 ♖e3 g5 14 ♗g3 f5 15 ♗e5 f4 16 ♖e1 ♗f6 17 ♗xf6 ♖xf6 18 h3 ♗h5 19 ♘e5! ± Browne-Murray, Vancouver 1971.

b12) 9...0-0 10 h3 (10 ♖b1!? is another possibility) 10...♗e6 11 ♖e1 ♕d7 12 ♗f4 ♖fe8 13 ♖b1 ♖ab8 14 ♖e3 ♗f6 15 ♘g5 ± Aronin-Zhilin, USSR 1959.

b2) 8...♗f5 9 ♕e1 0-0 10 ♘xe4 dxe4 11 ♗xe4 ♗b4 12 c3 ♖e8 13 ♗xf5 ♖xe1 14 ♖xe1 ♗d6 and now 15 ♗g5 gives White compensation, and so is an improvement over 15 ♘g5?! h6 16 ♘e4 ♗f8 17 ♗g4 ♘e7 18 ♘c5 b6 19 ♘d3 c5 ∓ Balashov-Yusupov, Minsk 1982.

A)

8 ♖e1 *(D)*

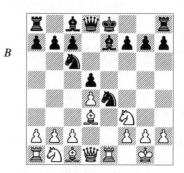

B

Attacking the e4-knight. Black's choice lies between simple defence and an attempt to counterattack d4:

A1: 8...♗f5   192
A2: 8...♗g4   196

The former is a solid move, but the latter is more active.

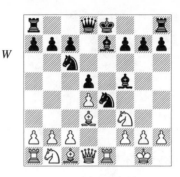

Or:

a) 8...♘f6 9 ♗f4 0-0 10 c3 ♗d6 11 ♘e5 ♖e8 12 ♘d2 ♗g4 13 ♘df3 ♘cxe5 14 dxe5 ♗c5 15 ♗g3 ♘h6 16 ♕c2 is much better for White, Tarrasch-Walbrodt, Nuremberg 1894.

b) 8...♘d6 9 ♗f4 (9 ♘c3 ♗e6 10 ♘e2 ± Steinitz) 9...0-0 10 c3 ♗e6 (10...♗g4 11 h3 ♗h5 12 ♘bd2 ♗g6, Lanka-Mikenas, Riga 1978, 13 ♗xg6 hxg6 14 ♕b3 ±) 11 ♘bd2 ♕d7 (or 11...♗f5 12 ♘f1 ♗xd3 13 ♕xd3 ♘c4 14 b3 ♘b6 15 ♘g3 ±) 12 ♘f1 f5?! (better is 12...♖fe8 ±) 13 ♕e2 ♘e4 14 ♘e5 ♘xe5 15 ♗xe5 ♗f6 16 ♗xf6 ♖xf6 17 f3 ± Byrne-Reshevsky, USA 1972.

c) 8...f5 9 c4 ♗e6 (9...♘b4 10 cxd5 {10 ♗f1 ±} 10...♘xd3 11 ♕xd3 0-0 12 ♘c3 ± Solomon-Singh, Thessaloniki OL 1988) 10 cxd5 ♗xd5 11 ♘c3 ♘xc3 12 bxc3 0-0 13 ♗f4 (13 ♘e5!? ♘xe5 14 ♖xe5 ± intending ♕e2 – Maroczy) 13...♗d6 14 ♗xd6 ♕xd6 15 ♘e5 ± Löwenthal-Morphy, London (3) 1858.

A1)
8...♗f5 *(D)*
9 c4

White has a number of other ideas, although of these only line 'e' presents any sort of challenge for Black:

a) 9 a3 0-0 10 c4 ♗f6 (10...♖e8!? 11 ♘c3 ♘xc3 12 bxc3 ♗xd3 13 ♕xd3 dxc4 14 ♕xc4 ♗d6 =) and here:

a1) 11 cxd5 ♕xd5 12 ♗xe4 (12 ♘c3 ♘xc3 13 bxc3 ♖fe8 14 ♗f4 ♖xe1+ 15 ♘xe1 ♘xd4! ∓ Liang Jinrong-Zarnicki, Manila OL 1992) 12...♗xe4 13 ♘c3 ♗xf3 14 ♘xd5 ♗xd1 =.

a2) 11 ♘c3 ♘xc3 12 bxc3 ♗xd3 13 ♕xd3 dxc4 14 ♕xc4 ♘a5 15 ♕a4 and now:

a21) 15...b6 16 ♗f4 ♕d5 (16...c5 17 dxc5! ♗xc3 18 ♖ad1 ♕c8 19 ♖e3 ±) 17 ♗xc7 ♖ac8 18 ♗e5 ♖xc3 19 ♗xf6 gxf6 20 ♖ac1 ± Kavalek-Karpov, Turin 1982.

a22) 15...c5 (Wedberg-Schüssler, Eksjö 1982) 16 ♗e3 cxd4 17 ♗xd4 ♘c6 18 ♖ab1 ♘xd4 19 cxd4 b6 =.

b) 9 c3 0-0 10 ♕c2 ♖e8 (alternatively, 10...♗g6!? 11 ♘bd2 ♘xd2 12 ♗xd2 ♗d6 13 ♗xg6 hxg6 14 c4 dxc4 15 ♕xc4 ♕d7 16 ♗c3 ♘e7 = Tsariov-S.Ivanov, Tuzla 1989) 11 ♗f4 ♗d6 12 ♗xd6 ♕xd6 13 ♘bd2 ♘xd2 14 ♕xd2 ♗xd3 = Fedorowicz-Reshevsky, USA Ch (South Bend) 1981.

c) 9 ♘c3 ♘xc3 (9...♗b4 10 ♗d2 ♗xc3 11 bxc3 0-0 12 c4 ±) 10 bxc3 ♗xd3 and now:

c1) 11 ♕xd3 0-0 12 c4 (12 ♖b1 ♖b8) 12...dxc4 (12...♗f6!? intending 13 ♗a3? ♘xd4! Adorjan) 13 ♕xc4

♗d6 14 a4 ♖e8 15 ♗b2 ♕d7 16 d5 ♘b4 ∞ Velimirović-Mihailović, Yugoslavia 1991.

c2) 11 cxd3 0-0 12 ♖b1 (12 ♕b3 ♖b8 13 ♘e5 ♘xe5 14 ♖xe5 c6 =) 12...♖b8 13 ♕a4 (13 ♗f4 ♗d6 14 ♗g3 ♗xg3 = Suetin-Makarychev, Moscow 1982) 13...a6 (13...♖e8 14 ♗f4 ♕d7 15 h3 b6 16 c4 dxc4 17 dxc4 ♖bd8 18 d5 with a slight advantage for White, Moiseev-Mathe, Kecskemet 1991) 14 c4 ♖e8 15 ♗f4 dxc4 16 dxc4 ♘xd4 17 ♘xd4 ♕xd4 ∞ Kapengut-Andrianov, USSR 1982.

d) 9 ♗b5!? and now:

d1) 9...0-0 10 ♗xc6 bxc6 11 ♘e5 ♗h4 12 ♗e3 ♖e8! (12...♕d6?! 13 ♕h5! ♕f6 14 ♘f3 g5 15 ♘bd2 ♗g6 16 ♕h6 ♘d6 17 ♗xg5 ♗xg5 18 ♕xg5 ♕xg5 19 ♘xg5 ± Timman-Portisch, Moscow 1981) 13 ♘xc6 ♕f6 14 ♘e5 ♘xf2 15 ♗xf2 ♗xf2+ 16 ♔xf2 ♗g4+ 17 ♘f3 ♗xf3 18 ♖xe8+ ♖xe8 19 gxf3 ♕h4+ 20 ♔g2 ♖e1 21 ♕d2 ♕e7 22 ♔f2 ♕h4+ = Makarychev.

d2) 9...♗f6! 10 ♘bd2 (10 c4 0-0 =; 10 ♘e5 ♗xe5 11 dxe5 0-0 12 f3 ♘c5 ∞; 10 ♗f4 0-0 11 ♗xc6 bxc6 12 ♗e5 ♗e7 ∓) 10...0-0 11 ♘f1 ♘e7 12 c3 ♘g6 13 ♗d3 ♘d6 14 ♗xf5 ♘xf5 15 ♕b3 b6 16 ♕b5 a6 = Karpov-Korchnoi, Merano Wch (4) 1981.

e) 9 ♘bd2 ♘xd2 (9...♘d6 10 ♘f1 0-0 11 ♘g3 ♗g6 12 c3 ♗f6 13 ♗f4 ± Akopian-Sorokin, USSR 1985) 10 ♕xd2 ♗xd3 (10...♗g4? 11 ♕g5 ♗xf3 12 ♕xg7 ♖f8 13 ♗h6 +−; 10...♕d7 11 ♗xf5 ♕xf5 12 ♘e5 ±; 10...♗e6 11 c3 ± intending ♘g5 and ♕c2, or ♘e5) 11 ♕xd3 0-0 (White's modest plan cannot possibly lead to any more than a

very slight advantage, although it is easy for Black to slip up and fall into an unpleasantly passive position) 12 c3 *(D)* (12 ♗f4 a6 13 ♕f5 ♗f6 14 c3 ♘e7 15 ♕c2 ♘g6 16 ♗g3 c6 = Ljubojević-Timman, Lucerne Wcht 1989) and then:

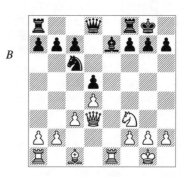

B

e1) 12...♕d6 13 ♕f5 (13 ♗g5 ♖fe8 14 ♗xe7 ♘xe7 15 ♖e3 ♘g6 16 ♖ae1 ♕d7 17 g3 ♖xe3 18 ♖xe3 ♖e8 is level, Chandler-Speelman, Brighton 1981) 13...♖ad8 14 ♗f4 ± ½-½ Adorjan-Hübner, Bad Lauterberg Ct (8) 1980.

e2) 12...♕d7 13 ♗f4 and then:

e21) 13...♗d6?! 14 ♘g5! g6 15 ♗xd6 ♕xd6 16 ♕h3 h5 17 ♕f3 ♕d7 18 ♘h3! ♖ae8 19 ♘f4 ± Lukov-Govedarica, Belgrade 1982.

e22) 13...♖fe8 14 h3 (14 ♕b5!?) 14...a6 15 ♖e3 ♗d6 16 ♘g5 g6 17 ♗xd6 ♕xd6 18 ♖ae1 ♕d7 19 ♘f3 ♖xe3 20 ♕xe3 ± Adorjan-Hübner, Bad Lauterberg Ct (10) 1980.

e23) 13...a6 14 ♖e3 ♖ae8 15 ♖ae1 ♗d8 and here:

e231) 16 ♖xe8 ♖xe8 17 ♖xe8+ ♕xe8 18 ♕f5 ♘e7 19 ♕g4 ♘g6 = Ljubojević-Christiansen, Mar del Plata 1981.

e232) 16 ♘e5 ♘xe5 17 dxe5 ♕b5 = Kavalek-Smyslov, Amsterdam 1981.

e233) 16 ♕e2 ♖xe3 17 ♕xe3 ♕f5 is equal.

e234) 16 h3 ♖xe3 17 ♖xe3 (17 ♕xe3 ♕f5 =) 17...f6 (17...♖e8 18 ♕f5 ♖e6 ±) 18 ♖e2 (18 ♘d2 ♘e7 19 ♘b3 ♕f5 20 ♕xf5 ♘xf5 21 ♖e2 b6 ½-½ Golubević-Stević, Pula 2000) 18...♖f7 (18...♖e8?! 19 ♖xe8+ ♕xe8 20 ♕f5 ±) 19 ♘d2 ♗e7 20 ♘f1 ♗f8 21 ♕f3 ♘d8 (21...♖e7? 22 ♘e3 ♘d8 23 ♗xc7! ± Kasparov-Karpov, Moscow 1981) 22 ♘e3 c6 and now White should prefer 23 h4 ± over 23 ♗g3 ♖e7 24 h4 ♘f7 = intending ...♖e8 and ...♗d6.

We now return to 9 c4 (D):

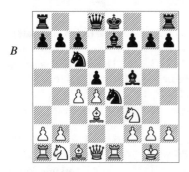

9...♘b4

Or 9...0-0, and then:

a) 10 cxd5 ♕xd5 11 ♘c3 (11 ♕e2 ♘f6 12 ♘c3 ♗xd3 13 ♕xd3 ♕d7 =; 11 ♗xe4 ♗xe4 12 ♘c3 ♗xf3 13 ♘xd5 ♗xd1 14 ♘xe7+ ♘xe7 15 ♖xe7 ♖fe8 =) 11...♘xc3 12 bxc3 and now:

a1) 12...♗xd3?! 13 ♕xd3 b5 (alternatively, 13...♗f6 14 ♗f4 ±) 14 ♗f4 ♗d6 15 ♘g5 g6 16 ♕h3 h5 17 ♘e4 ♔g7 18 ♕e3 ± Abramović-Radulov, Vrnjačka Banja 1983.

a2) 12...♖fe8 13 ♗f4 ♗xd3 (not 13...♗d6? 14 ♖xe8+ ♖xe8 15 c4 ♕a5 16 ♗d2 ♗b4 17 ♗xb4 ♘xb4 18 ♗xf5 ♕xf5 19 ♕a4 ♘c6 20 d5 +-) 14 ♕xd3 ♕d7 15 ♖ab1 b6 16 d5 ♖ad8 17 c4 ± Matulović-Capelan, Vršac 1985.

a3) 12...♗f6 13 ♗f4 ♖ac8 14 ♖b1 is slightly better for White.

a4) 12...b5!? ∞.

b) 10 ♘c3 ♘xc3 11 bxc3 ♗xd3 12 ♕xd3 dxc4 13 ♕xc4 ♗d6 (13...♕d7 14 ♖b1 b6 15 d5 ♘a5 16 ♕d3 ♖fe8 17 ♗f4 ±) 14 ♖b1 (14 ♕b5 ♖b8 15 ♖b1 a6 = Yudasin-Kholmov, Lvov 1983) 14...♖e8 15 ♗e3! (15 ♖xe8+ ♕xe8 16 ♗d2 h6 17 ♕d3 b6 18 ♖e1 ♕d7 19 ♕e4 ♖d8 20 c4 ♗b4! = Chandler-Van der Sterren, Lucerne OL 1982) and then:

b1) 15...♕f6 16 ♕a4 b6 17 ♗g5 ♕g6 18 g3 ♘e7 19 ♗xe7 ♖xe7 (Timman-Van der Sterren, Dutch Ch (Hilversum) 1983) 20 ♕c6! ♖d8 21 ♔g2 ♖xe1 22 ♖xe1 h6 23 c4 intending c5 ± Timman.

b2) 15...♕d7 16 ♕b5 (16 ♖xb7? ♘a5 17 ♕b5 ♕c8 -+) 16...b6 17 c4 a6 18 ♕h5 ♗f8 19 d5 ♘a5 20 ♘e5 ± Gongora-Ro.Perez, Santa Clara Garcia mem 2000.

10 ♗f1 (D)

10 cxd5 ♘xf2 11 ♕a4+ (11 ♗b5+ c6 12 dxc6 bxc6 13 ♗xc6+ ♘xc6 14 ♔xf2 0-0 ∓) 11...♗d7 12 ♗b5 ∞ Herrera-Perez, Cuba 2000.

10...0-0

10...dxc4?! is risky when Black's king is still in the centre. 11 ♘c3! gives Black problems:

a) 11...♘xc3 12 bxc3 ♘d5 (the alternatives are 12...♘d3? 13 ♗xd3 cxd3

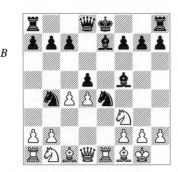

B

14 ♗a3 +− and 12...♘c2? 13 ♖e5 ♕d7 14 ♕e2 {or 14 ♖b1 ±} 14...♘xa1 15 ♗a3 ±) 13 ♗xc4 ♗e6 (13...c6 14 ♗xd5 ±) 14 ♕b3! ± Karpov.

b) 11...♘f6 12 ♗xc4 0-0 13 a3 ♘c6 (13...♘c2? 14 ♘h4 +−) 14 d5 ♘a5 15 ♗a2 c5 16 ♗g5 ♖e8 17 ♕a4 ± ♗d7 18 ♕c2 h6 19 ♗h4 ♘xd5 20 ♘xd5 ♗xh4 21 ♖xe8+ ± Karpov-Portisch, Tilburg 1982.

11 a3 ♘c6 12 ♘c3

Or 12 cxd5 ♕xd5 13 ♘c3 ♘xc3 14 bxc3 ♗f6 (14...♗g6?! 15 c4 ♕d7 16 d5 ♗f6 17 ♖a2 ♘a5 18 ♗f4 is much better for White, Karpov-Portisch, Lucerne OL 1982; 14...♕d6 15 a4 ♖fe8 16 ♕b3 b6 17 ♗a3 ♕f6 18 ♗xe7 ♖xe7 19 ♖xe7 ♕xe7 20 ♖e1 ♕f6 21 ♕d5 ♖d8 22 ♘d2!, Lobron-Schüssler, Bundesliga 1982/3, 22...♔f8!? 23 ♕f3 ♗d7 24 ♕g3 ♕d6 25 ♘h4 ♕h6 ± Lobron) 15 ♗f4, and now:

a) 15...♖ac8 16 ♖c1!? (16 ♘e5 ♘xe5 17 ♗xe5 ♕c6 18 ♕b3 ♗e6 19 c4 ♗xe5 20 ♖xe5 ♕d6 21 ♕e3 ½-½ Am.Rodriguez-Garcia Gonzales, Cuban Ch 1983; 16 ♖e3!? ♘a5 17 ♘e5 c5 18 g4 ♗g6 19 ♗g2 ♕d8 20 dxc5 ± Tal-Garcia Gonzales, Jurmala 1983) 16...♖fd8 17 h3 a6 18 g4 ♗g6 19 ♗g2

♕d7 20 d5 ♘a5 21 c4 b6 22 ♗e5 ♗e7 (not 22...♗xe5? 23 ♘xe5 ♕d6 24 c5 bxc5 25 ♕a4 ♘b7 26 ♘c6 +−) 23 ♗b2 ♗d6 24 ♘e5 ± Anand-Karpov, Frankfurt rpd 1999.

b) 15...♕d7!? 16 ♖a2!? (16 h3!?; 16 ♗g5 ♗xg5 17 ♘xg5 ♖ae8 18 ♕b3 ♘a5 19 ♕b4 b6 20 ♘f3 f6 = Glek-Antonov, USSR 1984) 16...♖ad8 17 ♖d2 ♘e7 and now 18 ♘e5 ± or 18 ♗e5 ± (Yusupov).

12...♘xc3 13 bxc3 dxc4

Or:

a) 13...♗e6? 14 cxd5 ♗xd5 15 ♘d2! ±.

b) 13...♗f6 14 ♗f4 dxc4 15 ♗xc4 ♕d7 and then:

b1) 16 ♕d2 is met by 16...♖ae8.

b2) 16 ♘g5 ♘a5 (16...h6? 17 ♘e4 ±; 16...♗xg5?! 17 ♗xg5 is good for White since 17...♗e6?? loses to 18 d5 ♘a5 19 dxe6 +−) 17 ♗a2 c5 18 ♖c1 (18 ♘e4!? ♗xe4 19 ♖xe4 ♖fe8 20 ♗e5 ±) 18...c4! 19 ♘e4 ♗e7 20 a4 ♖fe8 21 ♖b1 (21 f3 ♗e6 22 ♖b1 ♘b3 ∞) 21...♗xe4 22 ♖xe4 ♗d6 = Yurtaev-Makarychev, Tallinn 1983.

b3) 16 ♖a2!? ♘a5 17 ♗d3 ±.

b4) 16 ♗a2!? ♖fe8 17 ♘g5!? (17 ♕d2 b5 18 ♗g5 ♗g6 19 ♗xf6 gxf6 20 ♘h4 ± Adams-Karpov, Dortmund 1999) 17...♖xe1+ 18 ♕xe1 ♗xg5 19 ♗xg5 ♖e8 20 ♕d2 h6 21 ♗f4 ♘d8 22 d5 b5 ±.

14 ♗xc4 (D)

This is a typical pawn-structure for this variation. The struggle often revolves around whether White can push his mobile pawns forward by c4 and d5. If he can achieve this, then Black's pieces may be driven away and White

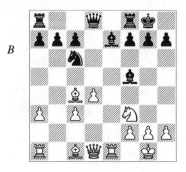

will be able to secure a space advantage. However, it is usually hard to achieve this without careful preparation, as Black's pieces are quite active and White must be sure not to allow a tactical counterblow.

14...♗d6

Or:

a) 14...♘a5!? 15 ♗a2 c5 16 ♘e5 ♗f6 17 g4! ♗d7 (17...♗e6!?) 18 ♗f4 ♗xe5 19 ♖xe5 cxd4 20 cxd4 ♘c6 21 ♖d5 ± Ehlvest-Khalifman, USSR Ch (Minsk) 1987.

b) 14...♗f6 15 ♗f4 – *13...♗f6 14 ♗f4 dxc4 15 ♗xc4*.

15 ♗g5 ♕d7 16 ♘h4 ♘a5

16...♗g4 gives White a choice between 17 ♕b1!? ♘a5 18 ♗d3 ± and 17 f3 ♗h5 18 g4 ±.

17 ♗a2 b5

17...♗g4 18 ♕d3!? (18 f3 ♗e6 19 d5 ♗f5 =; 18 ♕c2 ♖ae8 19 h3 ∞ Ljubojević-Yusupov, Barcelona 1989) 18...♖fe8 19 h3 ♗h5 20 ♕f5 ±.

The text-move is designed to prevent White's pawns from rolling forward with c4 and d5. This is normally such a strong threat that Black does not mind the slight weakening of his queenside resulting from ...b5.

18 a4

White tries to remove Black's b-pawn and release the c- and d-pawns for action. Now:

a) 18...a6 19 axb5 axb5 20 ♘xf5 ♕xf5 21 ♗e7 ♖fb8 (21...♖fc8 22 ♗b1 ♕d7 23 ♕f3 g6 24 ♗a2 +−; 21...♖fe8 22 ♗xd6 cxd6 23 ♗b1 ♕h5 24 ♖xe8+ ♖xe8 25 g4 ♕h3 26 ♖xa5 ♕xc3 27 ♖a2! +−; 21...♗xe7 22 ♖xe7 c6 23 ♕e2 ♘c4 24 ♖e1 ♕d5 25 ♗b3 ±) 22 g4!! ♕d7 (22...♕f4 23 ♗xd6 ♕xd6 24 ♕f3 ♕d7 25 ♖e2 ♘c6 26 ♖ae1 ±) 23 ♗xf7+ and White wins, Karpov-Portisch, Turin 1982.

b) 18...bxa4!? 19 c4 (19 ♗d5!? ♖ae8 20 ♖xe8 ♖xe8 21 ♘xf5 ♕xf5 22 ♕xa4 ♖b8 23 ♖e1 ±/± Karpov) 19...c5 20 ♘xf5 ♕xf5 21 h4 ♘b3 22 ♗b1 ♕d7 23 dxc5 ♘xc5 24 ♖a2 ± Karpov.

A2)
8...♗g4 *(D)*

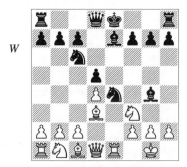

The main reply, playing for a counterattack against d4. Now White has two principal continuations, typifying his two different strategies in this line:

A21: 9 c3 197
A22: 9 c4 207

If 9 ♗xe4, then 9...dxe4 10 ♖xe4:

a) 10...f5?! 11 ♖e1 ♗xf3 12 ♕xf3 ♘xd4 13 ♕xb7 0-0 14 ♗e3 ♗f6 (14...♘xc2?? 15 ♕b3+ +−; 14...♔h8 15 ♗xd4 ♕xd4 16 ♘c3 +− Schallop-Showalter, Nuremberg 1896) 15 ♗xd4 ♗xd4 16 c3 ♖b8 17 ♕f3 ♗f6 18 ♕e2 ± Zinkl-Weiss, 1986.

b) 10...♗xf3 11 ♕xf3 (11 gxf3? f5 12 ♖f4 0-0 13 d5 ♗g5 14 ♖a4 ♗xc1 15 ♕xc1 ♕xd5 ∓) 11...♘xd4 12 ♕d3 (12 ♕c3?! ♘e6 13 ♘d2 0-0 14 ♘f3 ♗f6 15 ♕e1 ♕d5 ∓ Barry-Napier, Cambridge Springs 1904) 12...♘e6 13 ♕e2 0-0 14 ♘c3 ♗f6 15 ♗d2 c6 = Langenberg-Düsselford, corr. 1875.

A21)

9 c3

Securing the d4-pawn and forcing Black to deal with the attack against e4.

9...f5 *(D)*

The passive 9...♘f6 is dubious in view of 10 ♗g5:

a) 10...♕d7 11 ♘bd2 0-0-0 (11...0-0 12 ♕c2 ± intending ♗xf6 or ♘e5) 12 ♕a4 h6 13 ♗h4 g5 14 ♗g3 ♗xf3 15 ♘xf3 g4 16 ♘e5 ♘xe5 17 ♗f5! ♕xf5 18 ♖xe5 ± Keres-Alexander, Hastings 1954/5.

b) 10...0-0 11 ♘bd2 ♗h5 12 ♕b3 ♘a5 13 ♕c2 ♗g6 14 ♘e5 ♗xd3 15 ♕xd3 ♖e8 16 ♖e3 ♘c6 (16...♘h5 17 ♕f5 ♗xg5? 18 ♕xf7+ ♔h8 19 ♕xh5 ♖xe5 20 ♖xe5 ♗xd2 21 ♖xd5 +−) 17 ♘xc6 bxc6 18 ♖ae1 ± Sax-Capelan, Vršac 1981.

The text-move is necessary if Black is to keep his knight at e4, but it weakens the squares along the e-file, with

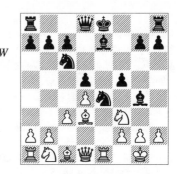

e5 being an especially sensitive spot. Thus Black is now committed to dynamic play, making use of the active e4-knight, to compensate for the positional concessions involved in pushing his f-pawn.

10 ♕b3

Other continuations pose less of a threat to Black:

a) 10 ♗b5?! 0-0 11 ♗f4 ♗d6 12 ♗xd6 ♕xd6 13 ♕d3 ♗xf3 14 ♕xf3 ♖f6 15 ♘a3 ♖h6 16 h3 ♘g5 ∓ Torre-Handoko, Indonesia 1983.

b) 10 b4 a6 11 ♕b3 0-0 12 ♘bd2 ♔h8 ∓ Krieger-Bösken, Bundesliga 1986/7.

c) 10 ♗e2 ♕d6 ∓.

d) 10 ♗f4?! ♗d6 11 ♗xd6 ♕xd6 12 h3 ♗h5 13 ♘bd2 0-0 14 ♖c1 ♘xd2 ∓ Pereira-Handoko, Dubai OL 1986.

e) 10 ♘bd2 and then:

e1) 10...0-0 is best met by 11 ♕b3 − *10 ♕b3 0-0 11 ♘bd2*, rather than 11 ♘f1?! ♗d6!? 12 ♘e3? (12 h3 ♗h5 ∓) 12...♗xh2+! 13 ♔xh2 ♘xf2, which is winning for Black, Janowski-Schlechter, Karlsbad 1902.

e2) 10...♕d6!? and here:

e21) 11 ♘f1 0-0-0! 12 ♘e3 h5 13 h3 g6 14 ♗e2 ♗xf3 15 ♗xf3 ♗h4 16

♖e2 ♘e7 17 ♘f1 ♗f6 18 ♖c2 ♔b8 ∓ Adams-Makarychev, Oviedo rpd 1992.

e22) 11 ♕c2 0-0 12 b4 ♗f6 13 a4 (13 b5?! ♘e7 14 a4 c5 ∓) 13...♖ae8 14 ♗a3 ♕f4! (14...♘xd2 15 ♖xe8 ♘xf3+ 16 gxf3 ♖xe8 17 fxg4 ♕f4 18 ♗xf5 ±) 15 b5 ♘e7 16 ♗c1 ♕d6 17 ♘e5 (17 ♗a3 = Lau-Yusupov, Skien jr Wch 1979) 17...♗xe5 18 dxe5 ♕g6 ∞.

e23) 11 c4!? ♘xd4 12 ♕a4+ ♘c6 13 cxd5 ♕xd5 14 ♗c4 ♕a5 ∞.

f) 10 h3 ♗xf3 11 gxf3 (11 ♕xf3 0-0 =) 11...♘f6! (11...♘d6?! 12 ♕b3 ±) 12 ♗xf5 0-0 and then:

f1) 13 ♕d3 ♗d6 14 ♗g5 ♘e7 15 ♘d2 (15 ♗xf6? ♖xf6 16 ♗xh7+ ♔f7 with an initiative for Black; 15 ♗e6+? ♔h8 16 ♘d2 ♘g6 17 ♗f5 ♗f4! ∓ Enklaar-Dvoretsky, Wijk aan Zee 1975) 15...♘xf5 16 ♕xf5 ♔h8 gives Black compensation.

f2) 13 f4 ♗d6 14 ♗e3 ♕e8 15 ♘d2 ♘e4 16 ♗xe4 dxe4 17 ♕g4 ♖f6 18 f5 ♕f7 19 ♘xe4 ♖xf5 20 ♖ad1 ♖f8 gives Black compensation, Vasiukov-Kaunas, Riga 1975.

f3) 13 ♘d2!? could be considered.

g) 10 c4 *(D)* (White is hoping that the move ...f5 will prove more of an asset for White than for Black, but the loss of time is an important factor) and now:

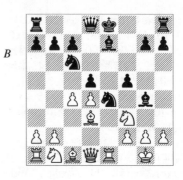

g1) 10...♘xd4? 11 ♗xe4 dxe4 12 ♕xd4 exf3 13 ♕xg7 +−.

g2) 10...♗xf3?! 11 gxf3 ♘f6 12 cxd5 ♕xd5 13 ♘c3 ♕d7 14 ♗b5! ±.

g3) 10...0-0 11 cxd5 ♕xd5 (Black should avoid 11...♘xd4? 12 ♗xe4 fxe4 13 ♕xd4 ±) 12 ♘c3 ♘xc3 13 bxc3 ♗d6 (13...♗xf3 14 ♕xf3 ♕xf3 15 gxf3 ♗d6 16 ♖b1 ♖ab8 17 ♖b5 ±

Maroczy-Pillsbury, Monte Carlo 1902) 14 ♕b3 (14 c4 ♕f7 ∞) 14...♕xb3 15 axb3 f4 16 ♗e4 and White is slightly better.

g4) 10...♗h4!? and here:

g41) 11 ♖f1?! dxc4 12 ♗xc4 ♕f6 13 ♘c3 0-0-0 ∓.

g42) 11 ♗e3?! 0-0 12 cxd5 (12 g3 f4 13 gxf4 ♘xf2 14 ♗xf2 ♗xf2+ 15 ♔xf2 ♖xf4 with a dangerous attack) 12...♘b4 13 d6 (13 ♘c3 ♗xf3 14 gxf3 ♘g5 ∓) 13...♘xd3 14 ♕xd3 ♗xf3 15 gxf3 ♘xd6 ∓.

g43) 11 ♗xe4?! dxe4 12 d5 ♘e5 13 ♕a4+ (13 ♗f4 ♘g6 ∓) 13...b5! 14 ♕xb5+ c6 15 dxc6 ♘xf3+ 16 gxf3 ♗xf2+ 17 ♔xf2 ♕h4+ 18 ♔f1 0-0 ∓.

g44) 11 cxd5 ♗xf2+ 12 ♔f1 ♗xe1 13 dxc6 ♗xf3 14 gxf3 (14 ♕xf3 ♕xd4 15 cxb7 ♖d8 16 ♗b5+ c6 17 ♗xc6+ ♔e7 18 ♗xe4 fxe4 19 ♗g5+ ♔e8 20 ♕e3 ♖f8+ −+) 14...♕xd4 15 ♕e2 0-0-0 16 cxb7+ (16 ♗c2 ♗a5 17 fxe4 ♗b6 −+ Ernst-L.Schneider, Sweden 1986; 16 ♗a6 ♗h4 ∓) 16...♔b8 17 ♔xe1 ♘c5! −+.

g45) 11 g3 and then:

g451) 11...♘xd4 12 ♗xe4 dxe4 13 ♕xd4 ♗xf3 14 ♕e5+! (14 ♕xg7 ♗f6 15 ♕h6 ♕e7 ∓) 14...♕e7! 15 ♕xf5 g6

16 ♕h3 ♗g5 17 ♗xg5 ♕xg5 18 ♕e6+ ♔f8 =.

g452) 11...♗f6 12 cxd5 ♘xd4 13 ♕a4+ (13 ♗xe4 0-0! ∓) 13...♕d7 14 ♕xd7+ ♔xd7 15 ♘xd4 ♗xd4 16 ♗xe4 ♖ae8 ∓.

g5) 10...dxc4 11 ♗xc4 (11 ♗xe4 fxe4 12 ♖xe4 ♕d7 intending ...0-0-0 ∓) and here:

g51) 11...♗xf3 12 gxf3 ♕xd4 (not 12...♘f6? 13 d5 ♘b8 14 ♕b3 ±) 13 ♕xd4 ♘xd4 14 fxe4 ♘c2 15 ♖e2 ♘xa1 16 exf5 ♖d8!? (16...0-0-0 17 ♖xe7 ♖d1+ 18 ♔g2 ♖xc1 19 ♘c3 ±) 17 ♘c3 c6! 18 ♗g5 (18 b3 b5 19 ♗e6 b4 −+) 18...♖d7 ∓/∓ intending ...♔d8.

g52) 11...♕d6 12 ♘c3 0-0-0 (or 12...♗xf3 13 gxf3 ♘xf2 14 ♕e2! ♘h3+ 15 ♔g2 ♘f4+ 16 ♗xf4 ♕xf4 17 ♘d5 ♕g5+ 18 ♔h1 ♕d8 19 ♖g1 ♕h4 20 ♖xg7 ±) and now:

g521) 13 ♘b5 ♕b4 14 b3 a6 15 ♗a3 ♕a5 ∓.

g522) 13 ♘xe4 fxe4 14 ♖xe4 ♕g6 15 ♖f4?! (15 ♖xg4 ♕xg4 16 ♗e3 ♗f6 17 ♕b3 ♖d6 ∓) 15...♘xd4! 16 ♖xd4 ♖xd4 17 ♕xd4 ♗xf3 18 ♗f1 ♖d8 19 ♕e3 ♗xg2! 20 ♕xe7 ♗xf1+ 21 ♕g5 ♖d1! −+ Kholmov-Mikhalchishin, Minsk 1985.

g523) 13 ♗e3!? ♕g6 14 d5!? ♗f6 15 ♖c1 ∞ Yusupov.

We now return to the position after 10 ♕b3 (D):

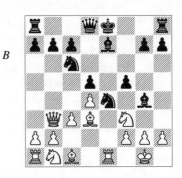

10...0-0

Or:

a) 10...♘a5? 11 ♕a4+ c6 12 ♘e5 and White is much better.

b) 10...♖b8 should be met by 11 ♘fd2! intending f3, rather than 11 ♘bd2?! 0-0 12 h3 ♗h5 13 a4 ♔h8 14

♕c2 ♗d6 = Planinc-Benko, Hastings 1974/5.

c) 10...♕d7 11 ♘fd2 (11 ♕xb7 ♖b8 12 ♕a6 ♖b6 13 ♕a4 ♗xf3 14 gxf3 0-0 gives Black the initiative) 11...0-0-0 12 f3 ♘xd2 13 ♘xd2 ♗h5 14 ♕a4! (14 ♕c2 ♖df8 15 b4 f4 16 ♘b3 g5 17 b5 ♘d8 18 ♖e5 ♔b8 ∞ Sax-Mikhalchishin, Sarajevo 1985; 14 ♘f1 ♗f7 15 ♘g3 g6 16 ♗f4 ♗d6 =) and then:

c1) 14...♖de8 15 ♘b3 ♗d6 (another possibility is 15...a6!?) 16 ♗d2 ♖xe1+ 17 ♖xe1 ♖e8 18 ♘c5 ♗xc5 19 dxc5 ♖xe1+ 20 ♗xe1 g5 21 ♗f2 with a slight advantage for White, Oll-Mikhalchishin, Kuibyshev 1987.

c2) 14...♖he8 15 ♘b3 a6 16 ♗d2 ♗g6 17 ♗f4 ♘b8 18 ♕xd7+ ♘xd7 19 ♔f2 ♗f6 20 g3 ♖f8 21 a4 ♖f7 22 a5 h6 23 ♘c5 ± Ehlvest-Yusupov, Rotterdam 1989.

d) 10...♕d6 and here:

d1) 11 ♘e5 ♘xe5 12 dxe5 ♕xe5 13 f3 (13 ♕xb7 0-0 14 c4 ♗c5 15 ♗e3 ♘xf2! 16 ♔xf2 ♗xe3+ 17 ♖xe3 ♕f4+ 18 ♖f3 ♗xf3 19 gxf3 ♕d4+ −+ Gizunsky-Heinze, Halle 1985) 13...♗d6 ∓ intending 14 fxg4 ♕xh2+ 15 ♔f1 0-0-0.

d2) 11 ♕xb7 ♖b8 12 ♕a6 ♗xf3!
(12...0-0 13 ♘bd2 ♖f6 14 ♗f1 ♖g6 15
♕d3 ♖f8 16 b4 ♗g5 ∞ Yagupov-Sin-
kevich, St Petersburg Petroff mem
2000) 13 gxf3 ♕g6+ 14 ♔f1 0-0 15
♗c2 (15 fxe4 fxe4 16 ♗xe4? ♖xf2+!
17 ♔xf2 ♗h4+ ∓) 15...♗h4 16 ♖e2
♖f6 17 fxe4 fxe4 18 ♗e3 ♘xd4 19
♕xf6 ♕xf6 20 cxd4 (Hübner-Borik,
Bundesliga 1980/1) 20...c5! ∓.
    d3) 11 ♘bd2 0-0-0 12 ♗b5 ♗f6 13
♕a4 (13 ♗xc6? ♕xc6 14 ♘e5 ♗xe5
15 dxe5 ♖hf8 16 ♕b4 ♕g6 17 ♘xe4
fxe4 ∓ Arboleda-Garcia Gonzales,
Medellin 1987) and then:
    d31) 13...♖he8 14 ♗xc6 ♕xc6 and
here:
    d311) 15 ♕xc6 bxc6 16 ♘xe4 ♖xe4
17 ♗g5 ♖de8 18 ♗xf6 (18 ♖xe4?!
fxe4 19 ♗xf6 gxf6 20 ♘h4 ♔d7 and
Black is slightly better, Pokojowczyk-
Sinkovics, Budapest 1985) 18...♗xf3
19 ♖xe4 ♗xe4 =.
    d312) 15 ♕xa7!? should be com-
pared with *13...♖de8 14 ♗xc6 ♕xc6
15 ♕xa7*.
    d32) 13...♖de8 14 ♗xc6 ♕xc6 15
♕xa7 ♘xf2 16 ♔xf2 ♖e1 17 ♘xe1
♖e8 18 ♘df3 (18 ♘ef3!? ∞) 18...♕b5
19 c4 ♕xc4 20 ♗e3 ♗xf3 21 ♘xf3
♕c2+ 22 ♗d2 (22 ♘d2 f4 ∓) 22...♗g5
23 ♕a8+ ♔d7 24 ♕a5 ♗e3+ 25 ♔g3
f4+ −+.
    d33) 13...♘xd2! and here:
    d331) 14 ♗xd2 ♗xf3 15 gxf3 a6 16
♗d3?! (16 ♗f1!?; 16 ♗xc6!?) 16...♗b8
(16...♗h4!) 17 ♗xf5? (17 b4 is unclear) 17...♗h4 18 ♗h3 ♕f6 19 ♗g2
♘e7 ∓ Mukhin-Dolmatov, USSR 1977.
    d332) 14 ♘xd2 ♖he8 15 ♖f1 ♗e2
16 ♗xe2 ♖xe2 17 b4 (17 ♘b3 a6 18

♘c5 ♘b8 =) 17...♘xd4 is equal, Mes-
tel-Wolff, London Lloyds Bank 1985.
    d4) 11 ♘fd2! *(D)* and then:

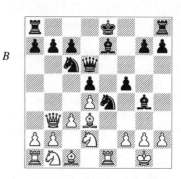

B

    d41) 11...♘xd2 12 ♘xd2 0-0 13
♕xb7 ♖ab8 14 ♕a6 f4 15 ♗e2 f3?! 16
♘xf3 ♗xf3 17 ♗xf3 ♘xd4 18 ♗xd5+
♕xd5 19 cxd4 ♗d6 20 ♕e2 ♕xd4 21
♕e6+ ♔h8 22 ♗e3 ♕xb2 23 ♗xa7
♖a8 24 ♗e3 ± Ernst-Schüssler, Malmö
1987/8.
    d42) 11...♗h5 12 f3 ♘xd2 13 ♘xd2
0-0 14 ♘f1 f4 15 ♕xb7 ♖ab8 16 ♕a6
♗h4 17 ♖e2 ♗g6 18 ♗xg6 ♘xd4 19
♗xh7+ ♔h8 20 ♗d3 ♖b6 (White wins
after 20...♘xe2+!? 21 ♗xe2 ♕c5+ 22
♔h1 ♕f2 23 ♗d2 ♖xb2 24 ♗d3 ♖xd2
25 ♘xd2 ♕xd2 26 ♕g6) 21 ♕a4
♘xe2+ 22 ♗xe2 ♕c5+ 23 ♗e3! ±
Ehlvest-Forintos, Tallinn 1986.
    d43) 11...0-0-0 12 f3 and now:
    d431) 12...♗h3 13 ♖e2 ♕g6 14
♘f1 ♗g5 (14...♘g5? 15 ♗xg5 ♕xg5
16 ♔h1 +− Ernst-L.Schneider, Swedish Ch (Norrköping) 1988) 15 ♕c2
♖he8 16 ♘a3 ♗xc1 17 ♖xc1 ♘g5 18
♔h1 ±.
    d432) 12...♗h4 and here:
    d4321) 13 ♖e2!? ♗h5 14 fxe4 fxe4
(14...♗xe2 15 ♗xe2 {15 e5? ♕h6}

15...fxe4 16 ♘f1 ±) 15 ♘xe4 (15 ♗b5 ♗xe2 16 ♗xe2 ♖hf8 −+) 15...dxe4 16 ♖xe4 ♖de8 17 ♘d2! ∞.

d4322) 13 ♖f1 and then:

d43221) 13...♗h5 14 fxe4 fxe4 15 ♗xe4! dxe4 16 ♘xe4 ♕g6 17 ♘c5 b6 18 ♕e6+ +−.

d43222) 13...♖hf8 14 ♕c2 ♗h3 15 ♘b3 ♕g6 16 ♘a3 ♖de8 17 ♗f4 ♘d8 18 ♔h1 ♘e6 19 ♗e5 is winning for White, Borriss-Camejo, Santiago jr Wch 1990.

d43223) 13...♗h3 14 ♕c2! (intending ♘b3; 14 gxh3 ♕g6+ 15 ♔h1 ♘f2+ 16 ♖xf2 ♗xf2 17 ♕d1 ♖de8 −+; 14 ♕d1 ♕g6 15 ♕e2 ♘xc3! 16 bxc3 ♖de8 −+; 14 ♘xe4 fxe4 15 fxe4 dxe4 16 ♗xe4 ♖hf8 17 ♘d2 ♖de8 18 ♕b5 ♖xf1+ 19 ♕xf1 ♗d7 gives Black compensation, Woda-Ostrowski, Poznan 1987) 14...♕g6 15 ♘b3 ♖hf8 16 ♘a3 ♖de8 17 ♗f4! (17 ♔h1? ♘f2+ 18 ♖xf2 ♗xg2+ 0-1 Ivanchuk-Anand, Reggio Emilia 1988/9) 17...♗g5 18 ♗xg5 ♘xg5 19 gxh3 ♘e6+ 20 ♔h1 ♘f4 21 ♖ae1 +−.

d43224) 13...♗f2+ 14 ♖xf2 ♘xf2 15 ♔xf2 ♕xh2 16 ♘f1 ♕h4+ 17 ♔g1 ♖hf8 18 ♕c2 ♗h5 19 ♗e3 f4 20 ♗f2 ♕g5 21 ♘bd2 ♖d6 22 ♖e1 ± Ernst-L.Schneider, Gothenburg 1988.

We now return to 10...0-0 *(D)*:

11 ♘bd2

Other moves are bad:

a) 11 ♗f4? ♗xf3 12 gxf3 ♘g5 13 ♔g2 ♕d7 14 ♕c2 ♘e6 15 ♗c1 ♗d6 16 ♘d2 ♖ae8 ∓ Lasker-Pillsbury, St Petersburg 1895/6.

b) 11 ♘fd2? ♘xf2! 12 ♔xf2 (12 ♗f1 ♘e4 13 ♕xb7 ∓) 12...♗h4+ 13 g3 (13 ♔f1 ♗xe1 14 ♔xe1 ♕h4+ 15

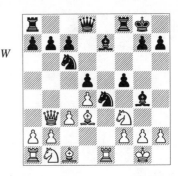

W

♔f1 ♖ae8 −+) 13...f4 14 ♔g2 (14 gxh4 ♕xh4+ 15 ♔f1 f3 −+; 14 ♔g1 fxg3 15 h3 ♗xh3 16 ♗e4 g2 17 ♕xd5+ ♔h8 18 ♕xd8 ♖axd8 19 ♖d1 ♗g4 20 ♗c2 ♖de8 −+) 14...fxg3 15 ♗e4 (15 hxg3 ♕d6! 16 gxh4 ♖f2+ 17 ♔xf2 ♕h2+ 18 ♔e3 ♕g3+ 19 ♘f3 ♖e8+ 20 ♔d2 ♖xe1 21 ♕xd5+ ♗e6 −+) 15...♗h3+! 16 ♔g1 gxh2+ 17 ♔xh2 ♕d6+ 18 ♔h1 ♗xe1 −+ Ljubojević-Makarychev, Amsterdam 1975.

c) 11 ♕xb7?! ♗xf3 12 gxf3 (12 ♕xc6 ♖f6 13 ♕a4 ♖g6 ∓) 12...♘xf2! 13 ♔xf2 ♗h4+ 14 ♔f1 ♗xe1 15 ♔xe1 ♕d6! 16 ♔d1 ♖ab8 17 ♕a6 ♖f6 18 ♘d2 ♕xh2 19 ♕a4 h5 20 b4 (Browne-Viner, Australia 1971) 20...♖e8! 21 b5 ♖e3 22 ♔c2 ♘d8 23 ♕xa7 ♘e6 ∓ Gutman.

We now return to 11 ♘bd2 *(D)*:

This is the principal position of this variation. Black now has two main continuations at his disposal:

A211: 11...♘a5 202
A212: 11...♔h8 204

The latter move has been considered the main line for some decades. Black offers his b-pawn, and is prepared to make further sacrifices to break through on the kingside. The enormous

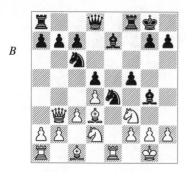

B

complications that result have not been fully resolved. The former has become increasingly popular in recent years; Black offers no immediate sacrifice, but he is still committed to the attack because of the weaknesses created by ...f5.

Other moves are less important:

a) 11...♖b8 12 ♘xe4 ♘a5 13 ♕a4 fxe4 (13...♗xf3? 14 ♘g3 +−) 14 ♘e5 exd3 15 ♘xg4 ♘c4 16 ♕d1 ♗g5 ± Ernst-Forintos, Malmö 1988/9.

b) 11...♘xd2 12 ♘xd2 ♔h8 13 ♕xb7 ♖f6 14 ♕b3 ♗d6 15 ♘f1 ♖g6 16 g3 ♘e7 17 ♘e3 ± Thipsay-Le Blancq, London 1986.

A211)
11...♘a5 12 ♕a4

12 ♕b5!? deserves serious attention: 12...c5!? (12...c6 13 ♕a4 b5 14 ♕c2 and rather than 14...♗d6?! 15 ♘e5 ±, Botvinnik recommended 14...♘c4!? =) 13 ♘e5 (13 dxc5 a6 14 ♕a4 ♗xc5 15 ♘d4 b5! 16 ♕c2 ♗xd4! 17 cxd4 ♖c8 ∓; 13 h3?! ♗h5! intending ...♗e8; 13 b4 cxb4 14 cxb4 ♘c6 15 ♕xb7 ♘xb4) 13...♗h5 (13...a6 14 ♕d7!) 14 ♕a4! (14 dxc5 ♗e8 −+; 14 b4 cxb4 15

cxb4 ♘c6; 14 ♕d7 cxd4) 14...cxd4 15 cxd4 ♗e8 16 ♕d1 ♘c6 17 ♘df3 ± Analysis.
   12...♘c6 13 ♗b5 *(D)*

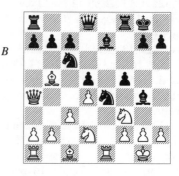

B

13...♗h4
Or:

a) 13...♖f6 14 ♗xc6 ♖xc6 15 ♘e5 ♖a6 16 ♕c2 ♗h5 17 f3 ±.

b) 13...♘xd2 14 ♘xd2 ♕d6 and then:

b1) 15 ♘f1 is well met by 15...f4!.

b2) 15 f3 ♗h4!? (15...♗h5!?) 16 ♖e2 ♗h5 17 ♘b3 (17 ♘f1?! f4! ∓) 17...♖ae8 18 ♖xe8 ♖xe8 19 ♗d2 and now Black can try 19...♗xf3 20 gxf3 ♕g6+ 21 ♔h1 (21 ♔f1 ♕h5 22 ♗e2? ♗g3!) 21...♕h5, when 22 ♖f1? loses to 22...♗g3 −+, while 22 ♔g2 gives Black a choice between 22...♕g6+ = and 22...♖e6!? − Analysis. However, 22 ♗f1! makes it harder for Black to justify his sacrifice.

b3) 15 ♘b3 ♗h4! and here:

b31) 16 g3 f4 17 gxh4 ♕h6 −+.

b32) 16 ♘c5 and then:

b321) 16...f4!? 17 ♘xb7 ♕g6 18 ♗d3 (18 ♗xc6 ♗f3 −+) 18...♖xd3 19 ♕xc6 ♖ae8! 20 ♕xe8 (20 ♗xf4 ♗xf2+! 21 ♔xf2 ♕d2+! −+; 20 ♗d2

♗xf2+ 21 ♔xf2 ♕xd2+ 22 ♔f1 f3
forces mate) 20...♖xe8 21 ♖xe8+ ♔f7
22 ♖e1 ♕c2! 23 g3 (23 ♖f1 ♗e2 ∓)
23...fxg3 24 hxg3 ♗xg3! ∓ with the
point that 25 fxg3? loses to 25...♗f3.

b322) 16...♗xf2+ 17 ♔xf2 ♕xh2
18 ♗xc6 (18 ♘e6 f4 19 ♘xf4 ♖xf4+
20 ♗xf4 ♖f8 −+) 18...bxc6 19 ♕xc6
(19 ♘e6 f4 ∓) 19...f4 20 ♕xd5+ ♔h8
∓.

b33) 16 ♖f1! ♕g6!? (16...f4 17 f3
♗f5 18 ♘c5 ♕g6 19 ♕d1! ♗h3 20
♕d2 ♖ae8 21 ♘d3 a6 ∞ Anand-Yusupov, Linares 1993) 17 ♗f4 ♗h3 18 g3!
(18 ♗g3? f4 19 gxh3 fxg3 20 hxg3
♗xg3 21 fxg3 ♕xg3+ 22 ♔h1 ♕xh3+
23 ♔g1 ♕g3+ 24 ♔h1 ♖f3 wins for
Black) 18...♗g5 19 ♗xg5 ♗xf1 20
♗xf1! (20 ♖xf1 ♕xg5 21 ♗xc6 bxc6
22 ♕xc6 f4 ∓) 20...♕xg5 21 ♘c5 ∓.

b4) 15 h3!! (this preliminary move
has two benefits; first of all, the e6-
square is accessible in some lines, and
secondly in some tactical continuations Black's queen will not arrive at h2
with the capture of a pawn) and then:

b41) 15...♗h4 16 hxg4 fxg4 17
♖f1! ± has the point 17...♗xf2+ 18
♖xf2 ♖xf2 19 ♔xf2 ♖f8+ 20 ♔e2
♕g3 21 ♔d1! +−.

b42) 15...♗h5 16 ♘b3 ♗h4 17
♘c5 and now:

b421) 17...♗xf2+? 18 ♔xf2 ♕h2
(thanks to White's preliminary h3, this
does not take the h-pawn) 19 ♗xc6
bxc6 (19...f4 20 ♗xd5+ ♔h8 21 ♘d3!
f3 22 ♘f4 ♖xf4 {22...fxg2 23 ♗xg2
♖xf4+ 24 ♗xf4 ♖f8 25 ♖e4 +−} 23
♗xf4 ♕xg2+ 24 ♔e3 +−) 20 ♕xc6 f4
21 ♕xd5+ ♔h8 22 ♕xh5 f3 (22...♕g3+
23 ♔f1 f3 24 gxf3 ♖xf3+ 25 ♔e2 +−)

23 ♕xf3! +− Anand-Kramnik, Tilburg
1998.

b422) 17...f4 18 ♖e6! (and here
White makes use of the e6-square)
18...♕d8 19 ♘d3!? (19 ♗f1 and 19 f3
are both slightly better for White according to Anand) 19...f3 20 ♗xc6 (20
g3? ♕c8! ∓) 20...bxc6 21 g3 (Anand)
is probably good for White.

We now return to 13...♗h4 (D):

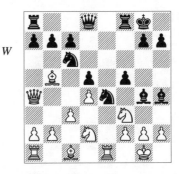

14 g3
14 ♖f1 ♘xd2 15 ♘xd2 ♘e7 =.
14...♗f6
14...♘xd2 15 ♘xh4! ±.
15 ♗xc6 bxc6 16 ♕xc6 ♖e8
Black has sufficient compensation.
17 ♘e5 ♗xe5 18 dxe5 ♘g5
18...♖xe5 19 ♘b3! ♖e8 20 ♗f4 ±.
19 f4
19 c4 ♖e6 20 ♕xd5 ♕e8 21 h4
♘h3+ 22 ♔g2 ♖d8 23 ♕c5 ♕h5 24
♘f3?! f4 gives Black compensation,
Ponomariov-Pavasović, Batumi Echt
1999.
19...♘h3+!
19...♖e6?! 20 ♕c5 ♘e4? (20...♘h3+!
21 ♔g2 ±) 21 ♘xe4 dxe4 (21...fxe4 22
c4 ±) 22 ♗e3 ± Shirov-Kramnik, Belgrade ECC 1999.

20 ⌸g2

20 ⌸f1 ⌸b8 is also fine for Black.

20...⌸b8 21 c4 dxc4!

21...⌸h8 22 c5! gives White a slight advantage.

22 ⌸xc4 ⌸d3

Black has compensation. 23 ⌸e3?! ⌸xb2+ 24 ⌸xb2 ⌸d2+ 25 ⌸h1 ⌸f2+ 26 ⌸g1 ⌸h3+ 27 ⌸h1 ⌸f2+ ½-½ Anand-Kramnik, Wijk aan Zee 1999.

A212)

11...⌸h8 (D)

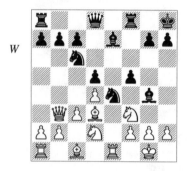

Offering the b-pawn is critical. According to current theory, Black can obtain adequate compensation, although the play is extremely complicated.

12 ⌸xb7

White is now committed to taking the b7-pawn, and the only real question is whether it is better to play h3 first:

a) 12 ⌸e5? ⌸xe5 13 dxe5 ⌸c5 14 ⌸f1 ⌸h4 −+.

b) 12 ⌸f1?! ⌸xf3 (12...⌸d7?! 13 ⌸3d2 ⌸xd2 14 ⌸xd2 f4 15 f3 ± Capablanca-Kostić, Havana 1919) 13 gxf3 ⌸xf2! (13...⌸g5?! 14 ⌸xg5 ⌸xg5 15 ⌸e6!) 14 ⌸xf2 ⌸h4+ 15 ⌸g3 f4 ∓ Capablanca.

c) 12 ⌸e2 ⌸a5 (12...⌸b8!?) 13 ⌸a4 and now 13...⌸c6!? ∞ is an improvement over 13...c5?! 14 ⌸e5 ± Stein-Anikaev, Kislovodsk 1972.

d) 12 h3 (on the available evidence, it seems that this interpolation only makes life somewhat easier for Black) 12...⌸h5 (12...⌸xf3 13 ⌸xf3 ⌸b8 14 ⌸f4 ⌸d6 15 ⌸xd6 ⌸xd6 16 ⌸e2 ±) 13 ⌸xb7 ⌸f6! (13...⌸a5?! 14 ⌸a6 c5 15 ⌸e2 ⌸b8 ± Ligterink-Dvoretsky, Wijk aan Zee 1975) 14 ⌸b3 and then:

d1) 14...⌸d6?! 15 ⌸b5 ⌸b8 16 ⌸a4 ±.

d2) 14...g5!? and then:

d21) 15 ⌸e5 ⌸xe5 16 dxe5 ⌸xf2!? (16...⌸b6 17 ⌸c2 intending c4) 17 exf6?! (White should prefer 17 ⌸xf2! ⌸c5+ and now both 18 ⌸g3 and 18 ⌸f1 are unclear) 17...⌸c5 18 ⌸e2? ⌸e4+ 19 ⌸h1 ⌸g3+ 20 ⌸h2 ⌸d6 21 ⌸f3 ⌸f1++ 0-1 Macagno-Tempone, Moron 1981.

d22) 15 ⌸xe4 fxe4 16 ⌸xg5 ⌸b8 17 ⌸c2 ⌸f8 (17...h6!? ∞) 18 ⌸f1 ⌸g6 ∞ intending ...e3 and ...h6.

d3) 14...⌸g6 15 ⌸e2 (D) and here:

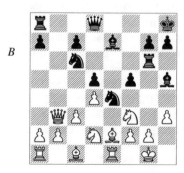

d31) 15...♘xf2? 16 ♔xf2 ♗h4+ 17 ♔f1 ♗xe1 18 ♘xe1 ♗xe2+ 19 ♔xe2 ♕e7+ 20 ♔f1 ♖e8 21 ♕d1 +–.

d32) 15...♕d6? 16 ♘e5 ±.

d33) 15...♗h4? 16 ♖f1 ♗xf3 17 ♘xf3 ♗xf2+ 18 ♖xf2 ♘xf2 19 ♔xf2 ♕d6 20 ♘g5! +– Karpov-Korchnoi, Moscow Ct (6) 1974.

d34) 15...♖b8 16 ♕d1 ♗d6 17 ♘xe4! fxe4 18 ♘e5 ♘xe5 19 ♗xh5 ♘d3 20 ♗xg6 ♕f6 ± Stieg-Mende, corr. 1976.

d35) 15...♗d6! 16 ♘e5 (Black has compensation after 16 ♕d1 ♕f6, 16 ♘f1 ♖b8 17 ♕c2 ♗xf3 18 ♗xf3 ♕h4 or 16 ♔f1!? ♗f4!? intending 17...♗xd2 18 ♘xd2 ♕g5) 16...♘xe5 17 ♗xh5 (17 ♘xe4? ♘f3+) 17...♖xg2+ 18 ♔xg2 ♕g5+ and then:

d351) 19 ♗g4 fxg4! 20 ♘xe4 gxh3+ 21 ♔f1 ♕g2+ 22 ♔e2 ♕f3+ 23 ♔f1 (23 ♔d2 ♕d3#) 23...h2 24 ♘g3 ♘d3 –+.

d352) 19 ♔f1 ♕h4 and then:

d3521) 20 ♖e2? ♘xd2+ 21 ♖xd2 ♕xh3+ 22 ♔e1 ♕h1+ –+.

d3522) 20 ♖xe4? fxe4 21 dxe5 ♗c5! ∓.

d3523) 20 ♘xe4 ♕xh3+ 21 ♔g1 (21 ♔e2?? ♕d3#) 21...♘f3+ 22 ♗xf3 ♗h2+ =.

12...♖f6 *(D)*

Other moves are bad: 12...♘xd2? 13 ♗xd2 ♗xf3 14 ♕xc6 ♖f6 15 ♖e6 ± Garbisu-Abell, Spanish jr Ch 1992; 12...♕d6? 13 ♗b5! ♘a5 14 ♕a6 ♘xd2 15 ♘xd2 c6 16 ♗f1 +– Petrushin-Timofeev, USSR 1979.

13 ♕b3

There is nothing better than simply withdrawing the queen.

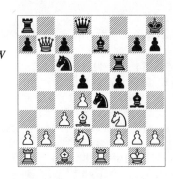

W

13...♖b8

Or:

a) 13...♕d6? 14 ♗b5! ♖af8 15 ♗xc6 ♕xc6 16 ♘e5 ♕d6 17 f3 +– Losev-Bianchi, Moscow 1991.

b) 13...♗d6 14 g3 ♕g8?! 15 ♗e2 ♖e8 16 ♘xe4 ♖xe4 17 ♗e3 f4 18 ♘g5! ± Blatny-Kuczynski, Groningen jr Ech 1985/6.

c) 13...♖g6 and then:

c1) 14 ♘e5? ♘xe5 15 dxe5 ♘xf2! 16 ♔xf2 ♗c5+ 17 ♔f1 ♕h4 –+.

c2) 14 ♔f1? ♖b8 15 ♕c2 ♗d6 16 h3 ♗h5 17 a3? (17 ♗e2!) 17...♕f6 18 ♘e5? ♘xe5 19 dxe5 ♕xe5 20 ♘f3 ♗xf3 21 gxf3 (Showalter-Pillsbury, Cambridge Springs 1904) 21...♘g3+! –+.

c3) 14 ♗f1 f4!? and now White should play 15 ♕c2 ∞, rather than 15 ♘xe4? dxe4 16 ♘e5 ♘xe5 17 dxe5 e3! ∓ Muchnik-Chekhova, Minsk 1981.

c4) 14 ♗e2 ♕d6! 15 ♘f1 f4 16 ♘3d2 ♘xf2 (16...♗h4!?) 17 ♗xg4 ♖xg4 (17...♘xg4!?) 18 ♖xe7?! (18 ♖e2 ♘e4 gives Black compensation) 18...♘xe7! 19 ♔xf2 ♕g6 20 g3 ♖f8 21 ♘f3 fxg3+ 22 hxg3 ♕h5! 23 ♕d1 ♘g6 with an initiative – Dvoretsky.

c5) 14 ♗b5!? and here:

c51) 14...♕d6? 15 ♗xc6 ♗h3 16 ♘xe4 ♖xg2+ 17 ♔h1 fxe4 18 ♘e5 +−.

c52) 14...♖b8?! 15 ♕a4 ♕d6 16 ♗xc6 ♗h3 17 g3! ♘xg3 18 fxg3 ♖xg3+ 19 ♔f2 ♖g2+ 20 ♔e3 f4+ 21 ♔d3 ♗f5+ 22 ♘e4 ±.

c53) 14...f4?! (Dreev-Wolff, Bucaramanga jr 1983) 15 ♗xc6! ♘xd2 (15...♗h3? 16 ♘xe4! ♗xg2 17 ♘e5 +−) 16 ♘e5! ♘xb3 17 ♘f7+ ♔g8 18 ♘xd8 ♖xd8 (18...♘xa1 19 ♗xa8 ♗xd8 20 ♖e8+ +−) 19 axb3 ♔f8 20 ♗b5 ±.

c54) 14...♘xd2 15 ♘xd2 ♗d6! (15...f4?! 16 ♗d3 ♖h6 17 ♗e2 ♖b8 18 ♕d1 ♗xe2 19 ♕xe2 ♗d6 20 ♘f3 ± De Jong-P.Müller, Hamburg jr 1989) 16 g3 (16 ♗xc6 ♗xh2+! 17 ♔xh2 {17 ♔f1? ♖xc6 ∓} 17...♕h4+ 18 ♔g1 ♖h6 was given as winning for Black by Dreev and Dvoretsky, but 19 f3 ♕xe1+ 20 ♘f1 ♖h1+ 21 ♔xh1 ♕xf1+ 22 ♔h2 ♗xf3, with a draw, appears to be a forced continuation) 16...♘e7 ± (Dreev and Dvoretsky).

We now return to the position after 13...♖b8 *(D)*:

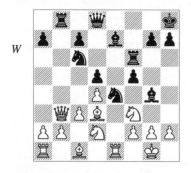

W

14 ♕c2
Or:

a) 14 ♕d1 ♖g6 15 ♘f1 (Ribli-Bonner, Skopje OL 1972) 15...♗d6 gives Black compensation.

b) 14 ♕a4 ♗d6 15 h3 (15 ♗e2 ♖g6 16 ♘xe4 fxe4 17 ♘g5 ♕d7 18 ♗g4 ♕xg4 19 g3 ♖f8 20 ♕xc6 ♕f5 ∓ Losev-Baikov, Moscow 1985) and now:

b1) 15...♗h5 16 ♗e2 ♖g6 (16...♗e8 17 ♕c2 ♖g6 18 ♘f1 ♗d7 19 ♘e3 ♗e6 20 ♗f1 f4 21 ♘c4 ♗xh3 22 ♖xe4 dxe4 23 ♕xe4 ♕d7 24 ♘xd6 cxd6 25 ♕xf4 ∞ Arlandi) and then:

b11) 17 ♘xe4 fxe4 (17...dxe4 18 ♘g5 ♖xg5 19 ♗xg5 ♕xg5 20 ♕xc6 ♗e8 21 ♕d5 e3 22 ♕f3 ±) 18 ♘g5!? ♖xg5 19 ♗xg5 ♕xg5 20 ♗xh5 ♘e7! 21 ♕d1 g6 22 ♗g4 h5! 23 ♗d7 ♖d8 ∞.

b12) 17 ♔f1!? ♗f4 18 ♘b3 ♗xc1 19 ♖axc1 ♕d6 20 ♖c2 ♕f4 21 ♗d1 ♖e8 is unclear, Ivanchuk-Shirov, Dortmund 1998.

b2) 15...♘xd2!? 16 hxg4 (16 ♘xd2 ♗xh3 17 gxh3 ♖g6+ 18 ♔f1 ♕g5 19 ♕xc6 ♕g2+ 20 ♔e2 ♗g3 −+ Ernst-Storland, Gausdal 1987) 16...♘xf3+ 17 gxf3 fxg4 18 fxg4 ♖f3! 19 ♕xc6 ♕h4 20 ♖e8+ ♖xe8 21 ♕xe8+ ♖f8 22 ♕e3 ♕xg4+ 23 ♔f1 is analysis by Ernst. Now Black should take a draw by 23...♕d1+, etc., since the move recommended by Ernst, 23...♗g3?, is strongly met by 24 ♗f5!.

14...♗d6 15 ♗f1

15 ♘f1 ♖g6 16 ♔h1 ♕f6 gives Black compensation, Arakhamia-Cholushkina, Kiev 1984. However, 15 h3!? deserves very serious attention, as it rules out the sacrifice on f2.

15...♘xd2 16 ♘xd2 ♗xh2+ 17 ♔xh2 ♖h6+ 18 ♔g1 ♕h4 19 f3 ♕xe1 20 ♘b3 ♖h5 21 ♗f4

21 ♕d2?? ♖h1+! (21...♕h4?! 22 ♕f4 ♘e7! 23 ♗d2 ♘g6 24 ♕xc7 ♖f8 25 ♗e2, Barua-Arlandi, Manila OL 1992, 25...♗h3! 26 ♕h2 ♗xg2 27 ♕xg2 ♘f4 28 ♗xf4 ♕xf4 −+) 22 ♔xh1 ♕xf1+ 23 ♔h2 ♖e8 24 ♕f4 ♖e2 25 ♕g3 ♗xf3 −+ Arlandi.

21...♕h4 22 ♕e2! g5 23 ♗e5+ ♔g8 24 fxg4 fxg4 25 ♗xc7 ♖f8 26 ♕e6+ ♖f7

With a draw by perpetual check.

A22)
9 c4 *(D)*

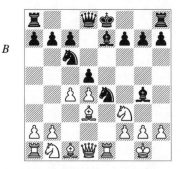

This move offers White fair prospects of a slight advantage, and it is less double-edged than 9 c3. It almost always leads to an isolated d-pawn position, in which White has good piece-play and some attacking chances, while Black hopes to exploit White's weak pawn in an endgame.

9...♘f6

Other moves are unattractive:

a) 9...♘xd4?? 10 ♗xe4 dxe4 11 ♕xd4 +−.

b) 9...f5?! 10 cxd5 ♕xd5 11 ♘c3 ♘xc3 12 bxc3 ♗xf3 13 ♕xf3 ♕xf3 14 gxf3 ±.

c) 9...♗xf3 10 ♕xf3 ♘xd4 11 ♕e3 ♘f5 (11...c5? 12 cxd5 ♘f6 13 ♘c3 ♕d7 14 ♗d2 ± Vecsey-Androvitsky, corr. 1971) 12 ♕h3! ♘fd6 13 cxd5 ♘f6 14 ♗g5 ♕d7 (14...♘xd5? 15 ♘c3 ♔f8 16 ♖xe7! ♘xe7 17 ♘d5 ± Lobron-Handoko, Indonesia 1983) 15 ♕h4 0-0-0 16 ♘c3 h6 17 ♕d4! ♔b8 18 ♗e3 b6 19 a4 ± Chigorin-Schiffers, St Petersburg 1879.

Now (after 9...♘f6):

A221: 10 ♘c3 207
A222: 10 cxd5 214

The second of these appears to be White's best chance for an advantage.

A221)
10 ♘c3 *(D)*

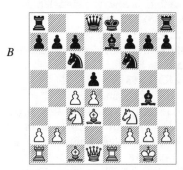

The main defect of this move is the transpositional possibility given in line 'b' just below.

10...dxc4

Or:

a) 10...0-0 11 cxd5 ♘xd4?! (Black should prefer 11...♘xd5! – *10 cxd5 ♘xd5 11 ♘c3 0-0*) 12 ♗xh7+ ♘xh7 13 ♕xd4 ♗xf3 14 gxf3 ♘f6 15 ♕d3 (15 ♕c4 ♕d7 16 ♗f4 ♕h3 ∞) 15...♕d7 16 ♗f4 ♖ad8 17 ♖ad1 ±.

b) Black's best option is 10...♗xf3!
11 ♕xf3 ♘xd4 – 6...♘c6 7 0-0 ♗g4 8
c4 ♘f6 9 ♘c3 ♗xf3 10 ♕xf3 ♘xd4 11
♖e1+ ♗e7, which is a satisfactory line
for Black.

11 ♗xc4 0-0 12 d5
Or:

a) 12 ♗g5 ♘d5 13 ♗xe7 ♘cxe7 14
h3 ♗h5 15 g4 ♗g6 16 ♘e5 c6 17 ♕f3
♔h8 18 h4 f6 = Hübner-P.Nikolić,
Wijk aan Zee 1984.

b) 12 ♗e3 ♗xf3 13 ♕xf3 ♘xd4 14
♗xd4! (14 ♕xb7 ♘c2 15 ♖ad1 ♗d6!
16 ♖e2 ♘xe3 17 ♖xe3 ♖b8 is level)
14...♕xd4 15 ♖xe7 ♕xc4 16 ♕xb7 c6
17 ♕b3 ♕xb3 18 axb3 ♖ab8 (not
18...♖fe8? 19 ♖b7! ±) 19 ♖a3 ♖fe8 20
♖xe8+ ♖xe8 21 ♔f1 ♖e7 22 ♖a6 ♖c7
23 ♔e2 (Ljubojević-Schüssler, New
York 1985) 23...♔f8 ±.

12...♘a5 13 ♗d3 c6
Black must not delay in rescuing
the offside knight.

14 h3 ♗xf3
Or 14...♗h5, and then:

a) 15 ♗g5!? cxd5 16 ♖e5 ♗xf3
(16...d4? 17 ♗xf6 ♗xf3 18 ♗xh7+!
{18 ♕xf3 ± J.Polgar-Kamsky, Las Palmas 1994} 18...♔xh7 19 ♕d3+ ♔g8
20 ♗xe7 ♕c7 21 ♖xa5 ♕xa5 22 ♗xf8
+−) 17 ♕xf3 ♘c6 18 ♗xf6 ♗xf6 19
♖xd5 ±.

b) 15 ♖e5! ♗g6 (15...cxd5? 16
♘xd5! ±) 16 ♗xg6! (16 ♗g5?! ♗d6
17 ♖e2 ♗b4 ∞ Kasparov-Timman,
Amsterdam 1994) 16...hxg6 17 d6
♗xd6 18 ♖xa5 ♕xa5 19 ♕xd6 ♖ad8
20 ♕f4 ±.

15 ♕xf3 cxd5
15...♘xd5 16 ♘xd5 cxd5 17 ♖e5 is
much better for White.

**16 ♗g5 ♘c6 17 ♗xf6 ♗xf6 18
♘xd5**
White is slightly better, Gutman-
Hergott, Graz 1987. White's advantage is based on his slightly more active pieces and the fact that Black's
queen has no obviously good square.
However, the opposite-coloured bishops will exert a drawish tendency.

A222)
10 cxd5 (D)

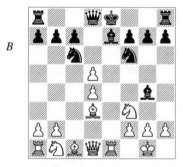

10...♘xd5
10...♕xd5?! is dubious in view of
11 ♘c3:

a) 11...♕d8 12 ♗b5 0-0 13 ♗xc6
bxc6 14 h3 ± Browne-Meduna, Las
Palmas 1974.

b) 11...♕h5 12 ♗b5 ♗xf3 (12...♖d8
13 ♗f4 ±) 13 gxf3 ♘d5 14 ♕a4 ♘xc3
15 bxc3 ♔f8 16 ♗xc6 ♕g6+ 17 ♔f1 ±
Vitolinš-Heida, Riga 1972.

c) 11...♗xf3 12 ♘xd5 ♗xd1 is the
key tactical line, but it favours White:

c1) 13 ♘xf6+!? gxf6 14 ♖xd1
♘xd4 15 ♗e3 and here:

c11) 15...c5 16 ♗xd4 cxd4 17
♗b5+ ♔f8 18 ♖ac1! (18 ♖xd4?! ♖d8
19 ♖xd8+ ♗xd8 20 ♖d1 ♔g7 21 ♖d7

♗b6 and now both 22 ♖xb7 ♖c8 and 22 ♗c4 ♖d8 are equal) 18...a6 19 ♗e2 ± intending 20 ♖c7 – Analysis.

c12) 15...♘e6 16 ♗e4 c6 17 ♖ac1 ±/± (intending ♖xc6) King-Bex, Berne 1986.

c2) 13 ♘xc7+ ♔d7 14 ♗f4 (14 ♘xa8? ♗g4 ∓) 14...♗g4 (14...♘h5 15 ♗f5+ ♔d8 16 ♖axd1 ♘xf4 17 ♘xa8 ±) 15 d5! ♘d4 16 ♘xa8 ♖xa8 17 ♗e5 (17 ♖ac1?! ♘xd5 18 ♗e5 ♘c6 19 ♗xg7 ♖g8 20 ♗h6 ♗b4! 21 ♖f1 ♗f3 ∓ Panchenko-Makarychev, USSR 1975) 17...♗f5! (17...♗c5 18 h3 ♗h5 19 ♖ac1 ♗b6 20 ♖c4 ♖e8 21 ♔f1 ±) 18 ♗f1 and then:

c21) 18...♗c5 19 ♖ad1 ♘c2 20 ♗b5+ ♔e7 21 ♗d4+ ♔d6 22 ♗e5+ ♔e7 23 ♖e2 ♔f8 24 d6 ♖d8 25 d7 ♘xd7 26 ♗xd7 ♗g4 27 ♗d6+ ♗xd6 28 ♗xg4 ± Makarov-Rozentalis, USSR 1982.

c22) 18...♘c2 19 ♗b5+ ♔d8 20 d6 ♘xe1 21 ♖xe1 ♗e6 22 dxe7+ ♔xe7 23 ♗d4 ± Kavalek-Toth, Haifa OL 1976.

11 ♘c3 0-0 *(D)*

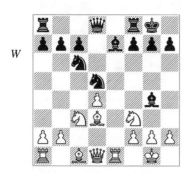

12 ♗e4

A thematic move, fighting for control of the key blockading square d5.

White has tried two other moves at this point:

a) 12 ♘xd5 ♕xd5 13 ♗e4 ♕d6 and then:

a1) 14 ♕d3?! ♗xf3 15 ♗xf3 ♗f6 16 ♗xc6 bxc6 ∓ Mitsousek-Toth, Italy 1973.

a2) 14 d5 ♘e5 15 h3 ♘xf3+ 16 ♗xf3 ♗xf3 17 ♕xf3 ♕f6 18 ♕b3 b6 19 ♗f4 ♕xf4 20 ♖xe7 ♖fe8 = Richardson-Morgado, corr. 1978.

a3) 14 ♗xc6 bxc6 (White inflicts doubled pawns on Black, but White lacks the development tempo he needs to exploit them) 15 ♖e4 ♗e6 16 ♗g5 ♗xg5 17 ♘xg5 ♗d5 18 ♖e3 and now:

a31) 18...♕f4 19 ♖e5! ♖ab8 (not 19...f6?? 20 g3 +–, but 19...h6 20 g3 ♕f6 21 ♘e4 ± is possible) 20 g3 ♕f6 21 b3 h6 (21...♖fd8 22 ♕e2 h6 23 ♘e4 ♕g6 24 ♘c5 ± Zapata-Lima, Bogota 1992) 22 ♘e4 ♗xe4 23 ♖xe4 ♖fd8 24 ♖c1 ♖d6 ±.

a32) 18...h6 19 ♘e4 ♗xe4 20 ♖xe4 ♖ab8 (20...♖fe8 21 ♖xe8+ ♖xe8 22 ♕a4 ±) 21 ♕e2 (21 b3 ♖fe8 is equal) 21...♖b4 =.

b) 12 h3 is a major alternative, but on current evidence it doesn't give White any advantage:

b1) 12...♗h5? 13 ♗xh7+! ♔xh7 14 ♘g5+ ♔g6 15 ♕d3+ f5 16 ♘e6 ♕d6 17 ♘xd5 +– F.Olafsson-Persitz, Hastings 1955/6.

b2) 12...♗xf3?! 13 ♕xf3 ♘db4 14 ♗b1 (14 d5!?) 14...♖e8 (14...♗f6 15 a3 ♘a6 16 d5 ♘d4 17 ♕d3 g6 18 ♗h6 ♘c5 19 ♕c4 ♖e8 20 ♗a2 ♕d6 21 ♖ad1 a5 22 ♗e3 b5 23 ♘xb5 ± A.Sokolov-Yusupov, Moscow Ch 1981) 15 d5 ♗d6 16 ♖xe8+ ♕xe8 17 ♗e3 ♘e5 18

♕e4 ♘g6 19 a3 ♘a6 20 ♗c2 ♕xe4 21 ♘xe4 ♗e5 22 ♗d3 ± Dolmatov-Yusupov, USSR Ch (Frunze) 1981.

b3) 12...♗e6 *(D)* and here:

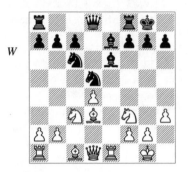

b31) 13 ♘e4 h6!? 14 a3 should be answered by 14...♘f6!? =, rather than 14...♖e8?! 15 b4 ♘f6 16 ♘c5!? (16 ♗b2?, J.Polgar-Hort, Monaco (Veterans vs Ladies) 1994, 16...♘xe4! 17 ♗xe4 ♗d5 =) 16...♗xc5 17 dxc5 ±.

b32) 13 ♕c2 ♘f6!? and here:

b321) 14 ♘g5!? h6 (14...♘xd4 15 ♗xh7+ ♔h8 16 ♕b1 ±) 15 ♘xe6 fxe6 16 ♘e2 (16 ♗e3 ♘xd4 17 ♗xd4 ♕xd4 18 ♖xe6 =) 16...♘b4 17 ♕b1 ♘xd3 18 ♕xd3 ♘d5! 19 ♘g3 (19 ♗xh6 gxh6 20 ♕g6+ ♔h8 =) 19...♗g5! =.

b322) 14 ♗f5 ♘b4 15 ♕b1 ♗xf5 16 ♕xf5 g6 17 ♕b1 ♖e8 18 a3 (18 ♗f4!? intending ♗e5) 18...♘bd5 19 ♗g5 c6 = L.Schneider-Vladimirov, Gausdal 1991.

b33) 13 a3 and now:

b331) 13...♘xc3?! 14 bxc3 ♗f6 15 ♖b1! b6 16 ♖b5! and here:

b3311) 16...a6 17 ♖h5 g6 18 ♘g5!! ♗xg5 (18...gxh5 19 ♕xh5 ♖e8 20 ♖xe6! ♗xg5 21 ♕xh7+ ♔f8 22 ♕h8#; 18...♗d5 19 ♘xh7! gxh5 20 ♕xh5 ♖e8

21 ♘xf6+ ♕xf6 22 ♕h7+ wins for White) 19 ♗xg5 (1-0 Gipslis-Rothflus, Schwäbisch Gmünd 1996) 19...♕d5 20 ♗e4 ♕b3 21 ♕d2 (intending ♗f6) 21...f6 22 ♗xc6 gxh5 23 ♗h6 +−.

b3312) 16...♗d5 17 ♘e5! ♗xe5 (17...♘xe5 18 dxe5 c6 19 ♖xd5! +−; 17...♘e7 18 ♘g4 ±) 18 dxe5 ♘e7 19 ♗g5! c6 20 ♖b4 ±.

b332) 13...♖e8 14 ♕c2 h6 15 ♗e3 a6?! 16 ♕d2 ♗f8 17 ♗c2 ♘xc3 18 bxc3 ♗d5 19 ♘h2 ± Pyhälä-Handoko, Thessaloniki OL 1988.

b333) 13...♕d7 14 ♕c2 h6 15 ♘e5 and White is slightly better.

b334) 13...a6 14 ♕c2!? (14 ♗c2 ♖e8 15 ♗e3 ♕d7 16 ♕d2 ♖ad8 17 ♖ad1!? ♘xc3 18 bxc3 ♗xa3 19 ♗g5 ♗e7 20 ♕f4! ♗d5 21 ♗xe7 ♖xe7, Timman-Yusupov, Dortmund 1994, 22 ♘e5 ♕e8 23 ♕h4 h6 24 f4 gives White compensation) 14...h6 15 ♗e3 ♗f6 16 ♖ad1 ± Lutz-Yusupov, Nussloch 1996.

b335) 13...♗f6 *(D)* and now:

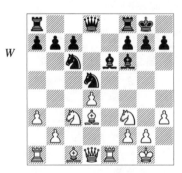

b3351) 14 ♗b5 ♘xc3 15 bxc3 ♘e7 16 ♘g5 ♗f5 17 ♘e4 ♗xe4! 18 ♖xe4 c5 19 ♗e3 ♘d5 = Lukin-Yusupov, USSR 1981.

b3352) 14 ♘a4 ♘xd4! 15 ♘xd4 ♗xd4 16 ♗xh7+ ♔xh7 17 ♕xd4 b6 18 ♘c3 ½-½ Psakhis-Karpov, USSR Ch (Moscow) 1983.

b3353) 14 ♗c2 ♘b6!? (14...♘de7!? 15 ♗e3 ♘f5) 15 ♘e4 ♗f5 16 ♗e3 (16 d5?! ♘xd5 17 ♗b3 ♗xe4 18 ♖xe4 ♘ce7 19 ♘e5 ♕d6 20 ♕e2 c6 ∓ Tal-Schüssler, Tallinn 1983) 16...♘c4 17 ♕d3 ♘xe3 18 fxe3 ♗g6 =.

b3354) 14 ♘e4 h6 15 ♘c5 (15 ♗c2 ♗f5 16 ♗b3 ♘b6 17 ♗f4 ♗xd4 18 ♕d2 ♗e6 19 ♗xe6 fxe6 20 ♘xd4 ♘xd4 21 ♗g3 ½-½ Gufeld-Kharitonov, Volgodonsk 1981) and then:

b33541) 15...♗c8!? 16 ♘e5 ♘xd4 (16...♗xe5 17 dxe5 b6 18 ♕a4 is much better for White, A.Sokolov-Andrianov, Sochi 1980) 17 ♗c4 ♗xe5 18 ♖xe5 ♘b6 19 ♗a2 ♘c6 20 ♕xd8 ♖xd8 21 ♖e1 gives White compensation.

b33542) 15...♘xd4 16 ♘xb7 ♕e7 (16...♕b8!? 17 ♘c5 ♕b6 ∞) 17 ♘xd4 (17 ♘a5!?) 17...♗xd4 18 ♗h7+ ♔xh7 19 ♕xd4 ♕f6 20 ♕d3+ ♕f5 21 ♕xf5+ ♗xf5 22 ♘c5 ±/=.

b3355) 14 ♗e4!? h6 (14...♘ce7 15 ♗g5 c6 16 ♕d2 ♕d6 17 ♗c2 ♕c7 18 ♗xf6 ♘xf6 19 ♘g5 ♗d5 20 ♖e5 ± Westerinen-Schüssler, Malmö 1986) 15 ♗c2 ♘de7 (15...♘ce7 16 ♘xd5 ♘xd5 17 ♕d3 ♘g6 18 ♘e5 ±; 15...♘b6 16 ♕d3 ±) 16 ♗e3 ♘f5 17 ♗xf5! ♗xf5 18 d5 ♘e5!? and then:

b33551) 19 ♘d4 ♗h7 20 ♕b3 ♘d3 21 ♖ed1 (21 ♕xb7?! ♘xe1 22 ♖xe1 ♖b8 23 ♕xa7 ♖xb2 24 ♘c6 ♕a8 ∓; 21 ♖e2 c5 22 ♘f3 ♕b6! 23 ♕xb6 axb6 ∓) 21...c5 22 ♘de2 ♕b6! 23 ♕xb6 axb6 ∓ Gipslis-Morgado, corr. 1996.

b33552) 19 ♘xe5! ♗xe5 20 ♗d4 ♗f6! =.

We now return to the position after 12 ♗e4 *(D)*:

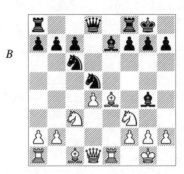

12...♗e6

Black should try to keep control of d5. The alternatives are:

a) 12...♗b4 13 ♕b3! (better than 13 ♘xd5 ♗xe1 14 ♕xe1 f5 15 ♗g5 ♕d7! 16 ♗c2 {16 ♘e7+ ♘xe7 17 ♗xe7 fxe4 ∓} 16...♗xf3 17 gxf3 ♘xd4 18 ♕d1 c5 ∞ Yuneev) is favourable for White, since 13...♗xf3 14 ♗xf3 ♘xc3 15 bxc3 ♘xd4 16 ♕xb4 ♘c2 17 ♖d1! gives White a clear advantage.

b) 12...♘xc3?! 13 bxc3 ♘a5 14 ♖b1 c6 15 h3 ♗e6 16 ♕c2 h6 17 ♘e5 ♕c7 18 ♕e2 ± (intending ♕e5) R.Haag-Copliw, corr. 1984-5.

c) 12...♘f6 13 ♗xc6 bxc6 14 h3 ♗xf3 (14...♗h5 15 g4 ♗g6 16 ♘e5 ±) 15 ♕xf3 ♘d5 16 ♘xd5 cxd5 17 ♗f4 gives White a slight advantage, Ljubojević-Christiansen, London 1982.

13 ♕c2

Or:

a) 13 ♕d3?! h6 (13...f5? 14 ♘xd5 ♗xd5 15 ♗xf5 ♗xf3 16 gxf3 ♘xd4 17 ♗xh7+ ♔h8 18 f4 is much better for White, Mortensen-Solomon, Thessaloniki OL 1984) and now:

a1) 14 ♕b5 ♘cb4! 15 ♕xb7 ♖b8 is level.

a2) 14 a3 ♗f6 – *13 a3 ♗f6 14 ♕d3 h6 =*.

a3) 14 ♗f5 ♘cb4 and now: 15 ♕e4 – *13 ♕c2 h6 14 ♗f5 ♘cb4 15 ♕e4*; 15 ♕b1 – *13 ♕c2 h6 14 ♗f5 ♘cb4 15 ♕b1*.

a4) 14 ♗h7+ ♔h8 15 ♗f5 ♘cb4 and now: 16 ♕e4?! – *13 ♕c2 h6 14 ♗h7+! ♔h8 15 ♗f5 ♘cb4 16 ♕e4?!*; 16 ♕b1 – *13 ♕c2 h6 14 ♗h7+! ♔h8 15 ♗f5 ♘cb4 16 ♕b1*.

b) 13 ♘a4 ♖e8 (13...♘f6?! 14 ♗xc6 bxc6 15 ♘e5 ♗d5 16 ♗g5 ♔h8 17 ♕c2 ± Schatzle-Morgado, corr. 1978) 14 ♘c5 ♗xc5 15 dxc5 ♘f6 =.

c) 13 a3 and then:

c1) 13...♕d7 14 ♗g5! f6 (14...h6? 15 ♗xd5 ±; 14...♖fe8 15 ♗xe7 ♖xe7 16 ♘g5 ±) 15 ♗h4 g6 16 ♗g3 ♖ac8 17 ♕e2 ♗f7 18 ♕b5! ± Sax-Kurajica, Vrbas 1980.

c2) 13...♖e8 14 ♕d3 h6 15 ♗h7+ ♔h8 16 ♗f5!? ±.

c3) 13...♗f6 and here:

c31) 14 ♘a4 ♗g4! and then:

c311) 15 h3 ♗xf3 16 ♕xf3 ♖e8 (16...♘ce7!? is possible) 17 ♗d2 ♘de7 (17...♘ce7? 18 ♗xd5 ♕xd5 19 ♖xe7 ♕xd4 20 ♘c3! ♕xa4 21 ♗xf6 ±) 18 d5 ♘e5 19 ♕b3 ♘c8! 20 g3 (20 ♕xb7? ♘d6 intending ...♘ec4 –+; 20 ♖ac1?! ♘d6 21 ♗b1 b5! is slightly better for Black, Ljubojević-Kovačević, Bugojno 1984) 20...♘d6 21 ♗g2 and White has a small advantage.

c312) 15 ♕d3 ♗xf3 16 ♕xf3 ♘ce7 (16...♘xd4 17 ♕h5 g6 18 ♕xd5 ♕xd5

19 ♗xd5 ♘c2 20 ♗h6 ♖fd8 21 ♗xb7 ♖ab8 22 ♗f3 ♘xa1 23 ♖xa1 ♖d4 =) 17 ♘c5 b6 18 ♕h3 ♘g6 19 ♘d7 ♖e8 20 ♗d2 c6 21 ♗xd5 ♖xe1+ 22 ♖xe1 cxd5 23 ♘xf6+ ½-½ Adorjan-Yusupov, Vrbas 1980.

c32) 14 ♕d3 h6 (14...g6?! 15 ♗h6 ♗g7 16 ♗xg7 ♔xg7 17 ♕b5 a6 18 ♕c5 ♘ce7 19 ♘g5 b6 20 ♕c4 ± Secchi-Garner, corr. Wch 1959-62) 15 ♗e3 (15 ♘a4 b6 16 ♘c3 ♖c8 17 ♗d2 ♘ce7 = Ljubojević-Henley, Indonesia 1983) 15...♘ce7 16 ♖ad1 c6 =.

13...h6 *(D)*

Black should avoid both 13...f5? 14 ♗d3 ♘db4 15 ♕e2 ♘xd3 16 ♕xe6+ ♔h8 17 ♖d1 ♘xc1 18 ♖axc1 ± Tseshkovsky-Dvoretsky, Vilnius 1975 and 13...g6?! 14 ♗h6 ♖e8 15 ♖ad1 ± intending ♘e5.

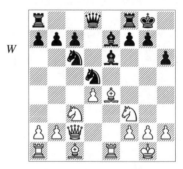

14 ♗h7+!

It is important to insert this check. The immediate 14 ♗f5 gives White nothing:

a) 14...♗f6? is no good at all here due to 15 ♖xe6! +–.

b) 14...♘db4? 15 ♕e4 ♗xf5 16 ♕xf5 ♗f6 17 a3! gives White a clear advantage.

c) 14...♕d7?! 15 ♗xe6 fxe6 16 ♕e2! ♗f6 (the alternatives are also good for White, e.g. 16...♖f6 17 ♘e4 ± or 16...♘xc3 17 bxc3 ♖f6 18 ♗b2 ±) 17 ♕xe6+ ♕xe6 18 ♖xe6 ♖ad8 19 ♖e4 ♘db4 20 ♗e3 ♘c2 21 ♖d1 ±.

d) 14...♗xf5 15 ♕xf5 ♘xc3 16 bxc3 ♗f6 and now White should play 17 ♖b1 ± or 17 ♗a3 ±, rather than 17 ♕g4?! ♕c8! 18 ♕g3 ♘e7! 19 ♘e5 ♗xe5 20 ♖xe5 ♘g6 ½-½ Kasparov-Yusupov, Leningrad 1977.

e) 14...♘cb4! 15 ♕b1 (15 ♕e4 ♘f6!) 15...♗xf5 16 ♕xf5 and then:

e1) 16...♘f6 17 ♗f4 (17 a3 ♘bd5 =) 17...♘bd5 18 ♗e5 c6 19 ♖e2 (Rozentalis-Arlandi, Debrecen Echt 1992) 19...♕c8 =.

e2) 16...♗f6!? 17 a3 ♘xc3 18 bxc3 ♕d5!? (18...♘d5 = Machulsky-Yusupov, Vilnius 1978) 19 ♕b1 (19 ♘e5 ♘c6 20 ♗f4 {20 ♗xh6?? ♗xe5 21 ♕g5 ♗xh2+ −+} 20...♖ad8!? is a little better for Black) 19...♘a6 20 ♗f4 c5 (20...♖fe8!?) 21 ♕b5 ♖fd8 = Analysis.

14...♔h8 15 ♗f5 ♗f6!?

This is a new move that I am recommending. To date, Black has tried:

a) 15...♘db4? 16 ♕e4! ♗c4 (alternatively, 16...♗xf5 17 ♕xf5 ♗f6 18 a3 ♘a6 19 ♕h5 ± Anton-Rozentalis, Moscow 1977) 17 ♕g4! (17 d5? ♗xd5 18 ♘xd5 ♕xd5 19 a3 ♕xe4 20 ♗xe4 f5!) 17...♘d3 18 ♖d1 ♘xc1 19 ♖axc1 ♘b4 (19...♗g5 20 ♘xg5 ♕xg5 21 ♕xg5 hxg5 22 b3 ±) 20 ♗b1 ± Beliavsky-Yusupov, USSR Ch (Frunze) 1981.

b) 15...♗xf5 16 ♕xf5 and here:

b1) 16...♘b6?! 17 ♗e3 (17 d5!?) 17...♗f6 18 ♘e4 ♘d5 19 ♖ad1 ♖e8

20 ♗c1 ♘ce7 21 ♕h5 ± Mihalko-Revesz, corr. 1983-4.

b2) 16...♘f6 17 ♗f4 ♗d6 18 ♗e5 ♘e7 19 ♕c2 (19 ♕h3 ♘g6 20 ♖ad1 ♖e8 21 ♖e3 ♔g8! 22 ♕g3 ♘h5 23 ♕g4 ♘f6 24 ♕g3 ♘h5 ½-½ Tal-Karpov, Moscow 1983) 19...♘g6 (19...♗xe5?! 20 dxe5 ♘fd5 21 ♖ad1 ±) 20 ♖ad1 ±.

c) 15...♘cb4!? 16 ♕b1 (16 ♕e4?! ♘f6 17 ♕b1 ♗xf5 18 ♕xf5 ♘bd5 = Hulak-Toth, Reggio Emilia 1983/4) 16...♗xf5 17 ♕xf5 (D) and then:

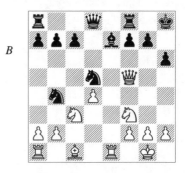

B

c1) 17...♕c8 18 ♕e4! (18 ♕h5?! ♘f6 19 ♕h4, Psakhis-Yusupov, Vilnius 1978, 19...♗d6! intending to meet 20 ♗xh6 with 20...♘g4!) 18...f5 19 ♕b1 ♗f6 20 a3 ♘xc3 21 bxc3 ♘d5 and now:

c11) 22 c4 is well answered by 22...♘c3!.

c12) 22 ♕d3 ♖e8!? 23 ♖xe8+ (23 c4?! ♖xe1+ 24 ♘xe1 ♘e7 intending ...c5; 23 ♘e5?! ♗xe5 24 ♖xe5 ♖xe5 25 dxe5 ♕e6 ∓) 23...♕xe8 24 c4 ♕e4! (24...♘e7 25 ♗f4 ±/±) 25 ♕b3 (25 ♕xe4 fxe4 26 ♘e5 {26 ♘d2? ♗xd4 27 ♖b1 ♘c3 −+} 26...♗xe5 27 dxe5 ♘b6 ∞) 25...♗xd4 26 ♗b2 ♘f4! (26...♗xb2 27 ♖e1! ♕f4 28 cxd5 ±/±) 27 ♖e1

♗xf2+ 28 ♔xf2 ♘d3+ 29 ♔f1 ♘xe1 30 ♕c3!? ♕d3+ 31 ♔xe1 ♖e8+ =.

c13) 22 ♕b3! ♕d7 23 c4 ♘e7 and now 24 ♗b2! ±/± is better than either 24 ♕xb7 ♖fb8 25 ♕a6 ♖b6 26 ♕a5 ♘c6 27 ♕a4 ♖d8! or 24 ♗f4?! c5! =.

c2) 17...♘f6 18 ♗f4 (18 ♗d2!? ♘bd5 19 ♘e5 ♕c8?! {19...♔g8!} 20 ♕f3 ± Mortensen-O.Jakobsen, Esbjerg 1984) and here:

c21) 18...c6 19 ♗g3!? ♔g8 20 ♖e2 ♘bd5 21 ♘e5 ♗b4 22 ♖c1 (22 ♕f3!?) 22...♘e7 23 ♕f3 ♕xd4 24 ♖d1 ♕b6 gives Black compensation, Klovans-Yusupov, Riga 1984.

c22) 18...♘bd5 19 ♗e5 (19 ♗g3!?) 19...c6 (Psakhis-Schüssler, Tallinn 1983) 20 ♖ad1 (20 ♕h3!? ♕c8 21 ♕g3 ♕d7 =) 20...♕c8 21 ♕xc8 (21 ♕c2!?) 21...♖axc8 22 ♗xf6 ♗xf6 23 ♘xd5 cxd5 = Makarychev.

We now return to 15...♗f6 (D):

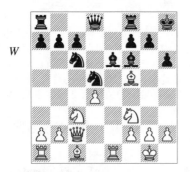

16 ♗xe6 fxe6 17 ♕e4!?
Or:

a) 17 ♖xe6 ♘xd4 =.

b) 17 ♗e3!? ♘xc3 18 bxc3 e5 19 ♖ad1 (19 dxe5 ♘xe5 20 ♘xe5 ♗xe5 21 ♗xh6 ♗xh2+ 22 ♔xh2 ♕h4+ 23 ♔g1 ♕xh6 24 ♖e7 ♖ad8 =) 19...exd4

20 cxd4 ♕d5 21 ♘e5 ♘xe5 22 dxe5 ♕xe5 23 ♗c5 (23 ♗xh6 is also met by 23...♕c3!) 23...♕c3 is at least OK for Black.

17...♖e8!
17...♘de7?! 18 ♗e3 ♘f5 19 ♖ad1 ♕e8 20 ♗f4 ±.

18 h4
A difficult move to find. Other moves give White no real advantage:

a) 18 ♗d2 ♘xc3 19 bxc3 (19 ♗xc3 ♕d5!) 19...♕d5 =.

b) 18 ♘e5 ♗xe5 19 dxe5 ♘xc3 (19...♘ce7!?) 20 bxc3 ♕d5 21 ♕h4 ♔h7 = intending 22 c4 ♕d4.

c) 18 ♕g4 ♘xc3 19 bxc3 e5 =.

d) 18 ♗e3 ♘xc3 19 bxc3 ♕d5 20 ♘d2 ♖ad8 =.

18...♘xc3 19 bxc3 ♕d5 20 g4!
White intends g5 and is slightly better – Analysis.

B)
8 c4 (D)

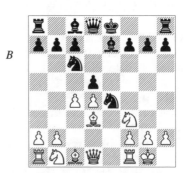

White plays his thematic card immediately, seeking to undermine the e4-knight as soon as possible. If Black avoids playing ...♘f6, then he may have to recapture on d5 with the queen. In this case White would like to chase the knight away with ♖e1, and then gain further time by attacking the queen with ♘c3. If White can achieve all this then he is very likely to gain an advantage, so Black's main replies all aim to prevent this plan in some way. In this chapter we consider:

The main line, 8...♘b4, is considered in the next chapter.

B1)

8...0-0 9 cxd5

Or:

a) 9 ♖e1 should be compared with *8 ♖e1*.

b) 9 ♘c3 ♘xc3 (*9...♘f6 – 8...♘f6 9 ♘c3 0-0*) 10 bxc3 ♗e6 11 cxd5 ♗xd5 – *8...♗e6 9 cxd5 ♗xd5 10 ♘c3 ♘xc3 11 bxc3 0-0*.

9...♕xd5 10 ♖e1

Or:

a) 10 ♘c3 ♘xc3 11 bxc3 ♗g4 – *8...♗g4 9 cxd5 ♕xd5 10 ♘c3 ♘xc3 11 bxc3 0-0*.

b) 10 ♗xe4?! ♕xe4 11 ♖e1 ♕g6! 12 d5 ♗h3 13 g3 ♖ad8 and now:

b1) 14 ♕b3 ♕f5!! 15 dxc6 ♖d3 16 ♘d4 ♖xd4 17 ♘d2 (17 ♖xe7 ♖d3 –+) 17...♖d3 18 ♕c4 ♗c5 19 ♕f4 ♕d5 20 ♕e4 bxc6 21 ♕xd5 cxd5 22 ♘b3 ♗b4! –+ Matulović-Udovčić, Zagreb 1961.

b2) 14 ♘c3 ♗f6 15 ♕a4 ♗xc3 16 bxc3 ♖xd5 ∓ Winawer-Schumov, St Petersburg 1875.

10...♘f6

10...♗f5 11 ♘c3 ♘xc3 12 bxc3 ♗f6 13 ♗f4 ♖ac8 14 ♖b1 ± Mikhalchishin.

11 ♘c3 ♕d6 12 h3 a6

12...♗e6!? intending ...♖ad8.

13 ♗g5 ♗e6

13...h6!? 14 ♗xf6 ♗xf6 15 ♘e4 ♕d8 is unclear, Kupreichik-Mikhalchishin, Minsk 1985.

14 ♗xf6 ♗xf6 15 ♘e4 ♕d8 16 ♘xf6+ ♕xf6 17 ♗e4 ♖fd8 18 ♗xc6 bxc6 19 ♖c1

White has chances for an advantage, as White wins a piece after 19...♗xa2? 20 b3 ♖ab8 21 ♖c3 c5 22 ♕e2 cxd4 23 ♖d3.

B2)

8...♗e6 (*D*)

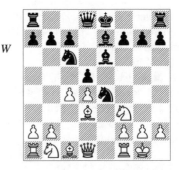

Preparing to recapture on d5 with the bishop.

9 cxd5

Or:

a) 9 ♕b3?! 0-0 10 ♗xe4 (not 10 ♕xb7? ♘b4 11 ♗xe4 ♖b8 12 ♕xa7 dxe4 13 ♘e5 ♖a8 14 ♕b7 ♕xd4 ∓) 10...dxe4 11 d5 exf3 12 dxc6 fxg2 13 ♖d1 ♗d6 14 cxb7 ♖b8 favours Black.

b) 9 ♖e1 ♘f6 10 c5 (10 cxd5 ♘xd5 11 ♘c3 0-0 is equal, Korzubov-Yuferov, Minsk 1982) 10...0-0 (10...b6? 11 ♖xe6! fxe6 12 ♕a4 wins for White) 11 ♘c3 ♗g4 12 ♗e3 ♗xc5! 13 dxc5 d4 14 ♗xd4 ♘xd4 15 ♗xh7+ ♔xh7 16 ♕xd4 ♗xf3 17 ♕xd8 ♖fxd8 18 gxf3 ♘g5 gives Black compensation, Short-Smyslov, Hastings 1988/9.

9...♗xd5 10 ♘c3

10 ♗e3 0-0 11 ♘c3 f5 (11...♘xc3 12 bxc3 ♗f6 13 ♘d2 ±) 12 ♘xd5 ♕xd5 13 ♗c2 ♔h8 14 ♗b3 ♕d6 15 d5 ♘a5 16 ♗d4 ♗f6 17 ♖e1 ♖ad8 18 ♗xf6 ♘xf6 19 ♘g5 ± Löwenthal-Morphy, London (5) 1858.

10...♘xc3

10...f5 11 ♕e2 ♘xc3 12 bxc3 0-0 13 ♖b1 ♕d7 14 ♗b5! ±.

11 bxc3 0-0

Black's problem is that the bishop is not a very good blockader on the d5-square since it is vulnerable to being chased away by c4.

12 ♗f4 h6

12...♗d6 13 ♗xd6 ♕xd6 (another idea is 13...cxd6!?) 14 ♘g5 f5 15 c4 ♗xg2 16 ♔xg2 ♕g6 17 f4 h6 18 d5 ♘d8 19 h4 hxg5 20 hxg5 ± Löwenthal-Morphy, London (13) 1858.

13 ♘e5 ♘xe5 14 ♗xe5 ♗f6 15 f4 ♗xe5 16 fxe5 ♕g5 17 ♕e2

± Jaenisch.

B3)

8...♗g4 *(D)*
9 cxd5

The alternatives are noteworthy:

a) 9 ♖e1 – *8 ♖e1 ♗g4 9 c4*, a line which offers White fair chances of a slight advantage.

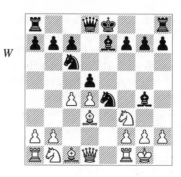

b) 9 ♘c3 and now:

b1) 9...♗xf3 10 gxf3! (10 ♕xf3 ♘xd4 11 ♕g4 h5! ∞) 10...♘f6 11 cxd5 ♘xd5 12 ♗e4 ♘xc3 13 bxc3 0-0 14 f4 ± Schiffers-Kulomzin, Russian Ch (Moscow) 1901.

b2) 9...♘f6 10 cxd5 ♘xd5 11 ♗e4 ♘f6 12 ♗xc6+ bxc6 13 h3 ♗xf3 14 ♕xf3 ♕d7 15 ♗f4 0-0 16 ♗e5 ♖ab8 17 b3 ♘e8 18 ♖fd1 f6 19 ♗g3 ♗a3 20 d5 c5 ± Chandler-Hort, Bundesliga 1988/9.

b3) 9...♘xc3 10 bxc3 0-0 11 ♖e1 dxc4 12 ♗xc4 and then:

b31) 12...♕d6?! 13 h3 ♗h5 14 ♖b1 a6? 15 ♖xb7 ♘a5 16 ♖b4 ♘xc4 17 ♖xc4 ± Diaz-Lepeshkin, Vraca 1975.

b32) 12...♘a5 13 ♗d3 c5 14 ♗a3 ♖c8?! (14...♖e8 15 ♗b5 ±) 15 ♕e2 (Ermenkov-Radulov, Vraca Z 1975) 15...♘c6 16 ♕e4 f5 17 ♕e6+ ♔h8 18 ♖ad1 ±.

b33) 12...♗d6 13 ♖b1 ♕d7 (the alternative 13...♕f6?! is answered by 14 ♗d5!? intending 14...♗xh2+ 15 ♔xh2 ♕d6+ 16 ♗e5 ♘xe5 17 dxe5 ♗xf3 18 ♕xf3 ♕xe5+ 19 ♗f4 ±) 14 h3 ♗h5 15 ♗d3 ♖ae8 16 ♗e3 ±.

9...♕xd5 10 ♘c3 *(D)*
10 h3 ♗xf3 11 ♕xf3 ♘f6 =.

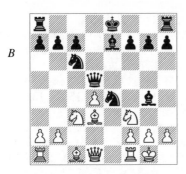

B

10...♘xc3 11 bxc3 0-0

11...♗xf3 12 ♕xf3 ♕xf3 13 gxf3 0-0-0 (13...0-0 14 ♖b1! ♘a5 15 ♖e1 ♗d6 16 ♗e3 b6 17 c4 ♖ad8 18 ♗f1 ♖fe8 19 c5 ± Byrne-Hector, Reykjavik 1984) 14 ♖b1!? (14 ♖e1 ♗d6 ± Tarrasch-Marshall, Ostend 1905) 14...g6 15 ♖e1 ♗d6 (15...♖he8 16 ♗c4 ♗d6 17 ♗g5 ±) 16 ♗g5 ♖de8 17 ♖e3 ± Sax-Insam, Lugano 1984.

12 ♖e1

Or:

a) 12 ♗f4 ♗d6 13 c4 ♕h5 14 ♗xd6 cxd6 =.

b) 12 c4!? ♕h5 and now White should settle for 13 ♗e2 =, rather than trying 13 ♗e4 ♖ad8 ∓.

c) 12 ♖b1!? ♖ab8 13 ♖e1 ♗xf3 14 ♕xf3 ♕xf3 15 gxf3 ♗d6 16 ♗e3 is slightly better for White.

12...♗xf3

12...♖fe8 13 ♗e4 ♕d6 14 ♖b1 ♖ab8 15 h3 ♗d7 16 ♕c2 h6 17 ♗h7+ ♔h8 18 ♗f5 ± Matulović-Capelan, Vršac 1981.

13 ♕xf3 ♕xf3 14 gxf3

White's active bishops provide quite good compensation for his broken pawns and in fact it is Black who has to watch his step.

14...♗d6 15 ♗e3 ♖ad8

15...♘e7 16 c4 c6 17 ♖ab1 b6 18 a4 ♖ab8 19 ♖b3 h6 20 ♖eb1 ♖fd8 21 ♗c2 ♗c7 (Timman-Yusupov, Belfort 1988) 22 ♔g2 intending f4 and ♔f3 ±.

16 ♖ad1 b6 17 ♗g5 f6 18 ♗e3 ♘e7 19 c4 c6 20 ♗c2 ♘g6 21 c5 ♗c7 22 ♗c1 bxc5 23 dxc5 ♘e5 24 ♗b3+!

±; 24 ♔g2 ± Ehlvest-Yusupov, Saint John Ct (4) 1988.

B4)

8...♘f6 *(D)*

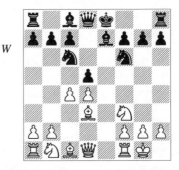

W

There are many similarities between this line and Line A22 above. The verdict is rather similar: White has reasonable prospects for an advantage.

9 ♘c3

Or:

a) 9 ♗g5 0-0 10 cxd5 ♘xd5 11 ♗xe7 ♘cxe7 12 ♘c3 h6 13 ♕b3 ♖b8 14 ♖fe1 ♗e6 15 ♕a4 a6 16 ♖ac1 ♘f4 17 ♗b1 c6 18 g3 ♘fd5 = Kamsky-Yusupov, Tilburg 1993.

b) 9 ♗e3 dxc4 (Black could try 9...♗g4!? or 9...0-0!?) 10 ♗xc4 ♗g4 11 ♘c3 ♗xf3 12 ♕xf3 ♘xd4 13 ♕xb7 0-0 (= Bilguer) 14 ♖ad1 ±.

c) 9 c5 0-0 10 ♗b5 ♗g4 (10...♘b8 11 ♘e5 c6 12 ♗d3 b6 13 cxb6 gives White a slight advantage, Chekhover-Kamyshov, Leningrad 1938) 11 ♗xc6 bxc6 12 ♘bd2 ♘e4 13 ♕a4 and now Black should play 13...♗f6 ∞, rather than 13...♘xd2 14 ♘xd2 ♕d7 15 ♘b3 ± Browne-Segal, Winnipeg 1974.

9...0-0

9...♗e6 10 c5 (10 cxd5 ♘xd5 11 a3 ♕d7!? 12 ♗b5 f6 13 ♖e1 a6 14 ♗a4 ♗f7 15 ♕e2 b5 16 ♗c2 0-0 17 ♘xd5 ♗xd5 18 ♕d3 g6 = Karpov-Larsen, Bugojno 1980) 10...0-0 (10...♗g4 11 ♗b5 ±) 11 h3 ±.

10 h3

Or:

a) 10 ♖e1 ♗g4 – 8 ♖e1 ♗g4 9 c4 ♘f6 10 ♘c3 0-0.

b) 10 cxd5 is a major alternative:

b1) 10...♘b4 and here:

b11) 11 ♗c4 ♘bxd5 12 ♘e5 (12 ♖e1!?) 12...♗e6 13 ♕b3 ♘xc3 14 bxc3 ♗xc4 15 ♘xc4 ♕d5 16 ♗f4 ♘h5 (Dvoirys-Rozentalis, Beersheba 1997) 17 ♗e3 ♖fe8 =.

b12) 11 ♖e1 ♘bxd5 12 ♕b3 c6 13 ♗g5 ± Beliavsky-Mascariñas, Lvov 1981.

b2) 10...♘xd5 (D) and then:

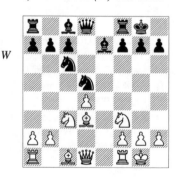

b21) 11 ♕b3 ♗e6 ∞.

b22) 11 h3 ♗f6 12 ♗e4 ♗e6 13 ♕d3 h6 14 ♕b5?! a6 ∓ Rogulj-Pavasović, Bizovac 2000.

b23) 11 a3 ♗f6 12 ♗e4 ♗e6 13 ♕d3 h6 14 ♗e3 ♘ce7 15 ♖ac1 c6 16 ♖fd1 ♘b6 17 ♗h7+ ♔h8 18 ♘e4 ♘f5 19 ♘eg5!? ♗xg5 20 ♗xf5 (20 ♗xg5? ♕c8! –+; 20 ♘xg5 hxg5 21 ♗xf5 ♗xf5 22 ♕xf5 f6 ∞) 20...♗xf5 21 ♕xf5 ♗f6 22 ♗f4 ♘d5 23 ♗e5 ♗g5 24 ♖c2 ♕c8 = Renet-Arlandi, Manila OL 1992.

b24) 11 ♗e4 ♗e6 12 ♕d3 f5! 13 ♗xd5 (13 ♘xd5 fxe4 14 ♘xe7+ ♘xe7 15 ♕xe4 ♗d5 ∓) 13...♗xd5 14 ♘xd5 ♕xd5 15 ♗f4 ♗d6 =.

b25) 11 ♖e1 ♗e6 12 a3 (12 ♘e4 h6 13 a3 a6 14 h3 ♕d7 = W.All-A.Shaw, corr. 1988-91) 12...♗f6 13 ♗e4 (13 ♘e4 ♗f5! =) and now:

b251) 13...♘de7?! 14 ♗g5 ♗xg5 15 ♘xg5 ♗f5? (15...h6! ±) 16 d5 ♗xe4 17 ♖xe4 ♘b8 18 ♕h5 h6 19 ♖ae1 ♘xd5 20 ♘xf7 +– Kudrin-Wolff, USA 1985.

b252) 13...♘ce7 14 ♘g5 ♗xg5 15 ♗xg5 f6 16 ♗d2 ♕d7 ± Geller-Anand, Coimbatore 1987.

b253) 13...♘xc3?! 14 bxc3 ♗d5 15 ♗f4 ♗xe4 16 ♖xe4 ♘e7 17 ♖b1 ♘d5 18 ♗d2 ♘b6 19 ♕b3 ± Korzubov-Yuferov, Minsk 1983.

b254) 13...h6 and then:

b2541) 14 ♗b1 ♘ce7 and now 15 ♘xd5 ± is better than 15 ♘e5 ♗f5 16 ♗xf5 ♘xf5 17 ♕g4 ♘de7 18 ♘e4 ♗xe5 19 dxe5 ♕c8 = Pyhälä-Schüssler, Pohja 1985.

b2542) 14 ♕d3 ♘ce7 15 ♗d2 c6 16 ♘e2 and here Black should prefer

16...♕d6 = over 16...♘c7?! 17 ♘f4 ♘ed5 18 ♘xe6 ♘xe6 19 g3 ♖e8 20 h4 ± Renet-Arlandi, Debrecen Echt 1992.

b2543) 14 h3 ♕d7 15 ♗c2 ♗f5 16 ♘e4 ♖fe8 (16...♖ae8!? 17 ♘xf6+ ♘xf6 18 ♖xe8 ♖xe8 19 ♗a4 ♕d6 20 ♗e3 ♖e7 21 ♖c1 ♘d5 22 ♗xc6 bxc6 23 ♘e5 ♘xe3 24 fxe3 ♗e4 25 ♕g4 ½-½ Topalov-Yusupov, Moscow OL 1994) 17 ♕d3 ♖e6 18 ♗b3 ♗e7 19 ♘e5 ♘xe5 20 dxe5 ♖d8 21 g4 ♖g6 22 ♕f3 ♗e6 23 ♘g3 ♘b6 24 ♗c2 ♗d5 25 ♕e2 ♗c4 26 ♕f3 ♗d5 ½-½ Hraček-Yusupov, Germany 1996.

b2544) 14 ♗c2 ♘ce7 (14...♘de7 15 ♗e3 ♘g4 16 h3 ♗h5 17 ♕d3 ♗g6 18 ♘e4 ± Hübner-Yusupov, Nussloch 1996) 15 ♘e5 ♗f5 16 ♗b3 ♗e6 17 ♘e4 ♗xe5 18 dxe5 b6 19 ♕f3 c6 20 ♗c2 ♘f5 21 ♖d1 ± Hraček-Yusupov, Nussloch 1996. White's bishop-pair and dark-square pressure give him a slight advantage.

We now return to the position after 10 h3 *(D)*:

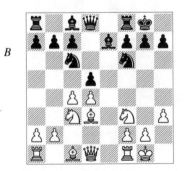

10...♘b4

Or 10...dxc4 11 ♗xc4 ♘a5 (11...♗f5 12 a3 ♘e4 13 ♘d5!? ±) 12 ♗d3, and now:

a) 12...♖e8!? 13 ♖b1 (13 ♖e1!?) 13...♘c6 14 a3 a6 15 b4 ♗e6 16 ♖e1 ♕d7 17 b5 axb5 18 ♖xb5 ♗xa3 19 d5! and then:

a1) 19...♗xc1 20 dxe6 fxe6 (not 20...♖xe6? 21 ♗f5) 21 ♗xh7+ ♔xh7 22 ♕xc1 gives White compensation.

a2) 19...♘xd5 20 ♘xd5 ♗xc1 21 ♖xe6! fxe6 (21...♖xe6? 22 ♘f6+ ♖xf6 23 ♗xh7+ ♔xh7 24 ♕xd7 ±) 22 ♘b6! ♕d6 23 ♘xa8 ♖xa8 24 ♗xh7+ ♔xh7 25 ♕xc1 gives White compensation, Becerra Rivero-Morena, Havana 1996.

b) 12...♗e6 13 ♖e1 (13 ♗e3 ♘c4 14 ♕c2 ♘xe3 ∞) 13...♘c6 (13...c5 14 ♗g5 h6 15 ♗h4 c4 16 ♗xf6 ♗xf6 17 ♗e4 ±) 14 a3 and here:

b1) 14...♖e8 15 ♗b5 ♕d6 (15...a6 16 ♗xc6 bxc6 17 ♘e5 c5 18 ♘c6 ♕d6 19 ♘xe7+ ♕xe7 20 d5 ♖ad8 21 ♗g5 h6 22 ♕c1 ±) 16 ♗g5! ♖ed8 (16...♖ad8 17 ♘e5 ♕xd4 18 ♗xc6 bxc6 19 ♘xc6 ♕xd1 20 ♖axd1 ♖xd1 21 ♘xe7+ ♖xe7 22 ♖xd1 ±) 17 ♗xf6! ♗xf6 18 ♘e4 ♕f4 19 ♗xc6 bxc6 20 ♕c1! and White has a clear advantage, Lobron-Handoko, Zagreb 1985.

b2) 14...a6 15 ♗f4 (15 ♗e3 ♘d5 16 ♕c2 h6 17 ♖ad1 ♗d6 = Ivanchuk-Rokhmanov, USSR 1985) 15...♘d5 (15...♕d7 16 ♘e5 ♘xe5 17 dxe5 ♘d5 18 ♘xd5 ♗xd5 19 ♕c2 g6 20 ♖ad1 ±/± Kasparov-Karpov, Moscow Wch (48) 1984/5) 16 ♗g3 ♗f6 17 ♗e4!? (17 ♗c2 ♘ce7 18 ♘e4 ♗f5 19 ♘xf6+ ♘xf6 20 ♗b3 c6 21 ♘e5 ♘fd5 is equal, Gufeld-Schüssler, Havana 1985) 17...♘ce7 18 ♕c2 g6 19 ♗e5 ♗xe5 20 dxe5 c6 with a slight advantage for White, Jodice-Battistini, corr. 1990.

11 ♗e2 *(D)*

11 cxd5?! ♘xd3 12 ♕xd3 ♘xd5 13 ♗d2 ♗e6 14 ♖fe1 ♗f6 = Anderssen-Barnes, London 1862.

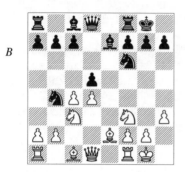

11...dxc4

Or:

a) 11...c5?! 12 a3 ♘c6 13 dxc5 dxc4 14 ♗e3 ± Velimirović-Schüssler, Smederevska Palanka 1979.

b) 11...c6 12 c5 a5 13 a3 ♘a6 14 ♘a4 ♘d7 15 ♖e1 ♗f6 16 ♗d2 ♘c7 17 ♕b3 ♘e6 18 ♗c3 ± Tolnai-Briffel, Lucerne Wcht 1989.

c) 11...♗f5!? and then:

c1) 12 ♗g5!? dxc4 13 ♗xc4 c6 14 ♖e1 b5?! 15 ♗f1 ♖e8 (15...♘c2 16 ♘h4!) 16 ♖c1 ± Schlechter-Barry, Cambridge Springs 1904.

c2) 12 a3 ♘c6 13 ♖e1 (13 ♗f4!? dxc4 14 ♗xc4 ± Dolmatov-Kärner, Tallinn 1985) and here:

c21) 13...h6 14 cxd5 (14 ♗f4!?; 14 ♘e5 dxc4 15 ♘xc6 bxc6 16 ♗xc4 ♕d7 =) 14...♘xd5 15 ♕b3 ±.

c22) 13...♗e6!? 14 ♘g5 ♗f5 15 ♗f1 h6 16 ♘f3 dxc4 (16...♗e6 17 b3 ±) 17 ♗xc4 ♗d6 18 d5 ♘e7 19 ♘d4 ± Nisipeanu-Khalifman, Las Vegas FIDE 1999.

12 ♗xc4 ♘bd5

Or:

a) 12...♘fd5?! 13 ♖e1 ♘b6 14 ♗b3 ♗f5 15 ♘e5 ♘4d5 16 ♕h5 ♗g6 17 ♕f3 ± G.Hartmann-P.Grün, Bundesliga 1986/7.

b) 12...c6 and now:

b1) 13 ♗g5 ♘bd5 14 ♕b3 ♘b6 15 ♗d3 ♗e6 16 ♕c2 h6 17 ♗d2 ♘bd5 18 ♘a4 ♕c8 19 ♘e5 ♖d8 20 ♘c5 ♗xc5 21 dxc5 ♗xh3!? ∞ Gufeld-Andrianov, Krasnoiarsk 1980.

b2) 13 ♘e5 ♘bd5 14 ♗g5 ♗e6 15 ♗b3 (15 ♕b3!?) 15...♖e8 16 ♖e1 h6 17 ♗h4 ♘d7 18 ♗g3 ♘xe5 19 ♗xe5 ♘xc3 20 bxc3 ♗f6 with an equal position, Lanka-Arlandi, Debrecen Echt 1992.

b3) 13 ♖e1 is best answered by 13...♘bd5 – 12...♘bd5 13 ♖e1 c6, rather than 13...♗f5?! 14 a3 ♘c2 15 ♘h4! (15 ♖e5 ♗g6 16 ♖a2 c5 17 dxc5 ± G.Hartmann-G.Röder, Bundesliga 1985/6) 15...♘xd4 16 ♖xe7 ±.

13 ♖e1 c6 *(D)*

Again we have a typical isolated d-pawn position. To some extent the evaluation of such a position is a matter of taste, but objectively speaking White is probably a little better here since all the minor pieces are still on the board.

14 ♕b3

Or:

a) 14 a3 ♗e6 15 ♗d3 h6 16 ♗d2 (16 ♖xe6!? fxe6 17 ♕e2 ♕d6 18 ♗d2 ♗d8! 19 ♖e1 ♗b6 is unclear) 16...♖e8 (16...♕c8!? 17 ♕c2 ♖e8 18 ♘e2!? ♗d6 19 ♘e5 ∞) 17 ♖xe6!? fxe6 18 ♗g6 ♖f8 19 ♕e2 gives White compensation, Bologan-Rozentalis, Belfort 1999.

b) 14 ♗g5 ♗e6 15 ♕b3 (15 ♕d2 ♘xc3 intending to meet 16 ♗xe6 with 16...♘ce4; 15 ♗b3 ♖e8 16 ♕d2 h6 17 ♗h4 ♘d7 18 ♗g3 ♘f8 19 ♖ad1 ♗b4 20 ♘e5 a5 21 ♘d3 ♗xc3 22 bxc3 a4 ½-½ Pinter-Smyslov, Szolnok 1975) 15...♖b8 (15...♕b6!?; 15...♖e8? 16 ♗xf6 gxf6 17 ♘xd5 cxd5 18 ♗b5 ± Ornstein-Valkesalmi, Järvenpää 1985) 16 ♘e5 ♖e8 17 ♖ad1 ♕d6 18 ♗h4! ± Hulak-Toth, Budva 1981.

14...♘b6 15 ♗d3 ♗e6 *(D)*

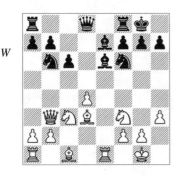

16 ♕c2

16 ♖xe6 fxe6 17 ♘g5 ♕xd4! has the point that 18 ♘xe6? is met by 18...♕xd3 intending ...♕c4.

16...h6 17 ♗d2 ♘bd5

Black could also try 17...♖e8!?, intending ...♗f8 =, or 17...♗d6!?.

18 a3 ♖c8! *(D)*

18...♘xc3? 19 bxc3 c5?! (19...♕c8 20 c4 ±) 20 ♖xe6! fxe6 21 ♖e1 is distinctly better for White, Anand-Yusupov, Dortmund 1998.

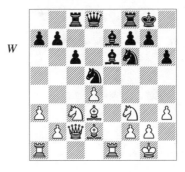

19 ♘a4

19 ♖ad1 ♖e8 20 ♘a4 ♖c7 21 ♘e5 ♗f8 22 ♗a5 b6 23 ♗d2 ♕c8 with equality, Ivanchuk-Yusupov, Frankfurt 2000.

19...♖c7! 20 ♖e2 ♗d6 21 ♖ae1 ♘h5 22 ♗h7+ ♔h8 23 ♗f5 ♘hf4 24 ♗xf4 ♘xf4 25 ♖e3 ♘d5 26 ♖3e2 ♘f4 27 ♖e3

½-½ Gelfand-Yusupov, Istanbul OL 2000.

11 The Main Line: 7 0-0 ♘c6 8 c4 ♘b4

1 e4 e5 2 ♘f3 ♘f6 3 ♘xe5 d6 4 ♘f3 ♘xe4 5 d4 d5 6 ♗d3 ♗e7 7 0-0 ♘c6 8 c4 ♘b4 *(D)*

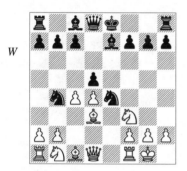

W

Now:

A: 9 cxd5   222
B: 9 ♗e2   227

Line A leads to tactical complications, while Line B is a more positional approach.

9 ♖e1 can be met by 9...♘xd3 10 ♕xd3 c6 11 cxd5 cxd5 12 ♕b5+ ♕d7 13 ♕b3 0-0 14 ♘c3 ♘xc3 15 bxc3 ♖d8 16 ♗a3 (16 ♘e5 ♕c7 17 ♗f4 ♗f6! 18 ♗g3 ♕a5 =) 16...♗f6 17 ♖e3 ♕c6 18 ♗e7 ♖e8 19 ♖ae1 ♗xe7 20 ♖xe7 ♗d7 21 h3 f6 22 ♕a3 a6 23 ♘d2 ♖xe7 24 ♖xe7 ♖e8 25 ♘f1 ♖xe7 26 ♕xe7 ♕e6 = Topalov-Kramnik, Las Vegas FIDE 1999.

A)

9 cxd5 ♘xd3 10 ♕xd3 ♕xd5

10...♘f6?! is suspect in view of 11 ♕b5+ ♗d7 12 ♕b3 0-0 13 ♘c3 b5 14 ♗g5 b4 15 ♗xf6 gxf6 16 ♘e4 ♔h8 17 ♖fe1 a5 18 ♖ac1 ♗b5 19 ♘h4, which is much better for White, Timman-V.Kovačević, Zagreb 1985.

11 ♖e1 ♗f5 *(D)*

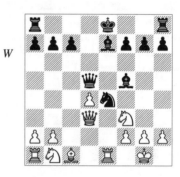

W

If Black is allowed to complete his development in peace then he will have no problems, so White must act at once. The options are:

A1: 12 ♘c3   223
A2: 12 ♘e5   224
A3: 12 g4   225

The third of these possibilities has become fashionable recently; hitherto, the other two continuations were more popular.

A1)

12 ♘c3 ♘xc3 13 ♕xc3 ♗e6

This move, offering the c7-pawn, is clearly best. Otherwise:

a) 13...♕d6? 14 d5! 0-0? 15 ♗f4? (15 ♕e5! wins for White) 15...♕xf4 16 ♖xe7 ♖ac8 17 ♘d4 ♖fe8 (17...♗g6 18 ♘e6! +−) 18 g3 ♕g5 19 ♖xe8+ ♖xe8 20 ♕xc7 ♗h3 21 ♕c4 ± G.M.Todorović-D.Lalić, Kladovo 1990.

b) 13...c6? is met by the startling and effective idea 14 ♗h6!:

b1) 14...gxh6 15 ♖e5 ♕d7 16 ♖ae1 ♗e6 17 d5! cxd5 18 ♖xe6 fxe6 19 ♕xh8+ ♗f8 20 ♕f6 +−.

b2) 14...♖g8 15 ♖e5 ♕d7 16 ♖ae1 ♗e6 17 ♘g5! 0-0-0 (17...♗xg5 18 ♗xg5 h6 19 ♗h4 g5 20 ♗g3 0-0-0 21 d5! ♗xd5 22 ♖e7 +−; 17...gxh6 18 ♘xe6 fxe6 19 ♖xe6 ♖g7 20 d5 ♔f8 21 ♕g7+! +−) 18 ♘xf7! ♗xf7 19 ♖xe7 ♕xd4 20 ♖xf7 ♕xc3 21 bxc3 gxh6 22 ♖b1 ♖g5 23 h4 +− Browne-Bisguier, USA 1974.

b3) 14...♗e4 15 ♗xg7 ♖g8 16 ♖xe4! ♕xe4 17 ♖e1 ♕xe1+! 18 ♕xe1 ♖xg7 19 ♕e5 ± Byrne and Mednis.

14 ♖e5

Or:

a) 14 ♗g5 ♗d6! 15 ♗h4 0-0 16 a3 ♖fe8 ∓ Zapata-Am.Rodriguez, Cali Z 1990.

b) 14 ♕xc7 (few players have cared to accept Black's offer) 14...♗d6 15 ♕c2 0-0 16 ♗d2 (16 ♗e3 ♖ac8 17 ♕e2 a6 with compensation for Black) 16...♗f5 17 ♕b3 ♕xb3 18 axb3 f6 19 ♗c3 ♔f7 gives Black compensation, Hübner-Smyslov, Velden Ct (3) 1983.

14...♕c6

Or:

a) 14...♕c4?! 15 ♕xc4 ♗xc4 16 b3 ♗e6 17 d5 ±.

b) 14...♕d7!? and now:

b1) 15 ♘g5 0-0-0 16 ♘xe6 fxe6 17 ♗e3 ♗d6 18 ♖e4 ♖hf8 =.

b2) 15 d5 ♗xd5 16 ♖xe7+ ♕xe7 17 ♗g5 f6 18 ♖e1 ♗e6 19 ♘d4 (19 ♗f4 c5! −+) 19...0-0-0 with equality, Glek-Baikov, Moscow 1982.

b3) 15 ♗g5 f6 (15...c6 16 ♗xe7 ♕xe7 17 ♘g5 ±) 16 ♖e2 fxg5 17 ♖ae1 0-0-0 18 ♖xe6 ♗f6 19 ♖6e4 with equality, Schulte Berthold-Schwartzman, Dortmund 1989.

15 ♕e1 0-0-0

Black has solved his problems and White has nothing better than to head for equality.

16 ♗g5 ♗xg5

16...♖he8!?.

17 ♘xg5

17 ♖xg5 ♗d5 18 ♘e5 ♕b6 (alternatively, 18...♕h6!? 19 ♖g3 f6 ∞) 19 ♖xg7 ♖hg8 20 ♖g3 (Van der Wiel-Short, Biel IZ playoff 1985) 20...♖xg3 21 hxg3 ♕xd4 ∞.

Now (after 17 ♘xg5):

a) 17...♖xd4 18 ♘xe6 fxe6 19 ♖xe6 is slightly better for White.

b) 17...♗d5 18 ♖c1 ♕b6 19 ♖e7 ♔b8 20 ♖cxc7! (20 ♕c3 ♖c8 21 b3 h6!? 22 ♘f3 {22 ♘xf7 ♕g6 23 ♕g3 ♗xf7 24 ♖cxc7 ♔a8! −+} 22...♖he8 ∓) 20...♕xd4 21 h3 ♕f4 22 ♘xf7 ♖c8 23 ♖xc8+ (23 ♖cd7!? is an interesting alternative) 23...♖xc8 24 ♕e5+ ♕xe5 25 ♘xe5 ♖c1+ 26 ♔h2 ♖c2 27 ♔g3 ♖xb2 28 ♖xg7 ♖xa2 29 ♖xh7 ♖e2 ± Am.Rodriguez.

c) 17...♖he8!? 18 ♖c1 ♕d7 19 ♘xe6 ♖xe6 20 ♖xe6 fxe6! (20...♕xe6?! 21

♕a5 ♕b6 22 ♕f5+ ±) 21 ♕e5 c6 22 g3 ♕xd4 23 ♕xe6+ ♔c7 = A.Grosar-Pavasović, Maribor 1996.

A2)
12 ♘e5 *(D)*

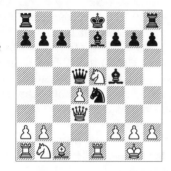

By interrupting the line between queen and bishop, White sets up the threat of 13 ♘c3.

12...g6

Of the alternatives, line 'e' deserves the closest examination:

a) 12...♗h4? 13 g3 ♘xg3 14 ♕f3! ♘e4 15 ♘c3 ♘xc3 16 bxc3 ♕xf3 17 ♘xf3+ ♗e7 18 ♗a3 +− Zuidema-Barendregt, Amsterdam 1966.

b) 12...♘d6?! 13 ♘c3! ♕a5 (not 13...♕xe5 14 dxe5 ♗xd3 15 exd6 cxd6 16 ♘d5 +−) 14 ♕f3 0-0 15 ♗f4! ±.

c) 12...0-0 13 ♘c3 ♘xc3 14 ♕xf5 g6 (14...♘b5? 15 ♘g6! +−) 15 ♕d7 ♕xd7 16 ♘xd7 ♖fd8 17 ♖xe7 ♘d5 18 ♘f6+ ♘xf6 19 ♖xc7 with a slight advantage for White.

d) 12...0-0-0 13 ♕f3 (13 ♘c3? ♕xe5) 13...g6 14 g4 ♗h4 (14...♗b4!? 15 ♖e3 ♕xd4 ∞) and here:

d1) 15 ♖e2?! ♖hg8 16 gxf5 ♕xd4 17 ♔f1? ♕xe5 18 ♖xe4 ♕b5+ 19 ♖e2 ♖d1+ 20 ♔g2 gxf5+ −+ Halasz-Arkhipov, Kecskemet 1984.

d2) 15 ♘d3?! ♘xf2! 16 ♕xd5 ♘h3+ 17 ♔g2 ♖xd5 18 gxf5 ♗xe1 19 ♘xe1 ♖e8! ∓.

d3) 15 ♔g2 ♗xf2! 16 ♖e2 ♗xd4 17 gxf5 ♕xe5 18 ♕xe4 ♕c5! gives Black compensation − Arkhipov.

d4) 15 ♘c3! ♘xc3 16 bxc3 ♗e6 and then:

d41) 17 ♕xd5 ♗xd5 (17...♖xd5 18 g5 ±) 18 c4 (18 g5 f6) 18...f6 19 cxd5 fxe5 20 dxe5 ♖xd5 (20...♖hf8!?) 21 ♖e2 (21 ♗h6!?) 21...♔d7 22 f4 ♔e6 = Hazai-Tischbierek, Leipzig 1986.

d42) 17 g5!? ♖he8! (17...f6? 18 gxf6 ♖hf8 19 ♕xd5 ♗xd5 20 f7 ±) 18 c4! (18 ♖e4?! ♗f5 19 ♖xh4 ♖xe5 ∓) 18...♕xd4 19 ♖b1 and now:

d421) 19...♗d5 20 cxd5 ♖xe5 21 ♖xe5 ♕xe5 22 d6 (22 ♕g4+? ♕f5 23 ♕xf5+ gxf5 24 ♖b4 ♗xg5 25 ♗xg5 ♖g8 −+) and now 22...c6? 23 ♕xf7 ♖d7 was given as equal by Yusupov, but White has a clear win: 24 ♕f8+! ♖d8 25 d7+! ♔c7 26 ♕f4! +−. Black should probably try 22...♕e1+ 23 ♔g2 ♖xd6, though his position remains treacherous.

d422) 19...c6 20 ♗f4 ♕c5 with an unclear position, Wahls-Yusupov, Bundesliga 1992/3.

e) 12...f6!? and then:

e1) 13 ♕f3 g6 and now:

e11) 14 g4 fxe5 15 gxf5 gxf5 has the point 16 ♕xf5 ♖g8+ 17 ♔f1 ♕c4+ −+, as in Wit-Wolf, corr. 1987.

e12) 14 ♘d2 fxe5 15 ♘xe4 (15 dxe5?? 0-0-0 and Black wins) 15...0-0-0 16 ♘g5 ♕xf3 17 gxf3 (17 ♘xf3 e4 ∓) 17...♖xd4 ∓.

e13) 14 ♘d3 ♖d8 15 ♗e3 ♘c3! 16 ♘d2 ♕xf3 17 ♘xf3 ♘e2+! 18 ♖xe2 ♗xd3 19 ♖d2 ♗e4 ∓ Carvalho-da Costa Junior, corr. 1985.

e2) 13 ♘c3 ♘xc3 14 ♕xf5 ♘b5 (now White is virtually committed to a sacrifice, but it is doubtful if he can achieve more than a draw) 15 ♕g4 (15 ♕h5+ g6 16 ♕h3 fxe5 17 ♖xe5 ♕xd4 18 ♕e6! ♕d1+ 19 ♖e1 ♕d7 20 ♗g5 0-0-0 21 ♕xe7 ♖de8 22 ♕xd7+ ♔xd7 = Makropoulos-Toth, Budva 1981) 15...♘xd4 (15...fxe5? 16 ♖xe5 ♕xd4 17 ♖xe7+! ♔xe7 18 ♗g5+ ♔d6 19 ♖d1 c5 20 ♗e3 ♕xd1+ 21 ♕xd1+ ♔c7 22 ♕c2 b6 23 b4 ± Vaulin-Glianets, USSR 1986) 16 ♘d3 and then:

e21) 16...♘c2? 17 ♘b4! ♘xb4 18 ♕xb4 ♕d7! (18...c5 19 ♕g4 ♔f7 20 ♗h6! gxh6 21 ♖ad1 +− de Firmian-Plaskett, Copenhagen 1985) 19 ♗f4! ♔f7 20 ♕b3+ ±.

e22) 16...♔f7! 17 ♖xe7+ (17 ♗e3!?) 17...♔xe7 18 ♘b4 (18 ♕xg7+ ♕f7 19 ♕g4 ♖ad8 20 b3 ♕g6 21 ♕xg6 hxg6 22 ♗a3+ ♔f7 −+ Ulybin-Sorokin, Sochi jr 1986) and now 18...♕c4!? appears strong, as 19 ♕xg7+ ♔e6 20 ♗d2 is met by 20...♘f3+!.

We now return to 12...g6 *(D)*:

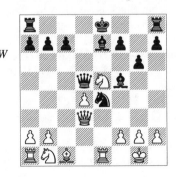

13 ♕f3

Or:

a) 13 g4? ♘xf2 14 ♕g3 ♘e4 ∓.

b) 13 ♘c3 ♘xc3 14 ♕xc3 0-0-0 =.

c) 13 f3 ♘f6 14 ♕e3 0-0-0 15 ♘c3 ♕xd4 16 ♕xd4 ♖xd4 17 ♗e3 ♖b4 18 b3 ♗e6 19 ♗f2 ♗d6 20 ♘d3 ♖d8 21 ♘xb4 ♗xb4 22 ♖ec1 ♗xc3 23 ♖xc3 ♘d5 24 ♖d3 b6 25 ♖ad1 ½-½ Anand-Kramnik, Linares 2000.

13...♕xd4 14 ♘c3 ♕xe5

Taking everything is the way to proceed. White should now be satisfied with equality, as attempts to play for a win can easily rebound.

15 ♗f4

15 ♘xe4 0-0 (15...0-0-0!? 16 ♗f4 ♕d5 17 ♖ac1 c6 ∞) 16 ♗h6 ♖fe8 =.

15...♕a5

Now:

a) 16 ♘xe4 0-0 17 ♘g3 ♗e6 ∓.

b) 16 ♖xe4!? ♗xe4 17 ♕xe4 ♕f5! (17...♕b4 18 ♕e5 f6 19 ♕xc7 ♖d8 20 ♖e1 gives White compensation, Moreno Ramon-Espinoza, Havana 1994) 18 ♕d4 0-0 19 ♘d5 ♖fe8 20 ♗h6 f6 21 g4 c5! ∓.

c) 16 b4!? ♕a3! 17 ♘d5 (17 ♘xe4? ♕xf3 ∓) 17...♕xf3 18 gxf3 ♗d8! 19 fxe4 ♗e6 20 ♘xc7+ ♗xc7 21 ♗xc7 f6 22 a3 ♖c8 23 ♖ac1 ♔f7 ½-½ Beliavsky-Smyslov, Reggio Emilia 1986/7.

A3)

12 g4 *(D)*

Anand's idea, which has been investigated extensively in recent years. White's aim is to stop Black castling by preventing the bishop from retreating to e6. The defect is that White seriously weakens his kingside, so that if

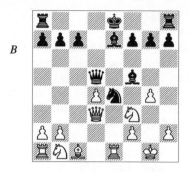

Black can safeguard his king at the cost of a pawn he is likely to have full compensation for the material.

12...♗g6 13 ♘c3 ♘xc3 14 ♕xc3 f6!

Preparing ...♔f7 at the cost of the c7-pawn. The alternatives are:

a) 14...♔f8 15 ♗f4 (15 ♕xc7 ♗d6 16 ♕c3 h5 gives Black compensation) 15...c6 (15...h5 16 ♘e5! ± intending to meet 16...hxg4?! with 17 ♕xc7 ♗b4 18 ♘xg6+ fxg6 19 ♖e5) 16 ♖xe7! ♔xe7 17 ♕b4+ and then:

a1) 17...c5 18 dxc5 ♔d8 (18...♕c6 19 ♘e5) 19 c6 b6 (19...bxc6 20 ♕b7 ♖c8 21 ♗g5+ f6 22 ♕xg7) 20 ♖e1 ♖e8 21 c7+ ♔d7 22 ♘e5+ and White wins.

a2) 17...♔d8 18 ♕xb7 ♖c8 19 ♗g5+ f6 20 ♕xg7 fxg5 21 ♕xh8+ ♔c7 22 ♕e5+ +− Anand-Kramnik, Frankfurt rpd 1999.

b) 14...♕d6!? (a playable alternative to the text-move) 15 ♕e3 (15 ♕b3?! 0-0 intending to answer 16 ♕xb7? with 16...♖fb8; 15 ♗g5!? f6 16 ♗h4 ♕d7 17 ♖xe7+ ♔xe7 18 ♘e5 ♕d6 19 ♖e1 ♔d8 20 ♕b3 gives White compensation) 15...♔f8!? 16 ♘e5 f6 17 ♕f3 ♖d8! 18 ♗f4 ♕d5 19 ♕xd5

(½-½ Anand-Kramnik, Frankfurt rpd 1999) 19...♖xd5 20 ♘xg6+ hxg6 21 ♗xc7 ♖xd4 22 ♖ad1 ♖xd1 23 ♖xd1 ♔f7 =.

We now return to the position after 14...f6 (D):

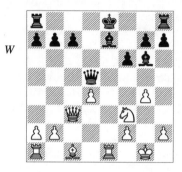

15 ♕xc7

15 ♗f4!? ♔f7 (15...♕d7!? 16 h3 ∞) 16 ♕xc7 ♖he8 17 ♘d2 (17 ♖e3 ♗e4! intending ...♖ac8) 17...♖ad8 18 ♖ac1 (not 18 ♘c4? ♖d7 19 ♘d6+ ♖xd6 20 ♖xe7+ ♖xe7 21 ♕xd6 ♕f3! −+ intending ...♗e4) 18...♖d7 19 ♕c4 ♕xc4 20 ♖xc4 ♗d3 gives Black compensation, Bisby-Lalić, Coulsdon 1999.

15...0-0!

This is the tactical justification for Black's play. White can win the g7-pawn, but Black is saved by the weakness of White's own kingside.

16 ♖xe7 ♕xf3 17 ♖xg7+ ♔h8 18 ♗h6 ♕xg4+ 19 ♕g3 ♕xd4 20 ♖xg6!

20 ♖xb7 ♖g8 21 ♖e1 ♕d5! (not 21...♗f7? 22 ♖xf7 ♖xg3+ 23 hxg3 ±) 22 ♖ee7 ♕d1+ 23 ♔g2 ♗e4+! 24 ♖xe4 ♖xg3+ 25 hxg3 ♕d5 26 ♖be7 f5 and Black wins.

20...hxg6 21 ♕h3 ♔g8 22 ♗xf8 ♖xf8 23 ♕b3+ ♖f7 24 ♖d1 ♕g4+ 25

♔f1 ♚g7 26 h3! ♕e4 27 ♕d5 ♕c2 28 ♖d2 ♕c1+ 29 ♔g2 ♖e7 30 ♕d8 ♕c6+ 31 ♕d5 ♕xd5+

½-½ Anand-I.Sokolov, Dortmund 1999.

B)

9 ♗e2 *(D)*

This more positional approach was first used by Karpov. White preserves his bishop, hoping to drive Black's knights back with gain of time. White usually does not want to play a3 to force the knight back. In that case Black will have gained time because the move a3 is almost useless, so he will have driven the bishop from d3 to e2 without loss of time. Instead, White would prefer to play ♘c3 and somehow force Black to take on c3. Then the knight will have to retreat from b4 without White having to spend a tempo on a3. Thus a kind of waiting game often arises, with White attempting to delay a3 while Black tries to avoid playing ...♘xc3.

9...0-0

Black has also played 9...dxc4 10 ♗xc4 0-0, even though the resulting isolated d-pawn position probably does not give him full equality:

a) 11 ♘e5 ♘d6! (11...♘c6?! 12 ♘xc6 bxc6 13 ♘c3 ♘d6 14 ♗b3 ♘f5 15 d5 c5 16 ♖e1 ♘d4 17 ♗e3 ± Sindik-Jansson, Italy 1983; 11...c6 12 ♘c3 ♘xc3 13 bxc3 ♘d5 14 ♕d3 ±) 12 ♗b3 ♘f5 13 a3 ♘d5 14 ♘c3 ♗e6 15 ♖e1 c6 16 ♗c2 ♘c7 = Sindik-Zysk, Baden-Baden 1985.

b) 11 ♘c3 and then:

b1) 11...♘xc3 12 bxc3 ♘d5 13 ♘e5 (13 ♕d3 c6 14 ♗b3 ♖e8 15 ♘e5 ♗f8 16 ♗d2 ♗e6 17 ♖ae1 ± Popović-Capelan, Vršac 1989) 13...c6 14 ♕f3 ♗e6 15 ♖e1 ♕c7 (15...♗g5 16 ♗a3 is much better for White, Emms-Rubio, Benidorm 1992) 16 ♗b3 ±.

b2) 11...♘d6 12 ♗b3 and here:

b21) After 12...♗g4 13 h3 ♗h5 14 g4! ♗g6 15 ♘e5 ± White intends f4.

b22) 12...♔h8!? deserves attention: 13 a3!? (13 h3!?; 13 ♘e5?! f6 14 ♘f3 ♗g4 15 h3 ♗h5 16 ♗e6? ♗xf3 17 gxf3 {17 ♕xf3 ♘c2} 17...♕e8 18 ♗f4 f5 19 ♔h2 ♕g6 20 ♗b3 ♗g5 ∓ Mnatsakanian-Diaz, Varna 1985) 13...♘c6 14 h3! ± Zagrebelny-Rodriguez, Lucerne Wcht 1993.

b23) 12...♗f6 and now:

b231) 13 h3 ♗f5 14 ♗e3 ♖e8 15 a3 ♘d3 16 ♖b1 c5 17 dxc5 ♘e4 (not 17...♘xb2 18 ♖xb2 ♗xc3 19 cxd6 ♗xb2 20 ♗xf7+ ♔xf7 21 ♕d5+ +–) 18 ♗c2! ♘xb2 19 ♕xd8 ♖axd8 20 ♖xb2 ♗xc3 21 ♖xb7 ♘xc5 22 ♗xc5 ♗xc2 23 ♖xa7 ± Karpov-Kasparov, Moscow Wch (41) 1984/5.

b232) 13 ♘e5! and then:

b2321) 13...♘f5? 14 ♘xf7! ♖xf7 15 ♗xf7+ ♔xf7 16 ♕b3+ ±.

b2322) 13...♗xe5? 14 dxe5 ♘f5 15 ♗xf7+! ±.

b2323) 13...♘c6 14 ♗f4 ♘f5 15 ♘xc6 bxc6 16 d5 c5 (16...♗b7 17 ♖c1 ♘d4 18 ♗e3 ♘b5 19 ♘xb5 cxb5 20 ♖c2 ±) 17 ♘a4 ♗a6 18 ♖e1 c4 (not 18...♗e7? 19 ♖c1 ♗d6 20 ♗g3 ♘xg3 21 hxg3 ♖b8 22 ♘xc5 +– A.Sokolov-Agzamov, USSR Ch (Riga) 1985) 19 ♗c2 ±.

b2324) 13...c5 14 ♗f4 c4! (Black should avoid 14...cxd4? 15 ♕xd4 ♘c6 16 ♘xc6 ♗xd4 17 ♘xd8 ♖xd8 18 ♖ad1 ♘e8 19 ♘d5 +–) 15 ♘xc4 ♘xc4 16 ♗xc4 ♗xd4 (16...♕xd4? 17 ♕xd4 ♗xd4 18 ♗d6 +–) 17 ♘b5 ♘c6 18 ♘xd4 (18 ♗d6 a6! 19 ♘xd4 ♕xd6 20 ♘xc6 ♕xc6 =) 18...♘xd4 ± Kuznetsov-Matsukevich, corr. 1985.

We now return to the position after 9...0-0 (D):

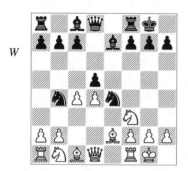

10 ♘c3

White has also tried 10 a3!? (White should really be trying to avoid this; while there is some merit in trying to clarify the position, this move appears too simple to succeed) 10...♘c6 11 cxd5 ♕xd5 12 ♘c3 ♘xc3 13 bxc3 ♗f5 (13...♘a5!?), and now:

a) 14 ♘d2 ♘a5 15 ♗f3 ♕d7 16 ♖e1 ♖ad8 17 ♘e4 ∓/= Liss-Av.Bykhovsky, Herzliya 1998.

b) 14 c4 ♕d6!? 15 ♖a2 (15 ♗e3!? ♗f6 16 ♕b3 b6 17 ♖fd1 ♖ad8 is unclear) 15...♗f6 16 ♗e3 (Steingrimsson-Mikhalchishin, Kecskemet 1991; 16 d5 ♘e5 17 ♘d4 ♗d7 18 ♗e3 c5 ∞) 16...b6! 17 d5 ♘a5 18 ♘d4 ♗d7 = intending ...c5.

c) 14 ♗f4 ♘a5 15 ♗xc7 ♖ac8! 16 ♗xa5 ♕xa5 17 c4 ♗f6! (17...♖fd8 18 ♖a2! ±) and then:

c1) 18 ♖a2 ♖fe8 gives Black compensation.

c2) 18 ♗d3 ♖fd8! 19 ♗xf5 ♕xf5 20 ♕a4 a6 (20...♗xd4 21 ♘xd4 ♖xd4 22 ♕xa7 ♖d7 23 ♖fd1 ♖dc7 = Sakaev) 21 c5 g6 22 ♖ab1 ♕d5 23 ♖b4 ♔g7 24 ♖fb1 ♖c7 = Palac-Ferčec, Pula 2000.

c3) 18 ♕b3 ♕b6 (½-½ Svidler-Sakaev, Russian Ch (St Petersburg) 1998) 19 ♕xb6 (19 ♕c3 ♖fe8 gives Black compensation) 19...axb6 20 ♖a2 (20 ♖ad1 ♖fd8 21 ♘e5 ♗c2 22 ♖d2 ♗xe5 23 ♖xc2 =) 20...♖fd8 21 d5 (21 ♖d1 ♗e4 22 d5 b5 =) 21...b5 is equal – Sakaev.

Now:

B1: 10...♗e6   228
B2: 10...♗f5   236

B1)

10...♗e6 (D)

There is no particular threat behind this move, but it challenges White to find a constructive move other than a3. If White does play a3, Black will be ready to recapture on d5 with his bishop later on. Now:

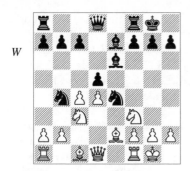

B11: 11 ♗e3   229
B12: 11 ♘e5   235

Or:

a) 11 ♖e1 ♗f5 (this may look odd, but the point is that 10...♗f5 is met by 11 a3, when 11...♘xc3 12 bxc3 ♘c2 13 ♖a2 only leads to the knight being trapped; in this position, with the rook on e1, White is unable to play a3) 12 ♘xd5 ♘xd5 13 cxd5 ♗b4 14 ♖f1 ♕xd5 15 ♕a4 ♗e7 16 ♗f4 c6 17 ♖fe1 ♗f6 = Sherzer-Anand, London Lloyds Bank 1987.

b) 11 cxd5 ♘xc3 12 bxc3 ♘xd5 and then:

b1) 13 ♕c2 c5 14 c4 (14 ♗d3 h6 15 ♖e1 cxd4 16 ♘xd4 ♘b4!? 17 ♗h7+ ♔h8 18 ♕e4 ♘d5 19 ♘xe6 fxe6 20 ♗g6 ♗c5 ∓ Perpinya-Casilas, Spanish jr Ch 1992) 14...♘b4 15 ♕e4 ♕d7 (15...♗f6!? 16 ♗e3 ♕c8 ∓) 16 dxc5? (16 ♗b2! =) 16...♗f5 17 ♕d4 ♕e6 18 ♗b2 ♗f6 19 ♕d2 ♗xb2 20 ♕xb2 ♘c2 and Black wins, Ljubojević-Seirawan, Brussels 1986.

b2) 13 ♗d2 ♘b6 14 ♕b1!? (14 ♕c2 ♗c4 is equal) 14...♖e8 15 a4 ♕c8 16 ♗d3 (Becerra-Ro.Perez, Cuba 1995) 16...g6! =.

c) 11 a3 (once again, this simplistic move doesn't offer White any advantage) 11...♘xc3 12 bxc3 ♘c6 13 cxd5 ♗xd5 (this is the point behind 10...♗e6; Black avoids having to recapture on d5 with the queen) 14 ♗e3 (14 ♕c2 ♕d6 15 ♖e1 ♖ae8 16 ♗d3 ♗xf3 17 gxf3 ♔h8 = Nunn-Khalifman, Groningen 1988; 14 ♖e1 ♘a5 15 ♗d2 ♗f6 ½-½ Short-Seirawan, Biel IZ 1985) 14...♗f6 (14...♘a5!? intending 15 ♕a4?! c6 16 c4? b5! −+) 15 ♖b1 a6!? (15...♖b8 16 ♘d2 ♗e6 17 ♗f3 ± Saltaev-Tolstykh, Volgograd 1994) 16 ♘d2 (16 c4 ♗xf3 17 ♗xf3 ♘xd4 18 ♗xb7 ♖b8 is level) 16...b5 17 a4 ♘a7 18 axb5 axb5 19 ♘b3 (19 ♗xb5 ♘xb5 20 ♖xb5 c6 gives Black compensation) 19...c6 20 ♘c5 ♘c8 =.

d) 11 ♗f4 c5 12 ♖e1 ♗f6 and here:

d1) 13 ♘b5? dxc4 14 ♘c7 (14 ♗f1 ♗d5 15 ♘c7 ♖c8 16 ♘xd5 ♕xd5 17 a3 ♘d3 18 ♗xd3 cxd3 19 ♕xd3 ♖fe8 ∓ intending 20 ♖ad1 cxd4 21 ♘xd4 ♘c5 −+) 14...♘d5! 15 ♘xe6 fxe6 16 ♗g3 (Adams-Shirov, Dortmund 1998; 16 ♗xc4 ♘xf2 17 ♔xf2 ♘xf4! 18 dxc5 ♕a5 ∓) 16...♘xg3! 17 hxg3 b5! 18 a4 cxd4 19 ♘xd4 ♕b6! 20 ♘f3 (20 ♘xb5? ♕xf2+ 21 ♔xf2 ♗d4#) 20...♗xb2 21 ♖b1 ♘c3! 22 ♕c2 ♘xa4 23 ♖xb2 ♘xb2 24 ♕xb2 ♖ac8 ∓ Shirov.

d2) 13 a3 ♘xc3 (13...♘c6 14 ♘xd5 ∞) 14 bxc3 ♘c6 =.

B11)

11 ♗e3 *(D)*
Now:
B111: 11...f5   230
B112: 11...♗f5   232

B

Or:

a) 11...♘f6 12 a3 ♘c6 13 b3 ♘e4 14 ♘xe4 dxe4 15 d5 exf3 16 ♗xf3 ♗d7 17 dxc6 ♗xc6 18 ♗xc6 bxc6 19 ♕f3 ♕d3 20 ♖ab1 ± A.Sokolov-Smyslov, Moscow rpd 1987.

b) 11...♘xc3 12 bxc3 ♘c6 13 cxd5 ♗xd5 and then:

b1) 14 c4 ♗xf3 15 ♗xf3 ♗f6 is equal.

b2) 14 ♘d2!? ♗e6!? 15 f4 ♕d7 16 ♘f3 ♖ad8 17 c4?! (17 ♖b1!) 17...♗f6 ∓ Poli-G.David, Italian corr. Ch 1989.

b3) 14 ♕c2!? ♗f6 15 ♘d2 ♖e8 16 ♖ae1 ♗e6 (16...♘e7 17 c4 ±) 17 ♗d3 g6 18 ♗f4 ♗g7 (18...♘a5!?) 19 ♘e4 ♗d5 20 ♘c5 ±/± Ehlvest-Yusupov, Saint John Ct (2) 1988.

c) 11...♗f6!? and now:

c1) 12 cxd5 ♘xc3 13 bxc3 ♘xd5 is slightly better for Black.

c2) 12 a3 ♘xc3 13 bxc3 ♘c6 14 cxd5 ♗xd5 = Gipslis-Smyslov, Moscow 1991.

c3) 12 ♕b3 a5 13 ♖ad1 (13 ♘xe4?! dxe4 14 ♘e1 ♗xd4 15 a3 ♗xe3 16 ♕xe3 ♘c6 17 ♕xe4 ♕f6 18 ♘f3 ♗f5 ∓ Kuczynski-Garcia Gonzales, Polanica Zdroj 1987) 13...♘xc3 14 bxc3 dxc4 15 ♗xc4 ♗xc4 16 ♕xc4 ♘d5 17

♖b1 ±/= Bauer-Burrows, New York 2000.

c4) 12 ♕a4 ♘xc3 13 bxc3 ♘c6 14 ♖ab1 ♖b8 15 ♖fd1 ♖e8 16 cxd5 ♗xd5 17 c4 ♗e4 18 ♖bc1 ½-½ Chandler-Ribli, Bundesliga 1986/7.

c5) 12 ♖c1!? c5 13 a3 cxd4 14 ♘xd4 ♗xd4 15 ♗xd4 ♘xc3 16 ♖xc3 ♘c6 17 cxd5 ♘xd4 18 dxe6 and now the best way to limit the damage is 18...♘xe6 ±, rather than 18...fxe6? 19 ♗d3 ♖f7 20 ♕d2 ♕f6 21 ♖fc1 ± Ljubojević-Christiansen, Linares 1985.

c6) 12 ♘xe4 dxe4 13 ♘e1 c6 14 ♕b3 ♕e7 15 a3 ♘a6 16 ♘c2 ♖fd8 17 ♖fd1 ♖ac8 18 ♕a4 c5 19 ♖ac1 cxd4 20 ♘xd4 ♘c5 21 ♕xa7 ♘d3 22 ♗xd3 ♗xd4 23 ♗xd4 exd3 24 ♖xd3 ♖xc4 ± Ljubojević-Karpov, Bugojno 1986.

B111)
11...f5 *(D)*

W

This is a committal and double-edged move. Although it appears very weakening, it does give Black active play and so far White has not found a really promising reply. One word of warning: although ...f4 is a natural follow-up, it is not always a good idea to push the pawn straight away as this advance can create further weaknesses.

12 a3

Or:

a) 12 ♞e5 and here:

a1) 12...f4 13 ♗c1! c6 (13...♞xc3?! 14 bxc3 ♞c6 15 ♗g4! ♗xg4 16 ♕xg4 ♞xe5 17 dxe5 dxc4 18 ♗xf4 ±; however, 13...♗d6!? is possible) 14 a3 (14 c5!?) 14...♞a6 15 cxd5 cxd5 16 ♕b3 and White has a slight advantage.

a2) 12...dxc4!? 13 ♞xe4 fxe4 14 ♗xc4 ♗xc4 15 ♞xc4 ♕d5 =.

b) 12 cxd5 ♞xd5 13 ♞xd5 (13 ♞xe4 fxe4 14 ♞d2 ♞xe3 15 fxe3 ♗g5 =) 13...♗xd5 14 ♗f4 c6 15 ♗e5 and now Black should choose between 15...♗d6!? = and 15...♕e8!? intending ...♕g6, rather than 15...♕b6?! 16 ♕c2 ± Dvoirys-Sorokin, Cheliabinsk 1989.

c) 12 ♕b3!? ♞xc3 13 bxc3 dxc4 14 ♗xc4 ♗xc4 15 ♕xc4+ ♕d5 16 ♕e2 ♞c6 17 c4 ♕e4 = Zagrebelny-Agzamov, Tashkent 1988.

12...♞xc3 13 bxc3 ♞c6 14 ♕a4

Or:

a) 14 ♖b1 and then:

a1) 14...f4?! 15 ♗c1 ♖b8 16 cxd5! ♗xd5 17 ♖e1 ♔h8 (17...♗f6 18 ♗xf4 ♗xd4 19 ♗xc7 ♕xc7 20 ♞xd4 ±) 18 ♗d3 ♗f6 (18...♕d7?! 19 c4 ♗xf3 20 ♕xf3 ♞xd4 {20...♕xd4? 21 ♗b2 +−} 21 ♕e4 ± Anand-Yusupov, Munich 1993) 19 ♗c2! ±.

a2) 14...♖b8!? 15 cxd5 (15 ♕a4 f4 and now 16 ♗d2 ♔h8 – *14 ♕a4 f4 15 ♗d2 ♔h8 16 ♖ab1 ♖b8*; 16 ♗c1 ♔h8 – *14 ♕a4 f4 15 ♗c1 ♔h8 16 ♖b1 ♖b8*) 15...♗xd5 16 c4 (16 ♗f4 ♗d6 =) 16...♗e4 ∞ Makarychev.

b) 14 cxd5 ♗xd5 and here:

b1) 15 ♗f4 g5! 16 ♗c1 (16 ♗e5? g4 ∓) 16...♗f6 ∓ Makarychev.

b2) 15 c4 ♗xf3 16 ♗xf3 f4 17 ♗d5+ ♔h8 18 ♗c1 ♞xd4! (18...♗f6 19 ♗b2 ♞xd4 {19...♞e7 20 ♗e4 ±} 20 ♗xd4 ♗xd4 21 ♕xd4 c6 22 ♖ad1 ±) 19 ♖b1 (19 ♕xd4? ♗f6 −+; 19 ♗b2 c5 =) 19...♗c5 20 ♖xb7 (20 ♗b2 ♕f6! is equal) 20...f3! 21 ♗xf3 (21 ♗e3?! ♞e2+ 22 ♔h1 ♗xe3 23 fxe3 ♞c3 ∓) 21...♞xf3+ ½-½ Hübner-Yusupov, Rotterdam 1988.

b3) 15 ♕c2 ♔h8 16 ♖fd1 ♕d7! (16...♗f6? 17 ♞e5! ±) 17 ♗f4 ♗d6 and now White should settle for 18 ♗xd6 =, rather than 18 ♞e5?! ♗xe5 19 dxe5 ♕e6 20 c4 ♗e4 21 ♕c3 ♞e7 22 ♖d4 ♖ae8 ∓ Beliavsky-Yusupov, Barcelona 1989.

We now return to 14 ♕a4 *(D)*:

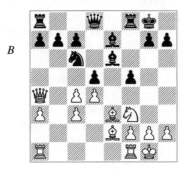

14...f4

Or:

a) 14...♖b8!? 15 cxd5 ♗xd5 16 ♗c4 ♗f6 17 ♗xd5+ (17 ♗f4!? is slightly better for White) 17...♕xd5 18 c4 ♕a5 19 ♕c2 f4 20 ♗d2 ♕h5 21 ♗c3 b5 with an unclear position, Madl-Solomon, Sydney 1990.

b) 14...♔h8!? 15 ♖ab1 ♖b8 16 ♖fe1! f4 (16...a6?! 17 ♗f4! ♗d6 18 ♗g5! ♗e7 19 ♗f1! ± Ljubojević-Beliavsky, Belgrade 1995) 17 ♗c1 – *14...f4 15 ♗c1 ♔h8 16 ♖b1 ♖b8 17 ♖e1.*

15 ♗c1

15 ♗d2 ♔h8 16 ♖ab1 (16 ♖fe1 dxc4 17 ♗xc4 ♗g4 18 ♗e2 a6 19 h3 ♗h5 20 ♘h2 ♗xe2 is equal, Böhnisch-Tischbierek, E.German Ch (Zittau) 1989) 16...♖b8 17 ♖fe1 dxc4 18 ♗xc4 ♗g4 19 ♗e2 a6! (Black defends the b5-square and prevents White's rook manoeuvre; this move is better than 19...♗d6?! 20 h3 ♗h5 {20...♗f5!?} 21 ♖b5! ♗e8 {21...♗g6 22 c4 ±} 22 ♕c2 a6 23 ♖f5! ♖xf5 24 ♕xf5 ♗g6 25 ♕g4 ♕f6 26 ♗c4 ± Karpov-Seirawan, Brussels 1986) 20 h3 ♗h5 and then:

a) 21 ♘g5?! ♗xe2! 22 ♘e6 ♕d5 23 ♘xf8 (23 ♖xe2 f3 24 ♖ee1 fxg2 25 ♘xf8 ♖xf8 26 ♕d1 ♕f5 –+ Rohde-Seirawan, USA Ch (Estes Park) 1986) 23...f3 24 gxf3 ♗b5! 25 c4 ♕xd4 26 ♕d1 ♕xc4 27 ♘e6 ♗d6 gives Black good compensation.

b) 21 ♖bd1 ♗d6 with an equal position.

15...♔h8 16 ♖b1 ♖b8

Black has sufficient piece activity to justify the advance of his f-pawn.

17 ♖e1 dxc4

17...a6 18 ♗d3 ♗g4 (18...dxc4? 19 ♗xh7 ±) 19 cxd5 ♗xf3 20 gxf3 ♕xd5 21 ♗e4 ♕h5 22 ♔h1 (22 ♗xc6? ♕g6+ –+) 22...♗d6 23 ♖g1 (23 ♗xc6? bxc6 24 ♖xb8 ♕xf3+ ∓) 23...b5 24 ♕d1 ♘e7 with an unclear position, Benjamin-Zarnicki, Manila OL 1992.

18 ♗xc4

Now:

a) 18...♗xc4 19 ♕xc4 ♗d6 20 d5 ♘e7 21 ♕d3 ♕d7 22 c4 c6?! 23 ♗b2 ± Garriero-Battistini, corr. 1990.

b) 18...♗f5!? 19 ♖b2 a6 20 ♗f1 (20 ♗xa6?! ♖a8 21 ♖xb7 ♕d6 gives Black compensation) 20...b5 21 ♕b3 ♗g4 22 ♖e4 ♗d6 23 ♘e5 ♘xe5 24 dxe5 ♗c5 (Zapata-Garcia Gonzales, Santa Clara 1990) 25 ♖xf4 ♖xf4 26 ♗xf4 ♕f8 gives Black compensation.

c) 18...♗g4!? and now:

c1) 19 d5 is best met by 19...♕d6!, with the point that 20 dxc6? fails to 20...♗xf3.

c2) 19 ♗e2 a6 20 ♕d1 b5 21 d5 ♗f5 22 ♖a1 ♘a5 23 ♗xf4 ♗e4 24 ♗g3 (Shmuter-Tolstykh, Volgograd 1994) 24...♗xd5 25 ♗xc7 ♕xc7 26 ♕xd5 ♗f6 ∞.

B112)

11...♗f5 *(D)*

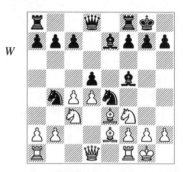

Playing the bishop to e6 and then to f5 may appear strange, but the point is that the position of the bishop on e3 allows Black to meet a3 by ...♘xc3 followed by ...♘c2.

12 ♖c1

Or:

a) 12 a3 ♘xc3 13 bxc3 ♘c2 14 ♖a2 ♘xa3 (14...♘xe3 15 fxe3 ±) 15 ♖xa3 ♗xa3 16 c5 b5!? (16...♗b2?! 17 ♕b3 ♗xc3 18 ♕xc3 c6 19 ♖a1 ♖e8 20 ♖a3 ♕c7 21 ♘d2 b5 22 ♖a6 ± Al.Ivanov-Arkhipov, USSR 1985) 17 ♕b3 (17 ♗xb5?! ♖b8 18 ♕a4 ♗b2 19 ♗d2 ♗c2!? ∓) 17...♗xc5 18 dxc5 c6 19 ♘d4 ♗d7 20 ♗f4 a5 21 ♗d6 ♖e8 is unclear.

b) 12 ♘e5 and here:

b1) 12...♗f6? 13 g4! ♗e6 14 f4 ♘xc3 15 bxc3 ♘c6 16 ♗f3 ± Short-Anand, Amsterdam 1993.

b2) 12...♘xc3 13 bxc3 ♘c2 14 ♖c1 ♘xe3 15 fxe3 ♗e4 (15...♗e6!?) 16 cxd5 and now Black should certainly go for 16...♗a3!?, rather than 16...♗xd5 17 ♗d3 ±/±.

b3) 12...f6 13 ♘d3 (13 g4? ♗e6 ∓) 13...♘xc3 14 bxc3 ♘xd3 15 ♗xd3 ♗xd3 16 ♕xd3 ♕d7 17 cxd5 ♕xd5 with equality, Popović-Mikhalchishin, Yugoslavia 1993.

c) 12 ♕b3!? *(D)* is an important alternative, which can lead to tactical complications. In some lines White gives up his queen for three minor pieces, while in others he sacrifices the exchange. Although the play is quite interesting, objectively speaking Black is able to maintain the balance. The possible replies are:

c1) 12...dxc4 13 ♗xc4 a5 14 a3 ♘d2!? (14...♘xc3 15 axb4! b5 16 bxa5! bxc4 17 ♕xc3 ♗d3 18 ♖fe1 ± Timman-Hjartarson, Rotterdam 1989) and then:

c11) 15 ♗xd2 ♗c2 16 axb4! (16 ♗xf7+ ♖xf7 17 ♕e6 ♗f5 18 ♕b3 ♗c2 = Efimenko-Vzdvizhkov, corr.

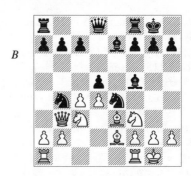

B

1989) 16...♗xb3 17 ♗xb3 ♗xb4 18 ♗g5 ±.

c12) 15 ♘xd2!? ♗c2 16 axb4 ♗xb3 17 ♘xb3 axb4 18 ♘d5 ±.

c2) 12...c6 and then:

c21) 13 ♖ac1 dxc4 14 ♗xc4 b5 (not 14...a5? 15 a3 ♘xc3 16 axb4 ♘b5 17 bxa5 ♖xa5 18 d5 ♗e4 19 dxc6 ♗xf3 20 ♗xb5 bxc6 21 ♗xc6 ± Adams-Christiansen, Cannes tt rpd 1992) and here:

c211) 15 ♗e2 ♗e6 16 ♕d1 ♘xc3 17 ♖xc3 (17 bxc3 ♘xa2 18 ♖c2 b4 ∓) 17...♗xa2 18 b3 a5 intending ...a4 ∓.

c212) 15 ♗xf7+ ♖xf7 16 ♘e5 ♘d5! 17 ♘xe4 (17 ♘xc6 ♘exc3! 18 ♘xd8 ♘e2+ 19 ♔h1 ♘xc1 ∓) 17...♗xe4 18 ♖xc6 ♕e8 ∓ Khalifman-Arkhipov, Moscow 1985.

c22) 13 cxd5 cxd5 14 ♖fc1 (14 ♖ac1 a5 15 a3 ♘xc3 16 bxc3 a4 17 ♕b2 ♘d3 ∓) 14...a5 15 a3 ♘xc3 16 ♖xc3 (16 ♕xc3?! ♖c8 17 ♕d2 ♘c2 ∓) 16...a4 17 ♕d1 ♘c6 18 ♖ac1 (18 ♗b5 ♕b6 19 ♗xa4 ♕xb2 20 ♖b3 ♕c2 ∓) 18...♕b6 =.

c23) 13 c5!? ♘xc3 14 bxc3 ♘c2 15 ♕xb7!? (15 ♖ad1 ♘xe3 16 fxe3 ♖b8 17 c4 ♗e6 18 ♕c2 ♕c7 19 ♗d3 f5 20 g3 g6 ∞ de Firmian-Schwartzman,

USA Ch (Chandler) 1997) 15...♘xa1 16 ♖xa1 and then:

c231) 16...♗f6?! 17 ♕xc6 ♖e8 18 ♕a4 h5 (18...♖xe3 19 fxe3 ♕e7 20 ♖e1! ♕xe3+ 21 ♔h1 ♕xc3 22 ♗c4 ♖f8 23 ♗xd5 ♗g4 24 ♕e8! and White wins) 19 ♗b5 and now Black should try 19...♖e6!, with the point that 20 ♗c6 is met by 20...♗c2, instead of 19...♗e4?! 20 ♗c6! ♖c8 21 c4 ♖g4 22 ♗xd5 ♖xc5 23 dxc5 ♗xa1 24 ♕xa7 ♗e6 25 h3 ♖g6 26 c6 ♕f6 27 c7 1-0 de Firmian-Marciano, Elista OL 1998.

c232) 16...♕d7!? 17 ♕xd7 ♗xd7 18 ♘e5 ♗e8 19 ♗a6 ♖b8 20 ♘d3 g5! is unclear.

c233) 16...♕e8 17 ♕a6 (17 ♘e5!?) 17...f6 18 ♘e1 ♕c8 ∞ Topalov-Kramnik, Tilburg 1998.

We now return to 12 ♖c1 (D):

12...dxc4

12...♘xc3 13 bxc3 ♘xa2 14 ♖c2 ♗xc2 15 ♕xc2 ♘xc3 16 ♕xc3 c6 17 ♖b1 a5 18 ♖xb7 a4 19 ♘e5 ♗d6 20 ♘xc6 ♕c8 21 ♖b6 ± Short-Timman, Hilversum (6) 1989.

13 ♗xc4 c6

13...♘xc3 14 bxc3 ♘d5 15 ♕b3 (or 15 ♘e5 ♘b6 16 ♗b3 ♘d5 with a

slight advantage for White, Smirin-Ristić, Geneva 1992) 15...♗e6 16 ♘e5 ♖b8 (16...f6?! 17 ♘d3 ♔h8 18 ♖fe1 ± Kundin-Ribshtein, Givataim 1998) 17 ♗xd5 ♗xd5 (17...♕xd5 18 ♕xd5 ♗xd5 19 ♘d7 ±) 18 c4 ♗e4 ±.

14 ♘e5

14 ♕b3 – 12 ♕b3 c6 13 ♖ac1 dxc4 14 ♗xc4.

14...♘xc3 15 bxc3 ♘d5

Black's position is very solid and he can maintain the balance.

16 ♕f3

Or:

a) 16 ♖e1? ♗a3 wins for Black, Timman-Bareev, Linares 1993.

b) 16 ♕b3 f6! (16...♖b8!? =) 17 ♘f3 (17 ♕xb7? fxe5 18 ♕xc6 ♗e4 −+) 17...b5 (17...♕d7!? 18 ♖fe1 ♔h8 19 ♗d2 ♗d6 20 ♗f1 ♘f4 21 ♘h4 ∞) 18 ♗e2 ♔h8 19 ♗d2 ♘b6 (19...♗d6!? intending ...♘f4) 20 ♖fe1 ♕d7 21 c4 bxc4 22 ♗xc4 ♘xc4 23 ♕xc4 ♖fc8 24 ♘h4 ♗f8 = Ki.Georgiev-Ivanchuk, Debrecen Echt 1992.

16...♗e6 (D)

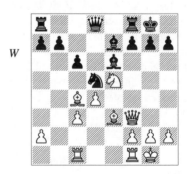

Now:

a) 17 ♗d3 ♗d6 (17...♘xe3 18 fxe3 ♗d6 19 ♘c4 ♗c7 20 e4 ±) 18 ♗d2 (18

♖fe1 ♗xe5 19 dxe5 ♘xe3 20 ♖xe3 ♕g5 =) 18...♕h4! 19 ♖fe1 ♘f6 20 a4 (20 h3 ♗d5 21 ♕f5 ♗e6 22 ♕g5 ♕xg5 23 ♗xg5 ♘d5 =) 20...♘g4 21 ♗f4 ♘xe5 22 ♗xe5 ♗d5 23 ♕f5 ♗xe5 24 ♖xe5 g6 25 ♕d7 and now 25...b6! = is better than 25...♖ab8? 26 ♖b1 ♖fd8 27 ♕c7 ♕g4 28 ♗f1 ♕d7 29 ♖e7 ± Hübner-Timman, Sarajevo Ct (4) 1991.

b) 17 ♖fe1 ♘xe3 18 ♕xe3 (18 ♗xe6? fxe6 19 ♕xe3 ♗g5 20 ♕h3 ♗xc1 21 ♕xe6+ ♔h8 22 ♖xc1 ♕f6 ∓; 18 fxe3 ♗xc4 19 ♘xc4 ♕d5 20 ♕xd5 cxd5 =) 18...♗xc4 19 ♘xc4 ♗f6 20 ♖b1 b6 21 ♕f3 ♖c8 22 ♘e3 g6 23 d5 ♗g5! 24 dxc6 ♗xe3 25 ♖xe3 ♕d6 = Kamsky-Anand, Sanghi Nagar FIDE Ct (8) 1994.

c) 17 ♗d2 f6!? (17...♗g5 18 ♗xg5 ♕xg5 19 ♖fe1 ± Topalov-Akopian, Linares 1995) 18 ♘d3 ♕d7 19 ♖fe1 (19 ♗b3 should be met by 19...b5! =, rather than 19...♗g4?! 20 ♕g3 ♔h8 21 c4 ♗d6 22 ♘c5 ♗xc5 23 dxc5 ♘e7 24 ♗f4 ± Shirov-Kramnik, Monaco Amber blindfold 2000) 19...♗d6 20 h3 ♗f7 (20...b5!? 21 ♗b3 ♖fe8 =) 21 ♗b3 ♖ae8 22 ♕g4 ♖xe1+ 23 ♖xe1 ♖d8 24 ♕xd7 ♖xd7 25 ♘e5 ♗xe5 26 dxe5 fxe5 27 ♖xe5 ♘f6 with an equal position, Topalov-Ivanchuk, Novgorod 1996.

B12)

11 ♘e5 (D)

The latest fashion, and currently the biggest headache for Black.

11...f6

This forces White to retract his previous move, but the price is high. The bishop is no longer secure on e6, and

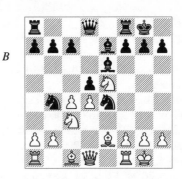

the f6-square is not available to the black pieces. The alternatives are:

a) 11...c6 12 f3 ♘xc3 13 bxc3 f6 14 ♘g4 ♘a6 15 cxd5 ♕xd5 16 ♗f4 is much better for White, Yu Xiadong-Shu Yinmin, China tt 1987.

b) 11...c5 12 ♘xe4 dxe4 13 d5 ♗d6 and then:

b1) 14 f4!? exf3 (14...♗c8!? 15 a3 ♘a6 16 ♗d2 f6 17 ♘g4 ♗xg4 18 ♗xg4 f5 19 ♗e2 ♘c7 20 ♗c3 ±/±) 15 ♘xf3 and now 15...♗f5! should be preferred to 15...♗g4 16 a3 ± Milos-Zarnicki, Cascavel tt 1995.

b2) 14 a3 ♗xe5 (14...♘a6 15 f4 ±) 15 axb4 ♗d7 16 bxc5 and now:

b21) 16...f5 17 f4 exf3 18 ♖xf3 ♕c7 (18...f4 19 ♖aa3 ♗g4?! 20 ♖f1 f3 21 ♗xf3 ♕h4 22 g3 ♗xg3 23 hxg3 ♕xg3+ 24 ♗g2! +−) 19 d6! ♕xc5+ 20 ♗e3 ♕c6 21 c5 f4 22 ♗c4+ ♔h8 23 ♗d5 ♕b5 24 ♗d4 ± Nadyrkhanov-Maiorovas, Krasnodar 1994.

b22) 16...♕c7 17 ♗e3! (17 d6 ♕xc5 18 ♗e3 ♕b4 is equal) 17...♗xh2+ (17...♗xb2 18 ♖b1 ±) 18 ♔h1 ♗e5 19 ♗d4 ♖fe8 20 b4 ♕d8 21 ♗xe5 ♖xe5 22 ♖a3! ♕h4+ 23 ♔g1 ♖g5 24 f4! exf3 25 ♖fxf3! ± Wahls-Pavasović, Dresden Z 1998.

12 ♘f3

12 ♗g4!? is interesting:

a) 12...♕c8? 13 ♘xd5!.

b) 12...♗c8 13 ♗xc8 ♖xc8 14 ♘f3 and then:

b1) 14...♘xc3?! 15 bxc3 ♘c6 16 ♕a4 dxc4 17 ♖b1 ♖b8 18 ♕xc4+ ♔h8 19 ♖e1 ♗d6 (19...♘a5 20 ♕e6 ♗d6 21 c4 ♖e8 {21...b6 22 ♗d2 ±} 22 ♕xe8+ ♕xe8 23 ♖xe8+ ♖xe8 24 c5 ♗f8 25 ♗d2 ±) 20 ♕a4 ♖e8 21 ♗e3 a6 22 c4 ± A.Sokolov-Mikhalchishin, Berne 1994.

b2) 14...c5!? 15 ♕e2!? (15 ♗e3!? cxd4 16 ♘xd4 ♕d7 17 ♘xd5 ♘xd5 18 cxd5 ♕xd5 19 ♘b3 ±/= A.Sokolov-J.Horvath, Mulhouse ECC 1997) 15...cxd4 16 ♘xd4 ♖e8 (Anand-Kramnik, Frankfurt rpd 1998) 17 ♗e3 ♗c5 18 ♖ad1 ±.

c) 12...♗xg4!? 13 ♘xg4 dxc4 (not 13...♕d7 14 ♖e1 ♘xc3 15 bxc3 ♘c6 16 cxd5 ♕xd5 17 c4 ±) 14 ♘xe4 f5 15 ♘d2 fxg4 16 ♘xc4 c5 17 a3 ♘c6 18 dxc5 (18 d5 ♘d4 19 d6 ♗xd6 20 ♘xd6 ♕xd6 21 ♕xg4 ♕e6 with an equal position) 18...♕xd1 19 ♖xd1 ♗xc5 20 ♗e3 ♗xe3 21 ♘xe3 h5 22 ♖d5 ½-½ Anand-Kramnik, Frankfurt rpd 1998.

We now return to 12 ♘f3 *(D)*:

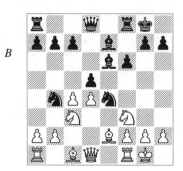

12...♔h8

Or 12...c5 13 ♗e3 ♖c8, and then:

a) 14 a3 ♘xc3 15 bxc3 ♘c6 16 cxd5 should be met by 16...♗xd5! =, rather than 16...cxd4?! 17 ♘xd4 ♗xd5 18 ♘f5 ± J.Polgar-Marciano, Batumi Echt 1999.

b) 14 dxc5 ♗xc5 15 ♗xc5! (15 ♘d4 ♘xc3 16 bxc3 ♗xd4 17 ♗xd4 ♘c6 18 c5 ♗f7 19 ♖e1 ♖e8 = Leko-Anand, Wijk aan Zee 2000) 15...♖xc5 16 ♕b3 (Black has no satisfactory reply) 16...a5 (16...♘xc3 17 ♕xc3 ♘c6 18 b4 ± Lutz-Kutuzović, Pula Z 2000) 17 ♖ad1 ♕e8 (17...♕e7 18 ♘a4 is much better for White, Khalifman-Karpov, Bali 2000) 18 ♘xd5 ♗xd5 19 cxd5 ♕f7 20 a3 ♘xd5 21 ♗c4 ♖d8 22 ♖d4 ± Torre-Handoko, Bali 2000.

13 ♕b3 ♘xc3 14 bxc3 dxc4 15 ♗xc4 ♗xc4 16 ♕xc4 ♕d5 17 ♕b3 ♕xb3 18 axb3 ♘d5 19 ♖e1 ♖fe8 20 ♗d2

White has a slight advantage, Leko-Timman, Wijk aan Zee 2000. White's more centralized pawn-structure gives him an edge.

B2)

10...♗f5 *(D)*

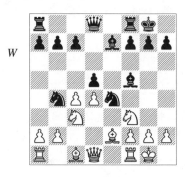

This is a more straightforward option. The threat is 11...♘xc3 12 bxc3 ♘c2 13 ♖b1 ♘xd4, so White is forced to play a3 in order to free a2 for his rook. Black's only real problem is that he will have to take back with his queen on d5, when White can gain time by chasing the queen.

11 a3 ♘xc3 12 bxc3 ♘c6 (D)

W

13 ♖e1

It is useful to keep Black guessing by playing some essential developing moves, and only then deciding whether to take on d5. Other possibilities:

a) 13 ♗e3 dxc4 14 ♗xc4 ♗f6 15 ♗d3 ♕d7 16 ♖b1 b6 = Schmittdiel-Panzer, Bundesliga 1990/1.

b) 13 cxd5 ♕xd5 – *10 a3!? ♘c6 11 cxd5 ♕xd5 12 ♘c3 ♘xc3 13 bxc3 ♗f5*.

13...♗f6 14 ♗f4 ♘a5

Or:

a) 14...♘e7 15 ♕b3 b6 16 cxd5 ♘xd5 17 ♗e5! ±/± Kasparov-I.Sokolov, Sarajevo 2000.

b) 14...♖c8!? 15 ♕a4 a6 16 ♕b3?! ♘a5 17 ♕b4 c5 18 dxc5 ♘c6 19 ♕b3 ♘a5 ½-½ Ljubojević-Yusupov, Belgrade 1989.

15 cxd5 ♕xd5 16 ♘d2

Or:

a) 16 ♗xc7 ♖ac8 gives Black compensation.

b) 16 ♕a4!? b6 17 ♗xc7 ♖fc8 18 ♗e5 ♕b3 19 ♕b4 (Benjamin-P.H.Nielsen, Las Vegas FIDE 1999) 19...♗xe5 20 ♘xe5 ♖xc3 ∞.

c) 16 ♗f1!?.

16...♕d7 17 ♗f3 ♖fe8 (D)

17...♖ae8!?.

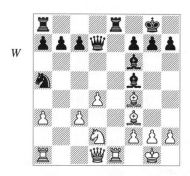

W

18 ♘e4 ♗e7 19 ♘g3 ♗g6 20 ♗g4 ♕c6 21 ♗f3

21 d5 ♕c4.

21...♕d7 22 ♖a2 ♗f8

22...♗d6 23 ♗xd6 ♖xe1+ 24 ♕xe1 ♕xd6 25 h4 ∞.

23 ♖ae2

∞ J.Polgar-P.H.Nielsen, Las Vegas FIDE 1999.

Index of Variations

1: Unusual Third Moves for White
1 e4 e5 2 ♘f3 ♘f6 *6*
A: 3 ♗c4 *6*
B: 3 ♘c3 *10*
C: 3 d3 *16*

2: 3 d4 without 3...♘xe4
1 e4 e5 2 ♘f3 ♘f6 3 d4 *17*

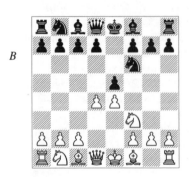

B

**3...exd4 4 e5 ♘e4 5 ♕xd4 d5 6 exd6
    ♘xd6** *20*
A: **7 ♗d3** *21*
B: **7 ♘c3** *24* **7...♘c6 8 ♕f4** *24*